WORLD

HISTORY

Cultures, States, and Societies
to 1500

Eugene Berger, Ph.D. | George L. Israel, Ph.D. | Charlotte Miller, Ph.D.
Brian Parkinson, Ph.D. | Andrew Reeves, Ph.D. | Nadejda Williams, Ph.D.

ISBN: 978-1-940771-10-6

Produced by:
University System of Georgia

Published by:
University of North Georgia Press
Dahlonega, Georgia

Cover Design and Layout Design:
Corey Parson

For more information, please visit http://ung.edu/university-press
Or email ungpress@ung.edu

TABLE OF CONTENTS

CHAPTER FOUR: CHINA AND EAST ASIA TO THE MING DYNASTY — 111

CHAPTER FIVE: THE GREEK WORLD FROM THE BRONZE AGE TO THE ROMAN CONQUEST — 171

1

Prehistory

Eugene Berger

1.1 CHRONOLOGY

8 – 6 million years ago	Bi-pedal hominids in Africa
2.6 million years ago	*Homo habilis* begin to use tools
43,000 BCE	*Homo sapiens* expand out of Africa
50,000 – 10,000 BCE	*Homo sapiens* complete their migration to all continents
22,000 – 14,000 BCE	Last Glacial Maximum
c. 9,000 BCE	Younger Dryas event
c. 9,000 BCE	Jericho reaches its height
c. 7,000 BCE	Çatalhüyük reaches several thousand inhabitants
2,000 BCE	Paleo-Eskimos appear in the Arctic
2,000 BCE	Humans begin to make pottery

1.2 INTRODUCTION

> In 1952, at the age of 77 and suffering with an abdominal hernia long overdue for surgery, Sellards returned to Vero to collect charcoal or bone suitable for the newly invented technique of radiocarbon dating. … His longtime field assistant Glen Evans accompanied him, having left Texas with careful instructions from Sellard's physician about what to do if the hernia suddenly bulged. It did, and Sellards collapsed unconscious at the excavation. … But the moment Sellards regained consciousness he insisted on continuing to excavate.[1]

The above case of Florida State Geologist Elias Sellards demonstrates that the study of "human antiquity" or man's earliest origins is one surrounded by passion, controversy, and a deep well of curiosity. Our curiosity about our earliest origins has not only given birth to fictional characters like Indiana Jones and Captain Kirk, but also is largely responsible for the growth of archaeology in the early twentieth century. Western scholars and explorers were

---

[1] David J. Meltzer, *The Great Paleolithic War: How Science Forged an Understanding of America's Ice Age Past* (Chicago: University of Chicago Press, 2015), 1.

not content with simply reaching remote places; they were curious about their earliest human inhabitants. While the motives of early excavators may have been quite simple (Well-known paleoanthropologist Richard Leakey got his start collecting stones as a child), archaeologists and paleoanthropologists eventually created an entirely new field of historical investigation: prehistory. Multiple pioneers have hacked through underbrush or spent months excavating **Paleolithic** sites. Not until recently, however, have scientific advances, local knowledge, and anthropological theory merged with the curiosity of western explorers to craft a more accurate version of human origins and evolution.

Written texts are the primary sources most historians are trained to work with and are those they are most comfortable using. However, if we are to understand humanity's origins, we have to recognize that written language is a relatively recent invention (around 5,000 years old); therefore, much of what we know about human beginnings must be borrowed from the findings of colleagues in other disciplines like geology, botany, and archaeology. In all of the regions mentioned below, archaeologists have excavated and analyzed physical evidence relating to our pre-historic ancestors. Up until recent times, though, it was difficult to understand migration patterns and chronology without a method to determine the age of anything from a human skull to a cutting tool. Archaeologists in the 1930s and 40s used imprecise terms like "stone bowl cultures," a nomenclature that referred more to the details of the articles unearthed than their historical context.[2] This began to change with the advent of radiocarbon dating or C14 dating in the 1940s. Through this method, we were able to place thousands of organic archaeological materials in their proper historical context even without textual evidence. For artifacts over 40,000 years old, the amount of radioactive carbon we can recover doesn't permit accurate measurement. However, we do have a number of techniques to trace human origins even further back, including aerial photography, side-scanning radar, and potassium-argon dating. All these techniques get around the lack of radioactive carbon in that they don't date the organic material, but instead the terrain in which they were found, allowing us to trace human origins back millions of years to the beginnings of bipedalism.

The goal of this chapter, though, is not to trace human evolution from its beginnings, but to set the scene for the beginnings of civilization. In this chapter we will explore why hominids moved, how they survived, and how they came to develop agriculture. We also hope to lay out why humans in far flung parts of the world responded similarly to changing conditions around them and hence developed civilizations at roughly the same time.

This chapter begins at the origins of bipedalism some eight million years ago and brings us up to eight thousand years ago with the the **Neolithic** Era or "new stone age." Bipedal hominids would develop during the Pliocene era and our closest ancestors during the more recent **Pleistocene**. Finally, modern ***Homo sapiens*** would appear during the **Holocene**. During the **Holocene** humans would perfect tool usage during the **Paleolithic** Era, and would usher in agriculture during the Neolithic. Our chapter ends as humans prepare to enter the Bronze and Iron Ages.

---

2   J.E.G Sutton, "Archeology and Reconstructing History in the Kenya Highlands: The Intellectual Legacies of G.W.B. Huntingford and Louis S.B. Leakey," *History in Africa* 34, (2007): 313.

1.3 QUESTIONS TO GUIDE YOUR READING

1. What were some factors that led to hominid bipedalism?

2. How did climate affect hominid development?

3. How and why did *Homo sapiens* expand out of Africa?

4. How and when did *Homo sapiens* populate the Americas?

5. What was a hunter-gatherer existence like?

6. Why did *Homo sapiens* start to prefer agriculture?

7. How did agriculture start to change human relationships?

1.4 KEY TERMS

- Abu Hureya
- Beringia
- Çatalhüyük
- Dolni Vetoniçe
- Holocene
- *Homo erectus*
- *Homo habilis*
- *Homo sapiens*

- Ice Age
- Jericho
- Natufians
- Neanderthals
- Neolithic
- Oldowan Industry
- Paleolithic
- Pleistocene

1.5 HUMAN BEGINNINGS IN AFRICA

The fossil record in Africa clearly establishes that a human lineage diverged there from African apes sometime between eight to six million years ago. Beginning as far back as eight million years ago, various species of hominids (the ancestors of modern humans or *Homo sapiens*) began to walk upright. This bipedalism would allow these hominids to use their hands to develop, craft, and use tools. Bipedalism would also eventually contribute to a move out of forests into the savanna and turn hominids into big game hunters and gatherers. Paleoanthropologists once theorized that hominids became bipedal to adapt to life in the grasslands. However, the fact that fossils of bipedal hominids were found alongside fossil remains of wood, seeds, and other forest dwellers has cast some doubt on that theory. In fact, bipedal hominids may have lived in the forest for some time. While some bipedal hominids may have stayed in the forest, climate changes did drive others to move into new areas within Africa and beyond it.

1.5.1 Climate, Hominin in Evolution, and Migrations

As far as thirty million years ago hominids were reacting to changes in their environment. ("Hominids" refers to all Great Apes including humans and their ancestors. "Hominins" is often used when speaking more specifically about modern humans and their more recently extinct ancestors. We will use "hominids" here because it covers all of the groups we will reference including modern humans). The earth cooled, producing more fragmented environments. As already mentioned, some hominids may have stayed in the trees, but those that left the forest began to thrive in grasslands. These savannas and prairies expanded during the Miocene, the geologic era lasting from 24 – 2 million years ago. This grassland expansion prompted baboons and hominids to move out of the forest.

During the Pliocene epoch (5 – 1.6 million years ago), another series of environmental changes made these grasslands even more prevalent, leading to a transformation that geologists call the "turnover-pulse hypothesis." Animals with adaptations such as angled knee joints and arched feet survived on the grasslands, while those with longer arms or curved fingers who were better suited to the woodlands did not. For hominids, this favorable grassland environment meant the "development of several closely related species. Large-toothed hominids known as robust australopithecines appeared in Southern and Eastern Africa."[3] Towards the end of the Pliocene, around 2.4 million years ago, the first members of our genus—*homo* (***Homo habilis***)—appeared, the first hominid to make stone tools.

The **Pleistocene** epoch (1.6 million – 10,000 years ago) saw at least twenty-five periods of glaciation and warming. Glaciation resulted from dips in global temperature which had two

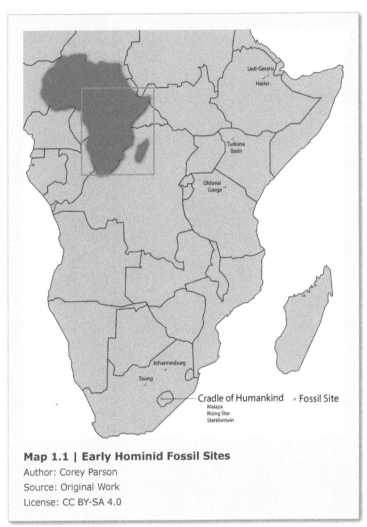

Map 1.1 | Early Hominid Fossil Sites
Author: Corey Parson
Source: Original Work
License: CC BY-SA 4.0

---

[3]   Lauren Ristvet, *In the Beginning: World History from Human Evolution to the First States* (Boston: McGraw Hill, 2007), 4.

major effects on hominid development. First, with sea levels dropping due to glaciation, hominids migrated to Australia and the Americas for the first time. Second, while many migrated out of colder climates, those that remained developed physical adaptations. *Homo neanderthalensis* (Neaderthals), a hominid that disappeared 28,000 years ago, became stockier and more powerful to deal with the difficulties of this icy climate.

While not as dramatic as previous developments, the current **Holocene** period has seen its share of significant climatic events. The Younger Dryas event (c. 12,000 BCE) was a drop in global temperatures accompanied by a corresponding change in vegetation distribution. Reduced rainfall from 2200 – 1900 BCE made conditions very difficult for civilizations in the Eastern Mediterranean. Finally, the Medieval Warm Period represents "one of the most recent periods of climate change."[4]

Like *neanderthalensis*, **Homo sapiens, Homo erectus, Homo habilis**, and other hominids all reacted to changing climate conditions. *Homo erectus and Homo habilis* migrated, hunted, and used fire, while *neanderthalensis* had some use of language and tools and buried their dead. For millions of years, in fact, hominids had been using slivers of volcanic stone and cutters probably to hack through animal skin. The cutters were often found close together, suggesting that early hominids even had a division of labor between hunters who would have to pursue their prey and butchers who could wait nearby at the butchering site. There is even evidence of task division by gender among *neanderthalensis*. Multiple sites in Europe show different patterns of wear on male and female teeth, indicating a gendered task division in tasks where teeth were used to hold, break, or strip objects.[5]

However, by 25,000 years ago all other hominins were extinct; only *Homo sapiens sapiens*, our species, survived. Paleoanthropologists attribute this survival to larger brains, durability, and ability to adapt to changing environmental conditions. Based on migration patterns and archaeological evidence, *Homo sapiens sapiens* appear to have been the only hominids to build sea-worthy boats, create art, have organized religion, and live in any climate.[6]

1.5.2 *Homo sapiens* Migration

While *Homo sapiens* were decidedly more advanced than other hominids, when they first moved out of Africa some 45,000 years ago, they were only equipped with stone tools for hunting and cutting. Despite those initial limitations, 30,000 years later *Homo sapiens* would inhabit almost every environment on earth and had a presence in every continent except Antarctica. *Homo sapiens* in fact moved further and faster than all other hominids. While it is hard to attribute a single factor to all *Homo sapiens* migration, we do see that multiple human societies required migration to arrive at a more sophisticated level of development. *Homo sapien* migration accelerated close to 40,000 years ago, where humans reached continental Eurasia.

Modern humans (50,000 – 10,000 years ago) completed the migration to all the continents except Antartica, moving first into Australia, Eastern Siberia, the Pacific margins, Japan, and the

---

4   Ibid., 3-5.
5   Almudena Estalrrich and Antonio Rosas, "Division of Labor by Sex and Age in Neandertals: An Approach Through the Study of Activity-Related Dental Wear," *Journal of Human Evolution* 80, (March 2015): 51-63.
6   Ristvet., 24-26.

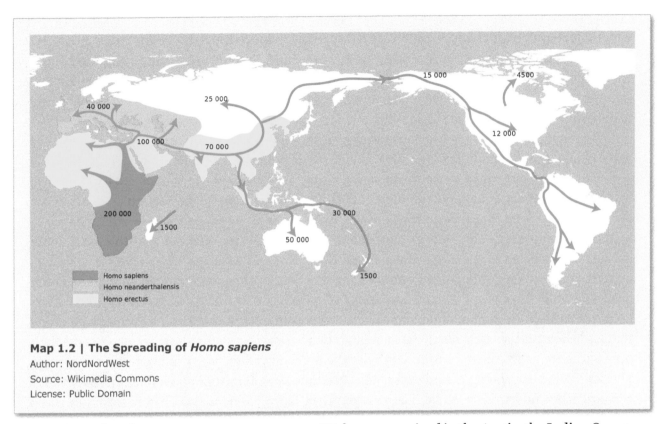

Map 1.2 | The Spreading of *Homo sapiens*
Author: NordNordWest
Source: Wikimedia Commons
License: Public Domain

Americas. Then from 10,000 years ago to 1,500 CE, humans arrived in the Arctic, the Indian Ocean, the deep Pacific, and tropical rain forests. Migration occurred in a "staccato" pattern with "easiest" areas colonized quickly, while more "difficult" areas remained uninhabited for thousands of years. A region's "easiness" is calculated from estimates about available plant and animal biomass and net productivity—that is, how quickly it returns—in each habitat. For example, tropical savannas and grasslands of East Africa were colonized first as the biomass there sustained the first bipedal hominids.

Hominids first left "sub-Saharan Africa ... through the northern savannahs, up the Nile corridor or across the straits of Bab el Mandeb to the Arabian Peninsula."[7] Evidence exists of *Homo erectus* in Morocco, Chad, and Algeria, and it appears that they eventually left Africa via the Arabian Peninsula. After leaving Africa about 1.5 million years ago, choppers, handaxes, and spheroids found at sites like Ubeidiya in Israel put *Homo erectus* in the Levant. Some scholars argue for the existence of a second migration out of Africa and into the Jordan Valley 500 to 600 thousand years ago.

Asia

Some evidence suggests the presence of *Homo ergaster* and *Homo erectus* as having occurred in Java over a million years ago. Chinese *Homo erectus* fossils date between 800,000 to 400,000 years ago. *Homo sapiens* began to leave Africa around 40,000 years ago, and hunter gatherers appeared in China by the end of the last **Ice Age** (36,000 to 16,000 BCE) as continental ice in central Asia began to melt.

---

7   Clive Gamble, *Timewalkers: Prehistory of Global Colonization* (Bath, Avon: The Bath Press, 1993), 125-128.

Europe

Animal bones and pebble tools place hominids near Rome just before the beginning of the Middle **Pleistocene** (730,000 years ago). This seems to be the first hominid incursion into Europe. Hominid remains in Spain suggest colonization in Iberia up to two million years ago, but there are not nearly enough remains (no more than twenty inhabitants in any given site) to provide any certainty in terms of which hominids they correspond to or when they lived there. Either way, colonization of Europe can be considered "late." This tardiness may have been related to a lack of animal food sources. Not until around 500,000 years ago did "new species of deer, bovid, rhino, and horse appear"[8] in Europe. Around the same time, the cheetah, saber-tooth tiger, and dirk-tooth cat declined in the region, making more carcasses from the aforementioned species available to hominid foragers.

Australia, Papua New Guinea, Sahul

Evidence of tools from 30,000 years ago exists in Australia, and from even longer in New Guinea. The lack of "a dry land crossing to Sahul" (the land mass that once connected New Guinea and Australia) meant that an ocean journey of somewhere between sixty-five and 100 kilometers was required from mainland Asia. This made Australians and New Guineans the first sea-going colonizers. Once in Sahul, how humans populated Australia is still the subject of some debate between those who support the "coastal hugger" theory and those who support the idea of population by "overlanders." The more difficult of the two means of populating Australia is overland, as it is more arid than the coasts, and the evidence for tools overland is not as advanced as that for the coast.

Peopling the New World

North and South America were the last continents to be settled by humans. Most scholars think that the Americas were populated from **Beringia** over land. Around 12,000 years ago, mammoth hunting became more common and supported larger populations on both the Asian and American sides of **Beringia**, a landmass (now divided by the Bering Strait) which at that time connected North America and Asia. On the Asian side, outlines of houses with stone-lined hearths have been found, remnants indicating permanent settlement that didn't necessarily have colonization as an end goal. But colonize they did, one group pushing southward between 10,000 and 3,000 years ago and establishing settlements that would become the origins of modern Korean, Japanese, Chinese, and Inuit populations. Another group migrated southeastward through Alaska, their descendants making it as far as Chile and Argentina.

While we know about when American colonization began, the pace and means of colonization are still debated. Complicating the discussion of timing is the fact that the Late Wisconsin Ice sheet blocked the overland route from about 30,000 years ago, when two sheets merged, up until about 12,000 years ago, when they opened after a thaw. At this point in time, only a handful of sites support possible pre-10,000 BCE occupation: Monte Verde in Chile, Meadowcraft near Pittsburgh, and Page-Ladson in Florida. As recently as 2015, excavations at Monte Verde and

---

8   Ibid., 135.

Chinchihuapi have strengthened the "possibility of an earlier human presence on the continent" to as far back as 17,000 BCE. This date has continued to move back in time as archeologists consider evidence of more mobile humans who did not leave large artifact clusters because of their ephemeral nature, but nonetheless may have been present before more sedentary groups.

For now, however, the clearest evidence for when the Americas were widely populated comes through the Clovis point, a specific arrowhead shape that was unique in its ubiquity and sophistication. The Clovis point was also found in mammoths that had grown extinct by 10,500 years ago, this discovery meaning that humans were common in North America by then. From Beringia, humans moved at a rate of roughly 10 miles a year until they reached Tierra del Fuego and fully populated the Americas (with the exception of some tropical areas mentioned above).[9]

Map 1.3 | Geomorphological Context of the Monte Verde Site
Author: Tom Dillehay
Source: PLOS
License: CC BY 4.0

The Arctic

The first Paleo-Eskimo populations appeared around 4,000 years ago after arriving from Eastern Siberia, populations that were left behind by the American colonists already mentioned. The Arctic climate is harsh, to say the least, and these populations needed sophisticated weapons and tools to be able to survive it, which explains their late arrival.

The Arctic colonists expanded rapidly across Alaska, through Canada, and into Greenland, assisted by their arctic "small tool kits" that included the important toggle headed harpoons to kill walrus and seal.

Polynesian origins

The origins of Polynesian humans are still very much in doubt. Groups of Polynesian mariners had existed 50,000 years ago, but they were not colonizers. In fact, many scholars argue that eventual colonization actually began as exploration. Around 2,500 years ago, we see more permanent settlements in Fiji, Tonga, and other areas of the "remote" Pacific, as remnants of pottery

---

9   Dillehay TD, Ocampo C, Saavedra J, Sawakuchi AO, Vega RM, Pino M, et al. (2015) "New Archaeological Evidence for an Early Human Presence at Monte Verde, Chile," PLoS ONE 10(11): e0141923. doi:10.1371/journal.pone.0141923: 208.

have been found there. Based on linguistic and technological similarities among Polynesian cultures, some scholars argue that Fiji, Somoa, and Tonga were a crucible of sorts where Polynesians were "made" from groups from throughout Asia. Once these cultural groups had a certain identity, they began to colonize Easter Island, Hawaii, and New Zealand about and beyond 1,000 CE.

We can't use land migration patterns to understand oversea migration. The Pacific was somewhat of a highway, where currents and winds were well-known and frequently used by mariners. Migrating humans were much more likely to wander aimlessly on land than they were to let currents take them to unknown parts of the ocean. Pacific mariners tacked to use the winds in their favor and, despite population pressures, Pacific mariners were too adept at

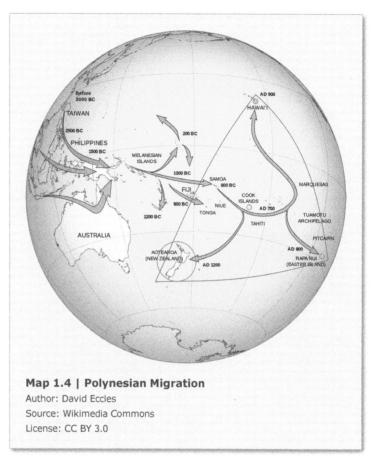

Map 1.4 | Polynesian Migration
Author: David Eccles
Source: Wikimedia Commons
License: CC BY 3.0

seafaring to suggest a simple casting out of people into the Pacific in hopes of finding something. Once Pacific colonization did commence, settlers were very deliberate about it, taking with them families, and plants, and animals. It seems that they had every intention of recreating "home." In sum, the exploration was neither extremely heroic nor extremely risky but instead was calculated and not left to chance.

1.5.3 Hunter-gatherers

Chapter Two explores the importance of farming to the creation and expansion of early civilizations. However, farming was only invented 13,000 years ago, meaning that for most of human history, our food has come through foraging. Early hominids like australopithecines, *Homo habilis*, and *Homo erectus* ate mostly plant food. *Homo sapiens* became more sophisticated foragers as they began to fish with hooks and, more recently, nets, and as they used stone grinding tools to produce flour.

As food gathering techniques evolved for these Paleolithic foragers, so did their behavior as organized groups. Modern humans became mobile to prevent resource depletion; they controlled population through dispersion or infanticide, and they began to "live and work cooperatively." Modern foragers also began to divide tasks and share food with others, a feature that distinguishes them from other animals like chimpanzees that live in communities but feed individually.

Sharing food is, of course, much easier to do when there is a surplus, and, with increasing tool use, Paleolithic humans became even more adept at foraging, leading to the higher likelihood of food surpluses.

Tool use not only helped humans live cooperatively, but it also may have helped hominids develop abstract thought—evidence of tool use may give us a clue as to when this development began. We know that other animals use tools, but even as long as 2.6 million years ago, we see evidence of the creative thinking required to make more effective tools. **Homo habilis** in fact takes its name ("handy man") from the fact that they were the first known hominid tool-makers. Soon after individual tools appeared, the **Oldowan** Industry became the first widely used toolset,

Figure 1.1 | Paleolithic Chopper
Author: User "Archaeodontosaurus"
Source: Wikimedia Commons
License: CC BY-SA 4.0

"consisting of flaked and smashed quartz riverside pebbles made into poorly formed choppers and sharp stone flakes, [and] lasted for 1 million years with little change [from 2.6 to 1.5 million years ago]."[10] The Oldowan were followed about 1.5 million years ago by hand axes that remained unchanged for more than a million years. Many scholars argue that these smaller-brained hominids like *Homo habilis, homo ergaster, and Australopithecus* were both unable and unwilling to innovate much beyond their simple but effective tools, especially considering how harsh their environment could become. Fire was another important tool, first used by *Homo erectus* about 1.6 million years ago. Fire would become important to migrants to colder climes in Europe and Asia and to foragers who could now eat foods that were poisonous if ingested raw. *Homo erectus* also cooked foods they had previously eaten raw, thereby expanding their lifespan by eliminating toxins found in raw meats.

Homo sapiens would add more meat to their diet when advances in tool-making led to an increase in big game hunting during the late Pleistocene. For example, excavations near **Dolni Vetoniçe** in the Czech Republic have helped reveal a society that "used mammoth remains not only for meat, but for fuel, construction, jewelry, and portable art." The inhabitants of Dolni Vetoniçe also made thousands of ceramic figurines, bird bone flutes, and ivory carvings of human heads. The cave paintings of Lascaux also reflect this increased skill as hunters and painters both. The colors and types of paint they used were vibrant and durable, and the scenes they depicted demonstrated their use of diverse hunting techniques. There we see depictions of humans hunting not only deer, but also woolly rhinoceros and mammoths.

---

10   Ristvet, 17-22.

Also at Lascaux, we see evidence that hunter-gatherers had both religious beliefs and gender specific tasks, reflecting a sophistication that we usually only attribute to sedentary humans. The fact the humans and animals were depicted together so often at Lascaux may be evidence of a belief that man descended from these animals. Or perhaps the bison, rhinoceri, and birds were painted on the walls to produce "hunting magic" designed to make expeditions more successful. Finally, it was mostly men depicted in these higher-risk hunting activities, suggesting that women were the artists, participated less in the hunt, or both.

Closer to the Neolithic era, societies began to experience a growing role for women reflected through their representation in "Venus" statuettes. (See Figure 1.5) As we get closer to the Neolithic era, we see the relative role of women increasing; their place in ritual increases, their stature increases, their economic importance increases, and their childbearing uniqueness becomes more greatly emphasized.

Increased sophistication was not limited to big game hunters, however. Campsites, rock art, and burial sites near Lake Mungo in Australia reveal how these early humans used pottery for cooking and had a diverse diet of birds, fish, and shellfish, a diet that seems to have kept them well-nourished. [11] Australia was a society of hunter-gatherers until European colonization. Mobility was essential, with the continent's lack of widespread rainfall and rich soil. As a result, aboriginal Australians needed an extensive knowledge of

Figure 1.2 | Bull, Bird, and Human from Lascaux Cave
Author: User "Peter80"
Source: Wikimedia Commons
License: CC BY-SA 2.5

their terrain and where to move when. Tasmanians would ambush wallabies at their seasonal grazing territory, while aborigines in the central deserts had to know when water holes would go dry. We also learn from the remains of Australian aborigines that foragers could be quite complex if they continued to hunt and gather for thousands of years. Aborigines painted, developed advanced weapons like the boomerang, warred against one another, developed creation myths, passed down oral histories, and played musical instruments.

---

11   Ibid., 27-30.

1.6 AGRICULTURE AND THE "NEOLITHIC REVOLUTION"

Historian Lauren Ristvet defines agriculture as the "'domestication' of plants... causing it to change genetically from its wild ancestor in ways [that make] it more useful to human consumers."[12] She and hundreds of other scholars from Hobbes to Marx have pointed to the **Neolithic Revolution**, that is, the move from a hunter-gatherer world to an agricultural one, as the root of what we today refer to as civilization. Without agriculture we don't have empires, written language, factories, universities, or railroads. Despite its importance, much remains unclear about why and where agriculture began. Instead, scholars hold a handful of well-regarded theories about the roots (pun intended) of agriculture.

Most scholars agree that the Ice Age played a fundamental role in the rise of agriculture, in the sense that it was impossible during the much colder and often tundra-covered period of the Pleistocene, but inevitable during the Holocene thawing. Only 4,000 years before the origins of agriculture, the planting of anything would have been an exercise in futility. During the Last Glacial Maximum (24,000 – 16,000 years ago), average temperatures dropped "by as much as 57° F near the great ice sheets..."[13] This glaciation meant not only that today's fertile farmlands of Spain or the North American Great Plains were increasingly covered in ice, but also that other areas around the world could not depend on constant temperatures or rainfall from year to year. Pleistocene foragers had to be flexible. The warming trend of the Holocene, by contrast, resulted in consistent rainfall amounts and more predictable temperatures. The warming also altered the habitats of the megafauna that humans hunted, alterations that in some cases contributed to their extinction. Therefore, as animal populations declined, humans were further encouraged to plant and cultivate seeds in newly-thawed soil.

When we start to examine other factors that allowed humans to transition to agriculture, we find that the climate factor looms even larger. For example, agriculture was usually accompanied by sedentarism, but we see communal living and permanent settlements among multiple groups of hunter-gatherers. *Homo sapiens* had also begun to domesticate animals and plants alike during the Pleistocene. Humans were already being buried alongside dogs as early as 14,000 years ago.[14] As we'll see below, gatherers were developing an increasing taste for grains long before they would abandon a foraging lifestyle. Essentially, humans were ready for agriculture when climate permitted it.

We discuss elsewhere the timing of agriculture's appearance in all of the continents, but generally speaking by about 8,000 years ago, farmers in West Asia were growing rye, barley, and wheat. In northern China, millet was common 8,500 years ago. In the Americas, the domestication of maize began around 8,000 years ago in Mesoamerica, while at about the same time, Andean residents began cultivating potatoes. Once all of these areas realized agriculture's potential as a permanent food source, they began to adapt their societies to increase their crop consistency and crop yields. We'll discuss how agriculture affected societal development below.

---

12   Ibid., 36.
13   Ibid., 36-37.
14   Chris Scarre, ed. *The Human Past: World Prehistory and the Development of Human Societies.* 2nd ed. (London: Thames & Hudson, 2009), 183-84.

1.6.1 First farmers of West Asia [or the Fertile Crescent]

In later chapters we will discuss Mesopotamia, the area between the Euphrates and Tigris Rivers that agriculture would make the "cradle of civilization." (See Map 2.1). However, the incubator of Mesopotamian and Fertile Crescent agriculture and cultural patterns dated back to the foragers of the nearby Eastern Mediterranean, thousands of years before. The rye, barley, and wheat in West Asia were first harvested by late Pleistocene foragers called the Kebarans who ground wild wheat and barley into a porridge.[15] Kebarans consumed the porridge as part of their broad spectrum diet that also included land mammals, birds, and fish. Advancing into the Holocene we see the **"Natufian Adaptation,"** where residents of this same area began to see the benefits of sedentary living in a precursor to the advent of agriculture. The Natufians consumed the same rye, barley, and wheat that their Kebaran predecessors had, but because their teeth were well-worn it appears they ate relatively more of it. Having a constant source of these grains enabled their eschewing long hunting or gathering soujourns; instead, the Natufians drew more of their meat from in and around Lake Huleh in modern Israel. Near Lake Huleh was Ain Mallaha, one of the earliest examples of year-round human settlement and an important precursor to sedentary agriculture.

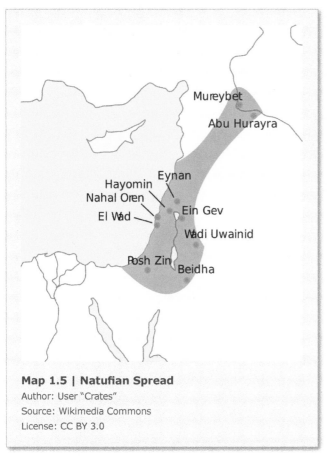

Map 1.5 | Natufian Spread
Author: User "Crates"
Source: Wikimedia Commons
License: CC BY 3.0

Another permanent settlement in Southwest Asia seems to have been more directly responsible for the decision to actually domesticate grain, rather than simply cultivate wild varieties. Abu Hureya in Syria was deeply affected by the Younger Dryas event of 11,000 years ago, an event which caused many of their wild food staples to disappear. Rather than migrating out of the area, the Abu Hureyrans cultivated rye. Soon afterward, other sites in the Levant began to see the planting of barley, while wheat was cultivated in both the Levant and Anatolia.[16]

1.6.2 First Permanent Settlements in West Asia [of the Fertile Crescent]

The transition from foraging, to collecting to cultivating took place over several centuries, but these gradual changes did serve to mark a very distinct era of permanent settlement during the Neolithic Period. Increased rainfall around 9600 BCE meant that the Jordan River would swell

---

15   Ristvet, 41.
16   Ristvet, 41-42.

yearly, in the process depositing layers of fertile soil along its banks. This fertile soil allowed locals to rely on agriculture for survival. Soon after they founded **Jericho** just north of the Dead Sea: "perhaps the very first time in human history that a completely viable population was living in the same place at the same time."[17] By Jericho's height, around 9000 BCE, the settlements population reached the hundreds. This increase cannot be considered an urban boom of course, and the transition away from foraging occurred gradually. For example, excavations from this area have unearthed no separation of tasks or dwellings by gender or skill. However, by the end of Jericho's development, maintaining large populations in one place would prove to produce other extensive adjustments.[18]

Jericho's residents did distinguish themselves from their hunter-gatherer predecessors, however, through their relatively extensive construction projects. They used mud bricks to build a wall that encircled the settlement probably for flood control, a tower, and separate buildings for grain storage.

Map 1.6 | The Jordan River
Author: User "Interiot"
Source: Wikimedia Commons
License: Public Domain

The former foragers now living at Jericho could rely on fish or other aquatic creatures for meat as they experimented with permanent settlement, but those foragers living further away from large bodies of water would need another source of meat. This need increasingly was met by animal domestication. Domestication would prove to be a slow process, as humans learned the hard way that zebras bite, impalas are claustrophobic, and bighorn sheep do not obey orders. In other words, some animals cannot be domesticated, but this is information only understood through trial and error. By about 7,500 BCE, however, humans in the Taurus and Zagros mountains employed selective breeding to eventually domesticate mountain sheep and goats. The temperament and size of pigs and cows delayed their domestication until the 6,000s BCE, but this process proved equally, if not more important, than that of sheep and goats.

As agriculture and animal domestication progressed, settlements around the Mediterranean became larger and more sophisticated. By 7,000 BCE on the Anatolian plateau, Çatalhüyük reached several thousands of inhabitants. The residents at Çatalhüyük buried their dead, constructed uniform adjacent houses with elaborate designs painted on their interior walls, and had multiple workshops where (among other activities) they wove baskets, and made obsidian mirrors as well as daggers with "carved bone handles."[19] Catalhüyük denizens wove wool into

---

17   Steven Mithen, *After the Ice: A Global Human History, 20,000 – 5,000 BC.* (London: Weidenfeld & Nicolson, 2003), 59.
18   Robert Strayer, *Ways of the World: A Brief Global History with Sources,* 2nd ed (New York, Bedford St. Martins, 2013), 40
19   Mithen, 94.

cloth; developed a varied diet of peas, nuts, vegetable oil, apples, honey, and the usual grains; and improved weapons technology with sharper arrows added to their use of daggers and lances. These gains may seem modest by our standards, but the legacy of communal living and, ultimately, political centralization that they introduced was extraordinary.

Figure 1.3 | Çatalhüyük at the Time of the First Excavations
Author: Omar Hoftun
Source: Wikimedia Commons
License: CC BY-SA 3.0

Jericho and Çatalhüyük were surely some of the most notable early settlements, but they were not alone. The appearance of these two settlements was accompanied by the increasing presence of village life across the world. Most early agricultural villages in Southwest Asia and around the world were very similar in appearance; they had around twenty residents and were organized around grain cultivation and storage. Small huts were organized in a "loose circle," and grain silos were placed between each hut. Labor was a communal activity, and village members all spent time hoeing the fields or hunting. The most valuable asset to a community was the grain itself, but neither it nor the land where it grew it belonged to one individual.

This model existed for hundreds and even thousands of years in some areas, until the villages stopped hunting and domesticated animals. For many scholars, the abandonment of hunting represents the "real" Neolithic Revolution. As communities completely abandoned hunting and gathering, they dedicated more energy to warfare, religion, and construction; in consequence, dwellings and settlements grew, along with a concomitant focus on tool and weapon making.[20]

1.6.3 Leaving Paleolithic Culture Behind

While the Neolithic Era is described in greater detail elsewhere, it is important to understand Paleolithic and Neolithic differences in order to convey a sense of just how revolutionary the shift to agriculture was for humanity. For example, agriculture contributed to (along with religion and trade) the development of class. Before agriculture, hunter-gatherers divided tasks like seed gathering, grinding, or tool-making. However, without large scale building projects like aqueducts or canals required for agriculture, hierarchies were much less pronounced. The intensification of agriculture during the Neolithic required irrigation, plowing, and terracing, all of which were labor intensive. The amount of labor required could not be met through simple task division; someone had to be in charge. This meant the establishment of ruling elites, a societal grouping that had not existed during the Paleolithic.

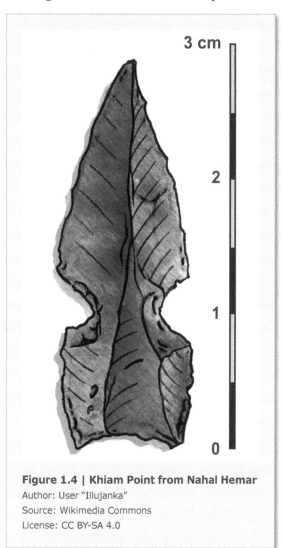

Figure 1.4 | Khiam Point from Nahal Hemar
Author: User "Illujanka"
Source: Wikimedia Commons
License: CC BY-SA 4.0

While violence certainly existed during the Paleolithic period, organized warfare was an invention of the Neolithic. Agriculture meant larger populations and settlements that were more tightly packed and closer to one another. These closer quarters created new social and economic pressures that could produce organized violence. Agricultural intensification produced stores of food and valuables that could be seized by neighbors. During the 9,000s BCE, settlements like Jericho began to build defensive walls, while skeletons unearthed in the area reveal wounds from new types of projectiles (like the Khiam Point) developed during the era.[21]

Family life also changed significantly during the Neolithic. Sedentary communities invested more time and resources into the construction of permanent homes housing nuclear families. People spent less time with the community as a whole and within homes it became easier to accumulate wealth and keep secrets.

The shift in gender roles after agriculture seems to be even more pronounced, as the role of women became more important as humans moved out of the Paleolithic and into the Neolithic era.

20   Ristvet, 66.
21   Scarre, 192, 215.

During the Paleolithic Era, and until recently in fact, a child would be breastfed until he or she was three or four years old, a necessity preventing mothers from joining long-distance hunting expeditions without their toddlers. However, a breastfeeding woman could complete tasks that "don't require rapt concentration, are relatively dull and repetitive; they are easily interrupted, don't place the child in danger, and don't require the participant to stray far from home."[22] Spinning, weaving, and sewing were

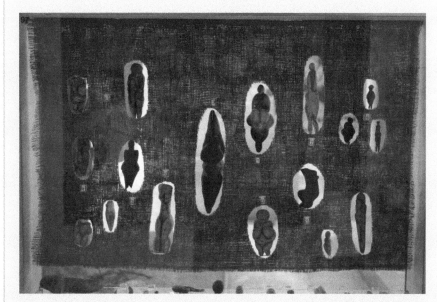

Figure 1.5 | Different types of carved Venus figurines, Anthropos Museum, Brno, Czech Republic
Author: Mercy from Wikimedia Commons
Source: Wikimedia Commons
License: CC BY-SA 3.0

some of these tasks. Also, the essential tasks of preparing food and clothing could be accomplished with a nursing toddler nearby. These tasks that may be consigned as "women's work" today are among the most important tasks (and very time consuming ones before the industrial revolution) that a human could perform. In fact, they were so time consuming that women would spend most of their day on them, often being assisted by men.

Over time, Paleolithic women gathered new species of berries as well as bird eggs, and learned which mushrooms were nontoxic. Women also were the principal gatherers of mosses for sleeping mats and other plants for shelter. When men returned with a kill, the women then began an involved process of dressing and butchering it. Sinews from animals and fibers from plants became rope to tie or fasten the hides as well as baskets. Women thus were essential to any kind of productivity or progress associated with hunting. Women used sinews and fibers to create netting for transport and for hunting and fishing. In hunting societies with elements of horticulture, women were responsible for, and could provide, such food as legumes, eggs, and grains. Food gathering and weaving, especially in the dry Mediterranean, was an outdoor and community activity that also served as a preschool and apprentice system for children. So women were also community educators.

Neolithic Women

While Paleolithic women certainly had important responsibilities, the added tasks of herding and animal domestication expanded their roles tremendously in the Neolithic era. Neolithic

---

22   Elizabeth Wayland Barber, Women's Work: The First 20,000 Years – Women, Cloth and Society in Early Times, (New York: Norton, 1995), 30.

survival required not only effective food storage, but also increased production. Children on a farm can be more helpful and put in less danger than those on a hunt. Neolithic women increasingly bore more children, either because of increased food production or to help augment it. This increase in child bearing may also have offset an increase in mortality due, for example, to disease. Because dangers from disease grew in new villages due to the ease with which deadly diseases spread in close quarters, and nearby domesticated animals whose diseases spread from animal to humans, more children would be necessary to replace those who had succumbed to illness.

While Neolithic women carried an increased child-bearing responsibility, their other responsibilities did not necessarily wane. Though women may not have fired pottery when it began to appear some 6,000 years ago, they appeared on it in decorative symbols of female fertility. Around 4,000 BCE, gendered tasks shifted again with the domestication of draft animals. Food production once again became men's domain, as herding was incompatible with childrearing. Later, in Neolithic herding societies, women were often responsible for the actual domestication of feral babies, nursing them and raising them. Men would shear sheep, help weave, market the textiles, and cultivate the food that was prepared in the home.

We should say that this was not the case with all agricultural societies, as many horticulturalists who were able to cultivate crops closer to home were able to remain matrilineal. For example, we have the case of Minoan women on the Mediterranean island of Crete that we discuss in more detail in Chapter Five. On Crete's hilly terrain, women were able to cultivate terraced horticulture and keep herds of sheep and goats nearby. Therefore, as women lost power and influence elsewhere due to more intensive agriculture, Minoan women actually expanded their control over Crete's economic and cultural life and would help give rise to Classical Greece.

1.6.4 Toward First Civilizations

We will discuss the Bronze Age elsewhere, but we should mention here that new pursuits like mining added to the domestic burden on women. The advent of the Bronze Age led to far-spread searching and mining for copper and other metals like arsenic or tin to harden it and create the bronze alloy. Mining consequently become a male pursuit. Between 9,000 and 4,000 BCE, as metal become a source for wealth and subsistence, men's roles shifted from being secondary to being both the food collectors and the economic backbone of individual families and societies.

These Neolithic developments in sedentary agriculture and village life would be the foundation for an explosion of cultural development three thousand years later in Egypt and Mesopotamia (addressed later in this text). By the Age of Exploration in the 1500s CE, most of the world had adopted agriculture as a primary means of subsistence, and the foundation of great civilizations.

1.7 SUMMARY

The story of world civilizations really begins six to eight million years ago when ancestors of modern humans began to walk upright. Millions of years of evolutionary response to changing climates and environment led to the existence of our species, *Homo sapiens*. While other hominids migrated out of Africa, had language, and made fire and tools, it was *Homo sapiens* who were able to navigate open oceans and eventually populate the entire planet. Over the last 50,000 years or so, *Homo sapiens* became modern humans by improving their hunting, their building techniques, their community living, and their food gathering and storage. About 10,000 years ago, the Neolithic Era began. Humans began to live in larger, permanent settlements where a permanent food source needed to be nearby. These were the beginnings of agriculture. This "agricultural revolution" deeply affected gender relationships, class distinctions, and economic priorities as most humans left their foraging days behind them, the importance of which will be discussed in later chapters.

1.8 WORKS CONSULTED AND FURTHER READING

Bradley, Bruce and Dennis Stanford. "A Possible Paleolithic Route to the New World." *World Archaelolgy* 36 no. 4 (Dec., 2004): 459-478.

Dillehay TD, Ocampo C, Saavedra J, Sawakuchi AO, Vega RM, Pino M, et al. (2015) "New Archaeological Evidence for an Early Human Presence at Monte Verde, Chile." PLoS ONE 10(11): e0141923. doi:10.1371/journal.pone.0141923 http://journals.plos.org/plosone/article?id=10.1371/journal.pone.0141923

Estalarrich, Almudena and Antinio Rosas. "Division of Labor by Sex and Age in Neandertals: An Approach Through the Study of Activity-Related Dental Wear." *Journal of Human Evolution* 80 (March 2015): 51-63.

Fawcett, Percy. *Exploration Fawcett: Journey to the Lost City of Z.* New York: The Overlook Press, 2010.

Gamble, Clive. *Timewalkers: Prehistory of Global Colonization.* Bath, Avon: The Bath Press, 1993.

Grann, David. *The Lost City of Z: A Tale of Deadly Obsession in the Amazon.* New York: Vintage Books, 2010.

Mithen, Steven. *After the Ice: A Global Human History, 20,000-5,000 BC.* London: Weidenfeld & Nicolson, 2003.

Ristvet, Lauren. *In the Beginning: World History from Human Evolution to the First States.* Boston: McGraw Hill, 2007.

Scarre, Chris, ed. *The Human Past: World Prehistory and the Development of Human Societies.* 2nd ed. London: Thames & Hudson, 2009.

Smithsonian Institution, Human Origins Initiative. http://humanorigins.si.edu/evidence/human-fossils/species/homo-habilis

Sutton, J.E.G. "Archeology and Reconstructing History in the Kenya Highlands: The Intellectual Legacies of G.W.B. Huntingford and Louis S.B. Leakey." *History in Africa* 34 (2007), pp. 297-320.

Strayer, Robert. *Ways of the World: A Brief Global History with Sources, 2nd. Ed.* New York, Bedford St. Martins, 2013.

Wayland Barber, Elizabeth. *Women's Work: The First 20,000 Years – Women, Cloth and Society in Early Times.* New York: Norton, 1995.

1.9 LINKS TO PRIMARY SOURCES

Bering Land Bridge National Preserve

https://www.nps.gov/nr/travel/cultural_diversity/Bering_Land_Bridge_National_Preserve.html

Oldowan & Acheulean Stone Tools

https://anthromuseum.missouri.edu/minigalleries/handaxes/intro.shtml

Dolni Vetoniçe

http://australianmuseum.net.au/dolni-vstonice-archaeological-site

Natufian site of Eyan/Ain Mallaha

http://www.metmuseum.org/toah/hd/eyna/hd_eyna.htm

Çatalhüyük

http://whc.unesco.org/en/list/1405

2 Early Middle Eastern and Northeast African Civilizations

Charlotte Miller

2.1 CHRONOLOGY

Ancient Mesopotamia

c. 10,000 BCE	Beginnings of the Agricultural Revolution
c. 3500 BCE	Appearance of Sumerian city-states in lower Mesopotamia
c. 3200 BCE	Early use of cuneiform
c. 2900 BCE	Production of bronze
2334 – 2100 BCE	Akkadian Empire
c. 2000 BCE	Gilgamesh first recorded in cuneiform
1792 – 1595 BCE	Babylonian Empire
1792 – 1750 BCE	Reign of Hammurabi
900 – 612 BCE	Assyrian Empire
626 – 539 BCE	New Babylonian Empire
605 – 562 BCE	Reign of Nebechadnezzar

Ancient Israel

c. 1300 – 1200 BCE	Israelites leave Egypt (following Moses)
c. 1050 – 1010 BCE	Israelites establish a kingdom
c. 1000 – 970 BCE	Reign of King David
c. 979 – 930 BCE	Reign of King Solomon
931 BCE	Israel divides into two kingdoms
586 – 539 BCE	Babylonian captivity of Israelites

Northeast Africa (Egypt and Nubia)

c. 7000 BCE	Beginnings of Agricultural Revolution in Northeast Africa
c. 6000 – 3500 BCE	Desiccation of the Sahara Desert pushed people towards Nile River Valley

c. 4000 BCE	Towns and villages grew along the Nile River
c. 3100 BCE	Unification of Egypt
3100 – 2600 BCE	Egyptian Archaic Period
2660 – 2160 BCE	Egyptian Old Kingdom
2400 – 1450 BCE	The Kingdom of Kerma
2040 – 1640 BCE	Egyptian Middle Kingdom
1640 – 1570 BCE	Egypt's Second Intermediate Period (Egypt under Hyksos Rule)
1530 – 1070 BCE	Egyptian New Kingdom
1350 – 1325 BCE	Amarna Period (under Pharaoh Akhenaten)
1040 – 332 BCE	Egyptian Late Period
750 – 656 BCE	The Kingdom of Kush ruled Egypt, creating the "Ethiopian Dynasty"
750 – 593 BCE	Kingdom of Kush (with capital at Napata)
656 – 639 BCE	Assyrians occupied Egypt
593 BCE	Egyptian army sacked Napata, the capital of Kush
593 BCE	The Kingdom of Kerma moved its capital to Meroe
525 BCE	Persian conquest of Egypt
323 BCE	Alexander the Great conquered Egypt/Ptolemaic Kingdom of Egypt
30 BCE	Roman conquest of Egypt

2.2 INTRODUCTION: DEFINING CIVILIZATION

The term **civilization** often elicits mostly idealized images of ancient empires, monumental architecture, and the luxurious lives of ruling classes. Civilization, however, is a tricky term. In the United States, students of history studied Western Civilization, almost exclusively, through the 1950s. In their studies, civilizations were advanced societies with urban centers, rooted in European or Middle Eastern culture. America's origins in these western civilizations was used to explain our own high level of development. However, more recent scholars have definitely broadened the geographical focus by recognizing that worldwide from 3500 to 1000 BCE at least seven independent civilizations emerged in different regions. These recent scholars also continue to debate the definition of civilization, and the current compromise amongst World Historians is to recognize characteristics that civilizations tended to share. Common characteristics of civilizations included food surpluses, higher population densities, social stratification, systems of taxation, labor specialization, regular trade, and accumulated learning (or knowledge passed down from generation to generation). The list here is not all-inclusive by any means, but it indicates the complexity of the societies that scholars have labeled civilizations.

In addition to heated debates about its exact definition, civilization is a loaded term, meaning that it can contain a value judgment. If we use the term carelessly, it seems to indicate that some societies are deemed civilized and worthy of inclusion, while others are uncivilized and thus not worth our study. In part, our sensitivity to this issue is a response to the tendency of past historians, including many of those working in Europe in the 1800s, to assume that there was a natural progression from an uncivilized state to civilization. These historians viewed people who had values, ways of living, and religious beliefs different than theirs as uncivilized. They further believed that these allegedly uncivilized peoples were behind or needed to catch up with those who were civilized. Today, World Historians try to appreciate the great diversity of human experiences and consciously remove these sorts of value judgments. World Historians avoid assumptions that some societies in the past were better or further along than others. Therefore, many World Historians remain wary of the uncritical use of the term civilization.

For our purposes, let us leave aside any value judgments. Societies labeled as civilizations were not inherently better than any others. In fact, as we will see, civilizations demonstrated various vulnerabilities. Considering things like war, slavery, and the spread of diseases, there were sometimes advantages to living outside the nexus of civilizations. For example, in comparing societies, scholars have found that in many instances people residing in decentralized states were healthier and lived longer than did their counterparts in early civilizations. However, people living in societies with social stratification, labor specialization, and trade usually left more written records and archeological evidence, which historians can analyze to narrate our past. The available resources mean that civilizations tend to be better represented in the written historical records. As you read about past civilizations, keep in mind that historians are currently enhancing our understanding of societies that perhaps remained mobile, rejected hierarchies, or preserved their histories orally. These societies were also part of our shared past, even if they are harder to study or have received less scholarly attention.

This chapter focuses on early civilizations in the Fertile Crescent and Northeast Africa. The civilizations in these regions left written records. They also all initially had economies based on farming and developed alongside rivers. Their locations alongside rivers allowed populations in the Fertile Crescent and Northeast Africa to grow the surplus food that they used to support urbanization, social stratification, labor specialization, and trade.

2.3 QUESTIONS TO GUIDE YOUR READING

1. Explain why the Tigris and Euphrates Rivers were significant for ancient Mesopotamians.

2. Describe the characteristics of civilizations that were found in ancient Mesopotamia.

3. What does the *Epic of Gilgamesh* tell scholars about Mesopotamian values, views of the environment, and conceptions of the afterlife?

4. How did the rulers of ancient Mesopotamian empires attempt to bring together and control the people within their realms?

5. Describe the legacies of the civilization in ancient Mesopotamia.

6. Explain the central beliefs of Judaism that are evident in the early written tradition.

7. How did the United Kingdom of Israel develop and who were its key leaders?

8. Describe how the Israelites and their traditions have been influential.

9. How did the Nile River and the region's climate and geography influence the development of Egyptian civilization?

10. Which characteristics of civilizations were seen in Ancient Egypt?

11. What major continuities were evident throughout Dynastic Egypt?

12. Describe Egypt's intermediate periods.

13. Explain the significance of pyramids.

14. Describe the major innovations of the New Kingdom.

15. What are the legacies of Ancient Egypt?

16. Compare the civilizations of Mesopotamia and Egypt.

17. What were the defining features of Nubian civilization?

18. Describe Kerma and Kush's relationship with Egypt.

2.4 KEY TERMS

- Amarna Period
- Assyrian Empire
- Aten
- Cataract
- City-states
- Civilization
- Covenant
- Cuneiform
- Desiccation
- Divine kingships
- Empire
- Exodus
- Hammurabi's Code

- Hieroglyphics
- Kerma
- Kush
- Levant
- Meroe
- Meroitic
- Mesopotamia
- Middle Kingdom
- Monotheism
- Nebuchadnezzar II
- New Kingdom
- Nile River
- Nubia

- Old Kingdom
- Ostraca
- Palette of Narmer
- Polytheistic
- Prophets
- Pyramids

- Sargon of Akkad
- Sumerian King List
- The Ten Commandments
- Valley of Kings
- Western Deffufa
- Ziggurat

2.5 ANCIENT MESOPOTAMIA

Mesopotamia is located in an area known as the Fertile Crescent. Archeologists have found some of the earliest known sites of agricultural production in the Fertile Crescent. Although much of this region received little or irregular rainfall, the Tigris and Euphrates Rivers provided large amounts of freshwater, facilitating agricultural production and the development of early civilizations. The Greeks later recognized the significance of the river systems to these ancient societies and referred to the region as "the Land between the Rivers" or **Mesopotamia**.

The Tigris and Euphrates Rivers both originate in the Taurus Mountains of eastern Anatolia and flow southward to empty into the Persian Gulf. The rivers carry and deposit silt downstream, enriching the soil. In general, the richer soils and availability of water in areas that in the north otherwise had little rain, or else towards the south had concentrated months of rainfall followed by long, dry spells, encouraged settlement near the rivers. The areas closer to the Persian Gulf, known as Lower Mesopotamia, in particular, were attractive to early settlers because they had extremely fertile soils. People built some of the earliest cities, including Uruk, Eridu, and Ur, in Lower Mesopotamia.

While the Tigris and Euphrates Rivers did provide water to the region, their floods were unpredictable and could even be catastrophic when they washed away entire settlements. In response, the

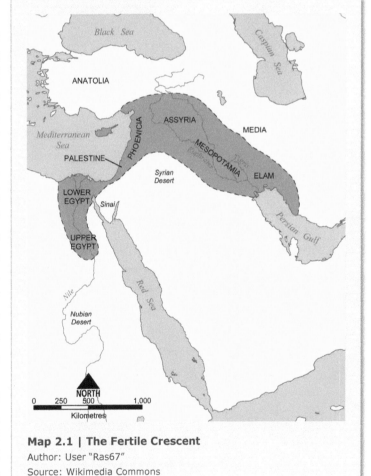

Map 2.1 | The Fertile Crescent
Author: User "Ras67"
Source: Wikimedia Commons
License: CC BY-SA 3.0

region's residents created irrigation canals and drainage ditches to control the flow of water. They also stored water in reservoirs to use during the dry months of the year. Additionally, in parts of Lower Mesopotamia, the courses of the rivers and their tributaries changed frequently, so people either had to move to follow the water's new path or divert a river to continue supplying water for their settlement. As regular access to water supported agricultural surpluses and population growth, people tended to fare better against the unpredictability of the floods, seasonal changes, and the rivers' changing courses when they lived in settlements capable of maintaining irrigation canals, drainage ditches, and water reservoirs.

The rivers offered another benefit to ancient Mesopotamians. Just as the rivers were definitely important to meet people's everyday needs for water and for agricultural production, so they also facilitated trade. While people made use of local resources, like mud to build their homes, in general, Lower Mesopotamia lacked other desired resources, including wood, stone, and precious metals. Traders were able to use the rivers to bring in these resources from Assyria, Anatolia, the Levant, and areas adjacent to the Persian Gulf. Early Mesopotamians also obtained

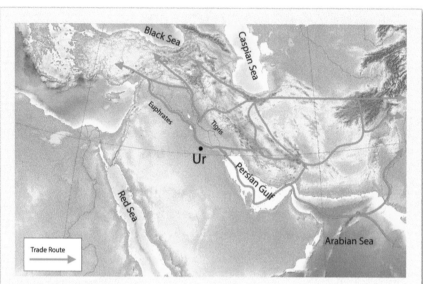

Map 2.2 | Trade Routes in Early Mesopotamia | In the third millennium BCE, people in Lower Mesopotamia used river routes to trade northward. They also used sea routes through the Persian Gulf, and they connected with traders to the east by crossing the Iranian Plateau.
Author: Corey Parson
Source: Original Work
License: CC BY-SA 4.0

goods from as far away as what today are northern Pakistan and India. Merchants used overland routes that crossed the Iranian Plateau and sea routes, exchanging Mesopotamian products like grains and textiles for luxury goods from the east. Royal cemeteries show that by 2500 BCE Mesopotamian elites were buried with a variety of imports, including beads brought from the Indus River Valley. The rivers and the overland trade routes also facilitated communication and, with it, the sharing of ideas and technologies.

2.6 SUMERIAN CITY-STATES

Lower Mesopotamia, or the southern areas of Mesopotamia towards the Persian Gulf, drew settlers, who moved to take advantage of rich soils and the availability of water in the area commonly known as Sumer. The people who lived in Sumer are generally referred to as

Sumerians. Prior to 3,000 BCE, Sumerians, whose origins remain a subject of debate, founded a number of independent cities in Lower Mesopotamia. In these cities, Sumerians had organized religions, centralized governments, social hierarchies, and access to trade networks. As these cities expanded, their leaders claimed control over adjacent territories, forming at least a dozen **city-states**, which became the basic organizational structure of Sumerian civilization in the third millennium BCE. By incorporating the surrounding territories into city-states, urban centers were able to draw on more resources.

Sumerian cities had certain characteristics in common. First, a temple complex or a ziggurat was usually the visual focus of the urban landscape. Sumerians believed that their entire city belonged to its main deity, and built a massive temple, the most important building in the city, to be the dwelling place of their city's main god or goddess. A complex that comfortably housed many of the priests and priestesses who served the city's deity surrounded each temple. In addition to attending to the religious needs of the community, temples complexes also owned land, managed industries, were involved in trade, and acted as banks. Their wide-ranging roles meant that temples often had additional outbuildings, like granaries and storage sheds, in the surrounding countryside. Sumerians were **polytheistic**, meaning they worshipped multiple gods and goddesses. Because Sumerians believed each god had a family, they also built smaller shrines and temples dedicated to these divine family members. Therefore, each city would have a number of temples while many Sumerian homes had small altars dedicated to other gods. Sometimes, urban temples or ritual spaces were built atop a **ziggurat,** a solid rectangular tower made of sun-dried mud bricks.

Figure 2.1 | The Great Ziggurat of Ur | Located in what is today the Dhi Qar Province of Iraq, Sumerians originally built the ziggurat in the Third Dynasty of Ur (c. 2100 BCE). It has been restored several times since, including fairly recently in the 1980s.
Author: User "GDK"
Source: Wikimedia Commons
License: CC BY 3.0

Archaeological evidence shows that temple complexes were expanded and rebuilt over time and, by the late third millennium BCE, temples in many of the Sumerian city-states were raised on platforms or else situated on a ziggurat. The towering architecture of the ziggurat stressed the significance of the temple to the surrounding community. The best-preserved ziggurat, the Great Ziggurat of Ur, was constructed with an estimated 720,000 baked bricks and rose to a height of about 100 feet. The people of Ur constructed this ziggurat for their patron deity, the moon goddess Nanna. They likely brought regular offerings to Nanna and also received food rations from the Great Ziggurat of Ur.

Viewing nature as unpredictable, people brought offerings to their city's temple complexes or ziggurat, hoping to please the gods who controlled the natural forces of their world. Priests and priestesses collected and redistributed the offerings, demonstrating the vital roles they played in Sumerian society. The relatively privileged position of priests and priestesses at the temple complex also shows Sumerian social stratification (the development of a hierarchy) and how agricultural surpluses supported the specialization of labor. Some of the early leaders of Sumerian cities may have been "priest-kings," who attained elevated positions through their association with the temples. The later rulers of city-states definitely supported the temples, claiming to be acting on behalf of the gods who brought divine favor to their followers.

Sumerian city-states had local rulers, who lived in large palaces, but most of these local rulers were not considered kings. So far, archeologists have dated the earliest known royal palaces to c. 2600 BCE and conclude that Sumerian city-states had centralized governments with secular rulers by at least that timeframe. While there does seem to have been a sense of inhabiting a shared space in Southern Mesopotamia, referred to as "the Land" in written records, city-states had distinctive identities. In part, their distinctive identities revolved around their main deity. The rulers of city-states alternately supported, competed with, and fought against one another. The **Sumerian King List** (Figure 2.2), a manuscript that listed early kings and described their reigns (with some presumably fictive and exaggerated elements), provides evidence of these alliances, competition, and war. For example, it describes En-mebarages as the second to last king of the 1st Dynasty of Kish, "...who carried away as spoil the weapons of the land of Elam, became king, and reigned 900 years..."[1] Local rulers often came to power after proving themselves militarily.

Figure 2.2 | The Sumerian King List
Author: Taiwania Justo
Source: Wikimedia Commons
License: Public Domain

Furthermore, the Sumerian King List recognized only rulers who had established control over multiple city-states as kings (with the title of *lugal* in the Sumerian language) belonging to distinct dynasties. While it lasted, a dynasty generally passed down the kingship through the male line. According to the Sumerian King List, the seat of power, held by hereditary kings, shifted from city-state to city-state with the rise and fall of dynasties through the third millennium BCE. Significantly, the Sumerian King List began its recorded history "when kingship came down from heaven," legitimizing secular kings through their association with gods.[2] Sumerian kings, often along with more local rulers, led armies, collected taxes, organized labor for state projects, and meted out justice. At the top of the hierarchy and with control over

---

1   J.N. Postgate, *Early Mesopotamia: Society and Economy at the Dawn of History*, (London: Routledge, 1994): 28.
2   Ibid.

multiple city-states, kings expected obedience from local rulers and their subjects, and support from the priests and priestesses of the temples.

Kings, local rulers, priests, and priestesses held influential positions in Sumerian societies. However, farmers, taken as a whole, made up an estimated 90% of the population. Other skilled people included animal-breeders, merchants, craftspeople, fishermen, doctors, soldiers, architects, and scribes. Surplus agricultural production collected as tribute as well as wealth generated by trade supported such labor specialization. One important outcome of labor specialization was innovation in metalworking. In approximately 2900 BCE, metalworkers began producing bronze, which was stronger than copper. Stronger weapons and farming tools gave Sumerians advantages when it came to combat and agricultural production.

Social stratification is further evident as some Sumerians and even institutions, including temples, owned slaves. Slaves performed a variety of tasks like construction, weaving, agricultural and domestic labor, tending animals, and even administrative work as scribes. Some slaves were chattel slaves, meaning that society treated them as property with no rights. Usually, chattel slaves were prisoners of war or slaves bought from outside communities. They were branded by barbers or tattoo artists and forced to work at the will of their masters. If they tried to run away, the law required slaves to be returned. The more widespread type of servitude in most Sumerians societies was likely debt slavery, which was generally temporary until a debtor paid off a loan and its interest. Over the past century or so, archaeologists have added a great deal to our understanding of Sumerian social distinctions through their work at numerous excavation sites, but many gaps in our knowledge still exist.

The archaeological discovery of cuneiform tablets at these excavation sites has aided efforts to learn about this civilization. Sumerians developed **cuneiform**, a written script of wedge shaped marks, around 3200 BCE. Cuneiform was one of the earliest, if not the very first, written script in the world. The Sumerian King List, discussed above, was recorded in cuneiform. Merchants, scribes, administrators, priests, and others kept written records describing financial transactions, court proceedings, administrative decisions, and architectural plans.

Figure 2.3 | Cuneiform | Cuneiform script on a clay tablet currently housed at the National Archaeological Museum in Tehran.
Author: A. Davey
Source: Wikimedia Commons
License: CC BY 2.0

They also wrote legends, epic poems, chants, and prayers. Most people were not literate, so scribes—who had been specially trained in scribal schools—generated many of the records. While in school, in addition to copying written passages, scribes learned arithmetic. The Sumerians system of arithmetic was based on the number 60, which we still use to divide time into hours, minutes, and seconds. Scribes used styluses made of reed to write on clay tablets that were dried and could be stored. The discovery of cuneiform tablets has greatly aided archaeologists, but only a small percentage of the tablets found to date have been translated.

Using archaeological and written evidence, scholars have pieced together what they can about everyday life for Sumerians, though some questions remain. For instance, it has been a challenge to determine the layout of urban spaces beyond the prominence of the temples and the relative grandeur of palaces. From archaeological finds, scholars suspect that Sumerian cities were divided into neighborhoods by occupation and according to kinship groups, but uncertainties about specifics linger. Legal documents and tax records show that people owned property in both the cities and the countryside. Also, evidence suggests social stratification, as some Sumerians owned fairly large chunks of land, while others had much smaller plots or presumably no land at all. Wills, court proceedings, and temple documents show that land and temple offices were usually bought or else acquired through military or other service to the state. A man inherited land, property, offices, and their attendant obligations to the state (like reoccurring military service) from his father. The eldest son seems to have frequently inherited a larger share than younger brothers and have been given control over the family home. He was tasked with performing regular rituals to honor dead ancestors, who were usually buried underneath the home. From the written documents, we also get glimpses into other aspects of Sumerian life, like marriage and divorce.

Sumerians viewed marriage as a contract between two families and, as a result, the male heads of the two families arranged a couple's marriage. Documents show that both families contributed resources to seal the union or complete the marriage contract. The man's family gave gifts or money and hosted a feast, while the woman's family amassed a dowry. Although a woman did not automatically receive an inheritance upon the death of her father, she could expect (and use the court system to make sure she got) to receive a dowry, even if it came from her father's estate after his death. Divorce was possible but sometimes led to social ostracism or even punishment if there were accusations of misconduct, such consequences being especially the case for the woman. Records indicate that polygamy was not common, but wealthier men did keep slave-girls as concubines. Overall, Sumerians considered marriage an essential institution in that it brought families together and ensured the continuation of the family lineage.

Legends, myths, poems, and literary texts tell us about Sumerians, too. For example, we can explore their values and views of the afterlife through reading the *Epic of Gilgamesh*. The *Epic of Gilgamesh* relates the adventures of Gilgamesh, a legendary king, who may have lived around 2700 BCE. The epic has multiple versions and was told orally before it was first written down in cuneiform in about 2000 BCE. The epic follows the heroic exploits of Gilgamesh and his companion, Enkidu, to emphasize the importance of values such as loyalty and humility. In one section, the epic describes a very gloomy afterlife where "people see no light, they sit in darkness,"[3] reflecting Mesopotamian beliefs that the afterlife was miserable for all, even those who had lived virtuously. Additionally, it portrays the environment as potentially violent and hostile as in its

---

3   Excerpt from: *The Epic of Gilgamesh*, trans. Nancy Sandars (New York: Penguin Books, 1960), http://web.archive.org/web/20010217041824/http://www.humanities.ccny.cuny.edu/history/reader/gilgames.htm

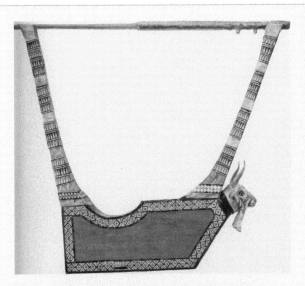

Figure 2.4 | The Queen's Lyre | The Queen's Lyre is a reconstructed musical instrument modeled after a lyre found by archaeologist Leonard Wooley in one of the graves at the Royal Cemetery of Ur. The original instrument has been dated to c. 2500 BCE. The reconstructed instrument is held at the British Museum in London.
Author: User "Fae"
Source: Wikimedia Commons
License: Public Domain

flood story, which in some ways resembles the account of Noah and the flood found in Genesis. Ultimately, Gilgamesh fails at his quest to find eternal life but learns to work for the glory of the gods and for worthwhile human achievements.

Other archaeological finds and the written documents also give some hint of the wider popular culture and artistic conventions in ancient Mesopotamia. For example, cuneiform tablets with pictures of dancers and singers, as well as instruments found in graves, suggest that Sumerians placed importance on music, using it for entertainment and ritual purposes. Trying to learn more about Sumerian music, scholars and other enthusiasts have replicated these instruments and presented their best estimation of Sumerian scales and tuning. The documentary evidence suggests that hymns from the ancient Sumerian city-states were shared with later Mesopotamian empires and even spread into the Mediterranean world.

2.7 MESOPOTAMIAN EMPIRES

In the second half of the third millennium BCE, Sumerian city-states fought each other, and dynasties rose and fell. Kings consolidated power over multiple city-states in the region. Then, King Sargon of Akkad enlarged the scale by conquering the Sumerian city-states and parts of Syria, Anatolia, and Elam. In doing so, he created one of the world's first empires in approximately 2334 BCE. For generations, Mesopotamian literature celebrated the Akkadian Empire (c. 2334 – 2100 BCE) that King Sargon founded. Like the Akkadian Empire, three subsequent empires, the Babylonian Empire (c. 1792 – 1595 BCE), the Assyrian Empire (c. 900 – 612 BCE), and the Neo-Babylonian Empire (c. 605 – 539 BCE), also ruled large parts of Mesopotamia and the Fertile Crescent.

2.7.1 The Akkadian Empire (c. 2334 – 2100 BCE)

Sargon of Akkad founded the first empire in Mesopotamia. Legends about Sargon of Akkad stress that he rose from obscurity to become a famous, powerful king. While the legends all tend to describe him as coming from humble origins and rising to the top using his own wits, there are many variations. One much later Babylonian tablet, from the seventh century BCE, describes his background as descendent of a high priestess and an anonymous father. His mother hid her pregnancy and the birth of Sargon, secreting him away in a wicker basket on a river, where he was

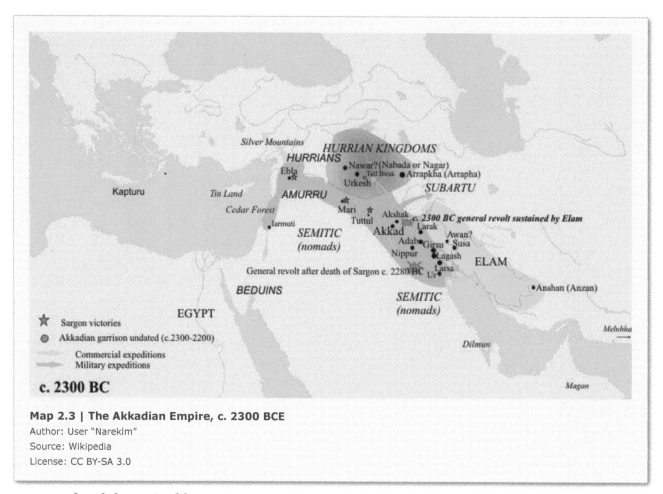

Map 2.3 | The Akkadian Empire, c. 2300 BCE
Author: User "Nareklm"
Source: Wikipedia
License: CC BY-SA 3.0

rescued and then raised by Aqqi, a water-drawer. This version of the legend links Sargon with a more elite family through his birth-mother, a high priestess, but also shows how he had to advance himself up to king after being adopted by the rather more humble figure of a water-drawer.

From his allegedly humble origins, Sargon of Akkad conquered Sumerian city-states one by one, creating an **empire,** or a large territory, encompassing numerous states, ruled by a single authority. It's quite possible that Sargon of Akkad's predecessor, who claimed to rule over the large region stretching from the Mediterranean Sea to the Persian Gulf, began the process of building the empire, but Sargon is remembered for accomplishing the task. One of the reasons we attribute the empire to him is his use of public monuments. He had statues, stellae (tall, upright pillars), and other monuments built throughout his realm to celebrate his military victories and to build a sense of unity within his empire. Archaeologists have not found the empire's capital city, Akkad. However, from the available information, archaeologists have estimated its location, placing it to the north of the early Mesopotamian city-states, including Ur and Sumer. It is clear that Sargon of Akkad turned the empire's capital at Akkad into one of the wealthiest and most powerful cities in the world. According to documentary sources, the city's splendor stood as another symbol of Sargon's greatness. The city grew into a cosmopolitan center especially because of its role in trade. Akkadian rulers seized and taxed trade goods, with trade routes extending as far as India. Sargon ruled the empire for over fifty years. His sons, grandson, and great grandson attempted to hold the empire together. After about 200 years, attacks from neighboring peoples caused the empire to fall. After the fall of the Akkadian Empire, Hammurabi founded the next empire in the region in 1792 BCE.

2.7.2 The Babylonian Empire (1792 – 1595 BCE)

Hammurabi, who aspired to follow Sargon's example, created the next empire in the region, the Babylonian Empire. With well-disciplined foot soldiers armed with copper and bronze weapons, he conquered Mesopotamian city-states, including Akkad and Sumer, to create an empire with its capital at Babylon. Although he had other achievements, Hammurabi is most famous for the law code etched into a stele that bears his name, the Stele of Hammurabi.

The Stele of Hammurabi records a comprehensive set of laws. Codes of law existed prior to Hammurabi's famous stele, but **Hammurabi's Code** gets a lot of attention because it is still intact and has proven very influential. As seen in Figure 2.5, the upper part of the stele depicts Hammurabi standing in front of the Babylonian god of justice, from whom Hammurabi derives his power and legitimacy. The lower portion of the stele contains the collection of 282 laws. One particularly influential principle in the code is the law of retaliation, which demands "an eye for an eye, a tooth for a tooth." The code listed offenses and their punishments, which often varied by social class. While symbolizing the power of the King Hammurabi and associating him with justice, the code of law also attempted to unify people within the empire and establish common standards for acceptable behavior. An excerpt of Hammurabi's Code appears below:

6. If anyone steal the property of a temple or of the court, he shall be put to death, and also the one who receives the stolen thing from him shall be put to death.

8. If any one steal cattle or sheep, or an ass, or a pig or a goat, if it belong to a god or to the court, the thief shall pay thirtyfold therefore; if they belonged to a freed man of the king he shall pay tenfold; if the thief has nothing with which to pay he shall be put to death.

Figure 2.5 | The Stele of Hammurabi
Author: User "Mbzt"
Source: Wikimedia Commons
License: CC BY 3.0

15. If any one receive into his house a runaway male or female slave of the court, or of a freedman, and does not bring it out at the public proclamation of the major domus, the master of the house shall be put to death.

53. If any one be too lazy to keep his dam in proper condition, and does not so keep it; if then the dam break and all the fields be flooded, then shall he in whose dam the break occurred be sold for money, and the money shall replace the corn which he has caused to be ruined.

108. If a tavern-keeper (feminine) does not accept corn according to gross weight in payment of drink, but takes money, and the price of the drink is less than that of the corn, she shall be convicted and thrown into the water.

110. If a "sister of god" open a tavern, or enter a tavern to drink, then shall this woman be burned to death.

127. If any one "point the finger" (slander) at a sister of a god or the wife of any one, and can not prove it, this man shall be taken before the judges and his brow shall be marked. (by cutting the skin or perhaps hair)

129. If a man's wife be surprised (in flagrante delicto) with another man, both shall be tied and thrown into the water, but the husband may pardon his wife and the king his slaves.

137. If a man wish to separate from a woman who has borne him children, or from his wife who has borne him children: then he shall give that wife her dowry, and a part of the usufruct of field, garden, and property, so that she can rear her children. When she has brought up her children, a portion of all that is given to the children, equal as that of one son, shall be given to her. She may then marry the man of her heart.

195. If a son strike his father, his hands shall be hewn off.

196. If a man put out the eye of another man his eye shall be put out. (An eye for an eye)

197. If he break another man's bone, his bone shall be broken.

198. If he put out the eye of a freed man, or break the bone of a freed man, he shall pay one gold mina.

199. If he put out the eye of a man's slave, or break the bone of a man's slave, he shall pay one-half of its value.

202. If any one strike the body of a man higher in rank than he, he shall receive sixty blows with an ox-whip in public.

203. If a free-born man strike the body of another free-born man or equal rank, he shall pay one gold mina.

205. If the slave of a freed man strike the body of a freed man, his ear shall be cut off.[4]

Hammurabi also improved infrastructure, promoted trade, employed effective administrative practices, and supported productive agriculture. For example, he sponsored the building of roads and the creation of a postal service. He also maintained irrigation canals and facilitated trade all along the Persian Gulf. After Hammurabi's death, his successors lost territory. The empire declined, shrinking in size. The Hittites, from Anatolia, eventually sacked the city of Babylon in 1595 BCE, bringing about the official end of the Babylonian Empire.

2.7.3 The Assyrian Empire (c. 900 – 612 BCE)

The **Assyrian Empire**, which saw its height of power at the end of the first millennium to the seventh century BCE, was larger than any empire that preceded it.

Dominating the region, its well-equipped soldiers used their stronger iron weapons to extend the empire's control through Mesopotamia, Syria, parts of Anatolia, Palestine, and up the Nile into Egypt. They used siege warfare, along with battering rams, tunnels, and moveable towers, to get past the defenses of cities. The Assyrians had a large army (with perhaps as many as 150,000 soldiers) that utilized a core of infantry, a cavalry, as well as chariots. As part of their military strategy, the Assyrians purposefully tried to inspire fear in their enemies; they decapitated conquered kings, burnt cities to the ground, destroyed crops, and dismembered defeated enemy soldiers. One Assyrian soldier claimed:

> In strife and conflict I besieged [and] conquered the city. I felled 3,000 of their fighting men with the sword...I captured many troops alive: I cut off of some of their arms [and] hands; I cut off of others their noses, ears, [and] extremities. I gouged out the eyes of many troops. I made one pile of the living [and] one of heads. I hung their heads on trees around the city.[5]

The Assyrians expected these methods to deter potential rebellions and used their spoils of war, like precious metals and livestock, to finance further military campaigns. After conquering an area, they conscripted men into their army, and employed resettlement and deportation as techniques to get laborers where they wanted them and deal with communities who opposed

---

4   "The Code of Hammurabi, c. 1780 BCE." *Ancient History Sourcebook.* Fordham University. https://legacy.fordham.edu/halsall/ancient/hamcode.asp#text

5   Quoted in Erika Belibtreau, "Grisly Assyrian Record of Torture and Death," http://faculty.uml.edu/ethan_Spanier/Teaching/documents/CP6.0AssyrianTorture.pdf

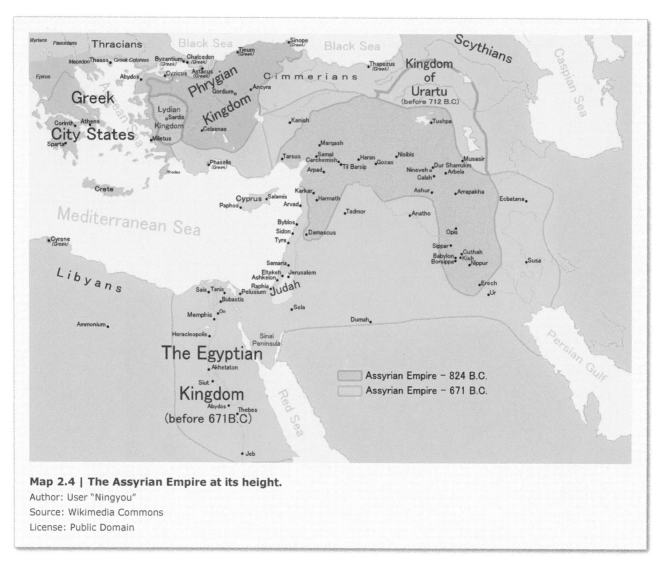

Map 2.4 | The Assyrian Empire at its height.
Author: User "Ningyou"
Source: Wikimedia Commons
License: Public Domain

their regime. They also collected annual tributes that were apparently high enough to, at least occasionally, spur rebellions despite the Assyrians' reputation for violent retribution.

In addition to its military strength, the Assyrian empire also stands out for the size of its cities and its administrative developments. The empire's biggest cities, such as Nineveh and Assur, each had several million people living within them. Administratively, kings ruled Assyria, appointing governors to oversee provinces and delegates to keep tabs on the leaders of allied states. There were between 100 and 150 governors, delegates, and top officials entrusted by the king with ruling in his place and helping him maintain the empire. In the later centuries of the Assyrian Empire, kings chose these officials on the basis of merit and loyalty. Kings met with large groups of officials for rituals, festivals, and military campaigns. Evidence of such meetings has led some scholars to propose the possibility that the king and his officials might have worked together in something resembling a parliamentary system, though there is no scholarly consensus on the point. Ultimately, the Assyrian Empire became too large to control; rebellions occurred with more frequency and were difficult for its overextended military to quell. The empire fell after the conquest of Nineveh in 612 BCE.

2.7.4 The New Babylonian Empire (c. 626 – 539 BCE)

With the weakening of the Assyrian Empire, the New Babylonian Empire began to dominate Mesopotamia. Lasting for less than 100 years, the New Babylonian Empire is best known for its ruler, **Nebuchadnezzar II**, and its great architectural projects. As described in the Hebrew Scriptures (also known as the Old Testament), Nebuchadnezzar II, who ruled from 605 – 562 BCE, was a ruthless leader. He gained notoriety for destroying the city of Jerusalem and deporting many of the city's Jews to Babylon. The captive Jews suffered in exile, as they were not allowed to return to their homeland. Nebuchadnezzar II also rebuilt Babylon with fortresses, temples, and enormous palaces. He associated the New Babylonian Empire with the glory of ancient Babylonia by reviving elements of Sumerian and Akkadian culture. For example, he had artists restore ancient artwork and celebrated the kings of old, like Hammurabi. Nebuchadnezzar is often also credited with rebuilding the city's ziggurat, *Etemanaki*, or the "Temple of the Foundation of Heaven and Earth." When completed, the ziggurat rose several stories above the city and seemed to reach to the heavens. Some scholars claim that the Babylonian ziggurat was the famous Tower of Babel described in the Old Testament. Another one of Nebuchadnezzar's purported projects, the Hanging Gardens of Babylon, was considered by the later Greek historian Herodotus to be one of the Seven Wonders of the World. According to legend, Nebuchadnezzar had the hanging gardens built for his wife. He made the desert bloom to remind her of her distant homeland; the elaborate gardens planted on rooftops and terraces were designed so that the plants' leaves would spill down high walls. Since definitive archaeological evidence of the Hanging Gardens of Babylon has not been found, scholars continue to debate its most likely location and even its very existence. After the death of Nebuchadnezzar II, outside military pressures as well as internal conflict weakened the empire until the much larger Persian Empire conquered the New Babylonian Empire in 539 BCE.

2.8 THE SIGNIFICANCE OF MESOPOTAMIA FOR WORLD HISTORY

Mesopotamia saw the emergence of some of the first cities and the world's first empires. The city-states of the region flourished from about 3000 to 2300 BCE. Then, Sargon of Akkad and subsequent rulers built empires, expanding their control and influence over even larger territories.

There were cultural links and commonalities found in the Sumerian city-states of the third millennium BCE. With agricultural production dependent on access to water, cities initially grew in Southern Mesopotamia near rivers, namely the Tigris and Euphrates Rivers and their tributaries. Sumerians tried to control their environment using irrigation, drainage ditches, water reserves, and other methods. With unpredictable floods and other environmental challenges, the Sumerians viewed nature as hostile and their expectations of the afterlife tended to be pessimistic. Their understanding of nature as unpredictable also spurred engineering innovations as Sumerians prepared for floods, water shortages, and other natural events. While farming was the mainstay of their economies, city-states were also involved in robust long-distance trade networks, which allowed them to garner the many resources not available in their region. These city-states alternately allied with, competed against, and waged war on one another, with kingship emerging as rulers dominated multiple city-states. As evidenced by the centrality of temples and the belief that kingship came from heaven, religion was of fundamental importance to these societies. Archaeologists have also uncovered ample evidence of social stratification and labor specialization in these ancient city-states. Archeologists have been able to recognize Sumerian developments, in part, because the Sumerians left behind a wealth of information documented in cuneiform, one of the world's first written scripts. Scholars have begun to describe life in ancient Sumerian societies and appreciate the many Sumerian achievements, like those in math, where they introduced a computation system based on 60 (which we still use to divide time and in geometry as a circle has 360°). Overall, Sumerians were innovators, with some of the first cities, one of the first systems of writing, notable achievements in engineering and architecture, the creation of larger political entities, and more.

Starting with the Akkadian Empire, four empires controlled vast territories in Mesopotamia and the Fertile Crescent. Over a period of almost 1800 years, these empires brought together diverse communities, often by military conquest and force. The empires facilitated trade, and spread ideas and culture. Their rulers developed administrative, military, and other techniques to try to ensure compliance and recognition of their authority. As intended, the rulers and the cities they built live on in legends, even though their empires eventually withered and fell.

2.9 THE ISRAELITES AND ANCIENT ISRAEL

The Israelites, "or children of Israel," were Semetic-speakers who lived in Canaan and traced their descent back to Abraham through his grandson Israel. Hebrew tradition begins their history with Abraham's departure from Ur in southern Mesopotamia (see Map 2.1). Therefore, Abraham is important in Jewish tradition, as he has been recognized as the first Jew, the patriarch from whom all Jews trace their descent, and a role model. As described in the Hebrew Scriptures, known to Christians as the Old Testament, Abraham also made a covenant with God, which blessed his descendants. Jews, Christians, and Muslims of today all recognize Abraham as a significant figure, though these major monotheistic religions view him a little differently. Respect for Abraham by believers in all three of these religions is just one indication that the world's three major monotheistic religions are connected. Examining these connections reveals the extraordinary contributions that the Israelites made to World History. The Israelites were highly influential in developing the idea of **monotheism**, or belief in one god. Furthermore, they recorded their history orally at first, until their tradition was written down in the Hebrew Scriptures (alternatively referred to as the Tanakh, the Hebrew Bible, or the Old Testament of the Christian Bible). The Hebrew Scriptures has been one of the most important texts ever written.

Eventually, by the end of the second millennium BCE (likely between 1200 and 1000 BCE), the Israelites established small kingdoms in the **Levant**. The Levant refers to areas adjacent to the eastern Mediterranean; in the ancient world, it comprised roughly the area from southern Anatolia through coastal areas of the eastern Mediterranean south and westward to the Egyptian delta. The Israelite kingdoms were concentrated along the Mediterranean coast in what are today Israel and the contested territory of the West Bank/Palestine.

Much debate exists amongst scholars about the sources used to reconstruct the history of the Israelites with much of the debate revolving around the use and interpretation of religious texts, particularly the Hebrew Scriptures. Right now, scholars rely fairly heavily on the Hebrew Scriptures to discuss periods before about 1200 BCE because other sources just do not exist. Some main points of contention have centered on dates, the purpose of religious texts, the reality that the Hebrew Scriptures were written centuries after the events they described, and the relationship between the scriptures and historical fact. Additionally, there has been back and forth discussion about whether archaeological finds confirm or disprove the narrative in the religious texts. These heated debates have led some scholars to question whether it is even possible to write a history of the ancient Israelites. For our purposes, this section will give an overview of Hebrew tradition and, using archaeological and collaborating evidence when possible, describe the development of the Israelite civilization.

2.10 EARLY ISRAELITES

By leading people out of Ur, his homeland in Southern Mesopotamia, to eventually settle in Canaan, later called Palestine, Abraham began the traditional history of the Israelites. According to Hebrew tradition, even before leaving Ur, Abraham taught his followers about the existence of a single, creator god and rejected the idol-worship and sin of Ur. The narrative continues to explain how when Abraham agreed to God's directive to leave his homeland, God blessed him and all of his descendants. God entered into a **covenant** with Abraham, saying, "...And I will make you into a great nation, and I will bless you, and I will make your name great...and by you all the families of the earth shall bless themselves."[6] Jews recognize this covenant as indicating their special relationship with God, and it remains one of the most important aspects of the Jewish faith.

Tradition recounts how several generations later Abraham's grandson, Israel (also called Jacob), had twelve sons, who became the ancestors of the Twelve Tribes of Israel. One of these twelve sons, Joseph, led followers from Canaan during a famine to settle in Egypt. As the biblical text describes, the Israelites were prosperous at first and were becoming powerful, leading the Egyptian pharaoh to fear their influence. To try to stem the Israelite influence, the pharaoh put restrictions on births and forced them into slave labor. Then, Moses, whose mother had secreted him away in a waterproof basket on the Nile River, played an important role in delivering his people from subjugation. According to Hebrew tradition, God tasked Moses with leading his people out of Egypt, a flight to freedom called **Exodus**. Moses led "the children of Israel" into Sinai, where they entered into the Sinai Covenant. This covenant bound all Israelites into a pact with God. Israelites agreed to worship God alone and obey his law, while God confirmed the place of the Israelites as his "Chosen People," whom he would protect. As part of the covenant, Israelites agreed to follow **the Ten Commandments**. According to Hebrew tradition, God gave the Ten Commandments to the Israelites at Mount Sinai, instructing the Israelites to worship only him, keep the Sabbath, and honor their parents. The Ten Commandments also prohibit idolatry, blasphemy, murder, adultery, theft, dishonesty, and coveting.

---

6   As quoted in "Abraham and the Covenant," Israel and Judaism Studies. http://www.ijs.org.au/Abraham-and-the-Cove-nant/default.aspx

These written traditions established important elements of the Jewish faith. For example, the Hebrew Scriptures trace Jewish descent from the Hebrew patriarchs: Abraham, Isaac, Israel (alternatively known as Jacob), and the twelve sons of Israel. They also describe the transition to monotheism and the covenant relationship between God and "the children of Israel." Israelites believed in one god, Yahweh, who created and ruled over everything in the universe, and overall, they perceived Yahweh as being just and merciful. The ideas that there is a single, universal god and that his laws apply to everyone have been defining tenets of other monotheistic religions. Subsequent written and oral traditions, like the Talmud, reflect further development of Jewish beliefs, ethics, laws, and practice.

2.11 THE UNITED KINGDOM OF ISRAEL

After Exodus, the Israelites resettled in Canaan and in time began to unify. They formed kingdoms in the Levant just prior to 1000 BCE. King Saul (c. 1030 – 1009 BCE), a member of one of the Twelve Tribes of Israel, established the first Israelite monarchy, but ruled over a fairly limited territory and died in battle with the Philistines. He was crowned king and began the process of unification, but did not completely defeat his enemies and finish unification before he died. His son, King David, (d. 969 BCE), is often portrayed as Israel's greatest ruler or a model king. He established the United Kingdom of Israel, with its capital at Jerusalem. King David's successor, his son Solomon, further shaped the kingdom.

In popular memory, King David is probably most remembered for defeating Goliath. Historical traditions also celebrate him for expanding the borders of a newly unified Israel, contributing to the Book of Psalms, and, in Christian tradition, for being a forbear of Jesus. David was a "warrior king," who defeated both internal and external enemies to unite Israel. He maintained a large standing army that helped extend his influence and create neighboring tributary states. With control of trade routes and tribute coming in from neighboring territories, Israel became a wealthy state under David. With this wealth, David began to build Jerusalem into the capital city of the Israelites, with further plans to build a temple to house the Ark of the Covenant (which according to Hebrew tradition held the Ten Commandments). David died before building this temple, but tradition credits him with other achievements, including composing many of the hymns and prayers in the Book of Psalms. Like Abraham, David is considered an important figure by Jews, Christians, and Muslims.

King Solomon, David's son, ruled a mostly peaceful realm. He accomplished his father's goal of building the first Jewish temple in Jerusalem. The temple exemplified monumental architecture and became a focal point for the Jews of Jerusalem. Its ruins, known as the Western Wall or the Wailing Wall, are still a site of Jewish prayer and pilgrimage. Solomon also directed the building of a royal palace, a defensive wall around the city of Jerusalem, and fortresses along the kingdom's frontier. Administratively, Solomon set up twelve districts, overseen by purveyors, who collected tribute in kind (usually as crops or foodstuffs). Each of the twelve districts was charged with supplying the king and the court for one month a year. Finally, Solomon used treaties and reciprocal trade agreements to maintain relatively peaceful relationships with Israel's neighbors. He also forged diplomatic relations through marriage; according to scripture, he had 700 wives! After Solomon's death, what had been the United Kingdom of Israel split into two pieces: Israel and Judah. Over the long term, some of Solomon's policies, including forced labor and tributary payments, likely contributed to the divide.

After the decline of the United Kingdom of Israel, Hebrew tradition describes the significance of great **prophets** or teachers, who spoke on behalf of god and set moral and ethical standards for the whole community. Yahweh sent these prophets to warn the Israelites that they were not abiding by their covenant. The prophets during this later period, especially Jeremiah and Second Isaiah, cultivated a new conceptualization of the covenant, which was much more personal as it was a relationship between Yahweh and each individual.

The Assyrians and later the Greeks and then the Romans brought parts of the former United Kingdom of Israel under their rule. These conquests and persecution forced members of the Jewish population into exile. This conceptualization of being members of a **diaspora,** that is, a scattered people who desire to return to their homeland, has played an important part in the

Map 2.5 | The United Kingdom of Israel | The map shows the unified state in blue, as well as the surrounding territories that paid tribute to the United Kingdom of Israel.
Author: Regno di Davide
Source: Wikimedia Commons
License: CC BY-SA 3.0

formation of a Jewish identity. Also, in part, due to this history, preservation of cultural and religious heritage has become an enduring objective of Jews.

2.12 THE IMPORTANCE OF THE ISRAELITES AND ANCIENT ISRAEL

The Israelites left an extraordinary religious and ethical legacy. They were some of the first monotheists, worshipping a single god, whom they referred to as Yahweh. Their religious texts from the ancient world, including the Hebrew Scriptures, served as the foundational texts of Judaism. The Hebrew Scriptures were also the basis of the Christian Old Testament, and Islam recognizes parts of the scriptures as divine revelations. There were other, widespread religious influences as well. For example, Christians and Muslims consider many of the figures, including Abraham, Moses, and David, and teachings, like the Ten Commandments, from the Hebrew Scriptures to be very important. Furthermore, the Hebrew Scriptures contained the idea that everyone, regardless of status, was bound to obey the law.

The United Kingdom of Israel was a "golden age," associated with the creation of a unified, wealthy state with its new capital in Jerusalem. This civilization had well-developed religious traditions, political power vested in a king, monumental architecture, and administrative innovations. It also maintained a strong military, multiple tributary states, long-distance trade networks, and well-established diplomatic relationships with foreign states.

2.13 ANCIENT EGYPT

In our study of World History, ancient Egypt serves as an excellent example of a complex society with cross-cultural connections, adaption to and control over changing environments, and sophisticated political and religious developments. All of these themes are evident in an examination of the origins of Egypt. Egyptian leaders unified Upper and Lower Egypt around 3100 BCE, creating a powerful ancient state. Developments in the millennia preceding unification, including the sharing of innovations and responses to environmental change, set the stage for the emergence of the Egyptian civilization.

Cross-cultural connections introduced the people of Northeast Africa to domesticated wheat and barley, two of the crops that they grew and whose surpluses supported the process of social differentiation and eventually the pharaonic, elite, and skilled classes of ancient Egypt. People in Northeast Africa had likely been gathering wild barley since before 10,000 BCE. However, sharing in the knowledge spreading from the Fertile Crescent around 7,000 BCE, they began cultivating wheat and barley and also keeping domesticated animals, including sheep and goats. At that time, agricultural production and herding were possible in areas that are today part of the Sahara Desert. The period was much wetter than now. People in the region settled into small communities, and archaeological evidence of hearths, grinding stones, and storage silos show the growth of settlements in areas that today are not well watered enough for agricultural production. The presence of crocodile bones, along with similar pottery styles, also suggest a history of contact between communities emerging along the Nile River and these settlements farther west. However, environmental change was leading to the **desiccation** or drying out of areas not adjacent to the Nile River, and by about 5,000 BCE, it was no longer possible to farm much beyond the floodplain of the Nile River. Many people adapted by moving towards the Nile River, and the Nile River became increasingly important to Egypt's populations.

The **Nile River** flows south to north, fed by two main river systems: the White Nile and the Blue Nile. The White Nile flows steadily throughout the year and has its origins in the Great Lakes Region of East Africa. The Blue Nile originates in the Ethiopian highlands, and brings floodwaters up past the first **cataract** in the summers. (The first cataract lies roughly at Aswan on the map in Map 2.6.) Cataracts are generally considered impassable by boat due to their shallows, rocks, and rapids. Comparatively, the flood plain of the Nile River is narrow, leading, especially with the desiccation of the surrounding areas, to high population densities close to the river. The winds also blow north to south, in the opposite direction of the river flow, thus facilitating trade and contact between Upper Egypt (to the south) and Lower Egypt (to the north). Upper and Lower Egypt lie north of the first cataract, usually allowing river traffic to proceed uninterrupted throughout the territory. Egyptian views of the Nile generally recognized the river's centrality to life as demonstrated in the "Hymn to the Nile," dated to approximately 2100 BCE. The praise-filled ode to the Nile River begins, "Hail to thee, O Nile! Who manifests thyself over this land, and comes to give life to Egypt."[7] The course of the Nile River definitely impacted settlement patterns, while the river also allowed for trade and the development of larger agricultural communities.

At the tail end of that era of desiccation, from about 3600 to 3300 BCE, complex societies formed in areas adjacent to the Nile River. These communities exerted increased influence over their environments, exhibited social differentiation, and showed evidence of labor specialization. For example, people in the settlements of Naganda and Hierakonpolis in Upper Egypt cleared trees and built dykes, canals, and early irrigation systems. By about 3500 BCE, they used these methods to quadruple the amount of cleared, arable land and could support population densities of up to one thousand people per square mile. Just as one example, recent archaeological finds at Hierakonpolis also show evidence of both social differential and specialization with separate burials for the settlement's elite, the oldest known painted tomb, and the remnants of a large-scale brewery, capable of producing up to 300 gallons of beer a day. It is believed that early leaders in Naganda, Hierakonpolis, and similar communities cemented their roles by claiming control over the environment as rainmakers or commanders of the floods. Over time, some of these leaders created **divine kingships**, asserting their right to even more power and access to resources, power that they legitimized by claiming

Map 2.6 | The Path of the Nile | The White Nile originates near Lake Victoria, in the Great Lakes region of East Africa. The Blue Nile flows from the Ethiopian Highlands. Both rivers merge at Khartoum, in present day Sudan, and flow northward to empty into the Mediterranean Sea.
Author: User "Hel-hama"
Source: Wikimedia Commons
License: CC BY-SA 3.0

---

7   "Hymn to the Nile, c. 2100 BCE." *Ancient History Sourcebook* Fordham University. http://legacy.fordham.edu/halsall/ancient/hymn-nile.asp

special relationships with, or even descent from, gods. Once Egypt was unified, pharaohs ruled as divine kings, as the personification of the gods. They promised order in the universe. When things went well, the pharaohs were credited with agricultural productivity and the success of the state. There was no separation between religion and the state in ancient Egypt.

The **Palette of Narmer** (see Figure 2.6 and Figure 2.7), which is used to date the unification of Egypt, shows signs that King Narmer legitimized his rule, in part, by claiming a special relationship with the gods. King Narmer, who is referred to in some text as Menes, is commonly recognized as the first unifier of Upper (to the south) and Lower (to the north) Egypt in approximately 3100 BCE (see Map 2.7). Unification brought together Egypt from the first cataract at Aswan to the Nile Delta. The Palette of Narmer, which was found in Hierakonpolis, shows King Narmer's conquest of both regions. The right side in Figure 2.6 shows him slaying an enemy of Upper Egypt. The largest figure, Narmer is wearing the crown of Upper Egypt and beheading a rival king, while standing atop conquered enemies. The left side also shows him as a conqueror, wearing the crown of Lower Egypt and directing flag bearers to mark his victory. Religious imagery appears in the inclusion of the goddess Hathor at the top of the palette as well as the falcon, a reference to Horus, the patron god of Hierakonpolis, who later in dynastic Egypt became the god of sun and kingship.

Figure 2.6 | Both Sides of the Palette of Narmer
Author: User "Jean88"
Source: Wikimedia Commons
License: CC0 1.0

Figure 2.7 | Detail of Palette of Narmer | Close-up of the left side of the Palette of Narmer. Note the larger figure of King Narmer, with celebratory flag bearers preceding him.
Author: User "NebMaatRa"
Source: Wikimedia Commons
License: CC BY-SA 3.0

Both sides of the Palette of Narmer also have some of the earliest known hieroglyphs. **Hieroglyphics** emerged as written text, combining pictograms (a pictorial symbol for a word or phrase) and phonograms (a symbol representing a sound), during the period of unification. Tax assessment and collection likely necessitated the initial development of Hieroglyphics. Ancient Egyptians eventually used three different scripts: Hieroglyphic, Hieratic, and Demotic. Hieroglyphics remained the script of choice for ritual texts. Students of Egyptian history are most familiar with hieroglyphics as they were usually what artists used to record the history of Egypt's elite. For example, skilled artisans used hieroglyphs to chronicle glorified accounts of their patrons' lives on the sides of their tombs. The Egyptians developed Hieratic and Demotic, the two other scripts, slightly later and used them for administrative, commercial, and many other purposes. The Egyptian administration tended to use ink and papyrus to maintain its official records. On the other hand, literate people used **ostraca,** pieces of broken pottery and chips of limestone, for less formal notes and communications. Over the past decades, archaeologists have uncovered a treasure trove of ostraca that start to tell us about the lives of the literate elite and skilled craftsmen. Just like Mesopotamia, ancient Egypt had one of the oldest written scripts found anywhere in the world.

In addition to one of the earliest writing systems and Egyptian paper (papyrus), archaeologists have credited ancient Egyptians with a number of other innovations. For construction purposes, ancient Egyptians invented the ramp and lever. They also developed a 12-month calendar with 365 days, glassmaking skills, arithmetic (including one of the earliest decimal systems) and geometry, and medical procedures to heal broken bones and relieve fevers. Finally, Egyptians used stone-carving techniques and other crafting skills and tools that were shared throughout the Mediterranean.

2.14 DYNASTIC EGYPT

Scholars break the 1500 years following unification, a time known as dynastic Egypt, into three main periods: the Old Kingdom (c. 2660–2160 BCE), the Middle Kingdom (c. 2040 – 1640 BCE), and the New Kingdom (c. 1530–1070 BCE). There is some disagreement about the exact dates of the periods, but, in general, these spans denote more centralized control over a unified Egypt. During dynastic Egypt, pharaohs ruled a united Upper and Lower Egypt. In between these periods of centralized control were intermediate periods, during which the Egyptian pharaohs had less authority. The intermediate periods were characterized by political upheaval and military violence, the latter often at least partially resulting from foreign invasions.

Striking continuities existed in Egypt throughout the Old Kingdom, the Middle Kingdom, and the New Kingdom. Egypt had stable population numbers, consistent social stratification, pharaohs—who exercised significant power—and a unifying religious ideology, which linked the pharaohs to the gods. As Egypt transitioned from the period of unification under King Narmer to the Old Kingdom, the pharaohs and the elite became increasingly wealthy and powerful. They further developed earlier systems of tax collection, expanded the religious doctrine, and built a huge state bureaucracy.

Social distinctions and hierarchies remained fairly consistent through all of dynastic Egypt. Most people were rural peasant farmers. They lived in small mud huts just above the flood plain and turned over surplus agricultural produce to the state as taxes. When they weren't farming, they were expected to perform rotating service for the state, by, for example, working on a pharaoh's tomb, reinforcing dykes, and helping in the construction of temples. The labor of the majority of the population supported the more elite and skilled classes, from the pharaoh down through the governing bureaucrats, priests, nobles, soldiers, and skilled craftspeople, especially those who worked on pyramids and tombs. (Visit the following link for a diagram of the Egyptian social hierarchy: http://dgh. wikispaces.com/file/view/who6fs_ c04000006a.jpg/76595189/385x235/ who6fs_c04000006a.jpg.)

Another continuity in dynastic Egypt was the relative equality of women to men. At least compared to women in other ancient societies, women in ancient Egypt had considerable legal rights and freedoms. Men and women did generally have different roles; Egyptian society charged men with providing for the family and women with managing the home and children. Society's ascribed gender roles meant that women were usually defined primarily by their husbands and children, while men were defined by their occupations. This difference could leave women more economically vulnerable than men. For example, in the village of craftspeople who worked on the pharaoh's tomb at Deir el Medina, houses were allocated to the men who were actively employed. This system of assigning housing meant that women whose husbands had died would be kicked out of their homes as replacement workers were brought in. Despite some vulnerability, Egyptian law was pretty equal between the sexes when it came to many other issues. Egyptian women could own property, and tax records show that they did. Egyptian women could also take cases to court, enter into legally binding agreements, and serve actively as priestesses. There were also female pharaohs, most famously Hatshepsut

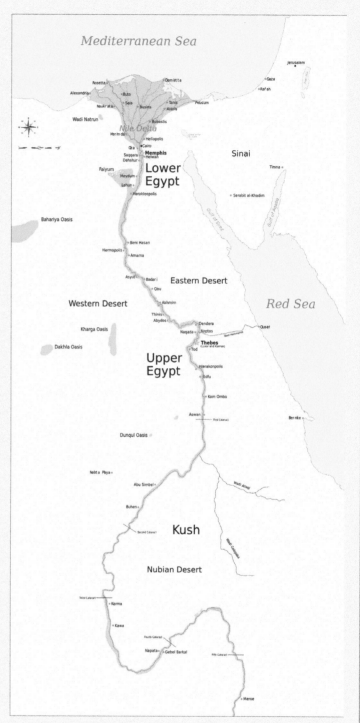

Map 2.7 | Upper and Lower Egypt | Note the narrowness of the floodplain, marked in green. The narrow floodplain, usually not more than 15 miles wide and often considerably less, encouraged high population densities close to the Nile River.
Author: Jeff Dahl
Source: Wikimedia Commons
License: CC BY-SA 4.0

who ruled for twenty years in the fifteenth century BCE. One last, perhaps surprising, legal entitlement of ancient Egyptian women was their right to one-third of the property that a couple accumulated over the course of their marriage. Married women had some financial independence, which gave them options to dispose of their own property or divorce. Therefore, while women did face constraints in terms of their expected roles and had their status tied to the men in their families, they nevertheless enjoyed economic freedoms and legal rights not commonly seen in the ancient world.

While scholars working over the past several decades have used artwork, archeology, and the surviving legal documents to draw conclusions about women's roles in ancient Egypt, there is much ongoing debate about the

Figure 2.8 | Female figurines from ancient Egypt | These figurines show some of the everyday tasks carried out by women. They made bread, brewed beer, and prepared for family meals.
Author: Andreas Praefcke
Source: Wikimedia Commons
License: Public Domain

prevalence of slavery within this society. Part of the disagreement stems from how various scholars define slavery. There is also great uncertainty about the number of slaves within the Egyptian population. The emerging consensus suggests that Egyptians increasingly used slaves from the Middle Kingdom onward. The majority of the slaves in these later dynasties were either prisoners of war or slaves brought from Asia. Slaves performed many tasks. For example, they labored in agricultural fields, served in the army, worked in construction, helped their merchant owners in shops, and were domestic servants for the Egyptian elite. Slaves were branded and, if possible, would be captured and returned to their masters if they tried to escape. Some masters undoubtedly abused their slaves, though the image of thousands of slaves sacrificed to be buried with pharaohs incorrectly depicts dynastic Egypt. Manumission (freeing a slave) was seemingly not very common, but if they were freed, former slaves were not stigmatized; instead, they were considered part of the general free population. These new scholarly conclusions about the relatively small numbers of slaves in Egypt, especially during the Old Kingdom, have impacted our understanding of how pyramids, tombs, and temples were constructed during dynastic Egypt.

The **Old Kingdom** saw pharaohs harness their influence to build **pyramids** to emphasize their relationship to the divine and facilitate their ascent to the gods after their earthly deaths. Pyramids, with their distinctive shape, which you can see in Figure 2.9, contained tombs for the pharaohs and their wives. They were marvels of engineering, built on a massive scale to honor the pharaohs and usher them into the afterlife. Pharaohs were mummified to preserve their bodies and were buried with everything considered necessary for the afterlife, including furniture, jewelry, makeup, pottery, food, wine, clothing, and sometimes even pets. The most recognizable pyramids from the Old Kingdom are the three pyramids at the Giza complex, which were built for a father (Egyptian pharaoh Khufu), and his son and grandson, who all ruled during the fourth dynasty.

The Great Pyramid of Giza, built for Pharaoh Khufu, is the largest of the three pyramids. Still largely intact today, it was the largest building in the world until the twentieth century. Over 500 feet high, it covered an area of 200 square yards, and was built with over 600 tons of limestone. Recent studies on the construction of the pyramids have put much more emphasis on the roles of skilled craftsmen—who might work at multiple pyramid sites over the course of their lifetimes—and rotating groups of unskilled workers than on slaves. These studies suggest that skilled craftsmen and local labor forces of Egyptians were the primary builders of the pyramids, including the Great Pyramid of Giza. The Great Pyramid of Giza took an estimated 20 years to construct and employed skilled stonemasons, architects, artists, and craftsmen, in addition to the thousands of unskilled laborers who did the heavy moving and lifting. The construction of the Great Pyramid of Giza was an enormous, expensive feat. The pyramid stands as testimony to the

Figure 2.9 | The Great Pyramid at Giza
Author: User "Jeancaffou"
Source: Wikimedia Commons
License: CC BY-SA 3.0

increased social differentiation, the great power and wealth of the Egyptian pharaohs, and the significance of beliefs in the afterlife during the Old Kingdom.

In addition to the construction of pyramids, the Old Kingdom saw increased trade and remained a relatively peaceful period. The pharaoh's government controlled trade, with Egypt exporting grain and gold (the latter from Nubia to the south) and importing timber, spices, ivory, and other luxury goods. During the Old Kingdom, Egypt did not have a standing army and faced few foreign military threats. Lasting almost 400 years, the Old Kingdom saw the extension of the pharaoh's power, especially through the government's ability to harness labor and control trade.

However, the power of the pharaohs began to wane in the fifth dynasty of the Old Kingdom. Continuing environmental change that led to droughts and famine, coupled with the huge expense of building pyramids likely impoverished pharaohs in the last centuries of the Old Kingdom. Additionally, the governors known as *nomes*, who administered Egypt's 42 provinces from the fifth dynasty onward, became more independent and took over functions that had been overseen by the state. As an added blow, the pharaohs lost control of trade. While dynastic leaders still referred to themselves as pharaohs, they lacked central authority over a unified Egypt by 2180 BCE.

Following the decentralized First Intermediate Period of roughly 150 years, Pharaoh Mentohotep II reunified Egypt to found the **Middle Kingdom**. The Middle Kingdom saw the reorganization of the state's bureaucratic apparatus to control the *nomes*. To further strengthen their authority, the pharaohs also moved their capital from the Old Kingdom capital of Thebes south to Lisht, halfway between Upper and Lower Egypt. With military expeditions, they extended the boundaries of the state north to Lebanon and south to the second cataract of the Nile into a region known as Nubia. With this extension of territory, Egypt had access to more trade goods, and the organization of trade shifted so that professional merchants took a leading role in developing new trade routes. These professional merchants paid taxes to the state, supporting further consolidation of power by the pharaohs and also infrastructural improvements like irrigation. During the Middle Kingdom, the pharaohs focused less on the building of massive pyramids and more on administrative reorganization, military expeditions, and the state's infrastructural repair.

Disputes over succession and ineffectual rulers led into the Second Intermediate Period. Most notably, Egypt was invaded from both the north and the south during this period. The Hyksos invaded from the north in 1670 BCE. They brought bronze and horse-drawn chariots, which allowed them to conquer parts of Lower Egypt and establish their own kingdom, one lasting about 100 years in the Nile Delta region. From the south, the Kingdom of Kush, based in Nubia, invaded and temporarily established control over Upper Egypt to Aswan. Thus, foreign rulers dominated much of Egypt during the Second Intermediate Period.

The **New Kingdom** of reunified Egypt that began in 1530 BCE saw an era of Egyptian imperialism, changes in the burial practices of pharaohs, and the emergence of a brief period of state-sponsored monotheism under the Pharaoh Akhenaten. In 1530 BCE, the pharaoh who became known as Ahmose the Liberator (Ahmose I) defeated the Hyksos and continued sweeping up along the Eastern Mediterranean. By 1500 BCE, the Egyptian army had also pushed into Nubia, taking Kush southward to the fourth cataract of the Nile River (see Map 2.8). As pharaohs following Ahmose I continued Egypt's expansion, the Imperial Egyptian army ran successful campaigns in

Palestine and Syria, along the Eastern Mediterranean. Furthermore, by expanding into Kush, Egypt controlled trade routes into Sub-Saharan Africa. Adopting the Hyksos' chariot military and metal technologies contributed to the Egyptian ability to strengthen its military. Egypt maintained a large standing army and built an expansive empire during the New Kingdom.

Egypt saw many other developments during the New Kingdom, especially when it came to burial practices and religion. During the New Kingdom, pharaohs and Egyptian elites used the **Valley of Kings**, located across the Nile River from Thebes, as their preferred burial site. They desired tombs that were hidden away and safe from tomb robbers. Therefore, instead of pyramids, they favored huge stone tombs built into the mountains of the Valley of the Kings. Nearly all of the tombs in the Valley of Kings were raided, so the fears of the pharaohs were well founded. Tomb raiding

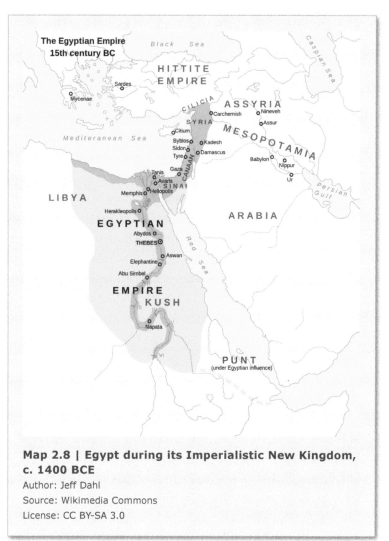

Map 2.8 | Egypt during its Imperialistic New Kingdom, c. 1400 BCE
Author: Jeff Dahl
Source: Wikimedia Commons
License: CC BY-SA 3.0

was even common during dynastic Egypt. King Tutankhamen's tomb has become one familiar exception. His tomb fared unusually well over the millennia, and King Tutankhamen's image is well known to us because his tomb was found mostly intact in 1922.

Throughout dynastic Egypt, much continuity existed in religious beliefs, causing scholars to characterize Egyptian society as conservative, meaning that Egyptians shied away from change. In general, Egyptian religious beliefs emphasized unity and harmony. Throughout the dynastic period, Egyptians thought that the soul contained distinct parts. They believed that one part, the *ka,* was a person's lifeforce and that it separated from the body after death. The Egyptians carried out their elaborate preservation of mummies and made small tomb statues to house their *ka* after death. The *ba,* another part of the soul, was the unique character of the individual, which could move between the worlds of the living and the dead. They believed that after death, if rituals were carried out correctly, their ka and ba would reunite to reanimate their *akh,* or spirit. If they observed the proper rituals and successfully passed through Final Judgment (where they recited the 42 "Negative Confessions" and the god Osiris weighed their hearts against a feather), Egyptians believed that their resurrected spirit, their *akh,* would enter the afterlife. In contrast to Mesopotamian society,

Egyptians conceptualized the afterlife as pleasant. In the afterlife, they expected to find a place with blue skies, agreeable weather, and familiar objects and people. They also expected to complete many of the everyday tasks, such as farming, and enjoy many of the same recognizable pastimes. Throughout the centuries, the Egyptians conceptualized the afterlife as a comfortable mirror image of life.

One change that occurred over time was the "democratization of the afterlife." As time progressed through the Middle Kingdom and into the New Kingdom, more and more people aspired to an afterlife. No longer was an afterlife seen as possible for

Figure 2.10 | Tombs at the Valley of the Kings
Author: User "Karmosin"
Source: Wikimedia Commons
License: CC BY-SA 3.0

only the pharaoh and the elite of society. Instead, just about all sectors of society expected access, as evident in the increased use of funeral texts, like the *Book of the Dead*. People of varying means would slip papyrus with spells or prayers from the *Book of the Dead* (or a similar text) into coffins and burial chambers. They intended these spells to help their deceased loved ones make it safely through the underworld into the pleasant afterlife. Conceptualizations of the afterlife consistently emphasized its familiarity and beauty, while more people looked forward to this continued existence after their earthly deaths.

As they developed religious doctrine and came into contact with new deities, Egyptians integrated new gods and goddesses into their religious beliefs. Like ancient Mesopotamians, Egyptians were polytheistic. Some of the roles and back-stories of the deities did change over time; nevertheless, over the millennia they remained quite consistent. For example, Re, Osiris, Horus, and Isis, just to name a few deities in the Egyptian pantheon, stayed significant throughout dynastic Egypt. Re was the

Figure 2.11 | Golden Mask of Tutankhamun | Because his tomb was found mostly intact in 1922, King Tutankhamen (or King Tut) has become one of our most familiar images from dynastic Egypt.
Author: Carsten Frenzl
Source: Wikimedia Commons
License: CC BY 2.0

sun god, Osiris was the god of the afterworld, who also controlled nature's cycles (like the all important flooding of the Nile), Horus became a god of war and protection, and Isis was a goddess associated with healing and motherhood. During the Middle Kingdom, Amun, initially a patron saint of the city of Thebes and later recognized as the father of the pharaoh, was combined with Re, the sun god, to become Amun-Re the supreme god of the Egyptian pantheon. Amun-Re retained this place at the top of the Egyptian pantheon through most of the New Kingdom. One major exception occurred during the reign of Pharaoh Akhenaten.

Pharaoh Akhenaten started what is known as the **Amarna Period**. The Amarna Period, which lasted from approximately 1350 to 1325 BCE, stands out for its state-sponsored monotheism. Akhenaten introduced radical changes to Egyptian society, moving the capital to Tell el Amarna, a new settlement in the middle of the desert that was devoted to the worship of Aten and the recognition of the pharaoh's superiority over everyone else. **Aten**, who had been one of many deities worshipped during the Middle Kingdom, was elevated to the creator god associated with sunlight, the foundation of all life. The "Great Hymn to Aten" explains the god Aten's association with the sun as, like the sun, his "rays embraced the lands" of Egypt.[8] Akhenaten had the Great Temple of Aten built in the middle of the new capital, and, unlike previous temples, this one had no roof and was open to sunlight. Akhenaten further modified Egyptian religious doctrine to identify himself as the son of Aten. According to the new religious ideology, Akhenaten alone was able to ensure access to the afterlife and communicate with Aten, the sole god. To reinforce Aten's singularity, Akhenaten withdrew financial support from temples dedicated to other deities and defaced the temples dedicated to Amun, who had previously been the most dominant Egyptian deity. The prominence of Aten and Akhenaten's exclusive access to him define the Amarna Period.

Why did Akhenaten introduce these radical changes? At least in part, Akhenaten wanted to break with the priests in Thebes who controlled the temples dedicated to Amun because he believed that these priests had become too powerful. Additionally, by taking on the role of the son of Aten and regulating entry into the afterlife, Akhenaten certainly attempted to reformulate beliefs to emphasize his own importance.

Akhenaten's radical changes were likely troubling for most of the Egyptian population. They had previously found comfort in their access to deities and their regular religious rituals. The worship of Aten as the only Egyptian god did not last more than a couple of decades, floundering after the death of Akhenaten. Pharaohs who ruled from 1323 BCE onward tried not only to erase the religious legacies of the Amarna Period, but also to destroy the capital at Tell el Amarna and remove Akhenaten from the historical record. Archaeologists have not found Akhenaten's tomb or burial place. Scholars continue a long-standing debate about how this brief period of Egyptian monotheism relates (if at all) to the monotheism of the Israelites. Despite such uncertainties, study of the Amarna period does indicate that Egyptians in the fourteenth century BCE saw the fleeting appearance of religious ideology that identified Aten as the singular god.

Some of the strongest rulers of the New Kingdom, including Ramses I and Ramses II, came to power after the Amarna Period. These pharaohs expanded Egypt's centralized administration and its

---

8   "The Great Hymn to Aten." http://web.archive.org/web/19990221040703/http://puffin.creighton.edu/theo/simkins/tx/Aten.html

control over foreign territories. However, by the twelfth century BCE, weaker rulers, foreign invasions, and the loss of territory in Nubia and Palestine indicated the imminent collapse of the New Kingdom. In the Late Period that followed (c. 1040 to 332 BCE), the Kingdom of Kush, based in Nubia, invaded and briefly ruled Egypt until the Assyrians conquered Thebes, establishing their own rule over Lower Egypt. Egyptian internal revolts and the conquest by Nubia and the Assyrian Empire left Egypt susceptible to invasion by the Persians and then eventually the 332 BCE invasion of Alexander the Great.

The ancient Egyptians made numerous contributions to World History. We remember them for mummification, their pharaohs, and the pyramids. Certainly, in this era, Egypt stands out for its ability to produce agricultural surpluses that supported the elites, priests, and skilled craftspeople. While we tend to focus on the bureaucratic, religious, and artistic contributions of these classes, all Egyptians played crucial roles in creating and maintaining this sophisticated civilization. Additionally, the innovations

Figure 2.11 | Panel with adoration Scene of Aten | Pharaoh Akhenaten with his wife and children making offerings to Aten, the divine incarnation of the sun during the monotheistic Amarna Period.
Author: Jean-Pierre Dalbéra
Source: Wikimedia Commons
License: CC BY 2.0

of Egyptians, such as their stone-carving techniques, hieroglyphics, the use of papyrus, their knowledge of the length of a solar year, and their construction methods, influenced the ancient world and still inspire awe. Overall, the ancient Egyptians created a vibrant civilization, while they also found comfort in the familiar and traditional.

2.15 NUBIA: THE KINGDOMS OF KERMA AND KUSH

The region south of Aswan, at the first cataract of the Nile River, is commonly called **Nubia**. Nubia is notable for its long-term, dynamic relationship with ancient Egypt. Just as importantly, Nubia was also the site of an early civilization. The kingdoms of Kerma (c. 2400 BCE to 1500 BCE) and Kush (c. 1000 BCE to 300 CE) emerged along the Nile River. These kingdoms prospered especially due to their productive agriculture and the region's copious natural resources. At certain points, both Kerma and Kush were strong enough to successfully invade Egypt. These kingdoms in Nubia also developed their own religious and cultural traditions, including a written script, Meroitic. While the people of this region, known collectively as Nubians, borrowed heavily from the Egyptians, Nubians also had distinctive practices that set their civilization apart from that of their northern neighbors.

Scholars generally link the origins of ancient Kerma (in present-day Sudan) back to the desiccation of the Sahara Desert and the rise of dynastic Egypt. Similarly to ancient Egypt, the drying out of the region encouraged people to move closer to the Nile River in the years between 5,000 and 4,000 BCE. Rock paintings, showing cattle in areas that have been desert for thousands of years, attest to the environmental changes in Nubia and also the development of a cattle culture that dates back to at least the fourth millennium BCE. Just as in Egypt, the desiccation of the Sahara desert drew together people from all directions. As people settled closer to the Nile River in Nubia, they brought their cattle, their agricultural traditions, and their languages, building settlements with higher population densities.

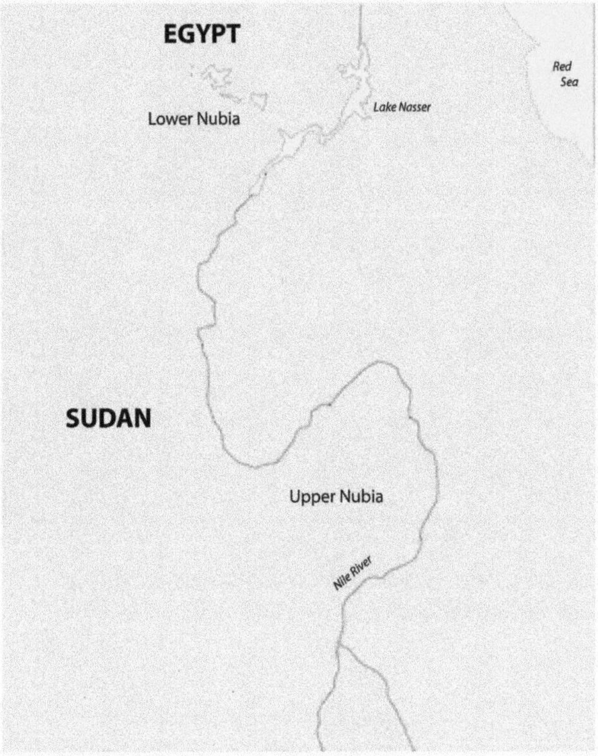

Additionally, Egyptian elites desired ivory, animal skins, incense, and other luxury goods prompting trade between Nubia and Egypt that pre-dated the unification of Egypt. With increased demand for luxury goods as social stratification grew, the Egyptians even ran military forays into Nubia. After unification, the Egyptians continued to invade Nubia to trade and raid for slaves and cattle. Likely, Nubian desires to control trade and protect themselves from Egyptian raids further compelled state formation in Nubia. Without Nubian records from the third millennium BCE, it is difficult to identify additional reasons why the state arose. However, archeological evidence does clearly indicate that by about 2400 BCE, Nubians had formed the Kingdom of Kerma between the third and fourth cataracts of the Nile River.

Map 2.9 | A map of ancient Nubia
Author: Mark Dingemanse and Corey Parson
Source: Wikimedia Commons
License: CC BY 2.5

2.15.1 Kerma (c. 2400 BCE to c. 1500 BCE)

Kerma endured in Upper Nubia for almost a thousand years. The kingdom is named after its capital city at Kerma at the third cataract, but excavations at other sites (where similar pottery styles and burial sites have been found) suggest that at its height Kerma's reach may have extended more than 200 miles southward past the fifth cataract of the Nile River. So far, archaeological evidence indicates that, with the exception of the capital and perhaps one or two other cities, most of the people in Kerma lived in smaller villages. They grew crops like barley, and kept goats, sheep, and cattle, sending tribute to their capital. The people of Kerma also developed industries, especially in mining, metalworking, and pottery. Kerma was linked inter-regionally through trade to its tributary villages, to dynastic Egypt, and to sub-Saharan Africa. Egyptian pharaohs and elites wanted the gold, copper, slaves, ivory, exotic animals, and more that they obtained from Kerma.

The people of Kerma also made use of their location on the Nile and proximity to Egypt as they imported textiles, jewelry, and other manufactured goods. Presumably, one reason that Nubian leaders built their ancient capital at Kerma was to oversee river trade. At the impassable cataract, boat owners unloaded their cargo and took it overland past the shallows and rocks before again proceeding on the water. This location at the cataract gave the leaders at Kerma the chance to tax, divert, and register goods being transported between Kerma and Egypt.

Agricultural surpluses and other tributary payments supported the rulers and elites of the capital. Archaeologists have shown that the capital had defenses, including ditches, ramparts, and massive walls with towers. There were also palaces within the city and on its outskirts. However, the most famous structure is the **Western Deffufa** (Figure 2.13) made of mud-bricks, which likely served as a temple. Two other deffufa, large mud-brick structures with spaces for rituals on top, have been at least partially excavated within the vicinity of Kerma. Another notable archaeological find is the Eastern Cemetery, which lies a couple of miles to the east of the city. It served as the burial site for Kerma's rulers for almost a thousand years and contains over 30,000 tombs. Some of the tombs were covered with large mounds. Demonstrating the cattle culture of the region, dozens of cattle skulls encircle a number of the tombs. Tombs also contain the remains of human sacrifices and other symbols of wealth and status, like jewelry made of gold and silver. The largest tomb found to date is 300 feet in diameter and covered with black granite, white quartz pebbles, and a marble top. Its interior burial suite contains semi-precious stones, bronze weapons, and lavish furniture. In the corridor leading into the underground burial site,

Figure 2.13 | The Western Deffufa at Kerma
Author: Walter Callens
Source: Wikimedia Commons
License: CC BY 2.0

archaeologists unearthed the remains of horses, dogs, and about 400 human sacrificial victims. The cattle skulls, mounds, and the remains of human sacrifices have led scholars to suggest that the Kerma elite had their own styles for monumental structures like the Western Deffufa and their tombs, even though they sometimes employed Egyptian artisans to complete the construction of these grand projects.

It appears that Kerma was strongest when neighboring Egypt was weak. As a case in point, during Egypt's Second Intermediate Period, Kerma, at the height of its power, successfully invaded parts of Upper Egypt and established diplomatic relations with the occupying Hyksos. Once reunified during the New Kingdom, Egypt retaliated by conquering Kerma to the fourth cataract. Then, Egypt occupied Kerma for the next 500 years. During the Egyptian occupation, the elite classes of Kerma adopted many elements of Egyptian culture, including Egyptian gods, styles of dress, Hieroglyphics, and the Egyptian language. However, scholars believe that the Nubian masses retained their own distinctive identity with their local language and customs.

2.15.2 The Kingdom of Kush

As Egypt entered its Third Intermediate Period, Nubians gradually established their independence, eventually creating a new state, the Kingdom of **Kush** in the eighth century BCE. The initial capital of the Kingdom of Kush was Napata (c. 750 BCE to 593 BCE). From Napata, the Nubians took control of Upper Egypt, establishing the "Ethiopian Dynasty," which ruled for 60 years from Thebes. Assyrian invasions destabilized the Nubian rulers in Thebes, causing the last pharaoh of the Ethiopian Dynasty to flee to Napata. Then, once strengthened, the Egyptians pushed back. The Egyptian army sacked Napata in 593 BCE and, in response, the Nubian rulers moved their capital farther south to Meroe. (See Map 2.9.) At this southern location, they further developed their civilization, which lasted until the fourth century CE.

With the new capital at **Meroe**, a location with well-watered farmland and some distance between it and Egypt, the Kingdom of Kush flourished. Meroe got more rainfall than Napata and was not as dependent on the Nile floods. Nubians were able to extend the areas under cultivation and grow a wider variety of crops, like cotton, sorghum, and millet. They were also able to easily graze their livestock and, as a result, during this period cattle became even more important as a symbol of their culture and wealth.

After moving the capital to Meroe, the culture of Kush showed more independence from Egypt as well. Particularly as Egypt's power declined, the people of Kush put more emphasis on their own deities and pushed Egyptian gods to the background. For example, temples devoted to a Nubian war god, Apedamak, "the Lion of the South," received more support and even used live lions for rituals. Gold had long been mined in the region and remained important while the people of Kush continued to develop additional industries. The area was rich in iron ore and the hardwoods used to make charcoal, which encouraged the growth of a booming iron industry. They made iron weapons and tools that they used for defense and to increase their crop yields. They were able to trade their agricultural surpluses, iron, cattle, and exotic things like elephants from sub-Saharan Africa, with Egypt, Greece, Rome, and India, bringing great wealth and

Figure 2.14 | Pyramids at Meroe
Author: B. N. Chagny
Source: Wikimedia Commons
License: CC BY-SA 1.0

prestige to Meroe. Also, the rulers of Meroe commissioned pyramids but had them built in a local style. As evident in Figure 2.14, their pyramids were smaller and had a unique shape. Kush burial practices were different than those used in dynastic Egypt, as corpses were not always mummified and were buried in the fetal position. Finally, a new locally-created written script, **Meroitic**, replaced the use of Egyptian Hieroglyphics by 300 BCE. Modern scholars have not yet translated Meroitic, and students of their culture will surely learn even more about the Kingdom of Kush once scholars have done so. As for now, we know that very productive agriculture, local rituals and burial practices, the growth of industries, social stratification facilitated by Meroe's wealth and extensive trade networks, and the written script Meroitic, were some of the distinctive elements of the civilization at Kush.

While the Greeks and Romans occasionally sent raiding parties into Nubia, for a while, Meroe's southern location helped isolate it from conquest. Legends also emphasize the strength of Meroe's army and the physical prowess of its soldiers. Environmental changes, internal rivalries, and the rise of Axum (a new state to the East) likely all contributed to the fairly abrupt collapse of Meroe in the fourth century CE.

Egyptian sources were generally very derogatory in their portrayal of Nubians and even a few early twentieth century archaeologists carelessly (and incorrectly) identified these Nubian kingdoms as slave colonies of the Egyptians. However, the kingdoms of Kerma and Kush were known in the ancient world for their wealth and industries. The wealth garnered through productive agriculture and trade supported a ruling class, great artists, and monumental architecture. Egyptian culture was influential, but Nubians adapted Egyptian practices to meet their own needs and sensibilities. Often entangled with Egypt and sometimes defending themselves from other invaders as well, these two kingdoms persisted for hundreds of years, creating an independent civilization along the southern stretches of the Nile River.

2.16 SUMMARY

Between about 4000 and 3000 BCE, civilizations emerged in the fertile river valleys of Mesopotamia and Northeast Africa. These civilizations had common elements, including food surpluses, higher population densities, social stratification, systems of taxation, labor specialization, regular trade, and written scripts.

In areas adjacent to the Tigris and Euphrates Rivers, Mesopotamians built city-states by 3500 BCE. While Sumerian traditions influenced developments throughout the region, other cities emerged and refined their own institutions and beliefs. Archaeological finds and records in the *cuneiform* script show the significance of the temple complex and religious leaders throughout Mesopotamia. Kingship, with hereditary rulers who claimed control over multiple city-states and special relationships with the gods, was just one significant political innovation in the region. History credits Sargon of Akkad with founding the first empire in Mesopotamia. Thereafter, a succession of empires rose and fell, demonstrating the dynamic nature of Mesopotamian societies.

According to Hebrew Tradition, Abraham led his followers from the city of Ur in Mesopotamia and they eventually settled in the Levant. Several generations later, according to Hebrew Tradition, the Israelites went to Egypt where they suffered persecution and enslavement, until Moses liberated them. Upon their return to Canaan, the Israelites built kingdoms just prior to 1000 BCE. Their kingdoms formed complex administrations and were unified by powerful kings, such as the well-known King Solomon. Historians also recognize countless other contributions made by the Israelites, especially as regards monotheistic religious traditions and western understandings of justice.

The unification of Egypt in approximately 3100 BCE evidenced the emergence of one civilization in Northeast Africa. In Nubia to the south of Egypt, Africans built another civilization with the kingdoms of Kerma and Kush. The people in each of these civilizations made good use of the agriculturally productive floodplains of the Nile River. Egypt and the kingdoms in Nubia influenced one another; they traded and intermittently claimed control over each other's territory. While we may be more familiar with the pharaohs, pyramids, and religious beliefs of ancient Egypt, Nubians made their own contributions, like the Merotic script and unique architectural styles, to World History.

2.17 WORKS CONSULTED AND FURTHER READING

Civilizations

Brown, Cynthia Stokes. "What is a Civilization, Anyway?" *World History Connected* (October 2009) http://worldhistoryconnected.press.illinois.edu/6.3/brown.html

Bellows, Sierra. "The Trouble with Civilization," *UVA Magazine* (Fall 2010) http://uvamagazine.org/articles/the_trouble_with_civilization/

Mesopotamia

Belibtreu, Erika. "Grisly Assyrian Record of Torture and Death." http://faculty.uml.edu/ethan_Spanier/Teaching/documents/CP6.0AssyrianTorture.pdf

History Department, University College London. "Assyrian Empire Builders." http://www.ucl.ac.uk/sargon/

International World History Project. "The Akkadians." http://history-world.org/sargon_the_great.htm

Khan Academy. "Ziggurat of Ur." https://www.khanacademy.org/humanities/ancient-art-civilizations/ancient-near-east1/sumerian/a/ziggurat-of-ur

Kilmer, Anne. "The Musical Instruments from Ur and Ancient Mesopotamian Music." *Expedition*. The Penn Museum. 40, 2 (1998): 12-18. http://www.penn.museum/documents/publications/expedition/PDFs/40-2/The%20Musical1.pdf

Kramer, Samuel. *The Sumerians: Their History, Culture, and Character.* Chicago: Chicago University Press, 1963.

Leick, Gwendolyn. *Mesopotamia: The Invention of the City.* London: Penguin Books, 2004.

Mitchell, William. "The Hydraulic Hypothesis: A Reappraisal." *Current Anthropology*. Vol. 15. No. 5. (Dec. 1973): 532-534.

Postgate, J.N. *Early Mesopotamia: Society and Economy at the Dawn of History.* London: Routledge, 1994.

Spar, Ira. "Gilgamesh." In *Heinbrunn Timeline of Art History*. New York: The Metropolitan Museum of Art, 2000. (April 2009). http://www.metmuseum.org/toah/hd/gilg/hd_gilg.htm

University of Pennsylvania Museum of Archaeology and Anthropology. "Iraq's Ancient Past: Rediscovering Ur's Royal Cemetery." http://www.penn.museum/sites/iraq/

The Israelites and Ancient Israel

Baden, Joel. *The Historical Hero: the Real Life of an Invented Hero.* New York: Harper One, 2014.

Dever, William. *The Lives of Ordinary People in Ancient Israel: Where Archaeology and the Bible Intersect.* Grand Rapids, MI: William B. Eerdman's Publishing Company, 2012.

Guisepi, Robert (ed). "Civilization of the Hebrews: Along the Banks of the Rivers." World History International. http://history-world.org/Hebrews.htm

Hawkins, Ralph. *How Israel Became a People.* Nashville, TN: Abingdon Press, 2013.

Milstein, Mati. "King Solomon's Wall Found – Proof a Bible Tale?" National Geographic (Feb. 2010): http://news.nationalgeographic.com/news/2010/02/100226-king-solomon-wall-jerusalem-bible/

Shanks, Hershel (ed). *Ancient Israel: From Abraham to the Roman Destruction of the Temple.* 3e. Washington, D.C.: Biblical Archaeology Society, 2010.

Ancient Egypt

Australian Museum. "The Underworld and the Afterlife in Ancient Egypt." (Australian Museum, 2015) http://australianmuseum.net.au/the-underworld-and-the-afterlife-in-ancient-egypt

David, Rosalie. *The Pyramid Builders of Ancient Egypt: A Modern Investigation of Pharaoh's Workforce.* New York: Routledge, 1997.

Dollinger, Andre. "Slavery in Ancient Egypt." (February 2011) http://www.reshafim.org.il/ad/egypt/timelines/topics/slavery.htm

Hierakonoplis Expedition, Hierakpopolis-online. http://www.hierakonpolis-online.org/

Johnson, Janet. "Women's Legal Rights in Ancient Egypt." Fathom Archive, Digital Collections. University of Chicago Library: 2002. http://fathom.lib.uchicago.edu/1/777777190170/

McDowell, A.G. *Village Life in Ancient Egypt: Laundry Lists and Love Songs.* Oxford: Oxford University Press, 1999.

Pinch, Geraldine. *Egyptian Mythology: A Guide to the Gods, Goddesses, and Traditions of Ancient Egypt.* Oxford: Oxford University Press, 2004.

Shaw, Ian. *The Oxford History of Ancient Egypt.* Oxford: Oxford University Press, 2004.

Shillington, Kevin. *History of Africa.* 2nd e. Oxford: Macmillan Education, 2005.

Smith, Jeffrey. "The Narmer Palette," Yale 2013 PIER Summer Institutes, http://www.yale.edu/macmillan/pier/classroom-resources/The%20Narmer%20Palette%20-%20by%20Jeff%20Smith%20.pdf

Teeter, Emily. *Religion and Ritual in Ancient Egypt.* Cambridge: Cambridge University Press, 2011.

Tyldesley, Joyce. *Daughters of Isis:Women in Ancient Egypt.* New York: Penguin History, 1995.

Ancient Nubia

Afolayan, Funso. "Civilizations of the Upper Nile and North Africa." In *Africa, Volume 1: African History Before 1885.* Toyin Falola (ed.) (73-108) Durham, North Carolina: Carolina Academic Press, 2000.

British Museum. "The Wealth of Africa: The Kingdom of Kush." Student Worksheets. www.britishmuseum.org

Louis, Chaix; Dubosson, Jerome; and Matthieu Honegger. "Bucrania from the Eastern Cemetery at Kerma (Sudan) and the Practice of Cattle Horn Deformation." *Studies in African Archaeology,* 11. Poznan Archeological Museum, 2012. www.academia.edu

Collins, Robert and James Burns. *A History of Sub-Saharan Africa.* Cambridge: Cambridge University Press, 2008.

Ehret, Christopher. *The Civilizations of Africa: A History to 1800.* Charlottesville, VA: University Press of Virginia, 2002.

Garlake, Peter. *Early Art and Architecture of Africa.* Oxford: Oxford University Press, 2002.

Trigger, Bruce. "Kerma: The Rise of an African Civilization." *International Journal of African Historical Studies.* Vol. 9, no. 1 (1976): 1-21.

2.18 LINKS TO PRIMARY SOURCES

"The Sumerian King List."

http://www.csun.edu/~hcfll004/sumking.html

The Epic of Gilgamesh. Nancy Sandars (trans.). New York: Penguin Books, 1960.

http://web.archive.org/web/20010217041824/http://www.humanities.ccny.cuny.edu/history/reader/gilgames.htm

"The Flood." Excerpted from S. Dalley. *Myths from Mesopotamia*. New York: Oxford University Press, 1991.
http://web.archive.org/web/19990221091328/http://puffin.creighton.edu/theo/simkins/tx/Flood.html

"The Code of Hammurabi, c. 1780 BCE." *Ancient History Sourcebook*. Fordham University.
https://legacy.fordham.edu/halsall/ancient/hamcode.asp#text

"Hymn to the Nile, c. 2100 BCE." *Ancient History Sourcebook*. Fordham University.
http://legacy.fordham.edu/halsall/ancient/hymn-nile.asp

Exodus. Revised Standard Version of the Bible. *Ancient History Sourcebook*, Fordham University.
http://legacy.fordham.edu/Halsall/ancient/exodus-rsv.asp

"The Egyptian Negative Confession."
https://d628e93a87508d390763-57cef68fda4fc1e410cee0eeddd485c4.ssl.cf5.rackcdn.com/42_
confessions.pdf

"The Great Hymn to Aten."
http://web.archive.org/web/19990221040703/http://puffin.creighton.edu/theo/simkins/tx/Aten.html

3 Ancient and Early Medieval India

George L. Israel

3.1 CHRONOLOGY

2600 – 1700 BCE	Harappan/Indus Valley Civilization
1700 – 600 BCE	Vedic Age
1700 – 1000 BCE	Early Vedic Age
1000 – 600 BCE	Later Vedic Age
321 – 184 BCE	Mauryan Empire
c. 2nd century BCE to 3rd century CE	Kushan Kingdom
c. 320 – 550 CE	Gupta Empire
600 – 1300 CE	Early Medieval India
1206 – 1526 CE	Delhi Sultanate

3.2 INTRODUCTION: A POLITICAL OVERVIEW

Our knowledge of the ancient world has been radically altered by impressive archaeological discoveries over the last two centuries. Prior to the twentieth century, for instance, historians believed that India's history began in the second millennium BCE, when a people known as Indo-Aryans migrated into the Indian subcontinent and created a new civilization. Yet, even during the nineteenth century British explorers and officials were curious about brick mounds dotting the landscape of northwest India, where Pakistan is today. A large one was located in a village named Harappa (see Figure 3.1). A British army engineer, Sir Alexander Cunningham, sensed its importance because he also found other artifacts among the bricks, such as a seal with an inscription. He was, therefore, quite dismayed that railway contractors were pilfering these bricks for ballast. When he became the director of Great Britain's Archaeological Survey in 1872, he ordered protection for these ruins. But the excavation of Harappa did not begin until 1920, and neither the Archaeological Survey nor Indian archaeologists understood their significance until this time. Harap-

Figure 3.1 | Archaeological Site for Harappa | Excavation of this ancient city began in 1920.
Author: Hassan Nasir
Source: Wikimedia Commons
License: CC BY-SA 3.0

pa, it turned out, was an ancient city dating back to the third millennium BCE, and only one part of a much larger civilization sprawling over northwest India. With the discovery of this lost civilization, the timeline for India's history was pushed back over one thousand years.

The Indus Valley civilization (2600 – 1700 BCE) now stands at the beginning of India's long history. Much like the states of ancient Mesopotamia and Egypt, the foundations for that history were established by Paleolithic foragers who migrated to and populated the region, and then Neolithic agriculturalists who settled into villages. During the third millennium BCE, building on these foundations, urban centers emerged along the Indus River, along with other elements that contribute to making a civilization.

This civilization, however, faded away by 1700 BCE, and was followed by a new stage in India's history. While it declined, India saw waves of migration from the mountainous northwest, by a people who referred to themselves as Aryans. The Aryans brought a distinctive language and way of life to the northern half of India and, after first migrating into the Punjab and Indus Valley, pushed east along the Ganges River and settled down into a life of farming and pastoralism. As they interacted with indigenous peoples, a new period in India's history took shape. That period is known as the Vedic Age (1700 – 600 BCE).

During the long course of the Vedic Age, states formed in northern India. The surplus from farming and pastoralism allowed people to engage in a multitude of other occupations and made for a lively trade. Villages thus grew in number and some became towns. Consequently, there was a need for greater leadership, something that was provided by chieftains of the many Aryan clans. Over time, higher levels of political organization developed, and these chieftains became kings or the leaders of clan assemblies. By the end of the Vedic Age, northern India was divided up by sixteen major kingdoms and oligarchies.

The ensuing three centuries (c. 600 – 321 BCE) were a time of transition. These states fought with each other over territory. The most successful state was the one that could most effectively administer its land, mobilize its resources and, by so doing, field the largest armies. That state was the kingdom of Magadha which, by the fourth century BCE, had gained control of much of northern India along the Ganges River.

In 321 BCE, the last king of Magadha was overthrown by one of his subjects, Chandragupta Maurya, and a new period in India's history began. Through war and diplomacy, he and his two successors established control over most of India, forging the first major empire in the history of South Asia: the Mauryan Empire (321 – 184 BCE). Chandragupta's grandson, King Ashoka, ended the military conquests and sought to rule his land through Buddhist principles of non-violence and tolerance. But after his time, the empire rapidly declined, and India entered a new stage in its history.

After the Mauryan Empire fell, no one major power held control over a substantial part of India for five hundred years. Rather, from c. 200 BCE to 300 CE, India saw a fairly rapid turnover of numerous, regional kingdoms. Some of these were located in northern India, along the Ganges River, but others grew up in the south—the Indian Peninsula—for the first time. Also, some kingdoms emerged through foreign conquest. Outsiders in Central Asia and the Middle East saw India as a place of much wealth, and sought to plunder or rule it. Thus, throughout its history, India was repeatedly invaded by conquerors coming through mountain passes in the northwest. Many of these, like King Kanishka of the Kushan Empire (c. 100 CE), established notable kingdoms that extended from India into these neighboring regions from which they came.

Even after 300 CE and up to the fifteenth century, India was never again unified for any length of time by one large empire. For that reason, historians highlight those kingdoms that became substantial regional powers and contributed in other important ways to India's civilization. The period 300 – 600 CE, for instance, is often referred to as the Gupta Period and Classical Age. The Guptas (c. 320 – 550) were rulers who forged an impressive empire in northern India. As their empire flourished, Indian intellectuals were also setting standards for excellence in the fields of art, architecture, literature, and science, in part because of Gupta patronage. But important kingdoms also developed in south India.

The last period covered in this chapter is early medieval India (c. 600 – 1300 CE). After the Gupta Empire, and during the following seven centuries, the pattern of fragmentation intensified, as numerous regional kingdoms large and small frequently turned over. Confronting such an unstable and fluid political scene, medieval kings granted land to loyal subordinate rulers and high officers of their courts. The resulting political and economic pattern is referred to as Indian feudalism. Also, kings put their greatness on display by waging war and building magnificent Hindu temples in their capital cities. And, during the medieval period, a new political and religious force entered the Indian scene, when Muslim Arab and Turkic traders and conquerors arrived on the subcontinent.

This overview briefly summarizes major periods in India's political history. But the history of a civilization consists of more than just rulers and states, which is why historians also pay close attention to social, cultural, and economic life every step of the way. This attention is especially important for India. Although the Asian subcontinent sees a long succession of kingdoms and empires and was usually divided up by several at any particular point in its history, peoples over time came to share some things in common. Socially, the peoples of India were largely organized by the caste system. Culturally, the peoples of India shared in the development of Hinduism and Buddhism, two major religious traditions that shaped people's understanding of the world and their place in it. Finally, throughout the ancient and medieval periods, India flourished as a civilization because of its dynamic economy. The peoples of India shared in that too, and that meant they were linked in networks of trade and exchange not only with other parts of South Asia but also with neighboring regions of the Afro-Eurasian world.

3.3 QUESTIONS TO GUIDE YOUR READING

1. How did the geography of South Asia (India) impact its history?

2. What are the limits of our knowledge of Harappan Civilization?

3. How did kingdoms form during the Vedic Age?

4. Describe the *varna* and caste systems.

5. Explain the early historical origins and basic beliefs of Hinduism and Buddhism. How do these religious traditions change over time?

6. How was the Mauryan Empire governed?

7. How was India impacted by other regions of Afro-Eurasia, and how did it impact them?

8. Why is the Gupta period sometimes described as a classical age?

9. What are the characteristics of early medieval India?

10. Explain the history of the formation of Muslim states in India.

3.4 KEY TERMS

- *Arthashastra*
- Aryabhata
- Ashoka (Mauryan Empire)
- *Atman*
- Ayurveda
- Bay of Bengal
- *Bhagavad-Gita*
- *Brahman*
- Brahmanism
- Caste and *Varna*
- Chandragupta I (Gupta Empire)
- Chandragupta Maurya
- Chola Kingdom
- Coromandel Coast
- Deccan Plateau
- Delhi Sultanate
- Dharma (Buddhist and Hindu)
- Dharma Scriptures
- Four Noble Truths
- Ganges River
- Guilds
- Gupta Empire

- Harappan/Indus Valley Civilization
- Hindu Kush
- India
- Indian Feudalism
- Indo-Europeans
- Indus River
- Indo-Gangetic Plain
- Kalidasa
- Kanishka
- Karma
- Kushan Kingdom
- Magadha
- Mahayana Buddhism
- Malabar Coast
- Mahmud of Ghazna
- Mehrgarh
- Mohenjo-Daro

- Pataliputra
- Punjab
- *Ramayana*
- Samudragupta
- Satavahana Kingdom
- Seals (Harappan/Indus Valley Civilization)
- Siddhartha Gautama/Buddha
- Sindh
- South Asia
- Sri Lanka
- Theravada Buddhism
- Transmigration
- Tributary Overlordship
- *Upanishads*
- Vedic Age

3.5 WHAT IS INDIA? THE GEOGRAPHY OF SOUTH ASIA

India's dynamic history, then, alternated between periods when the subcontinent was partially unified by empires and periods when it was composed of a shifting mosaic of regional states. This history was also impacted by influxes of migrants and invaders. In thinking about the reasons for these patterns, historians highlight the size of India and its diverse geography and peoples.

It is important to remember that "**India**" can mean different things. Today, India usually designates the nation-state of India (see Map 3.1). But modern India only formed in 1947 and includes much less territory than India did in ancient times. As a term, India was first invented by the ancient Greeks to refer to the **Indus River** and the lands and people beyond it. When used in this sense, India also includes today's nation of Pakistan. In fact, for the purpose of studying earlier history, India can be thought of as the territory that includes at least seven countries today: India, Pakistan, Bhutan, Bangladesh, Nepal, Sri Lanka, and the Maldives. This territory is also referred to as **South Asia** or the Indian subcontinent.

The Indian subcontinent is where Indian civilization took shape. But that civilization was not created by one people, race, or ethnic group, and it doesn't make sense to see India's history as the history of one Indian people. Rather, the history of this region was shaped by a multitude of ethnic groups who spoke many different languages and lived and moved about on a diverse terrain suited to many different kinds of livelihood.

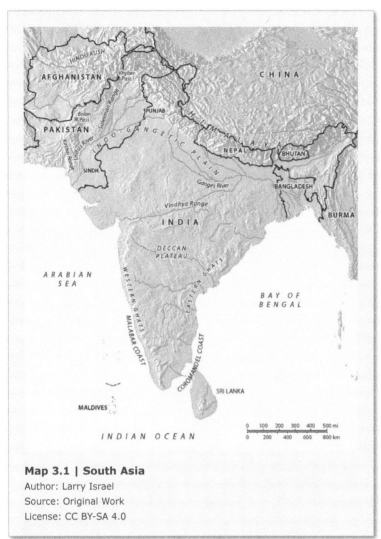

Map 3.1 | South Asia
Author: Larry Israel
Source: Original Work
License: CC BY-SA 4.0

Large natural boundaries define the subcontinent. Mountain ranges ring the north, and bodies of water surround the rest. To the east lies the **Bay of Bengal**, to the south the Indian Ocean, and to the west the Arabian Sea. The largest mountain range is the Himalaya, which defines India's northern and northeastern boundary. A subrange of the Himalaya—the **Hindu Kush**—sits at its western end, while a ridge running from north to south defines the eastern end, dividing India from China and mainland Southeast Asia. To the northwest, the Suleiman Range and Kirthar Range complete what might seem like impassable barriers. Yet, these ranges are punctuated by a few narrow passes that connect India to Central Asia and West Asia.

To the south of the mountain ranges lie **the Indo-Gangetic Plain** and the two great rivers of northern India that comprise it: the Indus River and the **Ganges River**. These rivers originate in the Himalaya and are regularly fed by snow melt and monsoon rains. The Indus River, which is located in the northwest and drains into the Arabian Sea, can be divided into an upper and lower region. The region comprising the upper Indus and its many tributary rivers is called the **Punjab**, while the region surrounding the lower Indus is referred to as the **Sindh**. The Ganges River begins in the western Himalaya and flows southeast across northern India before draining into the Bay of Bengal. Because they could support large populations, the plains surrounding these river systems served as the heartland for India's first major states and empires.

Peninsular India is also an important part of the story because over time great regional kingdoms will also emerge in the south. The peninsula is divided from northern India by the Vindhya Mountains, to the south of which lies the **Deccan Plateau**. This arid plateau is bordered by two coastal ranges—the Western Ghats and Eastern Ghats, beyond which are narrow coastal plains, the **Malabar Coast** and the **Coromandel Coast**. This nearly 4600 miles of coastline is important to India's history because it linked fishing and trading communities to the Indian Ocean and, therefore, the rest of Afro-Eurasia. **Sri Lanka** is an island located about thirty kilometers southeast of the southernmost tip of India, and also served as an important conduit for trade and cultural contacts beyond India.

3.6 INDIA'S FIRST MAJOR CIVILIZATION: THE INDUS VALLEY CIVILIZATION (2600 BCE – 1700 BCE)

A century of archaeological work in India that began in 1920 not only revealed a lost civilization but also a massive one, surpassing in size other major early riverine civilizations of Afro-Eurasia, such as ancient Egypt and the Mesopotamian states. In an area spanning roughly a half million square miles, archaeologists have excavated thousands of settlements (see Map 3.2). These can be envisioned in a hierarchy based on size and sophistication. The top consists of five major cities of roughly 250 acres each. One of those is Harappa, and because it was excavated first the entire civilization was named **Harappan Civilization**. The bottom of the hierarchy consists of fifteen thousand smaller agricultural and craft villages of about 2.5 acres each, while between the top and bottom lie two tiers with several dozen towns ranging in size from 15 to 150 acres. Because the

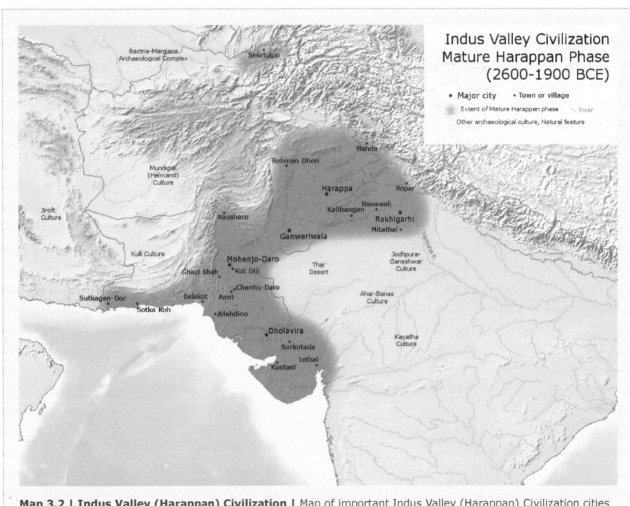

Map 3.2 | Indus Valley (Harappan) Civilization | Map of important Indus Valley (Harappan) Civilization cities and towns during its most developed period.
Author: User "Avantiputra7"
Source: Wikimedia Commons
License: CC BY-SA 3.0

majority of these settlements were situated near the Indus River in the northwestern region of the subcontinent, this civilization is also called the Indus Valley Civilization.

As with ancient Egypt and Mesopotamia, archaeologists have been able to sketch out how this civilization evolved out of the simpler agricultural villages of the Neolithic period. On the subcontinent, farming and the domestication of animals began c. 7000 BCE, about two thousand years after they did in the Fertile Crescent. To the west of the Indus River, along the foothills of Baluchistan, the remains of numerous small villages have been found that date back to this time (see Map 3.3). One of these is **Mehrgarh**. Here, villagers lived in simple mud-brick structures, grew barley and wheat, and raised cattle, sheep, and goats.

Over the course of the next three thousand years, similar Neolithic communities sprang up not only in northwest India but also in many other locations on the subcontinent. But it was to the

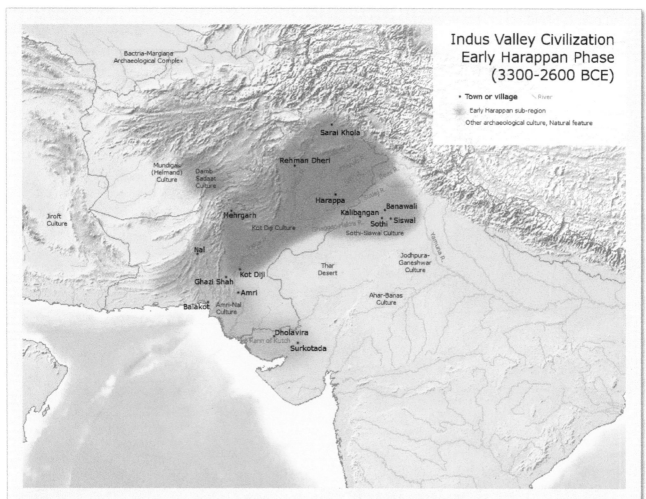

Map 3.3 | Archaeological sites dating to northwest India's Neolithic period and the Indus Valley Civilization | Agricultural village societies first emerged to the west of the Indus and then spread to the Indus River and its many tributaries, as well as the Ghaggar-Hakra River (running parallel to and east of the Indus), which has since dried up. These provided the foundation for the emergence of towns and cities.
Author: User "Avantiputra7"
Source: Wikimedia Commons
License: CC BY-SA 3.0

west of the Indus River and then throughout neighboring fertile plains and valleys of the Punjab and Sindh that we see the transition to a more complex, urban-based civilization. Excavations throughout this region show a pattern of development whereby settlements start looking more like towns than villages: ground plans become larger, include the foundations of houses and streets, and are conveniently located by the most fertile land or places for trade. Similar artifacts spread over larger areas show that the local communities building these towns were becoming linked together in trade networks. Archaeologists date this transitional period when India was on the verge of its first civilization from 5000 to 2600 BCE. The mature phase, with its full-blown cities, begins from 2600 BCE, roughly four centuries after the Sumerian city-states blossomed and Egypt was unified under one kingdom.

The ruins of **Mohenjo-Daro** and other Indus cities dating to this mature phase suggest a vibrant society thriving in competently planned and managed urban areas. Some of the principal purposes of these urban settlements included coordinating the distribution of local surplus resources, obtaining desired goods from more distant places, and turning raw materials into commodities for trade. Mohenjo-Daro, for instance, was located along the lower reaches of the Indus (see Figure 3.2). That meant it was conveniently built amidst an abundance of resources: fertile flood plains for agriculture, pasture for grazing domesticated animals, and waters for fishing and fowling. The city itself consisted of several mounds—elevated areas upon which structures and roads were built. A larger mound served as a core, fortified area where public functions likely took place. It contained a wall and large buildings, including what archaeologists call a Great Bath and Great Hall. Other mounds were the location of the residential and commercial sectors of the city. Major avenues laid out on a grid created city blocks. Within a block, multistory dwellings opening up to interior courtyards were constructed out of mudbricks or bricks baked in

Figure 3.2 | Great Bath at Mohenjo-Daro | View of the Great Bath at Mohenjo-Daro, an Indus Valley city located along the lower reaches of the Indus River. This section was part of the largest mound at the site. The higher structure in the rear is a Buddhist stupa dating to a later period in India's history.
Author: Saqib Qayyum
Source: Wikimedia Commons
License: CC BY-SA 3.0

kilns. Particular attention was paid to public sanitation. Residences not only had private wells and baths, but also toilets drained by earthenware pipes that ushered the sewage into covered drains located under the streets.

Artifacts tell of city life. Farmers and pastoralists brought their grain and stock to the city for trade or to place it in warehouses managed by the authorities. Laborers dug the wells and collected trash from rectangular bins sitting beneath rubbish chutes. Craftsmen worked copper and tin into bronze tools, fired ceramics, and manufactured jewelry and beads out of gold, copper, semi-precious stones, and ivory. Merchants travelling near and far carried raw materials and

Figure 3.3 | Seals from Indus Valley cities | These were made from fired steatite and used to imprint the identity of owners on goods.
Author: User "MrABlair23"
Source: Wikimedia Commons
License: Public Domain

finished goods by bullock carts or boats to the dozens of towns and cities throughout the region.

Some goods also went to foreign lands. Harappan cities located along the coast of the Arabian Sea engaged in coastal shipping that brought goods as far as the Persian Gulf and the delta of the Tigris and Euphrates Rivers. In Mesopotamian city-states, Harappan seals and beads have been found, and Mesopotamian sources speak of a certain place called "Meluhha," a land with ivory, gold, and lapis lazuli. That was the Indus Valley Civilization. Cities like Mohenjo-Daro were linked in networks of exchange extending in every direction.

But unlike ancient Egypt and Sumer, this civilization has not yet provided sources we can read, and this poses major problems of interpretation. True, over four thousand inscribed objects with at least four hundred different signs recurring in various frequencies have been found on clay, copper tablets, and small, square **seals** excavated primarily at the major cities (see Figure 3.3). But the heroic efforts of philologists to decipher

Figure 3.4 | Indus Priest/King Statue | 17.5 cm tall sculpture found at Mohenjo-Daro. The dignified appearance and headband and cloak of this man suggest that he was an important political or religious leader in the city.
Author: Mamoon Mengal
Source: Wikimedia Commons
License: CC BY-SA 1.0

the language have failed to yield results. Thus, some historians call this civilization proto-historic, distinguishing it from both prehistoric cultures that have no writing and historic ones with written sources that we can read.

This proto-historical state of the evidence leaves many questions concerning Harappan people's political organization and beliefs unanswered. On the one hand, much uniformity in the archaeological record across the region suggests coordination in planning—cities and towns were similarly designed, fired bricks had the

Figure 3.5 | Unicorn Seal | Mold from a "unicorn seal" from Mohenjo-Daro depicting a mythical animal standing over an altar or trough, with writing above.
Author: User "Ismoon"
Source: Wikimedia Commons
License: CC0 1.0

Figure 3.6 | Dancing Girl of Mohenjo-daro
Author: Joe Ravi
Source: Wikimedia Commons
License: CC BY-SA 3.0

same dimensions, and weights were standardized. On the other hand, the ruins lack structures that can be clearly identified as palaces, temples, or large tombs. In other words, there is little evidence for either a central political authority ruling over an empire or for independent city-states. One intriguing artifact found in Mohenjo-Daro is a small sculpture of a bearded man made of soapstone (see Figure 3.4). The dignified appearance suggests he may have been a priest or king, or even both. Perhaps he and other priests purified themselves in the Great Bath for ritual purposes. Yet, this is purely speculation, as the sculpture is unique. He may also have been a powerful landowner or wealthy merchant who met with others of a similar status in assemblies convened in the Great Hall of the citadel. Perhaps local assemblies of just such elites governed each city.

Religious beliefs are also difficult to determine. Again, some of the principal evidence consists of small artifacts such as figurines and the square seals. The seals were carved out of a soft stone called steatite and then fired so they would harden. They contain images of animals and humans, typically with writing above. Mostly, they were used to imprint the identity of a merchant or authorities on goods. However, some of the images may have had religious significance. For example, hundreds of "unicorn seals" display images of a mythical animal that resembles a species of cattle (see Figure 3.5). These cattle are usually placed over an object variously interpreted as a trough or altar. Perhaps these were symbols of deities or animals used for sacrificial rituals. Equally as interesting are the numerous female clay figurines. These may have been used for fertility rituals or to pay homage to a goddess (see Figure 3.6).

The decline of Harappan civilization set in from 1900 BCE and was complete two hundred years later. Stated simply, the towns and cities and their lively trade networks faded away, and the region reverted to rural conditions. Likely causes include geologic, climatic, and environmental factors. Movement by tectonic plates may have led to earthquakes, flooding, and shifts in the course of the Indus. Less rainfall and deforestation may have degraded the environment's suitability for farming. All of these factors would have impacted the food supply. Consequently, urban areas and the civilization they supported were slowly starved out of existence.

3.7 THE LONG VEDIC AGE (1700 – 600 BCE)

By 1700 BCE, Harappan Civilization had collapsed. In northwest India, scattered village communities engaging in agriculture and pastoralism replaced the dense and more highly populated network of cities, towns, and villages of the third millennium. The rest of northern India too (including the Ganges River), as well as the entire subcontinent, were similarly dotted with Neolithic communities of farmers and herders. That is what the archaeological record demonstrates.

The next stage in India's history is the **Vedic Age** (1700 – 600 BCE). This period is named after a set of religious texts composed during these centuries called the Vedas. The people who composed them are known as the Vedic peoples and **Indo-Aryans**. They were not originally from India, and rather came as migrants travelling to the subcontinent via mountain passes located in Afghanistan and Pakistan. The Aryans first settled in the Punjab, but then they pushed east along the Ganges, eventually impressing their way of life, language, and religious beliefs upon much of northern India. The course of India's history was completely changed during this period. By the end of the Vedic Age, numerous states had emerged and **Hinduism** and the *varna* **social system** were beginning to take shape.

3.7.1 The Early Aryan Settlement of Northern India (1700 – 1000 BCE)

The early history of the Vedic Age offers the historian little primary source material. For example, for the first half of the Vedic Age (1700 – 1000 BCE), we are largely limited to archaeological sites and one major text called the ***Rig Veda***. This is the first of four *Vedas*. It consists of 1028 hymns addressed to the Vedic peoples' pantheon of gods. But it wasn't actually written down until after 500 BCE. Rather, from as early as the beginning of the second millennium BCE, these hymns were orally composed and transmitted by Aryan poet-seers, eventually becoming the preserve of a few priestly clans who utilized them for the specific religious function of pleasing higher powers. Thus, these hymns only offer certain kinds of information. Yet, despite these limits, historians have been able to sketch out the Aryan's way of life in these early centuries, as well as to make solid arguments about how they came to India.

The Indo-Aryans were pastoralists who migrated to India in waves beginning c. 1700 BCE (see Map 3.4). They referred to themselves as Aryans, a term meaning "noble" or "respectable." They spoke **Sanskrit**, and used it to transmit their sacred hymns. At first, in search of land, they settled along the hills and plains of the upper reaches of the Indus River and its tributaries, bringing with them their pastoral and farming way of life. In their hymns, the Aryans beseech the gods to bless them with cattle, bounteous harvests, rain, friends, wealth, fame, and sons. From these, it is clear that herding was the principal occupation and cows were especially prized. But the Aryans also farmed, as apparent in hymns that speak of plough teams and the cutting and threshing of grain.

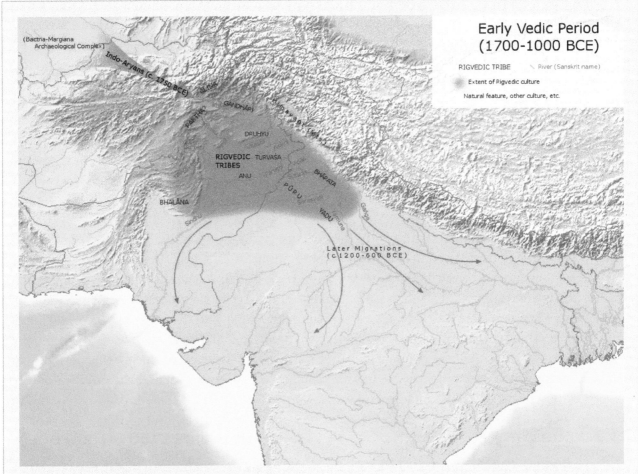

Map 3.4 | Early Vedic Culture (1700-1000 BCE) | The early Vedic Age, showing the Aryan's migration routes and the areas where they first resided in the Punjab.
Author: User "Avantiputra7"
Source: Wikimedia Commons
License: CC BY-SA 3.0

During these early centuries, led by their pastoral chiefs, some Aryans retained a semi-nomadic way of life, living in temporary dwellings and then moving about with their herds or migrating further. Others settled down in villages. In both cases, kinship was especially valued. At the simplest level, society consisted of extended families of three generations. Fathers were expected to lead the family as patriarchal heads, while sons were expected to care for the herds, bring honor through success in battle, and sacrifice for the well-being of their fathers' souls after death. They also inherited the property and family name. This suggests that, as is so often the case for ancient societies, men were dominant and women were subordinate. Yet, women's roles weren't as rigidly defined as they would be in later times, and they had some choice in marriage and could remarry.

Several extended families, in turn, made up clans, and the members of a clan shared land and herds. Groups of larger clans also constituted tribes. The *Vedas* speak of rajas who, at this point, are best understood as clan or tribal chieftains. These men protected their people and led in times of battle, for the clans and tribes fought with each other and with the indigenous villagers living in the northwest prior to the Aryan migrations. In times of war, these chiefs would rely on priests who ensured the support of the gods by reciting hymns and sacrificing to them. At assemblies of kinsmen and other wealthy and worthy men from the clan, the rajas distributed war booty. Sudas, for example, was the chief of the Bharata clan. After settling in the Punjab, the Bharatas were attacked by neighboring clan confederacies, but drawing on his skills in chariot warfare and the support of priests, Sudas successfully fought them off.

More than anything else, the *Rig Veda* reveals the Aryan's religious ideas. For them, the universe was composed of the sky, earth, and netherworld. These realms were populated by a host of divinities and demons responsible for the good and evil and order and disorder blessing and afflicting the human world. Although one Vedic hymn gives a total of thirty-three gods, many more are mentioned. That means early Vedic religion was polytheistic. These human-like powers lying behind all those natural phenomena so close to a people living out on the plains were associated with the forces of light, good, and order. By chanting hymns to them and sacrificing in the correct way, the Aryan priests might secure blessings for the people or prevent the demons and spirits on earth from causing sickness and death. They might also ensure that the souls of the dead would successfully reach the netherworld, where the spirits of righteous Fathers feasted with King Yama, the first man to die.

Approaching the gods required neither temples nor images. Rather, a fire was lit in a specially prepared sacrificial altar. This might take place in a home when the family patriarch was hoping for a son or on an open plot of land when the clan chieftain wished to secure the welfare of his people. Priests were called in to perform the ceremony. They would imbibe a hallucinogenic beverage squeezed from a plant of uncertain identity and chant hymns while oblations of butter, fruit, and meat were placed in the fire. The gods, it was believed, would descend onto grass strewn about for them and could partake of the offerings once they were transmuted by the fire.

Indra was among the most beloved of the Vedic gods. As a god of war and the storm, and as king of the gods, Indra exemplified traits men sought to embody in their lives. He is a great warrior who smites demons and enemies but who also provides generously for the weak. Agni, another favorite, was god of fire and the household hearth. Agni summons the gods to the sacrifice and, as intermediary between gods and humans, brings the sacrificial offering to them.

3.7.2 The Origins of the Aryan People and the Indo-European Hypothesis

Because the Aryans came to India as migrating pastoralists from mountainous regions to the northwest of the Indian subcontinent, historians have sought to understand their origins. Sanskrit has provided important clues because it contains features similar to languages spoken at some point in Europe, Iran, and Central Asia. For example, although they are vastly different languages, Latin, Persian, and Sanskrit share similar sounds, vocabulary, and grammar.

On the basis of these shared traits, linguists have constructed a kind of family tree that shows the historical relationship between these languages (see Figure 3.7). Sanskrit belongs to a group of languages used in northern India called Indo-Aryan. These languages are closely related to languages used throughout history in neighboring Iran. Together, all of these are called the Indo-

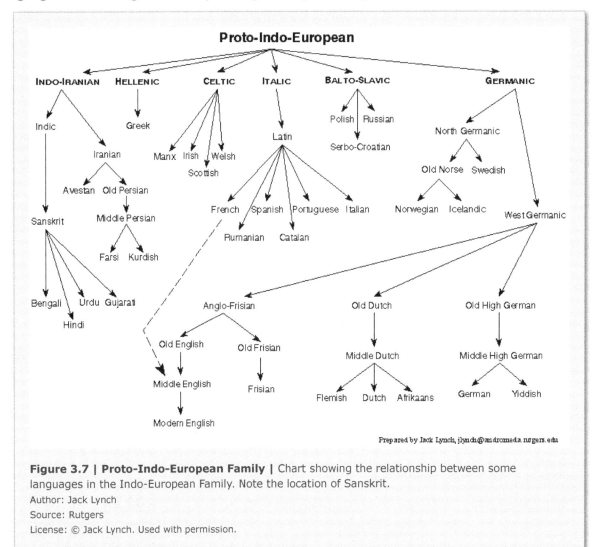

Figure 3.7 | Proto-Indo-European Family | Chart showing the relationship between some languages in the Indo-European Family. Note the location of Sanskrit.
Author: Jack Lynch
Source: Rutgers
License: © Jack Lynch. Used with permission.

Iranian language group. This language group is in turn one of nine branches of related language groups comprising the **Indo-European language family**.

Linguists assume these distantly-related languages share a common ancestor. They label that ancestral language proto-Indo-European and the people who spoke it Indo-Europeans. They posit a scenario whereby, in stages and over time, groups of these peoples migrated from their homeland to neighboring areas and settled down. Since this process happened over the course of many centuries and involved much interaction with other peoples along the way, the ancestral language evolved into many different ones while retaining some of the original features.

One question, then, is the location of this homeland and the history of the peoples who spoke these languages as they changed. Many places have been proposed, but at present the most widely accepted scenario puts this homeland in the steppe lands of southern Russia, just to the north of the Black Sea and Caspian Sea (see Map 3.5).

Evidence from archaeological sites suggests that during the third millennium an Indo-European people lived in this region as semi-nomadic pastoralists. They were likely the first to domesticate the horse and also improved the chariot by adding lighter, spoked wheels. They lived in tribes made up of extended families and worshipped numerous sky gods by offering sacrifices in fire altars.

At some point during this millennium and over the course of several centuries, groups of these peoples left their homeland and migrated south to the Iranian

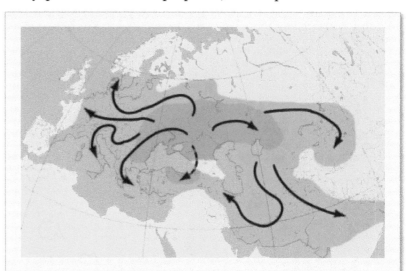

Map 3.5 | Indo-European Migrations | The area highlighted in pink, lying between the Black and Caspian Seas, is the suggested homeland for Indo-Europeans in the third millennium BCE. Arrows show the movement of speakers of Indo-European languages in the second millennium. The arrow showing movement to the southeast into India designates the Indo-Aryans, who began entering the Indo-Gangetic Plains from c. 1700 BCE.
Author: Larry Israel
Source: Original Work
License: CC BY-SA 4.0

Plateau. By 2000 BCE, Indo-Iranian speaking pastoralists were living on the Iranian Plateau and in Afghanistan. Some among these evolved into the Indo-Aryan speakers living to the northwest of the Indus. It is these peoples that began to arrive in the Punjab from c. 1700 BCE, with their Vedic religion, kinship-based social order, and pastoral and farming way of life.

3.7.3 The Later Vedic Age (1000 – 600 BCE)

During the early centuries of the Vedic Age, the world of the Aryan tribes was the rural setting of the Punjab. Some settlers, however, migrated east to the upper reaches of the Ganges River, setting the stage for the next period in India's history, the later Vedic Age. The later Vedic Age differs from the early Vedic Age in that during these centuries lands along the Ganges River were colonized by the Aryans and their political, economic, social, and religious life became more complex.

Over the course of these four centuries, Aryan tribes, with horses harnessed to chariots and wagons drawn by oxen, drove their herds east, migrating along and colonizing the plains surrounding the Ganges. Historians debate whether this happened through conquest and warfare or intermittent migration led by traders and people seeking land and opportunity. Regardless, by 600 BCE the Aryans had reached the lower reaches of the Ganges and as far south as the Vindhya Range and the Deccan Plateau. Most of northern India would therefore be shaped by the Aryan way of life. But in addition, as they moved into these areas, the Aryans encountered indigenous peoples and interacted with them, eventually imposing their way of life on them but also adopting many elements of their languages and customs.

During this time, agriculture became more important and occupations more diverse. As the lands were cleared, village communities formed. Two new resources made farming more productive: iron tools and rice. Implements such as iron axes and ploughs made clearing wilderness and sowing fields easier, and rice paddy agriculture produced more calories per unit of land. Consequently, population began to grow and people could more easily engage in other occupations. By the end of this period, the earliest towns had started to form.

Political changes accompanied economic developments. Looking ahead at sixth-century northern India, the landscape was dominated by kingdoms and oligarchies. That raises the question of the origins of these two different kinds of states, where different types of central authority formally governed a defined territory. Clearly, these states began to emerge during the later Vedic Age, especially after the eighth century.

Prior to this state formation, chiefs (rajas) and their assemblies, with the assistance of priests, saw to the well-being of their clans. This clan-based method of governing persisted and evolved into oligarchies. As the Aryans colonized new territory, clans or confederacies of clan would claim it as their possession, and name it after the ruling family. The heads of clan families or chiefs of each clan in a confederacy then jointly governed the territory by convening periodically in assembly halls. A smaller group of leaders managed the deliberations and voting, and carried out the tasks of day-to-day governing. These kinds of states have been called oligarchies because the heads of the most powerful families governed. They have also been called republics because these elites governed by assembly.

But in other territories clan chiefs became kings. These kings elevated themselves over kinsmen and the assemblies and served as the pivot of an embryonic administrative system. Their chief priests conducted grand rituals that demonstrated the king's special relation with the gods, putting the people in awe of him and giving them the sense that they would be protected. Treasurers managed the obligatory gifts kings expected in return. Most importantly, kingship became hereditary, and dynasties started to rule (see Map 3.6).

Society changed too. In earlier times, Aryan society was organized as a fluid three-class social structure consisting of priests, warriors, and commoners. But during the later Vedic Age, this social structure became more hierarchical and rigid. A system for classifying people based on

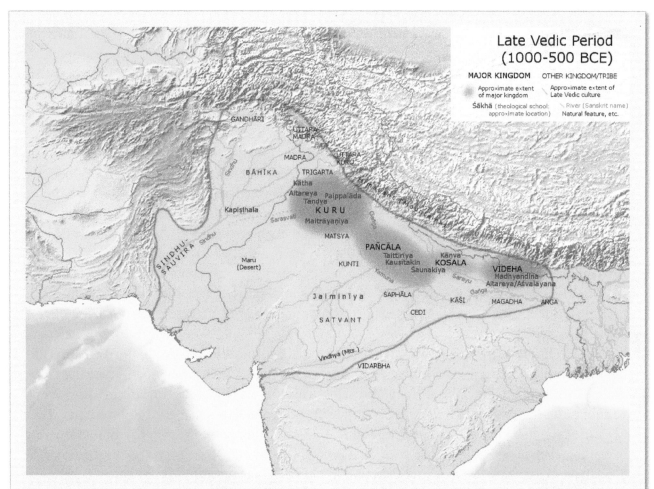

Map 3.6 | The Late Vedic Age (1000-600 BCE) | The area highlighted in pink, lying between the Black and Caspian Seas, is the suggested homeland for Indo-Europeans in the third millennium BCE. Arrows show the movement of speakers of Indo-European languages in the second millennium. The arrow showing movement to the southeast into India designates the Indo-Aryans, who began entering the Indo-Gangetic Plains from c. 1700 BCE.
Author: User "Avantiputra7"
Source: Wikimedia Commons
License: CC BY-SA 3.0

broad occupational categories was developed by the religious and political leaders in society. These categories are known as ***varnas***, and there were four of them: Brahmins, Kshatriya, Vaishya, and Shudra. The Brahmins were the priests, whose duty was to memorize and orally transmit the *Vedas* and perform sacrifices so as to maintain good relations with the gods. The Kshatriya were the chiefs and warriors, whose duty was to govern well and fight. The Vaishya were commoners who traded and farmed. They were responsible for society's material prosperity. The Shudras were servants who labored for others, usually as artisans or by performing menial tasks.

Varnas became hereditary social classes. That means a person was born into one of these and usually remained there for life, pursuing an occupation included in and marrying someone belonging to that *varna. Varna* has also been translated as ritual status. Your *varna* determined how pure or polluted you were, and thus what level of participation in rituals you would be allowed

Page | 79

and also who you could associate with. *Varna* thus defined a social hierarchy. The Brahmins were the purest and most honored. Warriors were respected for their leadership and supported the Brahmins, who affirmed their authority by carrying out royal ceremonies. Together, they dominated society. The Shudras (servants) were the most polluted and could not participate in any sacrifice or speak freely to members of other *varnas*. Over time, this way of organizing society came to be viewed as normal and natural.

During the later Vedic Age, the religion of the Aryans also developed in new directions. As one of the world's major religious traditions, **Hinduism** is multi-faceted and contains many layers of historical development. The earliest layer is called **Brahmanism**. Brahmanism begins with the *Rig Veda*, which presents a universe controlled by a host of divinities. During the early Vedic Age, the Aryans explained the world through myths about these higher powers, and their priests sought to influence them through sacrificial ceremonies. These priests become the Brahmin *varna*.

This early layer persisted and became even more elaborate. Three new *Vedas* were added to the *Rig Veda*, as well as two sets of texts called *Brahmanas* and **Upanishads**. Combined, this literature, which was composed in Sanskrit, constituted the full Vedic corpus, and became the preserve of the Brahmins.

The Brahmins weren't content with the 1028 hymns of the *Rig Veda*. Later Vedas set the hymns to music, added prose formulas that were to be uttered in the course of sacrificing to the divinities, and offered spells and incantations for achieving such goals as warding off disease and winning a battle. The *Brahmanas* were primarily handbooks of ritual for the Brahmins. They explained the meaning of the sacrifices and how to carry them out. Clearly, the Brahmins were becoming ever more conscious of their role in keeping the universe in good working order by pleasing and assisting the gods and consecrating kings. Their sacrificial observances became all the more elaborate, and an essential component of good kingship.

The *Upanishads*, however, added an entirely new set of ideas. The title means "sitting near" and points to a setting where sages conveyed spiritual insights to students through dialogue, stories, and analogies. The *Upanishads* are records of what was taught and discussed, the earliest dating to the eighth and seventh centuries BCE. These sages were likely hermits and wanderers who felt spiritually dissatisfied with the mythological and ritualistic approach of Brahmanism. Rather, they sought deeper insight into the nature of reality, the origins of the universe, and the human condition. The concepts that appear throughout these records of the outcome of their search are **brahman** (not to be confused with Brahmins), **atman**, **transmigration**, and **karma**.

According to these sages, human beings face a predicament. The universe they live in is created and destroyed repeatedly over the course of immense cycles of time, and humans wander through it in an endless succession of deaths and rebirths. This wandering is known as transmigration, a process that isn't random, but rather determined by the law of karma. According to this law, good acts bring a better rebirth, and bad acts a worse one. It may not happen in this lifetime, but one day virtue will be rewarded and evil punished.

Ultimately, however, the goal is to be liberated from the cycle of death and rebirth. According to Hindu traditions, the *Upanishads* reflect spiritual knowledge that was revealed to sages who undertook an inward journey through withdrawal from the world and meditation. What they discovered is that one divine reality underlies the universe. They called this ultimate reality *brahman*. They also discovered that deep within the heart of each person lies the eternal soul. They called this soul *atman*. Through quieting the mind and inquiry, the individual can discover *atman* and its identity with *brahman*: the soul is the divine reality. That is how a person is liberated from the illusion of endless wandering.

In conclusion, by the end of the Vedic Age, northern India had undergone immense changes. An Aryan civilization emerged and spread across the Indo-Gangetic Plains. This civilization was characterized by the Brahmin's religion (Brahmanism), the use of Sanskrit, and the *varna* social system. The simpler rural life of the clans of earlier times was giving way to the formation of states, and new religious ideas were being added to the evolving tradition known today as Hinduism.

3.8 TRANSITION TO EMPIRE: STATES, CITIES, AND NEW RELIGIONS (600 TO 321 BCE)

The sixth century begins a transitional period in India's history marked by important developments. Some of these bring to fruition processes that gained momentum during the late Vedic Age. Out of the hazy formative stage of state development, sixteen powerful kingdoms and oligarchies emerged. By the end of this period, one will dominate. Accompanying their emergence, India entered a second stage of urbanization, as towns and cities become a prominent feature of northern India. Other developments were newer. The caste system took shape as an institution, giving Indian society one of its most distinctive traits. Lastly, new religious ideas were put forward that challenged the dominance of Brahmanism.

3.8.1 States and Cities

The kingdom of **Magadha** became the most powerful among the sixteen states that dominated this transitional period, but only over time. At the outset, it was just one of eleven located up and down the Ganges River (see Map 3.7). The rest were established in the older northwest or central India. In general, larger kingdoms dominated the Ganges basin while smaller clan-based states thrived on the periphery. They all fought with each other over land and resources, making this a time of war and shifting alliances.

The victors were the states that could field the largest armies. To do so, rulers had to mobilize the resources of their realms. The Magadhan kings did this most effectively. Expansion began in 545 BCE under King Bimbisara. His kingdom was small, but its location to the south of the lower reaches of the Ganges River gave it access to fertile plains, iron ore, timber, and elephants. Governing from his inland fortress at **Rajagriha**, Bimbisara built an administration to extract these resources and used them to form a powerful military. After concluding marriage alliances with states to the north and west, he attacked and defeated the kingdom of Anga to the east. His son Ajatashatru, after killing his father, broke those alliances and waged war on the Kosala Kingdom and the Vrijji Confederacy. Succeeding kings of this and two more Magadhan dynasties continued to conquer neighboring states down to 321 BCE, thus forging an empire. But its reach was largely limited to the middle and lower reaches of the Ganges River.

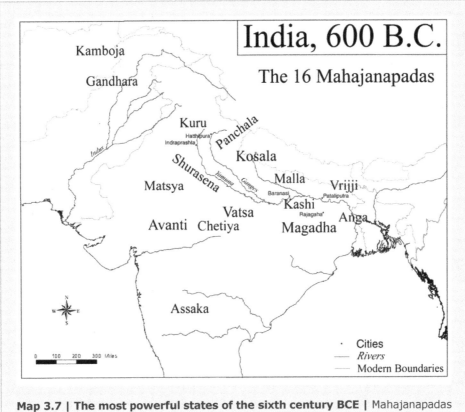

Map 3.7 | The most powerful states of the sixth century BCE | Mahajanapadas refers to the great kingdoms and oligarchies stretching along the Indo-Gangetic plains. The two capitals of Magadha–Rajagriha and Pataliputra–are also indicated.
Author: User "Kmusser"
Source: Wikimedia Commons
License: CC BY 2.5

To the northwest, external powers gained control. As we have seen, the mountain ranges defining that boundary contain passes permitting the movement of peoples. This made the northwest a crossroads, and, at times, the peoples crossing through were the armies of rulers who sought to control the riches of India. Outside powers located in Afghanistan, Iran, or beyond might extend political control into the subcontinent, making part of it a component in a larger empire.

One example is the Persian Empire (see Chapter 5). During the sixth century, two kings, Cyrus the Great and Darius I, made this empire the largest in its time. From their capitals on the Iranian Plateau, they extended control as far as the Indus River, incorporating parts of northwest India as provinces of the Persian Empire (see Map 3.8). Another example is Alexander the Great (also see Chapter 5). Alexander was the king of Macedon, a Greek state. After compelling other Greeks to follow him, he attacked the Persian Empire, defeating it in 331 BCE. That campaign took his forces all the way to mountain ranges bordering India. Desiring to find the end of the known world and informed of the riches of India, Alexander took his army through the Khyber Pass and overran a number of small states and cities located in the Punjab. But to Alexander's dismay, his soldiers refused to go any further, forcing him to turn back. They were exhausted from years of campaigning far from home and discouraged by news of powerful Indian states to the east. One of those was the kingdom of Magadha (see Map 3.9).

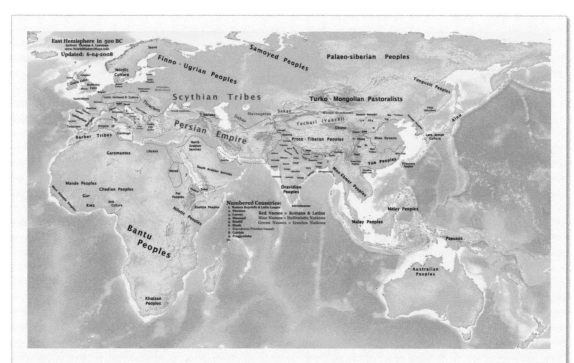

Map 3.8 | Afro-Eurasia in 500 BCE | Note how India is divided up among numerous polities, and how a large Persian Empire is reaching from the Middle East into northwest India.

Author: Thomas Lessman

Source: Talessman's Atlas of World History

License: © Thomas Lessman. Used with permission.

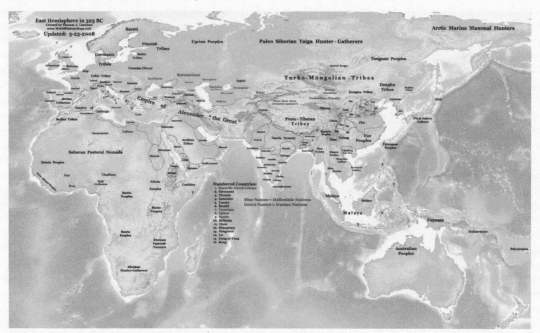

Map 3.9 | Afro-Eurasia in 323 BCE | By this time, Alexander the Great had defeated the Persian Empire and entered northwest India. The Nanda Dynasty (located along the Ganges River) was the last to rule Magadha.

Author: Thomas Lessman

Source: Talessman's Atlas of World History

License: © Thomas Lessman. Used with permission.

Magadha's first capital—Rajagriha—is one of many cities and towns with ruins dating back to this transitional period. Urban centers were sparse during the Vedic Age but now blossomed, much like they did during the mature phase of the Harappan Civilization. Similar processes were at work. As more forests were cleared and marshes drained, the agricultural economy of the Ganges basin produced ever more surplus food. Population grew, enabling more people to move into towns and engage in other occupations as craftsmen, artisans, and traders. Kings encouraged this economic growth as its revenue enriched their treasuries. Caravans of ox-drawn carts or boats laden with goods travelling from state to state could expect to encounter the king's customs officials and pay tolls. So important were rivers to accessing these trade networks that the Magadhan kings moved their capital to **Pataliputra**, a port town located on the Ganges (see Map 3.7). Thus, it developed as a hub of both political power and economic exchange. Most towns and cities began as one or the other, or as places of pilgrimage.

3.8.2 The Caste System

As the population of northern India rose and the landscape was dotted with more villages, towns, and cities, society became more complex. The social life of a Brahmin priest who served the king differed from that of a blacksmith who belonged to a town guild, a rich businessman residing in style in a city, a wealthy property owner, or a poor agricultural laborer living in a village. Thus, the social identity of each member of society differed.

In ancient India, one measure of identity and the way people imagined their social life and how they fit together with others was the *varna* system of four social classes. Another was **caste**. Like the *varnas*, castes were hereditary social classifications; unlike them, they were far more distinct social groups. The four-fold *varna* system was more theoretical and important for establishing clearly who the powerful spiritual and political elites in society were: the Brahmins and Kshatriya. But others were more conscious of their caste. There were thousands of these, and each was defined by occupation, residence, marriage, customs, and language. In other words, because "I" was born into such-and-such a caste, my role in society is to perform this kind of work. "I" will be largely confined to interacting with and marrying members of this same group. Our caste members reside in this area, speak this language, hold these beliefs, and are governed by this assembly of elders. "I" will also be well aware of who belongs to other castes, and whether or not "I" am of a higher or lower status in relation to them, or more or less pure. On that basis, "I" may or may not be able, for instance, to dine with them. That is how caste defined an individual's life.

The lowest castes were the untouchables. These were peoples who engaged in occupations considered highly impure, usually because they were associated with taking life; such occupations include corpse removers, cremators, and sweepers. So those who practiced such occupations were despised and pushed to the margins of society. Because members of higher castes believed touching or seeing them was polluting, untouchables were forced to live outside villages and towns, in separate settlements.

3.8.3 The Challenge to Brahmanism: Buddhism

During this time of transition, some individuals became dissatisfied with life and chose to leave the everyday world behind. Much like the sages of the *Upanishads*, these renunciants, as they were known, were people who chose to renounce social life and material things in order that they might gain deeper insight into the meaning of life. Some of them altogether rejected Brahmanism and established their own belief systems. The most renowned example is **Siddhartha Gautama** (c. 563 – 480 BCE), who is otherwise known as the **Buddha**.

Buddha means "Enlightened One" or "Awakened One," implying that the Buddha was at one time spiritually asleep but at some point woke up and attained insight into the truth regarding the human condition. His life story is therefore very important to Buddhists, people who follow the teachings of the Buddha.

Siddhartha was born a prince, son to the chieftain of Shakya, a clan-based state located at the foothills of the Himalaya in northern India. His father wished for him to be a ruler like himself, but Siddhartha went in a different direction. At twenty-nine, after marrying and having a son, he left home. Legends attribute this departure to his having encountered an old man, a sick man, a corpse, and a wandering renunciant while out on an excursion. Aging, sickness, and death posed the question of suffering for Siddhartha, leading him to pursue spiritual insight. For years, he sought instruction from other wanderers and experimented with their techniques for liberating the self from suffering through meditation and asceticism. But he failed to obtain the answers he sought.

Then, one day, while seated beneath a tree meditating for an extended period of time, a deepening calm descended upon Siddhartha, and he experienced *nirvana*. He also obtained insight into the reasons for human suffering and what was needful to end it. This insight was at the heart of his teachings for the remaining forty-five years of his life. During that time, he travelled around northern India teaching his dharma—his religious ideas and practices—and gained a following of students.

The principal teaching of the Buddha, presented at his first sermon, is called the **Four Noble Truths**. The first is the noble truth of suffering. Based on his own experiences, the Buddha concluded that life is characterized by suffering not only in an obvious physical and mental sense, but also because everything that promises pleasure and happiness is ultimately unsatisfactory and impermanent. The second noble truth states that the origin of suffering is an unquenchable thirst. People are always thirsting for something more, making for a life of restlessness with no end in sight. The third noble truth is that there is a cure for this thirst and the suffering it brings: *nirvana*. *Nirvana* means "blowing out," implying extinction of the thirst and the end of suffering. No longer striving to quell the restlessness with temporary enjoyments, people can awaken to "the city of nirvana, the place of highest happiness, peaceful, lovely, without suffering, without fear, without sickness, free from old age and death."[1] The fourth noble truth is the Eight-Fold Path, a set of practices that leads the individual to this liberating knowledge. The Buddha taught that through a program of study of Buddhist teachings (right understanding, right attitude), moral conduct (right speech, right action, right livelihood), and meditation (right effort, right

---

1   Rupert Gethin, *The Foundations of Buddhism* (Oxford University Press, 1998), 79.

concentration, right mindfulness), anyone could become a Buddha. Everyone has the potential to awaken, but each must rely on his or her own determination.

After the Buddha died c. 480 BCE, his students established monastic communities known as the Buddhist *sangha*. Regardless of their *varna* or caste, both men and women could choose to leave home and enter a monastery as a monk or nun. They would shave their heads, wear ochre-colored robes, and vow to take refuge in the Buddha, dharma, and *sangha*. Doing so meant following the example of the Buddha and his teachings on morality and meditation, as well as living a simple life with like-minded others in pursuit of *nirvana* and an end to suffering.

3.9 THE MAURYAN EMPIRE (321 – 184 BCE)

The kingdom of Magadha was the most powerful state in India when the Nanda Dynasty came to power in 364 BCE. Nine Nanda kings made it even greater, by improving methods of tax collection and administration, funding irrigation projects and canal building, and maintaining an impressive army of infantry, cavalry, elephants, and chariots.

But Nanda aspirations were cut short when they were overthrown by **Chandragupta Maurya** (r. 321 – 297 BCE), who began a new period in India's history. He and his son Bindusara (r. 287 – 273 BCE) and grandson **Ashoka** (r. 268 – 232 BCE) were destined to forge the first large empire in India's history, one that would inspire the imagination of later empire builders in South Asia. The **Mauryan Empire** included most of the subcontinent and lasted for 140 years (see Map 3.10)

Conflicting accounts make it difficult to say anything definitive about the first two kings. Chandragupta may have come from a Kshatriya (warrior) clan, or a Vaishya (commoner) clan of peacock-tamers. In his youth, he spent time in the northwest, where he encountered Alexander the Great. With the assistance of Kautilya, a disloyal

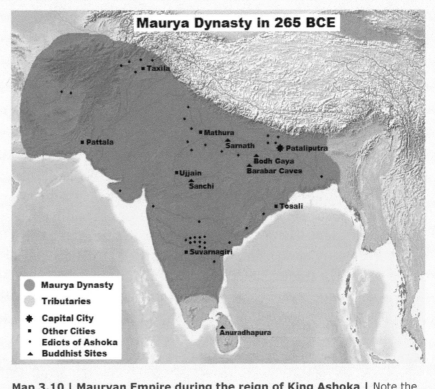

Map 3.10 | Mauryan Empire during the reign of King Ashoka | Note the location of the capital, Pataliputra.
Author: User "Vastu"
Source: Wikimedia Commons
License: CC BY-SA 3.0

Brahmin of the Nanda court, Chandragupta formed alliances with Nanda enemies, overthrowing them in 321 BCE. Thereafter, through diplomacy and war, he secured control over central and northern India.

Kautilya, whose advice may have been critical to Chandragupta's success, is viewed as the author of the **Arthashastra**, a treatise on statecraft. This handbook for kings covered in detail the arts of governing, diplomacy, and warfare. To help ensure centralization of power in the ruler's hands, it provided a blueprint of rules and regulations necessary to maintain an efficient bureaucracy, a detailed penal code, and advice on how to deploy spies and informants.

Chandragupta's campaigns ended when he concluded a treaty with Seleucus Nicator in 301 BCE. After Alexander the Great retreated from India and then died, a struggle for his empire broke out among his generals. Seleucus was one of them. He gained control of the eastern half and sought to reclaim northwest India. But he was confronted by Chandragupta, defeated, and forced to surrender the Indus Basin and much of Afghanistan, giving the Mauryan Empire control over trade routes to West Asia. The treaty, however, established friendly relations between the two rulers, for in exchange for hundreds of elephants, Seleucus gave Chandragupta a daughter in marriage and dispatched an envoy to his court. Hellenistic kings (see Chapter 5) maintained commercial and diplomatic ties with India.

Military expansion continued under Bindusara and Ashoka until all but the tip of the subcontinent came under the empire's control. With King Ashoka, however, warfare came to an end. We know far more about him because he left behind a fascinating record telling much about his ideas on governing. He had edicts inscribed on rocks throughout the realm and on sandstone pillars erected in the Ganges heartland (see Map 3.11).

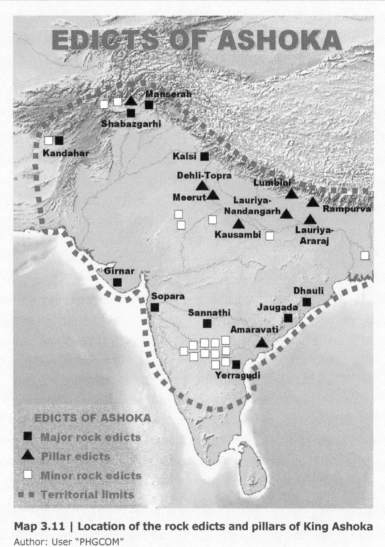

Map 3.11 | Location of the rock edicts and pillars of King Ashoka
Author: User "PHGCOM"
Source: Wikimedia Commons
License: CC BY-SA 3.0

He then placed them in populous areas where people usually gathered, so that his officials could read them to his largely illiterate subjects.

One rock edict speaks to why King Ashoka decided to renounce violence. While waging war against a small state located along the east coast, he was deeply disturbed by the amount of suffering and dislocation the war heaped upon innocent people's lives. This realization caused him to redouble his faith in the Buddha. Ashoka, it turns out, was a lay follower of Buddhism.

In his edicts, he proclaimed to his subjects that the sound of the drum would be replaced by the sound of the **dharma**. In ancient India, dharma meant universal law. For the Brahmin priests, for example, dharma meant a society and religious order founded on Vedic principles and the caste system. For Buddhists, dharma consisted of the truths taught by the Buddha. For kings, dharma was enlightened governing and just rule. Thus, Ashoka was proclaiming that he would now rule by virtue, not force.

Ashoka's kingly dharma was shaped by his personal practice of Buddhism. This dharma consisted of laws of ethical behavior and right conduct fashioned from Indian traditions of kingship and his understanding of Buddhist principles. To gain his subject's willing obedience, he sought to inspire a sense of gratitude by presenting himself in the role of a father looking out for his children. He told his subjects that he was appointing officers to tour his realm and attend to the welfare and happiness of all. Justice was to be impartially administered and medical treatment provided for animals and humans. A principle of non-injury to all beings was to be observed. Following this principle meant not only renouncing state violence, but also forbidding slaughtering certain animals for sacrifices or for cooking in the royal kitchen. Ashoka also proclaimed that he would replace his pleasure and hunting tours with dharma tours. During these, he promised to give gifts to Brahmins and the aged and to visit people in the countryside.

In return, Ashoka asked his subjects to observe certain principles. He knew his empire was pluralistic, consisting of many peoples with different cultures and beliefs. He believed that if he instilled certain values in these peoples, then his realm might be knit together in peace and harmony. Thus, in addition to non-injury, Ashoka taught forbearance. He exhorted his subjects to respect parents, show courtesy to servants, and, more generally, be liberal, compassionate, and truthful in their treatment of others. These values were also to be embraced by religious communities, since Ashoka did not want people fighting over matters of faith.

The king's writ shaped the government because kings were the heart of it. They were advised by a council of ministers and served by high officials who oversaw the major functions of the state. The Mauryans were particularly concerned with efficient revenue collection and uniform administration of justice. To that end, they divided the empire into a hierarchy of provinces and districts and appointed officials to manage matters at each level. But given such an immense empire spread over a geographically and ethnically diverse territory, the level of Mauryan control varied. Historians recognize three broad zones. The first was the metropolitan region—with its capital Pataliputra—located on the Ganges Plain. This heartland was tightly governed. The second zone consisted of conquered regions of strategic and economic importance. These provinces were placed under the control of members of the royal family and senior officials, but state formation was slower. That is, the tentacles of bureaucracy did not reach as deeply into local communities. Lastly, the third zone consisted of hinterlands sparsely populated by tribes of foragers and nomads. Here, state control was minimal, amounting to little more than establishing workable relations with chieftains.

After King Ashoka's reign, the Mauryan Empire declined. The precise reasons for this decline are unknown. Kings enjoyed only brief reigns during the final fifty years of the empire's existence, so they may have been weak. Since loyalty to the ruler was one element of the glue that held the centralized bureaucracy together, weak kings may explain why the political leaders of provinces pulled away and the empire fragmented into smaller states. Furthermore, the Mauryan court's demand for revenue sufficient to sustain the government and a large standing army may have contributed to discontent. In 184 BCE, the last king was assassinated by his own Brahmin military commander, and India's first major imperial power came to an end.

3.10 REGIONAL STATES, TRADE, AND DEVOTIONAL RELIGION: INDIA 200 BCE – 300 CE

After the Mauryan Empire fell, no one major power held control over a substantial part of India until the rise of the Gupta Empire in the fourth century CE. Thus, for five hundred years, from c. 200 BCE to 300 CE, India saw a fairly rapid turnover of numerous, competing regional monarchies. Most of these were small, while the larger ones were only loosely integrated. Some developed along the Ganges. Others were of Central Asian origins, the product of invasions from the northwest. Also, for the first time, states formed in southern India. Yet, in spite of the political instability, India was economically dynamic, as trade within and without the subcontinent flourished, and India was increasingly linked to other parts of the world in networks of exchange. And new trends appeared in India's major religious traditions. A popular, devotional form of worship was added to Buddhism and also became a defining element of Hinduism.

3.10.1 Regional States

The general who brought the Mauryan Empire to a close by a military coup established the Shunga Dynasty (c. 185 – 73 BCE). Like its predecessor, this kingdom was centered on the middle Ganges, the heartland of India's history since the late Vedic Age. But unlike it, the Shunga Kingdom rapidly dwindled in size.

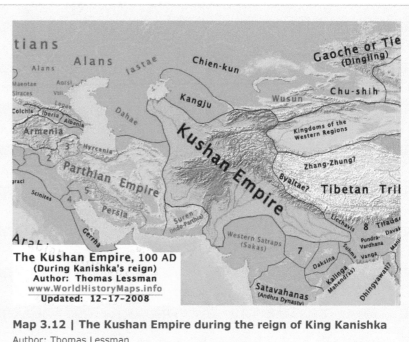

Map 3.12 | The Kushan Empire during the reign of King Kanishka
Author: Thomas Lessman
Source: Talessman's Atlas of World History
License: © Thomas Lessman. Used with permission.

Shunga rulers were constantly warring with neighboring kingdoms, and the last fell to an internal coup in 73 CE. Subsequently, during the ensuing half millennium, other regions of India played equally prominent roles.

The northwest remained a source of dynamism, as different peoples living beyond the Hindu Kush invaded India and established one kingdom after another. Most of this movement was caused by instability on the steppe lands of Central Asia, where competing confederations of nomadic pastoralists fought for control over territory.

The most powerful among this succession of states was the **Kushan Kingdom**, whose origins take us far away to the north of China. There, in the second century CE, nomadic groups struggling with scarcity moved west, displacing another group and forcing them into northern Afghanistan. Those peoples are known as the Yuezhi (yew-eh-jer), and they were made up of several tribes. In the first century CE, a warrior chieftain from one Yuezhi tribe, the Kushans, united them, invaded northwest India, and assumed exalted titles befitting a king. His

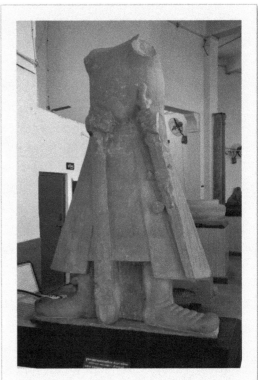

Figure 3.8 | Statue of King Kanishka | Statue of King Kanishka, second century CE. The head is missing.
Author: Biswarup Ganguly
Source: Wikimedia Commons
License: CC BY 3.0

successor, ruling from Afghanistan, gained control over the Punjab and reached into the plains of the upper Ganges River.

The greatest Kushan ruler, **King Kanishka**, furthered what these first two kings began, forging an empire extending from Central Asia across the mountain ranges of Afghanistan into much of northern India (see Map 3.12). Ruling the many peoples of such a sprawling territory required more than the periodic plundering campaigns of nomad chieftains. One sculpture of King Kanishka puts these Central Asian roots on display (see Figure 3.8). In it, he is wearing a

Figure 3.9 | Gold coins dating to the reign of King Kanishka | Each coin contains an image of Kanishka on one side, an image of a deity on the obverse, and inscriptions giving the names of both. Kanishka is depicted wearing a crown, beard, long tunic, trousers, and boots. He is holding a scepter or trident in the left hand and standing over an altar. Inscriptions recognize him as "King of kings." Flames arise from his shoulders. On the obverse side, the first coin displays the Buddha raising his right hand, symbolizing reassurance. Other Kushan coins display Greek, Indian, and Iranian deities.
Author: User "World Imaging"
Source: Wikimedia Commons
License: CC BY-SA 3.0

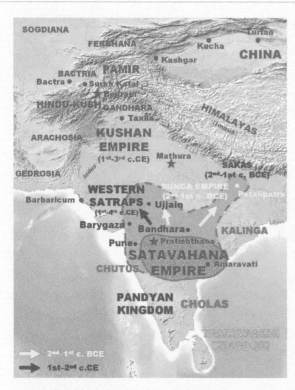

Map 3.13 | India in the second and first century CE | This map shows the location of the Shunga (Sunga), Satavahana, and Kushan Empires, demonstrating clearly that India was constituted by several greater and lesser regional powers during these centuries.

Author: User "PHG"

Source: Wikimedia Commons

License: Public Domain

belted tunic, coat, and felt boots, and carrying a sword and mace. Kushan gold coins, however, cast him and his two predecessors in another light: as universal monarchs (see Figure 3.9). On one side, the crowned kings are displayed along with inscriptions bearing titles used by the most powerful Indian, Persian, Chinese, and Roman emperors of that time. The obverse side contains images of both Indian and foreign deities. The Kushan rulers, it appears, solved the problem of ruling an extensive, culturally diverse realm by patronizing the many different gods beloved by the peoples living within it. Buddhists, for instance, saw King Kanishka as a great Buddhist ruler, much like they did King Ashoka. In fact, Kanishka supported Buddhist scholarship and encouraged missionaries to take this faith from India to Central Asia and China. But his coins also depict Greek, Persian, and Hindu deities, suggesting that he was open-minded, and perhaps strategic, in matters of religion.

After Kanishka's reign, from the mid-second century CE onwards, the empire declined. Like the other, larger Indian states during this time, only a core area was ruled directly by the king's servants. The other areas were governed indirectly by establishing tributary relations with local rulers. As Kushan power waned, numerous smaller polities emerged, turning northern and central India into a mosaic of states.

The Indian peninsula—the territory south of the Indo-Gangetic Plain and the Vindhya Mountain Range—also features more prominently after the fall of the Mauryan Empire. In the south, kingdoms emerged for the first time. The largest was the **Satavahana Kingdom**, which included most of the Deccan Plateau and lasted about three centuries. The first rulers were former Mauryan officials who capitalized on its dissolution, established their own state, and expanded to the north (see Map 3.13). To establish their legitimacy, Satavahana kings embraced Aryan civilization by allowing Brahmins to perform sacrifices at the court and by upholding the *varna* social order. They also prospered from a rich agricultural base and trade. However, like so many of the larger states during these centuries, this kingdom was only loosely integrated, consisting of small provinces governed by civil and military officers and allied, subordinate chieftains and kings.

3.10.2 Economic Growth and Flourishing Trade Networks

Gold coins discovered in Kushan territory provide much information about the rulers who issued them. The Satavahanas also minted coins. Additionally, Roman gold coins have been found at over 130 sites in south India. These were issued by Roman emperors at the turn of the Christian era, during the first century CE. These coins serve as a sign of the times. Indian monarchs issued coins because trade was growing and intensifying all around them and they wished to support and profit from it. Expanding the money supply facilitated trade and was one way to achieve that goal. Both Indian kingdoms were also geographically well positioned to take advantage of emerging global trade networks linking the subcontinent to other regions of Afro-Eurasia. This advantage provides one reason why they flourished.

The expansion of trade both within and without India is a major theme of these five centuries. Put simply, South Asia was a crossroads with much to offer. In market towns and cities across the subcontinent, artisans and merchants organized to produce and distribute a wide variety of goods. **Guilds** were their principal method of organization. A guild was a professional association made up of members with a particular trade. Artisan guilds—such as weavers and goldsmiths—set the prices and ensured the quality of goods. Operating like and sometimes overlapping with castes, guilds also set rules for members and policed their behavior. They acted collectively as proud participants of urban communities, displaying their banners in festive processions and donating money to religious institutions. Merchant guilds then saw to it that their artisan products were transported along routes traversing the subcontinent or leading beyond to foreign lands.

The lands and peoples surrounding India, and the many empires they lived under, are the topic of later chapters, but we can take a snapshot of the scene here (see Map 3.14). In the first century CE, India sat amidst trade networks connecting the Roman Empire, Persian Empire (Parthian), Chinese Empire, and a host of smaller kingdoms and states in Africa, Central Asia, and Southeast Asia. The major trade networks were the Silk Roads and the Indian Ocean maritime trade routes. Thus, for example, Greco-Roman traders plied the waters of the Arabian Sea, bringing ships filled with amphorae and gold coins to ports located along the west coast of India, and returning with spices, textiles, and gems. Indian traders sailed the waters of the Bay of Bengal, bringing cloth

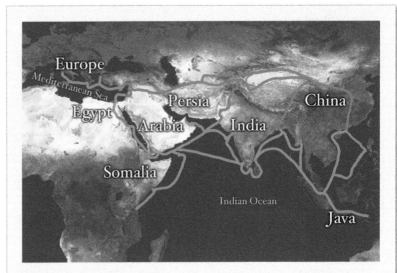

Map 3.14 | Trade Routes | Some of the major Indian Ocean and Silk Road trade routes that linked India to the rest of Afro-Eurasia
Author: User "Splette"
Source: Wikimedia Commons
License: Public Domain

and beads from the Coromandel Coast to Southeast Asia and returning with cinnamon cloves and sandalwood. In the northwest, a similar trade in a variety of goods took place along the Silk Roads. Indian traders, for instance, took advantage of the excellent position of the Kushan Empire to bring silk from Central Asia to the ports of northwest India, from where it could then be sent on to Rome. In sum, this vibrant international trade constituted an early stage of globalization. Combined with regional trade across the subcontinent, India saw an increase in travel in all directions, even as it remained divided among many regional kingdoms.

3.10.3 Religious Transformations: Buddhism and Hinduism into the Common Era

Aside from expanding trade, another theme during these centuries of political division is transformations in two of India's major religions traditions: Buddhism and Hinduism. In both cases, new religious ideas and practices were added that emphasized the importance of devotion and appealed to broader groups of people.

Buddhism thrived after the Buddha died in c. 480 BCE, all the more so during this period of regional states and the early centuries of the Common Era, at the very moment Christianity was spreading through the Roman Empire. In fact, it would not be exaggeration to say that Buddhism was the dominant public religion. The communities of monks and nuns (*sangha*) that formed after Buddha's time lived in monasteries built along trade routes, near towns, or in caves. To build these and survive, the *sangha* needed much support, which often came in the form of royal patronage. Kings such as Ashoka and Kanishka, for example, offered lavish support for Buddhist institutions. But over time, the contributions of merchants, women, and people from lower *varnas* became just as important. Unlike Vedic Brahmanism, which privileges the Brahmin *varna*, Buddhism was more inclusive and less concerned with birth and social class. After all, in theory, anyone could become a Buddha.

Buddhism also emphasized the importance of attaining good karma for better rebirths and a future enlightenment; one didn't need to be a monk to work at this. Rather, any ordinary layperson, regardless of their religious beliefs, could also take Buddhist vows and practice Buddhist ways. That meant not only leading a moral life but also supporting the *sangha*. By so doing, the good karma of the monks and nuns would be transferred to the community and oneself. This practice served to not only make the world a better place and to ensure a better future, but also to allow opportunities for publicly displaying one's piety. That is why kings, rich merchants, and ordinary people donated to the *sangha* and gave monks food.

With so much support and participation, Buddhism also changed. Every major world religion has different branches. Christianity, for example, has three major ones: the Roman Catholic, Eastern Orthodox, and Protestant churches. These branches share a common root but diverge in some matters of belief and practice. Buddhism has two major branches: Theravada and Mahayana Buddhism. **Theravada Buddhism** is early Buddhism, the Buddhism of the early *sangha*, and is based on the earliest records of the Buddha's teaching of the Four Noble Truths. A practitioner of this form of Buddhism sought to end suffering and attain *nirvana* by engaging the Eight-Fold

Path, a program of study, moral conduct, and meditation. Ideally, the practitioner pursued this program as a monk or nun in a monastic setting, and eventually became an "arhat," that is, a perfected person who is nearly or fully enlightened.

Mahayana Buddhism came later, during the early centuries of the Common Era. Mahayana means "Great Vehicle," pointing to the fact that this form of Buddhism offers multiple paths to enlightenment for people from all walks of life. This branch has no single founder and consists of a set of ideas elaborated upon in new Buddhist scriptures dating to this time. In one of these new paths, the Buddha becomes a god who can be worshipped, and by anyone. A monk or lay follower is welcome to make an offering before an image of the Buddha placed in a shrine. By so doing, they demonstrate their desire to end suffering and seek salvation through faith in the Buddha.

Furthermore, with the "Great Vehicle," the universe becomes populated with numerous Buddhas. Practitioners developed the idea that if anyone can become a Buddha over the course of many lifetimes of practice, then other Buddhas must exist. Also, the belief arose that some individuals had tread the path to Buddhahood but chose to forego a final enlightenment where they would leave the world behind so that they could, out of great compassion for all suffering people, work for their deliverance. These holy beings are known as Bodhisattvas, that is, enlightened persons who seek *nirvana* solely out of their desire to benefit all humanity. Buddhists also believed that the universe consisted of multiple worlds with multiple heavenly realms. Some of these Buddhas and Bodhisattvas created their own heavenly realms and, from there, offer grace to those seeking salvation through them. Through veneration and worship, the follower hopes to be reborn in that heavenly realm, where they can then finish the path to liberation. Seeking to become a Bodhisattva through a path of devotion was one of the new paths outlined by Mahayana scriptures.

Buddhism traveled out of India and had an impact on other parts of the world, making it a major world religion. This expansion resulted from the efforts of Buddhist missionaries and merchants, as well as kings who supported its propagation. Theravada Buddhism was carried to Sri Lanka and parts of Southeast Asia, where it remains a dominant religious tradition. Mahayana Buddhism spread to Central and East Asia, a process that was facilitated by the Silk Road and the support of kings like Kanishka of the Kushan Empire (see Map 3.15). However, Buddhism eventually declined in India, especially after the first millennium BCE. From that time, Hinduism and Islam increasingly won over the religious imagination of the peoples of India, with royal patronage and lay support following.

Hinduism also saw new developments during this period and throughout the first millennium CE. In fact, many scholars see these centuries as the time during which Hinduism first took shape and prefer using the term Vedic Brahmanism for the prior history of this religious tradition. Vedic Brahmanism was the sacrifice-centered religion of the Vedas where, in exchange for gifts, Brahmins performed rituals for kings and householders in order to ensure the favor of the gods. It also included the speculative world of the Upanishads, where renunciants went out in search of spiritual liberation.

But something important happened during these later centuries. An additional religious literature was compiled and shrines and temples with images of deities were constructed, pointing

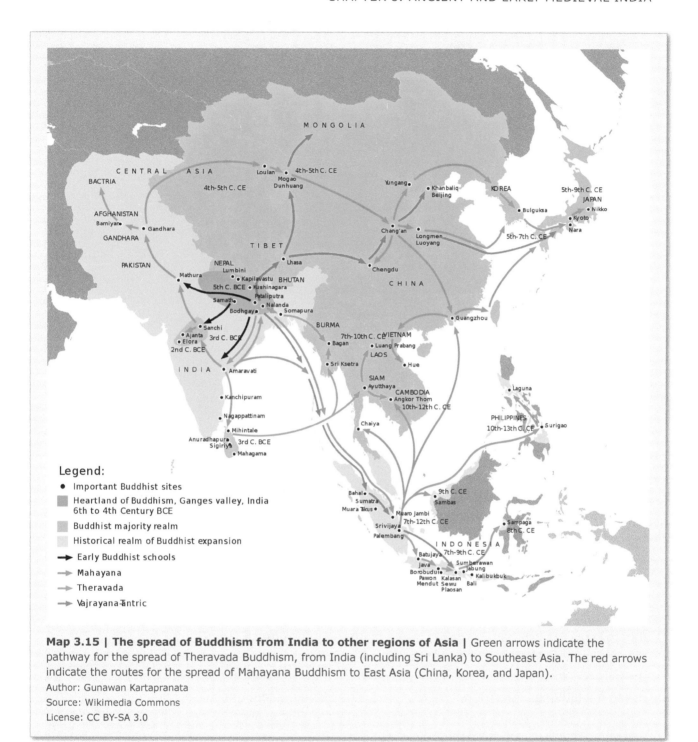

Map 3.15 | The spread of Buddhism from India to other regions of Asia | Green arrows indicate the pathway for the spread of Theravada Buddhism, from India (including Sri Lanka) to Southeast Asia. The red arrows indicate the routes for the spread of Mahayana Buddhism to East Asia (China, Korea, and Japan).
Author: Gunawan Kartapranata
Source: Wikimedia Commons
License: CC BY-SA 3.0

to the emergence of new, popular forms of devotion and an effort to define a good life and society according to the idea of **dharma**. With this transition, we can speak more formally of Hinduism.

One important set of texts is the **Dharma Scriptures**, ethical and legal works whose authority derived from their attribution to ancient sages. Dharma means "duty" or proper human conduct and so, true to their title, these scriptures define the rules each person must follow in order to lead a righteous and devout life and contribute to a good society. Most importantly, these rules were determined by the role assigned to an individual by the *varna* system of social classes, the caste system, and gender. For example, for a male, dharma meant following the rules for their caste and *varna* while passing through four stages in life: student, householder, hermit, and renunciant. In his youth, a man must study to prepare for his occupation and, as a householder, he must support his family and contribute to society. Late in life, after achieving these goals, he should renounce material desires and withdraw from society, first living as a hermit on the margins of society and then as a wandering renunciant whose sole devotion is to god.

A woman's roles, on the other hand, were defined as obedience to her father

Figure 3.10 | An early Hindu temple in Deogarh, India | This temple was erected to worship Vishnu during the Gupta period, c. 500 CE. Ruins from earlier temples dating to the period 200 BCE-300 CE are not well preserved.
Author: Byron Aihara
Source: Wikimedia Commons
License: CC BY-SA 2.0

in youth and faithful service to her husband as an adult. For this reason, historians see a trend in ancient Indian history whereby women became increasingly subservient and subordinate. Although women were to be honored and supported, the ideal society and family were defined in patriarchal terms. That meant men dominated public life, were the authority figures at home, and usually inherited the property. Also, women were increasingly expected to marry at a very young age—even prior to puberty—and to remain celibate as widows. In later centuries, some widows even observed the practice of burning themselves upon the funeral pyre of the deceased husband.

Famous Indian epics also illustrated the theme of duty. The ***Ramayana*** ("Rama's Journey") tells the story of Prince Rama and his wife Sita. Rama's parents—the king and queen—wished for him to take the throne, but a second queen plotted against him and forced him into exile for years. Sita accompanied him, but was abducted by a demon-king, leading to a battle in consequence. With the help of a loyal monkey god, Rama defeated the demon, recovered his wife, and returned with her to his father's kingdom, where they were crowned king and queen. In brief, throughout this long story, Rama exemplified the virtues of a king and Sita exemplified the virtues of a daughter and wife. They both followed their dharma.

A similar theme dominates the ***Bhagavad-Gita*** ("Song of the Lord"). This classic of Hindu scripture is included as a chapter in another Indian epic, the *Mahabharata* (*The Great Bharata*). It tells of wars between cousins who are fighting over the title to their kingdom's throne. As a battle was poised to commence, one of these cousins—Prince Arjuna—threw down his weapons and refused to fight because he did not wish to harm his kinsmen. But Krishna, his mentor and charioteer, delivered a speech on the nature of duty for a warrior like himself, one that illustrated

Figure 3.11 | Relief of Shiva and his wife Parvati in a rock-cut Hindu cave-temple (c. 800) | This relief also dates to a later age but well captures traditions of iconic representations of Hindu deities dating back to the early centuries CE.
Author: User "QuartierLatin1968"
Source: Wikimedia Commons
License: CC BY-SA 3.0

the religious basis for observing dharma. Arjuna was thus moved to action.

Religious texts and temples also signal the rise of a powerful devotional Hinduism centered upon a few supreme deities. Stone temples were erected for the purpose of housing representations of a god or goddess (see Figure 3.10). Peoples of all classes could go to the temple to view the deity, pray, and offer fruits and flowers. By so doing, they showed their love for this lord and their desire to be saved by his or her grace. The most popular deities were Shiva and Vishnu.

Growing up, devotees of these supreme deities would hear countless myths and legends about their origins, exploits, and powers from Brahmins at the temples or story-tellers in their hometown. Vishnu preserves the universe and watches over it; in times of unbridled evil, he assumes the form of an avatar to remove it and return the world to righteousness. King Rama of the *Ramayana* and Krishna of the *Bhagavad-Gita* are in fact two such incarnations of Vishnu. Shiva is both benevolent and protective but also destroys all things. Whereas Vishnu preserves the universe, Shiva destroys it at the end of a cycle. A third deity, Brahma, then recreates it. Combined, this Hindu trinity—Brahma the creator, Vishnu the preserver, and Shiva the destroyer—represent different facets of the one divine reality behind the great cosmic cycles and also life and death. They each have female counterparts. Shiva's wife Parvati, for instance, is a goddess of love and devotion (see Figure 3.11).

In sum, during this period and the first millennium CE, several elements come together to make up the religion outsiders later labeled Hinduism. These elements include the sacrificial religion of the Brahmins, the renunciants' spiritual pursuit of Self and divine reality (*atman* and *brahman*), a social order shaped by the *varna* and caste system, notions of law and duty embodied in each individual's dharma, and devotion to supreme deities and their avatars. Hinduism thus thoroughly shaped the social and spiritual life of the peoples of India and of Indian society. Therefore, the rulers of ancient India supported the Brahmins, built temples, upheld the *varna* system, and assumed titles declaring their devotion to the supreme deities. Hinduism became part of the king's dharma, and fulfilling that dharma brought the approval of his subjects.

3.11 THE GUPTA EMPIRE AND INDIA'S CLASSICAL AGE (300 – 600 CE)

The pattern of regional states characteristic of post-Mauryan times and the early centuries of the Common Era will persist in India until the sixteenth century. At any one time, India had many kings. But on occasion, one king might forge a substantial regional power and assume grand titles that elevated him over others. The political scene, therefore, consisted of not only a mosaic of royal powers but also a political hierarchy. Some rulers held power over others, making for a pattern of paramountcy and subordination among kings and princes of many different dynasties across the land. These paramount powers could then take advantage of the stability they established and the wealth they accrued to patronize the arts and promote a cultural renaissance. The **Gupta Empire** is the pre-eminent example of such a power during the period 300 – 600 CE; indeed, some historians see the time during which they dominated northern India as a classical age.

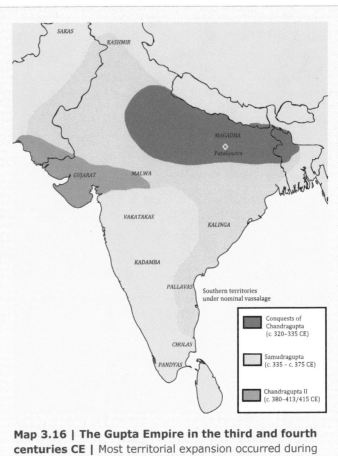

Map 3.16 | The Gupta Empire in the third and fourth centuries CE | Most territorial expansion occurred during the reign of Samudragupta, although many local rulers were left in place as subordinate kings.
Author: User "Javierfv1212"
Source: Wikimedia Commons
License: CC BY-SA 3.0

As is the case for so much of India's ancient political history, details concerning Gupta rulers have been reconstructed largely from coins, inscriptions, and seals. The dynasty begins in obscurity with two kings of a minor state located along the Ganges River, but then explodes on the scene with the next two kings: **Chandragupta I** (c. 320 – 335) and his son **Samudragupta** (c. 335 – 375). Through conquest and marital alliances, Chandragupta I forged a larger empire in the old Ganges heartland (see Map 3.16). A gold coin provides some of the evidence detailing the Gupta Empire. This coin displays Chandragupta standing next to a certain Queen Kumaradevi. He has taken the title "Great King of Kings," which signifies imperial power, while she is identified as the princess of a powerful neighboring kingdom (see Figure 3.12).

During his forty-year reign, Samudragupta made the empire great, a feat most forcefully evidenced by a royal eulogy inscribed on one of the old edict pillars of King Ashoka. This eulogy, which describes Samudragupta as "conqueror of the four corners of the earth," tells of how he subdued dozens of kings across the subcontinent. Closer to home, along the Ganges, many rulers were slain and their territory was annexed, while farther out across northern India and to the southeast, others were "captured and liberated." These captured and liberated kings were recognized as "servants," which meant they could continue to rule their own lands as subordinates, on the condition that they paid tribute and homage. Gupta rulers thus directly administered a core territory along the Ganges River while adopting a model of **tributary overlordship** for the rest. The Gupta imperial court in effect presided over a society of tributary rulers.

After Samudragupta's time, two more Gupta rulers enjoyed long reigns of forty years, with the empire reaching a peak of power and prosperity. But in the sixth century, decline set in. A series

Figure 3.12 | Gupta period coin depicting Chandragupta I and Queen Kumaradevi | This coin evidences a marital alliance between the Guptas and a powerful neighboring state.
Author: User "Uploadalt"
Source: Wikimedia Commons
License: CC BY-SA 3.0

of weaker rulers faced internal dissension at home and foreign invasion from abroad. A great nomadic power known as the Huns emerged out of Central Asia and invaded the northwest, destabilizing Gupta rule. Subordinate rulers then began to break away, and smaller kingdoms replaced the empire. After the sixth century, India entered a new stage in its history.

But there is more to these centuries than high politics. Again, the Gupta era is often labeled as a classical age for India. A period in the history of a civilization's being labeled as classical generally means it was a time of artistic and intellectual excellence, with its having attained standard-setting achievements in a number of fields. Classical also suggests a certain level of maturation for a civilization. It should be noted, however, that some scholars question the use of this term

Figure 3.13 | Gupta Period Buddhist sculpture (fifth century) showing the seated Buddha giving a sermon
Author: User "Tevaprapas"
Source: Wikimedia Commons
License: CC BY-SA 3.0

because all ages produce great works, and sometimes choosing one period as classical simply represents the biased judgment of a later time.

Yet, during the Gupta era, India did produce important scientific discoveries and works of art and literature. The exquisite sculptures of the Buddha portraying his serene enlightenment and teaching were the epitome of the classical achievement in art (see Figure 3.13). India also saw an outpouring of literary masterpieces. **Kalidasa** is one of India's greatest Sanskrit poets and playwrights. His play *The Recognition of Shakuntala*, a world masterpiece, tells the story of a girl who lived in a hermitage in the countryside after being abandoned by her parents. One day, a king was out hunting and chanced upon her. They fell in love and married. But then he hurried back to his palace and when she later came to him he no longer knew her because he had been cursed. The only solution for her dilemma was for her to present a ring he had left her. Unfortunately, it had slipped off her finger. The play tells of how this love story concluded, along with the involvement of many higher powers.

In the field of medicine, **Ayurveda** matured as more complete editions of ancient medical texts were compiled. Ayurveda (meaning "knowledge for longevity") is India's ancient medical science. It provides a systematic effort to explain the origins of diseases in dislocations of bodily humors (substances) and to prescribe cures for them. India also saw advancements in the fields of astronomy and mathematics. **Aryabhata** (476 – 550 CE), for instance, was the first astronomer to propose that the earth rotated on an axis and a scientific explanation for eclipses. He calculated *pi* to 3.1416 and the solar year to 364.3586805 days. His work demonstrates the contemporary use of a sophisticated system of decimal notation, which was also an ancient Indian discovery.

3.12 INDIA'S EARLY MEDIEVAL AGE AND THE DEVELOPMENT OF ISLAMIC STATES IN INDIA, 600 – 1300

The history of ancient India concludes with the decline of the Gupta Empire. The next major period, which lasts for roughly seven centuries (c. 600 – 1300), is the early medieval age. During these centuries, kingdoms in both the north and south proliferated and regularly turned over. Therefore, at any one time, India was fragmented by numerous regional kingdoms. As the rulers of these warred and formed alliances, they employed the system of paramountcy and subordination begun during the Gupta era, with some rulers being overlords and others vassals. Also, successful rulers demonstrated their power by granting land to officers, Brahmins, and temples. The outcome was a political pattern labeled **Indian feudalism**.

These rulers also demonstrated their power—and enhanced it—by patronizing Hindu institutions and developing local traditions in the regions where their courts resided. They adopted titles showing their devotion to the great Hindu deities, declared their intent to uphold dharma, built fabulous Hindu temples in urban centers, and charged Brahmins with attending to them and serving at their courts. One outstanding example of a feudal kingdom is the **Chola Kingdom** of southern India.

Lastly, at the end of this age, a new force appeared on the Indian scene. Muslim Arab and Turkic rulers of West and Central Asia made incursions into the subcontinent. Along with Arab traders arriving on India's west coast for trade, they brought a new religion and type of rule to the landscape of early medieval India and forged new connections between the subcontinent and the rest of Afro-Eurasia.

3.12.1 Indian Feudalism

Feudalism is a term historians first used to describe the political, social, and economic system of the European Middle Ages (see Chapter Twelve). That system was the world of lords, vassal knights, and serfs characteristic of Europe from the tenth to thirteenth centuries. In exchange for homage and military service, vassals received land from their lords. These lands became their manors, and serfs worked them. The lords and their vassals constituted a privileged nobility, while the serfs lived in a state of servitude.

Historians also use feudalism to describe India during the early medieval age. But the usefulness of this term is much debated, because conditions on the ground varied from place to place, not only in Europe but also in India. Therefore, historians now only use the term in a general sense while also describing specific variations. In general, feudalism designates a political and economic scene characterized by fragmented authority, a set of obligations between lords and vassals, and grants of land (including those who work it) by rulers in exchange for some kind of service.

Authority on the early medieval Indian subcontinent was indeed fragmented, not only by the many regional kingdoms that existed at any one time but also, more importantly, within kingdoms. Because kingdoms incessantly warred with one another, their boundaries were fluid. Rulers usually closely administered a core area near the capital with a civil administration, while granting feudatories on the periphery. Having defeated the ruling lineage of a powerful neighboring state—such as a king, prince, or chief, victorious kings might allow them to retain noble titles and their lands, on the condition that they demonstrate allegiance to him and even supply tribute and military service. The overlord could then wield the title "Great King of Kings," while the lesser rulers bore titles signifying their status as subordinate rulers who do obeisance.

Additionally, aside from granting these feudatories, medieval rulers also issued land grants to important persons and institutions in their realms, such as Brahmins, high officials, or temples. As opposed to receiving a cash salary, these recipients were permitted to retain revenue from villages on this land, as well as to exercise some level of judicial authority. Brahmins were so important to kings because they aided him in upholding the king's dharma. The king's duty was to protect the people, uphold the *varna* social order, sacrifice to the traditional Vedic deities, and show devotion to Shiva or Vishnu. As the religious leaders and intellectuals in the community, and the most prestigious *varna*, Brahmins could craft genealogies proving a king's illustrious origins in the heroic lineages of the epic stories of ancient times, perform the sacrifices, and maintain temples. So rulers often generously gifted land to them or to the magnificent temple complexes rulers built.

Medieval India, then, consisted of a multitude of kingdoms, each of which governed a part of their realms through feudal arrangements, by granting feudatories and issuing land grants to nobility or prestigious religious and political leaders, in exchange for allegiance and assisting the ruler in demonstrating his being worthy of his sacred role. In most instances, given that society was patriarchal, rulers were male, but in many cases queens inherited the throne. Rudramadevi, for instance, was chosen by her father to accede to the throne of a kingdom in central India, likely because he had no sons or living brothers. Inscriptions refer to her as a king; indeed, she is said to have donned male attire while leading soldiers into battle. She is also portrayed seated on a lion, with a dagger and shield in hand. Thus, she was conformed to the expected role of a warrior, male king. Clearly, preserving the dynastic line was more important than biological sex.

3.12.2 The Chola Dynasty

The Chola Kingdom illustrates well the grandeur of powerful regional states during the early medieval period. South India first came to prominence with the rise of the Satavahana Kingdom in the Deccan Plateau (c. the second century BCE). But even at that time, in the fertile hinterlands and along the seaboard of the southern tip of the subcontinent, Tamil states were forming. Tamil refers to the regional language spoken and written by Indian peoples of the far south, as well as to their local customs and culture. Powerful Tamil lineages divided up Tamil land among chiefdoms, and, over time, some evolved into small but impressive kingdoms. These Tamil states also adopted elements of the Aryan culture of the north, including the use of Sanskrit, the *varna* social system, Vedic Brahmanism, and the Hindu cults of Shiva and Vishnu.

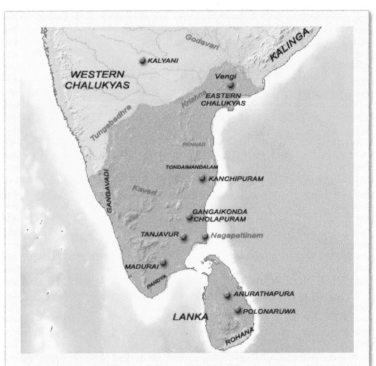

Map 3.17 | The Chola Kingdom during the reign of Rajaraja I (r. 985-1012) | The Brihadeshwara Temple was located in Tanjavur, the capital.
Author: User "Tevaprapas"
Source: Wikimedia Commons
License: CC BY-SA 3.0

The **Cholas**, for instance, date back to Satavahana times, but they don't become significant for India's political history until the ninth century CE, when they show up as a feudatory of a neighboring Tamil kingdom. Beginning with King Aditya I (r. 871 – 907), the Cholas began a process of expansion that would eventually make it the most powerful kingdom of the south up until the thirteenth century (see Map 3.17). Two of the most powerful Chola rulers were **Rajaraja I** (r. 985 – 1012) and his son Rajendra I (1012 – 1044). During their reigns, most of south India was conquered, including Sri Lanka, and a royal administration was built. Chola kings directly administered a core area of provinces and districts with royal officials, but also granted feudatories to allegiant chieftains and land grants to Brahmins. At the local level, these authorities worked with village assemblies and town associations, both of which were remarkable for the level of freedom they had to manage local affairs.

The Chola kings proved their greatness through not only the success of their imperial ambitions but also the temples they built. These temples, some of the most impressive structures in India, testify to the kings' piety. Eulogies to Chola kings describe them not only as great warriors and conquerors but also as protectors of the dharma, destroyers of evil,

Figure 3.14 | Brihadeshwara Temple | The temple was located in the Chola capital and dedicated to the Hindu god Shiva.
Author: User "Nirinsanity"
Source: Wikimedia Commons
License: CC BY-SA 4.0

and generous givers of gifts. Because they were built in honor of the great Hindu deities, temples put those latter qualities on display. In 1010 CE, Rajaraja I completed the Brihadeshwara Temple in Tanjavur, the Chola capital and ceremonial center (see Figure 3.14). Atop the main sanctuary stands a sixty-two meter tall tower carved out of a block of granite weighing eighty-one tons. Numerous representations portray the supreme lord Shiva in his various manifestations, including one located in the inner sanctuary. On the profusely ornamented tower, Shiva appears repeatedly in his form as destroyer of the cities of demons. Clearly, Rajaraja I wished to raise the cult of Shiva to a pre-eminent position in his kingdom, and built this temple to project Chola power.

Like other great regional powers with their unique histories and architectural traditions during the early medieval period, the Chola kingdom peaked for about two centuries and then declined. In the thirteenth century, neighboring kingdoms nibbled away at its power and it came to an end.

3.12.3 The Rise of Islamic States in North India

One of the most important developments during India's early medieval age is the arrival of Muslim Arab and Turkic traders and conquerors and the eventual establishment of Islamic states and communities in India. This story begins with the life of Muhammad (570 – 632 CE), the Prophet of Islam, whose revelations were recorded in the Quran (see Chapter 8). During his lifetime and after, an Arab community and state governed by the principles of Islam were founded in Arabia. Over the course of the seventh and eighth centuries, this Arab Islamic state grew into an empire that included much of West Asia and North Africa. This size meant that many different ethnic groups—Egyptians, Persians, and Turks, for instance—fell under its governing umbrella.

The ruler of this empire was the caliph, a man designated political successor to Muhammad, as the leader of the Islamic community. The caliph's government is called the caliphate. The first caliphs were friends and relatives of Muhammad, but eventually long-lasting dynasties formed that made the position hereditary. The first was the Umayyad Dynasty (661 – 750 CE) and the second the Abbasid Dynasty (750 – 1258 CE). It was during these caliphates that Islam and Islamic rule made their way into India.

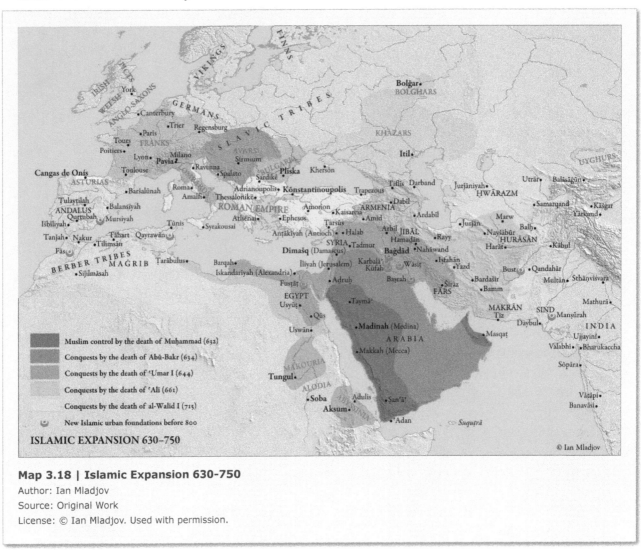

Map 3.18 | Islamic Expansion 630-750
Author: Ian Mladjov
Source: Original Work
License: © Ian Mladjov. Used with permission.

During the Umayyad Caliphate, systematic reconnaissance of the northwest coast of India was undertaken because conquests brought the empire just to the west of the Indian subcontinent. When pirates plundered an Arab vessel at the mouth of the Indus River, the caliph authorized punitive measures, and Umayyad rulers sent an invasion force. In 711, the Sindh (the lower Indus) was seized from a Hindu ruler and incorporated into the Islamic Empire. An Islamic community then began to set roots in this part of India.

The Umayyad Caliphate ruled from 661 – 750 CE. Note the inclusion of part of northwest India, near the Indus River. The next major event didn't transpire until the tenth century, at a time when Turkic peoples had become important to the history of Islamic states in India. By this time, the Abbasid Dynasty had replaced the Umayyad as the caliphs of the Islamic Empire. One method Abbasid rulers used to govern their large realm was to employ enslaved Turks as soldiers and administrators. Today, the word Turkic might normally be associated with the country of Turkey, but in fact Turkic peoples and their language family—Turkish—originated in Central Asia. That is where the expanding Islamic empire first encountered and began incorporating Turks into their governing.

The significance of these Turkic slave soldiers for India is that the Abbasids employed them as governors of the eastern end of their empire. This end included parts of Afghanistan, the neighbor to northwest India. In the tenth century, however, the caliphate was falling apart, and Turkic military governors took advantage of this dissolution by establishing an independent state in Afghanistan. The family that did so was the Ghaznavids. Ruling from a fortress in Ghazna, the Ghaznavids forged an empire that included much of Iran and northwest India (see Map 3.19).

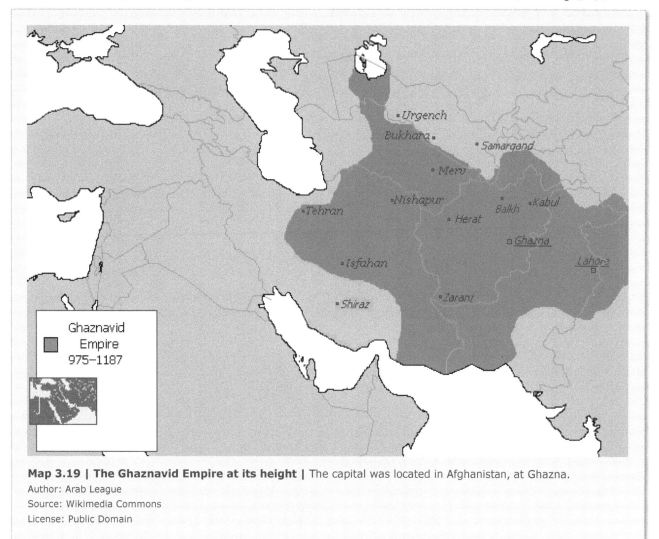

Map 3.19 | The Ghaznavid Empire at its height | The capital was located in Afghanistan, at Ghazna.
Author: Arab League
Source: Wikimedia Commons
License: Public Domain

The Ghaznavid ruler who first made forays into India was **Mahmud of Ghazna** (971 – 1030). In some historical writing, Mahmud has been portrayed as a brutal plunderer who descended on India seventeen times with hordes of Turkic cavalry, shocking wealthy cities of the north with the sword of Islam by destroying their Hindu temples and returning to his capital with their stolen wealth.

But the reality may have been otherwise. Recent work suggests that Mahmud was neither interested in spreading Islam nor caused massive destruction. Rather, northwestern India had always been closely linked to Central Asia, as well as being the location of both repeated invasions and kingdoms that crossed over into the mountains. Furthermore, by the tenth century, Muslim communities had already become a part of the Indian scene, along the west coast and in this region. Therefore, Mahmud's incursions were hardly something new. Nor were his motives. In medieval India, kings often waged war not only for revenue but also because such was their custom. Mahmud was likely no different. His empire was experiencing instability; he therefore sought to prove his mettle as a warrior ruler and to secure his legacy by using Indian wealth to build palaces and mosques in Ghazna.

Ghaznavid control over India didn't extend much beyond the Punjab, lasting less than two centuries. In 1186, Muhammad of Ghur—chieftain of a minor hill state in Afghanistan that was subordinate to the Ghaznavids—overthrew his overlords in Ghazna and proceeded to forge his own empire. Desiring to extend it across northern India, he found that his greatest foes were the Rajputs. The Rajputs were clans located in northern and central India that claimed descent from renowned Kshatriya (warrior) lineages of ancient times. While Muhammad of Ghuri was planning his military expeditions, the Rajputs were governing several regional Hindu kingdoms from large fortresses they had built. In 1192, Muhammad's forces defeated a confederation of Rajput rulers at the Battle of Tarain. His slave general and commander-in-chief, Qutb-ud-din Aybak, then achieved a string of victories across northern India, making it a part of the Ghurid Empire.

Muhammad of Ghur returned to his Afghan homeland, leaving northern India to Aybak, who then proceeded to set up his headquarters in Delhi, one of the most important cities in South Asia, and also the capital of today's nation of India. When Muhammad died in 1206, Aybak took control of these Indian possessions and established a state of his own called the **Delhi Sultanate** (see map 3.20). A sultanate is the government of a sultan, and a sultan is an Islamic ruler who governs a country largely independently of the caliphs, but without claiming their title. The Delhi sultans, then, were the sovereign rulers of the first major Muslim state in India, one that would last for three hundred years.

Looking ahead to our own time, the nation of India today is both culturally and religiously diverse. Approximately 80% of the population practices Hinduism while 15% practices Islam, making these the two largest religious traditions in India today. For this reason, relations between peoples adhering to these two different faiths have been an important issue in the history of South Asia. As we have seen, the history of Islam and Islamic communities in the subcontinent begins during the early medieval period. Therefore, historians pay close attention to how Delhi sultans governed an overwhelmingly Hindu population, as well as how Islamic communities fit into it.

Ruling as they were over an ancient and vast agrarian civilization, the Turkic sultans worked out an accommodation with India, adapting to the pattern of Indian feudalism. Outside the highest

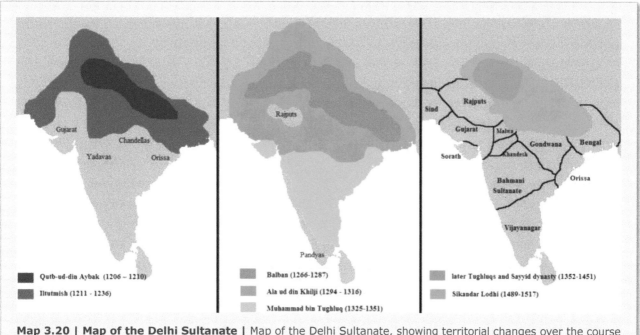

Map 3.20 | Map of the Delhi Sultanate | Map of the Delhi Sultanate, showing territorial changes over the course of three centuries and a series of ruling dynasties and their most important rulers.
Author: User "Javierfv1212"
Source: Wikimedia Commons
License: CC BY-SA 3.0

levels of government, Hindu society and its traditional leaders were largely left in place, so long as tax revenue was submitted. With a long history of conquest behind them, Islamic rulers had learned the benefits of adopting a pragmatic approach to non-Muslims, and these sultans were no exception. They had little interest in forcibly converting people to the faith, and rather adopted a principle from the Quran whereby non-Muslim peoples with a scriptural tradition of their own can live amidst the Islamic community and state so long as they pay a higher tax. At the highest levels, however, sultans placed Turkic military nobility and educated Persians in charge, often compensating them with land grants. In fact, because Persians became so important to Sultanate administration, Persian was adopted as the language of government.

This Muslim ruling elite attempted to retain their Turkic and Persian traditions, but also slowly adopted Indian customs in what was generally a tolerant atmosphere. At the lower levels of society, Muslim traders and artisans became an important presence in Indian towns and cities, as did Indian converts who saw an advantage to converting to this faith. Thus, Hindu and Muslim communities increasingly interacted with each other during the early medieval age, adopting elements of each other's way of life. For that reason, historians speak of a fusion of Islamic and Indian culture.

3.13 CONCLUSION

We have now passed through the long course of India's ancient and early medieval history. We began with the onset of India's Neolithic period in the seventh millennium BCE and saw how

India's first civilization—the Harappan Civilization (2600 – 1700 BCE)—emerged from it in the northwestern region of the subcontinent during the third millennium BCE.

We then examined the long course of the Vedic Age (1700 – 600 BCE). As Harappan Civilization declined, Indo-Aryans migrated from Central Asia into northern India, bringing with them their Vedic religion, Sanskrit language, and pastoral and farming way of life. As they settled down on the Indo-Gangetic Plains and interacted with indigenous peoples, new political, social, and religious institutions formed. Over the course of several centuries, Aryan clan and tribal organization developed into kingdoms and oligarchies. Also, a simpler society composed of priests, warriors, and commoners evolved into a more complex society organized by *varnas*, the system of four hereditary social classes. Finally, the Vedic religion of the Brahmin priests evolved into Brahmanism, the earliest stage in the development of Hinduism.

Next, we surveyed a transitional period in India's history that began in the sixth century and lasted until 321 BCE. Sixteen major kingdoms and oligarchies with roots in the late Vedic Age fought for control over territory in northern India. The kingdom of Magadha dominated. Accompanying this time of warring states, India entered a second stage of urbanization, as towns and cities became a prominent feature of the north. Alongside the *varnas*, the caste system began to form, organizing Indian society into a much larger number of social groups based on occupation, residence, language, and religious beliefs. Lastly, new religious ideas were put forward by the Buddha (c. 563 – 480 BCE) to challenge the dominance of Brahmanism, and Buddhist monastic communities began to form.

This transitional period ended when Chandragupta Maurya overthrew the last Magadhan dynasty in 321 BCE and established the Mauryan Empire (321 – 184 BCE). He and his successors built the first Indian state that included most of the subcontinent. Chandragupta's grandson, King Ashoka (r. 268 – 232), is famed for having tried to rule this large realm according to Buddhist principles.

We then saw how, for five centuries after the fall of the Mauryan Empire (c. 200 BCE – 300 CE), no one major power ruled India. The entire subcontinent saw instead a fairly rapid turnover of regional monarchies. Some developed along the Ganges River, while others, such as the Kushan Kingdom, were of Central Asian origins. Also, states such as the Satavahana Kingdom formed in southern India. Yet, in spite of the political instability, India was economically dynamic, as trade within and without the subcontinent flourished, and India was increasingly linked to other parts of the world in such networks of exchange as the Silk Road and Indian Ocean maritime trade. Lastly, new trends appeared in Buddhism and Hinduism, most notably a popular, devotional form of worship.

Although India remained a mosaic of states during the period 300 – 600 BCE, historians recognize this time as distinct because the Gupta Empire (320 – 550 CE) included much of northern India and facets of Gupta period society and culture suggest that Indian civilization had matured and entered a classical age. One facet was individual achievements in literature, the arts, and sciences. But equally as important, the lives of all members of society were now being shaped and given meaning by a political pattern, social institutions, religious traditions, and a culture with a deep history. That political pattern included, for example, notions of kingship and the king's dharma, as well as political hierarchy. Social institutions included the patriarchal family, *varna* and caste, and commercial associations in cities and towns. As for religious traditions, we have focused on the development of Hinduism and Buddhism and how they shaped the religious landscape with their long literary and scriptural traditions, notions of dharma, and monastic and temple life.

We ended this chapter by introducing early medieval India (c. 600 – 1300 BCE). The political scene remained one of powerful regional states, each with their unique local histories and traditions. The methods by which kings established relations with neighboring rulers and within their own lands has been described as Indian feudalism. Some kings, like the Cholas, buttressed their power by claiming to rule according to Hindu notions of dharma, by, for instance, building large Hindu temples and patronizing the Brahmins. Finally, during these centuries, Islamic rule, communities, and religion entered the South Asian landscape, changing the course of India's history.

3.14 WORKS CONSULTED AND FURTHER READING

Ali, Daud. *Courtly Culture and Political Life in Early Medieval India.* Cambridge: Cambridge University Press, 2004.

Asher, Catherine B. and Cynthia Talbot. *India before Europe.* Cambridge: Cambridge University Press, 2006.

Avari, Burjor. *India, The Ancient Past: A History of the Indian Sub-Continent from c. 7000 BC to AD 1200.* Routledge: New York and Oxon, 2007.

Basham, A.L. *The Origins and Development of Classical Hinduism.* Edited and Completed by Kenneth G. Zysk. Oxford: Oxford University Press, 1991.

Champakalakshmi, R. *Trade, Ideology, and Urbanization: South India 300 BC to AD 1300.* Oxford University Press, 1999.

Keay, John. *India: A History.* New York: Grove Press, 2000.

Khan, Omar. "Harappa.com," accessed October 15, 2014, http://www.harappa.com/.

Knott, Kim. *Hinduism: A Very Short Introduction.* Oxford: Oxford University Press, 2000.

Lal, Vinay. "Mans: India and its Neighbors," accessed November 10, 2015, https://www.sscnet.ucla.edu/southasia/index.html.

Singh, Upinder. *A History of Ancient and Medieval India: From the Stone Age to the 12th Century.* Pearson Education, 2008.

Talbot, Austin Cynthia. *Pre-Colonial India in Practice: Society, Religion, and Identity in Medieval Andhra.* Oxford: Oxford University Press, 2001.

Thapar, Romila. *Early India: From the Origins to AD 1300.* Berkeley: University of California Press, 2002.

Thapar, Romila. *Asoka and the Decline of the Mauryas.* Oxford: Oxford University Press, 1961.

Trautmann, Thomas R. *India: Brief History of a Civilization.* Oxford: Oxford University Press, 2011.

3.15 LINKS TO PRIMARY SOURCES

Websites with Collections of Documents

http://legacy.fordham.edu/Halsall/india/indiasbook.asp

http://www.sacred-texts.com/

Ashoka's Edicts

http://www.cs.colostate.edu/~malaiya/ashoka.html

Bhagavad Gita

http:www.sacred-texts.com/hin/#gita

Buddha's Early Teachings: "The Four Noble Truths"

http://acc6.its.brooklyn.cuny.edu/~phalsall/texts/bud-ser1.html

Dharma Scriptures (*Dharmashastra*): *The Laws of Manu*

http://www.sacred-texts.com/hin/manu.htm

Harappan Civilization Seals and other Artifacts

http://www.harappa.com/

Kalidasa's poems and plays, including *The Story of Shakuntala*

http://www.gutenberg.org/files/16659/16659-h/16659-h.htm

Ramayana

http:www.sacred-texts.com/hin/#rama

Samudragupta, stone pillar inscription eulogizing

http://www.sdstate.edu/projectsouthasia/upload/Allahabad-Posthumous.pdf

Upanishads

http:www.sacred-texts.com/hin/#upan

http://vivekananda.net/PDFBooks/The_Upanishads.pdf

Vedas

http:www.sacred-texts.com/hin/#vedas

4 China and East Asia to the Ming Dynasty

George L. Israel

4.1 CHRONOLOGY

China

8000 – 2000 BCE	Neolithic Cultures in China
5000 – 3000 BCE	Yangshao Culture
3000 – 1900 BCE	Longshan Culture
c. 1900 – 1600 BCE	Xia Dynasty
c. 1600 – 1046 BCE	Shang Dynasty
1045 – 256 BCE	Zhou Dynasty
1045 – 771 BCE	Western Zhou
770 – 256 BCE	Eastern Zhou
551 – 479 BCE	Confucius
475 – 221 BCE	Warring States Period
221 – 210 BCE	Qin Dynasty
221 – 210 BCE	First Emperor of Qin
202 BCE – 220 CE	Han Dynasty
141 – 87 BCE	Emperor Wu
220 – 589 CE	Period of Division
220 – 280 CE	Three Kingdoms Period
155 – 220 CE	Cao Cao
265 – 317 CE	Western Jin
317 – 589 CE	Northern and Southern Dynasties
581 – 618 CE	Sui Dynasty
618 – 907 CE	Tang Dynasty
960 – 1279 CE	Song Dynasty
1271 – 1368 CE	Yuan Dynasty
1215 – 1294 CE	Kublai Khan
1368 – 1644 CE	Ming Dynasty

Korea

c. 400 BCE – 313 CE	Early Historical Period
313 – 668 CE	Three Kingdoms
c. 37 BCE – 668 CE	Goguryeo Dynasty
668 – 892 CE	Silla Dynasty

Japan

11,000 – 500 BCE	Jōmon Period
500 BCE – 250 CE	Yayoi Period
250 – 600 CE	Mounded Tomb Period
600 – 800 CE	Asuka-Nara Period

4.2 INTRODUCTION

In 1974, farmers digging a well in a field located in northwest China uncovered fragments of a clay figurine. Little did they know, they had chanced upon what has turned out to be one of the most fascinating archaeological discoveries of the twentieth century. Subsequent excavation revealed that beneath the fragment lay a massive underground pit filled with over seven thousand terracotta figurines modeling archers, infantrymen, and charioteers. Another pit contained terracotta cavalry and infantry units that likely composed a military guard, while a third one contained high ranking officers and war chariots in what was

Figure 4.1 | Terracotta Soldiers | Excavated underground pit of the First Emperor of Qin, showing assembled infantry and horses pulling chariots.
Author: Aneta Ribarska
Source: Wikimedia Commons
License: CC BY-SA 3.0

perhaps a command post. These three pits are part of a much larger complex of underground vaults spread across twenty-two square miles. Most importantly, a large, forested burial mound towers over the neighboring fields containing these underground armies. This is where the First Emperor of Qin [cheen] was buried after he died in 210 BCE. Although it hasn't yet been excavated, experts believe the tomb is a microcosm of the emperor's palace, capital city, and empire. The pits, then, contained the army protecting his realm in the afterlife. With this discovery, our understanding of how China was unified under one empire after a long period of warfare was advanced immeasurably.

East Asia can be defined in two different ways. Geographically speaking, it can be defined as the eastern region of the Asian continent and the countries located there, principally China, North and South Korea, Taiwan, and Japan. But historians also define East Asia as a broader cultural realm, and include countries that both shared close historical relations with China and were impacted by China's political and legal institutions, and Confucian and Buddhist traditions. When defined in this way, Vietnam is also included. This chapter, however, as an introduction to the early history of East Asia, will focus on China, Korea, and Japan.

4.3 QUESTIONS TO GUIDE YOUR READING

1. During China's Neolithic Age, how did Longshan culture differ from Yangshao culture?

2. What kinds of evidence do we have to reconstruct the first dynasties in Chinese history—the Xia and Shang Dynasties? What can we learn from this evidence?

3. During the Western Zhou Dynasty, how did Zhou kings justify overthrowing the Shang Dynasty, and how did they govern newly-conquered lands?

4. During the Warring States Period, how did the nature of warfare change, and how did the demands of that changing warfare reshape Zhou feudal states?

5. Explain the major ideas of Confucius.

6. Explain the major ideas and practices of Daoism.

7. Why was the Qin Dynasty so important to the history of China? What did the First Emperor of Qin accomplish?

8. Describe prominent features of Han Dynasty society and governing.

9. How did Buddhism become a major religious tradition in China?

10. How was state development in Korea and Japan differently impacted by China?

11. What were the foundations of Tang Dynasty power in East Asia?

12. During the Song Dynasty, China was one of the most developed countries in the world. What features of that dynasty provide evidence supporting that judgment?

13. Describe the status of women during the Song Dynasty.

14. Explain the origins of the Yuan Dynasty and assess its impact on China.

4.4 KEY TERMS

- Anyang
- Asuka-Nara Period
- Cao Cao
- China proper
- Civil service examinations
- Commercialization
- Confucius and Confucianism
- Daoism
- East Asia
- Emperor Wu (Han Dynasty)
- Empress Suiko
- Equal fields system
- Footbinding
- Goguryeo Kingdom
- Imperial Confucianism
- Kublai Khan
- King Wu (Zhou Dynasty)
- Korean Peninsula
- Legalism
- Liu Bang
- Longshan culture
- Mandate of Heaven
- Mounded Tomb Period
- Neo-Confucianism
- North China Plain
- Northern and Southern Dynasties
- Oracle Bones
- Prince Shōtoku
- Qin Dynasty
- Scholar-officials
- Secondary state formation
- Shang Dynasty
- Shang Yang
- Shinto
- Silk Roads
- Silla Dynasty
- Tang Law Code
- Three Kingdoms period
- Xia Dynasty
- Yangshao culture
- Yangzi River
- Yayoi Period
- Yellow River
- Yellow Turbans
- Yuan Dynasty
- Zhao Kuangyin (Song Emperor Taizu)
- Zhou Dynasty and Western Zhou Dynasty
- Zhu Xi

4.5 GEOGRAPHY OF EAST ASIA

China's early historical development long predated Japan's and Korea's, which is why a chapter on East Asian history logically begins in the second millennium BCE with China's first dynasty. However, today's nation of China is much larger than China was in ancient times. In earlier times, the bulk of the Chinese population lived in **China proper**, by which we mean the historical heartland of ancient China (see Map 4.1). To the east, China proper is bounded by the Yellow Sea,

East China Sea, and South China Sea. To the south, it is bordered by the mountainous jungles of Southeast Asia. To the west and north, China is rimmed by a transitional frontier zone where land suited to agriculture gives way to mountains and plateau or vast expanses of steppe grasslands and desert. At times, the dynasties of China became actively involved in all of these neighboring areas, incorporating them directly into their expanding empires or indirectly as subordinate, tribute-paying states. Those areas include parts of the Korean Peninsula, Northeast China, Mongolia, Central Asia, and Vietnam.

Within China proper, two rivers were particularly important to the formation of agricultural communities that served as the building blocks of Chinese civilization. Those were the **Yellow River** and **Yangzi**

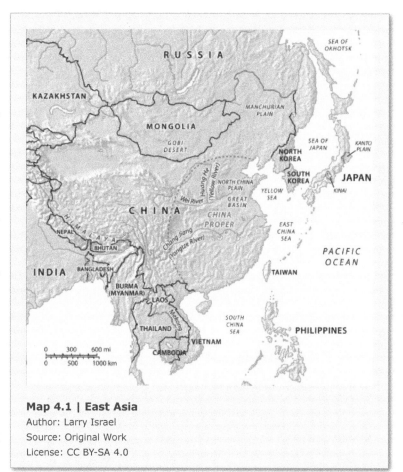

Map 4.1 | East Asia
Author: Larry Israel
Source: Original Work
License: CC BY-SA 4.0

River. The Yellow River meanders through the northern half of China, where a cool, dry climate is well-suited to wheat and millet farming. Beginning far to the west, this river meanders over dusty plateau, becomes muddied with silt, and then deposits this sediment along its middle and lower reaches. The plains surrounding these reaches are collectively referred to as the **North China Plain**. Historically, this was the heartland of Chinese civilization. However, the Yangzi River was just as important. Located in south China where the weather is relatively warmer and wetter, its long basin provided fertile soil for rice-paddy agriculture. Over time, the early dynasties expanded into and included the settled agricultural communities in this region.

Japan is an island country consisting of four main islands and many smaller ones located off the Pacific coast of the Asian continent. At 400,000 square kilometers, Japan is slightly smaller than California, although the terrain is more rugged. Because Japan is covered by mountains and traversed by numerous rivers, only fifteen percent of the land is suited to agriculture. Much of that was concentrated in two plains—the Kinai Plain and Kanto Plain—making them particularly important to Japan's early history. Japan is also located along the Pacific Ring of Fire, where tectonic plates composing the earth's crust frequently move and collide. That is why earthquakes and volcanic activity have been a constant threat to populations living on these islands.

The **Korean Peninsula** is the location of North and South Korea today. Prior to the twentieth century, however, it saw a long succession of Korean kingdoms. Extending roughly 1100 kilometers southward from the Asian landmass, the peninsula is bounded by seas to the east, west, and south, and defined by the Yalu River to the north. Beyond that lies Northeast China which was only periodically included in the territory of Chinese empires. Consequently, because the peninsula lies between China to the north and west and Japan to the east, Korean dynasties have been deeply impacted by these states' histories and cultures. Like Japan, Korea is also mountainous, although coastal areas and plains located to the west and south were well-suited to agriculture.

The countries of East Asia share in the region's temperate climate and summer monsoon season. During the summer months, warm and moist air originating from the Pacific flows from southeast to northwest, while during the winter months cold and dry air originating from Central Asia moves in the opposite direction. Thus, those areas of East Asia located further to the east and south are generally warmer and wetter, and for longer periods of time. That made them well-suited to rice-paddy agriculture, and rice consequently became the primary cereal crop in southern China, the Korean peninsula, and the islands of Japan. While growing rice is labor intensive, this grain also offers high yields per unit of land, so it has supported population growth in these countries and, therefore, the formation of vibrant civilizations.

4.6 CHINA FROM NEOLITHIC VILLAGE SETTLEMENTS TO THE SHANG KINGDOM

Chapters Two and Three covered the development of the first major civilizations of Mesopotamia, Egypt, and India. In each case, rivers were particularly important to that process because they offered a stable supply of water for agriculture. Similarly, in China, the first major states emerged along China's second longest river–the **Yellow River**. These states are the **Xia** [shee-ah] **Dynasty** (c. 1900 – 1600 BCE), **Shang** [shawng] **Dynasty** (1600 – 1046 BCE), and **Zhou** [joe] **Dynasty** (1045 – 256 BCE). Each of these kingdoms was ruled by a line of hereditary monarchs hailing from one lineage, which is why they are also referred to as dynasties.

Because written sources don't become available until the Shang

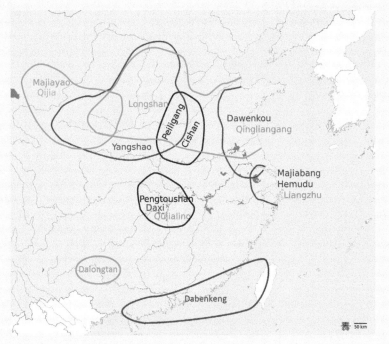

Map 4.2 | Neolithic cultures in China c. 4000 BCE | Note the location of Yangshao culture along the upper and middle reaches of the Yellow River, where nearly a thousand settlements have been identified by archaeologists.
Author: Lamassu Design
Source: Wikimedia Commons
License: CC BY-SA 3.0

Figure 4.2 | Neolithic cultures in China c. 4000 BCE | Note the location of Yangshao culture along the upper and middle reaches of the Yellow River, where nearly a thousand settlements have been identified by archaeologists.
Author: Lamassu Design
Source: Wikimedia Commons
License: CC BY-SA 3.0

Dynasty, historians have relied heavily on the archaeological record to reconstruct the process by which these states arose. Looking back at the end of the Paleolithic era (c. 10,000 BCE), East Asia was sparsely populated by bands of foragers living in temporary settlements. During the eighth millennium BCE, in China, some of these hunter-gatherers turned to domesticated cereals for a stable food supply and settled into villages so they could cultivate them. Thus, the Neolithic Age (8000 – 2000 BCE) commenced.

Over the course of those six millennia leading up to the Xia Dynasty, Neolithic communities became more diverse and complex. For instance, for the period 5000 – 3000 BCE, archaeologists have identified at least eight major regional Neolithic cultures located along rivers and coasts (see Map 4.2). They did so by examining pottery styles and village settlement patterns. One example is **Yangshao culture**, which was concentrated along the middle reaches of the Yellow River. Over one thousand sites left behind by millet-farming village communities have been discovered. Jiangzhai (c. 4000 BCE), for instance, was a moated village settlement that occupied roughly thirteen acres (see Figure 4.2). It was composed of related lineages and tribal in organization.

During the third millennium BCE, Yangshao culture was gradually supplanted by **Longshan culture** (c. 3000 – 1900 BCE), which emerged further to the east, along the middle and lower reaches of the Yellow River. In 1928, when archaeologists excavated a site near the town after which Longshan was named, they found evidence for a culture that had laid the foundations for the kingdoms that emerged in the second millennium BCE, including the ruins of numerous walled towns with cemeteries outside (see Map 4.3). Their rammed-earth walls protected urban areas with public buildings, roads, and drainage systems. The cemetery's arrangement suggests that people living in the towns were buried alongside clan members, but also that some members were wealthier and more powerful: while most graves had nothing but a skeleton, others contained numerous artifacts, such as pottery and jade.

Based on this evidence, archaeologists have concluded that, during the third millennium BCE, population grew and some of it shifted from villages to walled towns. These walled towns developed into political and economic centers exercising control over and serving as protection for surrounding communities. Individuals with more elaborate graves were likely political and

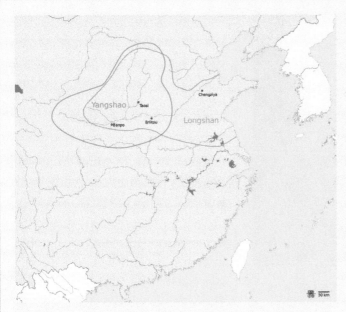

Map 4.3 | Location of Yangshao culture (5000-3000 BCE) and Longshan culture (3000-1900 BCE) | Note that they overlapped, but also that Longshan culture came later and eventually supplanted Yangshao culture.
Author: Lamassu Design
Source: Wikimedia Commons
License: CC BY-SA 3.0

religious leaders, and served as chieftains. Hence, numerous competing chiefdoms emerged, providing the foundation for more powerful kingdoms to follow.

Ancient Chinese histories identify the first major kingdom as the **Xia Dynasty** (c. 1900 – 1600 BCE). However, these were written many centuries after the kingdom about which they speak and, lacking written evidence from the dynasty itself, specialists have been unable to definitively establish its location. Nevertheless, most agree that the Xia capital was located along the Yellow River at Erlitou [are-lee-toe] (see Map 4.3). At its peak of activity from 1900 – 1600 BCE, this town looks like something more complex than a chiefdom. Erlitou included a central, walled palace complex (see Figure 4.3), workshops for the production of

bronze and pottery, and elite burials containing bronze weapons and jade, suggesting a socially stratified, Bronze Age civilization and kingdom. That is why many historians identify it as the capital of the Xia Dynasty.

With the **Shang Dynasty** (1600 – 1046 BCE), we formally step into China's historical period. In 1899, in an apothecary, a Chinese scholar came across mysterious bones that were being ground up for use as medicine. He immediately recognized that the Chinese characters inscribed on them were very ancient. Subsequently, the origin of these bones was traced to fields in **Anyang** [anne-yawng], China where, beginning in 1928, excavations were carried out.

Figure 4.3 | Bronze ritual vessel for heating and drinking wine found at Erlitou
Author: User "Editor at Large"
Source: Wikimedia Commons
License: CC BY-SA 2.5

Similar to the discovery of the Indus Valley Civilization, a lost civilization was revealed on the North China Plain, the one difference being that traditional histories of a later time had documented this one (see Map 4.4).

The findings were substantial. A diverse array of settlements with a royal capital at the center covered nearly thirty square kilometers (see Map 4.5). Archaeologists have identified 53 pounded earth foundations as the floors of royal palace-temples and the ruins in their vicinity as residential areas for elites and commoners; sacrificial pits; and workshops for the production of bronze, pottery, and stone. Also, a royal cemetery with eight large tombs and dozens of smaller ones lies to the northwest. The larger graves were roughly half the size of a

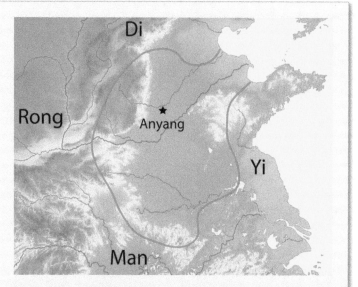

Map 4.4 | Shang Dynasty | This map of the Shang Dynasty shows its capital (Anyang) and boundaries. The Shang centered in the North China Plain, along the lower reaches of the Yellow River. The other labels indicate names given by the Shang rulers to tribal peoples surrounding the kingdom
Author: Corey Parson
Source: Original Work
License: CC BY-SA 4.0

Figure 4.4 | Royal Tomb of Lady Fu Hao | The royal tomb of Lady Fu Hao, principal consort to King Wu Ding. Shang royalty were buried with a rich assortment of personal belongings, bronzes, and servants.
Author: Chris Gyford
Source: Wikimedia Commons
License: CC BY-SA 3.0

football field, each accessible through four ramps whose orientation to the cardinal directions gives them the appearance of crosses. Deep down at the bottom of each tomb's central shaft, wooden chambers were built to house the dead bodies of Shang kings. Shockingly to us, dozens of human skeletons were placed above and below these, presumably as servants to accompany rulers in the afterlife (view reconstruction of a Xia Dynasty palace at Erlitou at the following link: http://www.waa.ox.ac.uk/XDB/images/world/tours/china-erlitou2.jpg).

Anyang, we now know, served as the last capital of the Shang Dynasty, from 1200 to 1046 BCE. It was at the center of a loosely governed territorial state located

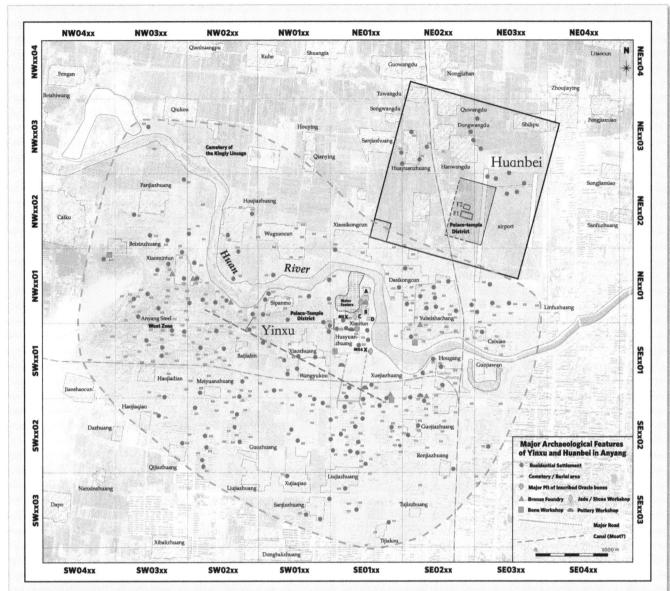

Map 4.5 | Shang Dynasty Site at Anyang | This map shows features of the Shang Dynasty site at Anyang, including the location of the palaces and temples of the last nine Shang kings. Yinxu is a Chinese term for Shang ruins.

Author: Zhichum Jing, Ph.D.

Source: Original Work

License: © Anyang Work Station of the Institute of Archaeology at the Chinese Academy of Social Sciences. Used with permission.

on the North China Plain. Shang kings directly governed the capital and its vicinity, but likely controlled areas farther out by building confederations with locally powerful lineage chieftains, and regularly hunting, warring, and carrying out rituals with them. Some of those leaders were directly related to the Shang kings, and some were allies by marriage.

The bones are the most important source for understanding this kingdom. Most of the two hundred thousand fragments found so far are either turtle plastrons or scapula from cows. Interestingly, these were used for divination, which is why they are called **oracle bones** (see

Figure 4.5 | Cache of oracle bones found at Anyang, China
Author: Xuan Che
Source: Wikimedia Commons
License: CC BY-SA 3.0

Figure 4.5). When Shang kings or his diviners sought to know the future, they would proceed to a temple erected in honor of a Shang deity or the spirits of deceased ancestors in the royal line. Before a stone tablet, they would make a statement about what might happen (for example, "It will rain," or "If we attack the Mafang [high god], Di will confer assistance on us"), and then apply heat to a hole bored into a bone until it cracked. The crack was viewed as the response from the god or spirit. The king would then determine whether or not it was auspicious, and a record would be inscribed on the bone, sometimes including the actual outcome (see Figure 4.6). From these, we know that Shang elites believed that a high god Di, nature gods, and the spirits of deceased kings controlled the future. That is why Shang kings had massive bronzes cast and carried out sacrifices for them. The bronzes were filled with food and placed at the temples, literally to feed the spirits. Likewise, the sacrificial pits show that a substantial shedding of blood for these higher powers was a regular occurrence. Shang elites worshipped their ancestors and frequently divined to determine their will.

4.7 THE LONG ZHOU DYNASTY (1046 – 256 BCE)

After the Xia and Shang, the next major dynasty in Chinese history is the **Zhou Dynasty** (1045 – 256 BCE). In 1046 BCE, a Zhou king overthrew the last Shang ruler and established control over much of north China. In the early centuries of Zhou rule, during the **Western Zhou** (1046 – 771 BCE), Zhou kings dispatched kinsmen to territories he granted to them (see Map 4.6). These nobles were allowed to rule their own lands hereditarily, so long as they observed certain obligations to their king.

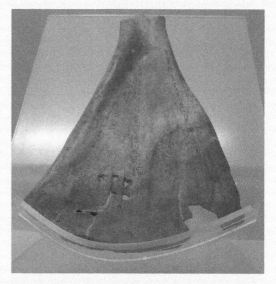

Figure 4.6 | An individual scapula showing the cracks made and Chinese characters inscribed during the divination process
Author: Herr Klugbeisser
Source: Wikimedia Commons
License: CC BY-SA 3.0

But over time, Zhou kings lost their ability to control these lords, and the lords became increasingly independent. In 771 BCE, in what became a telling sign of weakness, the Zhou king was murdered and his young successor was compelled to relocate farther east, to a capital closer to the heart of the North China Plain. This move marked the beginning of the Eastern Zhou (770 – 256 BCE). Over the long course of this half millennium, Zhou nobility engaged in escalating warfare with each other over matters small and large. As they did so, their lands evolved into powerful states (see Map 4.7). Eventually, the noble lords of the most powerful states also declared themselves kings, and fought to gain control over all of China. During the third century BCE, the Zhou Kingdom was destroyed and one of these warring states, the **Qin [Cheen] Dynasty**, prevailed over the rest.

But these centuries were not only marked by the growth of states and accelerating warfare between them. Burgeoning turmoil also inspired much thinking about what was needful to restore order and create a good society, as well as what defined the good life. Two major philosophical traditions emerged to address these issues: **Confucianism** and **Daoism**.

4.7.1 The Western Zhou Dynasty (1046 – 771 BCE)

In the eleventh century BCE, the Zhou state was a minor power on the western periphery of the Shang realm, located along the Wei [way] River. In 1059, upon witnessing five planets align, the Zhou ruler declared himself king and proceeded to engage in military conquests that made his kingdom a regional power to be reckoned with. This was King Wen ("Cultured King"), a ruler revered as the founder of the Zhou dynasty. But it was his son **King Wu** ("Martial King") who brought down the Shang Dynasty. He assumed the throne upon his father's death and, in 1046, led three-hundred chariots and 45,000 foot soldiers equipped with bronze armor and pole-mounted dagger-axes to a location just outside the Shang capital, where he met with and decisively defeated the last Shang king and his army.

King Wu then returned to his capital in the Wei River Valley, where he passed away in 1043 BCE. His young son took the throne, but was placed under the regency of Wu's capable brother, the Duke of Zhou. Now, the Zhou royal court was faced with the task of governing newly conquered territory, including the former lands of the Shang Dynasty. The king and his regent did so by implementing three policies. First, they established a secondary capital farther east at Luoyang [low-yawng], closer to the North China Plain. Second, they issued proclamations explaining to conquered peoples why they should accept Zhou rule. According to the Duke of Zhou, Heaven had decreed that Shang kings must fall and Zhou rulers should replace them. The Shang dynasty had begun with wise and benevolent rulers, but later kings were cruel and incompetent, and failed to see to the well-being of their subjects. Thus, a dynasty once sanctioned by Heaven had lost this sanction; now, Heaven had called upon Zhou rulers to overthrow the Shang dynasty and initiate a new era of just rule. This political theory, which is known as the **Mandate of Heaven**, would also be used by founders of later dynasties to justify their actions, as well as by theorists to explain the rise and fall of dynasties.

The third policy the Zhou court adopted was to dispatch royal kinsmen to strategically critical locations for the purpose of establishing colonies. At their royal palaces, Zhou kings conducted ceremonies of investiture during which they sacrificed to Heaven and the spirits of deceased ancestors, held banquets, and then bestowed noble titles and grants of land upon members of the royal family and relatives by marriage. Large bronzes were cast to commemorate these occasions (see Figure 4.7). These lords–dukes, marquis, earls, and barons–then took their families, contingents of soldiers, and emblems of nobility to the granted territory and set up palaces and ancestral temples in walled towns. From there, these illustrious lineages governed a predominantly rural population of farmers living in villages where life was not easy. Living in hovels and with little opportunity to leave their lord's manors, these farmers were required to work his lands and also to submit a portion of the harvest from their own small farms.

Historians call this method of governing **Zhou kinship feudalism**. Feudalism generally describes a political and economic system characterized by fragmented authority, a set of obligations (usually of a military nature) between lords and vassals, and grants of land ("fiefs") by rulers in exchange for some type of service (see Chapters Three and Twelve). Indeed, Zhou kings granted land and noble titles to kinsmen in exchange for

Figure 4.7 | Western Zhou Bronze Ritual Vessel | A Western Zhou bronze ritual vessel with an inscription commemorating events at the court of King Wu. The king had ordered the Duke of Zhou's son to assume new roles at the Zhou royal court, and the bronze was cast to celebrate his appointments
Author: User "Daderot"
Source: Wikimedia Commons
License: CC0 1.0

obedience, periodic visits to the king's palace, tribute, and military support. However, aside from the presence of royal overseers, a hereditary lord enjoyed relative sovereignty in his own domain. The glue that held the Zhou feudal order together was deference to the king and his Mandate and reverence for their shared history–including, most importantly, the deceased spirits of their related ancestors.

Over time, however, Zhou kinship feudalism failed to function as intended by the founding rulers. In brief, Zhou kings' ability to control the noble lords diminished over time, and their prestige suffered accordingly. There were two principal reasons for this. First, ties of kinship so crucial to the founding of Zhou lost their meaning over time. In later generations, lords simply became more interested in and identified with their own territories, and they had little sense of solidarity with what were at best distant cousins ruling neighboring feudal states. Hence, it is hardly surprising that histories inform us that the many lords ceased to pay visits to the king's court. Second, Zhou kings were unable to impose their will on feuding feudal lords and were even defeated by them in several military campaigns. In 771 BCE, for instance, King You [yo] was attacked by the allied forces of the lord of Shen and tribal peoples residing out west. The capital was sacked, and he was killed. Other states came to the rescue, relocating the king's son, Prince Ping, to the eastern capital at Luoyang. Zhou kings remained there for the next five hundred years, during the period called the Eastern Zhou.

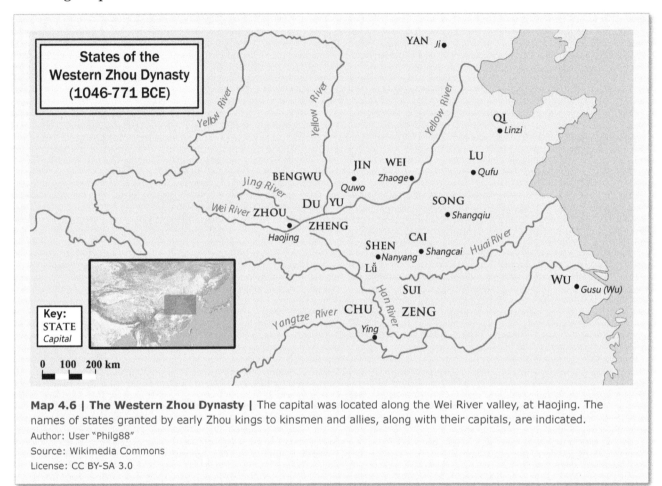

Map 4.6 | The Western Zhou Dynasty | The capital was located along the Wei River valley, at Haojing. The names of states granted by early Zhou kings to kinsmen and allies, along with their capitals, are indicated.
Author: User "Philg88"
Source: Wikimedia Commons
License: CC BY-SA 3.0

4.7.2 The Eastern Zhou Dynasty (770 – 256 BCE) and the Warring States Period (c. 475 – 221 BCE)

When King Ping was relocated to Luoyang, he ruled from a much smaller royal domain surrounded by approximately 150 feudal states and their lords. His and his successors' power was, however, much reduced. No longer able to impose their will on unruly noble lineages, Zhou kings failed to maintain a semblance of peace and order throughout the realm. Instead, this warrior nobility engaged in an escalating contest for power and prestige. By 475 BCE, in the wake of 540 wars fought over the course of two centuries, only fifteen states remained (see Map 4.7). But they fought even more fiercely. Over the next 250 years, during what is referred to as the **Warring**

States Period (475 – 221 BCE), these states averaged one major battle per year until, at the very end, only one remained standing. That was the state of **Qin** [cheen]. The Warring States period ended in 221 BCE when the Qin ruler defeated the remaining states and unified the former Zhou realm, initiating a new period in China's history. The line of Zhou kings had, however, already been extinguished in 256 BCE, so that date marks the end of the Eastern Zhou Dynasty.

As the frequency and scale of warfare escalated, and states gradually gobbled each other up, the way feudal lords governed their states and conducted military campaigns changed. Prior to the Warring States Period, Zhou kings were still accorded a level of respect, at least as symbols of unity and nominal heads of the Zhou feudal order. At this point, the many lords had no intention of toppling the king; rather, seeing his military weakness, the most powerful ones stepped in to enforce order. The first was Duke Huan of Qi [who-an of chee]. He held this title ("duke") and fief (Qi) because his distant ancestor had served as a commander under King Wu during the Zhou founding. Now, many generations later, his state was a formidable power on the east coast. In

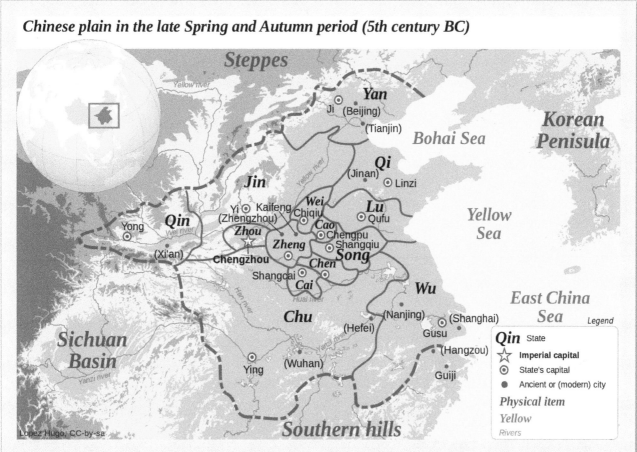

Map 4.7 | Eastern Zhou States (fifth century) | Map of the Eastern Zhou states as they looked during the fifth century BCE. The Zhou kingdom itself had relocated farther east, with its capital at Chengzhou. The map also highlights the state of Qin. This rising power to the west would eventually conquer all of China and establish an empire

Author: User "Yug"

Source: Wikimedia Commons

License: CC BY-SA 3.0

651 BCE, he convened an interstate meeting with other lords to discuss matters of order and security. Upon being elected as their leader, the Zhou king conferred the title of **hegemon**. In this capacity, Duke Huan had the authority to resolve disputes between nobles on behalf of the king.

Over the next two centuries, this title changed hands several times, going to the lord of the most powerful state. These hegemons periodically convened interstate meetings to manage such matters as misbehaving states or foreign invasions. Attending lords cemented their agreements by swearing oaths and drinking the blood of sacrificed animals. Yet, although hegemons maintained a semblance of order, warfare remained constant because it was a way of life for the illustrious lineages of the Zhou realm. Noble lords loved to demonstrate their prowess and raise their prestige through success in hunting and battling. A noble looked for a pretext to engage in a vendetta with another lord, at which point a battle was arranged and then carried out according to the protocols of chivalry. After announcing the impending campaign at the ancestral temple, a lord and his kinsmen, accompanied by farmer foot soldiers, would proceed in their chariots to a prearranged location and engage in a skirmish. In victory, a noble redressed matters of honor and brought glory to his ancestors, something symbolized by the mound of dead enemies placed by his ancestral temple.

However, with the onset of the Warring States Period in the fifth century BCE, the level of violence was no longer contained by the hegemon system and codes of chivalry. Both the purpose and conduct of warfare changed. Lords of the seven most powerful states lost respect for the Zhou kings and even assumed the same title, thus claiming the right to unify all of China under their rule. As opposed to serving a lesson to and resolving some dispute with another lord, these self-declared kings waged war to destroy them and take their land.

Hence, battles became increasingly bloody and bitter, and victory went to those kings who could field the most effective killing machines. Chariot-riding kinsmen and a few thousand foot soldiers no longer met that requirement. During the Warring States, rulers introduced large armies composed of mass infantry and cavalry. Soldiers were equipped with armor, crossbows, halberds, dagger-axes, and swords manufactured from bronze, iron, leather, and wood in royal workshops located at capital cities. (View the image of a Warring States Period soldier at the following link: http://brandonqindynasty.weebly.com/uploads/1/0/3/9/10391259/8580061.jpeg. One description of an elite soldier states that he wears heavy armor, shoulders a large crossbow and fifty arrows, straps a halberd to his back, buckles a helmet to his head, and places a sword to his side.) Kings also militarized their kingdoms' landscapes by building forts at strategically critical passes, walls to mark off boundaries, and watch towers to signal the enemy's approach. Finally, these rulers no longer relied solely on close kinsmen to wage war alongside them. Rather, they created a class of military commanders and specialists whose promotion was based on their ability to produce victories in the field. It is therefore not surprising that during this time some of China's greatest military treatises were written, most notably the ***Art of War*** by Master Sun [sue-in]. Master Sun was a military commander and strategist who served the lords of the state of Wu just prior to the onset of the Warring States period (c. fifth century BCE). The manual of military strategy and tactics attributed to him stresses the importance of formulating a strategy that insures victory prior to any campaigning. Stratagem is critical. "All warfare is deception," Master Sun states. "Hence, when able to attack, we must seem unable; when using our forces, we must seem inactive; when we are near, we must make the enemy believe we are far away; when far away, we must make him believe we are near."

To mobilize large numbers of men for war and supply them with weapons and grain, kings devised ways to make their realms more productive and compliant with their will. Prior to the Warring States Period, it was the norm for nobility to hand out land in their states to kinsmen, just as it had been for the king during the Western Zhou. This practice meant that lesser but related aristocratic lineages lived in estates across each noble's territory, while also serving as ministers at his court. For a king, however, these men might become an obstacle or pose a threat because they held this land hereditarily. Therefore, they devised better ways to control land in their realms. Whenever new territory was added or a noble line was extinguished, kings created counties and appointed magistrates to manage the villages and towns in that area. The magistrate's job would then be to register the population, maintain law and order, collect tax revenue, and conscript people for labor projects and military campaigns. And rather than give those posts to kinsmen, kings appointed men from the lower ranks of the nobility or commoners based on their loyalty and merit. Stated more simply, Warring States Period rulers created administrative units and a civil service. Their embryonic bureaucracies included such features as a system of official posts, salaries paid in grain and gifts, administrative codes, and methods for measuring a servant's performance. Thus, by the end of this period, largely owing to the demands of warfare, the Zhou feudal order had been supplanted by a small number of powerful territorial states with centralized monarchies. Among them, the most successful was the state of **Qin**, which eventually conquered all of China and became an empire. We return to that topic after reviewing the ideas put forward by philosophers in the context of these centuries of turmoil.

4.7.3 Philosophy in a Time of Turmoil: Confucianism and Daoism

China's three major pre-modern philosophical and religious traditions are Confucianism, Daoism, and Buddhism. The first two had their origins in the later centuries of the Eastern Zhou, while Buddhism only began to arrive from South Asia in the first century C.E. Confucianism and Daoism were both responses to the crisis presented by the breakdown of the Zhou feudal order and escalating warfare in China.

4.7.3.1: Confucius and Confucianism

Confucius lived just prior to the Warring States Period (551-479 BCE). What little we know about his life comes primarily from the *Analects*, a record of conversations Confucius held with his students compiled after he died. In later centuries, in China, Confucius was revered as a sage and teacher, and even today outside of China some people might think of him as a stern pedant, perhaps calling to mind sayings beginning with "The Master said." However, in the context of his time, Confucius was anything but stiff and rather a dynamic individual who believed he was mandated by Heaven to return the world to a more socially and politically harmonious time. The *Analects* not only shows a serious and learned man, but also someone capable in archery and horsemanship, who loved music and ritual, and who untiringly travelled the feudal states in the hopes of serving in a lord's retinue (see Figure 4.8). According to one passage, a lord once asked one of Confucius's students about his master, but the student fell silent. Later, Confucius asked him, "Why did you not say: As a man, when agitated in thought he forgets to eat, joyfully forgetting his cares, not realizing that old age is near at hand?"

Confucius was born to a family of minor nobility and modest means in the feudal state of Lu. His father died about the time Confucius was born, and he was raised by his mother, who also passed away when Confucius was young. Like other young men of similar background, he had access to an education and could aspire to serve in some capacity in a feudal state, perhaps at the lord's court, or as an official or soldier. Confucius chose to become learned and seek office. To his mind, he was living at a time when civilization was collapsing and society was decaying. He believed that, during the early Zhou, the nobility was honorable, observed moral codes, and upheld social standards. He believed that a golden age existed in the past and wished to transmit the ethical values of that time. However, in the course of doing so, he reinterpreted the past and imbued the virtues he stressed with rich, new meanings. Here are a few of the important statements Confucius made, and what they meant:

Figure 4.8 | Portrait of Confucius from the Tang Dynasty
Author: User "Louis le Grand"
Source: Wikimedia Commons
License: Public Domain

1. "The noble person is concerned with rightness, the small person is concerned with profit." (4.16) Confucius redefined the meaning of nobility. For him, nobility was defined not by birth but rather by character and conduct. A truly noble person is one who puts what is right before personal gain and the desire for wealth and fame.

2. "Young men should be filial at home and respectful to their elders when away from home." (1.6) Filial piety is central to Confucius's thought. He taught how a person becomes moral because a good society only develops when composed of and led by virtuous people. He saw the practice of morality in the family as the root. Should a young man learn to be respectful and reverent towards parents and elders, he will become a humane person, and humane people are far more likely to contribute in a positive way to society.

3. "The noble man does not abandon humaneness for so much as the space of a meal." (4.5) For Confucius, the highest virtue is humanity, and many of his conversations center upon defining what it is that makes a person humane. A person of humanity is, for instance, one who is capable of empathy and unselfish concern for the welfare of others. They know the golden rule: "what you would not want for yourself," he taught,

"do not do to others." (15.23) Confucius emphasized that a society cannot function if people are incapable of taking other's perspectives and doing their best for them. In addition, he insisted that such virtues as humanity are most fully demonstrated when individuals observe good etiquette. Decorum was important to Confucius.

4. "Heaven has given birth to the virtue that is in me."[1] (7.22) Interpreters of Confucius have rightly noted that he is quite silent about the supernatural and what happens after death, rather emphasizing the life we have and serving others. Yet, it would be wrong to conclude that he wasn't religious in any sense, because he frequently spoke of Heaven. He believed that Heaven ordains a certain course of life for each individual, including becoming a moral person. This Heaven, however, is less a deity than a higher moral order, a kind of beneficent presence.

5. "To govern is to rectify. If you lead the people by being rectified yourself, who will dare not be rectified?" (12.17) Confucius believed that good governing flows from good men. The first qualification for a ruler or one who serves is moral rectitude. If those who lead do so by virtue and conduct themselves according to rules of propriety, people will learn from them and develop a sense of honor and shame. Consequently, society will become more orderly.

The noble person, filial piety, humaneness, etiquette, Heaven, and government by men of virtue are just some of the ideas Confucius discussed as he traveled the feudal states seeking to advise their lords. However, he only managed to hold some minor offices in Lu and generally failed in his political aspirations. Instead, he gained an avid following of 70 students, whom he accepted regardless of their social status. After he died, they passed on his teachings, and a school of thought emerged from his teachings known as Confucianism. Those who belonged to it are **Confucians**—individuals distinguished by their commitment to the ideas articulated by Confucius, classical learning, and the value they place on character and conduct as the key to a good society and political order.

4.7.3.2: Philosophical and Institutional Daoism

During the turmoil of the Warring States period, however, other individuals developed a philosophy very different from Confucianism called **Daoism**. These Daoists largely rejected Confucian ideas about human moral development and social order as artificial constructs. Rather, they pointed to a natural condition that both individuals and society can recover, one that existed before desires trapped people in a world of strife. Their central concept is the Dao ("Way"). The Dao is mysterious: it is beyond sense perception and yet the source of life and the universe, the ultimate truth transcending the polarities that make up life and yet pervades them, empty and yet the mother of all things.

Paradoxically, although the Dao is indescribable and can't be seen or heard, the goal of the Daoist is to accord with and follow it. But this goal won't be accomplished through more seeking and

---

[1]   These selections from the *Analects* are translated in De Bary and Bloom, ed., *Sources of Chinese Tradition, Vol. 1: From Earliest Times to the Present*, 44-63.

Figure 4.9 | An image representing basic elements of Daoist cosmology | According to that cosmology, the yin and yang (at center, black and white) arise from one underlying primordial reality, and then differentiate into powers represented by eight trigrams (whose names are indicated in Chinese on the periphery)

Author: User "Pakua_with_name"

Source: Wikimedia Commons

License: CC BY-SA 2.5

more knowledge. Rather, the mind must be emptied out, calmed, and purified, until desires are absent and a primordial, natural condition is restored. At that point, when the individual is in accord with the ineffable Way, life becomes spontaneous, natural, and effortless.

The two most important early books belonging to this tradition are named after their putative authors: the *Laozi* ("Old Master") and *Zhuangzi* ("Master Zhuang"). Historians believe the "Old Master" was a fictional sage invented by Warring States Period philosophers who compiled the book attributed to him. Master Zhuang, however, lived during the fourth century BCE.

In later centuries, the Daoism of these early philosophers was taken in new directions. The definition of the Way was broadened to include the idea that individuals have a spiritual essence in need of harmonizing and liberation. By so doing, it was believed, one's health would be preserved and life prolonged. Daoists even entertained the idea that one could become immortal. To achieve these goals, techniques were developed, including special dietary regimens, yoga, Chinese boxing, meditation, and alchemy.

Over the course of the first millennium CE, Daoism also became a popular and institutionalized religion. Daoist masters, claiming divine inspiration, composed esoteric texts for their followers. These texts explained how the natural world originated from a primordial ether (*qi*) and its division into two polar forces: the *yin* and *yang* (see Figure 4.9). They presented a universe with multiple heavenly and hellish realms populated with divinities and demons. The principal purpose of these Daoists was to attend to a person's physical and psychological well-being. That involved not only teaching individual techniques for preserving the life spirit, but also the use of exorcism and faith healing to remove malevolent influences. Daoists also developed communal prayers and rituals that could cure illness, free souls from hell, win blessings from heaven, and eliminate sins from the community. Eventually, a Daoist church developed, with its own ordained priesthood, temples, and monasteries.

4.8 THE QIN DYNASTY AND THE TRANSITION FROM ANCIENT TO IMPERIAL CHINA

In 219 BCE, while touring his realm, the **First Emperor of Qin** [cheen] (259 – 210 BCE) erected a stone tablet atop a mountain with an inscription proclaiming:

They [the Qin ministers] recall and contemplate the times of chaos:
When [regional lords] apportioned the land, established their states,
And thus unfolded the pattern of struggle.
Attacks and campaigns were daily waged;
They shed their blood in the open countryside. . . .
Now today, the August Emperor has unified All-under-Heaven into one family—
Warfare will not arise again!
Disaster and harm are exterminated and erased,
The black-headed people live in peace and stability, benefits and blessings are lasting
and enduring.[2]

Indeed, just two years prior, in 221 BCE, the First Emperor had brought the Warring States Period to a close by defeating the last remaining state. Hence, he had realized the aspirations held by the many rulers he subjugated, that is, to unify the known world under one powerful monarch and, by so doing, to initiate an age of peace and prosperity, one rooted in obedience to a sagely ruler.

The title "First Emperor of Qin," however, was assumed by this conqueror only in the wake of his final victory, and it made sense. Having crushed the many warring kingdoms, the First Emperor did indeed create something new and more significant: an immense territorial

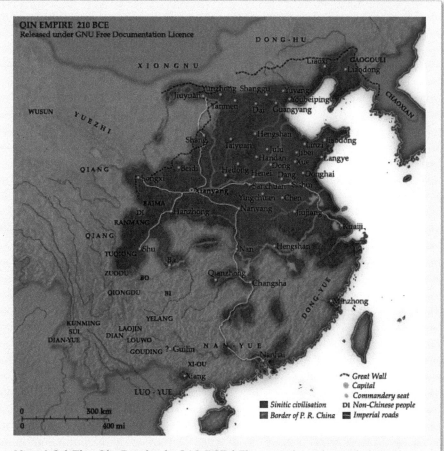

Map 4.8 | The Qin Empire in 210 BCE | The capital was located along the Wei River Valley at Xianyang.
Author: User "Itsmine"
Source: Wikimedia Commons
License: CC BY-SA 3.0

state centrally administered from his capital, by a monarch with unchallenged sovereignty (see Map 4.8). So how did his state–the Qin kingdom–prevail?

---

2   Adapted from a translation in Yuri Pines, "The Messianic Emperor: A New Look at Qin's Place in China's History," 264-265.

When the First Emperor inherited the Qin throne at the age of 13 in 246 BCE, he became King Zheng [jung], young ruler of the most powerful of the seven remaining Warring States. Looking back, he would understand that he had inherited a state whose origins dated back to the Western Zhou Period, when land to the west of the Zhou kings was granted as a fief to his chieftain forbears. The Qin star first rose when a Qin lord assisted King Ping in relocating to the eastern capital during the transition from the Western to the Eastern Zhou Period (c. 770 BCE). At that time, the old Zhou heartland was granted to him, and he was elevated to the status of a regional lord, the Duke of Qin.

The Dukes of Qin were important players throughout the centuries of warfare and alliances so characteristic of the Eastern Zhou, and especially after the reforms of Duke Xiao [she-ow] (r. 361 – 338). These reforms were based on the advice of his chancellor **Shang Yang** [shawng yawng], an individual famed for being one of the founders of another major intellectual tradition that developed during the Warring States Period: **Legalism**. The legalists were in tune with the efforts

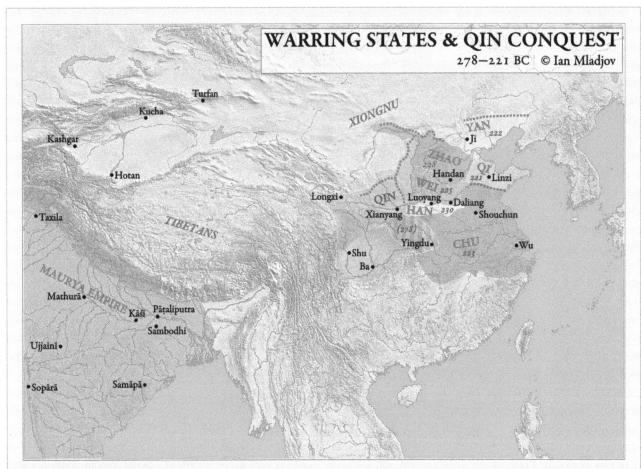

Map 4.9 | Warring States & Qin Conquest | This map shows states that yet remained at the end of the Warring States Period, when the state of Qin was unifying China through massive military campaigns. Dates for the fall of each state are indicated, the last being the state of Qi in 221 BCE
Author: Ian Mladjov
Source: Original Work
License: © Ian Mladjov. Used with permission.

rulers were putting forth to strengthen their states. Their goal was to devise the best techniques for organizing a state's territory and people so as to maximize a ruler's power and control in times of both war and peace. Legalists believed that the best way to do so was to concentrate authority in one central administration governed by an absolute monarch.

To these ends, Shang Yang introduced many measures, laying the foundations for future Qin greatness. He believed that the basis for state power lay with an obedient and disciplined farming population, because that was the principal source of revenue and conscripts for the army. So he organized villages across the land into units of five families each, and made the members of each unit responsible for each other. Every member would be rewarded based on the amount of grain the unit produced or the number of severed heads returned from the battlefield. For meritorious service to the state, a unit could advance along a system of ranks, each of which bestowed certain privileges. But should any member commit a crime, everyone would be severely punished. To make this more effective, the Qin state developed a legal code with clear lists of penalties for specific crimes, made it publicly available, and applied it uniformly to people regardless of their social status. Also, the Qin was among the most effective in establishing a civil service and county system to administer the law. Qin subjects lived under a regime with a transparent set of expectations, and also a system of rewards and punishments. Such rationality in matters of efficiently organizing a state through the uniform application of laws and regularizing administration, as implemented by Shang Yang, were a mark of legalist thinkers' methods.

After Duke Xiao's and Shang Yang's time, Qin rulers assumed the title of king and engaged in numerous battles, destroying several neighboring states. Some of these were major engagements. According to one account, after the Qin kingdom defeated the state of Zhao, a Qin general ordered 400,000 captured soldiers buried alive. Also, the Qin put an end to the Zhou royal line after conquering their territory in 256 BCE. Hence, King Zheng was heir to a kingdom whose success in battle derived in part from legalist reforms. In line with that tradition, he too employed a legalist advisor.

As of 230 BCE, only six other Warring States remained (see Map 4.9). Over the next decade, King Zheng led a series of massive campaigns each of which entailed both sides fielding over one hundred thousand

Figure 4.10 | Replica of the palace of the First Emperor of Qin
Author: User "kanegen"
Source: Wikimedia Commons
License: CC BY 2.0

soldiers. This was a bloody time, as one state after another fell. By 221 BCE, the Chinese realm was unified under Qin rule.

Although the Qin Dynasty (221 – 207 BCE) was brief-lived, it had a lasting effect on China because of the stable administrative foundation it laid. The First Emperor of Qin and his advisors invented the title used by all subsequent rulers. They made newly conquered territory a part of their centralized bureaucracy. From his royal court and central administration, the emperor governed a land organized into a hierarchical system of commanderies (provinces that began as military outposts) and counties. His regime standardized currency and the system of writing, and issued regulations for uniform weights and measures.

The emperor was also a great builder. Over 6800 kilometers of road were laid to connect the capital at Xianyang to each province and the northern border. Walls built by former northern states to protect against non-Chinese nomads to their north were linked together in an earlier version of the Great Wall. All of these measures served to facilitate communication and commerce across the land and, therefore, political stability and cultural unification. As a symbol of his power, the First Emperor also constructed an imposing palace (see Figure 4.10) and mausoleum (see Introduction). For all these reasons, historians mark Qin unification as the beginning of China's imperial era.

4.9 THE HAN DYNASTY, 202 BCE – 220 CE

After the First Emperor died in 210 BCE, the Qin Empire rapidly disintegrated. Historians debate causes but highlight weak successors manipulated by the intrigues of a high minister and court eunuch; excessive demands on the population for building projects, tax revenue, and military conscription; and a climate of fear created by the harshly punitive legal system. Regardless, by 207 BCE revolts were breaking out across the land, as rebels accrued armies, seized territory, and even declared themselves kings. China then fell into a state of civil war for five years until the intervention of **Liu Bang** [lee-oh bawng] (d. 195 BCE). A former farmer and village headman who rebelled and built an army and kingdom through his military acumen and charisma, Liu Bang defeated his adversaries and declared himself emperor of a new dynasty.

4.9.1 Government and Society during the Han Dynasty

The Han Dynasty, ruled by 24 successive emperors from the Liu imperial family, is normally divided into a Western Han (202 – 8 BCE) and Eastern Han (25 – 220 CE) because for a brief time an imperial in-law usurped the throne and established his own short-lived dynasty. This brief interregnum aside, the Han Dynasty lasted 400 years, making it second in length only to the Zhou Dynasty. So important was the Han to establishing a pattern in Chinese civilization distinguishing people belonging to it from those around them that Chinese people today refer to their ethnic group as Han Chinese. Also, after adopting the foundations laid by the Qin Dynasty, the Han further strengthened them, cementing an imperial pattern that persisted in China until the fall of the last dynasty (Qing) in 1911.

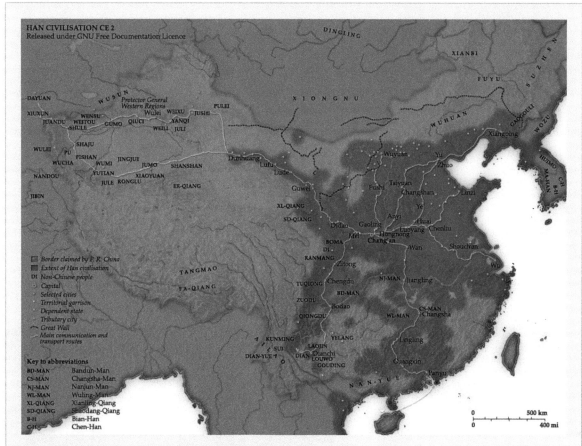

Map 4.10 | Map of the Han Dynasty in 2 CE | During the Western Han, the capital was located at Chang'an, while during the Eastern Han, it was located at Luoyang. Note the location of the Xiongnu confederation of nomadic pastoralists living on the steppe lands to the north of China. Han China also extended control far into Central Asia in order to secure the Silk Road trade routes. Most of the dependent states and tributary cities indicated by green and orange dots were brought under the control of China during the reign of Emperor Wu.

Author: Yeu Ninje

Source: Wikimedia Commons

License: CC BY-SA 3.0

As opposed to studying a chronology of important events during these centuries, let's consider the general picture for the political system and society of the Han Empire. The majority of people— as much as 90 percent of the population—were farmers, living out their lives in villages of a dozen to over 100 households. Some were independent farmers who owned small farms; some, tenants who leased land from owners of larger farms; and some, local magnates with large estates (see Figure 4.11). The government relied heavily on the first group for revenue and conscription and therefore tried to keep these owner-farmers in business with low taxes, relief in times of hardship, and improvement in their agricultural methods. Unfortunately, over the course of the dynasty, many farmers fell on hard times and were forced to sell their land to powerful landlords, thus becoming their tenants or even slaves. Landlordism thus became a major social and political problem, as local great families dominated ever more dependent poor, undermining the central government's revenue base.

The remaining ten percent of the population lived in urban areas–the towns and cities of Han China–as artisans and traders or officials and garrison soldiers. By some estimates, the total population during these centuries hovered at 60 million, which means about six million were urban residents. Many cities, such as the capitals of both the Western and Eastern Han, had over 100,000 residents (see Map 4.10). The first imperial capital, Chang'an [chawng-an] ("Forever Peace"), was a walled city with twelve gates, watchtowers, market places, residential wards, administrative buildings and, of course, the imperial palace. Some of the agricultural produce, manufactured goods, and raw materials filling up the marketplaces testify to what artisans and traders were busy making, buying, and selling: cooked meats, pickled vegetables, fish, and grains; utensils and tools made of wood, brass, and iron; lacquer ware, jade, and furs; and textiles fashioned from silk and hemp. Imperial highways and lesser byways, and canals and other waterways, provided the routes for moving these goods both within and beyond China. Ever suspicious of the profit motive and believing in the foundational importance of the farmer, government officials supervised city markets and established agencies to regulate the most important industries.

These commoner classes–farmers, artisans, and traders–were governed by a highly organized state and its corps of educated, professional civil servants. For administrative purposes, the empire was eventually divided into roughly 100 commanderies and 1300 counties. 130,000 officials constituted the bureaucracy. At the lowest level, working with village and town leaders, county magistrates handled such matters as tax collection, population registration, conscription for military service, law and order, and public works. They submitted reports to, and took orders from, commandery level military and civil officials, who then did the same with the nine ministries of the central government. These ministries handled such matters as revenue, justice, and foreign relations.

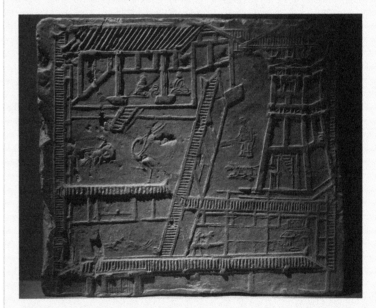

Figure 4.11 | Estate of a wealthy official during the Eastern Han Dynasty, as represented in the interior of his tomb
Author: User "Editor at Large"
Source: Wikimedia Commons
License: CC BY-SA 2.5

The heads of each of these ministries, as well as two chancellors, routinely held audiences with the emperor to decide all policy matters. An independent branch of government, the censorate, audited the rest and reported directly to the emperor.

From the outset, the Han Dynasty inherited the Qin legalist system of government, with its emphasis on rational and efficient methods of administration and use of systems of rewards and punishments to promote order. However, early in the Han, Confucian scholars criticized Qin governing for lacking humaneness, and Han rulers increasingly saw the benefit of Confucian ideas to governing. This change was particularly the case with **Emperor Wu** [woo] (r. 141 – 87 BCE). During his reign, Confucius's ideas were molded into an ideology that legitimated monarchy and a hierarchical social order. This ideology is called **Imperial Confucianism**. As an ideology, it simply provided a blueprint for how the political and social order should function.

Figure 4.12 | Painting depicting paragons of filial piety on a box excavated from a Han Dynasty tomb | During the Han Dynasty, Confucian values penetrated society, especially the idea that a child should actively demonstrate their reverence and respect for parents.
Author: User "PericlesofAthens"
Source: Wikimedia Commons
License: Public Domain

Rulers saw the benefit in having officials who were highly educated, loyal, of good character, and who understood the formalities of ritual and etiquette. An Imperial Academy was founded at the capital in 124 so that students could be educated in classical Confucian texts, including the *Analects*. Across the country, these students were nominated by local officials based on their learnedness and virtuous conduct. Successful graduates went on to serve as officials, and, because that conferred the highest prestige and status on an individual in Han China, Confucian values penetrated society. Texts were compiled explaining good etiquette, conduct, and ritual requirements for each family member and members of society based on their superior or subordinate status. Filial piety was celebrated in both art and texts (see Figure 4.12), and law codes reinforced social norms by, for example, supporting the authority of the family patriarch, division of property among sons, and arranged marriages. In brief, over the course of the Han Dynasty, Chinese increasingly identified themselves as defenders of a Confucian civilization.

The emperor was at the pinnacle of both Han society and the political system, while the imperial family and in-laws constituted a privileged aristocracy. The emperor's authority derived in theory from his having received the mandate of Heaven, his virtue, and his role as mediator between the celestial realms and human world; as such, he could expect his subjects' obedience and loyalty. He resided within the walls of the imperial palace at the capital city, attended by eunuchs who handled his personal needs, palace administration, and the imperial harem. Emperors had numerous consorts but also a principal wife–the empress–who held a special status and was quite influential, usually because she bore the heir to the throne, but also because she and her in-laws were an intimate part of the emperor's palace life. Often, the imperial family, imperial in-laws, eunuchs, and high officials broke apart into squabbling factions fighting for power and influence; this contention had deleterious consequences for the smooth functioning of the political system.

4.9.2 China and the Outer World during the Han Dynasty

Strengthened by its ever more confident political system and society, Han China also became an expansive empire, occupying and colonizing territory all along its borders. Sometimes this process was gradual: as migrants and merchants moved into neighboring areas, the government followed by setting up garrisons to protect them and eventually counties with civil servants to govern them. In other cases, armies were sent to subdue unstable borders or to secure trade routes. Regardless, as the dominant power in the region, China's actions profoundly influenced and shaped the history of peoples and states in neighboring areas of Central and East Asia.

Traditionally, the biggest threats to the settled agricultural population of China came from non-Chinese nomadic pastoralists scattered about the steppe lands along the northern border (see Chapter Ten). These skilled horsemen and hunters tended their herds from horseback, resided in mobile campsites made up of yurts, and organized as tribes. These tribes usually selected the most skilled male warriors as their chieftains and also periodically organized into confederations so as to raid Chinese villages and towns (see Chapter Ten). During the Han, the most threatening confederation was knit together by Xiongnu [she-ong-new] (see Map 4.10). The founding emperor, Liu Bang, sought to subdue them with his armies but was defeated and forced to pay tribute and offer imperial princesses in marriage to their chieftains. Emperor Wu, however, enjoying a stronger government, sent massive armies of over 100,000 soldiers campaigning deep into Xiongnu territory, breaking up their confederation and forcing them to relocate. Although his armies suffered great losses, Emperor Wu established garrisons across the northern border to consolidate his gains and protect China.

As Emperor Wu brought the Xiongnu under control, he became curious about Central Asian territories lying to the west of China. Interested in finding allies that might support him in his efforts to control nomad confederations, he sent envoys on exploratory missions. They returned with news of trade routes extending from oasis city-states ringing the forbidding deserts of the Taklamakan Desert to countries lying beyond the Pamir Mountains. What they were speaking of were the earliest **Silk Roads** (see Map 4.11). Merchants had been using camels to carry such goods as silk from China to distant civilizations while bringing back gold, horses, and various handicrafts and foodstuffs. For that reason, beginning in 104 BCE,

Emperor Wu dispatched armies to subdue the region as far as the Pamir Mountains, making the Han Dynasty overlords to Central Asian states, which were now obligated to send tribute and hostages. A frontier network of walls and watchtowers was then extended partway into the region. The Silk Roads were thus secured, and, because it could be conducted more safely, the volume of traffic grew. During the Han Dynasty, China demonstrated its intention of being a dominant player in Central Asia.

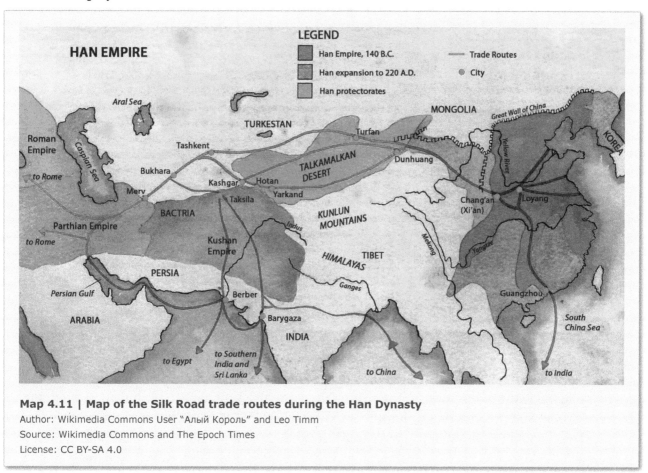

Map 4.11 | Map of the Silk Road trade routes during the Han Dynasty
Author: Wikimedia Commons User "Алый Король" and Leo Timm
Source: Wikimedia Commons and The Epoch Times
License: CC BY-SA 4.0

4.9.3 Conclusion: The Han Dynasty and Empires in History

These are some of the outstanding features of the Han Empire, and ones that can also be compared to other empires that existed at this time in other parts of the world, such as Mauryan Empire in India (see Chapter Three), Persian Empire in the Middle East (Chapter Five), or Roman Empire (see Chapter Six). Each empire conferred a special status on rulers, had an organized imperial administration with an educated civil service, maintained a large army to defend an expanding and increasingly well-defined territory, and developed an ideology and legal codes that justified authority and reinforced social order. Confident in the superiority of their organized governments, powerful militaries, and worldview, each of these empires proceeded to extend control over neighboring states and peoples.

4.10 THE PERIOD OF DIVISION, 220 – 589 CE

Like these other empires, the Han Dynasty also eventually fell. China was then divided up by independent, short-lived kingdoms until 589 CE, when the Sui Dynasty reunited most of the territory once controlled by the Han. Thus, for four centuries, during what is known as the Period of Division, China was politically unstable and racked by endemic warfare. Yet, in spite of the violence, these centuries also saw vibrant cultural developments, as Buddhism became an organized institutional religion reshaping the spiritual landscape.

4.10.1 Political History–From Three Kingdoms (220 – 280) and the Western Jin (265 – 317) to the Northern and Southern Dynasties (317 – 589)

During the second century CE, a combination of factors led to massive rebellions against the Han Dynasty by lower classes living in the countryside. Many once thriving, independent farmers who fell on hard times lost their land to powerful local families who used their political connections to amass large estates. A series of floods and droughts and the famines and epidemics they caused only worsened these farmers' plight, and the government was ineffective in providing relief. During the later Han, government revenue had fallen because local magnates kept their growing estates off the tax rolls. Also, many later Liu emperors were mere youths dominated by quarreling factions of imperial in-laws and eunuchs, so the quality of governing declined.

Desperate to escape poverty and starvation, many villagers fled their homes or joined roving bandit gangs. Some rallied behind individuals who promised the dawn of a new age, thereby becoming part of large, militarized religious societies with political goals. One was the **Yellow Turbans**, a society named after the yellow cloth members wrapped around their heads. The founder, Zhang Jue [jawng joo-eh], claimed he was a devoted follower of the legendary Daoist philosopher Laozi, who had by this time been deified and envisioned living in a Daoist heaven. Zhang accrued a following of disciples by instructing them in faith healing, establishing a rudimentary organization, and prophesying an impending apocalypse. He led his followers to believe that the apocalypse would be followed by an age of peace when the sky would turn yellow and all would be equal. The movement grew into the tens of thousands. Some followers proclaimed 184 CE was propitious, daubing the characters for that year in mud on the gates to government offices. The Yellow Turbans rebelled, and unrest spread across north China. Other similar millenarian religious movements followed.

The Han Dynasty was in crisis but lacked the strong leadership of earlier rulers like the founder Liu Bang or Emperor Wu. Youthful emperors were forced to rely on generals who commanded permanent standing armies around the empire as if they were private possessions. But by empowering military strongmen to suppress rebellions, Han rulers sealed the fate of the dynasty. Generals feuded amongst each other and competed to impose a military dictatorship on the court. Eventually, in 220 CE, one general deposed the Han emperor, but he failed to unite the realm because by that time the country had been divided up by three kingdoms and their rival warlords.

Within their realms, each warlord sought to strengthen his hand against the others by restoring order and establishing a functioning state. After all, they needed fighting men and revenue. **Cao Cao** (155 – 220 CE**)** was the most effective in achieving these goals. He was the adopted son of a Han court eunuch and eventually entered the military. As a commander, he earned his spurs leading Han armies against the Yellow Turbans. As the dynasty fell apart, he gained control over it and established a dictatorship in northern China. It was his son who removed the last Han ruler and established the Wei [way] Dynasty (220 – 265 AD), one of the **Three Kingdoms** (see Map 4.12).

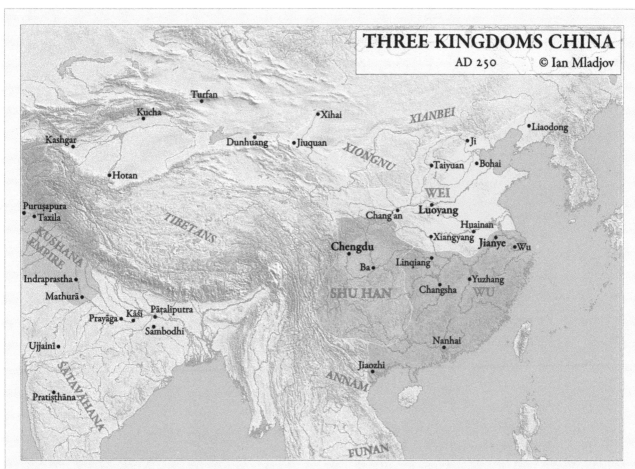

Map 4.12 | Map of the Three Kingdoms | These took shape as the Han Dynasty ended. Cao Cao was the founder of the northern state of Wei.
Author: Ian Mladjov
Source: Original Work
License: © Ian Mladjov. Used with permission.

By this time, as a result of the rebellions and civil wars, much land in north China had gone to waste. So Cao Cao turned it into huge state farms where he could settle his soldiers, landless poor, and, most importantly, tribes of nomadic herders from the steppe lands to the far north who had served him as he came to power. Thus, Cao rulers created colonies of farmers who supplied tax revenue

Map 4.13 | China during the Northern and Southern Dynasties | The Eastern Jin was the first of the southern dynasties, all of which had Jiankang as their capital. The north was divided up among shifting kingdoms established by non-Han chieftains. The names of these ethnic groups are indicated on the map.

Author: Paul Noll

Source: Original Work

License: © Paul Noll. Used with permission.

and, as hereditary military families, soldiers for Wei armies. Such state-owned land and hereditary soldiers became the mainstays of warlord dynasties throughout this time.

The two other kingdoms, Wu and Han, were located in the south. Over the course of decades, the ruling warlords of all three states fought each other in campaigns involving much treachery and stratagem. In 263 CE, the Han kingdom fell to the invading forces of Wei commanders. But then, just two years later, a powerful Wei family—the Sima—usurped the throne and changed the kingdom's name to Western Jin [jean] (265 – 317 CE). The Western Jin conquered Wu in 280 BCE, thereby bringing to an end the Three Kingdoms period.

The Western Jin had reunified China, but that unity wasn't to last. The policy of settling tribes of non-Chinese nomads in north China backfired. Among them, rebel chieftains rose up, carved out kingdoms of their own, and expanded their power all across the north. One Xiongnu chieftain, Liu Yuan [lee-oh you-anne], even declared he was a descendant of a Han Dynasty imperial princess and therefore had the right to restore the Han Empire. His son descended on the Western Jin court at Luoyang and eventually, in 317 CE, forced it to flee east to Jiankang [jee-an cawng] (today's city of Nanjing).

China was again divided up among competing dynasties, a state of affairs that would persist until 589 CE, during a time referred to as the **Northern and Southern Dynasties** (317 – 589). Six successive Southern Dynasties were all located at Jiankang, and had as their base of power the Yangzi River

Figure 4.13 | Terracotta figurine depicting a Northern Wei soldier on horseback | The Northern Wei was one of the Northern Dynasties

Author: Guillaume Jacquet

Source: Wikimedia Commons

License: CC BY-SA 3.0

basin (see Map 4.13). But their rulers were usually militarily weak and lacked revenue, due to southern China's comprising a colonial frontier dominated by powerful families with large estates and private armies. These families highly valued their pedigrees, intermarried, and saw themselves as the heirs to Confucian civilization. At the southern court, they dominated high offices, thus constituting a hereditary aristocracy. The ruling family was always limited in power by their influence.

The situation was even more complex in the north during those three centuries. The kingdom established by Liu Yuan along the Yellow River was just one of numerous short-lived Northern Dynasties established by non-Chinese chieftains of different eth-

Map 4.14 | Map of the Sui Dynasty | Map of the Sui Dynasty, which reunified China at the end of the Period of Division. Neighboring states and peoples in Sui times, as well as the boundaries of modern China, are also indicated.
Author: User "Arab Hafez"
Source: Wikimedia Commons
License: Public Domain

nicities. The Liu rulers, for instance, were Xiongnu, while others were of Turkic ancestry. At times, the north was divided among numerous, rival regimes, while, at others, it was unified. But all of these kingdoms shared similar characteristics. They were ruled by military dynasts who wanted to restore the Chinese empire. Their armies consisted of an elite, heavily armored cavalry drawn from aristocratic military families that was supplemented by Chinese foot soldiers (see Figure 4.13). They employed educated Chinese to serve as civil officials and administer their territories.

The Northern and Southern Dynasties came to an end in 589 CE after Yang Jian [yawng gee-an], a general hailing from the ruling clan of a northern kingdom, first established control over all of north China and then defeated the last southern dynasty. He ruled his new Sui [sway] Dynasty as Emperor Wen [one]. China was once again united under one dynasty (see Map 4.14).

4.10.2 China's Third Great Tradition: The Introduction of Buddhism to China

Aside from the shifting configuration of kingdoms, perhaps the most notable development during the Period of Division was the introduction of Mahayana ("Great Vehicle") Buddhism into

China (for the development of Mahayana Buddhism, see Chapter Three). Beginning from the second century CE, at the end of the Han Dynasty, Buddhist merchants and monks from India and Central Asia brought their faith and scriptures to China by the Silk Roads and maritime trading routes (see Map 4.15). The impact was immense and can be compared to the Christianization of the Mediterranean region and spread of devotional forms of Hinduism in South Asia during this same period of time (see Chapters Three and Six). Historians estimated that by the time the Sui Dynasty reunited China four centuries later, China had approximately 33,000 Buddhist temples and two million monks and nuns. Buddhism had become a large-scale religious organization with these temples, clerics, and scriptures (see Figure 4.14), as well as a widespread popular faith capturing the imagination of common people and rulers alike.

Figure 4.14 | Giant Buddhas
Author: User "WikiLaurent"
Source: Wikimedia Commons
License: CC BY-SA 3.0

Historians have also hypothesized why this spread occurred. First of all, Buddhism clearly met a spiritual need. During the Period of Division, turmoil from rapid political change and constant warfare brought much suffering and instability to people's lives. Now, here was a religion that explained their suffering with notions of karma and rebirth and also offered hope with paths to salvation and enlightenment. Buddhism placed the world amidst visions of multiple hells and heavens where merciful Buddhas and Bodhisattvas worked for the salvation of all beings.

Buddhism appealed to people in different ways. For scholarly elites living in capital cities or as hermits in mountain retreats, Buddhist doctrines about the nature of reality, self, and enlightenment were appealing because they seemed similar to concepts in Daoist philosophy. Both philosophies questioned the reality of ordinary understandings of the self and world, emphasized that our desires create an illusory world, and offered techniques for achieving liberation. Nirvana, for instance, was compared to the Dao (Daoist "Way").

For rulers, Buddhism served political purposes. Since the faith became so popular, rulers who took vows and sponsored temple construction and the ordination of monks looked good because they were upholding the dharma, that is, the Buddhist law. Some even went so far as to have monks recognize them as incarnate Buddhas. Lastly, Buddhist monks—whether foreign or Chinese—were some of the most educated people at their courts and could assist rulers with mundane matters, like international relations, but also esoteric ones, such as spells and divination. Monks won support by promising that their rituals and incantations had magical potency.

Lastly, for most people, Buddhism was a devotional religion. Buddhas and Bodhisattvas were merciful beings to be worshipped because their good karma redounded to the benefit of all beings. By going to a temple and burning incense or praying and making offerings before a Buddha statue, the faithful might have a simple wish granted: an illness cured, loved ones helped, or a better rebirth ensured.

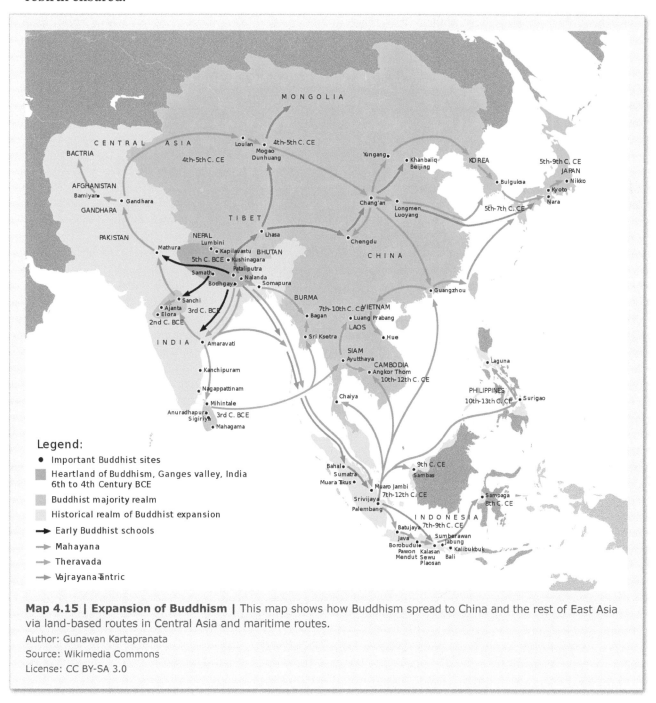

Map 4.15 | Expansion of Buddhism | This map shows how Buddhism spread to China and the rest of East Asia via land-based routes in Central Asia and maritime routes.

Author: Gunawan Kartapranata

Source: Wikimedia Commons

License: CC BY-SA 3.0

4.11 THE TANG DYNASTY AND THE EMERGENCE OF EAST ASIA

4.11.1 The Early Tang Dynasty

The Sui [sway] Dynasty did not last long (581 – 618 CE) and only had two emperors: Emperor Wen and Emperor Yang. Both envisioned recapturing the glory of the Han Dynasty; hence, they engaged in many construction projects and military campaigns. Immense capital cities were built at Chang'an and Luoyang and, in order to supply them with sufficient grain, a canal system was created to connect the Yellow River to the Yangzi River. These emperors also believed that Manchuria and the Korean Peninsula were properly Chinese territory; therefore, they repeatedly launched enormous military expeditions to attack the most powerful Korean kingdom located there. Emperor Yang's ground and naval campaign in 611 CE, for instance, required enlisting over one million combat troops and hundreds of thousands of additional men just to transport supplies. All of these campaigns met defeat.

What is more, that very same year, the Yellow River flooded, and rebellions broke out along it. Natural disasters combined with these emperors' heavy demands led to widespread unrest, and the Sui Dynasty unraveled. Bandit leaders, local officials, and local elites took matters into their own hands by organizing their communities for self-defense. After the emperor took flight to the south, General Li Yuan [lee you-an], who was stationed along the northern border to defend against the steppe nomads, marched into Chang'an, where he declared the founding of the Tang Dynasty (618 – 907 CE). Emperor Yang's life came to an end when he was assassinated by his own men.

Like the Han Dynasty, the Tang was one of the most dynamic and long-lived dynasties in China's history. That dynamism was made possible by how effectively early Tang rulers consolidated the empire internally and then engaged in military expansion (see Map 4.16). Consolidating the empire required first re-establishing solid political, economic, and military institutions. Fortunately, Tang rulers could draw upon nearly a millennium of historical experience going back to the Qin Dynasty, when a centralized monarchical political system governing all of China was first established. At the capital, Tang emperors had at their disposal sophisticated ministries that in

Figure 4.15 | Statue depicting a Tang Dynasty official holding a tablet with a report for his superiors | Giant Buddhas and other revered deities in Buddhism sculpted out of the walls of caves and cliffs in Longmen, China beginning from the Period of Division
Author: User "Editor at Large"
Source: Wikimedia Commons
License: CC BY-SA 2.5

turn oversaw a vast provincial and county administrative system. To serve in high office, a man usually had to come from one of a small number of highly prestigious families with illustrious family pedigrees. These families took pride in their superior education and manners and maintained their exclusiveness by intermarrying. Thus, the Tang Dynasty was dominated by an aristocracy. Nevertheless, some men from a larger pool of locally prominent families entered the civil service based on merit, by graduating from colleges located at the capitals or succeeding at civil service examinations (see Figure 4.15).

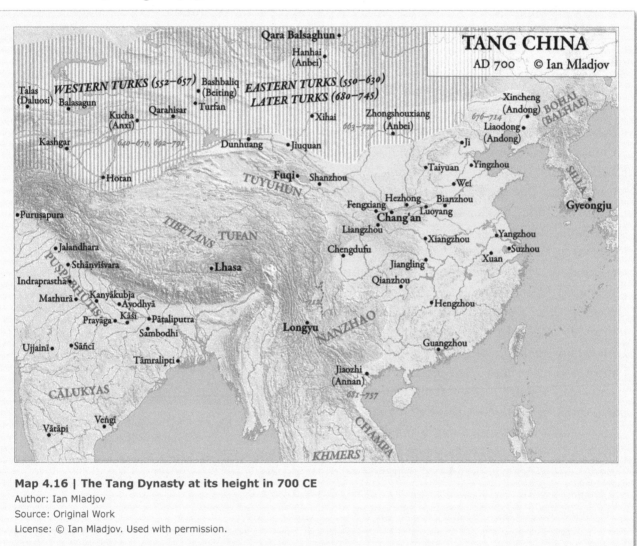

Map 4.16 | The Tang Dynasty at its height in 700 CE
Author: Ian Mladjov
Source: Original Work
License: © Ian Mladjov. Used with permission.

In earlier times, empires rarely flourished without a solid agricultural foundation and revenue base. To ensure sufficient grain and labor service, Tang rulers believed that land must be equitably distributed to farmers. So they implemented the **equal fields system**. In this system, each family was to receive an equal plot of land (adjusted for terrain and productivity) for life, as well as a smaller plot as a permanent possession. The former was for growing grain, and the latter, for hemp and mulberry trees. In exchange, each farming family had to pay a tax in grain and cloth and provide twenty days of labor service. To make this work, officials carried out censuses and land surveys and periodically redistributed land. Of course, this system was quite onerous and difficult to carry out in practice, but it did function well for about a century.

The Tang also flourished because special attention was paid to molding an orderly society through the promulgation of sophisticated law codes. From ancient times, in China, law was viewed as an expression of the will of the emperor, whose pronouncements defined illegal conduct and proper punishments for it. Also, law was critically important to maintaining order, not only in the social but also the natural world. Crimes committed both by subjects and the state could disturb the cosmos and lead to natural disasters. Thus, law maintained social and cosmic harmony. That is why codes were so important.

The **Tang Code** contains twelve sections, one addressing general principles, and the rest, administrative and penal law. Most of the statutes define criminal offenses and the punishment for each of them. The magistrate's role, then, was primarily to investigate and determine precisely the nature of the crime so that the proper punishment could be assigned. In Tang times, people believed that the severity of punishment should be based on the relative status of the perpetrator and victim. For instance, a crime committed against a family member was more serious than one committed against a stranger, and a crime committed against an official was more serious than one committed against a commoner. Within families, too, the status of members mattered. Whereas a father could flog his son without consequence, a son faced capital punishment should he beat his father. In brief, Tang laws encoded the status hierarchy and values of imperial Confucianism. The most serious crimes were those committed against the emperor, country, senior family members, and social superiors. Nevertheless, those of higher status were held accountable for their actions; a magistrate who failed to justly administer the law faced punishment. In fact, Tang monarchs were so concerned that justice might fail to be upheld that they often proclaimed amnesties, nullifying the sentences of all but the worst criminals.

Figure 4.16 | Relief of soldier and horse from the tomb of Emperor Taizong
Author: Yen Li-pen
Source: Wikimedia Commons
License: Public Domain

Lastly, Tang rulers established a formidable military. At first, the army consisted of six hundred militias stationed at headquarters located near the capitals and throughout the countryside, a large standing army located at the capital, and frontier garrisons strung out along the northern border. These forces were largely maintained by drawing men from a military population. That is, Tang rulers relied on a large number of families that maintained military traditions and provided sons for periods of service in lieu of paying taxes and providing labor service. As necessary, these men could be assembled into expeditionary armies consisting of heavy cavalry and marching infantry (see Figure 4.16).

Having laid these solid institutional foundations, the Tang Dynasty followed with military expansion. Offensives waged to the north divided up and subdued powerful Turkic khans and their confederations of steppe nomads. Tang imperial power was then projected deep into Central Asia, Manchuria, and northern Vietnam, making China the most dominant country in East Asia in the seventh and eighth centuries.

4.11.2 The Emergence of East Asia: The Case of Korea and Japan

In the introduction, we defined East Asia in both geographic and cultural terms, highlighting Korea and Japan. East Asia first emerges as an identifiable cultural sphere during the Tang Dynasty. By Tang times, kingdoms had already emerged on the Korean Peninsula and the main islands of Japan, but it was during the Tang that ruling elites in both of these states made extensive efforts to adapt components of the Chinese political, legal, and writing system, as well as of Chinese culture, to their own societies.

4.11.2.1: Korea's History from the Fourth Century BCE to 900 CE

We have already learned about China's history from the Han Dynasty (203 BCE – 220 CE) through the Period of Division (220 – 589 CE) and into the Tang Dynasty. During those same centuries, the first states formed on the Korean Peninsula, and historians generally organize that time into three periods: the early historical period (c. 400 BCE – 313 CE), **Three Kingdoms Period** (313 – 668 CE), and the **Silla Dynasty** (668 – 892 CE).

By the fourth century BCE, the peninsula had already long been populated by peoples who had migrated there from northeast Asia and settled into agricultural villages. These peoples were not originally speakers of Chinese; rather, they spoke languages belonging to the Altaic language family, which possibly includes Korean. This point is important because people unfamiliar with East Asia sometimes think that the languages *spoken* by Chinese, Koreans, Japanese, and Vietnamese are closely related, when in fact they are quite different. However, it is also important to note that in ancient times throughout East Asia, the Chinese writing system was adopted by literate elites for the purpose of writing their spoken languages. Only over time were native scripts developed out of it.

The political picture for the early historical period is complex because the peninsula and neighboring Manchuria looked like a mosaic of chiefdom confederations and petty kingdoms, each governed by elite families living in walled towns. These polities first took shape during these centuries. By the early centuries CE, three kingdoms extending from Manchuria to where Seoul lies today (the capital of South Korea) covered the northern half, while the southern half was divided up by confederations of chiefdoms. The most powerful kingdom was **Goguryeo** [Ko-goo-ryo] c. 37 BCE – 668 CE).

The Korean peninsula lies very close to China, with only Manchuria and the Yellow Sea dividing the two states. Long before Korea's early historical period, rulers of Chinese states had taken an interest in controlling both trade routes leading into this region and the peoples living there. In 108 BCE, during the Han Dynasty, Emperor Wu even sent expeditions into Manchuria and Korea.

Map 4.17 | A map of Korea during the early historical period |
After 108 BCE, Han China established commanderies in Korea. Lelang
was one of them and was located where the capital of North Korea–
Pyongyang–is today. The most powerful neighboring kingdom was
Goguryeo. Mahan and Jinhan were southern tribal confederations.
Author: User "Historiographer"
Source: Wikimedia Commons
License: CC BY-SA 3.0

He opened up a corridor leading from China through Manchuria into the peninsula and established four commanderies to control the area (see Map 4.17).

But Han China by no means colonized the entirety of this northeastern region. Kingdoms and tribal confederations remained to the east and south, most notably Goguryeo. After the Han Dynasty collapsed, northern China was in turmoil and unable to control these frontiers. In 313 CE, King Mich'on of Goguryeo, in an effort to expand the size of his kingdom, seized Chinese territory. That date marked the beginning of a new stage in Korean history referred to as the **Three Kingdoms period** (313 CE – 668 CE).

The Three Kingdoms were Goguryeo, Baekje [peck-jay], and **Silla** [she-la] (see Map 4.18). Like Goguryeo, the early histories of Baekje and Silla date back to the early historical period, during which time they were consolidated from southern chiefdom confederations (see Map 4.17). Each kingdom was dominated by a warrior elite composed of the ruling and aristocratic clans. For most of the Three Kingdoms period, Goguryeo was the dominant military and political power, spreading its control over much of Manchuria and northern Korea. During the fifth century CE, its capital was moved to Pyongyang, site of a former Han Commandery. This move made this city–the capital of North Korea today–important to Korean history. Murals on Goguryeo tombs located in the vicinity show what this kingdom's elites valued (see Figure 4.17). They are depicted as heavily-clad warriors fighting on horseback with bows and arrows, and swords and halberds. A cosmos depicts guardian spirits and nature gods belonging to a native Korean tradition of shamanism.

Given the geopolitical position of Korea, it is not surprising that all three kingdoms highly valued martial traditions. First of all, they fought with each other for control over territory and resources on the peninsula. Secondly, positioned as Korea is between China and Japan, those states often intruded upon peninsular conflicts. For all these reasons, Silla, Baekje, and Goguryeo monarchs readily borrowed ideas from China that might benefit their realms and give them more power. That borrowing included introducing elements of Chinese political institutions and legal traditions, as well as Buddhism and Confucianism. All of these kingdoms sent students to study in China and patronized Chinese Buddhist monks and learned Confucians who visited their courts. These visitors were knowledgeable in many fields of learning, including science and technology. As we have seen, Buddhism not only promised salvation but also magical powers of healing, and rulers could style themselves as living Buddhas. That is why they sponsored the building of temples and formation of a Buddhist religious order. Confucianism, on the other hand, provided models of civility, courtly etiquette, and bureaucratic governance for ruling elites, and rulers could style themselves in Chinese fashion as sovereign monarchs. Hence, Confucian academies were established to train students of aristocratic families for service.

Map 4.18 | Map of the Three Kingdoms Period in Korea, c. sixth century CE
Author: User "Chris 73"
Source: Wikimedia Commons
License: CC BY-SA 3.0

Figure 4.17 | Mural from a Goguryeo tomb, showing a warrior hunting
Author: User "Maksim"
Source: Wikimedia Commons
License: Public Domain

Towards the end of the Three Kingdoms period, however, it was not the great northeastern power of Goguryeo that unified the Korean Peninsula. This achievement went to the Silla Dynasty and did so for two reasons. First, Silla rulers were particularly effective in using Chinese political practices to centralize their power. They adopted Chinese-style titles, central government agencies, and law codes; made Buddhism a state-sponsored religion; and established an academy for studying Chinese classical texts, law, medicine, and astronomy. Second, Silla monarchs built alliances with Tang emperors that worked to their advantage. As we have seen, the Chinese Sui Dynasty fell because Sui rulers suffered terrible defeats at the hands of the armies of the great kingdom of Goguryeo. Tang Dynasty rulers continued the invasions but also failed. For that reason, they were open to building alliances with Silla and combining their military forces. Together, they defeated Baekje in 660 and Goguryeo in 668. Much to the Tang emperor's surprise, Silla then drove out Tang forces, preventing any efforts on China's part to control the Korean peninsula. The Silla Dynasty (668 – 892 CE) thus became the first one to unify the peninsula (see Map 4.16).

In sum, Goguryeo and the Silla Dynasty were, in succession, two of the most powerful kingdoms in ancient Korea. Their histories were deeply shaped by the intrusion of Chinese states into the region. For that reason, they can be categorized as instances of **secondary state formation**. Throughout history, some states developed and centralized their control over a territory largely in response to the impact of a powerful neighboring state that had developed before them. As they did so, they also borrowed ideas for how states should be organized from that neighboring power, even as native traditions and language are retained.

4.11.2.2 Japan from the Yayoi Period to the Seventh Century

Those who follow the history of World War II might know that, during those years, the highest authority in Japan was Emperor Hirohito. Even today, Japan has an emperor and empress, although they no longer have any formal political power in this now democratic nation and rather serve in a cultural and symbolic role. Interestingly, the Japanese monarchy is the oldest continuous one in the history of the world and traces its beginnings to at least the fourth century CE.

Japan's early historical development presents unique characteristics because of its geography. The island archipelago was close enough to Chinese and Korean states to borrow from them and benefit from migration and yet far enough away so that invasions were never a sudden impetus to change (see Map 4.1). Therefore, although we can also speak of **secondary state formation** for Japan, that is largely because of the conscious choice on the part of ruling elites to adopt political ideas and cultural patterns from China and Korea.

But even during the prehistoric period, geography impacted Japan's development in other ways. The first evidence for Paleolithic hunter-gatherers dates back to c. 30,000 BCE. In the resource-rich environments of mountainous and forested Japan, small bands of mobile,

Figure 4.18 | An earthenware "flame pot" from the Jōmon Period, dating to c. 3000 BCE
Author: User "Morio"
Source: Wikimedia Commons
License: CC BY-SA 3.0

Figure 4.19 | A reconstruction of Yoshinogari, a Yayoi Period chiefdom | It was located in northwest Kyushu and flourished c. first century BCE.
Author: User "Sanjo"
Source: Wikimedia Commons
License: Public Domain

multi-generational families were able to thrive on game, shellfish, fruits, tubers, and nuts. In fact, foraging strategies were so successful that even when sedentary village communities first formed, they thrived without agriculture. This period of time is known as the **Jōmon** [joe-moan] **Period** (c. 11,000 – 500 BCE). The archaeological record reveals that, up and down the archipelago, foragers had settled into permanent base camps. These were hamlet communities made up of pit dwellings for homes and raised floor structures for holding community functions. Jōmon, meaning "cord-marked," refers to the type of pottery they used (see Figure 4.18). This case is one of the few in prehistory where a culture invented and used pottery long before farming.

Farming began during the next stage in Japanese history–the **Yayoi** [ya-yo-ee] **Period** (500 BCE – 250 CE). The label refers to a site near Tokyo where artifacts were discovered evidencing new developments in Japan. Most importantly, rice-paddy agriculture and dry-field farming were introduced, techniques that supported population growth and the formation of more and larger village communities. The impetus to agriculture was likely earlier experimentation with simple horticulture, a warming climate, and migration from mainland East Asia. Those migrants also brought knowledge of iron- and bronze-working; hence, tools and weapons fashioned from metals became widespread.

During the early centuries of Yayoi, small village communities proliferated across the main islands of Japan, but, during the latter half, they evolved into something more substantial. Archaeologists have excavated the foundations of large settlements surrounded by moats and embankments (see Figure 4.19). These fortified bastions were home to up to two thousand residents and contained ceremonial centers, differentiated residences and burials, watchtowers, and palisades. Some

Page | 153

Map 4.19 | Map depicting extent of the Yamato Kingdom c. seventh century CE
Author: User "Morio"
Source: Wikimedia Commons
License: CC BY-SA 3.0

burials contained skeletons evidencing wounds or dismemberment. Combining this evidence with clues from contemporary Chinese historical sources, specialists have concluded that, by the end of the Yayoi period, powerful chiefdoms had emerged in Japan, and they were allying with and battling each other to control trade routes and territory.

In retrospect, the late Yayoi Period clearly was a transitional phase leading to the formation of the first kingdom in Japanese history. That happened in the next stage, the **Mounded Tomb Period** (250 – 600 CE). Among the warring chiefdoms, one emerged as dominant. Hailing from the Kinai region of Japan (see Map 4.1), Yamato chieftains expanded their power through force and diplomacy, and eventually forged a kingdom

(see Map 4.19). The principal evidence for their growing power are the massive, keyhole-shaped tombs giving this period its name (see Figure 4.20). In fact, nearly ten thousand tombs have been identified, but the largest ones belong to the Yamato rulers, the ancestors to the long-lived Japanese imperial line. Although the large royal ones have not yet been excavated, smaller tombs containing an abundance of horse trappings, iron weapons, and armor provide evidence that mounted warfare was introduced from the Korean peninsula, perhaps accelerating the pace of state formation.

As they conquered more territory, Yamato rulers devised strategies for strengthening their monarchy and incorporating leaders of the many powerful chieftain clans dominating local areas up and down the archipelago. For service at their royal court or as provincial officials, they granted them office and noble titles, thereby building a coalition of great clans. In addition, in the sixth century CE,

Figure 4.20 | The Daisen Tomb in Osaka, Japan, c. fifth century | At 486 meters in length, this is the largest of the keyhole tombs. It was the burial site for a Yamato king.
Author: Ministry of Land, Infrastructure and Transport Government of Japan
Source: Wikimedia Commons
License: © National Land Image Information (Color Aerial Photographs), Ministry of Land, Infrastructure, Transport and Tourism. Used with Permission.

Yamato rulers began to study the great Sui (581 – 618 CE) and Tang (618 – 907 CE) Dynasties in China and to introduce reforms based upon what they learned. The next two centuries in Japanese history, the **Asuka-Nara Period** (c. 600 – 800 CE), was defined by these Chinese-style reforms, although the name itself refers to the successive locations of the royal court.

Prince Shōtoku [show-toe-coo] (573 – 621 CE) and **Empress Suiko** [sue-ee-ko] (r. 593 – 628) led the way by sending several embassies to the capital of China and then remodeling their capital and court. In his "Seventeen

Figure 4.21 | The Grand Shrine at Ise | This Shinto Shrine was first built c. fourth century CE in honor of the Sun Goddess Amaterasu, progenitor of the Japanese imperial line. According to legends, it contains the Amaterasu's sacred mirror, which was handed down to the first emperors. The shrine has been rebuilt many times
Author: User "N yotarou"
Source: Wikimedia Commons
License: CC BY-SA 4.0

Article Constitution," Shōtoku called for the introduction of Buddhism and Confucian ethics. His articles, for instance, stated that the sovereign's relation to subjects was like Heaven's to the earth, and his or her commands should thus be obeyed. Empress Suiko adopted the title "Heavenly Monarch," thus shifting the character of the monarch from a martial king to a Chinese-style sovereign. In brief, they introduced a Confucian-oriented, emperor-centered state ideology that clearly established a hierarchical system of ranks and norms for court etiquette. For the remainder of this period, other reformers and monarchs would only deepen the reforms by introducing Chinese-style law codes. These laws reshaped the government and land according to a bureaucratic and administrative structure very similar to that of Tang China.

Nevertheless, distinctly Japanese patterns remained throughout this time. First, the royally-recognized great clans of earlier times evolved into an aristocratic class that dominated the court and the upper ranks of officialdom. Secondly, in addition to establishing a council to manage the growing numbers of Buddhist temples and clerics, the court established a Council of Kami Affairs to oversee native Japanese religious traditions. That tradition is known as **Shinto** [sheen-toe], or the "Way of the Kami."

Shinto began in prehistoric times as reverence for kami—spirits and deities associated with natural phenomena, such as the sun or moon. Really, anything mysterious might become a kami, including a mountain, charismatic ruler, or serpent. During the Yayoi and Mounded Tomb Periods, these kami became the subjects of myths that explained their origins and powers, and shrines were erected to house sacred objects symbolizing them. By properly purifying oneself, conducting rituals, and praying to a kami, an individual could avert a disaster and ensure his own or the community's well-being. Also, clans would claim important kami as their guardian spirits and fashion stories about how their ancestors descended from them. In fact, Yamato monarchs claimed they were descended from the Sun Goddess Amaterasu, and constructed a shrine at Ise [ee-say] to house her kami body (see Figure 4.21). Finally, during the Asuka-Nara Period, the Yamato court developed a centralized system to keep track of and regulate Shinto shrines throughout its realm, thereby harnessing higher powers to support its claim to rule the land.

In sum, like Korea, Japan's history was highly impacted by developments in China, even as native languages, traditions, and creative adaptation remained foundational to the unique identities of each. However, Korea was far more subject to the intrusion of Chinese states in the Korean Peninsula, something that did not happen in Japan. Rather, as the first state formed on the archipelago, ruling elites looked to China for ideas as to how the kingdom might be governed. In the course of doing so, they also introduced the great tradition of Mahayana Buddhism.

4.11.3 The Decline and Collapse of the Tang Dynasty

The Tang Dynasty reached its zenith during the eighth century under the reign of Emperor Xuanzong (r. 712 – 756 CE), but then went into decline. At first, the problem was overexpansion. Tang rulers had expanded the empire's boundaries in nearly every direction, including far into Central Asia. To defend the northwestern border, a system of regional frontier commands was established, each with its own commander and professional army. The earlier system of militias and garrisons manned by hereditary military families declined.

This decline turned out to be dangerous. After one general, An Lushan, butted heads with the emperor's chief minister, he marched his frontier army of 100,000 soldiers south to the capital, forcing the court to flee. An was eventually executed by his own men, and a Tang emperor returned to the throne, but the turmoil unleashed by this rebellion rendered the Tang Dynasty ineffective. During the ensuing turmoil, the empire shrank and Central Asia was lost (see Map 4.20). Also, both Tang supporters and pardoned rebels were granted military governorships, giving them control over provinces. Many then chose not to remit tax revenue to the central government, appointed their own subordinates, and designated their successors. They had, in effect, become warlords with their own loyal, regional bases.

Furthermore, as the political system decentralized in this way, the system of equitable land distribution collapsed. Thus, much like during the end of the Han Dynasty, landlords used their power and influence to build great estates. Large numbers of farmers ended up without land and survived only by joining bandit gangs or the ranks of warlord armies. When droughts and famine hit in the late ninth century, a massive rebellion broke out. The last Tang emperor was turned into a puppet by military commanders and eventually, in 907 CE, abdicated. China then entered yet another period of division until the Song Dynasty restored order in 960 CE.

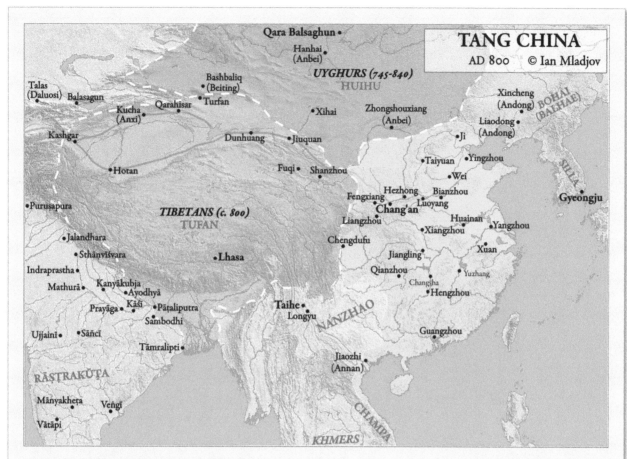

Map 4.20 | The Tang Dynasty in 800 CE | Note how Tang territory had shrunk after the An Lushan rebellion. Central Asia was now controlled by Tibetan and Turkic Uighur Empires

Author: Ian Mladjov

Source: Original Work

License: © Ian Mladjov. Used with permission.

4.12 THE SONG DYNASTY

Like every Chinese dynasty before it, the Song Dynasty (960 – 1279 CE) was born out of turmoil and warfare. After the Tang Dynasty fell, China was once again divided up by numerous, contending kingdoms. The founder of the Song, **Zhao Kuangyin** [j-ow kwong-yeen], was a military commander and advisor to the emperor of one of these kingdoms, but after he died and his six-year-old son came to the throne, Zhao staged a coup. He left the capital with his troops, ostensibly to fight enemies to the north. But just outside the capital, his troops instead proclaimed him emperor, a title he accepted only with feigned reluctance and after his followers promised obedience and to treat the child emperor and people living in the capital environs humanely. On February 3, 960, the child was forced to abdicate, and Zhao took the throne as Emperor Taizu [tie-dzoo]. He and his brother, the succeeding Emperor Taizong [tie-dzawng], ruled for the first forty years of a dynasty that would last over three hundred, laying the foundations for its prosperity and cultural brilliance. The Song Dynasty saw a total of eighteen emperors and is most notable for the challenges it faced from northern conquest dynasties, economic prosperity, **a civil service examination system** and the educated elite of **scholar-officials** it created, cultural brilliance, and **footbinding**.

During the Song, China once again confronted tremendous challenges from conquests by military confederations located along the northern border. So threatening and successful were these that the Song Dynasty counted as just one of many powerful players in a larger geopolitical system in Central and East Asia. The first two northern conquest dynasties, the Liao [lee-ow] and Jin [jean], emerged on the plains of Manchuria when powerful tribal leaders organized communities of hunters, fishers, and farmers for war (see Map 4.21).

As their power grew, they formed states and conquered territory in northern China, forcing the Chinese to pay them large subsidies of silk and silver for peace. So Chinese rulers and their councilors were in constant negotiations with peoples they viewed as culturally-inferior barbarians under conditions where they were forced to treat them as equals, as opposed to weaker

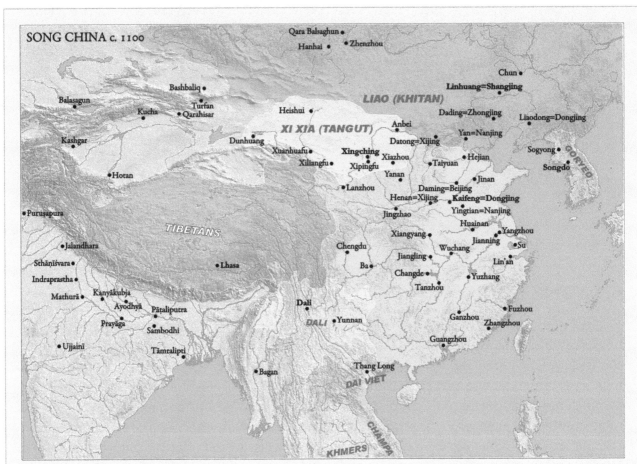

Map 4.21 | The Northern Song Dynasty in 1100 CE | Note that China (in yellow, with the capital at Kaifeng) was surrounded by powerful neighbors, such as the Khitan Liao state to the north. Khitan designates an ethnic group and Liao the name of their dynasty.

Author: Ian Mladjov

Source: Original Work

License: © Ian Mladjov. Used with permission.

tribute-paying states in a Chinese-dominated world. At first, they used a combination of defensive measures and expensive bilateral treaties, which did make for a degree of stability. But a high price was exacted. Halfway through the Song, the Jin Dynasty destroyed the Liao and occupied the entire northern half of China, forcing the Song court to move south (see Map 4.22). To rule Chinese possessions, Jin rulers even took on the trappings of Chinese-style emperors and developed a dual administrative system. Steppe tribes were ruled by a traditional military organization, while the farming population of China was governed with Chinese-style civilian administration. The Song Dynasty thus constantly faced the prospect of extinction and was challenged in its legitimacy by rival emperors claiming the right to rule the Chinese realm.

One reason Song monarchs were able to buy peace was the extraordinary prosperity during their rule and the resulting tax revenue made available. During those centuries, China was by many measures the most developed country in the world. In 1100 CE, the population was one hundred million, more than all of medieval Europe combined. That number doubled the population of

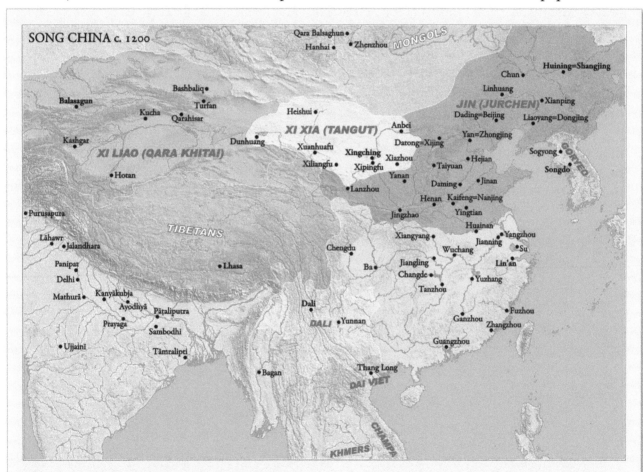

Map 4.22 | China during the Southern Song Dynasty, c. 1200 CE | Another military conquest dynasty, the Jin, had destroyed the Liao Dynasty and forced the Chinese emperor to relocate his capital further south, at Lin'an.

Author: Ian Mladjov

Source: Original Work

License: © Ian Mladjov. Used with permission.

750 CE, just three hundred years prior. The reason for such growth was flourishing agricultural production, especially rice-paddy agriculture. More drought-resistant and earlier-ripening strains of rice, combined with better technology, lead to higher yields per acre.

The impact was enormous. The productivity of farmers stimulated other industries, such as ironworking. Estimates place iron production at as high as twenty thousand tons per year. That amount made iron prices low and, therefore, such products as spades, ploughshares, nails, axles, and pots and pans more cheaply available. Seeing its profitability, wealthy landowning and merchant families invested in metallurgy, spurring better technology. Bellows, for instance, were worked by hydraulic machinery, such as water mills. Explosives derived from gunpowder were engineered to open mines. Similar development of textile and ceramic industries occurred.

Indeed, during the Song, China underwent a veritable economic revolution. Improvements in agriculture and industry, combined with a denser population, spurred the **commercialization** of the economy. A commercialized economy is one that supports the pursuit of profit through production of specialized products for markets. A Song farmer, for instance, as opposed to just producing rice to get by, might rather purchase it on a market and instead specialize in tea or oranges. Since markets were proliferating in towns and cities and transport via land and water was now readily available, farmers could rely on merchants to market their goods across the country. To support this economic activity, the government minted billions of coins each year as well as the world's first paper currency.

A denser population and sophisticated economy led to urbanization. During the Song, at a time when London had roughly fifteen thousand people, China had dozens of cities with over fifty thousand people and capitals with a half million. Song painted scrolls show crowds of people moving through streets lined with shops, restaurants, teahouses, and guest houses (see Figure 4.22).

Figure 4.22 | This section of a Song Dynasty period scroll depicts a bridge in Kaifeng, the first capital.
Author: User "Zhuwq"
Source: Wikimedia Commons
License: Public Domain

To manage their realm, Song rulers implemented a national **civil service examination** to recruit men for office. Prior dynasties had used written examinations testing knowledge of Confucian classics to select men for office, but only as a supplement to recommendation and hereditary privilege. During the collapse of the Tang Dynasty, however, aristocratic families that had for centuries dominated the upper echelons of officialdom disappeared. The first Song emperor, Zhao Kuangyin, rode to power with the support of military men; having largely unified China, he then sought to restore civil governance based in Confucian principles of humaneness and righteousness. So he invited senior commanders to a party and, over a cup of wine, asked them to relinquish their commands for a comfortable retirement. They obliged. He and his successors consequently made the examination system the pre-eminent route to office, even establishing a national school system to help young men prepare for and advance through it. Thus, during the Song Dynasty, civil offices came to be dominated by men who had spent years, even decades, preparing for and passing through a complex series of exams. Hence, they were both scholars and officials. Success in entering this class placed a person at the pinnacle of society, guaranteeing them prestige and wealth. These **scholar-officials**, and their Confucian worldview, dominated Chinese society until the twentieth century.

In theory, since any adult male could take the examinations, the system was meritocratic. But in reality, because they were so difficult and quotas were set, very few actually passed them. Estimates suggest that only one in one hundred passed the lowest level exam. This ratio meant that, in order to succeed, a young man had to begin memorizing long classical texts as a child and to continue his studies until he passed or gave up hope. Only affluent families could afford to support such an education.

Nevertheless, the meritocratic ideal inspired people from all classes to try and so promoted literacy and a literary revival during the Song Dynasty. As a part of this revival and to provide a curriculum for education, scholar-officials sought to reinvigorate Confucianism. The philosophical movement they began is known as **Neo-Confucianism**. By the Song Dynasty, whereas Confucianism largely shaped personal behavior and social mores, Buddhist and Daoist explanations of the cosmos, human nature, and the human predicament dominated the individual's spiritual outlook. Neo-Confucians responded to this challenge by providing a metaphysical basis for Confucian morality and governance. **Zhu Xi** (1130 – 1200), arguably the most important philosopher in later imperial Chinese history, produced a grand synthesis that would shape the worldview of the scholar-official class. He argued that the cosmos consists of a duality of principles and a material force composing physical things. One principle underlies the cosmos and individual principles provide the abstract reason for individual things. In human beings, principle manifests as human nature, which is wholly good and the origins of the human capacity to become moral persons. However, an individual's physical endowment obscures their good nature and leads to moral failings, which is why a rigorous Confucian curriculum of moral self-cultivation based in classical texts like Confucius' *Analects* is necessary. Most importantly, Zhu Xi argued, individual morality was the starting point for producing a well-managed family, orderly government, and peace throughout the world.

Furthermore, during the Song Dynasty, moveable-type printing also began to be widely used, contributing to an increase in literacy and broader exposure to these new ideas. Chinese characters were carved on wood blocks, which were then arranged in boxes that could be dipped in ink and printed on paper (see Figure 4.23). Books on a multitude of topics—especially classics and histories—became cheaply and widely available, fueling a cultural efflorescence at a time when education had become paramount to climbing the social ladder. Other inventions that made China one of the most technologically innovative during this time include gunpowder weapons (see Figure 4.24) and the mariner's compass.

Looked at from many angles, then, the Song was truly a dynamic period in China's history. However, some observers have bemoaned the fact that **footbinding** began during this dynasty and see that practice as a symbol of increasing gender oppression. Scholars believe footbinding

Figure 4.23 | A woodblock used to print one page of classical Chinese | The characters read from top to bottom and right to left. During the Song, individual, moveable woodblocks with one character were also carved and arranged in square frames.
Author: User "Vmenkov"
Source: Wikimedia Commons
License: CC BY-SA 3.0

began among professional dancers in the tenth century and was then adopted by the upper classes. Over time it spread to the rest of Chinese society, only to end in the twentieth century. At a young age, a girl's feet would be wrapped tightly with bandages so that they couldn't grow, ideally remaining about four-inches long. That stunting made walking very difficult and largely kept women confined to their homes. Eventually, the bound foot, encased in an embroidered silk slipper, became a symbol

Figure 4.24 | Buddhist scroll (c. 950) showing demons threatening the Buddha with a bomb and fire lance | During the Tang Dynasty, alchemists attempting to produce an elixir of immortality accidentally invented gunpowder when experimenting with saltpeter, sulfur, and charcoal. Gunpowder weapons first begin to be widely used in East Asia and during the Song Dynasty. The earliest evidence for their use is this scroll. The fire lance is a predecessor to the gun. Gunpowder and projectiles were placed in a tube and projected at the enemy. True guns and cannon are developed during the thirteenth century, towards the end of the Song Dynasty.
Author: User "Vmenkov"
Source: Wikimedia Commons
License: CC BY-SA 3.0

of femininity and also one of the criteria for marriageability (see Figure 4.25).

More generally, social norms and the law did place women in a subordinate position. Whereas men dominated public realms like government and business, women married at a young age and lived out most of their lives in the domestic sphere. Indeed, in earlier times, China was patriarchal, patrilineal, and patrilocal. It was patriarchal because the law upheld the authority of senior males in the household and patrilineal because one's surname and family property passed down the male line—though a wife did have control over her dowry. Importantly, ancestor worship, the pre-eminent social and religious practice in Chinese society, was directed toward patrilineal forbears. That is why it was important for the woman to move into the spouse's home, where she would live together with her parents-in-law. Patrilocal describes this type of social pattern. Marriages were almost always arranged for the benefit of both families involved, and, during the wedding ceremony, the bride was taken in a curtained sedan chair to the husband's home where she was to promise to obey her parents-in-law and then bow along with her husband before the ancestral altar. Ideally, she would become a competent household manager, educate the children, and demonstrate much restraint and other excellent interpersonal skills.

Although gender hierarchy was, therefore, the norm, other scholars have observed that ideals were not always reality and women did exercise their agency within the boundaries placed upon them. A wife could gain dignity

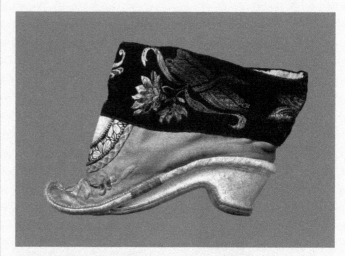

Figure 4.25 | Silk slipper for a bound foot, dating to a later Chinese dynasty.
Author: User "Vassil"
Source: Wikimedia Commons
License: CC0 1.0

Figure 4.26 | Painting of ladies at the Song court preparing silk.
Author: Museum of Fine Arts, Boston
Source: Wikimedia Commons
License: Public Domain

Figure 4.27 | A modern statue of Li Qingzhao placed in a museum built in her honor. | The museum is located in Jinan, China, her hometown.
Author: User "Gisling"
Source: Wikimedia Commons
License: CC BY 3.0

and a sense of self-worth by handling her roles capably; she would also earn respect. Song literature further reveals that women were often in the fields working or out on city streets shopping. Among the upper classes, literacy and the ability to compose essays or poetry made a woman more marriageable. For this reason, some women were able to excel. Li Qingzhao [lee ching-jow] (c. 1084 – 1155) is one of China's greatest poets (see Figure 4.27). She came from a prestigious scholar-official family. Her father was both a statesman and classical scholar, and her mother was known for her literary achievements. In her teens, Li began to compose poetry, and, over the course of her life, she produced many volumes of essays and poems. Poems to her husband even suggest mutual love and respect and treating her as an equal. In fact, throughout Chinese history, it was not unusual for women to challenge and transgress boundaries. At the highest level, during both the Han and Tang Dynasties, we find cases of empress dowagers dominating youthful heirs to the throne and even one case of an empress declaring her own dynasty.

4.13 THE YUAN DYNASTY

The last major dynasty prior to China's early modern period is the **Yuan** [you-an] **Dynasty**. Like earlier neighbors lying to the north of the Song, the Yuan was also a northern conquest dynasty. The key players here were steppe nomads living on the grasslands of Mongolia, known as Mongols, and their leader Genghis Khan. The story of their rise and how they created the largest territorial empire in the history of the world properly belongs to Chapter Eleven, which covers Central Asia, so we here only provide a brief introduction. The most important point to bear in mind is that the Mongols conquered many countries, including China, and incorporated them into a large Eurasian empire.

In the twelfth century CE, the Mongols were one of many tribes of nomadic pastoralists living on the steppes of Central Asia. Although these tribes were made up of peoples of differing ethnicity, they held in common a way of life. Since the steppe was unsuited to farming, they relied principally on their herds, but also on what they could obtain by trading with neighboring sedentary peoples. The nomads lived in temporary campsites, periodically breaking down their yurts and relocating as the seasons required. Since the tribes often fought with each other or turned to raiding, nomads were also excellent at mounted warfare. Their chieftain leaders–referred to as khans–were usually selected based on skill in battle and charisma.

Undoubtedly, the most famous khan in Central Asian history is Genghis Khan. In the late twelfth century, he accrued an army of loyal followers and began to subdue tribes across the Mongolian steppe. In 1206 CE, at a gathering of tribal leaders, he was proclaimed Universal Khan of a tribal confederation. Using a powerful military with a tight command structure, Genghis proceeded to unleash a wave of campaigning in northern China and Central Asia, thereby adding much territory to a growing Mongol Empire (see Map 4.23). After he died in 1227 CE, this empire was divided into four khanates, each of which went to one of his four sons as their territorial inheritance.

Tolui, Genghis Khan's youngest son, was granted the Mongol homeland as well as subjugated territory in northern China held by the Jin Dynasty. But this rugged warrior died in 1232 at the young

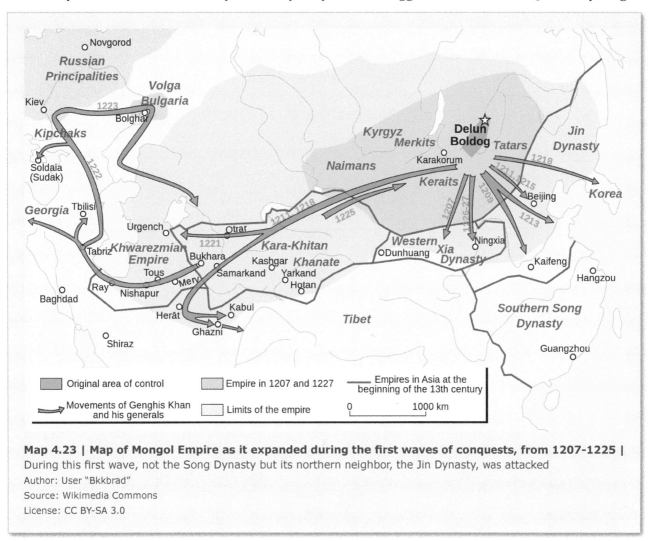

Map 4.23 | Map of Mongol Empire as it expanded during the first waves of conquests, from 1207-1225 | During this first wave, not the Song Dynasty but its northern neighbor, the Jin Dynasty, was attacked
Author: User "Bkkbrad"
Source: Wikimedia Commons
License: CC BY-SA 3.0

age of forty, so the task of managing Chinese territory fell to Tolui's capable wife Sorghagtani Beki and her second son, **Kublai Khan** (1215 – 1294 CE). Unlike his predecessors, who largely treated Chinese as chattel and ruthlessly exploited their towns and villages, Kublai saw the advantages of taking a more enlightened approach. With the advice of Chinese advisors, he adopted Chinese-style methods for governing China. In fact, after Kublai was elected as the fifth Universal Khan in 1260, he chose to move his capital from Mongolia to Beijing, making it the center of his khanate. He then took on the trappings of a Chinese-style sovereign and, in 1273, declared the founding of the Great Yuan Dynasty. Accordingly, he asserted that the Mandate of Heaven had been transferred to him from the Song Dynasty.

Figure 4.28 | Portrait of Kublai Khan
Author: User "Yaan"
Source: Wikimedia Commons
License: Public Domain

Kublai then engaged in a decade of conquest that concluded with the fall of the Song. This victory over the Song Dynasty, China required careful preparation. The Song was located in the southern two-thirds of China, where the terrain was matted with lakes, rivers, and canals. The Mongols had little experience with naval warfare, so they turned to Chinese advisors to build a navy. Mongol cavalry boarded the ships and floated down rivers leading to the Song capital, laying siege to cities along the way. When they reached it in 1276, Kublai's generals took the capital without bloodshed. The regent to the young Song emperor worked out conditions for surrender to them. Hence, the Mongol Yuan Dynasty had won control over China. After Kublai died, nine of his descendants ruled as emperors until the dynasty fell to native rebellions in 1368.

Historians differently assess the impact of Mongol Yuan rule on China. Earlier generations of historians judged that violent Mongol conquests devastated the land and led to a population drop. The Mongol style of rule was despotic. Rather than sustain the openness of Chinese society and use the merit-based examination system to bring talent into their government, Mongol rulers placed Chinese in rigid occupational categories and suspended the exams. Many capable men simply avoided official service and turned to other professions.

Recent studies, however, offer a more positive assessment. Because Yuan rulers followed the

Figure 4.29 | Blue and white porcelain plate manufactured during the Yuan Dynasty
Author: User "Yaan"
Source: Wikimedia Commons
License: Public Domain

counsel of Confucian advisors and adopted traditional Chinese methods for governing, for most Chinese life went on as before. Early on, much attention was also paid to the farming population. To promote agriculture, Yuan rulers provided relief measures and promoted the formation of rural cooperatives. Also, Mongols highly valued crafts and implemented policies that greatly benefited artisans and promoted their work. Hence, arts such as textiles and ceramics flourished (see Figure 4.28). Finally, the assessment of Yuan rule in China should be linked to a broader assessment of the impact of Mongol rule on world history (see Chapter Eleven). While duly acknowledging the devastation caused by Mongol conquests, historians also find much merit in Mongol patronage of arts and support for constructions projects and advancements in the areas of medicine and astronomy. Most importantly, the massive Eurasian empire they forged initiated a new era of trade and contacts between Europe and China, as well as the regions lying between.

4.14 CONCLUSION

We have now passed through nearly four millennia of East Asian history. We prefaced that history with the development of Neolithic cultures leading up to the second millennium BCE, at which point the first kingdoms in Chinese history emerged. Longshan culture (3000 – 1900 BCE) consisted of competing chiefdoms that laid the foundations for the emergence of the first major states.

The first major state was the Xia Dynasty (c. 1900 – 1600 BCE). Although historians debate whether or not it was legendary and lack written sources from that time, the archaeological evidence points to a Bronze Age civilization with a capital city at Erlitou. The next dynasty, the Shang (c. 1600 – 1046 BCE), brings us into history proper, because we have written evidence in the form of oracle bones and bronze inscriptions. The last Shang capital was located at Anyang on the North China Plain near the Yellow River. The dynasty's most important legacies were the earliest form of Chinese writing and ancestor worship. The oracle bones were used to divine the will of higher powers and the spirits of deceased Shang kings.

The next dynasty, the Zhou Dynasty (1045 – 256 BCE), began when chieftains to the west of the Shang declared themselves kings and overthrew it. They justified doing so with the Mandate of Heaven, which states that a higher power withdraws its support from corrupt ruling families and transfers it to righteous ones. Because it lasted eight hundred years and saw much change, the Zhou is divided into two major periods, the Western (1045 – 771 BCE) and Eastern Zhou (770 – 256 BCE). During the Western Zhou, Zhou kings ruled by granting land and noble titles to kinsmen and allies in exchange for loyalty and service. The resulting political system, which saw China divided up by over one hundred feudal states, is known as Zhou feudalism. During the Eastern Zhou, this nobility became increasingly independent and fought with each other for power and territory. A few declared themselves kings and forged powerful militaries by gearing their kingdoms for war. In the end, in 221 BCE, the state of Qin prevailed, initiating China's imperial era. Also, in the midst of the dislocation caused by Eastern Zhou instability, three of China's major philosophical traditions emerged: Confucianism, Legalism, and Daoism.

The short-lived Qin Dynasty was followed by the much longer lasting Han Dynasty (202 BCE – 220 CE). During the Han Dynasty, Confucianism was adopted as the governing philosophy and also penetrated society, shaping the Chinese worldview. The Han also became an empire, as borders were expanded in all directions. During the reign of Emperor Wu (141 – 87 BCE), China extended control over parts of Korea, northern Vietnam, and also much of Central Asia. The resulting stability and the productivity of the economy spurred the development of the Silk Routes.

After the Han dynasty fell, China was divided up by independent, short-lived kingdoms until 589 CE, when the Sui Dynasty reunited most of the territory once controlled by the Han. Thus, for four centuries, during what is known as the Period of Division (220 – 589 CE), China was politically unstable and racked by endemic warfare. Yet, in spite of the violence, these centuries also saw vibrant cultural developments, as Buddhism became an organized institutional religion reshaping the spiritual landscape.

The Tang Dynasty (618 – 907 CE) was yet another long-lived one in Chinese history. Tang rulers built an empire on the foundations of solid political and legal institutions, agricultural policy, and a formidable military. Also during the Tang Dynasty, East Asia first emerged as an identifiable cultural sphere. By Tang times, kingdoms had already formed on the Korean Peninsula and the main islands of Japan, but it was during the Tang that ruling elites in both of these states made extensive efforts to adapt components of the Chinese political, legal, and writing system, as well as of Chinese culture, to their own societies. During the seventh century CE, the Silla Dynasty unified the Korean Peninsula, and the Yamato heavenly sovereigns unified much of Japan. Two other unique East Asian civilizations had taken shape.

The last major dynasty surveyed was the Song Dynasty (960 – 1279 CE), one that is notable for the challenges it faced from northern conquest dynasties, its economic prosperity, and the civil service examination system and the educated elite of scholar-officials it created. Also, since footbinding developed during the Song, we considered the status of women in Chinese society, where gender hierarchy was the norm.

The Song Dynasty ended with Mongol conquests in 1279 CE. The Mongol Yuan Dynasty made China one part of a much larger Eurasian territorial empire. Mongol ruled lasted until 1368 CE, when native rebellions overthrew a faltering Yuan state, initiating a new period in Chinese history: the Ming Dynasty. This dynasty properly belongs to early modern history.

4.15 WORKS CONSULTED AND FURTHER READING

Barnes, Gina L. *State Formation in Japan: Emergence of a 4th Century Ruling Elite*. London and New York: Routledge, 2007.

Benn, Charles. *China's Golden Age: Everyday Life in the Tang Dynasty*. Cambridge: Oxford University Press, 2002.

Ebrey, Patricia. *The Inner Quarters: Marriage and the Lives of Women in the Sung Period*. Berkeley: University of California Press, 1993.

Ebrey, Patricia, James B. Palais, and Anne Walthall. *East Asia: A Cultural, Social, and Political History*. Boston: Houghton Mifflin Company 2006.

Hardy, Grant and Anne Behnke Kinney. *The Establishment of the Han Empire and Imperial China*. Westport, CT: Greenwood Press, 2005.

Hwang, Kyung Moon. *A History of Korea*. Palgrave Macmillan, 2010.

Keally, Charles. "Jōmon Culture." http://www.t-net.ne.jp/~keally/jomon.html

Keally, Charles. "Kofun Culture." http://www.t-net.ne.jp/~keally/kofun.html

Keally, Charles. "Yayoi Culture." http://www.t-net.ne.jp/~keally/yayoi.html

Kuhn, Dieter. *The Age of Confucian Rule: The Song Transformation of China*. Cambridge: Harvard University Press, 2009.

Lee, Ki-baik. *A New History of Korea*. Cambridge: Harvard University Press, 1984.

Lewis, Mark Edward. *China between Empires: The Northern and Southern Dynasties*. Cambridge: Harvard University Press, 2010.

Lewis, Mark Edward. *China's Cosmopolitan Empire: The Tang Dynasty*. Cambridge: Harvard University Press, 2009.

Lewis, Mark Edward. *Sanctioned Violence in Early China*. Albany: Statue University of New York Press, 1989.

Li Feng. *Early China: A Social and Cultural History*. Cambridge University Press, 2013.

Loewe, Michael. *Everyday Life in Imperial China*. Indianapolis: Hackett Publishing, 2005.

Mote, Frederick. *Imperial China,900 – 1800*. Cambridge: Harvard University Press, 1999.

Peers, C.J. *Soldiers of the Dragon: Chinese Armies 1500 BC – AD 1850*. Oxford: Osprey Publishing, 2006.

Pines, Yuri et al. eds. *Birth of an Empire: The State of Qin Revisited*. Berkeley: University of California Press, 2014.

Robinet, Isabelle. *Taoism: Growth of a Religion*. Stanford: Stanford University Press, 1997.

Rossabi, Morris. "The Mongols in World History." http://afe.easia.columbia.edu/mongols/index.html

Tanner, Harold M. *China: A History, Volume I: From Neolithic Cultures through the Great Qing Empire*. Indianapolis: Hackett Publishing Company, 2010.

Temple, Robert. *The Genius of China: 3,000 years of Science, Discovery and Invention*. Rochester: Inner Traditions, 2007.

Totman, Conrad. *A History of Japan*. Oxford: Blackwell Publishers, 2000.

4.16 LINKS TO PRIMARY SOURCES

China

http://afe.easia.columbia.edu/

Confucius – the *Analects* selections and complete online editions.

http://acc6.its.brooklyn.cuny.edu/~phalsall/texts/analects.html (selections)

http://www.olemiss.edu/courses/inst203/confucianthought.pdf (selections)

http://www.indiana.edu/~p374/Analects_of_Confucius_(Eno-2015).pdf (complete text)

Empress Wu Zetian and women during the Tang Dynasty

    http://www.womeninworldhistory.com/toc-06.html

The *Laozi* (*Dao de jing*) selections and complete online editions.

    http://afe.easia.columbia.edu/ps/cup/laozi_daodejing.pdf (selections)

    http://ctext.org/dao-de-jing (complete text)

    http://www.indiana.edu/~p374/Daodejing.pdf (complete text)

Mandate of Heaven

    http://acc6.its.brooklyn.cuny.edu/~phalsall/texts/shu-jing.html

    http://afe.easia.columbia.edu/ps/cup/classic_of_odes_king_wen.pdf

Mongols and the Mongol Yuan Dynasty

    http://afe.easia.columbia.edu/mongols/index.html

Oracle Bones of the Shang Dynasty

    http://afe.easia.columbia.edu/ps/cup/oracle_bone_general.pdf

Sunzi's (Master Sun's) *Art of War*

    http://afe.easia.columbia.edu/ps/cup/sunzi_art_of_war.pdf (selections)

    http://classics.mit.edu/Tzu/artwar.html (complete text)

Japan

Prince Shōtoku's Constitution

    http://afe.easia.columbia.edu/ps/japan/shotoku.pdf

Yoshinogari (a Yayoi Period archaeological site)

    http://www.yoshinogari.jp/en/

5 The Greek World from the Bronze Age to the Roman Conquest

Nadejda Williams

5.1 CHRONOLOGY

c. 3300 – 1150 BCE	Bronze Age
c. 1100 – 700 BCE	Dark Ages
c. 700 – 480 BCE	Archaic Period
480 – 323 BCE	Classical Period
431 – 404 BCE	The Peloponnesian War
323 – 146 BCE	Hellenistic Period

5.2 INTRODUCTION

Sometime in the eighth century BCE, an aristocratic resident of the Greek trading colony of Pithekoussai—located on the tiny island of Ischia just off the coast of Naples in Italy—held a symposium at his home. Most of what happened at the party stayed at the party, but what we do know is that it must have been a good one. One of the guests, presumably operating under the influence of his host's excellent wine, took the liberty of scratching the following ditty onto one of his host's fine exported ceramic wine cups: "I am the Cup of Nestor, good to drink from. Whoever drinks from this cup, straightaway the desire of beautifully-crowned Aphrodite will seize him."

While party pranks do not commonly make history, this one has: this so-called **Cup of Nestor** is one of the earliest examples of writing in the **Greek alphabet**, as well as the earliest known written reference to the Homeric epics. Overall, this cup and the inscription on it exemplify the mobility of the Ancient Greeks and their borrowing of skills and culture from others around the Mediterranean while, at the same time, cultivating a set of values specific to themselves. After all, just like the very residents of Pithekoussai, the cup had originally made the journey all the way from the island of Euboea, off the coast of Athens, to Pithekoussai, on the island of Ischia.

Furthermore, the new script, in which the daring guest wrote on the cup, had just recently been borrowed and adapted by the Greeks from the **Phoenicians**, a seafaring nation based in modern-

Figure 5.1a | "The Cup of Nestor" | Pythekoussai this so-called Cup of Nestor is one of the earliest examples of writing in the Greek alphabet, as well as the earliest known written reference to the Homeric epics.
Author: User "Antonius Proximo"
Source: Wikimedia Commons
License: CC BY-SA 3.0

Figure 5.1b | "The Cup of Nestor" | Detailed reconstruction of the inscription.
Author: User "Dbachmann"
Source: Wikimedia Commons
License: Public Domain

day Lebanon. Indeed, our clever poet wrote from right to left, just like the Phoenicians. Finally, the poem mentions Nestor, one of the heroes of **Homer's *Iliad***, an epic about the **Trojan War**, and a source of common values that all Greeks held dear: military valor, competitive excellence on both the battlefield and in all areas of everyday life, and a sense of brotherhood that manifested itself most obviously in the shared language of all the Greeks. That feeling of kinship facilitated collaboration of all the Greeks in times of crisis from the mythical Trojan War to the **Persian Wars**, and finally, during the Greeks' resistance against the Roman conquest.

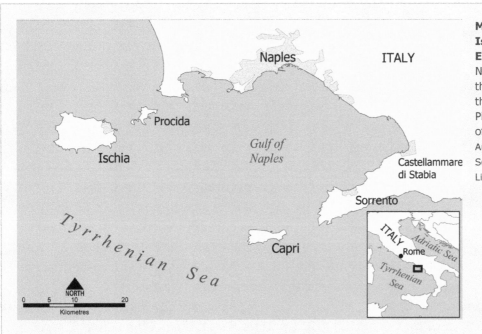

Map 5.1 | Map of the Island of Ischia and the Environs | The "Cup of Nestor" journeyed from the island of Euboea, off the coast of Athens, to Pithekoussai, on the island of Ischia.
Author: User "Norman Eistein"
Source: Wikimedia Commons
License: CC BY-SA 3.0

5.3 QUESTIONS TO GUIDE YOUR READING

1. In what ways did Greek geography and topography impact the history of the ancient Greek world?

2. What are the different periods of Greek history, and what are the chief defining characteristics of each period?

3. What primary sources are available for the study of Greek history, and what are the limitations of these sources?

4. What were the most important developments in the Greek world in the Archaic Period?

5. What was the significance of the Persian Wars for the subsequent history of the Greek World?

6. What were the stages of the Peloponnesian War? How did the outcome of the war impact Greece in the fourth century?

7. What were some of the most important contributions of Classical Athens in the areas of art, government and law, philosophy, and literature?

8. How and why did the Macedonians conquer the Greek world? Why did the empire conquered by Philip and Alexander disintegrate after Alexander's death?

9. What were some of the strengths and weaknesses of the Hellenistic kingdoms as political entities? Why did they prove to be inherently unstable?

10. What were some of the achievements and legacies of the Hellenistic period?

5.4 KEY TERMS

- Achaemenid Empire
- Alexander the Great
- Alexandria
- Antigonid dynasty
- Archaeological evidence
- Archaic Period
- Archidamian War
- Archimedes of Syracuse
- Aristophanes
- Aristotle
- Asia Minor
- Athenian democracy
- Athens
- Battle of Chaeronea
- Battle of Leuctra
- Battle of Marathon
- Battle of Thermopylae
- Bronze Age
- Chigi vase
- Classical Period

- Cleisthenes
- Cleopatra VII
- Crete
- "Cup of Nestor"
- Cynic philosophers
- Cyrus the Great
- Darius
- Dark Ages
- Decelean War
- Delian League / Athenian Empire
- Delphi
- *Ekklesia*
- Epicureanism
- Epidaurus
- Euripides
- First Peloponnesian War
- *Gerousia*
- Great Library of Alexandria
- Greek alphabet
- Greek colonization
- Hannukah
- Hellenistic Period
- Helots
- Herodotus
- Herophilus of Chalcedon
- Homer
- Homer's *Iliad*
- Hoplite phalanx
- Kingdom of Pergamon
- *Kleos*
- Isthmus of Corinth
- Linear A
- Linear B

- Macedonian Wars with Rome / Third Macedonian War
- Magna Graecia
- "Mask of Agamemnon"
- Mauryan Empire
- Megara Hyblaea
- Messenia
- Minoans
- Mycenaeans
- Oligarchy
- Olympic Games
- Orientalizing style
- *Othismos*
- Pan-Hellenic
- Peace of Nicias
- Peisistratus
- Peloponnese
- Peloponnesian War
- Pericles
- Persian Wars
- Pharos of Alexandria
- Philip II of Macedon
- Phoenicians
- Plato
- *Polis / poleis*
- Ptolemaic Egypt
- Ptolemy I Soter
- Pythia
- *Sarissa*
- Seleucid Empire
- Septuagint
- Sicilian Expedition
- Skepticism

- Socrates
- Solon
- Sophocles
- Sparta
- Spartan constitution
- Stoic philosophy
- Theban Hegemony
- Theban Sacred Band

- *Thetes*
- Thucydides
- Tyranny
- Tyranny of the Thirty
- Trojan War
- Tyrtaeus
- Wars of the *Diadochi*
- Xerxes

5.5 GEOGRAPHY AND TOPOGRAPHY

This chapter's title refers to the Greek World, rather than Greece. While Greece is a unified country today, the territory of the present-day country was not unified under one rule until the rise of the Macedonians in the fourth century BCE. Instead, the basic unit of organization in the period covered in this chapter was the **polis**, an independent city-state, which consisted of a walled city that controlled and protected the farmland around it. Historians estimate that close to 1,500 of these city-states dotted the ancient Greek landscape.

Each of these **poleis** (plural form of *polis*) possessed its own form of government, law-code, army, cults of patron gods, and overall culture that set it apart from the other city-states. While the two most famous *poleis*, **Athens** and **Sparta**, controlled vast territories of farmland, most city-states were quite small, with a population of just a few thousand citizens. Furthermore, the Greek world in antiquity encompassed much more than present-day Greece, extending as far as Italy in the West and the territories of modern-day Turkey and Ukraine in the East.

The geography and topography of the Greek mainland and the Mediterranean region surrounding it influenced the history of the Greek people in a number of crucial ways. First, the mountainous nature of mainland Greece, especially in the north, allowed different regions to remain somewhat isolated. The most isolated of all, Thessaly and Macedon, were viewed as uncivilized barbarians by the rest of the Greeks in the Archaic and Classical periods (one oft-mentioned example of their "barbarism" in Greek literature is that they drank their wine undiluted!)and largely kept to themselves until their rise to military prominence in the mid-fourth century BCE.

The mountains throughout the northern portion of mainland Greece, in addition to isolating regions from each other and promoting regional culture, also provided tactical defenses in the face of external attacks. Most famously, the Persians learned the hard way about the challenges of navigating the Greek landscape during the second Persian invasion of Greece in 480 BCE. Indeed, the story of the 300 Spartans who fought to the death at the **Battle of Thermopylae** addresses the challenge of the Persian army trying to cross the mountains to the north of Attica in order to invade Athens by land.

The **Isthmus**, a narrow strip of land controlled by Corinth, played a similar role in separating mainland Greece from the large peninsula of the **Peloponnese**. An inland city in southern

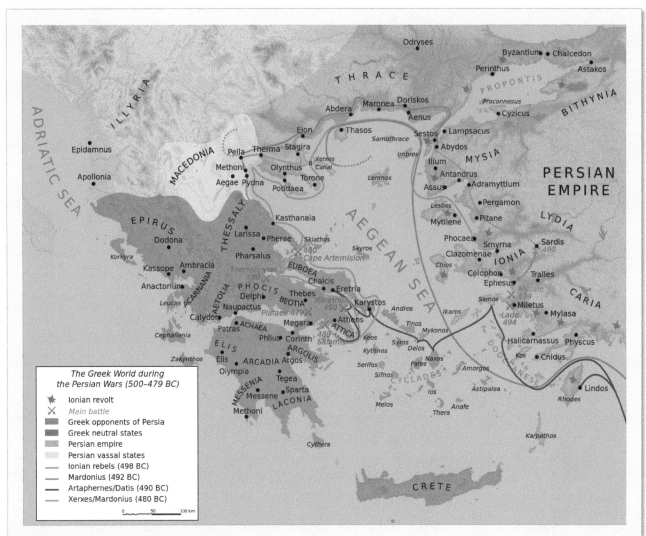

Map 5.2 | Map of the Ancient Greek city-states at the beginning of the Persian Wars | Historians estimate that close to 1,500 of these city-states dotted the ancient Greek landscape.

Author: User "Bibi Saint-Poi"

Source: Wikimedia Commons

License: CC BY-SA 3.0

Peloponnese, Sparta conquered **Messenia,** its surrounding region, early in its history and extended political control over much of the peninsula by early fifth century BCE. Unless the interests of Sparta herself were directly involved, Sparta practiced a policy of isolation and limited military intervention in other city-states affairs and wars, a practice enabled due to Sparta's far southern location in Peloponnese.

No less influential for the history of the Greek city-states than the topographical features were the resources that the land in different regions provided for agriculture and manufacturing. Mainland Greece was notoriously unsuitable for agriculture. Growing the grain staples wheat and barley in the rocky and clay-filled soil of Athens was especially difficult, while the mountainous regions across the entire mainland were optimal for herding, rather than agriculture. One notable exception, however, were olive trees, which grew abundantly. Olive oil, as a result, was ubiquitously used for eating, bathing, and lamps, and even as currency or prize for victors in athletic games. In addition, early on in their history, the inhabitants of Attica and Corinth found a way to profit from the clay in their soil by developing advanced ceramic pot-making and decorating techniques. Remains of Athenian and Corinthian wares have been found at archaeological sites all over the Mediterranean, attesting to their popularity abroad.

Finally, precious metals were in short supply in the mainland, but the few that were available had an impact on the history of their regions. Most famously, the discovery of the silver mines at Laurion in Attica contributed to the increased prosperity of Athens in the mid-fifth century BCE.

But the topography and geography of mainland Greece and the Peloponnese only

Figure 5.2 | Corinthian black-figure amphora, depicting the myth of Perseus and Andromeda c. 575-550 BCE, found in Cerveteri, Italy | The inhabitants of Attica and Corinth found a way to profit from the clay in their soil by developing advanced ceramic pot-making and decorating techniques. Remains of Athenian and Corinthian wares have been found at archaeological sites all over the Mediterranean, attesting to their popularity abroad.
Author: User "Butko"
Source: Wikimedia Commons
License: CC BY-SA 2.0

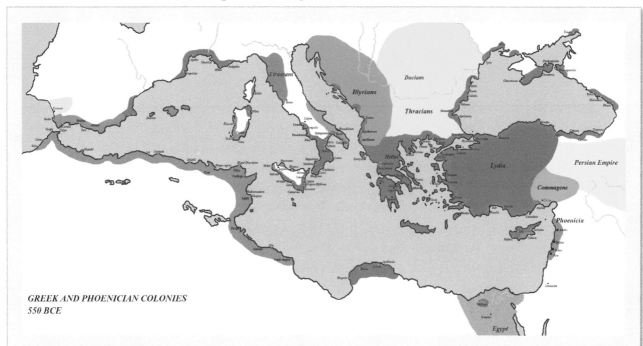

GREEK AND PHOENICIAN COLONIES
550 BCE

Map 5.3 | Map of the Greek (blue areas) and Phoenician city-states and colonies (red areas) c. 550 BCE.
Author: User "Javierfv1212"
Source: Wikimedia Commons
License: User "Javierfv1212"

tells us a part of the story. The Aegean is filled with islands, some of which remained autonomous, but most came under the control of the Athenian maritime empire in the fifth century BCE. In addition, the **Greek colonization** movement of the seventh and sixth centuries BCE resulted in the foundation of numerous Greek city-states in **Asia Minor** (modern-day Turkey), **Magna Graecia** (southern Italy), Sicily, and the Black Sea littoral.

The history of the Greek world from its earliest settlements to the Roman conquest, therefore, is inextricably tied together with the history of the Mediterranean as a whole. And since the Greek areas of influence overlapped with those controlled by the Phoenicians, Persians, and eventually the Romans, interactions, often warlike, were unavoidable as well. As the modern historians Peregrine Horden and Nicholas Purcell noted, the Mediterranean was "the Corrupting Sea"[1] whose inhabitants were like frogs around the pond, watching each other, and borrowing each other's cultural and technological achievements. As this chapter and the next will show, the Greeks and the Romans were the farthest-leaping frogs of all.

5.6 PERIODS OF GREEK HISTORY

Historians today separate Greek history into particular periods, which shared specific features throughout the Greek world:

The **Bronze Age** (c. 3,300 – 1,150 BCE) – a period characterized by the use of bronze tools and weapons. In addition, two particular periods during the Bronze Age are crucial in the development of early Greece: the Minoan Age on the island of **Crete** (c. 2,000 – 1,450 BCE) and the Mycenean period on mainland Greece (c. 1,600 – 1,100 BCE), both of them characterized by massive palaces, remnants of which still proudly stand today. The Minoan and Mycenaean civilizations had writing (dubbed **Linear A** and **Linear B**, respectively), which they used for keeping lists and palace inventories.

The **Dark Ages** (c. 1,100 – 700 BCE) – a period that is "dark" from the archaeological perspective, which means that the monumental palaces of the Mycenean period disappear, and the archaeological record reveals a general poverty and loss of culture throughout the Greek world. For instance, the Linear A and Linear B writing systems disappear. The Greeks do not rediscover writing until the invention of the Greek alphabet at the end of the Dark Ages or the early Archaic Period.

Archaic Period (c. 700 – 480 BCE) – the earliest period for which written evidence survives; this is the age of the rise of the Greek city-states, colonization, and the Persian Wars.

Classical Period (c. 480 – 323 BCE) – the period from the end of the Persian Wars to the death of **Alexander the Great**. One of the most important events during this period is the Peloponnesian War (431 – 404 BCE), which pitted Athens against Sparta, and forced all other Greek city-states to choose to join one side or the other. This period ends with the death of Alexander the Great, who had unified the Greek world into a large kingdom with himself at its helm.

Hellenistic Period (323 – 146 BCE) – the period from the death of Alexander to the Roman conquest of Greece; this is the age of the Hellenistic monarchies ruling over territories previously conquered by Alexander and his generals. Some historians end this period in 30

---

1   Peregrine Horden and Nicholas Purcell, *The Corrupting Sea: A Study of Mediterranean History* (Oxford: Wiley-Blackwell, 2000).

BCE, with the death of **Cleopatra VII**, the last surviving ruler of Egypt who was a descendant of one of Alexander's generals.

The rest of this chapter will be devoted to examining each of these periods in greater detail, covering chief political, military, and cultural developments.

5.7 METHODOLOGY: SOURCES AND PROBLEM

Before launching into the story of the early Greek world, it is important to consider the methodology that Greek historians utilize. In other words, how do we know what we know about the Greek world? Modern scholars of ancient history are notoriously obsessed with evaluating their primary sources critically, and with good reason. Studying Greek history, especially in its earliest periods, is like putting together a puzzle, most of whose pieces are missing, and some pieces from another puzzle have also been added in for good measure. Greek history requires careful consideration of a wide range of sources, which fall into two broad categories: literary sources (including both fiction and non-fiction), and material culture. The job of the historian, then, is to reconstruct the story of the Greek people using these very different sources.

While historians of the modern world rely on such archival sources as newspapers, magazines, and personal diaries and correspondence of individuals and groups, historians of the ancient world must use every available source to reconstruct the world in which their subject dwelled. Literary sources, such as epics, lyric poetry, and drama, may seem strange for historians to use, as they do not necessarily describe specific historical events. Yet, as in the case of other early civilizations, such sources are a crucial window into the culture and values of the people who produced them. For instance, the *Epic of Gilgamesh*, discussed in Chapter 2, is a key text for the study of early Mesopotamia.

The earliest literary sources for Greek history are the Homeric epics, *Iliad* and *Odyssey*. They are, however, one of the most challenging sources to interpret, with one modern historian dubbing them a "historian's headache."[2] Composed orally before the existence of the Greek alphabet, the epics were not written down until sometime in the sixth century BCE. The epics most likely do not reflect the society of any particular Greek city-state in any one period, but rather consist of an amalgam of features from the Bronze Age to the early Archaic Period. Their value for historians, as a result, rests more on their impact on subsequent Greek culture, rather than on their providing information about Bronze Age Greeks. More than any other literary source, the Homeric Epics influenced the mentality of the Greeks in thinking about war and what it means to be a hero.

Most other literary sources from the Archaic and Classical periods are easier to interpret than the Homeric Epics, as we often can date these later sources more precisely and thus know the period whose values or problems they reflect. There is, however, one important limitation to keep in mind: the overwhelming majority of surviving literature is from Athens, with very few sources from other city-states. Some of this distribution of evidence has to do with the differing values of the city-states themselves. For example, while Greeks of the Classical period considered Sparta to

---

2   Kurt Raaflaub, "A Historian's Deadache: How to Read 'Homeric Society'?" in N. Fisher and H. Van wees eds., Archaic Greece: New Approaches and New Evidence (London: Duckworth: 1998).

be as great a city as Athens, Spartans valued military valor over all else, so they did not cultivate arts and letters the way Athenians did. As a result, the only literary sources from Sparta are the works of two poets, Alcman and Tyrtaeus. Tyrtaeus' military elegies, like the Homeric epics, glorify heroic death in battle over life without honor and were likely sung by Spartan warriors as they marched into battle.

Several genres of non-fiction survive as well, allowing historians to study specific events and problems in the history of the Greek world, and especially Athens. The works of three major historians survive from Classical Athens. **Herodotus**, dubbed the Father of History, wrote the *Histories* about the Persian Wars in mid-fifth century BCE. **Thucydides**, an Athenian general in the Peloponnesian War, wrote a history of the Peloponnesian War over the course of the war (431 – 404 BCE). Finally, Xenophon wrote a history of the end of the Peloponnesian War, starting with 411 BCE, where Thucydides' work ended, and into the fourth century. In addition to the works of the historians, philosophical treatises – most notably, those of **Plato** and **Aristotle** – provide crucial insight into the political thought, moral values, and perceptions of the world in late fifth and fourth centuries BCE. The approximately 100 surviving courtroom speeches from the same period likewise provide us with a window into the Athenian legal system. Finally, the Hippocratic corpus, a series of medical treatises and physicians' journals from the Classical period, help us to understand the Greeks' views of the human body and diseases. But in addition to the geographical restrictions of these sources, which largely document Athens, it is also important to note two other key limitations of the available evidence. First, virtually all of the literary sources were written by men and provide very little evidence of the lives and perspectives of women in the Greek world, except as seen through the eyes of men. Second, most of the authors were wealthy and socially prominent individuals; thus, their perspective does not reflect that of less affluent citizens and slaves.

Archaeological evidence thankfully allows historians to fill some of the gaps in the literary evidence, but also comes with problems of its own. One joke that refers to the optimism of archaeologists reflects some of these problems of interpretation: whenever an archaeologist finds three stones that are together, he labels the find as a Minoan palace. Whenever he finds two stones that are together, he thinks he has found a city wall. Whenever he finds one building stone, he thinks he has found a house.

Still, archaeological sources provide us with key information

Figure 5.3 | Megara Hyblaea, main road, looking north | The careful planning of the road and the buildings is still evident, as the ruins on both sides of the road are perfectly aligned.
Author: User "Alun Salt"
Source: Wikimedia Commons
License: CC BY-SA 2.0

Figure 5.4 | Attic Black-Figure Hydria, c. 520 BCE | Shows women getting water from a public fountain.
Author: User "Jastrow"
Source: Wikimedia Commons
License: CC BY-SA 2.5

about different aspects of everyday life in different city-states. For example, the excavations of the sixth-century BCE colony **Megara Hyblaea** in Sicily shows that Greek colonists were interested in city planning and in equality of citizens, as demonstrated by the equal size of the lots.

Material finds, such as pottery remains, in different sites across the Mediterranean also allow historians to map trading routes – for instance, Figures 5.1 and 5.2 show vases that were made in Euboea and Corinth respectively, but were found in Greek colonies in Italy. In addition, images on pottery provide information about stories and myths that have entered popular culture and that sometimes reflect further aspects of everyday life. For instance, the prevalence of images of women gathering at public fountains on Athenian *hydriae* (water pots) from the late sixth century BCE shows the importance of the public fountains for the social life of women in Athens in the period.

Finally, written archaeological sources, such as inscriptions on stone or pottery shards from all over the Greek world, and papyri from Hellenistic Egypt, are the equivalent of documentary archives from the ancient world. The evidence from epigraphy (inscriptions) includes laws that were written on large stones and set up in public, such as the monumental law-code from Gortyn, Crete, and lists of war-dead, as well as private tomb inscriptions.

Papyri, on the other hand, include such private documents as prenuptial agreements (among the strangest are prenuptial documents for brother-sister marriages – legal

Figure 5.5 | The Gortyn Code (c. fifth century BCE) | Close-up of part of the inscription.
Author: User "Afrank99"
Source: Wikimedia Commons
License: CC BY-SA 2.5

in Egypt but nowhere else in the Greek world), divorce documents, loans, and village police reports (cattle theft appears to have been a serious problem in the Faiyum in the Hellenistic Period!).

Taken together, the literary and archaeological sources allow the historian to complete much more of the puzzle than would have been possible with just one of these types of sources. Still, significant gaps in knowledge remain nevertheless, and are, perhaps, one of the joys of studying ancient history: the historian gets to play the part of a sleuth, attempting to reconstruct the history of events based on just a few available clues.

5.8 FROM MYTHOLOGY TO HISTORY

The terms "mythology" and "history" may seem, by modern definitions, to be antithetical. After all, mythology refers to stories that are clearly false, of long-forgotten gods and heroes and their miraculous feats. History, on the other hand, refers to actual events that involved real people. And yet, the idea that the two are opposites would have seemed baffling to a typical resident of the ancient Mediterranean world. Rather, gods and myths were part of the everyday life, and historical events could become subsumed by myths just as easily as myths could become a part of history. For instance, Gilgamesh, the hero of the Sumerian *Epic of Gilgamesh*, was a real king of Uruk, yet he also became the hero of the epic. Each Greek city-state, in particular, had a foundation myth describing its origins as well as its own patron gods and goddesses. Etiological myths, furthermore, served to explain why certain institutions or practices existed; for instance, the tragic trilogy *Oresteia* of the Athenian poet Aeschylus tells the etiological myth for the establishment of the Athenian murder courts in the Classical period.

Yet, while the Greeks saw mythology and history as related concepts and sometimes as two sides of the same coin, one specific mythical event marked, in the eyes of the earliest known Greek historians, the beginning of the story of Greek-speaking peoples. That event was the Trojan War.

5.8.1 Homer and the Trojan War

It is telling that the two earliest Greek historians, Herodotus, writing in the mid-fifth century BCE, and Thucydides, writing in the last third of the fifth century BCE, began their respective histories with the Trojan War, each treating it as a historical event. The Homeric epics *Iliad* and *Odyssey* portray the war as an organized attack of a unified Greek army against Troy, a city in Asia Minor (see map 5.2). The instigating offense? The Trojan prince Paris kidnapped Helen, the most beautiful woman in the world, from her husband Menelaus, king of Sparta. This offense, interpreted as a slight to Menelaus' honor, prompted Agamemnon, king of Mycenae and Menelaus' brother, to raise an army from the entire Greek world and sail to Troy. The mythical tradition had it that after a brutal ten-year siege, the Greeks resorted to a trick: they presented the Trojans with a hollow wooden horse, filled with armed soldiers. The Trojans tragically accepted the gift, ostensibly intended as a dedication to the goddess Athena. That same night, the armed contingent emerged from the horse, and the city finally fell to the Greeks. Picking up the story ten years after the end of the Trojan War, the *Odyssey* then told the story of Odysseus's struggles to return home after the war and the changes that reverberated throughout the Greek world after the fall of Troy.

The Homeric epics were the foundation of Greek education in the Archaic and Classical periods and, as such, are a historian's best source of pan-Hellenic values. A major theme throughout both epics is personal honor, which Homeric heroes value more than the collective cause. For example, when Agamemnon slights Achilles' honor in the beginning of the *Iliad*, Achilles, the best hero of the Greeks, withdraws from battle for much of the epic, even though his action causes the Greeks to start losing battles until he rejoins the fight. A related theme is competitive excellence, with **kleos** (eternal glory) as its goal: all Greek heroes want to be the best; thus, even while fighting in the same army, they see each other as competition. Ultimately, Achilles has to make a choice: he can live a long life and die unknown, or he can die in battle young and have everlasting glory. Achilles' selection of the second option made him the inspiration for such historical Greek warriors and generals as Alexander the Great, who brought his scroll copy of the *Iliad* with him on all campaigns. Finally, the presence of the gods in the background of the Trojan War shows the Greeks' belief that the gods were everywhere, and acted in the lives of mortals. These gods could be powerful benefactors and patrons of individuals who respected them and sought their favor, or vicious enemies, bent on destruction. Indeed, early in the *Iliad*, the god Apollo sends a plague on the Greek army at Troy, as punishment for disrespecting his priest.

It is important to note that while the Homeric epics influenced Greek values from the Archaic period on, they do not reflect the reality of the Greek world in any one period. Furthermore, they were not composed by a single poet, **Homer**; indeed, it is possible that Homer never existed. Because the epics were composed orally by multiple bards over the period of several hundred years, they combine details about technological and other aspects of the Bronze Age with those of the Dark Ages and even the early Archaic Age. For instance, the heroes use bronze weapons side-by-side with iron. Archaeological evidence, however, allows historians to reconstruct to some extent a picture of the Greek world in the Bronze Age and the Dark Ages.

5.8.2 Greece in the Bronze Age, and the Dark Ages

While there were people living in mainland Greece already in the Neolithic Period, historians typically begin the study of the Greeks as a unique civilization in the Bronze Age, with the **Minoans**. The first literate civilization in Europe, the Minoans were a palace civilization that flourished on the island of **Crete** c. 2,000 – 1,450 BCE.

As befits island-dwellers, they were traders and seafarers; indeed, the Greek historian Thucydides credits them with being the first Greeks to sail on ships. Sir Arthur Evans, the archaeologist who first excavated Crete in the early 1900s, dubbed them Minoans, after the mythical Cretan king Minos who was best known for building a labyrinth to house the Minotaur, a monster that was half-man, half-bull. Bulls appear everywhere in surviving Minoan art, suggesting that they indeed held a prominent place in Minoan mythology and religion.

Four major palace sites survive on Crete. The most significant of them, Knossos, has been restored and reconstructed for the benefit of modern tourists.

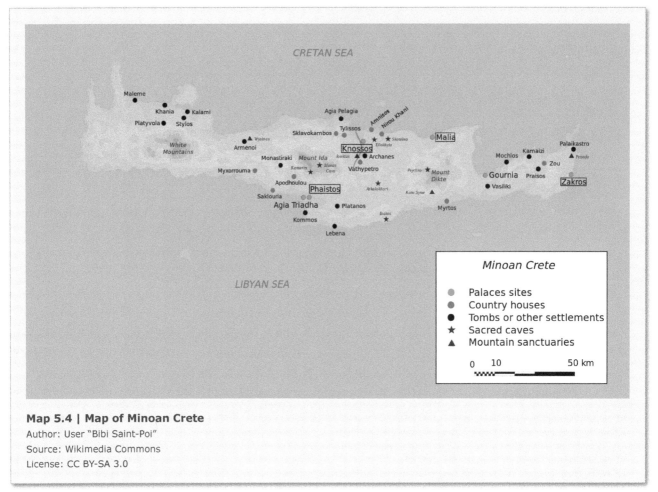

Map 5.4 | Map of Minoan Crete
Author: User "Bibi Saint-Poi"
Source: Wikimedia Commons
License: CC BY-SA 3.0

Historians hypothesize that the palaces were the homes of local rulers, who ruled and protected the surrounding farmland. The palaces seem to have kept records in two different writing systems, the earliest known in Europe: the Cretan hieroglyphic and Linear A scripts. Unfortunately, neither of these systems has been deciphered, but it is likely that these were palace inventories and records pertaining to trade. The palaces had no surrounding walls, suggesting that the Cretans maintained peace with each other and felt safe from outside attacks, since they lived on an island. This sense of security proved to be a mistake as, around 1,450 BCE, the palaces were violently destroyed by invaders, possibly the **Mycenaeans**

Figure 5.6 | The Bull-Leaping Fresco from Knossos
Author: User "Jebulon"
Source: Wikimedia Commons
License: CC0 1.0

who arrived from mainland Greece. Recent discoveries also suggest that at least some of the destruction may have been the result of tsunamis which accompanied the Santorini/Thera volcanic eruption in the 1600s BCE.

The Mycenaeans, similarly to the Minoans, were a palace civilization. Flourishing on mainland Greece c. 1,600 – 1,100 BCE, they received their name from Mycenae, the most elaborate surviving palace and the mythical home of Agamemnon, the commander-in-chief of the Greek army in the Trojan War. The archaeological excavations of graves in Mycenae reveal a prosperous civilization that produced elaborate pottery, bronze weapons and tools, and extravagant jewelry and other

Figure 5.7 | Reconstructed North Portico at Knossos
Author: User "Bernard Gagnon"
Source: Wikimedia Commons
License: CC BY-SA 3.0

objects made of precious metals and gems. One of the most famous finds is the so-called **"Mask of Agamemnon,"** a burial mask with which one aristocrat was buried, made of hammered gold.

The Mycenaeans also kept palace records in a syllabic script, known as Linear B. Related to the Cretan Linear A script, Linear B, however, has been deciphered, and identified as Greek.

Archaeological evidence also shows that sometime in the 1,200s BCE, the Mycenaean palaces suffered a series of attacks and were gradually abandoned over the next century. The period that begins around 1,000 BCE is known as the "Dark Ages" because of the notable decline, in contrast with the preceding period. The Mycenaean Linear B script disappears, and archaeological evidence shows a poorer Greece with a decline in material wealth and life expectancy. Some contact, however, must have remained with the rest of the Mediterranean, as shown by the emergence of the Greek alphabet, adapted from the Phoenician writing system towards the end of the Dark Ages or early in the Archaic Period.

5.9 ARCHAIC GREECE

The story of the Greek world in the Dark Ages could mostly be described as a story of fragmentation. With a few exceptions,

Figure 5.8 | Mask of Agamemnon, Mycenae
Author: User "Xuan Che"
Source: Wikimedia Commons
License: CC BY 2.0

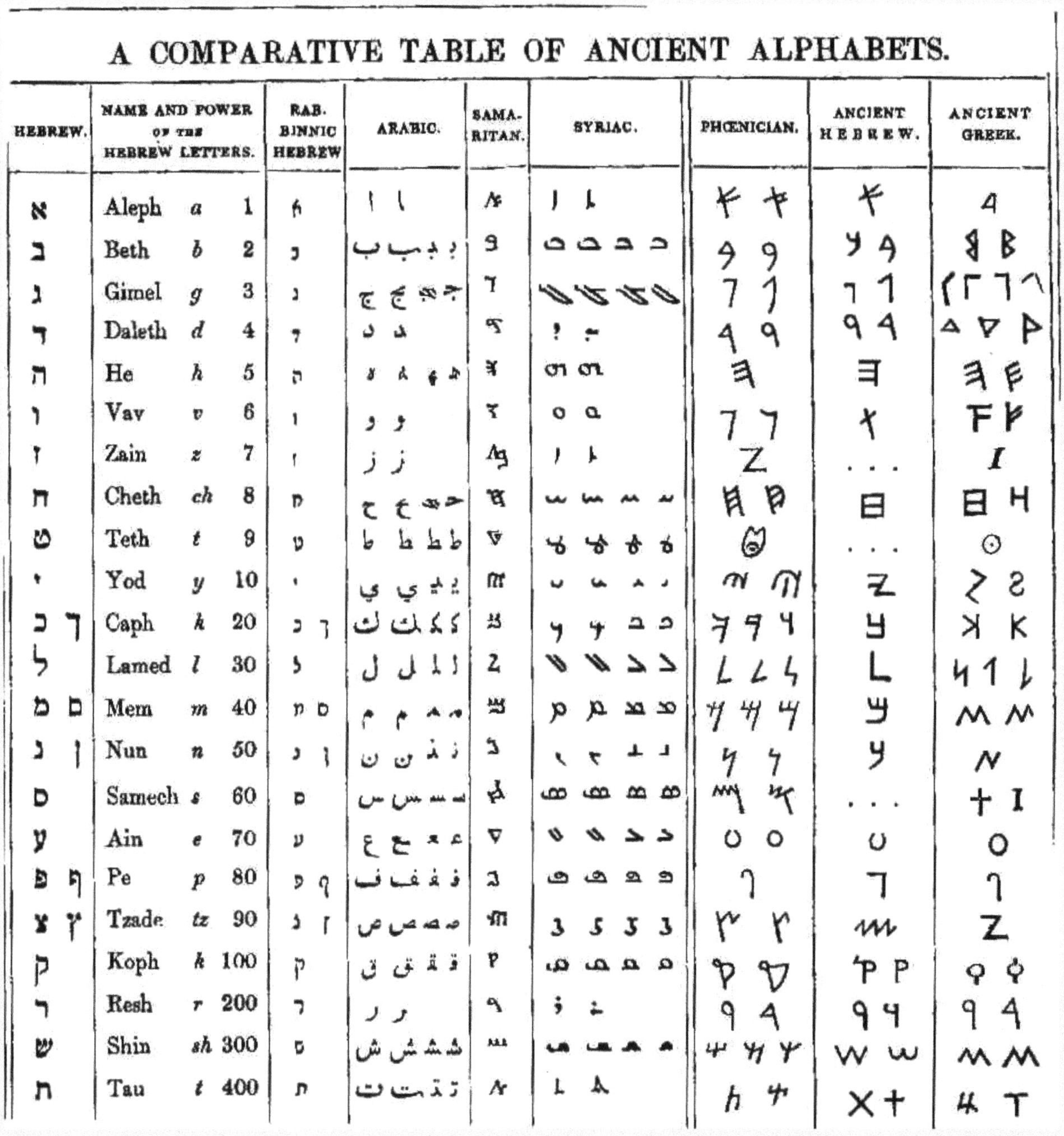

A COMPARATIVE TABLE OF ANCIENT ALPHABETS.

HEBREW.	NAME AND POWER OF THE HEBREW LETTERS.			RAB. BINNIC HEBREW	ARABIC.	SAMA-RITAN.	SYRIAC.	PHŒNICIAN.	ANCIENT HEBREW.	ANCIENT GREEK.
א	Aleph	a	1							
ב	Beth	b	2							
ג	Gimel	g	3							
ד	Daleth	d	4							
ה	He	h	5							
ו	Vav	v	6							
ז	Zain	z	7							
ח	Cheth	ch	8							
ט	Teth	t	9							
י	Yod	y	10							
כ ך	Caph	k	20							
ל	Lamed	l	30							
מ ם	Mem	m	40							
נ ן	Nun	n	50							
ס	Samech	s	60							
ע	Ain	e	70							
פ ף	Pe	p	80							
צ ץ	Tzade	tz	90							
ק	Koph	k	100							
ר	Resh	r	200							
ש	Shin	sh	300							
ת	Tau	t	400							

Figure 5.9 | Comparative chart of writing systems in the Ancient Mediterranean | As this chart shows, in addition to the influence of the Phoenician alphabet on the Greek, there were close connections between the Phoenician, Egyptian, and Hebrew writing systems as well.

Author: Samuel Prideaux Tregelles

Source: Google Books

License: Public Domain

individual sites had limited contact with each other. The Archaic period, however, appears to have been a time of growing contacts and connections between different parts of mainland Greece. Furthermore, it was a time of expansion, as the establishment of overseas colonies and cities brought the Greeks to Italy and Sicily in the West, and Asia Minor and the Black Sea littoral in the East. Furthermore, while Greeks in the Archaic period saw themselves as citizens of individual city-states, this period also witnessed the rise of a **Pan-Hellenic** identity, as all Greeks saw themselves connected by virtue of their common language, religion, and Homeric values. This Pan-Hellenic identity was ultimately cemented during the Persian Wars: two invasions of Greece by the Persian Empire at the end of the Archaic period.

5.9.1 Rise of the Hoplite Phalanx and the Polis

A Corinthian vase, known today as the **Chigi Vase**, made in the mid-seventh century BCE, presents a tantalizing glimpse of the changing times from the Dark Ages to the Archaic Period. Taking up much of the decorated space on the vase is a battle scene. Two armies of warriors with round shields, helmets, and spears are facing each other and appear to be marching in formation towards each other in preparation for attack.

Modern scholars largely consider the vase to be the earliest artistic portrayal of the **hoplite phalanx**, a new way of fighting that spread around the Greek world in the early Archaic Age and that coincided with the rise of another key institution for subsequent Greek history: the *polis*, or city-state. From the early Archaic period to the conquest of the Greek world by Philip and Alexander in the late fourth century BCE, the *polis* was the central unit of organization in the Greek world.

While warfare in the *Iliad* consisted largely of duels between individual heroes, the hoplite phalanx was a new mode of fighting that did not rely on the skill of individuals. Rather, it required all soldiers in the line to work together as a whole. Armed in the same way – with a helmet, spear, and the round shield, the *hoplon*, which gave the hoplites their name – the soldiers were arranged in rows, possibly as much as seven deep. Each soldier carried his shield on his left arm, protecting the left side of his own body and the right side of his comrade to the left. Working together as one, then, the phalanx

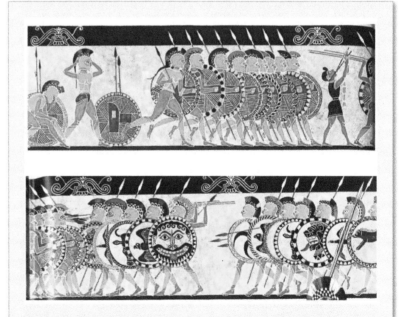

Figure 5.10 | "Unrolled" reconstructed image from the Chigi Vase
Author: User "Phokion"
Source: Wikimedia Commons
License: CC BY-SA 4.0

would execute the **othismos** (a mass shove) during battle, with the goal of shoving the enemy phalanx off the battlefield.

Historians do not know which came into existence first, the phalanx or the *polis*, but the two clearly reflect a similar ideology. In fact, the phalanx could be seen as a microcosm of the *polis*, exemplifying the chief values of the *polis* on a small scale. Each *polis* was a fully self-sufficient unit of organization, with its own laws, definition of citizenship, government, army, economy, and local cults. Regardless of the differences between the many *poleis* in matters of citizenship, government, and law, one key similarity is clear: the survival of the *polis* depended on the dedication of all its citizens to the collective well-being of the city-state. This dedication included service in the phalanx. As a result, citizenship in most Greek city-states was closely connected to military service, and women were excluded from citizenship. Furthermore, since hoplites had to provide their own armor, these citizen-militias effectively consisted of landowners. This is not to say, though, that the poorer citizens were entirely excluded from serving their city. One example of a way in which they may have participated even in the phalanx appears on the Chigi Vase. Marching between two lines of warriors is an unarmed man, playing a double-reed flute (seen on the right end of the top band in Figure 5.10). Since the success of the phalanx depended on marching together in step, the flute-player's music would have been essential to ensure that everyone kept the same tempo during the march.

5.9.2 Greek Religion

One theory modern scholars have proposed for the rise of the *polis* connects the locations of the city-states to known cult-sites. The theory argues that the Greeks of the Archaic period built city-states around these precincts of various gods in order to live closer to them and protect them. While impossible to know for sure if this theory or any other regarding the rise of the polis is true, the building of temples in cities during the Archaic period shows the increasing emphasis that the *poleis* were placing on religion.

It is important to note that Greek religion seems to have been, at least to some extent, an element of continuity from the Bronze Age to the Archaic period and beyond. The important role that the gods play in the Homeric epics attests to their prominence in the oral tradition, going back to the Dark Ages. Furthermore, names of the following major gods worshipped in the Archaic period and beyond were found on the deciphered Linear B tablets: Zeus, king of the gods and god of weather, associated with the thunderbolt; Hera, Zeus' wife and patroness of childbirth; Poseidon, god of the sea; Hermes, messenger god and patron of thieves and merchants; Athena, goddess of war and wisdom and patroness of women's crafts; Ares, god of war; Dionysus, god of wine; and the twins Apollo, god of the sun and both god of the plague and a healer, and Artemis, goddess of the hunt and the moon. All of these gods continued to be the major divinities in Greek religion for its duration, and many of them were worshipped as patron gods of individual cities, such as Artemis at Sparta, and Athena at Athens.

While many local cults of even major gods were truly local in appeal, a few local cults achieved truly Pan-Hellenic appeal. Drawing visitors from all over the Greek world, these Pan-Hellenic

Figure 5.11 | Themis and Aegeus | The Pythia seated on the tripod and holding a laurel branch – symbols of Apollo, who was the source of her prophecies. This is the only surviving image of the Pythia from ancient Greece
Author: User "Bibi Saint-Pol"
Source: Wikimedia Commons
License: Public Domain

cults were seen as belonging equally to all the Greeks. One of the most famous examples is the cult of Asclepius at **Epidaurus**. Asclepius, son of Apollo, was a healer god, and his shrine at Epidaurus attracted the pilgrims from all over the Greek world. Visitors suffering from illness practiced incubation, that is, spending the night in the temple, in the hopes of receiving a vision in their dreams suggesting a cure. In gratitude for the god's healing, some pilgrims dedicated casts of their healed body parts. Archaeological findings include a plentitude of ears, noses, arms, and feet.

Starting out as local cults, several religious festivals that included athletic competitions as part of the celebration also achieved Pan-Hellenic prominence during the Archaic period. The most influential of these were the **Olympic Games**. Beginning in 776 BCE, the Olympic Games were held in Olympia every four years in honor of Zeus; they drew competitors from all over the Greek world, and even Persia. The Pan-Hellenic appeal of the Olympics is signified by the impact that these games had on Greek politics: for instance, a truce was in effect throughout the Greek world for the duration of each Olympics. In addition, the Olympics provided a Pan-Hellenic system of dating events by Olympiads or four-year cycles.

Finally, perhaps the most politically influential of the Pan-Hellenic cults was the oracle of Apollo at **Delphi**, established sometime in the eighth century BCE. Available for consultation only nine days a year, the oracle spoke responses to the questions asked by inquirers through a priestess, named the **Pythia**. The Pythia's responses came in the form of poetry and were notoriously difficult to interpret. Nevertheless, city-states and major rulers throughout the Greek world considered it essential to consult the oracle before embarking on any major endeavor, such as war or founding a colony.

5.9.3 Maritime Trade and Colonization

The historian Herodotus records that sometime c. 630 BCE, the king of the small island of Thera traveled to Delphi to offer a sacrifice and consult the oracle on a few minor points. To his surprise, the oracle's response had nothing to do with his queries. Instead, the Pythia directed him to found a colony in Libya, in North Africa. Having never heard of Libya, the king ignored the advice. A seven-year drought ensued, and the Therans felt compelled to consult the oracle again. Receiving the same response as before, they finally sent out a group of colonists who eventually founded the city of Cyrene.

While this story may sound absurd, it is similar to other foundation stories of Greek colonies and emphasizes the importance of the Delphic oracle. At the same time, though, this story still leaves open the question of motive: why did so many Greek city-states of the Archaic period send out colonies to other parts of the Greek world? Archaeology and foundation legends, such as those recorded by Herodotus, suggest two chief reasons: population pressures along with shortage of productive farmland in the cities on mainland Greece, and increased ease of trade that colonies abroad facilitated. In addition to resolving these two problems, however, the colonies also had the unforeseen impact of increasing interactions of the Greeks with the larger Mediterranean world and the ancient Near East. These interactions are visible, for instance, in the so-called **Orientalizing style** of art in the Archaic period, a style the Greeks borrowed from the Middle East and Egypt.

As section 5.3.5 will show, however, the presence of Greek colonies in Asia Minor also played a major role in bringing about the Greco-Persian Wars.

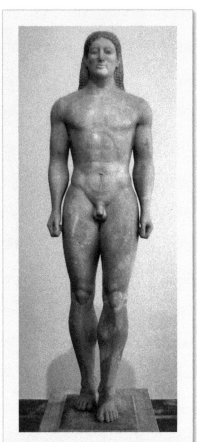

Figure 5.12 | Archaic *kouros* (youth) statue, c. 530 BC | Note the Egyptian hairstyle and body pose.
Author: User "Mountain"
Source: Wikimedia Commons
License: Public Domain

5.9.4. Aristocracy, Democracy, and Tyranny in Archaic Greece

Later Greek historians, including Herodotus and Thucydides, noted a certain trend in the trajectory of the history of most Greek *poleis*: most city-states started out with a monarchical or quasi-monarchical government. Over time the people gained greater representation, and an assembly of all citizens had at least some degree of political power—although some degree of strife typically materialized between the aristocrats and the poorer elements. Taking advantage of such civic conflicts, **tyrants** came to power in most city-states for a brief period before the people banded together and drove them out, thenceforth replacing them with a more popular form of government.

Many modern historians are skeptical about some of the stories that the Greek historians tell about origins of some *poleis*; for instance, it is questionable whether the earliest Thebans truly were born from dragon teeth. Similarly, the stories about some of the Archaic tyrants seem to belong more to the realm of legend than history. Nevertheless, the preservation of stories about tyrants in early oral tradition suggests that city-states likely went through periods of turmoil and change in their form of government before developing a more stable constitution. Furthermore, this line of development accurately describes the early history of Athens, the best-documented *polis*.

In the early Archaic period, Athens largely had an aristocratic constitution. Widespread debt-slavery, however, caused significant civic strife in the city and led to the appointment of **Solon** as lawgiver for the year 594/3 BCE, specifically for the purpose of reforming the laws. Solon created a more democratic constitution and also left poetry documenting justifications for his reforms—and different citizens' reactions to them. Most controversial of all, Solon instituted a one-time debt-forgiveness, *seisachtheia,* which literally means "shaking off." He proceeded to divide all citizens into five classes based on income, assigning a level of political participation and responsibility commensurate with each class. Shortly after Solon's reforms, a tyrant, **Peisistratus**, illegally seized control of Athens and remained in power off and on from 561 to 527 BCE. Peisistratus seems to have been a reasonably popular ruler who had the support of a significant portion of the Athenian population. His two sons, Hippias and Hipparchus, however, appear to have been less well-liked. Two men, Harmodius and Aristogeiton, assassinated Hipparchus in 514 BCE; then in 508 BCE, the Athenians, with the help of a Spartan army, permanently drove out Hippias. In subsequent Athenian history, Harmodius and Aristogeiton were considered heroes of the democracy and celebrated as tyrannicides.

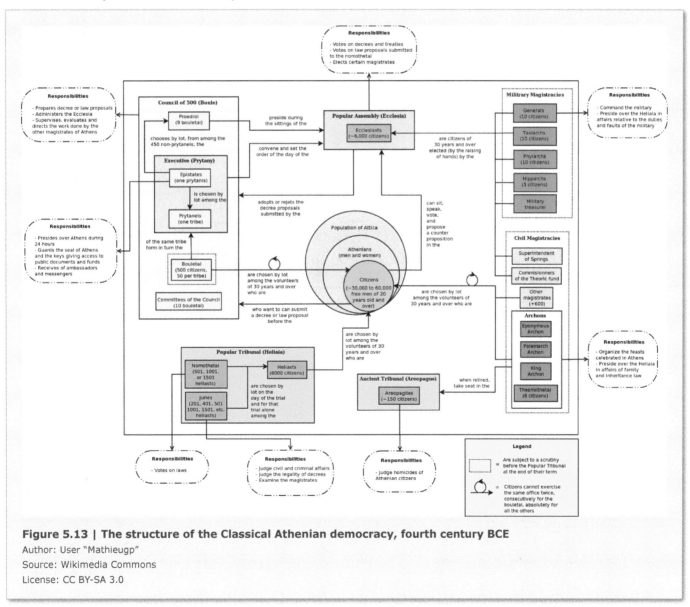

Figure 5.13 | The structure of the Classical Athenian democracy, fourth century BCE
Author: User "Mathieugp"
Source: Wikimedia Commons
License: CC BY-SA 3.0

Immediately following the expulsion of Hippias, Athens underwent a second round of democratic reforms, led by **Cleisthenes**. The Cleisthenic constitution remained in effect, with few changes, until the Macedonian conquest of Athens in the fourth century BCE and is considered to be the Classical **Athenian democracy**. Central to the democracy was the participation of all citizens in two types of institutions: the ***ekklesia***, an assembly of all citizens, which functioned as the chief deliberative body of the city; and the law-courts, to which citizens were assigned by lot as jurors. Two chief offices, the generals and the archos, ruled over the city and were appointed for one-year terms. Ten generals were elected annually by the *ekklesia* for the purpose of leading the Athenian military forces. Finally, the leading political office each year, the nine archons, were appointed by lot from all eligible citizens. While this notion of appointing the top political leaders by lot may seem surprising, it exemplifies the Athenians' pride in their democracy and their desire to believe that, in theory at least, all Athenian citizens were equally valuable and capable of leading their city-state.

Developing in a very different manner from Athens, Sparta was seen by other Greek *poleis* as a very different sort of city from the rest. Ruled from an early period by two kings – one from each of the two royal houses that ruled jointly – Sparta was a true oligarchy, in which the power

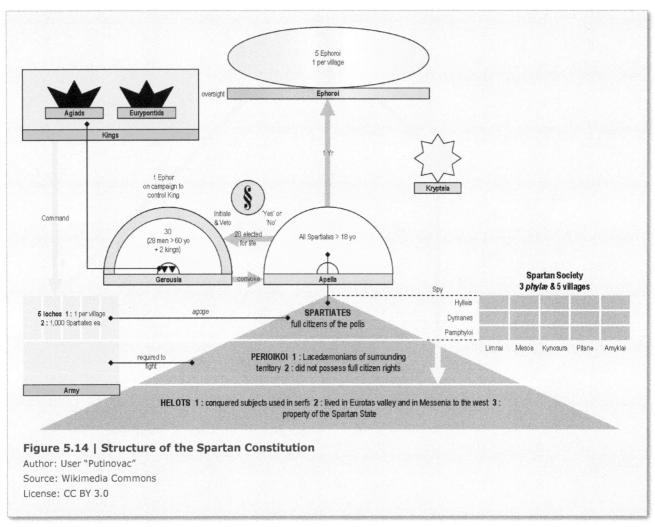

Figure 5.14 | Structure of the Spartan Constitution
Author: User "Putinovac"
Source: Wikimedia Commons
License: CC BY 3.0

rested in its **gerousia**, a council of thirty elders, whose number included the two kings. While an assembly of all citizens existed as well, its powers were much more limited than were those of the Athenian assembly. Yet because of much more restrictive citizenship rules, Spartan assembly of citizens would have felt as a more selective body, as Figure 5.14 illustrates.

A crucial moment in Spartan history was the city's conquest of the nearby region of Messenia in the eighth century BCE.

The Spartans annexed the Messenian territory to their own and made the Messenians **helots**. While the helots could not be bought or sold, they were permanently tied to the land in a status akin to medieval

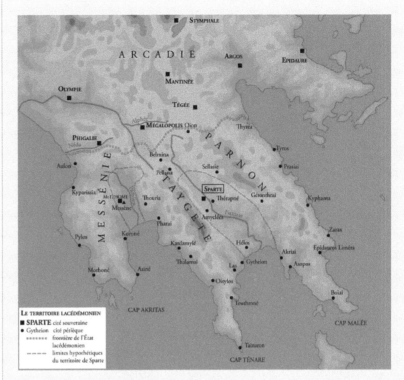

Map 5.5 | Map of Sparta and the Environs
Author: User "Marsyas"
Source: Wikimedia Commons
License: CC BY-SA 3.0

European serfs. The availability of helot labor allowed the Spartans from that point on to focus their attention on military training. This focus transformed Sparta into the ultimate military state in the Greek world, widely respected by the other Greek *poleis* for its military prowess. Other Greeks were fascinated by such Spartan practices as the communal bringing up of all children apart from their parents and the requirement that all Spartan girls and women, as well as boys and men, maintain a strict regimen of exercise and training.

But while Athens and Sparta sound like each other's diametrical opposites, the practices of both *poleis* ultimately derived from the same belief that all city-states held: that, in order to ensure their city's survival, the citizens must place their city-state's interests above their own. A democracy simply approached this goal with a different view of the qualifications of its citizens than did an oligarchy.

A final note on gender is necessary, in connection with Greek city-states' definitions of citizenship. Only children of legally married and freeborn citizen parents could be citizens in most city-states. Women had an ambiguous status in the Greek *poleis*. While not full-fledged citizens themselves, they produced citizens. This view of the primary importance of wives in the city as the mothers of citizens resulted in diametrically opposite laws in Athens and Sparta, showing the different values that the respective cities emphasized. In Athens, if a husband caught his wife with an adulterer in his home, the law allowed the husband to kill said adulterer on the spot. The adultery law was so harsh precisely because adultery put into question the citizenship status of potential children, thereby depriving the city of future citizens. By contrast, Spartan law allowed an unmarried man who wanted offspring to sleep with the wife of another man, with the latter's consent, specifically for the purpose of producing children. This law reflects the importance that Sparta placed on producing strong future soldiers as well as the communal attitude of the city towards family and citizenship.

5.9.5 The Persian Wars

Despite casting their net far and wide in founding colonies, the Greeks seem to have remained in a state of relatively peaceful coexistence with the rest of their Mediterranean neighbors until the sixth century BCE. In the mid-sixth century BCE, Cyrus, an ambitious king of Persia, embarked on a swift program of expansion, ultimately consolidating under his rule the largest empire of the ancient world and earning for himself the title "**Cyrus the Great.**"

Cyrus' **Achaemenid Empire** bordered the area of Asia Minor that had been previously colonized by the Greeks. This expansion of the Persian Empire brought the Persians into direct conflict with the Greeks and became the origin of the Greco-Persian Wars, the greatest military conflict the Greek world had known up until that point.

Over the second half of the sixth century, the Persians had taken over the region of Asia Minor, also known as Ionia, installing as rulers of these Greek city-states tyrants loyal to Persia. In 499 BCE, however, the Greek city-states in Asia Minor joined forces to rebel against the Persian rule. Athens and Eretria sent military support for this Ionian Revolt, and the rebelling forces marched on the Persian capital of Sardis and burned it in 498 BCE, before the revolt was finally subdued by the Persians in 493 BCE.

Seeking revenge on Athens and Eretria, the Persian king **Darius** launched an expedition in 490 BCE.

Map 5.6 | The Achaemenid Empire under the rule of Cyrus
Author: User "Gabagool"
Source: Wikimedia Commons
License: CC BY 3.0

Darius' forces captured Eretria in mid-summer, destroyed the city, and enslaved its inhabitants. Sailing a short distance across the bay, the Persian army then landed at Marathon. The worried Athenians sent a plea for help to Sparta. The Spartans, in the middle of a religious festival, refused to help. So, on September 12, 490 BCE, the Athenians, with only a small force of Plataeans helping, faced the much larger Persian army in the **Battle of Marathon**. The decisive Athenian victory showed the superiority of the Greek hoplite phalanx and marked the

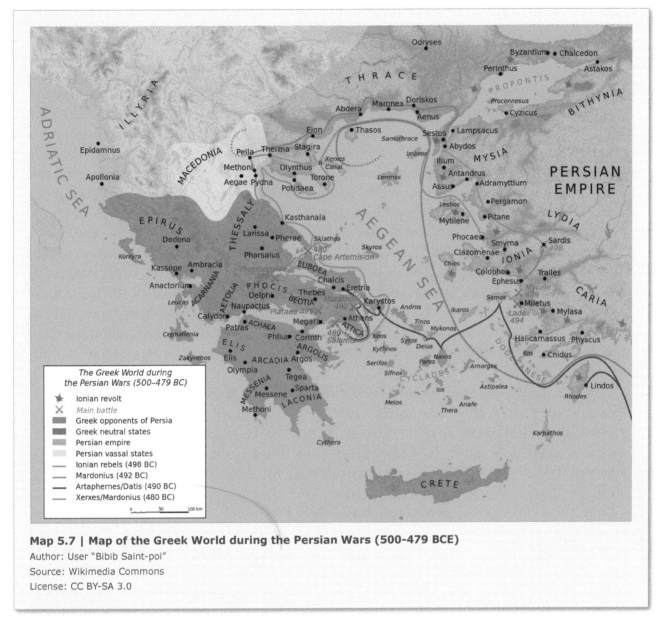

Map 5.7 | Map of the Greek World during the Persian Wars (500-479 BCE)
Author: User "Bibib Saint-poi"
Source: Wikimedia Commons
License: CC BY-SA 3.0

end of the first Persian invasion of Greece. Furthermore, the victory at Marathon, which remained a point of pride for the Athenians for centuries after, demonstrated to the rest of the Greeks that Sparta was not the only great military power in Greece.

Darius died in 486 BCE, having never realized his dream of revenge against the Greeks. His son, **Xerxes**, however, continued his father's plans and launched in 480 BCE a second invasion of Greece, with an army so large that, as the historian Herodotus claims, it drank entire rivers dry on its march. The Greek world reacted in a much more organized fashion to this second invasion than it did to the first. Led by Athens and Sparta, some seventy Greek *poleis* formed a sworn alliance to fight together against the Persians. This alliance, the first of its kind, proved to be the key to defeating the Persians as it allowed the allies to split forces strategically in order to guard against Persian attack by both land and sea. The few Greek city-states who declared loyalty to the

Persian Empire instead–most notably, Thebes–were seen as traitors for centuries to come by the rest of the Greeks.

Marching through mainland Greece from the north, the Persians first confronted the Spartans at the Battle of Thermopylae, a narrow mountain pass that stood in the way of the Persians' accessing any point south. In this now-legendary battle, 300 Spartans, led by their king Leonidas, successfully defended the pass for two days before being betrayed by a local who showed a roundabout route to the Persians. The Persians then were able to outflank the Spartans and kill them to the last man. This battle, although a loss for the Greeks, bought crucial time for the rest of the Greek forces in preparing to face the Persians. It is also important to note that although the Spartans were considered even in the ancient world to be the heroes of Thermopylae, they were also accompanied by small contingents from several other Greek city-states in this endeavor.

The victory at Thermopylae fulfilled the old dream of Darius, as it allowed access to Athens for the Persians. The Athenian statesman Themistocles, however, had ordered a full evacuation of the city in advance of the Persian attack through an unusual interpretation of a Delphic oracle stating that wooden walls will save Athens. Taking the oracle to mean that the wooden walls in question were ships, Themistocles built a massive fleet which he used to send all of the city's inhabitants to safety. His gamble proved to be successful, and the Persians captured and burned a mostly empty city.

The Athenians proceeded to defeat the Persian fleet at the Battle of Salamis, off the coast of Athens, thus shortly before winter turning the tide of the war in favor of the Greeks. Finally, in June of 479 BCE, the Greek forces were able to strike the two final blows, defeating the Persian land and sea forces on the same day in the Battle of Plataea on land and the Battle of Mycale on sea. The victory at Mycale also resulted in a second Ionian revolt, which this time ended in a victory for the Greek city-states in Asia Minor. Xerxes was left to sail home to his diminished empire.

It is difficult to overestimate the impact of the Persian Wars on subsequent Greek history. Seen by historians as the end-point of the Archaic Period, the Persian Wars cemented Pan-Hellenic identity, as they saw cooperation on an unprecedented scale among the Greek city-states. In addition, the Persian Wars showed the Greek military superiority over the Persians on both land and sea. Finally, the wars showed Athens in a new light to the rest of the Greeks. As the winners of Marathon in the first invasion and the leaders of the navy during the second invasion, the Athenians emerged from the wars as the rivals of Sparta for military prestige among the Greeks. This last point, in particular, proved to be the most influential for Greek history in the subsequent period.

5.10 THE CLASSICAL PERIOD

So far, the story of the Greek world in this chapter has proceeded from a narrative of the fragmented Greek world in the Dark Ages to the emergence and solidification of a Pan-Hellenic identity in the Archaic Period. The story of the Greeks in the Classical Period, by contrast, is best described as the strife for leadership of the Greek world. First, Athens and Sparta spent much of the fifth century BCE battling each other for control of the Greek world. Then, once both were weakened, other states began attempting to fill the power vacuum. Ultimately, the Classical

Period will end with the Greek world under the control of a power that was virtually unknown to the Greeks at the beginning of the fifth century BCE: Macedon.

5.10.1 From the Delian League to the Athenian Empire

In 478 BCE, barely a year after the end of the Persian Wars, a group of Greek city-states, mainly those located in Ionia and on the island between mainland Greece and Ionia, founded the **Delian League**, with the aim of continuing to protect the Greeks in Ionia from Persian attacks. Led by Athens, the league first met on the tiny island of Delos. According to Greek mythology, the twin gods Apollo and Artemis were born on Delos. As a result, the island was considered sacred ground and, as such, was a fitting neutral headquarters for the new alliance. The league allowed member states the option of either contributing a tax (an option that most members selected)

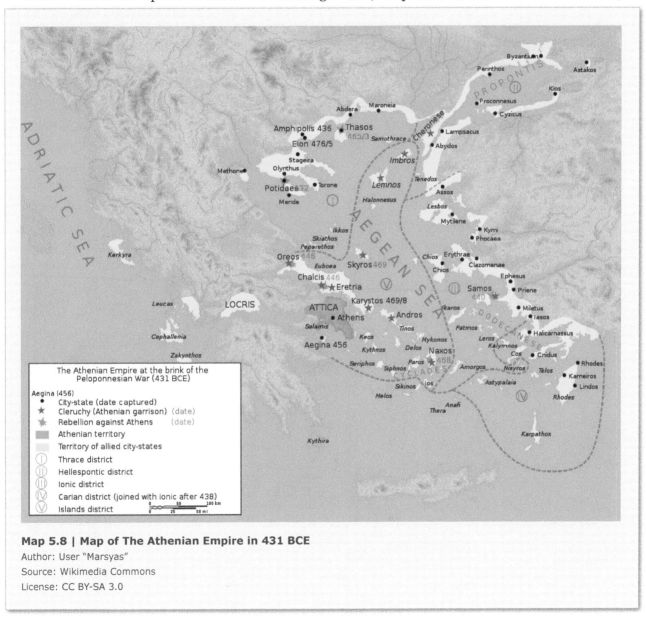

Map 5.8 | Map of The Athenian Empire in 431 BCE
Author: User "Marsyas"
Source: Wikimedia Commons
License: CC BY-SA 3.0

or contributing ships for the league's navy. The treasury of the league, where the taxes paid by members were deposited, was housed on Delos.

Over the next twenty years, the Delian League gradually transformed from a loose alliance of states led by Athens to a more formal entity. The League's Athenian leadership, in the meanwhile, grew to be that of an imperial leader. The few members who tried to secede from the League, such as the island of Naxos, quickly learned that doing so was not an option as the revolt was violently subdued. Finally, in 454 BCE, the treasury of the Delian League moved to Athens. That moment marked the transformation of the Delian League into the **Athenian Empire**.

Since the Athenians publicly inscribed each year the one-sixtieth portion of the tribute that they dedicated to Athena, records survive listing the contributing members for a number of years, thereby allowing historians to see the magnitude of the Athenian operation.

While only the Athenian side of the story survives, it appears that the Athenians' allies in the Delian League were not happy with the transformation of the alliance into a full-fledged Athenian Empire. Non-allies were affected a well. The fifth-century BCE Athenian historian Thucydides dramatizes in his history one particularly harsh treatment of a small island, Melos, which effectively refused to join the Athenian cause. To add insult to injury, once the treasury of the Empire had been moved to Athens, the Athenians had used some funds from it for their own building projects, the most famous of these projects being the Parthenon, the great temple to Athena on the Acropolis.

The bold decision to move the treasury of the Delian League to Athens was the brainchild of the leading Athenian statesman of the fifth century BCE, Pericles. A member of a prominent aristocratic family, Pericles was a predominant politician for forty years, from the early 460s BCE to his death in 429 BCE, and was instrumental in the development of a more popular democracy in Athens. Under his leadership, an especially vibrant feeling of Athenian patriotic pride seems to have developed, and the decision to move the Delian League treasury to Athens fits into this pattern as well. Shortly after moving the treasury to Athens, Pericles sponsored a Citizenship Decree in 451 BCE that restricted Athenian citizenship from thence onwards only to individuals who had two free-born and legitimately-wed Athenian parents, both of whom were also born of Athenian parents. Then c. 449 BCE, Pericles successfully proposed a decree allowing the Athenians to use Delian League funds for Athenian building projects, and, c. 447 BCE, he sponsored the Athenian Coinage Decree, a decree that imposed Athenian standards of weights and measures on all states that were members of the Delian League.

Figure 5.15 | Model of the Acropolis, with the Parthenon in the middle
Author: User "Benson Kua"
Source: Wikimedia Commons
License: CC BY-SA 2.0

Later in his life, Pericles famously described Athens as "the school of Hellas;" this description would certainly have fit Athens just as much in the mid-fifth century BCE as, in addition to the flourishing of art and architecture, the city was a center of philosophy and drama.

The growing wealth and power of Athens in the twenty or so years since the Persian Wars did not escape Sparta and led to increasingly tense relations between the two leading powers in Greece. Sparta had steadily consolidated the Peloponnesian League in this same time-period, but Sparta's authority over this league was not quite as strict as was the Athenian control over the Delian League. Finally, in the period of 460-445 BCE, the Spartans and the Athenians engaged in a series of battles, to which modern scholars refer as the **First Peloponnesian War**. In 445 BCE, the two sides swore to a Thirty Years Peace, a treaty that allowed both sides to return to their pre-war holdings, with few exceptions. Still, Spartan unease in this period of Athenian expansion and prosperity, which resulted in the First Peloponnesian War, was merely a sign of much more serious conflict to come. As the Athenian general and historian Thucydides later wrote about the reasons for the Great Peloponnesian War, which erupted in 431 BCE: "But the real cause of the war was one that was formally kept out of sight. The growing power of Athens, and the fear that it inspired in Sparta, made the war inevitable" (Thucydides, I.23).

5.10.2 The Peloponnesian War (431 – 404 BCE)

Historians today frown on the use of the term "inevitable" to describe historical events. Still, Thucydides' point about the inevitability of the Peloponnesian War is perhaps appropriate, as following a conflict that had been bubbling under the surface for fifty years, the war finally broke out over a seemingly minor affair. In 433 BCE, Corcyra, a colony of Corinth that no longer wanted to be under the control of its mother-city, asked Athens for protection against Corinth. The Corinthians claimed that the Athenian support of Corcyra was a violation of the Thirty Years Peace. At a subsequent meeting of the Peloponnesian League in Sparta in 432 BCE, the allies, along with Sparta, voted that the peace had been broken and so declared war against Athens.

At the time of the war's declaration, no one thought that it would last twenty-seven years and would ultimately embroil the entire Greek-speaking world. Rather, the Spartans expected that they would march with an army to Athens, fight a decisive battle, then return home forthwith. The long duration of the war, however, was partly the result of the different strengths of the two leading powers. Athens was a naval empire, with allies scattered all over the Ionian Sea. Sparta, on the other hand, was a land-locked power with supporters chiefly in the Peloponnese and with no navy to speak of at the outset of the war.

The Peloponnesian War brought about significant changes in the government of both Athens and Sparta, so that, by the end of the war, neither power looked as it did at its outset. Athens, in particular, became more democratic because of increased need for manpower to row its fleet. The lowest census bracket, the ***thetes***, whose poverty and inability to buy their own armor had previously excluded them from military service, became by the end of the war a full-fledged part of the Athenian forces and required a correspondingly greater degree of political influence. In the case of Sparta, the war had ended the Spartan policy of relative isolationism from the

Map 5.9 | Map of the Peloponnesian War Alliances at the Start and Contrasting Strategies, 431 BCE
Author: User "Magnus Manske"
Source: Wikimedia Commons
License: Public Domain

rest of the affairs of the Greek city-states. The length of the war also brought about significant changes to the nature of Greek warfare. While war was previously largely a seasonal affair, with many conflicts being decided with a single battle, the Peloponnesian War forced the Greek city-states to support standing armies. Finally, while sieges of cities and attacks on civilians were previously frowned upon, they became the norm by the end of the Peloponnesian War. In short, Thucydides's narrative of the war shows that the war had a detrimental effect on human nature, encouraging a previously unprecedented degree of cruelty on both sides. It is important to note, though, that as brutal as sieges could be during the Peloponnesian War, Greek siege warfare during the fifth century BCE was still quite primitive, as no tools existed for ramming or otherwise damaging the city gates or walls. Furthermore, catapults, so useful for targeting a city from the outside, first came into being in 399 BCE, five years after the war had ended.

Modern historians divide the Peloponnesian War into three distinct stages, based on the tactics used in each: the **Archidamian War**, the **Peace of Nicias**, and the **Decelean War**. The first stage, the Archidamian War (431 – 421 BCE), is named after the Spartan king Archidamus, who proposed the strategy of annual invasions of Attica at the beginning of the war. Beginning in late spring and early summer of 431 BCE, Archidamus led the Spartan army to invade Attica in order to devastate the agricultural land around the city. The Spartans thereby hoped to provoke the Athenians to a battle. Pericles however, refused to enter into battle against the Spartans, and instead ordered all inhabitants of Attica to retreat within the city. Pericles' decision was wise, as the Athenians would likely have lost a land battle against the Spartans. His decision, though, had unforeseen repercussions. In 430 BCE, the crowded conditions within Athens resulted in the outbreak of a virulent plague which by some estimates killed as much as twenty-five percent of the city's population over the following three years. Among the dead was none other than Pericles himself.

The plague had significant repercussions for Athens during the first phase of the war because of not only the loss of fighting men to disease and the consequent lowered morale in the city, but also the death of Pericles, the moderate leader. The subsequent leaders who emerged, such as

Cleon, were known as war-hawks. Meanwhile, the Spartans continued their annual invasions of Attica until 425 BCE, when luck was finally on the Athenians' side.

In 425 BCE, the Athenian fleet faced a new Spartan fleet in the Battle of Pylos in the Peloponnese. The Athenians won the battle and also managed to trap 420 Spartans on the tiny island of Sphacteria, just off the coast of Pylos. Sending shockwaves through the entire Greek world, the Spartans surrendered. By bringing the hostages to Athens, the Athenians put an end to the annual invasions of Attica. Finally, in 421 BCE, with the death of the most pro-war generals on both sides, the Athenians with their allies signed a peace treaty with Spartans and their allies. Named the "Peace of Nicias" after the Athenian general who brokered this treaty, it was supposed to be a fifty years' peace; it allowed both sides to return to their pre-war holdings, with a few exceptions. As part of the peace terms, the Spartan hostages from Pylos were finally released.

Despite its ambitious casting as a fifty years' peace, the Peace of Nicias proved to be a short and uneasy time filled with minor battles and skirmishes. One problem with the treaty was that while Athens and all of its allies signed the peace, several key allies of Sparta, including Corinth and Thebes, refused to do so. Furthermore, Athens made the disastrous decision during this stalemate to launch the **Sicilian Expedition**, a venture that took much of the Athenian fleet to Sicily in 415 BCE.

Syracuse, however, proved to be a difficult target, and the expedition ended in 413 BCE with a complete destruction of the Athenian navy. That same year, the Spartans renewed the fighting, launching the third and final phase of the Peloponnesian War.

In the third stage of the Peloponnesian war, also known as the Decelean War, the Spartans took the war to Attic soil by occupying Decelea, a village in Attica proper, and transforming it into a

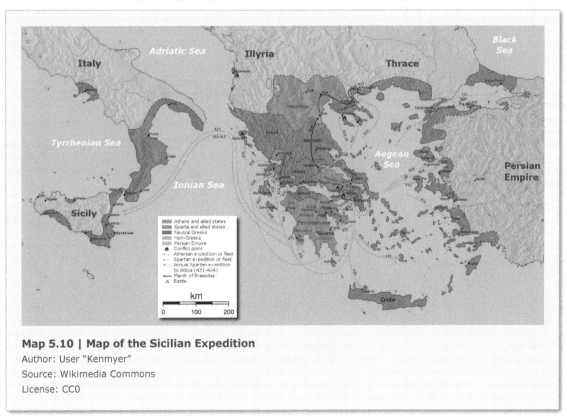

Map 5.10 | Map of the Sicilian Expedition
Author: User "Kenmyer"
Source: Wikimedia Commons
License: CC0

military fort. This occupation allowed the Spartans to prevent the Athenians from farming their land and cutting off Athens from most supply routes, effectively crippling the Athenian economy for the remainder of the war. Losing the Sicilian Expedition and the challenge of the Decelean War produced a high level of resentment towards the democratic leaders in Athens. Therefore in 411 BCE, an oligarchic coup briefly replaced the democracy with the rule of the Four Hundred. While this oligarchy was quickly overthrown and the democracy restored, this internal instability highlighted the presence of the aristocratic element in the city as well as the dissatisfaction of at least the aristocratic citizens with the long war.

Remarkably, in a testament to the resilience and power of the Athenian state, the Athenians managed to rebuild a navy after the Sicilian Expedition, and even managed to continue to win battles on sea during this final phase of the war. In 405 BCE, however, the Spartan general Lysander defeated Athens in the naval battle of Aegospotami. He proceeded to besiege Athens, and the city finally surrendered in 404 BCE. For the second time in a decade, the Athenian democracy was overthrown, to be replaced this time by the Spartan-sanctioned oligarchy known as the **Tyranny of the Thirty**. The rule of the Thirty proved to be a much more brutal oligarchy than that of the Four Hundred. A year later, an army formed largely of Athenian democrats in exile marched on the city and overthrew the Thirty. The democracy thus was restored in 403 BCE, and the painful process of recovery from the war and the oligarchic rule could begin.

5.10.3 Athenian Culture during the Peloponnesian War

Because it drained Athens of manpower and financial resources, the Peloponnesian War proved to be an utter practical disaster for Athens. Nevertheless, the war period was also the pinnacle of Athenian culture, most notably its tragedy, comedy, and philosophy. Tragedy and comedy in Athens were very much popular entertainment, intended to appeal to all citizens. Thus issues considered in these plays were often ones of paramount concern for the city at the time when the plays were written. As one character in a comedy bitterly joked in an address to the audience, more Athenians attended tragic and comic performances than came to vote at assembly meetings. Not surprisingly, war was a common topic of discussion in the plays. Furthermore, war was not portrayed positively, as the playwrights repeatedly emphasized the costs of war for both winners and losers.

Sophocles, one of the two most prominent Athenian tragedians during the Peloponnesian War era, had served his city as a general, albeit at an earlier period; thus, he had direct experience with war. Many of his tragedies that were performed during the war dealt with the darker side of fighting, for both soldiers and generals, and the cities that are affected. By tradition, however, tragedies tackled contemporary issues through integrating them into mythical stories, and the two mythical wars that Sophocles portrayed in his tragedies were the Trojan War, as in *Ajax* and *Philoctetes*, and the aftermath of the war of the Seven against Thebes, in which Polynices, the son of Oedipus, led six other heroes to attack Thebes, a city led by his brother Eteocles, as in *Oedipus at Colonus*. Sophocles' plays repeatedly showed the emotional and psychological challenges of war for soldiers and civilians alike; they also emphasized the futility of war, as the heroes of his plays, just as in the original myths on which they were based, died tragic, untimely deaths. Sophocles' younger contemporary, **Euripides**, had a similar interest in depicting the horrors of war and wrote a number of tragedies on the impact of war on the defeated, such as in *Phoenician Women* and *Hecuba*; both of these plays explored the aftermath of the Trojan War from the perspective of the defeated Trojans.

While the tragic playwrights explored the impact of the war on both the fighters and the civilians through narrating mythical events, the comic playwright **Aristophanes** was far less subtle. The anti-war civilian who saves the day and ends the war was a common hero in the Aristophanic comedies. For instance, in the *Acharnians* (425 BCE), the main character is a war-weary farmer who, frustrated with the inefficiency of the Athenian leadership in ending the war, brokers his own personal peace with Sparta. Similarly, in *Peace* (421 BCE), another anti-war farmer fattens up a dung beetle in order to fly to Olympus and beg Zeus to free Peace. Finally, in *Lysistrata* (411 BCE), the wives of all Greek city-states, missing their husbands who are at war, band together in a plot to end the war by going on a sex-strike until their husbands make peace. By the end of the play, their wish comes true. Undeniably funny, the jokes in these comedies, nevertheless, have a bitter edge, akin to the portrayal of war in the tragedies. The overall impression from the war-era drama is that the playwrights, as well as perhaps the Athenians themselves, spent much of the Peloponnesian War dreaming of peace.

While the playwrights were dreaming of the things of this world—most notably war—their contemporary, **Socrates**, was dreaming of difficult questions. One of the most prominent philosophers of the ancient world, Socrates has not left any writings of his own, but thoughts attributed to him survive in dialogues penned by his student, the fourth-century philosopher **Plato**. In Plato's writings, Socrates comes across as someone who loved difficult questions and who was not above confronting any passers-by with such questions as "What is courage?"; "What is moral?"; "What would the ideal city look like?" Using what became known ever since as the "Socratic method," Socrates continued to probe further every definition and answer that his conversation partners provided, guiding them to delve deeper in their reflections on the topics at hand than they had before. As a result of his love of such debates, Socrates was seen as connected to the Sophists, philosophical debate teachers, who (as Aristophanes joked) could teach anyone to convince others of anything at all, regardless of reality or truth. But Socrates radically differed from the Sophists by not charging fees for his teaching. Instead, as he himself is purported to have said, he was a pest-like gadfly that kept disturbing Athens from growing too content and encouraged all with whom he spoke to keep thinking and questioning.

5.10.4 The Fourth Century BCE

In 399 BCE, a seventy-year old Athenian was put on trial for impiety and for corrupting the youth, convicted, and speedily sentenced to death. The trial is especially shocking, since the man in question was none other than Socrates, the philosopher who had spent his life wandering the streets of Athens engaging in endless dialogues regarding the meaning of life. Why did the Athenians suddenly turn against this public teacher and judge him worthy of execution? The answer, most

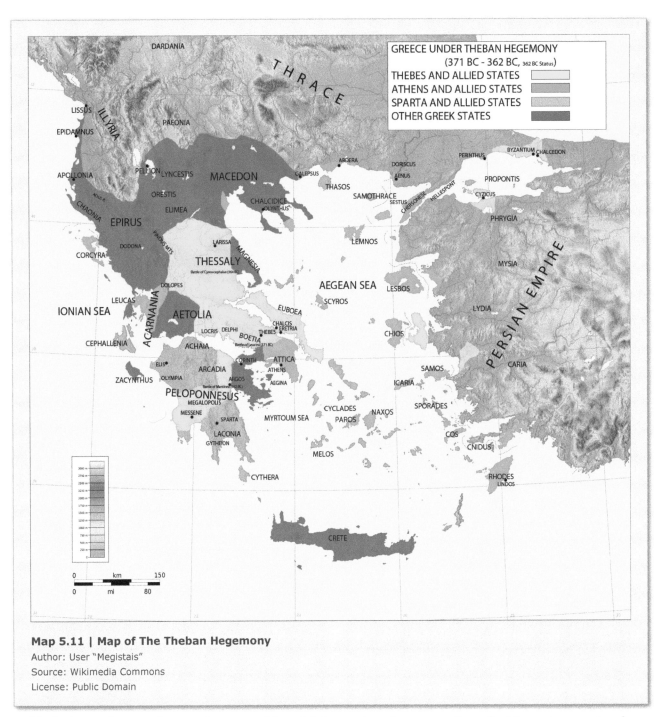

Map 5.11 | Map of The Theban Hegemony
Author: User "Megistais"
Source: Wikimedia Commons
License: Public Domain

likely, is not the openly-stated causes of the trial, but rather the connections that Socrates previously had to oligarchic leaders. In particular, Socrates had taught Critias, who became one of the Thirty in 404 BCE. Fueled by their hatred of all enemies of the democracy and anyone who had associated with the Thirty, the Athenians condemned Socrates to death. This trial shows how deeply the scars went in the collective psyche and how difficult it was for the Athenians to forget the terrible end of the Peloponnesian War. And while, as usual, more information survives about how the Athenians—more than any other *polis*—dealt with the aftermath of the war, it is clear that for the rest of the

Greek world, their life in the fourth century BCE was very much the result of the Peloponnesian War.

The early fourth century saw a power vacuum emerge in the Greek world for the first time since the early Archaic Period. Defeated in the war, Athens was no longer an Empire, while the winner, Sparta, had suffered a catastrophic decline in its population over the course of the Peloponnesian War. At the same time, Thebes had revamped its military, introducing the first two

Figure 5.16 | The Macedonian Phalanx | The wedge formation using the Macedonian sarissa, a spear about eighteen feet in length
Author: User "Alagos"
Source: Wikimedia Commons
License: Public Domain

significant changes to the hoplite phalanx way of fighting since its inception: slightly longer spears, and wedge formation. The final key to the Theban military supremacy was the **Theban Sacred Band**, formed in 378 BCE. An elite core of 300 warriors, the band consisted of 150 couples, based on the assumption that the lovers would fight most bravely in order not to appear to be cowardly to their beloved. In 371 BCE, the Thebans demonstrated the success of their military reforms by defeating the Spartans at the **Battle of Leuctra**. They continued an aggressive program of military expansion over the next decade, a period known as the **Theban Hegemony**.

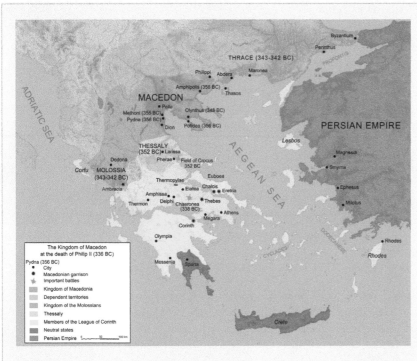

Map 5.12 | Map of the Conquests of Philip | The Kingdom of Macedon at the death of Philip II (336 BC)
Author: User "Marsyas"
Source: Wikimedia Commons
License: CC BY-SA 3.0

Sometime in the 360's BCE, a young Macedonian prince stayed for several years in Thebes as a hostage. While there, he caught the eye of the military reformer, Epaminondas, who took the prince under his wing. Circa 364 BCE, the prince returned to Macedon, and, in 359 BCE, he ascended to the throne as king **Philip II**. Up until that point in Greek history, the Macedonians had largely been known for two things: drinking their wine undiluted, which had marked them as complete and utter barbarians in the eyes of the rest of the Greeks, and being excellent horsemen. With Philip at the helm, this estimation was about to change. As soon as he came to the throne, Philip began transforming the Macedonian military into a more successful image of what he had seen at Thebes. Philip further lengthened the already longer spears used by the Thebans, creating the Macedonian *sarissa*, a spear of about eighteen feet in length, double that of the traditional Greek hoplite spear.

He retained the Theban wedge formation but also added heavy cavalry to the line, thus incorporating the Macedonians' strongest element into the phalanx. The results spoke for themselves, as over the next twenty years, Philip systematically conquered all of mainland Greece, with the exception of Sparta, which he chose to leave alone. Philip's final great victory, which he shared with his teenage son Alexander, was at the **Battle of Chaeronea** (338 BCE), in which the Macedonian armies defeated the combined forces of Athens and Thebes. Philip's conquest of the entire mainland was the end of an era, as for the first time, the entire territory was united under the rule of a king.

By all accounts, it appears that Philip was not going to stop at just conquering the Greek world. He did not, however, have this choice. In 336 BCE while on his way to a theatrical performance, Philip was assassinated by one of his own bodyguards. His son Alexander, then twenty years old,

Figure 5.17 | Alexander the Great | Alexander fighting Darius in the Battle of Issus (333 BCE). Mosaic from the House of the Faun, Pompeii. Note Alexander on the left side of the mosaic, fighting on horseback, while Darius, almost at the middle, charges in a chariot.
Author: User "Berthold Werner"
Source: Wikimedia Commons
License: CC BY-SA 3.0

succeeded and continued his father's ambitious program of conquests. Alexander's first target was the Persian Empire, motivated in part by his love of Homer's *Iliad*, and the perception among the Greeks that this new campaign was the continuation of the original, mythical war against Asia. Moving farther and farther East in his campaigns, Alexander conquered the Balkans, Egypt, and the territories of modern-day Lebanon, Syria, and Israel before he achieved a decisive victory over Darius III at the Battle of Gaugamela in 331 BCE.

Continuing to move eastwards, Alexander invaded India in 327 BCE, planning to conquer the known world and assuming that he was close to this achievement, since the Greeks of his day were not aware of China's existence. His war-weary troops, however, rebelled in 326 BCE and demanded to return home (see Chapter 3). It appears that this mutiny was not the first that occurred in Alexander's army; indeed, over the course of his rule, Alexander had also been the target of a number of failed assassinations. However, this mutiny forced Alexander to give in. Leaving several of his officers behind as satraps, Alexander turned back. In 323 BCE, he and his army reached Babylon, the city that he had hoped to make the new capital of his world empire. There, Alexander fell ill and died at the ripe old age of thirty-three.

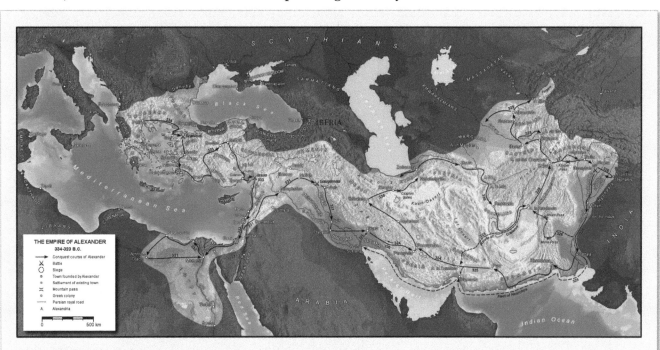

Map 5.13 | Map of the campaigns and conquests of Alexander
Author: User "IrakliGuna"
Source: Wikimedia Commons
License: CC BY-SA 3.0

While Alexander's rule only lasted thirteen years, his legacy reshaped Greece and the rest of ancient Eurasia for the next several centuries. A charismatic leader, albeit one prone to emotional outbursts, Alexander redefined what it meant to be king and general. His coinage reflects this reinvention. On one coin minted during his lifetime, for instance, appears Alexander dressed as the hero Heracles, while Zeus, whom Alexander alleged to be his real father, appears on the other side.

In addition, by conquering territories that were previously not part of the Greek world, Alexander spread Greek culture farther than had anyone else before him. At the same time, by marrying several non-Greek princesses and encouraging such marriages by his troops, Alexander also encouraged the creation of a "melting-pot" empire; he further cemented this creation by founding new cities named

Figure 5.18 | Silver coin of Alexander as Heracles
Author: User "World Imaging"
Source: Wikimedia Commons
License: CC BY-SA 3.0

after himself all over his new empire. In particular, Alexandria, the city that he founded in Egypt, became a center of Greek civilization—albeit with an Egyptian twist—was seen as a new Athens well into the Roman Empire. Alexander's brief time in India produced a significant impact as well, as in 321 BCE, Chandragupta Maurya was able to unify India into a single kingdom for the first time, establishing the **Mauryan Empire** (see Chapter Three). Finally, in the Middle East, North Africa, and the Greek world, Alexander's generals divided his conquests into several kingdoms that they and their descendants continued to rule until the Romans conquered these respective areas. It appears that Alexander's melting-pot empire, burning up as a phoenix upon his death, actually allowed several new empires and kingdoms to arise from its ashes.

5.11 HELLENISTIC PERIOD

Historians today consider the death of Alexander to be the end point of the Classical Period and the beginning of the Hellenistic Period. That moment, for historians, also marks the end of the *polis* as the main unit of organization in the Greek world. While city-states continued to exist, the main unit of organization from that point on was the great Hellenistic kingdoms. These kingdoms, encompassing much greater territory than the Greek world had before Alexander, contributed to the thorough Hellenization of the Eastern Mediterranean and the Middle East. The age of the Hellenistic kingdoms also coincided with the rise of Rome as a military power in the West. Ultimately, the Hellenistic kingdoms were conquered and absorbed by Rome.

5.11.1 Hellenistic Kingdoms

Although Alexander had several children from his different wives, he did not leave an heir old enough to take power upon his death. Indeed, his only son, Alexander IV, was only born several months after his father's death. Instead, Alexander's most talented generals turned against each other in a contest for the control of the empire that they had helped create.

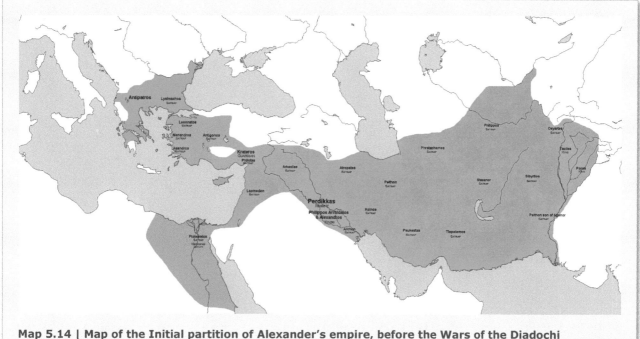

Map 5.14 | Map of the Initial partition of Alexander's empire, before the Wars of the Diadochi
Author: User "Fornadan"
Source: Wikimedia Commons
License: CC BY-SA 3.0

These **Wars of the Diadochi**, as they are known in modern scholarship, ended with a partition of Alexander's empire into a number of kingdoms, each ruled by dynasties. Of these, the four most influential dynasties which retained power for the remainder of the Hellenistic Age, were the following: Seleucus, who took control of Syria and the surrounding areas, thus creating the **Seleucid Empire**; Antigonus Monophthalmos, the One-Eyed, who took over the territory of Asia Minor and northern Syria, establishing the **Antigonid Dynasty**; the Attalid Dynasty, which took power over the **Kingdom of Pergamon**, after the death of its initial ruler, Lysimachus, a general of Alexander; and Ptolemy, Alexander's most influential general, who took control over Egypt, establishing the **Ptolemaic Dynasty**.

The most imperialistic of Alexander's successors, Seleucus I Nicator took Syria, swiftly expanding his empire to the east to encompass the entire stretch of territory from Syria to India. At its greatest expanse, this territory's ethnic diversity was similar to that of Alexander's original empire, and Seleucus adopted the same policy of ethnic unity as originally practiced by Alexander; some of Seleucus' later successors, however, attempted to impose Hellenization on some of the peoples under their rule. These successors had difficulties holding on to Seleucus' conquests. A notable exception, Antiochus III, attempted to expand the Empire into Anatolia and Greece in the early second century BCE but was ultimately defeated by the Romans. The empire's story for the remainder of its existence is one of almost constant civil wars and increasingly declining territories. The Seleucids seem to have had a particularly antagonistic relationship with their Jewish subjects, going so far as to outlaw Judaism in 168 BCE. The Jewish holiday **Hannukah** celebrates a miracle that occurred following the historical victory of the Jews, led by Judah

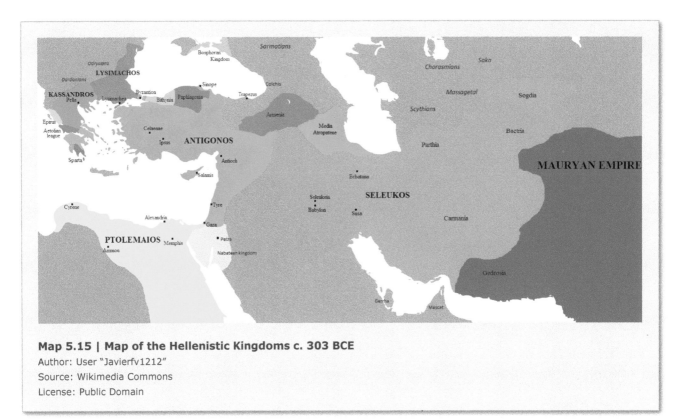

Map 5.15 | Map of the Hellenistic Kingdoms c. 303 BCE
Author: User "Javierfv1212"
Source: Wikimedia Commons
License: Public Domain

Maccabee, over the Seleucids in 165 BCE. Shortly afterwards, the Seleucids had to allow autonomy to the Jewish state; it achieved full independence from Seleucid rule in 129 BCE. In 63 BCE, the Roman general Pompey finally conquered the small remnant of the Seleucid Empire, making it into the Roman province of Syria.

Antigonus Monophthalmos, Seleucus' neighbor, whose holdings included Macedonia, Asia Minor, and the northwestern portion of Syria, harbored ambitious plans that rivaled those of Seleucus. Antigonus' hopes of reuniting all of Alexander's original empire under his own rule, however, were never realized as Antigonus died in battle in 301 BCE. The greatest threat to the Antigonids, however, came not from the Seleucid Empire, but from Rome with whom they waged three Macedonian Wars between 214 and 168 BCE. The Roman defeat of king Perseus in 168 BCE at the Battle of Pydna marked the end of the **Third Macedonian War**, and the end of an era, as control over Greece was now in Roman hands.

The smallest and least imperialistic of the successor states, the kingdom of Pergamon, was originally part of a very short-lived empire established by Lysimachus, one of Alexander's generals. Lysimachus originally held Macedonia and parts of Asia Minor and Thrace but had lost all of these territories by the time of his death in 281 BCE. One of his officers, Philetaerus, however, took over the city of Pergamon, establishing there the Attalid dynasty that transformed Pergamon into a small and successful kingdom. The final Attalid king, Attalus III, left his kingdom to Rome in his will in 133 BCE.

Lasting from the death of Alexander in 323 BCE to the death of Cleopatra VII in 30 BCE, the Ptolemaic kingdom proved to be the longest lasting and most successful of the kingdoms carved from Alexander's initial empire. Its founder, **Ptolemy I Soter**, was a talented general, as well as an astronomer, philosopher, and historian, who wrote his own histories of Alexander's campaigns. Aiming to make Alexandria the new Athens of the Mediterranean, Ptolemy spared no expense in building the Museum, an institution of learning and research that included, most famously, the **Great Library,** and worked tirelessly to attract scholars and cultured elite to his city. Subsequent Ptolemies continued these works so that Alexandria held its reputation as a cultural capital into Late Antiquity. One example of a particularly impressive scientific discovery is the work of Eratosthenes, the head librarian at the Great Library in the second half of the third century BCE, who accurately calculated the earth's circumference. But while the Ptolemies brought with them Greek language and culture to Egypt, they were also profoundly influenced by Egyptian customs. Portraying themselves as the new Pharaohs, the Ptolemies even adopted the Egyptian royal custom of brother-sister marriages, a practice that eventually percolated down to the general populace as well. Unfortunately, brother-sister marriages did not prevent strife for power within the royal family. The last of the Ptolemaic rulers, Cleopatra VII, first married and ruled jointly with her brother Ptolemy XIII. After defeating him in a civil war, she then married another brother, Ptolemy XIV, remaining his wife until his death, possibly from sisterly poisoning. Best known for her affairs with Julius Caesar and, after Caesar's death, with Marcus Antonius, Cleopatra teamed with Marcus Antonius in a bid for the Roman Empire. The last surviving ruler who was descended from one of Alexander's generals, she was finally defeated by Octavian, the future Roman emperor Augustus, in 30 BCE.

The history of the successor states that resulted from the carving of Alexander's empire shows the imperialistic drive of Greek generals, while also demonstrating the instability of their empires. Historians do not typically engage in counter-factual speculations, but it is very likely that, had he lived longer, Alexander would have seen his empire unravel, as no structure was really in place to hold it together. At the same time, the clash of cultures that Alexander's empire and the successor states produced resulted in the spread of Greek culture and language further than ever before; simultaneously, it also introduced the Greeks to other peoples, thus bringing foreign customs—such as the brother-sister marriages in Egypt—into the lives of the Greeks living outside the original Greek world.

5.11.2 Hellenistic Culture

The Hellenistic kingdoms spread Greek language, culture, and art all over the areas of Alexander's former conquests. Furthermore, many Hellenistic kings, especially the Ptolemies, were patrons of art and ideas. Thus the Hellenistic era saw the flourishing of art and architecture, philosophy, medical and scientific writing, and even translations of texts of other civilizations into Greek. The undisputed center for these advances was Alexandria.

Combining the practical with the ambitious, the **Pharos**, or Lighthouse, of Alexandria was one of the most famous examples of Hellenistic architecture and has remained a symbol of the city to the present day. Constructed in 280 BCE, it was considered to be one of the Seven Wonders of the Ancient World and was one of the tallest buildings in the world at the time. While its practical purpose was to guide ships into the harbor at night, it also exemplified the bold advances and experimental spirit of Hellenistic architecture. Indeed, it was located on a man-made mole off the coast of the city. The building comprised three layers, the top one of which housed the furnace that produced the light.

The structure of the Pharos shows an interest in straight lines and orderly shapes, while its function symbolized the ability of man to subdue the sea, even by night. Similarly, both the scientific and medical texts from the Hellenistic Period reveal a fascination with an ordered universe and an interest in discovering how it worked. **Herophilus of Chalcedon**, for instance, pioneered dissection in the early third BCE and was especially interested in the human brain and the nervous system. The mathematician Euclid, who lived and worked in Alexandria during the reign of Ptolemy I (323 – 283 BCE), wrote the *Elements*, an encyclopedic work of mathematics that effectively created the discipline of geometry. Going a step further than Euclid in his research, the third-century BCE scientist and inventor **Archimedes of Syracuse** specialized in applying mathematical concepts to create such devices as a screw pump and a variety of war machines, including the heat ray.

The same fascination with studying the order of the universe appears in Hellenistic philosophy and stems ultimately from the philosophy of Aristotle (384 – 322 BCE), considered to be the last Classical Greek philosopher. Aristotle was a prolific polymath, who wrote on political theory, poetry, music, and a variety of sciences, to list just some of his interests. Engrossed in seeing all disciplines as part of a larger world order, Aristotle specifically argued for empiricism, that is, the belief that knowledge is acquired from sensory experiences rather than from intuition. In the sciences, for instance, this approach required experiments and the careful gathering of data. While Aristotle's influence on the Hellenistic

Figure 5.19 | The Pharos, or Lighthouse, of Alexandria
Author: Emad Victor SHENOUDA
Source: Wikimedia Commons
License: © Emad Victor SHENOUDA. Used with permission.

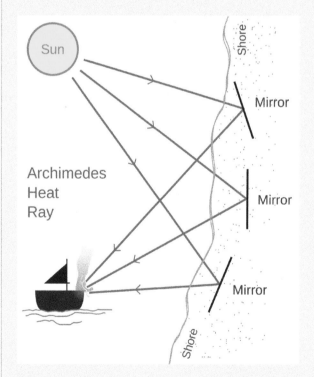

Figure 5.20 | The Archimedes Heat Ray
Author: User "Pbrokos13"
Source: Wikimedia Commons
License: CC BY-SA 3.0

philosophers is undeniable, the alternate theories that some of the philosophers developed regarding the structure of the universe and the place of humanity in it differs drastically from Aristotle's view. For instance, **Skepticism**, especially as formulated by Pyrrho in the third century BCE, argued that it was impossible to reach any accurate conclusions about the world and the key to happiness was to stop trying. **Cynic philosophers**, starting in the fourth century BCE, advocated the ascetic life of simplicity and freedom from possessions. A related philosophy, **Stoicism**, argued for letting go of all emotions and developing a self-control that would allow one to live in accordance to nature. On the other hand, the third-century philosophy of **Epicureanism** argued for the absence of pain as the ultimate goal in life and saw the universe as ruled by random chance, separate from the intervention of the gods. All of these philosophies, and many others that co-existed with them, aimed to provide a coherent system that made sense of the world and provided a purpose for human life.

Finally, in a testament to the deep influence of the Hellenistic language culture on the conquered regions, the Hellenistic Period saw the translation of texts of other civilizations into Greek. One particularly influential example was the translation of the Hebrew Old Testament into Greek. Jews formed a significant minority of the population of **Alexandria**, the capital of Ptolemaic Egypt, as well as other major cities around the Mediterranean, such as Antioch. By the third century BCE, these Jews appear to have largely lost the knowledge of Hebrew; thus, a translation of the sacred texts into Greek was necessary. In addition, as later legend has it, Ptolemy II Philadelphus allegedly commissioned seventy-two scholars to translate the Old Testament into Greek for his Royal Library. Whether indeed solicited by Ptolemy II or not, the translation was likely completed over the course of the third throughfirst centuries BCE. Named after the legendary seventy-two (or, in some versions, seventy) translators, the text was titled the ***Septuagint***. The completion of this translation showed the thorough Hellenization of even the Jews, who had largely kept themselves apart from mainstream culture of the cities in which they lived.

5.12 CONCLUSION

"Captive Greece has conquered her rude conqueror," the Roman poet Horace famously wrote in the late first century BCE. This comment about the deep influence of Greek culture on the Roman world, even after the Roman conquest of Greece was complete, continued to be the case well after the days of Horace. Ultimately, the impact of the Hellenization of the Mediterranean and the Middle East, which started with Alexander's conquests, lasted far beyond the Hellenistic kingdoms, as the Greek language continued to be the language of the Eastern Roman Empire and, subsequently, the Byzantine Empire up until the conquest of that territory by the Ottomans in 1453 CE. In some respects, this spread of the Greeks and their civilization ultimately changed what it meant to be Greek—or, rather, it created a more universal Greek identity, which largely replaced the *polis*-specific view of citizenship and identity that existed before Philip's conquest of Greece. And yet, certain cultural constants persisted.

The first of these was Homer, whose epics continued to be as great an inspiration to the Greeks of the Roman world as they were to their Archaic Age counterparts. For instance, the Homeric values were likely the reason for the minimal advances in military technology in the Greek world, as honor was more important than military success at all cost. The second cultural constant was the work of the philosophers Plato and Aristotle, in whose shadows all subsequent philosophers of the Greco-Roman world labored. Even as the Greek-speaking portions of the Roman Empire turned to Christianity, they could not abandon their philosophical roots, resulting, for instance, in the Gnostic heresies. Horace's cheeky comment thus proved to be true far longer than he could have expected.

5.13 WORKS CONSULTED AND FURTHER READING

Burkert, Walter. *The Orientalizing Revolution: Near Eastern Influence on Greek Culture in the Early Archaic Age*. Cambridge: Harvard University Press, 1998.

Bury, J. B. and Russell Meiggs. *A History of Greece to the Death of Alexander the Great*. New York: St. Martin's Press.

Cartledge, Paul. *Sparta and Laconia: A Regional History 1300 – 362 BC*. New York: Routledge, 2002.

Dickinson, Oliver. *The Aegean Bronze Age*. Cambridge: Cambridge University Press, 1994.

Gruen, Erich. *Diaspora: Jews amidst Greeks and Romans*. Cambridge: Harvard University Press, 2004.

Hanson, Victor Davis. *A War Like No Other: How the Athenians and Spartans Fought the Peloponnesian War*. New York: Random House Trade Paperbacks, 2006.

Horden, Peregrine and Nicholas Purcell, *The Corrupting Sea: A Study of Mediterranean History*. Oxford: Wiley-Blackwell, 2000.

Kagan, Donald. *The Archidamian War*. Ithaca: Cornell University Press, 1990.

———. The Fall of the Athenian Empire. Ithaca: Cornell University Press, 1991.

———. *The Outbreak of the Peloponnesian War*. Ithaca: Cornell University Press, 1989.

———. *The Peace of Nicias and the Sicilian Expedition*. Ithaca: Cornell University Press, 1991.

Lane Fox, Robin. *Alexander the Great*. New York: Penguin, 2004.

Lendon, J. E. *Soldiers and Ghosts: A History of Battle in Classical Antiquity*. New Haven: Yale University Press, 2006.

Lewis, Naphthali. *Greeks in Ptolemaic Egypt*. Durham: American Society of Papyrologists, 2001.

Long, A. A. *Hellenistic Philosophy: Stoics, Epicureans, Sceptics*. Berkeley: University of California Press, 1986.

Meiggs, Russell. *The Athenian Empire*. Oxford: Oxford University Press, 1979.

Morkot, Robert. *The Penguin Historical Atlas of Ancient Greece*. London: Penguin Books, 1997.

Murray, Oswyn. *Early Greece*. Cambridge: Harvard University Press, 1993.

Ober, Josiah. *Mass and Elite in Democratic Athens: Rhetoric, Ideology, and the Power of the People*. Princeton: Princeton University Press, 1991.

de Polignac, François. *Cults, Territory, and the Origins of the Greek City-State*. Chicago: University of Chicago Press, 1995.

Pomeroy, Sarah, Stanley Burstein, Walter Donlan, Jennifer Tolbert Roberts, and David Tandy. *Ancient Greece: A Political, Social, and Cultural History*. Oxford: Oxford University Press, 2011.

Walbank, F. W. *The Hellenistic World*. Cambridge: Harvard University Press, 1993.

5.14 LINKS TO PRIMARY SOURCES

Ancient History Sourcebook at Fordham University (collection of materials from all periods of Greek history)
http://legacy.fordham.edu/Halsall/ancient/asbook07.asp

Archimedes' Inventions
http://archimedesjack.weebly.com/discoveries-and inventions.html

Aristophanes, excerpt from *Clouds*, making fun of Socrates
http://www.thenagain.info/Classes/Sources/Aristophanes-Clouds.htm

Aristophanes, *Lysistrata*
http://drama.eserver.org/plays/classical/aristophanes/lysistrata.txt

Aristotle on Spartan Women
http://legacy.fordham.edu/Halsall/ancient/aristotle-spartanwomen.asp

Athens, photographic archive of archaeological materials
http://web.archive.org/web/20040607030018/www.stoa.org/athens/

Cyrene, primary sources on founding of the colony
http://legacy.fordham.edu/Halsall/ancient/630cyrene.asp

Euripides, *The Phoenician Women*
http://www.users.globalnet.co.uk/~loxias/phoenissae.htm

The Gortyn Code, selections
https://legacy.fordham.edu/halsall/ancient/450-gortyn.asp

Herodotus, *Histories*, excerpt on the Battle of Marathon
http://www.thenagain.info/Classes/Sources/Herodotus-Marathon.html

History of Greek Philosophy
http://faculty.washington.edu/smcohen/320/index.html
http://www.uh.edu/~cfreelan/courses/riceanc.html

Justin, on the beginning of the reign of Philip II of Macedon
http://legacy.fordham.edu/Halsall/ancient/justin-philip.asp

Linear B Writing
http://www.ancientscripts.com/linearb.html

Plutarch, *Lives*

http://classics.mit.edu/Browse/browse-Plutarch.html

Solon, selected fragments from political poems

http://homepage.usask.ca/~jrp638/DeptTransls/Solon.html

Sophocles, *Antigone*

http://www.stoa.org/diotima/anthology/ant/antigstruct.htm

Thucydides, Pericles' "Funeral Oration"

http://legacy.fordham.edu/Halsall/ancient/pericles-funeralspeech.asp

Thucydides, "Melian Dialogue" from the *History of the Peloponnesian War*

https://www.mtholyoke.edu/acad/intrel/melian.htm

Tyrants, primary sources documents

https://legacy.fordham.edu/Halsall/ancient/650tyranny.asp

Xenophon on the Battle of Leuctra

http://legacy.fordham.edu/Halsall/ancient/371leuctra.asp

Xenophon on the Spartan Constitution

http://legacy.fordham.edu/Halsall/ancient/xeno-sparta1.asp

6

The Roman World from 753 BCE to 500 CE

Nadejda Williams

6.1 CHRONOLOGY

753 BCE	Founding of Rome
c. 753 – 510 BCE	Regal Period
c. 510 BCE – 44 BCE*	Roman Republic
264 – 146 BCE	The Punic Wars
133 BCE – 44 BCE	The Late Republic
44 BCE – 476 CE	Roman Empire
44 BCE – 68 CE	Julio-Claudian Dynasty
69 CE	Year of the Four Emperors
69 CE – 96 CE	Flavian Dynasty
96 – 180 CE	The Five Good Emperors
235 – 284 CE	The Third Century Crisis
395 CE	Permanent division of the Empire into East and West

* See, however, explanation about possible dates proposed by scholars for the fall of the Roman Republic

6.2 INTRODUCTION

In 458 BCE, facing a military attack from the two neighboring tribes of the Aequi and the Sabines, the Roman Senate took a drastic measure, reserved for the direst of circumstances: they appointed a dictator, who would single-handedly lead the state in this time of trouble. As the Roman historian Livy tells it, **Cincinnatus**, the senator who was appointed dictator, received the news while working on his farm. Abandoning the plow, he immediately rushed to join the army, which he then led to a swift and brilliant victory. Then something astonishing happened: Cincinnatus resigned his extraordinary powers and returned to his farm. For the remainder of the Roman Republic, and well into the Imperial Period, Cincinnatus continued to be seen as the quintessential Roman cultural hero and model of virtue: an aristocratic man who was a talented soldier, general, and politician who put the interests of **Rome** first, above his own. While no other Roman politician displayed Cincinnatus' degree of self-sacrificing humility, the other Roman heroes of the Republic and the Empire were still uniformly male, predominantly aristocratic, and famed for military and political achievements.

But something happened to give rise to a rather different sort of cultural hero by the Late Roman Empire. In 203 CE, a young noblewoman and her slave were executed in Carthage, thrown into the arena with the

Figure 6.1 | Cincinnatus leaves the plow to accept the dictatorship
Author: User "Antonius Proximo"
Source: Wikimedia Commons
License: CC BY-SA 3.0

lions. Their crime? A stubborn faith: the belief that a Jewish man who lived in Judaea a century earlier was the son of God who had died on the cross and rose again. Eager to emulate his suffering in order to win eternal life with their God, the two women, **Perpetua and Felicity**, gave up a life of relative comfort and the chance to raise their babies—indeed, Felicity gave birth in prison mere hours before her execution!—placing their God above all else. They were not the only ones. Stories of martyrs abound in the Later Roman Empire and were told repeatedly by Christians, thus perpetuating the status of these martyrs as the new cultural heroes. But far from repelling others from imitating their example, these stories, rather, encouraged the rise of more willing martyrs to follow their suit. As a result of the spread of Christianity, therefore, the Roman cultural heroes of Late Antiquity were a far cry from Cincinnatus. Instead of aristocratic generals and politicians, they were nursing mothers and even slave-women who chose to die a humiliating and painful death for their faith and its promise of an eternal reward.

The story of the Roman world from the foundation of the city of Rome and to the fall of the Roman Empire in the West is, overall, a tale of two different transformations. The first of these is the dramatic transformation in cultural values and beliefs, a glimpse of which is reflected in the two stories above. The second is a similarly dramatic geographical transformation, which also brought about drastic clashes of cultures and a variety of changes throughout the entire Mediterranean world and beyond, that is, the transformation of a small village on the Tiber into one of the largest empires in all of world history, followed by a collapse of a part of that Empire, but a collapse from whose ashes arose what we now know as Europe.

6.3 QUESTIONS TO GUIDE YOUR READING

1. In what ways did the geography and topography of Rome and the Roman Empire impact the history of the ancient Roman world?

2. What are the different periods of Roman history, and what are the chief defining characteristics of each period?

3. What primary sources are available for the study of Roman history, and what are the limitations of these sources?

4. What were the stages of Roman expansion?

5. What were the key civic conflicts and civil wars of the Roman Republic? What did each of these conflicts demonstrate about the changing nature of Roman politics?

6. When and why did the Roman Republic fall? What were some key differences between the Roman Republic and the Age of Augustus?

7. What are some of the primary sources about the early Christians? What was revolutionary about early Christianity, from the Roman perspective?

8. What were some of the problems with which areas in the periphery of the Roman Empire had to deal in the second century CE?

9. What were the problems that the Roman Empire faced during the third-century crisis, and how did Diocletian attempt to resolve these?

10. What changes did the Roman Empire experience in the fourth century CE, and what were the causes of these changes?

11. How did the Romans' view of Rome in Late Antiquity differ from their view of Rome in earlier periods?

6.4 KEY TERMS

- Aedile
- Apuleius, *Metamorphoses*
- *ara pacis*
- *auctoritas*
- Augustine, *City of God*
- Augustus
- Battle of Lake Regillus
- Bithynia
- Caligula
- Carthage
- Catilina
- Cato the Elder, *Origins*

- Censor
- Centuriate Assembly
- Christianity
- Cincinnatus
- Claudius
- Cleopatra
- Conflict of the Orders
- Constantine
- Constantinople
- Consul
- Council of Nicaea
- Crassus
- *cursus honorum*
- *dignitas*
- Diocletian
- Etruscans
- Eusebius
- Five Good Emperors
- Flavian dynasty
- Gaius Gracchus
- *Gravitas*
- Josephus, *Jewish War*
- Julian the Apostate
- Julio-Claudians
- Julius Caesar
- Juno
- Jupiter Optimus Maximus
- Lex Hortensia
- Licinian-Sextian law
- Livy
- Lucretia
- Macedonian Wars
- Magna Graecia

- manipular legion and legion of cohorts
- Marcus Antonius
- Marius
- Mars
- Minerva
- *mos maiorum*
- Nero
- New Testament
- Numa Pompilius
- *Optimates*
- Ostia
- *paterfamilias*
- Patricians
- Paul
- *pax deorum*
- *Pax Romana*
- Perpetua and Felicity
- Plebeian Council
- Plebeians
- Plebeian tribune
- Pliny the Younger
- Plutarch
- Polybius
- Pompeii
- Pompey
- *Populares*
- Praetor
- Proscriptions
- Punic Wars
- Pyrrhus
- Quaestor
- *Res Gestae Divi Augusti*

- Roman Empire (period)
- Roman Republic (period)
- Rome
- Romulus and Remus
- Romulus Augustulus
- Samnite Wars
- Senate
- Social War
- Suetonius
- Sulla
- Tacitus
- Tarquin the Proud
- Tetrarchy
- Theodosius
- Third-Century Crisis
- Tiber
- Tiberius (emperor)
- Tiberius Gracchus
- Trajan
- Triumvirate (First and Second)
- Twelve Tables
- Veii
- Venus
- Vergil, *Aeneid*
- Vespasian
- Year of the Four Emperors (69 CE)

6.5 GEOGRAPHY AND TOPOGRAPHY OF ROME AND THE ROMAN EMPIRE

As the title of one recent textbook of Roman history puts it, Roman history is, in a nutshell, the story of Rome's transformation "from village to empire."[1] The geography and topography of Rome, Italy, and the Mediterranean world as a whole played a key role in the expansion of the empire but also placed challenges in the Romans' path, challenges which further shaped their history.

Before it became the capital of a major empire, Rome was a village built on seven hills sprawling around the river **Tiber**. Set sixteen miles inland, the original settlement had distinct strategic advantages: it was immune to attacks from the sea, and the seven hills on which the city was built were easy to fortify. The Tiber, although marshy and prone to flooding, furthermore, provided the ability to trade with the neighboring city-states. By the mid-Republic, requiring access to the sea, the Romans built a harbor at **Ostia**, which grew to become a full-fledged commercial arm of Rome as a result. Wheeled vehicles were prohibited inside the city of Rome during the day, in order to protect the heavy pedestrian traffic. Thus at night, carts from Ostia poured into Rome, delivering food and other goods for sale from all over Italy and the Empire.

One of the most surprising aspects of the history of early Rome is that, despite constant threats from its more powerful neighbors, it was never swallowed by them. The **Etruscans** dominated much of northern Italy down to Rome, while the southern half of Italy was so heavily colonized by the Greeks as to earn the nickname "**Magna Graecia**," meaning "Great Greece." In addition, several smaller tribes hemmed the early Romans, mainly, the Latins, the Aequi, and the Sabines.

---

1   Mary Boatwright, Daniel Gargola, Noel Lenski, and Richard Talbert. *The Romans: From Village to Empire: A History of Rome from Earliest Times to the End of the Western Empire* (Oxford: Oxford University Press, 2011).

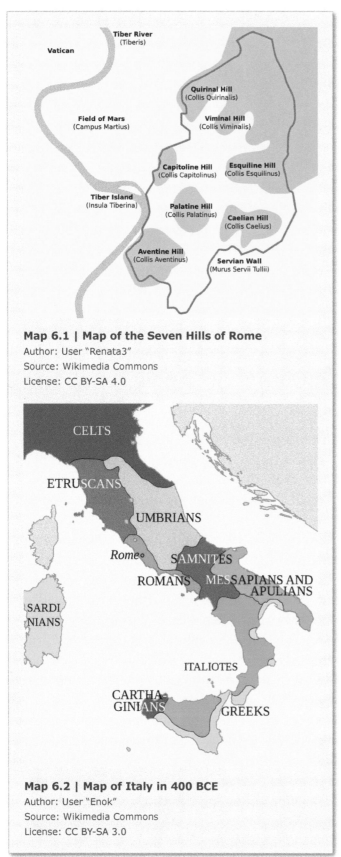

Map 6.1 | Map of the Seven Hills of Rome
Author: User "Renata3"
Source: Wikimedia Commons
License: CC BY-SA 4.0

Map 6.2 | Map of Italy in 400 BCE
Author: User "Enok"
Source: Wikimedia Commons
License: CC BY-SA 3.0

The topography of Rome—the advantage of the hills and the river—likely was a boon in the city's struggles against all of its neighbors. Likewise, the topography of Italy proper, with the Alps and the Appenines providing natural defenses in the north, hampered invasions from the outside. Indeed, the most famous example of an invasion from the north, that of Hannibal during the Second Punic War, is a case in point: he selected that challenging route through the Alps in order to surprise the Romans, and it proved even more destructive for his forces than he had anticipated.

As Rome built a Mediterranean empire, the city itself grew increasingly larger, reaching a population of one million by 100 CE. While Italy boasted fertile farmlands, feeding the city of Rome became a challenge that required the resources of the larger empire, and Egypt in particular became known as the breadbasket of Rome. As a result, emperors were especially cautious to control access to Egypt by prominent senators and other politicians, for fear of losing control over this key area of the Empire.

During the rule of the emperor Trajan in the early second century CE, the Roman Empire reached its greatest extent, stretching to Britain in the west, slightly beyond the Rhine and Danube river in the north, and including much of the Near East and north Africa.

Topography, however, played a role in the Romans' ultimately unsuccessful struggle to hold on to these territories after Trajan's death. The natural frontier offered by the Rhine and Danube rivers made it difficult for the Romans to maintain control over the territories on the other side of them. Struggling to fight off the warrior tribes in northern Britain, two second-century CE emperors—Hadrian, and later on Antoninus Pius—built

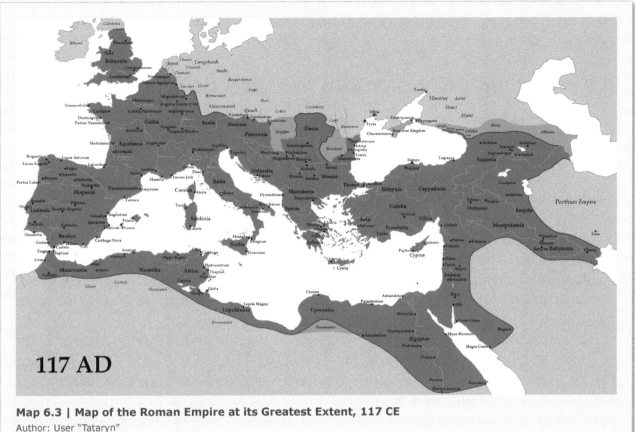

Map 6.3 | Map of the Roman Empire at its Greatest Extent, 117 CE
Author: User "Tataryn"
Source: Wikimedia Commons
License: CC BY-SA 3.0

successive walls, which attempted to separate the un-Romanized tribes from the territory under Roman control. Finally, a persisting challenge for Roman emperors was that of the location of the empire's capital. When the Roman Empire consisted of Italy alone, the location of Rome in the middle of the Italian peninsula was the ideal location for the capital. Once, however, the empire became a Mediterranean empire that controlled areas far in all directions, the location of Rome was a great distance from all the problem frontiers. As a result, emperors over the course of the second and third centuries spent increasingly less time in Rome. Finally, Diocletian's split of the Empire in 293 CE into four administrative regions, each with a regional capital, left Rome out, and in 330 CE, the emperor Constantine permanently moved the capital of the empire to his new city of Constantinople, built at the site of the older Greek city of Byzantium.

The large area encompassed by the empire required a sophisticated infrastructure of roads and sea routes, and the Romans provided both. By the first century CE, these roads and routes connected the center of the empire (Rome) to the periphery, providing ways for armies, politicians, traders, tourists, and students to travel with greater security and speed than ever before. As primary sources reveal, travel was never a fully safe undertaking, as bandits lurked on roads and pirates on seas, greedy locals were always eager to fleece unsuspecting tourists, and shipwrecks were an unfortunately common reality. Still, the empire created an unprecedented degree of networks and connections that allowed anyone in one part of the empire to be able to travel to any other part, provided he was wealthy enough to be able to afford the journey.

6.6 BASIC CHRONOLOGY AND PERIODS OF ROMAN HISTORY

According to Roman tradition, Rome was founded as a monarchy. That monarchy, however, was not long-lived, and its history is overshadowed by myth and legend. Historians of Rome have most often divided its history into two major periods, based on the type of government that Rome had at the time: the **Republic** (from the late sixth century BCE to the late first century BCE) and the **Empire** (from the late first century BCE to the fall of the Western half of the empire in the late fifth century CE). Indeed, as seen in the writings of the Roman historian Tacitus, already as early as the late first century CE, Romans themselves thought of their history in terms of those two periods. The basic difference between the two periods is quite simple. During the period of the Republic, Rome was ruled by a Republican government, which distributed power, in theory, among all Roman citizens. In practice, this was really an aristocratic oligarchy. By contrast, under the Empire, Rome was under one ruler, the Emperor.

Recent research, however, has challenged the over-simplification of Roman history that can be implied by thinking of it as comprising just two periods. The work of Harriet Flower has shown that the Roman Republic is best conceived of as a series of Republics, each with distinct features. The work of Peter Brown, furthermore, has challenged the myth of the "decline and fall" of the Roman Empire, first popularized by Edward Gibbon, a nineteenth-century British historian of Rome. Brown has shown that as a result of the Christianization of the Roman world, Roman culture in the Late Empire was quite different from that in the earlier periods, yet it was very much a flourishing culture.

This chapter proceeds chronologically, sub-dividing both the Republic and the Empire into early and late periods, while also devoting some attention to certain thematic topics that are key to understanding each period.

6.7 SOURCES AND PROBLEMS

One of the greatest challenges to modern historians of Rome is the Romans' own seeming lack of interest in writing their own history for their first 600 years. While, according to Roman legend, Rome was founded in 753 BCE, the first Roman history in Latin, *Origins*, composed by the Republican politician **Cato the Elder**, was not published until 149 BCE. A few senators had written about Roman history in Greek earlier on, and some aristocrats kept family histories, but Cato's work was truly the first Roman history on a large scale, as it narrated events from the foundation of the city to Cato's own death. Only fragments of Cato's history survive; they reveal that Cato's approach to the writing of history was rather unusual. Instead of referring to any individuals throughout Roman history by name, Cato referred to them by title or political position. As a result, his history was truly focused on Rome and aimed to glorify the accomplishments of Rome rather than individual Romans. Thankfully for modern historians, Cato's experiment of nameless history did not catch on with subsequent Roman historians. Modern historians are able to reconstruct the story of the Romans from a variety of written and archaeological sources, but some of these sources present problems of which the historian must be aware. Similarly to the challenges modern historians face when studying Greek history, historians of Rome must at times engage in educated guessing when attempting to reconstruct a picture of Rome and Romans based on the limited evidence that is available.

Because the genre of historical writing started so late in Rome, few histories survive from the period of the Republic. Of these, the most famous (and the most voluminous) is the work of **Livy**, who wrote his *Ab Urbe Condita* (From the Foundation of the City) in the late first century BCE. Livy was very much an "armchair historian," but he appears to have had access to a number of sources that are now lost, such as family histories from a number of aristocratic families. As the title indicates, Livy began his work with the legends about the founding of Rome. He continued his narrative down to his time, the age of Augustus, and the last known events in his work covered the year 9 BCE. Although Livy's work consisted of 142 books, only about a quarter survives, including the first ten books, covering the regal period and the early republic and the narrative of the first two Punic Wars. Other prominent historians of the Republic whose works survive include Sallust, a contemporary of Caesar who turned to writing moralistic history after a frustrating political career, and Caesar himself, who wrote two books about his own campaigns: the *Gallic Wars*, about his conquest of Gaul in the 50's BCE, and the *Civil War*, about his civil war against Pompey in 49 – 45 BCE.

The works of two prominent historians survive from the period of the Roman Empire. **Tacitus**, another politician-turned-historian, wrote in the early second century CE two works about the history of the Roman Empire in its first century of existence. The *Annals* covered the rule of the emperors Tiberius through Nero, while the *Histories* continued the narrative to the rule of the emperor Domitian. Significant portions of both works survive. Ammianus Marcellinus, a military officer writing in the late fourth century CE, saw himself as a successor of Tacitus, and composed a massive history of the Roman Empire from the end of Tacitus' work to his own day. In addition, the sensationalizing biographer **Suetonius**, a contemporary of Tacitus, composed tabloid-style biographies of the first twelve emperors (from Caesar to Domitian). The anonymous *Historia Augusta*, composed sometime in the late Empire, provides similarly sensationalizing biographies of Roman emperors and some usurpers from Hadrian in the early second century CE to Carinus in the late third century CE.

In addition to these Roman historians and biographers, a number of historical works in Greek survive from the late Republic and the Empire that cover topics related to Roman history. To mention just a few examples, in the late first century BCE, Diodorus of Sicily wrote a massive universal history that includes key events of Roman history, alongside Greek history and mythology. The Greek biographer **Plutarch**, writing in the first century CE, paired for the sake of comparison biographies of famous Greeks and Romans; one exemplary such pairing is that of Alexander the Great and Julius Caesar. **Josephus**, a Jewish rebel leader turned Roman citizen, wrote the ***Jewish War***, a detailed account of the disastrous Jewish revolt against Rome in the 60's CE.

Works of history, however, are only one type of source that modern historians of Rome use. Other written sources include poems, novels, letters of politicians and other prominent figures, military and farming manuals, cookbooks, etc. For instance, one of the best sources for the political ideology of the Augustan age is **Vergil**'s epic poem ***Aeneid***, which tells the story of the Trojan hero Aeneas and his struggle to reach Italy after the fall of Troy to found Rome. Arguably the single best source for everyday life in the Roman provinces under the Empire is **Apuleius**' novel ***Metamorphoses***, better known under the title *Golden Ass*. The novel is a fictional account of a man accidentally turned into a donkey, who tells the narrative of his travels through the Roman Empire in the late second century CE. And one of the best sources for the government of Roman provinces is the correspondence of Pliny the Younger, governor of the province of Bithynia on the shores of the Black Sea in 111 – 113 CE, with the emperor Trajan. To say the least, the job of the provincial governor, based on these letters, appears to have been decidedly unglamorous.

Early Christianity is one area of Roman history that has been especially well documented from its inception. The New Testament is an invaluable source, as it presents sources by early Christians about their own faith and its spread throughout the Roman Empire. A variety of popular heretical texts from the second and third centuries also survives and allows historians to reconstruct some of the dissent-ing views held in the early church. Writings in Greek and Latin by a number of influential figures in the early church, dubbed the Church Fathers, document the theological debates that resulted ultimately in the Nicene Creed. Starting in the second century CE, martyrdom accounts and saints' lives provide admittedly semi-fictional and stylized biographies of individual believers. Finally, two prominent theologians in the Late Empire attempted to write (or re-write) Roman history specifically through a Christian lens. **Eusebius**, the Bishop of Caesarea in the fourth century CE, wrote the *History of the Church*, focusing on the history of Christianity from its beginnings to his day. Then in the early fifth century CE, **Augustine**, Bishop of Hippo in North Africa, wrote the *City of God*, a massive work covering history and legends of Rome from its beginnings to his day, in an attempt to show that Rome's previous successes were due not to adherence to the pagan gods, but instead always to the Christian God's mercy.

Figure 6.2 | Reconstructed Roman Tombstone | Reconstructed Copy of a Tombstone for a Roman Soldier Stationed in Britain in the first century CE
Author: User "Chestertouristcom"
Source: Wikimedia Commons
License: CC BY-SA 3.0

In addition to written sources of various kinds, archaeological sources provide further insight into Roman life in different periods. Examples of sources that survive include inscriptions, especially gravestones; traded goods, such as lamps or bricks, which allow historians to reconstruct the movement of goods across the empire; and a number of Roman towns and military camps.

One example of the random nature of how some sources were able to survive is the ancient site of **Pompeii**. The eruption of Vesuvius in 79 CE caused volcanic ash to rain down on the resort Roman town of Pompeii and the nearby town of Herculaneum, effectively burying both towns and preserving them completely for

Figure 6.3 | Ruins of Pompeii | Ruins of Pompeii from above, with Vesuvius in the background
Author: User "ElfQrin"
Source: Wikimedia Commons
License: CC BY-SA 4.0

modern archaeologists. The tragedy for the Roman residents of the two towns at the time proved to be a modern archaeologist's dream.

While, as the above summary shows, abundant sources of different types survive from different periods of Roman history, certain perspectives are difficult to reconstruct from our sources. For instance, slaves in the Roman world were as archaeologically invisible as in the Greek world. Likewise, very little evidence documents women's lives before the rise of Christianity, and their voices are largely left out from Roman history. Other than epitaphs on their gravestones, most average Romans, in general, left no record of their lives, so our evidence is dominated by the history of the aristocracy. Still, the careful historian can gain at least some insight into these lesser-documented perspectives by gathering all references to them in sources that survive.

6.8 EARLY AND MIDDLE REPUBLIC

The period from the founding of Rome to the end of the Punic Wars is less documented than subsequent Roman history. Nevertheless, this period was the formative time during which Rome grew from a village on the Tiber to a pan-Mediterranean empire.

The process was as fascinating to consider for later Romans as for outsiders. The Greek politician-turned-historian **Polybius**, who spent seventeen years as a hostage in Rome and became quite a fan of the Roman military and political machine, put it simply in the prologue to his *Histories*, in which he documented the meteoric conquest of the Mediterranean world by the Romans:

> For who is so worthless or lazy as not to wish to know by what means and under what system of government the Romans in less than fifty-three years have succeeded in subjugating nearly the entire known world to their rule, an achievement unprecedented in history? (Polybius 1.1.5)

Map 6.4 | Map of the Roman Conquest of Italy | Stages of Early Roman Expansion from 500 BCE to 218 BCE.
Author: User "Javierfv1212"
Source: Wikimedia Commons
License: Public Domain

Polybius' question pointed to the answer that he subsequently proposed: part of the reason for the Romans' success was their adoption of the Republican government as replacement for their original monarchy. Polybius became increasingly convinced during his stay in Rome that the Romans' government was superior to all others in the Mediterranean at the time.

6.8.1 From Monarchy to Republic: Some Myths and Legends

"In the beginning, kings held Rome." Thus the late first-century CE Roman historian Tacitus opened his *Annals*, a history of the Empire under the rule of the emperors from Tiberius to Nero. Early Roman history is shrouded in myth and legend, but the beliefs of later Romans about their own past are important to consider, as these beliefs, whether truly grounded in reality or not, determined subsequent decisions and actions of the historical Romans later on. This tendency is especially true of the Romans' myths about the foundation of their city in 753 BCE and the kings who ruled it until the establishment of the Republic in 510 BCE.

According to myth, Rome received its name from its founder **Romulus**, the son of the war god Mars, and a descendant of the Trojan hero Aeneas. By linking themselves to the Trojans, the Romans were able to boast an ancient, reputable lineage, rivaling that of the Greeks, and a prominent place in the Greek heroic epic, Homer's *Iliad*. Furthermore, when embarking on a conquest of Greece later on, the Romans could claim to be seeking revenge for their Trojan ancestors' defeat and destruction by the Greeks during the Trojan War. Several generations removed from their heroic ancestor Aeneas, Romulus and his twin brother **Remus** were famously abandoned as infants and then nursed by a she-wolf, the sacred animal of their father Mars.

The sweetness of the story ends there, however. While Romulus was building Rome, Remus insulted the new city, and his brother killed him to avenge its honor. Later, after Romulus had completed the building of the new city with his band of soldiers, he realized the lack of women in the city, so Romulus and his supporters raided the neighboring tribe, the Sabines, and kidnapped their women.

It is telling that later Romans believed that their city was founded on fraternal bloodshed, as well as on rape and kidnapping. The stories of Romulus' accomplishments, while not laudatory, show an important Roman belief: the greatness of Rome sometimes required morally reprehensible actions. In other words, Rome came first, and if the good of the city required the sacrifice of one's brother, or required force against others, then the gods were still on the side of the Romans and ordained these actions.

Romans believed that, altogether, their city was ruled by seven different kings in succession. After Romulus, king **Numa Pompilius** regulated Roman religion and created many of the priestly colleges and positions that continued to exist thereafter. The seventh and final king, however, **Tarquin the Proud**, was known for his and his family's brutality. The final straw appears of have been the rape of a nobleman's wife, **Lucretia**, by the king's son. An aristocratic revolution ensued, which appears to have been largely bloodless, if Livy's account is to be trusted. The royal family was expelled from the city, and two consuls were immediately elected to govern the newly formed Republic. Or so, again, Livy tells us, based on Roman legend. The reality is likely to have been more complicated. Assuming there truly were seven kings who ruled the city, and assuming that the last of them was driven out by an aristocratic revolution, it appears that a period of transition ensued, as the Romans experimented with a variety of short-term solutions before arriving at the model of the Republican government that we

Figure 6.4 | She-Wolf Suckles Romulus and Remus | You can see a replica of this statue in Rome, Georgia.
Author: User "Nyenyec"
Source: Wikimedia Commons
License: Public Domain

know in the historical period. Furthermore, apparently what guided that gradual evolution of the government was the growing dissatisfaction of the plebeians, the lower socio-economic majority of the city, with their exclusion from the political process.

6.8.2 Early Republic: Conflict of Orders, the Twelve Tables, and Key Legislations

Roman sources from all periods, beginning already in the early Republic, reveal certain common values that all Romans held dear and considered to be foundational for their state. First, Romans had a strong respect for the past and were averse to change. Indeed, reformers had a difficult time passing their proposals in all periods of Roman history. The term for this reverence for the past, **mos maiorum**, "custom of ancestors" or "custom of elders," is telling. While innovation is a revered value in the modern world, Romans believed that innovation amounted to disrespect for their ancestors. Ancestral custom, which had first made Rome great, had to be respected, and successful reformers, such as the emperor Augustus, managed to phrase their reforms as a return to something old, rather than as something new. Three additional values that are key to understanding the Romans are **auctoritas**, "power" or "authority;" **dignitas**, roughly meaning "dignity;" and **gravitas**, "seriousness." Each citizen in the state had a degree of *auctoritas*, that intangible quality that made others obey him, but the degree of *auctoritas* varied, depending on one's social and political standing. Augustus, Rome's first emperor, would later describe his position in the state as having more *auctoritas* than anyone else. The other two qualities, *dignitas* and *gravitas*, were connected and reflected one's bearing and behavior as a true Roman. Jocularity was not valued, but seriousness reflected a particularly Roman conduct and determination. It is striking that Romans never smiled in portraits. The austere facial expression, instead, conveyed their power and superiority to others, whom they had conquered.

Figure 6.5 | Bust of an austere Roman, possibly Cato the Elder
Author: User "Shakko"
Source: Wikimedia Commons
License: Public Domain

While sharing common values, Romans were also deeply aware of social divisions between themselves. From its earliest time, Roman citizen population was divided into two orders: the **patricians**, defined as the descendants from the first one hundred senators appointed to the Roman aristocratic Senate by king Romulus, and the **plebeians**, that is, everyone who was not a patrician. The plebeians had their own political assembly, the **Plebeian Council**, while all Roman citizens also belonged to the **Centuriate Assembly**, which was responsible for annual elections for top political offices. The period of the early Republic, following the expulsion of the kings, was a time of conflict for the two orders, as patricians tried to establish a government that reserved all political power to themselves, whereas the plebeians fought for the opportunity to hold political and religious offices. Although they did not wield any political power at first, they discovered in the early fifth century that their most powerful weapon was secession, that is, departure en masse from the city, until the patricians acquiesced to a demand. While much about the **Conflict of the Orders**—just as anything else about the history of the early Republic—is shrouded in legend, it is possible to track its progress through the evidence of legislations that the Romans passed.

In 494 BCE, following the first plebeian secession, the Roman Senate allowed the plebeians to elect plebeian tribunes. An office that eventually was reserved for senators, it was originally merely an opportunity for plebeians to elect officers in the Plebeian Council, the assembly of all plebeian citizens, who would advocate for them. Plebeians next appear to have advocated for a public display of the laws, in order to protect the poor during lawsuits. The result was the first Roman legal code, the **Twelve Tables**, which was inscribed on twelve tables c. 450 BCE and displayed in public. One of the laws included was a ban on intermarriage between plebeians and patricians, showing a clear commitment on the part of the patricians to maintain the separation of the orders. It is important to note, however, that with the gradual decline in the number of patrician families over the course of the Roman Republic, most began to intermarry with prominent plebeian families.

The highest political office in the Republic, that of the consul, continued to be reserved solely for patricians until 367 BCE, when two senators sponsored the **Licinian-Sextian law**. The law required that one of the two consuls elected each year had to be plebeian. The phrasing of the law was significant, as it allowed the possibility that both consuls elected in a particular year could be plebeian, although this event did not happen in reality until 215 BCE. Finally, the legislation that modern historians have considered to have ended the early Republican Conflict of the Orders is the **Lex Hortensia** of 287 BCE. This law made all legislations passed by the Plebeian Council binding on all Romans, patricians and plebeians alike.

As historians connect the dots in the story of the Conflict of the Orders through these legislations, one trend that emerges is the gradual weakening of the patricians along with the growing influence of the plebeians on Roman government. Indeed, by the third century, a number of plebeian families were as wealthy and successful as patrician families, whereas some old patrician families had fallen on hard times.

6.8.3 Cursus Honorum and Roman Religion

The debate over plebeian access to political offices in general, and to the consulship in particular, resulted in the creation of a rigid *cursus honorum*, a sequence or ladder of political offices. The ultimate dream of every Roman who entered politics was to become a consul, but the narrowing pyramid that was the *cursus honorum* stood in his path. All offices were held for the term of one year, and, in order to prevent any one individual from amassing too much power, candidates had to wait ten years between consulships. Finally, each office had a minimum age requirement, with a special privilege for patricians to subtract two years from that minimum.

The prerequisite for holding any political office was ten years of military service. Thus, aspiring Roman politicians normally entered the army around eighteen years of age. Following ten years of distinguished service, candidates who were at least thirty years of age were allowed to run for the first office in the *cursus*: the quaestorship. The number of **quaestors** each year rose over time to twenty by the late Republic. Each quaestor was assigned to a particular duty for his year in office, varying from supervising the coin mint in Rome to serving as an assistant to a provincial governor or a consul in charge of a war.

While not officially part of the required *cursus honorum*, most ex-quaestors next ran for the office of the **plebeian tribune**, if they were plebeian, or an aedile. Ten plebeian tribunes were elected each year and were supposed to advocate for the benefit of the plebeians during Senatorial debates. Aediles—a term derived from the Latin "aedes," meaning "building" or "temple"—were in charge of public building projects and often also sponsored public entertainment.

The next step in the *cursus* was the praetorship. Similarly to the quaestors, the number of **praetors** rose over time, until topping at eight in the late Republic. Praetors could hold *imperium*, the right to command an army; thus, they often served in military roles or in administrative capacity by governing a province. Finally, one praetor each year, the *praetor urbanus*, was in charge of administering justice in the city of Rome and keeping track of legal cases and important decisions, which he issued at the end of the year as the Praetor's Edict.

Upon reaching the age of forty, candidates who had successfully held the praetorship ultimately could run for the consulship. Two **consuls** were elected annually, and this position change to "office" was the pinnacle of the Roman political career. Aristocratic families kept for centuries on display in their homes the ancestor masks of members of the family who had been consuls. Since ten years were required to elapse between successive consulships, very few individuals ever held more than one consulship, until several politicians in the late Republic broke the rules altogether. Last but not least, one additional office existed, for which ex-consuls could run: every five years, two **censors** were elected for a period of eighteen months for the purpose of conducting the census of citizens. While this structure of annually-elected offices was designed to prevent any one individual from usurping all political power in the state, the Senate also realized that, on rare occasions, concentrating all power in one set of hands was needed. Thus the Senate could appoint a dictator for a non-renewable period of six months in times of serious military emergency, such as in the already-mentioned case of Cincinnatus.

The *cursus honorum* is best visualized as a pyramid with a wide base and narrowing each step on the way up. While twenty men each year were elected to the quaestorship, only a fraction of them could ever achieve the praetorship, and a yet smaller fraction could rise to the consulship. Still, election to the quaestorship secured life-long membership in the Senate, the governing body of roughly 300 politicians—doubled in the first century BCE to 600—who effectively governed Rome under the Republic. The question remains, nevertheless: how did some men achieve political advancement while others never made it past the quaestorship? Part of the key to success, it appears, lay outside of politics proper, belonging instead to the realm of religion.

Roman religion, similarly to Greek, was traditionally polytheistic, with many myths and gods aligned to the Greek counterparts. Zeus, Greek king of the gods, became Jupiter, and was a patron

Figure 6.6 | The Capitoline Triad | Jupiter Optimus Maximus, with Juno and Minerva (known together as the Capitoline Triad). Note Juno's sacred goose at her foot, and Minerva's sacred owl next to her.
Author: User "Luiclemens"
Source: Wikimedia Commons
License: CC BY-SA 3.0

god of Rome under the title **Jupiter Optimus Maximus**, or Jupiter the Best and the Greatest.

His consort, Hera, became the Roman goddess **Juno** and was the patron goddess of marriage. The Greek Athena became Roman **Minerva** and was the patron divinity of women's crafts. In addition, both **Venus**, the goddess of love, and **Mars**, the god of war, had mythical family connections to Rome's human founders. Countless other divinities abounded as well; even the Roman sewer system, Cloaca Maxima, had its own patron goddess, Cloacina.

While Romans were expected to worship some of the gods in private, often making vows to them and promising gifts if the gods fulfilled a request, Roman religion also had a significant public component that was reserved for the priestly colleges. Although not limited to politicians, membership in these colleges was at times key for political advancement. One example of this phenomenon in action is the career of Julius Caesar, whose political career took off after his appointment to the religious office of ***pontifex maximus***, head of Roman religion. Ultimately, both public and private religion aimed at the same goal: keeping the ***pax deorum***, peace with the gods, upon which the success of their state rested, as the Romans believed. Put simply, as long as Romans maintained a respectful peace with their gods, they ensured Rome's success. Whenever any disasters befell the state, however, Romans typically assumed that *pax deorum* had been violated in some way. The gods then had to be appeased in order to end the disaster and prevent similar events from occurring in the future.

6.8.4 Roman Expansion to the End of the Punic Wars

While the legends about the kings of Rome suggest that they had significant military responsibilities, it appears that their military actions were largely defensive. Just a decade or so after the expulsion of the kings, shortly after 500 BCE, however, Roman expansion began in earnest. It is important to note here several key features of the early Roman military. First, until the late Republic, Rome did not maintain a standing army. Rather, a new army was raised for each campaign, and campaigns were typically launched in the spring and ended in the fall. The festival of the October Horse, one of the religious festivals the Romans celebrated each year, involved a ritual purification of the cavalry and originally was likely designed as the end point of the campaign season. Also, similarly to the Greek world, the Romans had minimum wealth requirements for military service, since soldiers supplied their own equipment. Finally, one significant trend to note in early Republican military history is the repeated nature of Roman conflicts with the same enemies, such as the three **Samnite Wars**, the three **Punic Wars**, and the four **Macedonian Wars**. This repetition suggests that, for whatever reason, the Romans did not aim to annihilate their opponents, unless absolutely pressed to do so.

It appears that the Roman expansion in the 490s BCE began as a defensive measure. In either 499 BCE or 496 BCE, the expelled seventh king of Rome, Tarquin the Proud, joined forces with the Latin League, a group of about thirty city-states around the area of Rome, and led them to attack the Romans. The result was the **Battle of Lake Regillus**, a decisive victory for Rome. The Romans signed an uneasy peace treaty with the Latins, but war broke out again in 340 – 338 BCE. The Roman victory this time resulted in the absorption of the Latin city-states into Rome as partial citizens.

The Latins were not the only enemies the nascent Roman Republic had to face. Romans fought and gradually conquered the Etruscan city-states to the north. One especially significant victory was over the powerful Etruscan city of **Veii** in 396 BCE. A legend preserved by Livy states that Romans were only able to conquer Veii after they performed the ceremony of *evocation*, "calling out." Fearing that their siege of Veii was not going well because Juno, the patron goddess of Veii, was not on their side, the Romans called Juno out of Veii; they promised her a nice new temple in Rome if she would switch sides. Shortly thereafter, the city fell to the Romans. When the Roman soldiers were packing up the cult statue of Juno from her temple in Veii for transportation to Rome, a cheeky Roman soldier asked Juno if she wanted to come to Rome. The statue enthusiastically nodded her head. Livy's history is full of similar tales of divine providence intervening on the side of the Romans. These legends show the Romans' own belief that throughout the process of expansion, the gods had protected them and guided them to success.

While still fighting the Latins, the Romans embarked upon what turned out to be a series of three wars with their neighbors to the east, the Samnites. Each of these wars, the last of which ended in 290 BCE, resulted in Roman territorial gains; by the end of the Third Samnite War, Rome controlled all of central Italy. It also appears that, at some point during the Samnite Wars, the Romans switched from fighting in the Greek hoplite phalanx fashion to a system of their own making, the **manipular legion**. This new system apparently allowed more flexibility in the arrangement of the troops on the battle-field; it also allowed using both heavy and light infantry as needed, instead of keeping them in a static formation for the duration of a battle.

Figure 6.7 | Two Roman Infantrymen and a Cavalryman, second century BCE
Author: User "ColderEel"
Source: Wikimedia Commons
License: Public Domain

While not much else is known about the manipular legion, it appears to have been an effective system for the Romans for much of the Republican period.

It is striking to consider that the Romans spent eighty of the hundred years in the third century BCE at war. They did not seem to have had the ambition to conquer the Greek city-states who were their neighbors in southern Italy; in 280 – 275 BCE, Rome nevertheless became embroiled in a war with **Pyrrhus**, king of Epirus in northern Greece, after providing help to Thurii in its dispute with Tarentum. Tarentum requested Pyrrhus' help, and he proceeded to invade Italy. The Romans fought three major battles against Pyrrhus, the first two of which he won at great cost to his army. Indeed, the term "Pyrrhic victory" in modern English refers to a

Map 6.5 | Roman Territories at the End of the Second Punic War |
Interactive Map Showing Stages of Roman Expansion in the Republic and Empire
Legend:
- Roman Republic: 510 BC - 40 BC
- Roman Empire: 20 CE - 360 CE
- Eastern Roman Empire: 405 CE - 1453 CE
- Western Roman Empire: 405 CE - 480 CE
Author: User "Semhur"
Source: Wikimedia Commons
License: CC BY-SA 3.0
NOTE: Interactive map requires Adobe Flash. Click the following link to view graphic on original website. https://commons.wikimedia.org/wiki/File:Roman_Republic_Empire_map.gif

victory that is so costly as to be truly a loss. The Romans finally defeated Pyrrhus at their third battle against him in 275 BCE, showing the superiority of the new Roman manipular legion even against the phalanx of the Macedonians, military descendants of Alexander the Great himself. This victory united most of Italy, except for the very northern portion, under Roman rule.

The war with Pyrrhus was the Romans' first serious conflict with the Greek world, but it was far from their last. The Romans' proximity to northern Greece, in particular, ensured an intersection of spheres of interest, thus also providing cause for continued conflict. Between 214 and 148 BCE, Rome fought four separate Macedonian Wars. During roughly the same period, from 264 and 146 BCE, the Romans also fought three Punic Wars against **Carthage**, originally a Phoenician colony that became a leading maritime power. Culminating with the Roman destruction of both Carthage and Corinth in 146 BCE, the eventual victory of the Romans over both powers allowed the Romans to gain full control over them and their previous land holdings. Their victory effectively put the entire Mediterranean world under Roman rule.

In 146 BCE, when the Romans found themselves in control of a Mediterranean empire, they appeared to foresee little of the consequences of such a rapid expansion on internal stability in Rome proper. A critical question nevertheless faced them: how would the Republic, whose system of government was designed for a small city-state, adapt to ruling a large empire? The preliminary answer on which the Romans settled was to divide the conquered territories into provinces, to which senatorial governors were assigned for terms that varied from one to five years. The system continued, with minor variations, into the Empire.

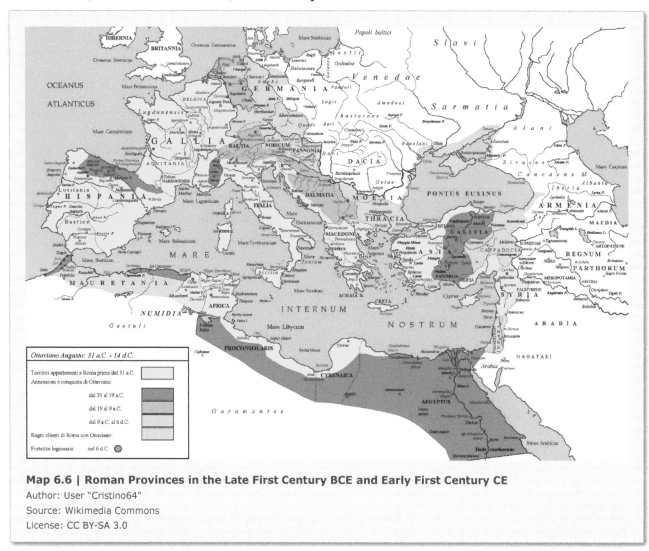

Map 6.6 | Roman Provinces in the Late First Century BCE and Early First Century CE
Author: User "Cristino64"
Source: Wikimedia Commons
License: CC BY-SA 3.0

The new availability of governor positions, however, only made the political competition in the Republic even stiffer than before. Senators competed for the most desirable positions; typically, these were provinces in which military action was on-going—since this provided the potential for winning military glory—or provinces that were wealthy, with the potential opportunity in governing them to acquire wealth.

6.9 FALL OF THE ROMAN REPUBLIC

The victory over Carthage in the Second Punic War allowed Rome to "close" the circle of the Mediterranean almost completely, acquiring control over all territories that had previously belonged to Carthage. The destruction of Carthage in the Third Punic War, while largely a symbolic gesture, further cemented Rome's control over the entire Mediterranean. The late Republican historian Sallust, though, grimly saw the Roman victory in the Punic Wars as the beginning of the end of the Republic. As Sallust and some other conservative politicians of his day believed, this victory corrupted the noble Roman character, traditionally steeled by privation. More importantly, the abundance of resources that flowed in following the victories over Carthage raised the question of distribution of this new wealth and land. The disagreements over this question dominated the politics of the Late Republic, creating two new political factions: the **Populares**, or those who protected the interests of the people, and the **Optimates**, or those who protected the interests of the best element of the populace—namely, themselves.

6.9.1 The Gracchi and the Beginning of Political Violence

It is striking to consider that political violence was minimal in the Roman Republic until 133 BCE. Indeed, if the legends are true, even the expulsion of the kings in 510 BCE was a bloodless event. Starting with 133 BCE, however, the final century of the Roman Republic was defined by political violence and civil wars.

In 133 BCE, **Tiberius Sempronius Gracchus**, a scion on his mother's side of one of the oldest and most respected families in Rome, the Cornelii Scipiones, was one of the ten annually elected plebeian tribunes. Alarmed that the lands acquired through recent Roman conquests had largely been taken over by rich landowners at the expense of poorer Romans, Gracchus proposed a land distribution law, known as the *Lex Sempronia Agraria*. Gracchus argued that the advantages of such land redistribution would have benefited the state, since land-ownership was a pre-requisite for military service. Aware that the Senate's Optimates faction opposed his proposal, Gracchus took his law directly to the Plebeian Council, which passed it. This measure resulted in escalating conflict between Gracchus and the rest of the Senate. At a meeting of the Senate, the *pontifex maximus*, who was Tiberius Gracchus' own cousin Publius Cornelius Scipio Nasica, ultimately argued that Gracchus had attempted to make himself king; thus, he had to be stopped. Since weapons were banned inside the Senate building, enraged Senators grabbed whatever was on hand, including chair and table legs, and clubbed Gracchus to death. As the biographer Plutarch states, this was the first instance of civic strife of this kind in ancient Rome.

The death of Tiberius Gracchus also meant the death of his proposed law. Ten years later, however, Gracchus' proposed reforms gained a second life in the hands of his younger brother, **Gaius Gracchus**, who was elected plebeian tribune in 123 BCE and served a second term in that office in 122 BCE. Gaius Gracchus' revived agrarian reform proposal was even more ambitious than his brother's a decade earlier. Especially controversial was Gaius Gracchus' proposal of granting full Roman citizenship to Rome's Italian allies. Finally, in 121 BCE, alarmed at Gaius Gracchus' popularity with the people, the consul Lucius Opimius proposed a new measure in the Senate: a *senatus consultum ultimum,* or the final decree of the Senate, which amounted to allowing the consuls to do whatever was necessary to safeguard the state. Realizing that the passing of this law amounted to his death sentence, Gaius Gracchus committed suicide.

The proposed reforms of Gaius Gracchus were overturned after his death, but the legacy of the Gracchi for the remainder of the history of the Roman Republic cannot be underestimated. First, their proposed laws showed the growing conflict between the rich and the poor in the Roman state. Second, the willingness on the part of prominent Senators to resort to violence to resolve matters set a dangerous precedent for the remainder of the Republic and fundamentally changed the nature of Roman politics. Finally, the support that the Gracchi received from the Roman people, as well as the residents of Italian cities who were not full citizens, showed that the causes that the Gracchi adopted were not going to go away permanently after their death. Indeed, Rome's Italian allies went to war against Rome in 90 – 88 BCE; the result of this **Social War**, after "socii," meaning "allies," was the grant of full Roman citizenship rights to Italians.

6.9.2 The Civil War of Marius and Sulla, and the Conspiracy of Catilina

The affair of the Gracchi was the first clear instance in the late Republic of Populares and Optimates in a violent conflict. Forty years later, a conflict between two politicians, representing different sides in this debate, resulted in a full-fledged civil war.

In 107 BCE, impatient over the prolonged and challenging war against the Numidian king Jugurtha, the Romans elected as consul Gaius **Marius**.

While Marius had already enjoyed a distinguished military career, he was a *novus homo,* or "new man," a term the Romans used to refer to newcomers to Roman politics, meaning individuals who have not had any family members elected to political office. Even more shockingly, Marius was not even from Rome proper, but from the town of Arpinum, located sixty miles south of Rome. Marius benefited from the sense of frustration in Rome over the length of the war and the perceived corruption of the aristocratic leaders abroad. Once elected, he took over the command in the war and passed the most comprehensive reforms to the Roman military since the Romans switched to the manipular legion. First, Marius abolished the property requirement for military

Figure 6.8 | Bust of Gaius Marius
Author: User "Direktor"
Source: Wikimedia Commons
License: Public Domain

service, allowing landless Romans to serve in the army for the first time in Roman history. A second and related change was the new commitment on the part of the Roman state to arm its troops and also pay them for service. Henceforth, the military became a profession, rather than a seasonal occupation for farmers. Finally, Marius changed the tactics of the legionary organization on the battlefield, changing the legion of maniples into a **legion of cohorts**.

Marius' reforms, while controversial, proved immensely successful, and he swiftly was able to defeat Jugurtha, ending the war in 104 BCE. As a result of his victories,

Figure 6.9 | Roman Soldiers with Aquilifer Signifer Centurio | The Cohortal Legion after Marius. Re-enactors Portraying Legion XV Appollinaris in the First Century CE
Author: User "MatthaisKabel"
Source: Wikimedia Commons
License: CC BY-SA 3.0

Figure 6.10 | Bust of Lucius Cornelius Sulla
Author: User "Direktor"
Source: Wikimedia Commons
License: Public Domain

Marius had gained unprecedented popularity in Rome and was elected to five more successive consulships in 104 – 100 BCE. While a law existed requiring ten years between successive consulships, Marius' popularity and military success, in conjunction with the Romans' fear of on-going foreign wars, elevated him above the law. While Marius began his military career fighting for Rome, though, he ended it by causing the worst civil war Rome had seen to that point.

In 88 BCE, the Roman Senate was facing a war against Mithridates, king of Pontus, who had long been a thorn in Rome's side in the Eastern provinces of the empire. Sensing that Marius was too old to undertake the war, the Senate appointed instead Lucius Cornelius **Sulla**, a distinguished general who had started his career as Marius' quaestor in the Jugurthine War and was now a consul himself. Marius, however, had another trick up his sleeve. Summoning the Plebeian Council, Marius overturned the decision of the Senate and drove Sulla out of Rome. Instead of going lightly into exile, however, Sulla gathered an army and marched on Rome—the first time in Roman history that a Roman general led a Roman army against Rome!

Sulla took over Rome, swiftly had himself declared commander of the war on Mithridates, and departed for the Black Sea. In 86 BCE, Marius was elected consul for the seventh and final time in his career then promptly died of natural causes, just seventeen days after taking office. The civil war that he started with Sulla, though, was still far from over.

In 83 BCE, victorious over Mithridates but facing a hostile reception from the Senate, Sulla marched on Rome for the second time. This time, he truly meant business. Declaring himself dictator for reforming the Roman constitution, Sulla ruled Rome as a dictator for the next three years. His reforms aimed to prevent the rise of another Marius so significantly curtailed the powers of the plebeian tribunes. In addition, he established the **proscriptions**—a list of enemies of the state, whom anyone could kill on sight, and whose property was confiscated. Incidentally, one name on Sulla's list was the young **Julius Caesar**, whose aunt had been married to Gaius Marius. While Caesar obviously survived the proscription, and went on to become a prominent politician himself, the confiscation of his property by Sulla ensured that he remained painfully strapped financially and in debt for the rest of his life.

After enacting his reforms, Sulla just as suddenly resigned from politics, retiring to a family estate outside of Rome in 79 BCE, where he appears to have drunk himself into an early grave—based on Plutarch's description of his death, the symptoms appear to fit with cirrhosis of the liver. Over the next several decades, some of Sulla's reforms were overturned, such as those pertaining to the plebeian tribunes. Most historians of the Republic agree, however, that the Republican constitution never afterward reverted to its old state. The Republic after Sulla was a different Republic than before him.

The civil war of Marius and Sulla showed the increasingly greater degree of competition in the Republic as well as the lengths to which some Roman politicians were willing to go to get power and hold on to it. Furthermore, it demonstrated one dangerous side effect of Marius' military reforms: before Marius, Roman farmer-soldiers did not feel a personal affinity for their generals. After Marius' reforms, however, because soldiers were paid by their generals, their loyalty was to their generals, as much or more than to the Roman state. Finally, Marius' incredible political success—election to a record-setting and law-breaking seven consulships over the course of his life—showed that military ability had somewhat leveled the playing field between old patrician families such as Sulla's—that had dominated the consulship for centuries—and the newcomers to Roman politics. This challenge by the newcomers to the old Roman political families was an especially bitter pill to swallow for some.

In 63 BCE, Lucius Sergius **Catilina**, a patrician who had unsuccessfully run for consulship and who was defeated that very year by another newcomer from Arpinum, Marcus Tullius Cicero, banded with other frustrated Senators to plan a conspiracy to assassinate the consuls and take over the state. Catilina's conspiracy failed, and modern historians can read Cicero's own reports to the Senate and the people about how he discovered and stopped this conspiracy. Catilina's frustration, just like that of Sulla twenty years earlier, nevertheless shows how difficult it was for Roman "old-school" political families to accept that their competition for the consulship now was not just against each other. Catilina's plan to resort to violence to achieve power also shows just how quickly political violence became the "normal" solution to problems in Roman Republican politics after the Gracchi.

6.9.3 The First Triumvirate, and the Civil War of Caesar and Pompey

The political careers of Marius and Sulla, as well as Catilina, show the increased level of competition in the late Republic and the ruthlessness with which some Roman politicians in the period attempted to gain the consulship. In 60 BCE, however, a group of three politicians tried to achieve its goals by doing something atypical of Roman politicians who had largely only looked out for themselves: the three formed an alliance in order to help each other. Spectacularly, their alliance even transcended the usual division of Populares and Optimates, showing that, for these three men at least, the thirst for political power was more important than any other personal convictions.

Marcus Licinius **Crassus** was the wealthiest man in Rome, son of a consul, and consul himself in 70 BCE. His colleague in the consulship in 70 BCE, Gnaeus **Pompey**, achieved military fame in his youth, earning him the nickname "Magnus," or "the Great," from Sulla himself.

By 60 BCE, however, both Crassus and Pompey felt frustrated with their political careers so joined forces with a relative newcomer to the world of politics, Gaius Julius Caesar. The three men formed their alliance, secret at first, an alliance which

Figure 6.11 | Bust of Pompey the Great | Pompey the Great with Alexander the Great's Hairstyle
Author: User "Robbot"
Source: Wikimedia Commons
License: Public Domain

Cicero later dubbed the **Triumvirate**. To cement the alliance, Caesar's daughter, Julia, married Pompey. Together, they lobbied to help each other rise again to the consulship and achieve desirable military commands.

The alliance paid immediate dividends for Caesar, who was promptly elected consul for 59 BCE and was then awarded Gaul as his province for five years after the consulship. Crassus and Pompey, in the meanwhile, were re-elected consuls for 55 BCE, and, in the same year, Caesar's command in Gaul was renewed for another five years. One modern historian has called it "the worst piece of legislation in Roman history," since the renewal did not specify whether the five-year clock started afresh in 55 BCE—in which case, Caesar's command was to end in 50 BCE—or if the five years were added to the original five-year term—in which case, Caesar's command would have ended in 48 BCE.

A talented writer, as well as skilled general, Caesar made sure to publish an account of his Gallic campaigns in installments during his time in Gaul. As a result, Romans were continually aware of Caesar's successes, and his popularity actually grew in his absence. His rising popularity was a source of frustration for the other two triumvirs. Finally, the already uneasy alliance disintegrated in 53 BCE. First, Julia died in childbirth, and her baby died with her. In the same year, Crassus was killed at the Battle of Carrhae, fighting the Parthians. With the death of both Julia and Crassus, no links were left connecting Caesar and Pompey; the two former family relations, albeit by marriage, swiftly became official enemies.

Late in 50 BCE, the Senate, under the leadership of Pompey, informed Caesar that his command had expired and demanded that he surrender his army. Caesar, however, refused to return to Rome as a private citizen, demanding to be allowed to stand for the consulship *in absentia*. When his demands were refused, on January 10th of 49 BCE, Caesar and his army crossed the Rubicon, a river which marked the border of his province. By leaving his province with his army against the wishes of the Senate, Caesar committed an act of treason, as defined in Roman law; the civil war began.

While most of the Senate was on Pompey's side, Caesar started the war with a distinct advantage: his troops had just spent a larger part of a decade fighting with him in Gaul; many of Pompey's army, on the other hand, was disorganized. As a result, for much of 49 BCE, Pompey retreated to the south of Italy, with Caesar in pursuit. Finally, in late 48 BCE, the two fought a decisive battle at Pharsalus in northern Greece. There, Caesar's army managed to defeat Pompey's much larger forces. After the defeat, Pompey fled to Egypt, where he was assassinated by order

Figure 6.12 | Bust of Cleopatra VII
Author: User "Louis le Grand"
Source: Wikimedia Commons
License: Public Domain

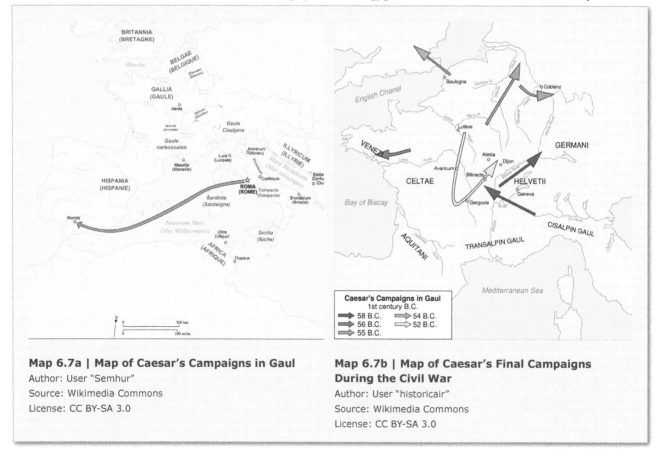

Map 6.7a | Map of Caesar's Campaigns in Gaul
Author: User "Semhur"
Source: Wikimedia Commons
License: CC BY-SA 3.0

Map 6.7b | Map of Caesar's Final Campaigns During the Civil War
Author: User "historicair"
Source: Wikimedia Commons
License: CC BY-SA 3.0

of Ptolemy XIII, who had hoped to win Caesar's favor by this action. When he arrived in Egypt in pursuit of Pompey, Caesar, however, sided with Ptolemy's sister **Cleopatra VII** and appears to have fathered a son with her, Caesarion.

With Pompey's death, the civil war was largely over, although Caesar still fought a number of battles across the Roman world with the remnants of the senatorial army. It is indeed striking to look at a map of Caesar's military career. While his military actions on behalf of Rome were largely limited to Gaul, with a couple of forays into Britain, his civil war against Pompey and his allies took Caesar all over the Roman world from 49 to 45 BCE.

6.9.4 Aftermath of the Civil War, the Second Triumvirate, and the Age of Augustus

Victorious in the civil war against Pompey and his supporters, Caesar was faced with the challenging question of what to do next. Clearly, he was planning to hold on to power in some way. Based on previous history, there were two options available to him: the Marius model of rule, meaning election to successive consulships, and the Sulla model, meaning dictatorship. Initially, Caesar followed the first model, holding the consulship first with a colleague in 47 BCE and 46 BCE then serving as sole consul in 45 BCE. By early 44 BCE, however, Caesar appears to have decided to

Figure 6.13 | Coin of Caesar from 44 BCE | Note Caesar's Image on One Side, and Venus on the reverse.
Author: User "Medium69"
Source: Wikimedia Commons
License: CC BY-SA 3.0

adopt the Sulla model instead. In February of 44 BCE, he took the title of ***dictator perpetuo***, or "dictator for life," and had coins minted with his image and new title. His was the first instance in Roman history of a living individual's placing his likeness on coinage.

This new title appears to have been the final straw for a group of about sixty senators who feared that Caesar aimed to make himself a king. On the Ides of March (March 15th) of 44 BCE, the conspirators rushed Caesar during a Senate meeting and stabbed him to death. But if the conspirators had thought that by assassinating Caesar they were going to restore the Republic, they turned out to be sorely mistaken.

Caesar's will, in which he left money to each resident of the city of Rome and donated his gardens for use by the public, only further increased his popularity among the people, and popular rioting ensued throughout the city. Since Caesar did not have legitimate sons who could inherit—Caesarion, his son with Cleopatra, was illegitimate—he adopted an heir in his will, a common Roman practice. The heir in question was his grand-nephew Gaius Octavius, whose name after the adoption became Gaius Julius Caesar Octavianus (or Octavian, in English). It is interesting to note that Caesar's will also named a back-up heir, in case the main heir would have died before inheriting. The back-up heir was none other than Brutus, one of Caesar's assassins.

Figure 6.14 | Statue of Augustus from the Villa of Livia at Prima Porta
Author: User "Soerfm"
Source: Wikimedia Commons
License: CC BY-SA 3.0

At the time of his adoption as Caesar's heir, Octavian was nineteen years old; thus, he was too young to have had much military or political experience. Quickly, though, he showed political acumen, initially using an alliance with two much more experienced former allies of Caesar: **Marcus Antonius** and Marcus Aemilius Lepidus. Forming what became known as the **Second Triumvirate**, the three men renewed the proscriptions in 43 BCE, aggressively pursuing the enemies of Caesar and also fighting a small-scale civil war with Caesar's assassins. The triumvirs defeated Caesar's assassins at the Battle of Philippi in northern Greece in 42 BCE; they then carved out the Roman world into regions to be ruled by each. Marcus Antonius, who claimed Egypt, although it was not yet a Roman province, proceeded to marry Cleopatra and rule Egypt with her over the following decade. Ultimately, however, another civil war resulted between Antonius and Octavian, with the latter winning a decisive victory in the Battle of Actium in 31 BCE. From that moment until his death in 14 CE, Octavian—soon to be named **Augustus** in 27 BCE, the name he subsequently used—ruled what henceforth was known as the Roman Empire, and is considered by modern historians of Rome to have been the first emperor.

While modern historians refer to Augustus as the first emperor of Rome, that is not the title that he himself had, nor would he have said that he was inaugurating a new form of government in Rome. Rather, throughout his time in power, Augustus claimed to have restored the Roman Republic, and, with the exception of a few elected offices, he did not have any official position. How did he manage to rule the Roman Empire for over forty years without any official position? Some answers can be found in the ***Res Gestae Divi Augusti***, an autobiography that Augustus himself composed in the year before he died and which he ordered to be posted on his Mausoleum in Rome, with copies also posted in all major cities throughout the Empire.

Reflecting on his forty-year rule in this document, Augustus described himself as the first citizen, or *princeps*, of the Roman state, superior to others in his *auctoritas*. In addition, he was especially proud of the title of "Pater Patriae," or "Father of the Fatherland," voted to him by the Senate and reflecting his status as the patron of all citizens. It is striking to consider that other than these honorary titles and positions, Augustus did not have an official position as a ruler. Indeed, having learned from Caesar's example, he avoided accepting any titles that might have smacked of a desire for kingship. Instead, he brilliantly created for himself new titles and powers, thoroughly grounded in previous, Republican tradition. In addition, he proved to be a master diplomat, who shared power with the Senate in a way beneficial to himself, and by all of these actions seamlessly married the entire Republican political structure with one-man rule.

The question remains: when did the Roman Republic actually fall? Different historians have proposed several possible answers. One minority position is that the Republic had fallen with the dictatorship of Sulla, since it fundamentally altered the nature of the Republican government and permanently destabilized it. Another possible answer is the assassination of Caesar in 44 BCE, since afterwards, the Republic was never quite the same as it had been before the civil war of Pompey and Caesar. Another possible answer is 27 BCE, when the Senate granted Octavian the title of Augustus, recognizing his albeit unofficial consolidation of

Figure 6.15 | Copy of the Res Gestae in Modern Ankara, Turkey
Author: User "Soerfm"
Source: Wikimedia Commons
License: CC BY-SA 3.0

power. Finally, yet another possible answer is the death of Augustus in 14 CE. Overall, all of these possible dates and events show the instability of the Roman state in the late first century BCE.

6.9.5 Roman Culture of the Late Republic and the Augustan Age

While the political structure of the Roman Republic in its final century of existence was becoming increasingly unstable, the period from the end of the Second Punic War on was actually one of increasing flourishing of entertainment culture and literary arts in Rome. Although much of Roman literary culture was based on Greek literature, the Romans adapted what they borrowed to make it distinctly their own. Thus, while adapting Greek tragedies and comedies and, in some cases, apparently translating them wholesale, Romans still injected Roman values into them, thus making them relatable to Roman Republican audiences. For example, in one fragment from a Roman tragedy, *Iphigenia at Aulis*, adapted by the Roman poet Ennius from the Greek tragedian Euripides' play by the same name, the chorus of frustrated Greek soldiers debates the merits of *otium*, or leisure, and *negotium*, or business (a specifically Roman concept). Similarly, while Roman philosophy and rhetoric of the Republic were heavily based on their Greek counterparts, their writers thoroughly Romanized the concepts discussed, as well as the presentation. For instance, Cicero, a preeminent rhetorician and philosopher of the late Republic, adapted the model of the Socratic dialogue in several of his philosophical treatises to make dialogues between prominent Romans of the Middle Republic. His *De Republica*, a work expressly modeled on Plato's *Republic*, features Scipio Aemilianus, the victor over Carthage in the Third Punic War.

While the late Republic was a period of growth for Roman literary arts, with much of the writing done by politicians, the age of Augustus saw an even greater flourishing of Roman literature. This increase was due in large part to Augustus' own investment in sponsoring prominent poets to write about the greatness of Rome. The three most prominent poets of the Augustan age, Virgil, Horace, and Ovid, all wrote poetry glorifying Augustan Rome. Virgil's *Aeneid*, finished in 19 BCE, aimed to be the Roman national epic and indeed achieved that goal. The epic, intended to be the Roman version of Homer's *Iliad* and *Odyssey* combined, told about the travels of the Trojan prince Aeneas who, by will of the gods, became the founder of Rome. Clearly connecting the Roman to the Greek heroic tradition, the epic also includes a myth explaining the origins of the Punic Wars: during his travels, before he arrived in Italy, Aeneas was ship-wrecked and landed in Carthage. Dido, the queen of Carthage, fell in love with him and wanted him to stay with her, but the gods ordered Aeneas to sail on to Italy. After Aeneas abandoned her, Dido committed suicide and cursed the future Romans to be at war with her people.

The works of Horace and Ovid were more humorous at times, but they still included significant elements from early Roman myths. They thus served to showcase the *pax deorum* that caused Rome to flourish in the past and, again now, in the age of Augustus. Ovid appears to have pushed the envelope beyond acceptable limits, whether in his poetry or in his personal conduct. Therefore, Augustus exiled him in 8 CE to the city of Tomis on the Black Sea, where Ovid spent the remainder of his life writing mournful poetry and begging unsuccessfully to be recalled back to Rome.

In addition to sponsoring literature, the age of Augustus was a time of building and rebuilding around Rome. In his *Res Gestae*, Augustus includes a very long list of temples that he had restored or built. Among some new building projects that he undertook to stand as symbols of renewal and prosperity ordained

Figure 6.16 | The Ara Pacis
Author: User "Manfred Heyde"
Source: Wikimedia Commons
License: CC BY-SA 3.0

by the gods themselves, none is as famous as the ***Ara Pacis***, or Altar of Peace, in Rome. The altar features a number of mythological scenes and processions of gods; it also integrates scenes of the imperial family, including Augustus himself making a sacrifice to the gods, while flanked by his grandsons Gaius and Lucius.

The message of these building projects, as well as the other arts that Augustus sponsored is, overall, simple: Augustus wanted to show that his rule was a new Golden Age of Roman history, a time when peace was restored and Rome flourished, truly blessed by the gods.

6.10 THE EARLY EMPIRE

The period from the consolidation of power by Augustus in 27 BCE to the death of the emperor Marcus Aurelius in 180 CE was one of relative peace and prosperity throughout the Roman Empire. For this reason, the Romans themselves referred to this time as the ***Pax Romana***, or Roman peace. During this period, the Empire became increasingly more of a smoothly run bureaucratic machine when commerce prospered, and the overall territory grew to its largest extent in the early second century CE. Of course, some of the Roman subjects did not feel quite as happy with this peace and what it brought to them. The Roman historian Tacitus narrates a speech of a British tribal rebel leader, Calgacus, to his men before they fought—and were defeated by—the Romans in 85 CE: "they (the Romans) make a desert, and call it peace." Other evidence from the territories in the periphery of the Empire also shows that Romanization was not absolute, as some remote rural areas in provinces far from Italy did not really feel the impact of the Empire. Finally, the period of the early Empire witnessed the rise of a new religion, **Christianity**. This new religion did not have a profound impact on the state yet at this point, but the seeds planted in this period allowed for fundamental changes to occur centuries later. This is, after all, one of the marvels of history. It can take centuries to see the long-term impact of events that seem so small and insignificant at first.

6.10.1 The Julio-Claudian Dynasty

The historian Tacitus describes in detail the emotions in the Roman Senate upon the death of Augustus. Some Senators were hoping for the return of the Republic, while others assumed that Augustus' stepson would inherit his nebulous yet amazingly powerful position. The scales were heavily weighed in favor of the latter option: as Tacitus points out, most Senators by 14 CE—fifty years after Caesar's assassination—had never lived under a Republic; thus, they did not really know what a true Republic looked like. Still, the question that all were pondering in 14 CE was: how do you pass on something that does not exist? After all, Augustus did not have any official position. The first succession was a test case to see if the imperial system of government would become the new normal for Rome or if Augustus would prove to have been an exception.

Augustus himself seems to have been worried about appointing a successor for his entire time in power. Because of untimely deaths of all other possible candidates, Augustus eventually settled on adopting his stepson **Tiberius** Claudius Nero (not to be confused with the later emperor Nero), son of his wife Livia from her first marriage. Over the final years of his life, Augustus gradually shared more of his unofficial powers with Tiberius, in order to smooth the process of succession. Augustus' plan appears to have worked, as after a brief conversation in the Senate, as Tacitus reports, the Senators conferred upon Tiberius all of Augustus' previous powers. Tiberius' succession is the reason for which historians refer to the first Roman imperial dynasty as the **Julio-Claudians**.

Tiberius, a decorated military general in his youth, appears in our sources as a sullen and possibly cruel individual, whose temperament made Augustus himself feel sorry for the Romans for leaving such a ruler in his stead—or so Suetonius tells us.

He also appears to have been a rather reluctant emperor, who much preferred life out of the public eye. Finally, in 26 CE, Tiberius retired to Capri for the final eleven years of his rule. It is a testament to the spectacular bureaucratic system that was the Roman Empire that the eleven-year absence of the emperor was hardly felt, one exception being a foiled plot against Tiberius by his chief trusted advisor in Rome, Sejanus.

Similarly to Augustus, Tiberius had a difficult time selecting a successor, as repeatedly, each relative who was identified as a candidate died an untimely death. Ultimately, Tiberius adopted as his successor his grandnephew Gaius **Caligula**, or "little boot," son of the popular military hero Germanicus, who died young.

While Caligula began his power with full support of both the people and the Senate, and with an unprecedented degree of popularity, he swiftly proved to be mentally unstable and bankrupted the state in his short rule of just under four years. In 41 CE, he was assassinated by three disgruntled officers in the Praetorian Guard, which ironically was the body formed by Augustus in order to protect the emperor.

Caligula's assassination left Rome in disarray. The biographer Suetonius reports that, while the

Figure 6.17 | Bust of the Emperor Tiberius
Author: User "Manfred Heyde"
Source: Wikimedia Commons
License: CC BY-SA 3.0

Figure 6.18 | Bust of the Emperor Caligula
Author: User "Manfred Heyde"
Source: Wikimedia Commons
License: CC BY-SA 3.0

Figure 6.19 | Bust of the Emperor Claudius
Author: User "Direktor"
Source: Wikimedia Commons
License: CC BY-SA 2.5

Figure 6.20 | Sketch of an Ancient Graffito of the Emperor Nero
Author: User "Shakko"
Source: Wikimedia Commons
License: Public Domain

confused Senate was meeting and planning to declare the restoration of the Roman Republic, the Praetorian Guard proclaimed as the next emperor **Claudius**, uncle of Caligula and the brother of Germanicus.

While Claudius was a member of the imperial family, he was never considered a candidate for succession before. He had a speech impediment; as a result, Augustus considered him an embarrassment to the imperial family. Claudius proved to be a productive emperor, but his downfall appears to have been pretty women of bad character, as he repeatedly weathered plots against his life by first one wife and then the next. Finally, in 54 CE, Claudius died and was widely believed to have been poisoned by his wife, Agrippina the Younger. Since the cause, as Suetonius tells us, was mushrooms, a popular joke thereafter in Rome was that mushrooms were the food of the gods—a reference to the deification of most emperors after their death.

Although Claudius had a biological son from an earlier marriage, that son was poisoned soon after his death. His successor instead became **Nero**, his stepson, who was only sixteen years old when he gained power.

Showing the danger of inexperience for an emperor, Nero gradually alienated the Senate, the people, and the army over the course of his fourteen-year rule. He destroyed his own reputation by performing on stage—behavior that was considered disgraceful in Roman society. Furthermore, Nero is believed in 64 CE to have caused the great fire of Rome in order to free up space in the middle of the city for his ambitious new palace, the Domus Aurea, or Golden House.

The last years of Nero's reign seem to have been characterized by provincial rebellions, as a revolt broke out in Judea in 66 CE, and then the governor of Gaul, Gaius Julius Vindex, also rebelled against Nero. The revolt of Vindex ultimately proved to be the end of Nero, since Vindex convinced the governor of Spain, Servius Sulpicius Galba, to join the rebellion and, furthermore, proclaim himself emperor. While the rebellion of Vindex was quickly squashed, and Vindex himself committed suicide, popular support for Galba grew just as quickly. Finally, terrified by rumors of Galba marching to Rome, Nero committed suicide in June of 68 CE. His death marked the end of the Julio-Claudian dynasty.

6.10.2 The Year of the Four Emperors, the Flavian Dynasty, and the Five Good Emperors

The year and a half after Nero's death saw more civil war and instability throughout the empire than any other period since the late Republic. In particular, the year 69 CE became known as the year of the four emperors, as four emperors in succession came to power: Galba, Otho, Vitellius, and Vespasian. Each challenged his predecessor to a civil war, and each was as swiftly defeated by the next challenger.

In the process, as the historian Tacitus later noted, the year of the four emperors revealed two key secrets that continued to be a factor in subsequent history of the Empire. First, emperors

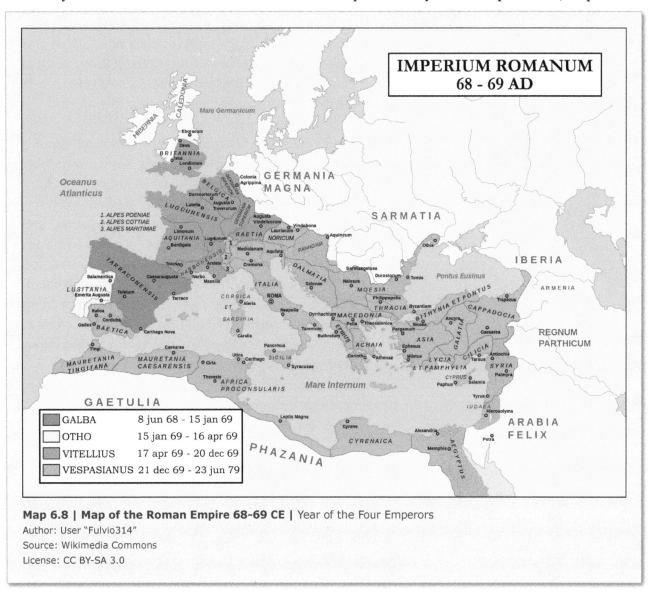

Map 6.8 | Map of the Roman Empire 68-69 CE | Year of the Four Emperors
Author: User "Fulvio314"
Source: Wikimedia Commons
License: CC BY-SA 3.0

could now be made outside of Rome, as seen, for example, with Galba's proclamation as emperor in Spain. Second, the army could make emperors; indeed, each of the four emperors in 69 CE was proclaimed emperor by his troops. These two *arcana imperii*, or "secrets of empire," as Tacitus dubbed them, continued to play a strong role in subsequent history of the Roman Empire. Their unveiling showed the declining importance of Rome as the center of political power and the concomitant decline in the importance of the Senate, once an advisory body to the entire empire, but now increasingly confined in its authority to Rome proper alone.

Several reasons caused **Vespasian**, a mere son of a tax-collector, to be the only successful emperor of 69 CE and the founder of the **Flavian dynasty**. First, a talented military commander, Vespasian

Figure 6.21 | Arch of Titus | Arch of Titus, celebrating his victory over Judaea, and featuring images of war spoils on the inside.
Author: User "Jebulon"
Source: Wikimedia Commons
License: CC0 1.0

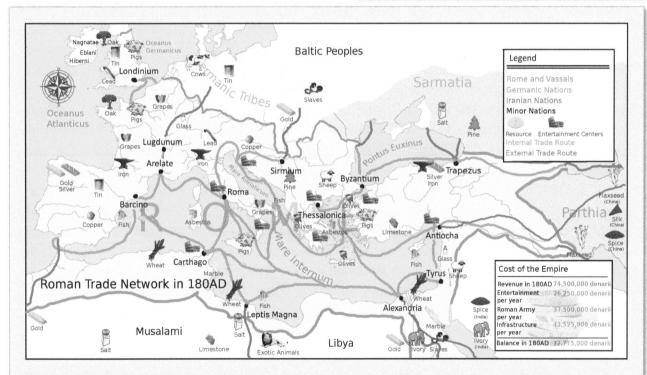

Map 6.9 | Map of Roman Trade Routes | This map of Roman trade routes c. 180 CE shows the economic prosperity in the urban centers.
Author: User "Adhavoc"
Source: Wikimedia Commons
License: CC BY-SA 3.0

proved to be already in command of a major military force in 69 CE, since he had been working on subduing the Jewish Revolt since 67 CE. Ironically, Nero had originally appointed him to command the Jewish War because of Vespasian's humble family origins—which to Nero meant that he was not a political threat. Second, Vespasian was the only one of the four emperors of 69 CE who had grown sons, and thus obvious successors. Furthermore, his older son, Titus, was already a popular military commander in his own right and cemented his reputation even further by his conquest of Jerusalem in 70 CE.

The Flavian dynasty did not last long, however, as it ended in 96 CE with the assassination of Emperor Domitian, Vespasian's younger son. The period from 96 CE to 180 CE saw a different experiment in determining imperial succession, instead of establishing traditional dynasties in which sons succeeded their fathers. Known as the period of the "**Five Good Emperors**," the trend in the second century CE was for each emperor to adopt a talented leader with potential as his successor. The result was what Edward Gibbon, the nineteenth-century British historian of Rome, called "the happiest age" of mankind. But was life everywhere in the Roman Empire in the second century equally happy for all? The evidence suggests that while Rome and other major urban centers flourished, life in the periphery could be a very different experience.

6.10.3 Center Versus Periphery in the Roman Empire: the Evidence of Pliny and Apuleius

Much of extant evidence from the Roman Empire comes from Rome and Italy. As is so often the case with empires, though, life in Rome was not representative of everyday life in the empire. The problems with which residents of Rome had to contend were a far cry from those with which residents of distant provinces had to deal. Careful examination of two sources from the second century CE reveals that the relationship of the Roman Empire to the provinces in the periphery was often uneasy. Writing about two different provinces within a half-century of each other, the two sources, Pliny the Younger and Apuleius, show the complicated blessings of living in a province far away from Rome that was yet under Roman rule.

It is shocking to consider today that most Roman governors setting out for the job received just one type of personnel to assist them with their duties: a flute-player, whose job was to play during sacrifice ceremonies. Since military forces were expensive to maintain and needed for emergencies in those areas of the Empire considered to be the most at risk for rebellion or outside attack, most governors did not have a legion stationed in their province. So how did governors resolve problems, and what resources did they find when they arrived? The single best sources of information about Roman provincial government is the prolific letter-writer Pliny the Younger, who served as governor of the province of **Bithynia** on the shore of the Black Sea in 111 – 113 CE. Pliny was a cautious and conscientious governor, and thus believed in consulting the emperor **Trajan** on every single issue that he encountered in his province. Luckily for us, their correspondence survives.

Pliny's letters reveal a myriad of problems that the governor was expected to solve: staffing personnel for prisons (is it acceptable to use slaves as prison guards?), building repairs and water supply, abandoned infants and their legal status (should they be considered slave-born or free?), fire brigades (are they a potential security risk to the Empire?) and, most famously, what to do with Christians in the province. The emperor Trajan patiently responded to each letter that he received from Pliny and appears to have placed stability and peace in the province foremost in his concerns. Thus, for instance, with regard to the issue of Christians in Bithynia, Trajan recommends that Pliny not worry about tracking down Christians in his province, as they were not a threat.

Another perspective from the periphery comes from the novel *Metamorphoses* or *Golden Ass*, written by the North African intellectual Apuleius sometime in the later part of the second century CE. The protagonist of the novel, Lucius, is a curious intellectual who is traveling through Greece and, through a magic experiment gone wrong, accidentally is turned into a donkey. For the remainder of the novel, Lucius, in his donkey form, is repeatedly stolen, traded, beaten, and abused, until finally being rescued at the end of the novel by the Egyptian goddess Isis, whose service he then enters as a priest. Throughout his travels, though, Lucius' observations reveal the limits of Romanization in the remote parts of Greece. Law and order are largely absent, highway robbery is simply a normal part of life, and on the one occasion when a poor farmer runs into a Roman soldier on the road, the soldier forcibly requisitions the farmer's sole possession: his donkey. Overall, the picture that Apuleius paints reveals the dark side of the *Pax Romana*. Yes, the Empire was at peace, and few attacks were happening on the frontiers. Yet life in the provinces was anything but truly peaceful.

6.10.4 Early Christianity in the Context of the Roman Empire

One of the problems that arose in Bithynia during Pliny's time as governor in 111 – 113 CE involved procedural questions on how to treat Christians in the province. Pliny does not seem to have much knowledge about them but is struck by what he describes as their stubbornness in clinging to their faith even when threatened with death. As he points out in his letter on the subject to Trajan, he has judged this stubbornness alone sufficient to merit punishment, presumably because it showed a dangerous level of disrespect towards Roman rule. Pliny's perspective is one of the earliest non-Christian sources about the new religion and shows how quickly it had spread over the Empire. But how and why did the new religion spread so rapidly over the Empire, and why was it so attractive to different populations? After all, quite a number of different cults and self-proclaimed prophets periodically appeared in the Roman world, yet none had the long-term impact of Christianity, which just two centuries after Pliny's day became the religion of the Roman emperor himself.

Early Christianity is, in some ways, an ancient historian's dream: for few other topics in Roman history do we have so many primary sources from both the perspective of insiders and outsiders, beginning with the earliest days of the movement. The **New Testament**, in particular, is a collection of primary sources by early Christians about their movement, with some of the letters composed merely twenty-five years after Jesus' crucifixion. It is a remarkably open document, collecting theological beliefs and stories about Jesus on which the faith was built. At the same time, however, the New Testament does not "white-wash" the early churches; rather, it documents their failings and short-comings with remarkable frankness, allowing the historian to consider the challenges that the early Christians faced from not only the outside but also within the movement.

The story of the origins of the faith is explained more plainly in the four Gospels, placed at the beginning of the New Testament. While different emphases are present in each of the four Gospels, the basic story is as follows: God himself came to earth as a human baby, lived a life among the Jews, performed a number of miracles that hinted at his true identity, but ultimately was crucified, died, and rose again on the third day. His resurrection proved to contemporary witnesses that his teachings were true and inspired many of those who originally rejected him to follow him. While the movement originated as a movement within Judaism, it ultimately floundered in Judea but quickly spread throughout the Greek-speaking world—due to the work of such early missionaries as **Paul**. (Visit the following link to view a map of Paul's missionary journeys: http://www.allaboutturkey.com/highres/paulsjourneys.jpg.)

It would be no exaggeration to call the early Christian movement revolutionary. In a variety of respects, it went completely against every foundational aspect of Roman (and, really, Greek) society. First, the Christian view of God was very different from the pagan conceptions of gods throughout the ancient Mediterranean. While in traditional Roman paganism the gods had petty concerns and could treat humans unfairly, if they so wished, Christianity by contrast presented the message that God himself became man and dwelt with men as an equal. This concept of God incarnate had revolutionary implications for social relations in a Christian worldview. For early Christians, their God's willingness to take on humanity and then sacrifice himself for the sins of the world served as the greatest equalizer: since God had suffered for all of them, they were all equally important to him, and their social positions in the Roman world had no significance in God's eyes. Finally, early Christianity was an apocalyptic religion. Many early Christians believed that Jesus was coming back soon, and they eagerly awaited his arrival, which would erase all inequality and social distinctions.

By contrast, traditional Roman society, as the conflict of the orders in the early Republic showed, was extremely stratified. While the conflict of the orders was resolved by the mid-Republic, sharp divisions between the rich and poor remained. While social mobility was

Figure 6.22 | Christ as the Good Shepherd in a Third-Century CE Catacomb Painting
Author: User "Wafflws9761"
Source: Wikimedia Commons
License: Public Domain

possible—for instance, slaves could be freed, and within a generation, their descendants could be Senators—extreme mobility was the exception rather than the rule. Furthermore, gender roles in Roman society were extremely rigid, as all women were subject to male authority. Indeed, the **paterfamilias**, or head of the household, had the power of life or death over all living under his roof, including in some cases adult sons, who had their own families. Christianity challenged all of these traditional relationships, nullifying any social differences, and treating the slave and the free the same way. Furthermore, Christianity provided a greater degree of freedom than women had previously known in the ancient world, with only the Stoics coming anywhere close in their view on gender roles. Christianity allowed women to serve in the church and remain unmarried, if they so chose, and even to become heroes of the faith by virtue of their lives or deaths, as in the case of the early martyrs. Indeed, the *Passion of the Saints Perpetua and Felicity*, which documents the two women's martyrdom in Carthage in 203 CE, shows all of these reversals of Roman tradition in practice.

The Passion of the Saints Perpetua and Felicity was compiled by an editor shortly after the fact and includes Perpetua's own prison diary, as she awaited execution. The inclusion of a woman's writings already makes the text unusual, as virtually all surviving texts from the Roman world are by men. In addition, Perpetua was a noblewoman, yet she was imprisoned and martyred together with her slave, Felicity. The two women, as the text shows, saw each other as equals, despite their obvious social distinction. Furthermore, Perpetua challenged her father's authority as *paterfamilias* by refusing to obey his command to renounce her faith and thus secure freedom. Such outright disobedience would have been shocking to Roman audiences. Finally, both Perpetua and Felicity placed their role as mothers beneath their Christian identity, as both gave up their babies in order to be able to be martyred. Their story, as those of other martyrs, was truly shocking in their rebellion against Roman values, but their extraordinary faith in the face of death proved to be contagious. As recent research shows, conversion in the Roman Empire sped up over the course of the second and third centuries CE, despite periodic persecutions by such emperors as Septimius Severus, who issued an edict in 203 CE forbidding any conversions to Judaism and Christianity. That edict led to the execution of Perpetua and Felicity.

Most of the early Christians lived less eventful (and less painful) lives than Perpetua and Felicity, but the reversals to tradition inherent in Christianity appear clearly in their lives as well. First, the evidence of the New Testament, portions of which were written as early as the 60s CE, shows that the earliest Christians were from all walks of life; Paul, for instance, was a tent-maker. Some other professions of Christians and new converts that are mentioned in the New Testament include prison guards, Roman military officials of varying ranks, and merchants. Some, like Paul, were Roman citizens, with all the perks inherent in that position, including the right of appeal to the Emperor and the right to be tried in Rome. Others were non-citizen free males of varying provinces, women, and slaves. Stories preserved in *Acts* and in the epistles of Paul that are part of the New Testament reveal ways—the good, the bad, and the ugly—in which these very different people tried to come together and treat each other as brothers and sisters in Christ. Some of the struggles that these early churches faced included sexual scandal (the Corinthian church witnessed the affair of a stepmother with her stepson), unnecessary quarrelling and litigation between members, and the challenge of figuring out the appropriate relationship between the requirements of Judaism and Christianity (to circumcise or not to circumcise? That was the question. And then there were the strict Jewish dietary laws). It is important to note that early Christianity appears to have been predominantly an urban religion and spread most quickly throughout urban centers. Thus Paul's letters address the churches in different cities throughout the Greek-speaking world and show the existence of a network of relationships between the early churches, despite the physical distance between them. Through that network, the churches were able to carry out group projects, such as fundraising for areas in distress, and could also assist Christian missionaries in their work. By the early second century CE, urban churches were led by bishops, who functioned as overseers for spiritual and practical matters of the church in their region.

6.11 THE THIRD-CENTURY CRISIS, AND LATE ANTIQUITY

While the second century CE was a time when the Empire flourished, the third century was a time of crisis, defined by political instability and civil wars, which ultimately demonstrated that the Empire had become too large to be effectively controlled by one ruler. Furthermore, the increasing pressures on the frontiers, which required emperors to spend much of their time on campaigns, resulted in the decline of the importance of the city of Rome. By the end of the third century, an experiment with dividing the empire showed a different model of rule, one which lasted, albeit with some interludes, until the last Western emperor, **Romulus Augustulus**, was deposed in 476 CE. While the political narrative of the third century and Late Antiquity could be described as a story of decline and fall of the Roman Empire (as the British historian Gibbon famously called it), nevertheless, it was a period in which culture, and especially Christian culture, flourished and replaced the traditional Roman pagan mode of thinking. Far from being culturally a time of "decline and fall," Late Antiquity, rather, was looking forward to the world of the Middle Ages. It was also the period of Roman history that produced some of its most influential leaders, most notably, Constantine.

6.11.1 The Third-Century Crisis and Diocletian

Although composed during a time of prosperity in the Empire, Apuleius' novel *Metamorphoses* showed tensions in the provinces, indicative of the failure of Empire to govern all portions equally effectively. While not visible in the larger urban centers until the third century CE, these tensions manifested themselves clearly during the third-century crisis, a period of almost fifty years (235 – 284 CE) that was characterized by unprecedented political, social, and economic upheaval across the Empire. In effect, the **third-century crisis** was the year 69 CE repeated, but this time it stretched over half a century. The same secrets of power that 69 CE revealed for the first time—that armies could make emperors and that emperors could be made outside of Rome—were now on display yet again.

In 235 CE, the emperor Severus Alexander was assassinated by his troops on campaign, who then proclaimed as emperor their general Maximinus Thrax. Over the subsequent half-century, twenty-six emperors were officially recognized by the Roman Senate, and a number of others

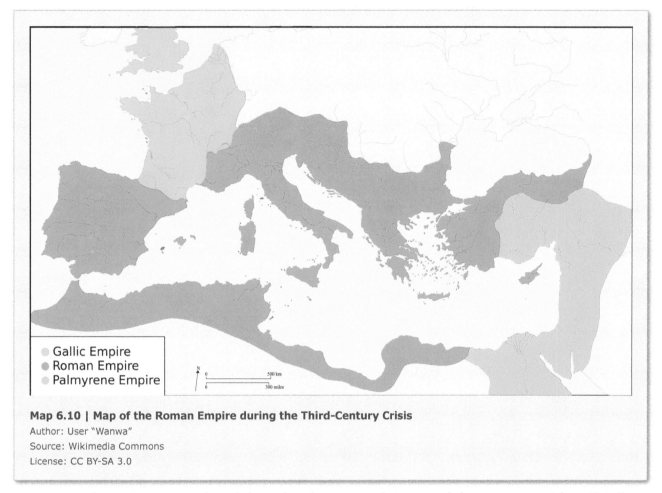

Map 6.10 | Map of the Roman Empire during the Third-Century Crisis
Author: User "Wanwa"
Source: Wikimedia Commons
License: CC BY-SA 3.0

were proclaimed emperors but did not live long enough to consolidate power and be officially accepted as emperors by the Senate. Most of these new emperors were military generals who were proclaimed by their troops on campaign. Most of them did not have any previous political experience and thus had no clear program for ruling the empire. The competing claims resulted in the temporary breaking away from the Roman Empire of regions to the East and the Northwest.

The political instability that resulted was not, however, the only problem with which the Empire had to contend. In addition to political upheaval and near-constant civil wars, the Empire was also dealing with increasing pressures on the frontiers, a plague that devastated the population, a famine, and rampant inflation. Roman emperors, starting with Nero, had been debasing the Roman coinage, but not until the third-century crisis did the inflation hit in full force.

The third-century crisis showed that a single emperor stationed in Rome was no longer equipped to deal with the challenges of ruling such a vast territory. And, indeed, so recognized the man who ended the crisis: the emperor **Diocletian**. Born to a socially insignificant family in the province of Dalmatia, Diocletian had a successful military career. Proclaimed emperor by his troops in 284 CE, Diocletian promptly displayed a political acumen that none of his predecessors in the third century possessed. Realizing that, as the third-century crisis showed, a single emperor in charge of the entire empire was a "sitting duck," whose assassination would throw the entire empire into yet another civil war, Diocletian established a new system of rule: the **Tetrarchy**, or the rule of four. He divided the empire into four regions, each with its own capital.

It is important to note that Rome was not the capital of its region. Diocletian clearly wanted to select as capitals cities with strategic importance, taking into account such factors as proximity to problematic frontiers. Of course, as a Dalmatian of low birth, Diocletian also lacked the emotional connection to Rome that the earliest emperors possessed. Two of the regions of the Tetrarchy were ruled by senior emperors, named Augusti ("Augustus" in the singular), and two were ruled by junior emperors, named Caesares ("Caesar" in the singular). One of the Augusti was Diocletian himself, with Maximian as the second Augustus. The two men's sons-in-law, Galerius and Constantus Chlorus, became the two Caesares. Finally, it is important to note that in addition to reforming imperial rule, Diocletian attempted to address other major problems, such as inflation, by passing the Edict of Maximum Prices. This edict set a maximum price that could be charged on basic goods and services in the Empire. He also significantly increased the imperial bureaucracy.

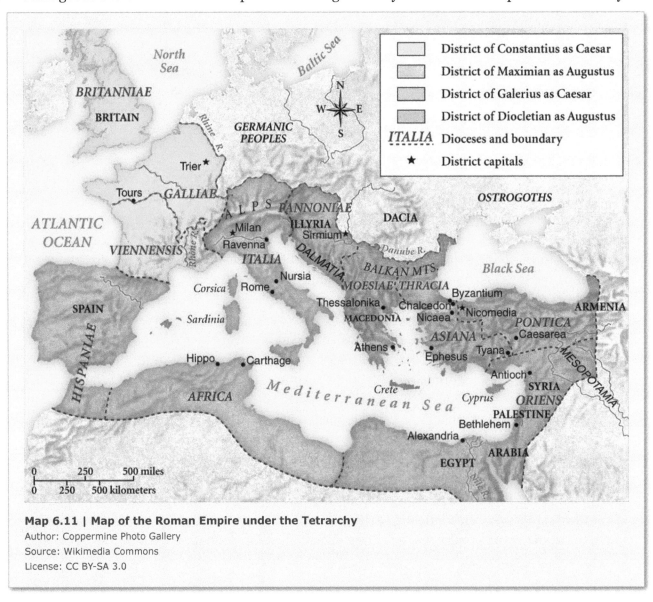

Map 6.11 | Map of the Roman Empire under the Tetrarchy
Author: Coppermine Photo Gallery
Source: Wikimedia Commons
License: CC BY-SA 3.0

In a nutshell, as some modern historians have described him, Diocletian was the most significant Roman reformer since Augustus.

Diocletian's political experiment was most clearly successful in achieving one goal: ending the third-century crisis. The four men were able to rule the empire and restore a degree of political stability. A statue column of the Tetrarchs together displays their message of unity in rule: the four men are portrayed identically, so it is impossible to tell them apart. Showing their predominantly military roles, they are dressed in military garb, rather than the toga, the garb of politicians and citizens, and each holds one hand on the hilt of his sword and hugs one of the other Tetrarchs with the other.

While it succeeded in restoring stability to the Empire, inherent within the Tetrarchy was the question of succession, which turned out to be a much greater problem than Diocletian had anticipated. Hoping to provide for a smooth transition of power, Diocletian abdicated in 305 CE and required Maximian to do the same. The two Caesares, junior emperors, were promptly promoted to Augusti, and two new Caesares were appointed. The following year, however,

Figure 6.23 | State Column of the Tetrarchs
Author: Nino Barbieri
Source: Wikimedia Commons
License: CC BY-SA 3.0

Constantius Chlorus, a newly minted Augustus, died. His death resulted in a series of wars for succession, which ended Diocletian's experiment of the Tetrarchy. The wars ended with Constantius' son, **Constantine**, reuniting the entire Roman Empire under his rule in 324 CE. In the process, Constantine also brought about a major religious shift in the Empire.

6.11.2 From Constantine to the Last Pagans of Rome

While traditional Roman religion was the ultimate melting pot, organically incorporating a broad variety of new cults and movements from the earliest periods of Roman expansion, Christianity's monotheistic exclusivity challenged traditional Roman religion and transformed Roman ways of thinking about religion in late antiquity. By the early fourth century CE, historians estimate that about ten percent of those living in the Roman Empire were Christians. With Constantine, however, this changed, and the previously largely underground faith grew exponentially because of the emperor's endorsement. The emperor's conversion must have seemed nothing short of miraculous to contemporaries, and a miracle is told to explain it in contemporary sources. Before a major battle in 312

CE, Constantine reportedly had a dream or a vision in which Christ himself told Constantine to place the Greek letters X and P (Chi, Rho, the first two letters of Christ's name in the Greek alphabet) on his soldiers' shields in order to assure victory.

Grateful for his subsequent victory, Constantine proceeded to play a major role in the government of the church over the course of his rule, although he was not baptized himself until he was on his deathbed. Constantine, for instance, summoned the First **Council of Nicaea** in 325 CE, which gathered major bishops from all over the Empire. The Council settled, among other issues, the question of the relationship of God the Father and God the Son, declaring them to have been one being from the creation of the world, thus affirming the doctrine of the Trinity. The Council set a significant precedent for communication of bishops in the Empire. It ended up being merely the first

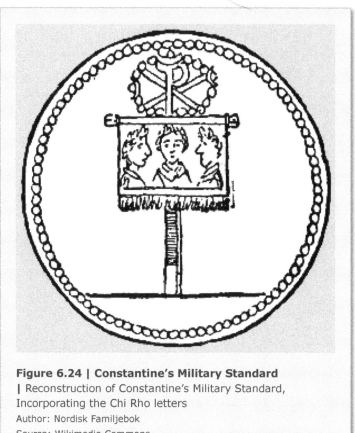

Figure 6.24 | Constantine's Military Standard
| Reconstruction of Constantine's Military Standard, Incorporating the Chi Rho letters
Author: Nordisk Familjebok
Source: Wikimedia Commons
License: Public Domain

of seven major ecumenical councils, the last of them being the Second Council of Nicaea in 787 CE. The councils allowed the increasingly different churches of the Eastern and Western parts of the Roman Empire to work together on key doctrines and beliefs of the church.

Last but not least, Constantine's rule marked the end of the city of Rome as the capital of the Roman Empire. Upon reuniting the Empire in 324 CE, Constantine established his capital at the old location of the Greek city of Byzantium, but renamed it **Constantinople** (the location of Byzantium appears on Map 6.11). The location had strategic advantages for the Empire at that stage. First, it had an excellent harbor. Second, it was close to the Persian frontier, as well as the Danube frontier, a trouble area that required attention from the emperor. Finally, building this new city, to which he also referred as "New Rome," allowed Constantine to send the message that his rule was a new beginning of sorts for the Roman Empire, which was now to be a Christian empire.

With the Emperor's backing, Christianity seems to have grown exponentially over the course of the fourth century CE, much to the chagrin of **Julian the Apostate**, Rome's final pagan emperor, who tried hard to restore traditional Roman paganism during his brief rule (361 – 363 CE). Finally, the Emperor **Theodosius** gradually banned paganism altogether by 395 CE. Thus a mere eighty-three years after Constantine's initial expression of support for Christianity, it became the official religion of Rome. Paganism continued to limp on for another century or so, but without state support, it slowly died out.

6.11.3 The Decline of the Empire—Looking Forward while Looking Back with Augustine and the Last Pagans of Rome

Imagine that you are a citizen of the greatest empire on earth. In fact, you reside in the greatest city of the greatest empire on earth. You feel protected by the pact that was made between the founders of your state and the traditional gods. The *pax deorum*, or peace with the gods, struck a clear bargain: as long as you and your state worshipped the gods and maintained peace with them, they would make it prosper. And prosper it did! Starting out as a tiny village on the marshes of the Tiber, the Roman Empire at its height encircled the entire Mediterranean, extending to Britain and the Rhine and Danube frontiers to the north, and including a wide strip of North Africa in its southern half. But something went so terribly wrong along the way, testing the gods' patience with Rome. A new sect started out in Judaea in the first century CE, one which followed a crucified Messiah. Spreading outward like a wildfire to all parts of the empire, this sect challenged and gradually replaced the worship of the traditional gods, bringing even the emperors into its fold, starting with Constantine in the early fourth century CE. This outright violation of the thousand-year old pact between the Romans and their gods could have only one outcome:

Figure 6.24 | Fresco Painting of Augustine, Sixth Century CE
Author: User "Mladifilozof"
Source: Wikimedia Commons
License: Public Domain

the ultimate punishment would come from the gods upon this rebellious state. And come it did; in 410 CE, the unthinkable happened. The city of Rome, untouched by foreign foe since the early days of the Republic, was sacked by the Goths, a Germanic tribe, led by the fearsome Alaric. How could something so terrible happen? And how could the Roman Empire recover from it? Such was the thought process of the typical Roman pagan, and especially the pagan aristocrat, as few of those as were left by 410 CE. And it was in response to these questions that Augustine, veteran theologian, philosopher, and bishop of Hippo in North Africa, wrote the final *magnum opus* of his career, the monumental twenty-two-book effort that he appropriately titled *De Civitate Dei Contra Paganos*, or On the **City of God** against the Pagans.

It is no coincidence that Peter Brown, the scholar credited with creating the academic field of study of Late Antiquity, began his career as a researcher by writing a biography of Augustine. Indeed, no other figure exemplifies so clearly the different culture that emerged in Late Antiquity, a culture of rethinking the Roman past, with an eye to a future in which Rome no longer existed as the capital of the Roman Empire. Born in North Africa in 354 CE, Augustine was educated in Rome and Milan, and, after a wild youth—about which he tells us in his *Confessions*—he rose to the post of the Bishop of Hippo in 396 CE. A famous figure by 410 CE, he was ideally suited to address the tragedy of the sack of Rome and the concerns that this event inspired in Christians and pagans alike.

In his book, Augustine presented an argument that challenged the core of Roman traditional beliefs about the state. Challenging the fundamental Roman pagan belief that Roman success was the result of the *pax deorum*, Augustine effectively argued that there was nothing special about Rome. It only prospered in its earlier history because God allowed it to do so. Furthermore, argued Augustine, obsession with Rome, emblematic of obsession with the earthly kingdom and way of life, was the wrong place for turning one's attention. The City of God was the only place that mattered, and the City of God was most definitely not Rome. By turning away from this world and focusing on the next, one could find true happiness and identity as a citizen of God's kingdom, which is the only city that is everlasting and free from threat of invasion or destruction.

Augustine's message would have made the Republican hero Cincinnatus weep. For Cincinnatus, nothing was more valuable than Rome. For Augustine, however, nothing was less valuable than Rome.

6.12 CONCLUSION: FROM LATE ANTIQUITY TO THE MIDDLE AGES

After the death of the Emperor Theodosius in 395 CE, the Roman Empire became permanently divided into Eastern and Western Empires, with instability and pressures on the frontiers continuing, especially in the West.

The sack of Rome by the Goths in 410 CE, which so shocked Augustine's contemporaries, was followed by an equally destructive sack of Carthage by the Vandals in 439 CE, as well as continuing raids of Roman territories by the Huns, a nomadic tribe from Eastern Europe, the Caucasus region, and south-east-

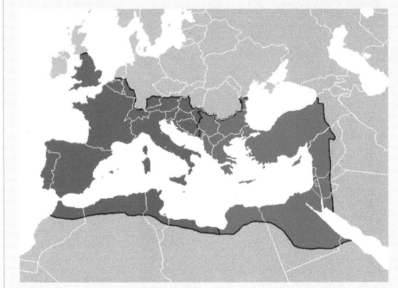

Map 6.12 | The Eastern and Western Roman Empires in 395 CE
Author: User "Geuiwogbil"
Source: Wikimedia Commons
License: CC BY-SA 3.0

ern China. The Huns experienced an especially prolific period of conquest in the 440s and early 450s CE under the leadership of Attila. While they were not able to hold on to their conquests after Attila's death in 453 CE, their attacks further destabilized an already weakened Western

Roman Empire. Finally, the deposition of the Emperor Romulus Augustulus in 476 CE marked the end of the Roman Empire in the West, although the Eastern half of the Empire continued to flourish for another thousand years.

The fall of the Roman Empire in the West, however, was not really as clear and dramatic a fall as might seem. A number of tribes carved out territories, each for its own control. Over the next five hundred years, led by ambitious tribal chiefs, these territories coalesced into actual kingdoms. Rome was gone, yet its specter loomed large over these tribes and their leaders, who spoke forms of Latin (albeit increasingly barbaric versions of it), believed in the Christian faith, and dreamed of the title of Roman Emperor.

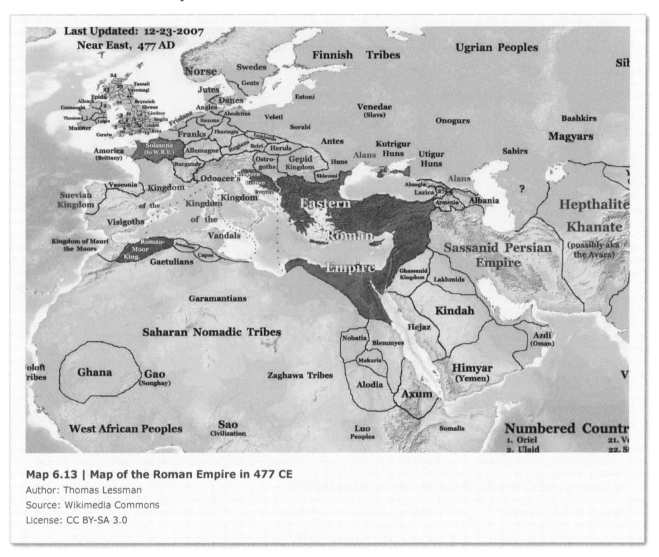

Map 6.13 | Map of the Roman Empire in 477 CE
Author: Thomas Lessman
Source: Wikimedia Commons
License: CC BY-SA 3.0

6.13 WORKS CONSULTED AND FURTHER READING

Beard, Mary, John North, and Simon Price. *Religions of Rome* (vol. 1 and vol. 2). Cambridge: Cambridge University Press, 1998.

Boatwright, Mary, Daniel Gargola, Noel Lenski, and Richard Talbert. *The Romans: From Village to Empire: A History of Rome from Earliest Times to the End of the Western Empire.* Oxford: Oxford University Press, 2011.

Brown, Peter. *Augustine of Hippo: A Biography.* Berkeley: University of California Press, 2013.

———. *The World of Late Antiquity: AD 150 – 750.* New York: W.W. Norton & Company, 1989.

Cameron, Alan. *The Last Pagans of Rome.* Oxford: Oxford University Press, 2010.

Champlin, Edward. *Nero.* Cambridge, MA: Belknap Press, 2005.

Coarelli, Filippo. *Rome and Environs: An Archaeological Guide.* Berkeley: University of California Press, 2014.

Faulkner, Neil. *Rome: Empire of the Eagles, 753 BC – AD 476.* New York: Routledge, 2009.

Flower, Harriet. *Ancestor Masks and Aristocratic Power in Roman Culture.* Oxford: Clarendon Press, 1996.

———. *Roman Republics.* Princeton: Princeton University Press, 2011.

Galinsky, Karl. *Augustan Culture.* Princeton: Princeton University Press, 1998.

Gruen, Erich. *The Last Generation of the Roman Republic.* Berkeley: University of California Press, 1995.

Harper, Kyle. *From Shame to Sin: The Christian Transformation of Sexual Morality in Late Antiquity.* Cambridge, MA: Harvard University Press, 2013.

Meeks, Wayne. *First Urban Christians: The Social World of the Apostle Paul.* New Haven: Yale University Press, 2003.

Morgan, Gwyn. *69 AD: The Year of Four Emperors.* Oxford: Oxford University Press, 2005.

Potter, David. *Constantine the Emperor.* Oxford: Oxford University Press, 2012.

———. *The Roman Empire at Bay: AD 180 – 395.* New York: Routledge, 2014.

Scullard, H. H. *From the Gracchi to Nero: A History of Rome from 133 BC to AD 68.* New York: Routledge, 1982.

Southern, Pat. *The Roman Army: A Social and Institutional History.* Oxford: Oxford University Press, 2007.

Stark, Rodney. *The Rise of Christianity: How the Obscure, Marginal Jesus Movement Became the Dominant Force in the Western World in a Few Centuries.* San Francisco: Harper, 1997.

Syme, Ronald. *The Roman Revolution.* Oxford: Oxford Paperbacks, 2002.

Wilken, Robert. *The Christians as the Romans Saw Them.* New Haven: Yale University Press, 2003.

6.14 LINKS TO PRIMARY SOURCES

Appian, Selections from *Civil Wars* on the Gracchi

http://legacy.fordham.edu/Halsall/ancient/appian-civwars1.asp

Apuleius, Resources and Selections from Writings

http://faculty.georgetown.edu/jod/apuleius/

Augustus, *Res Gestae Divi Augusti*

http://classics.mit.edu/Augustus/deeds.html

Caesar, *Gallic Wars* and *Civil War*

> http://mcadams.posc.mu.edu/txt/ah/Caesar/index.html

Cicero, First Oration Against Catiline

> http://www.bartleby.com/268/2/11.html

Etruscans (descriptions from Herodotus and Livy)

> http://legacy.fordham.edu/Halsall/ancient/etrucans2.asp

Livy, The Rape of Lucretia and Roman way of declaring war

> http://legacy.fordham.edu/Halsall/ancient/livy-rape.asp
> http://legacy.fordham.edu/Halsall/ancient/650livy1-34.asp

Passion of the Saints Perpetua and Felicity

> http://legacy.fordham.edu/halsall/source/perpetua.asp

Pliny, Correspondence with Trajan about Christians in Bithynia

> http://faculty.georgetown.edu/jod/texts/pliny.html

Pliny, Letters

> https://legacy.fordham.edu/halsall/ancient/pliny-letters.asp

Polybius, *Histories*, Books I and VI

> http://penelope.uchicago.edu/Thayer/E/Roman/Texts/Polybius/1*.html
> http://legacy.fordham.edu/Halsall/ancient/polybius6.asp

Polybius, Comparison of the Roman Maniple with Macedonian Phalanx

> http://legacy.fordham.edu/Halsall/ancient/polybius-maniple.asp

Sallust, *The Conspiracy of Catiline*

> http://www.forumromanum.org/literature/sallust/catilinae.html

Slavery in the Roman Republic: collected documents

> http://legacy.fordham.edu/Halsall/ancient/slavery-romrep1.asp

Suetonius, *Lives*

> http://legacy.fordham.edu/Halsall/ancient/suetonius-index.asp

Tacitus, *Annals* and *Histories*

> http://classics.mit.edu/Tacitus/annals.html
> http://classics.mit.edu/Tacitus/histories.html

The Twelve Tables

> http://avalon.law.yale.edu/ancient/twelve_tables.asp

7 Western Europe and Byzantium circa 500 - 1000 CE

Andrew Reeves

7.1 CHRONOLOGY

410 CE	Roman army abandons Britain
476 CE	The general Odavacar deposes last Western Roman Emperor
496 CE	The Frankish king Clovis converts to Christianity
500s CE	Anglo-Saxons gradually take over Britain
533 CE	Byzantine Empire conquers the Vandal kingdom in North Africa
535 – 554 CE	Byzantine Empire conquers the Ostrogothic kingdom in Italy
560s CE	Lombard invasions of Italy begin
580s CE	The Franks cease keeping tax registers
597 CE	Christian missionaries dispatched from Rome arrive in Britain
610 – 641 CE	Heraclius is Byzantine emperor
636 CE	Arab Muslims defeat the Byzantine army at the Battle of Yarmouk
670s CE	Byzantine Empire begins to lose control of the Balkans to Avars, Bulgars, and Slavs
674 – 678 CE	Arabs lay siege to Constantinople but are unsuccessful
711 CE	Muslims from North Africa conquer Spain, end of the Visigothic kingdom
717 – 718 CE	Arabs lay siege to Constantinople but are unsuccessful
717 CE	Leo III becomes Byzantine emperor. Under his rule, the Iconoclast Controversy begins.
732 CE	King Charles Martel of the Franks defeats a Muslim invasion of the kingdom at the Battle of Tours
751 CE	The Byzantine city of Ravenna falls to the Lombards; Pepin the Short of the Franks deposes the last Merovingian king and becomes king of the Franks; King Pepin will later conquer Central Italy and donate it to the pope
750s CE	Duke of Naples ceases to acknowledge the authority of the Byzantine emperor
770s CE	Effective control of the city of Rome passes from Byzantium to the papacy
c. 780 – 840 CE	The Carolingian Renaissance

782 CE	Charlemagne crushes a Saxon rebellion
787 CE	Second Council of Nicaea authorizes the use of icons in worship
793 CE	Viking raids begin
800 CE	Charlemagne crowned Roman emperor by Pope Leo III
830 CE	Abbasid caliph Al-Mamun founds the House of Wisdom in Baghdad
843 CE	In the Treaty of Verdun, Charlemagne's three sons, Lothar, Louis, and Charles the Bald, divide his empire among themselves
843 CE	Final resolution of the Iconoclast Controversy under Empress Theodora
846 CE	Muslim raiders from Aghlabid North Africa sack the city of Rome
c. 843 – 900 CE	Macedonian Renaissance
Mid-800s: CE	Cyril and Methodius preach Christianity to the Slavic peoples
864 CE	Conversion of the Bulgars to Christianity
867 CE	Basil I murders the reigning Byzantine emperor and seizes control of the Empire
871 – 899 CE	Alfred the Great is king of England. He defeats Norse raiders and creates a consolidated kingdom.
899 CE	Defeated by the Pechenegs, the Magyars begin moving into Central Europe
955 CE	Otto the Great, king of East Francia, defeats the Magyars in battle
976 – 1025 CE	Basil II is Byzantine Emperor
988 CE	Vladimir, Grand Prince of Kiev, converts to Christianity

7.2 INTRODUCTION

It was Christmas day in Rome in the year 800 CE. The cavernous interior of St. Peter's Church smelled faintly of incense. Marble columns lined the open space of the nave, which was packed with the people of Rome. At the eastern end of the church, which was the most prestigious in Western Europe, King Charles of the Franks knelt before the pope. A tall man when standing, the Frankish king had an imposing presence even on his knees. He wore the dress of a Roman patrician: a tunic of multi-colored silk, embroidered trousers, and a richly embroidered cloak clasped with a golden brooch at his shoulder. As King Charles knelt, the pope placed a golden crown, set with pearls and precious stones of blue, green, and red, on the king's head. He stood to his full height of six feet and the people gathered in the church cried out, "Hail Charles, Emperor of Rome!" The inside of the church filled with cheers. For the first time in three centuries, the city of Rome had an emperor.

Outside of the church, the city of Rome itself told a different story. The great circuit of walls built in the third century by the emperor Aurelian still stood as a mighty bulwark against attackers. Much of the land within those walls, however, lay empty. Although churches of all sorts could be found throughout the city, pigs, goats, and other livestock roamed through the open fields and streets of a city retaining only the faintest echo of its earlier dominance of the whole of the Mediterranean world. Where once the Roman forum had been a bustling market, filled with merchants from as far away as India, now the crumbling columns of long-abandoned temples looked out over a broad, grassy field where shepherds grazed their flocks.

The fountains that had once given drinking water to millions of inhabitants now went unused and choked with weeds. The once great baths that had echoed with the lively conversation of thousands of bathers stood only as tumbled down piles of stone that served as quarries for the men and women who looked to repair their modest homes. The Coliseum, the great amphitheater that had rung with the cries of Rome's bloodthirsty mobs, was now honeycombed with houses built into the tunnels that had once admitted crowds to the games in the arena.

And yet within this city of ruins, a new Rome sprouted from the ruins of the old. Just outside the city walls and across the Tiber River, St. Peter's Basilica rose as the symbol of Peter, prince of the Apostles. The golden-domed Pantheon still stood, now a church of the Triune God rather than a temple of the gods of the old world. And, indeed, all across Western Europe, a new order had arisen on the wreck of the Roman state. Although this new order in many ways shared the universal ideals of Rome, its claims were even grander, for it rested upon the foundations of the Christian faith, which claimed the allegiance of all people. How this post-Roman world had come about is the subject to which we shall turn.

Ever since the fifteenth century, historians of Europe have referred to the period between the fall of the Western Roman Empire and the Italian Renaissance (which took place in the fifteenth and sixteenth centuries) as the Middle Ages. The term has problems, but it is still useful because it demonstrates that Europe was undergoing a transitional period: it stood between, in the middle of, those times that we call "modern" (after 1500 CE) and what we call the ancient world (up to around 500 CE). This Middle Age would see a new culture grow up that combined elements of Germanic culture, Christianity, and remnants of Rome. It is to the political remnants of Rome that we first turn.

7.3 QUESTIONS TO GUIDE YOUR READING

1. How did the Germanic peoples of Western Europe relate to the former Roman territories over which they had taken control?

2. Which of Justinian's policies had the longest-lasting effects?

3. What crises did the Byzantine Empire face during the reign of Heraclius?

4. What was a way that the Byzantine state reorganized itself to face the challenges of seventh- and eighth-century invasions?

5. Why did the Iconoclast emperors believe that using images in worship was wrong?

6. How did the Church provide a sense of legitimacy to the kings of the Franks?

7. How did the majority of people in Europe and the Byzantine Empire live in the Early Middle Ages (i.e., *c.* 500 to 1000 C.E.)?

8. How did East Francia and England respond to Viking attacks?

7.4 KEY TERMS

- Al-Andalus
- Alcuin of York
- Anglo-Saxons
- Avars
- Balkans
- Battle of Tours
- Body of Civil Law/Justinian Code
- Bulgars
- Byzantine Empire/Byzantium
- Capitularies
- Carolingians
- Carolingian Renaissance
- Cathedral Church
- Charlemagne
- Charles Martel
- Constantinople
- Cyrillic
- Demonetization
- Dependent farmers
- Donation of Constantine
- Eastern Orthodox
- Exarch
- Hagia Sophia
- Iconoclast Controversy
- Iconoclasts
- Iconophiles
- Idolatry
- Kievan Rus
- Lateran
- Lombards
- Macedonian Dynasty
- Magnaura
- Mayor of the Palace/Major Domo
- Merovingians
- Ostrogoths
- Papal States
- Pillage and Gift
- Pope
- Romance Languages
- Ruralization
- Rus
- Scriptorium
- Slavs
- Slavonic
- Tagmata
- Themes
- Vandals
- Vikings
- Visigoths

7.5 SUCCESSOR KINGDOMS TO THE WESTERN ROMAN EMPIRE

The Germanic peoples who had invaded the Roman Empire over the course of the fifth century had, by the early 500s, established a set of kingdoms in what had been the Western Empire. The **Vandals** ruled North Africa in a kingdom centered on Carthage, a kingdom whose pirates threatened the Mediterranean for nearly eighty years. The **Visigoths** ruled Spain in a kingdom that preserved many elements of Roman culture. In Italy, the Roman general Odavacar had established his own kingdom in 476 before being murdered by the **Ostrogoth** king Theodoric, who established a kingdom for his people in Italy, which he ruled from 493 to his death in 526. Vandal, Visigoth, and Ostrogoth peoples all had cultures that had been heavily influenced over decades or even centuries of contact with Rome. Most of them were Christians, but, crucially, they were not Catholic Christians, who believed in the doctrine of the Trinity, that God is one God but three distinct persons of the Father, the Son (Jesus Christ), and the Holy Spirit. They were rather Arians, who believed that Jesus was lesser than God the Father (see Chapter Six). Most of their subjects, however, were Catholics.

The Catholic Church increasingly looked to the bishop of Rome for leadership. Over the fifth century, the bishop of Rome had gradually come to take on an increasing level of prestige among other bishops. Rome had been the city where Peter, whom tradition regarded as the chief of Christ's disciples, had ended his life as a martyr. Moreover, even though the power of the Western Roman Empire crumbled over the course of the 400s, the city of Rome itself remained prestigious. As such, by the fourth and fifth centuries, the bishops of Rome were often given the title of *papa*, Latin for "father," a term that we translate into **pope**. Gradually, the popes came to be seen as

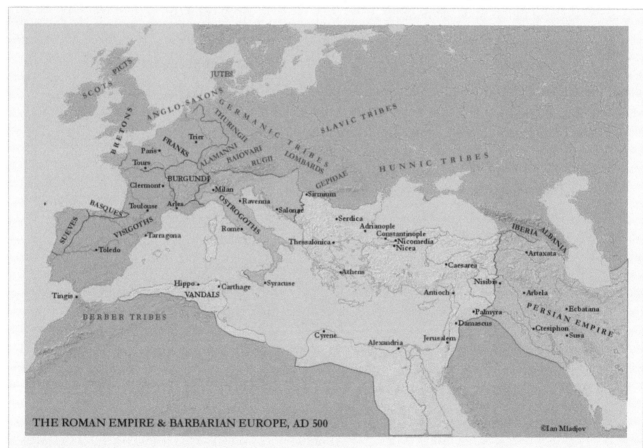

THE ROMAN EMPIRE & BARBARIAN EUROPE, AD 500   ©Ian Mladjov

Map 7.1 | The Roman Empire and Barbarian Europe 500 CE
Author: Ian Mladjov
Source: Original Work
License: © Ian Mladjov. Used with permission.

having a role of leadership within the wider Church, although they did not have the monarchial authority that later popes would claim.

In the region of Gaul, the Franks were a Germanic people who had fought as mercenaries in the later Roman Empire and then, with the disintegration of the Western Empire, had established their own kingdom. One key reason for the Frankish kingdom's success was that its kings received their legitimacy from the Church. In the same way that the Christian Church had endorsed the Roman Emperors since Constantine and, in return, these emperors supported the Church, the Frankish kings took up a similar relation with the Christian religion. King Clovis (r. 481 – 509) united the Franks into a kingdom, and, in 496, converted to Christianity. More importantly, he converted to the Catholic Christianity of his subjects in post-Roman Gaul. This would put the Franks in sharp contrast with the Vandals, Visigoths, and Ostrogoths, all of whom were Arians.

In none of these kingdoms, Visigothic, Ostrogothic, Frankish, or Vandal, did the Germanic peoples who ruled them seek to destroy Roman society—far from it. Rather, they sought homelands and to live as the elites of the Roman Empire had done before them. Theodoric, the king of the Ostrogoths (r. 493 – 526), had told his people to "obey Roman customs... [and] clothe [them] selves in the morals of the toga."[1] Indeed, in the generations after the end of the Western Empire in the late 400s, an urban, literate culture continued to flourish in Spain, Italy, and parts of Gaul. The Germanic peoples often took up a place as elites in the society of what had been Roman provinces, living in rural villas with large estates. Local elites shifted their allegiances from the vanished Roman Empire to their new rulers. In many ways, the situation of Western Europe was analogous to that of the successor states of the Han Dynasty such as Northern Wei, in which an invader took up a position as the society's new warrior aristocracy (see Chapter Four).

But even though the Germanic kings of Western Europe had sought to simply rule in the place of (or along with) their Roman predecessors, many of the features that had characterized Western Europe under the Romans—populous cities; a large, literate population; a complex infrastructure of roads and aqueducts; and the complex bureaucracy of a centralized state—vanished over the course of the sixth century. Cities shrank drastically, and in those regions of Gaul north of the Loire River, they nearly all vanished in a process that we call **ruralization.** As Europe ruralized and elite values came to reflect warfare rather than literature, schools gradually vanished, leaving the Church as the only real institution providing education. So too did the tax-collecting apparatus of the Roman state gradually wither in the Germanic kingdoms. The Europe of 500 may have looked a lot like the Europe of 400, but the Europe of 600 was one that was poorer, more rural, and less literate.

7.6 BYZANTIUM: THE AGE OF JUSTINIAN

An observer of early sixth-century Italy would have thought that its Ostrogothic kingdom was the best poised to carry forward with a new state that, in spite of its smaller size than the Roman Empire, nevertheless had most of the same features. But the Ostrogothic kingdom would only last a few decades before meeting its violent end. That end came at the hands of the Eastern

---

1   Cassiodorus, *Variae*, trans. Thomas Hodgkin, in *The Medieval Record: Sources of Medieval History*, ed. Alfred J. Andrea (New York: Houghton Mifflin, 1997), 58.

Roman Empire, the half of the Roman Empire that had continued after the end of the Empire in the West. We usually refer to that empire as the **Byzantine Empire** or **Byzantium**.

The inhabitants and rulers of this Empire did not call themselves Byzantines, but rather referred to themselves as Romans. Their empire, after all, was a continuation of the Roman state. Modern historians call it the Byzantine Empire in order to distinguish it from the Roman Empire that dominated the Mediterranean world from the first through fifth centuries. The Byzantine Empire or Byzantium is called such by historians because Byzantium had been an earlier name for its capital, **Constantinople.**

By the beginning of the sixth century, the Byzantine Army was the most lethal army to be found outside of China. In the late fifth century, the Byzantine emperors had built up an army capable of dealing with the threat of both Hunnic invaders and the Sassanids, a dynasty of aggressively expansionist kings who had seized control of Persia in the third century. Soon this army would turn against the Ostrogothic kingdom of Italy.

Figure 7.1 | Mosaic of Justinianus I from the Basilica San Vitale
Author: Petar Milosevic
Source: Wikimedia Commons
License: CC BY-SA 3.0

The man who would destroy the Ostrogrothic as well as the Vandal kingdom was the emperor Justinian (r. 527 – 565). Justinian had come from the ranks not of the aristocracy of the Eastern Roman Empire, but rather from the Army. Even before the death of his uncle, the emperor Justin I (r. 518 – 527), Justinian was taking part in the rule of the Empire. Upon his accession to the imperial throne, he carried out a set of policies designed to emphasize his own greatness and that of his empire.

He did so in the domain of art and architecture, sponsoring the construction of numerous buildings both sacred and secular. The centerpiece of his building campaign was the church called **Hagia Sophia**, Greek for "Divine Wisdom." His architects placed this church in the central position of the city of Constantinople, adjacent to the imperial palace. This placement was meant to demonstrate the close relationship between the Byzantine state and the Church that legitimated that state. The Hagia Sophia would be the principle church of the Eastern Empire for the next thousand years, and it would go on to inspire countless imitations.

This Church was the largest building in Europe. Its domed roof was one hundred and sixty feet in height, and, supported by four arches one hundred and twenty feet high, it seemed to float in the diffuse light that came in through its windows. The interior of the church was burnished with gold, gems, and marble, so that observers in the church were said to have claimed that they could not tell if they were on earth or in heaven. Even a work as magnificent as the Hagia Sophia, though, showed a changed world: it was produced with mortar rather than concrete, the technology for the making of which had already been forgotten.

While Justinian's building showed his authority and right to rule which came from his close relations with the Church, his efforts as a lawmaker showed the secular side of his authority. Under his direction, the jurist Tribonian took the previous 900 years' worth of Roman Law and systematized it into a text known as the ***Body of Civil Law*** or the **Justinian Code**. This law code, based on the already-sophisticated system of Roman law, would go on to serve as the foundation of European law, and thus of much of the world's law as well.

Although the Justinian Code was based on the previous nine centuries of gathered law, Roman Law itself had changed over the course of the fifth century with the Christianization of the Empire. By the time of Justinian's law code, Jews had lost civil rights to the extent that the law forbade them from testifying in court against Christians. Jews would further lose

Figure 7.2 | Haga Sophia Interior
Author: Andreas Wanhra
Source: Wikimedia Commons
License: Public Domain

civil rights in those Germanic kingdoms whose law was influenced by Roman law as well. The reason for this lack of Jewish civil rights was that many Christians blamed Jews for the execution of Jesus and also believed that Jews refused out of stubbornness to believe that Jesus had been the messiah. A Christian Empire was thus one that was often extremely unfriendly to Jews.

As Byzantine emperor (and thus Roman emperor), Justinian would have regarded his rule as universal, so he sought to re-establish the authority of the Empire in Western Europe. The emperor had other reasons as well for seeking to re-establish imperial power in the West. Both Vandal Carthage and Ostrogoth Italy were ruled by peoples who were Arians, regarded as heretics by a Catholic emperor like Justinian.

During a dispute over the throne in the Vandal kingdom, the reigning monarch was overthrown and had fled to the Eastern Empire for help and protection. This event gave Justinian his chance. In 533, he sent his commander Belisarius to the west, and, in less than a year, this able and capable general had defeated the Vandals, destroyed their kingdom, and brought North Africa back into the Roman Empire. Justinian then turned his sights on a greater prize: Italy, home of the city of Rome itself, which, although no longer under the Empire's sway, still held a place of honor and prestige.

In 535, the Roman general Belisarius crossed into Italy to return it to the Roman Empire. Unfortunately for the peninsula's inhabitants, the Ostrogothic kingdom put up a more robust fight than had the Vandals in North Africa. It took the Byzantine army nearly two decades to destroy the Ostrogothic kingdom and return Italy to the rule of the Roman Empire. In that time, however, Italy itself was irrevocably damaged. The city of Rome had suffered through numerous sieges and sacks. By the time it was fully in the hands of Justinian's troops, the fountains that had provided drinking water for a city of millions were choked with rubble, the aqueducts that had supplied them smashed. The great architecture of the city lay in ruins, and the population had shrunk drastically from what it had been even in the days of Theodoric (r. 493 – 526).

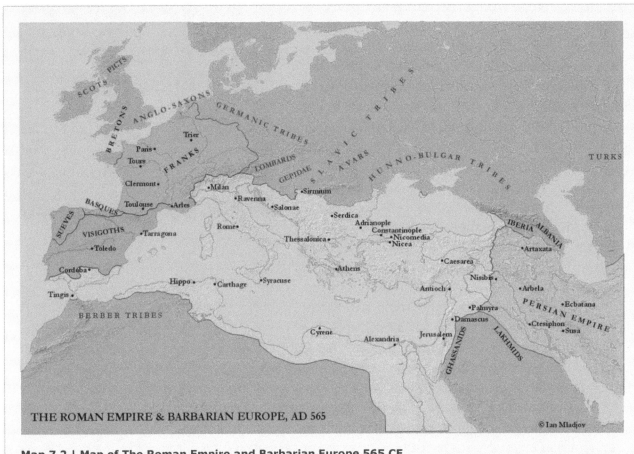

Map 7.2 | Map of The Roman Empire and Barbarian Europe 565 CE
Author: Ian Mladjov
Source: Original Work
License: © Ian Mladjov. Used with permission.

7.6.1 The Aftermath of Justinian

Justinian's reconquest of Italy would prove to be short-lived. Less than a decade after restoring Italy to Roman rule, the **Lombards**, another Germanic people, invaded Italy. Although the city of Rome itself and the southern part of the peninsula remained under the rule of the Byzantine Empire, much of northern and central Italy was ruled either by Lombard kings or other petty nobles.

But war was only one catastrophe to trouble Western Europe. For reasons that are poorly understood even today, the long-range trade networks across the Mediterranean Sea gradually shrank over the sixth and seventh centuries. Instead of traveling across the Mediterranean, wine, grain, and pottery were increasingly sold in local markets. Only luxury goods—always a tiny minority of most trade—remained traded over long distances.

Nor was even the heartland of Justinian's empire safe from external threat. The emperor Heraclius (r. 610 – 641) came to power in the midst of an invasion of the Empire by the Sassanid Persians, who, under their king Khusrau (see Chapter Eight), threatened the Empire's very existence, his armies coming within striking range of Constantinople itself. Moreover, Persian armies had seized control of Egypt and the Levant, which they would hold for over a decade. Heraclius thwarted the invasion only by launching a counter-attack into the heart of the Persian Empire that resulted, in the end, in a Byzantine victory. No sooner had the Empire repelled one threat than another appeared that would threaten the Empire with consequences far more severe.

Under the influence of the Prophet Muhammad, the tribes of the Arabian deserts had been united under first the guidance of the Prophet and then his successors, the caliphs and the religion founded by Muhammad, Islam (see Chapter Eight). Under the vigorous leadership of the first caliphs, Arab Muslim armies invaded both Sassanid Persia and the Byzantine Empire. At the Battle of Yarmouk in 636, although the Byzantines and Arabs were evenly matched, the Byzantine field army was badly beaten. In the aftermath, first Syria and Palestine and then Egypt fell from Christian Byzantine rule to the cultural and political influence of Islam.

The seventh century also saw invasions by various semi-nomadic peoples into the **Balkans**, the region between the Greek Peloponnese and the Danube River. Among these peoples were the Turkic **Bulgars**, the **Avars** (who historians think might have been Turkic), as well as various peoples known as **Slavs**. The Avars remained nomads on the plains of central Europe, but both Bulgars and Slavs settled in Balkan territories that no longer fell under the rule of the Byzantine state. Within a generation, the Empire had lost control of the Balkans as well as Egypt, territory comprising an immense source of wealth in both agriculture and trade. By the end of the seventh century, the Empire was a shadow of its former self.

Indeed, the Byzantine Empire faced many of the social and cultural challenges that Western Europe did, although continuity with the Roman state remained. In many cases, the cities of the Byzantine Empire shrank nearly as drastically as did the cities of Western Europe. Under the threat of invasion, many communities moved to smaller settlements on more easily defended hilltops. The great metropolises of Constantinople and Thessalonica remained centers of urban life and activity, but throughout much of the Empire, life became overwhelmingly rural.

Even more basic elements of a complex society, such as literacy and a cash economy, went into decline, although they did not cease. The Byzantine state issued less money and, indeed, most transactions ceased to be in cash at this time. The economy was **demonetized**. Even literacy rates shrank. Although churchmen and other elites would often still have an education, the days of the Roman state in which a large literate reading public would buy readily-available literature were gone. As in the west, literacy increasingly became the preserve of the religious.

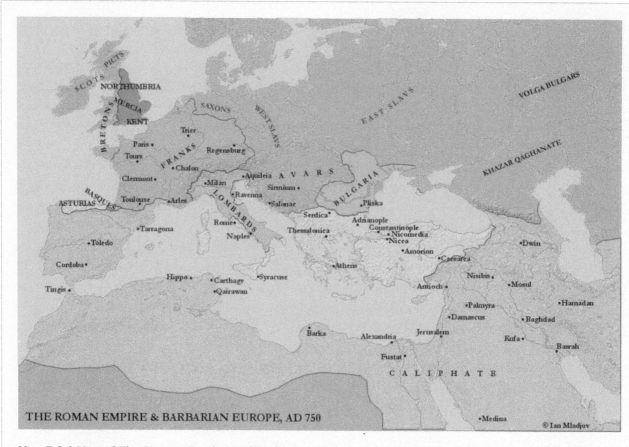

Map 7.3 | Map of The Roman Empire and Barbarian Europe 750 CE
Author: Ian Mladjov
Source: Original Work
License: © Ian Mladjov. Used with permission.

7.7 PERSPECTIVES: POST-ROMAN EAST AND WEST

In many ways, the post-Roman Germanic kingdoms of Western Europe and the Byzantine Empire shared a similar fate. Both saw a sharp ruralization, that is, a decline in the number of inhabited cities and the size of those cities that were inhabited. Both saw plunges in literacy. And both saw a state that was less competent—even at tax collection. Moreover, the entire Mediterranean Sea and its environs showed a steady decline in high-volume trade across the ocean, a decline that lasted for nearly two and a half centuries. By around the year 700, almost all trade was local.

But there remained profound differences between Byzantium and the Germanic kingdoms of Western Europe. In the first place, although its reach had shrunk dramatically from the days of Augustus, the imperial state remained. Although the state collected less in taxes and issued less money than in earlier years, even in the period of the empires' greatest crisis, it continued to mint some coins and the apparatus of the state continued to function. In Western Europe, by contrast, the Germanic kingdoms gradually lost the ability to collect taxes (except for the Visigoths in Spain). Likewise, they gradually ceased to mint gold coins. In Britain, cities had all but vanished, with an island inhabited by peoples living in small villages, the remnants of Rome's imperial might standing as silent ruins.

The post-Roman world stands in contrast to post-Han China. Although the imperial state collapsed as it had in Rome, in China, literacy never declined as drastically as it had done in the Roman Empire, and the apparatus of tax collection and other features of a functional state remained in the Han successor states to an extent that they did not in either Rome or Byzantium.

7.8 THE BRITISH ISLES: EUROPE'S PERIPHERY[2]

Figure 7.3 | Manuscript of Bede's *History of the English Church and People*
Author: User "Apex infinity"
Source: Wikimedia Commons
License: Public Domain

In many of the lands that had been part of the Roman Empire, the Germanic peoples who had taken over western Europe built kingdoms. Although not as sophisticated as the Roman state, they were still recognizable as states. This situation stood in sharp contrast to Britain. To the northwest of Europe, the Roman Army had abandoned the island of Britain in 410. The urban infrastructure brought about by the Roman state began to decay almost immediately, with towns gradually emptying out as people returned to rural lifeways that had existed prior to Rome's arrival.

At nearly the same time that the Roman Army withdrew from Britain, a group of Germanic peoples known as the Anglo-Saxons were moving into the island from the forests of Central Europe that lay to the east, across the ocean. Unlike the Franks, Visigoths, and Ostrogoths, each of whom had kingdoms, the social organization of the Anglo-Saxons was comparatively unsophisticated. They were divided up among chiefs and kings who might have only had a few hundred to a few thousand subjects each.

Over the period between about 410 and 600, the Anglo-Saxons gradually settled in and conquered much of southeastern Britain, replacing the Celtic-speaking peoples and their language. The island of Britain was one that was completely rural. All that remained of the state-building of the Romans was the ruins of abandoned cities.

---

2   Although the British Isles were peripheral to global affairs and even those of Western Europe, people at the time did regard these islands as part of the world that people of the Middle East and Mediterranean regarded as "civilized" (if only as its westernmost periphery). The ninth-century Arabic writer Harun ibn Yahya said of the British that "They are the last of the lands of the Greeks, and there is no civilization beyond them," quoted in Caitlin R. Green, "Britain, the Byzantine Empire, and the concept of an Anglo-Saxon 'Heptarchy': Harun ibn Yahya's ninth-century Arabic description of Britain," The Personal Website and Blog of Dr. Caitlin R. Green, http://www.caitlingreen.org/2016/04/heptarchy-harun-ibn-yahya.html (accessed 26 June 2016).

And yet, it would be England (called England because the name is derived from the word Anglo-Saxon) and the island of Ireland to its west that would lead to an increase of schools and literacy across Western Europe. In the fifth century, Christian missionaries traveled to Ireland and converted many of its peoples. In the early 600s, Pope Gregory the Great sent missionaries to the island of Britain. The English peoples adopted Christianity (usually under the initiative of their kings) over the course of the next several decades, which in turn led to the founding of monasteries. These monasteries would usually have attached schools so that those seeking to live as monks could have access to the texts of the Bible, the **liturgy**, and the writings of other churchmen. English churchmen like Benedict Biscop (c. 628 – 690) traveled south to Rome and returned to England with cartloads of books. English and Irish monks would often copy these books in their own monasteries.

Indeed, England saw not only the copying of older books, but also the composition of original literature, which was rare elsewhere in Western Europe of this time. The English churchman Bede (672 – 735) composed a history of England's people. He wrote this history to show how the Anglo-Saxons had adopted Christianity. Within a few decades of the island's peoples converting to Christianity, English and Irish monks were traveling to Western Europe, either to establish monasteries in lands already Christian or to serve as missionaries to those still-pagan peoples in the forests of central Europe.

7.9 BYZANTIUM: CRISIS AND RECOVERY

Although the Byzantine Empire was a remnant of the Roman state, by the eighth century it was much weaker than the Roman Empire under Augustus or even than the Eastern Empire under Justinian. After their conquest of Egypt, the forces of the caliphate had built a navy and used it to sail up and lay siege to Constantinople itself in two sieges lasting from 674 to 678 and from 717 to 718. On land, to the northwest, the Empire faced the threat of the Bulgars, Slavs, and Avars. The Avars, a nomadic people, in particular demanded that the Byzantine state pay them a hefty tribute to avoid raids. At the very moment that the Empire was in greatest need of military strength, it was a poorer empire than it had ever been.

The solution was a reorganization of the military. Instead of having a military that was paid out of a central treasury, the emperors divided the Empire up into regions called **themes**. Each theme would then equip and pay soldiers, using its agricultural resources to do so. Themes in coastal regions were responsible for the navy. In many ways, the **theme** was similar to the way that other states would raise soldiers in the absence of a strong bureaucratic apparatus. One might liken it to what we call feudalism in Zhou China, Heian Japan, and later Medieval Europe.

The greatest crisis faced by the Byzantine Empire in these years of crisis was the so-called **Iconoclast Controversy**. From the fourth and fifth centuries, Christians living in the Eastern Mediterranean region had used **icons** to aid in worship. An icon is a highly stylized painting of Christ, the Virgin Mary (his mother), or the saints. Often icons appeared in churches, with the ceiling painted with a picture of Christ or with an emblem of Christ above the entrance of a church.

Other Christians opposed this use of images. In the Old Testament (the term Christians use to refer to the Hebrew Bible), the Ten Commandments forbid the making of "graven images" and using them in worship (Exodus 20:4-5). Certain Christians at the time believed that to make an image even of Jesus Christ and his mother violated that commandment, arguing that to paint such pictures and use them in worship was **idolatry,** that is, worshiping something other than God. Muslims leveled similar critiques at the Christian use of icons, claiming that it showed Christians had fallen from the correct worship of God into idolatry.

Emperor Leo III (r. 717 – 41) accepted these arguments; consequently, in his reign he began to order icons removed (or painted over) first from churches and then from monasteries as well as other places of public display. His successors took further action, ordering the destruction of icons. These acts by Leo led to nearly a century of controversy over whether the use of icons in worship was permissible to Christians. The **iconophiles** argued that to use a picture of Christ and the saints in worship was in line with the Christian scriptures so long as the worshiper worshiped God with the icon as a guide, while the **icolono-clasts** proclaimed that any use of images in Christian worship was forbidden.

Figure 7.4 | Icon of the Virgin Mary
Author: User "Myrabella"
Source: Wikimedia Commons
License: Public Domain

In general, monks and civilian elites were iconophiles, while iconoclasm was popular with the army. In Rome, which was slipping out from under the jurisdiction of the Byzantine emperors, the popes strongly rejected iconoclasm. Some historians have argued that Leo and his successors attacked icon worship for reasons other than religious convictions alone, including the fact that monks who venerated icons had built up their own power base; more importantly, in confiscating the wealth of iconophile monasteries, the emperor would be able to better fund his armed forces.

The iconophile empress Irene, ruling on behalf of her infant son Constantine V (r. 780 – 797), convoked a new church council to bring an end to the controversy. At the 787 Second Council of Nicaea, the Church decreed that icons could be used in worship. Final resolution of the Iconoclast Controversy, however, would have to wait until 843, when the empress Theodora at last over-turned iconoclastic policies for good upon the death of her husband, the emperor Theophilus (r. 829 – 843). From this point forward, historians usually refer to the Greek-speaking churches of the eastern Mediterranean and those churches following those same patterns of worship as **Eastern Orthodox**.[3]

Although the iconoclast emperors had made enemies in the Church, they were often effective military commanders, and they managed to stabilize the frontiers with Arabs, Slavs, and Bulgars. In spite of the fact that the Byzantine armies of the eighth century would have some successes against Arabs and Slavs, it was during the eighth century that Byzantium increasingly lost control of Italy. While a Byzantine **exarch**, or governor, in Ravenna (in northeastern Italy) would rule the city of Rome, even these Italian territories were gradually lost. Ravenna fell to the Lombards in 751; the duke of Naples ceased to acknowledge the authority of the emperor in Constantinople in the 750s; and the popes in Rome, long the de facto governors of the city, became effectively independent from Byzantium in the 770s. The popes in particular would increasingly look to another power to secure their city: the Franks.

7.10 WESTERN EUROPE: THE RISE OF THE FRANKS

At the west end of the Mediterranean and in northern Europe, the kingdom of the Franks would become the dominant power of the Christian kingdoms. Justinian's armies had destroyed the Ostrogothic kingdom in Italy in the sixth-century Gothic War. A century and a half later, in 711, Arab Muslim invaders from North Africa conquered the Visigoth kingdom in Spain and established Muslim rule. From that time on, we refer to Muslim-ruled Spain of the early Middle Ages as **al-Andalus**. The destruction of these two kingdoms left the Franks as the dominant power of Western Europe. They were already the premier power in northern Gaul, but as the seventh century went on, they established themselves in southern Gaul as well, gradually subordinating other Germanic peoples to their rule.

The first dynasty of Frankish kings was known as the **Merovingians**, so named for Merovech, a possibly legendary ancestor of Clovis, the first Christian king of the Franks. The Franks' power grew in Western Europe for several reasons. In the first place, the Frankish monarchy had fewer civil wars than did that of the Visigoths. The Frankish kingdom did face the weakness that it was sometimes divided among a king's sons at his death (since Germanic peoples often looked at a kingdom as the king's personal property), with warfare resulting within the divided kingdom. Nevertheless, although the kingdom might be split by inheritance and later reunited, there existed in general a strong sense of legitimate dynastic succession. In addition, the Catholic Church provided the Frankish monarchs with a sense of legitimacy as it had since the days of Clovis.

But as the Frankish kingdom expanded, many elements of what had characterized the Roman state continued to wither. One reason for this decline was that the nature of warfare had changed in Western Europe. Soldiers were no longer paid out of a government treasury; instead, they were rewarded with lands whose surplus they would use to outfit themselves with military equipment. The soldiers thus served as a warrior aristocracy. Even those families who had been Roman elites took up

---

3   Modern historians use this label for convenience. At the time, both Churches in the Greek-speaking eastern Mediterranean and those following the pope would have said that they were part of the Catholic Church (the word catholic comes from a Greek word for "universal"). The churches in the eastern Mediterranean and Eastern Europe were coming to differ enough in terms of practice, worship, and thought that we can refer to them as distinct from the Catholic Church of Western Europe.

a military lifestyle in order to prosper in the new order. In addition, the Frankish kings increasingly made use of a **pillage and gift** system. In a pillage and gift system, a king or other war leader rewards his loyal soldiers by granting them gifts that came from the plunder of defeated enemies. With armies financed either by pillage and gift or by the wealth of an individual aristocrat's lands, the Frankish kingdom had little reason for maintaining taxation. Moreover, the kingdom's great landowners who supported the monarchy had a strong interest in seeing that they were not taxed efficiently; by the 580s, the Frankish government had simply ceased to update the old Roman tax registers.

One particular role that would gain prominence among the Frankish monarchy was that of the **Major Domo**, or **Mayor of the Palace**. The Mayor of the Palace was a noble who would grant out lands and gifts on behalf of the king and who would, in many cases, command the army. Gradually, one family of these Mayors of the Palace would rise to prominence above all other noble families in the Frankish kingdom: the **Carolingians.**

This dominant family's more prominent members were named Charles, which in Latin is Carolus, hence the name Carolingians. By the mid-seventh century, the Carolingians had come to hold the position of Mayor of the Palace as a hereditary one. Over the early eighth century, the Carolingian Mayors of the Palace had become the actual rulers of the Frankish realm, while the Merovingian kings had little or no actual power. The earliest significant Carolingian major domo to dominate the Carolingian court was **Charles Martel** (r. 715 – 741). He was an able and effective military commander who—even though he rewarded his troops with lands taken from the Church—was able to show himself a defender of the Christian religion by defeating a Muslim attack on Gaul from al-Andalus in 732 at the **Battle of Tours** and by defeating the Saxons, who were at this point still largely pagans living in the forests to the northeast of the Frankish kingdom, in 738. These victories over both pagan and Muslim allowed for Martel to present his family as defenders of the Church and of the Christian religion in general.

Martel's successor, Pepin the Short (r. 741 – 68), would take the final step towards wresting power away from the Merovingians and making his family the kings of the Franks. He followed in Martel's footsteps in using the Church to shore up his legitimacy. He wrote to Pope Zachary I (r. 741 – 752), asking whether one who exercised the power of a king should have that power, or if instead the person with the name of king should have that power. Pope Zachary answered that kingship should rest with the person exercising its power—because a king ruled the earth on behalf of God, so a king who was not properly ruling was not doing his God-given duty. Thus the last Merovingian king was deposed by the combined powers of the Carolingian Mayors of the Palace and the popes. This close cooperation between Church and crown would go on to be a defining feature of the Frankish monarchy.

The relationship between the papacy and the Carolingians not only involved the popes legitimating Pepin's coup d'état, but also included the Carolingian monarchs providing military assistance to the popes. Shortly after Zachary's letter allowing Pepin to seize power, Pepin marched south to Italy to give the pope military assistance against the Lombards. He took control of several cities and their surrounding hinterlands and gave these cities as a gift to the papacy. The popes would thus rule a set of territories in central Italy known as the **Papal States** from Pepin's day until the mid-nineteenth century.

The greatest of the Carolingians was the figure we refer to as **Charlemagne**, whose name means Charles the Great. As king of the Franks, he spent nearly the entirety of his reign leading his army in battle. To the southeast, he destroyed the khanate of the Avars, the nomadic people who had lived by raiding the Byzantine Empire. To the northeast of his realm, he subjugated the Saxons of Central Europe and had them converted to Christianity—a sometimes brutal process. When the Saxons rebelled in 782, he had 4,000 men executed in one day for having returned to their old religion. To the south in Italy, Charlemagne militarily conquered the Lombard kingdom and made himself its king. The only area in which he was less successful was in his invasion of al-Andalus. Although his forces seized control of several cities and fortresses in northeastern Spain (to include places like Barcelona), he was, on the whole, less successful against Spain's Umayyad emirs. One reason for this lack of success was that, compared to Charlemagne's other

foes, al-Andalus was organized into a sophisticated state, and so better able to resist him.

By the end of the eighth century, Charlemagne ruled nearly all of Western Europe. Indeed, he ruled more of Western Europe than anyone since the Roman emperors of four centuries before. In the winter of 800, a mob expelled Pope Leo III from Rome. Charlemagne took his troops south of the Alps and restored the pope to his position in the **Lateran** palace, the palace complex to the northeast of Rome where the popes both lived and conducted most of their business.

On Christmas Day in 800, Charlemagne was attending worship at St. Peter's Church. During that ceremony, the pope placed a crown upon Charlemagne's head and declared him to be Roman emperor. Historians are not sure whether Charlemagne had planned this coronation or had simply gone up to the pope for a blessing and was surprised by this crown. The question of who had planned this coronation is controversial because the pope's crowning the emperor could have been interpreted to mean that the crown was the pope's to confer.

Indeed, it was around this time that a document known as the **Donation of Constantine** appeared in Western Europe. This document was a forgery—to this day, scholars do not know who forged it—that claimed to have been written by the Roman emperor Constantine (see Chapter Six). According to this forged document, the emperor Constantine had been cured of leprosy by Pope Sylvester I and, in thanks,

Figure 7.5 | Painting of Charlemagne |
Charlemagne as imagined by Albrecht Dürer in the fifteenth century.
Author: Albrecht Dürer
Source: Wikimedia Commons
License: Public Domain

had given the popes authority over all of the Western Empire. Although false, this document would go on to provide the popes with a claim to rule not just central Italy, but Western Europe as a whole.

Charlemagne's coronation by the pope marked the culmination of the creation of a new society built on the wreck of the Western Roman Empire. This new society would be Christian and based on close cooperation of Church and State—although each would regard the others' sphere of influence as separate.

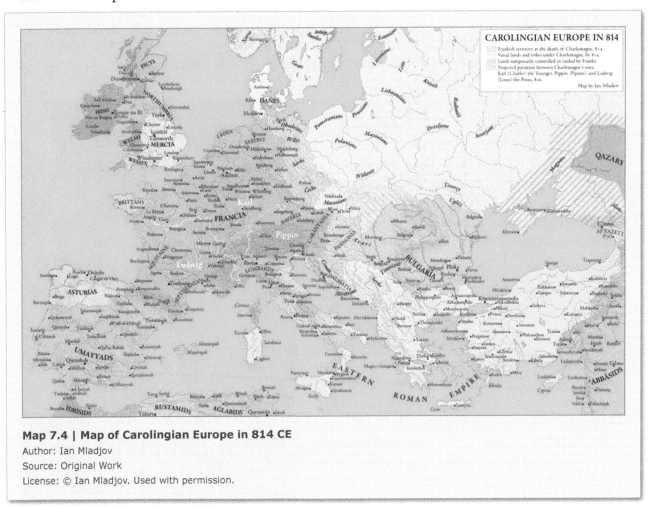

Map 7.4 | Map of Carolingian Europe in 814 CE
Author: Ian Mladjov
Source: Original Work
License: © Ian Mladjov. Used with permission.

7.11 GLOBAL CONTEXT

Although Charlemagne possessed one of the most powerful armies in Europe, the Mediterranean, and the Middle East, his empire was hardly a state compared to Tang China, the Abbasid Caliphate, or the Byzantine Empire. Compared to the armies of the Byzantine Emperors, the Abbasid Caliphs, and above all, the Tang emperors, Charlemagne's army was merely a very large war band, financed not by a state with a working system of taxation and treasury, but rather by the plunder of defeated enemies. Although he issued decrees known as **capitularies** through the agencies of Church and state, the realm had little in the way of either bureaucracy or infrastructure, save for the decaying network of the Roman Empire's roads. Indeed, although Charlemagne had sought to have a canal dug between the Rhine and Danube rivers, this project failed—a fitting illustration of the gap between the ambitions of Charlemagne and the reality.

7.11.1 The Carolingian Renaissance

In those territories that had been part of the Western Roman Empire, most of the people had spoken Latin, and Latin was the language of literature. By the time of the Carolingians, Latin was starting to change into the languages that would eventually become French, Spanish, Italian, and Portuguese, languages that we call **Romance** because they are descended from Latin, the language of the Romans. The Bible, the liturgy, and writings of theology and on saints, however, were still in Latin, although the skill in reading and writing Latin possessed by what few people remained literate had decreased, and in a less literate society, there were fewer books of Roman literature available in Western Europe. The copying of books had gradually dwindled with literacy.

The Carolingians were known not only for their conquests and attempted revival of the Roman Empire, but also for their efforts to improve the state of learning in the Carolingian Empire, particularly with respect to the Bible, theology, and literature of Ancient Rome. They also sought to increase the number of schools and books in the realm. Historians refer to this effort as the **Carolingian Renaissance**. Historians call it the Carolingian Renaissance in order to distinguish it from the later Italian Renaissance, an effort by northern Italian intellectuals of the fourteenth and fifteenth centuries to restore teaching and learning of the literature of Ancient Greece and Rome.

Charlemagne and his successors sponsored an increase in learning by the Church in order to promote moral reform. Charlemagne, like his predecessors and successors, considered himself a defender and protector of the Christian religion. As such, he wanted to make sure that the Church was promoting a reform of morality.

Figure 7.6 | The Chapel of Charlemagne's Palace at Aachen
Author: CEphoto, Uwe Aranas
Source: Wikimedia Commons
License: CC BY-SA 3.0

Moral reform would need to start with clergy, and these clergy would need to be able to adequately read the text of the Bible and of the writings of other churchmen (and –women).

Charlemagne's efforts would be centered on schools and centers of book production, what scholars of medieval Europe call **scriptoria** (singular **scriptorium**). He had help in that there were already many high quality schools attached to monasteries that had been founded in his empire by English and Irish monks. The main school of his empire was the school in his palace at Aachen. His palace itself was based on Roman and Byzantine architecture, as a demonstration that he possessed the same sort of legitimacy as the Roman Emperors. He then invited some of the best scholars of Western Europe to his court—including **Alcuin of York** (735 – 804), a monk from England—in order both to supervise his own court school and to direct the Church of the Frankish Empire to improve learning.

This improvement of learning included the establishment of new cathedral schools, schools attached to a **cathedral church** (i.e., a church where the bishop of a diocese—the basic geographic division of the Church—has his seat). These schools trained not only men and women from the church, but also the children of Frankish aristocrats, and in some cases women as well as men. As a result, an increasing number of Frankish nobles would be literate or at least would sponsor efforts by schools to further train people.

Likewise, under the guidance of Charlemagne and the Frankish church, scriptoria throughout his empire launched on a massive new effort to copy new books. Many of these books were religious in character, although Carolingian monks (and nuns) would also copy books from Ancient Rome that had been written by pagans; many of these ancient books, like the poetry of Virgil (see Chapter Six), would serve as the basis of the curriculum of Western Europe's schools as they had since the Roman Empire. A Christian of the eighth century would believe that even works by pagans would nevertheless afford their readers education and, thus, self-improvement.

7.11.2 The Macedonian Renaissance

The Byzantine Empire had been that half of the Roman Empire where the language of life and culture was not Latin, but Greek. At around the same time as the Carolingians' efforts, the Byzantine Empire also saw close cooperation of Church and State to revive the study of ancient literature and improve learning. The Byzantine Empire had suffered from a collapse of literacy, which, while not as severe as Western Europe's, had still resulted in a much less literate population. As such, an effort similar to that of the Carolingians was necessary in the Greek-speaking Eastern Mediterranean. We call this effort the **Macedonian Renaissance** because it reached its fullest expression under a dynasty of Byzantine emperors that we call the **Macedonian Dynasty** (867 – 1056).

The efforts of the Macedonian Dynasty, however, had begun earlier. The efforts to improve the availability of books and to

Figure 7.7 | Paris Psaulter |
Picture from a Byzantine Greek manuscript written during the Macedonian Renaissance
Author: User "Neuceu"
Source: Wikimedia Commons
License: Public Domain

increase learning began during the Iconoclast Controversy as both Iconophiles and Iconoclasts had sought to back up their positions by quoting from the Bible and the Church Fathers. Emperor Theophilus (r. 829 – 842), one of the last Iconoclast emperors, had had Leo the Mathematician found a school in the emperor's palace in Constantinople, a palace known as the **Magnaura**. Like Charlemagne's palace at Aachen, this school would go on to serve as the foundation for a revived learning among elites, only this learning was in Greek, rather than Latin.

Following the final triumph of the Iconophiles, these efforts continued with Photius, patriarch of Constantinople from 858 to 867 and then from 877 to 886, as a particular sponsor of monastic schools in the Byzantine Empire and of the copying of books in Ancient Greek, particularly works like those of Plato's philosophy and the epic poetry of Homer.

7.11.3 Comparisons with the Abbasids

We should also note the global context of both the Carolingian and the Macedonian Renaissance. Carolingian and Macedonian Emperors were not the only ones seeking to increase the availability of ancient texts from the time of the Greeks and Romans. The Abbasid Caliphs under al-Mamun (r. 813 – 883) and his successors also sponsored the work of the House of Wisdom, whose scholars translated the philosophy of the Ancient Greeks into Arabic. Like the Christians of the Carolingian and Byzantine Empires, the Muslims of the Caliphate believed that one could learn from pagan writers even if they had not believed in the one Creator God.

7.12 DAILY LIFE IN WESTERN EUROPE AND THE BYZANTINE EMPIRES

In both Western Europe and Byzantium, the vast majority of the population was made up of farmers. In Western Europe, some of these were what we call **dependent farmers**, living on the lands of aristocrats and giving over much of their surplus to their landlords. But in many villages, the majority of farmers might live on their own land and even enjoy a form of self-government. Although some slavery existed—especially in zones of conflict like the Mediterranean—compared to the days when vast estates had been worked by unfree labor (see Chapter Six), the workers on the estates of the Frankish aristocracy or those free and independent farmers enjoyed greater freedom than had their Roman counterparts. But their life was precarious. Crop yields were low, at ratios of around 3:1—meaning only giving back about three times as much as was planted—and the average Carolingian farmer frequently did not get adequate calories.

So too did most of the population of the Byzantine Empire live in small villages, living at a subsistence level, and selling what rare surplus they had. Byzantium, like its Western European counterpart, was fundamentally rural.

The nobles of Western Europe were generally part of a warrior aristocracy. These aristocrats often outfitted and equipped themselves based on the wealth of their lands. Their values were those of service to their king and loyalty and bravery in battle. Nobles would often not live on their lands but follow the royal court, which would itself travel from place to place rather than having a fixed location. Battle may have been frequent, but until Charlemagne, the scale of battle was often small, with armies numbering a few hundred at most.

Along with its warrior aristocracy, gender roles in the Frankish kingdom—like those of the Roman Empire that came before it—reflected a patriarchal society. The Christian religion generally taught that wives were to submit to their husbands, and the men who wrote much of the religious texts often thought of women in terms of weakness and temptations to sexual sin. "You," an early Christian writer had exclaimed of women, "are the devil's gateway...you are the first deserter of the divine law...you destroyed so easily God's image, man..."[4] The warlike values of the aristocracy meant that aristocratic women were relegated to a supporting role, to the management of the household. Both Roman and Germanic law placed women in subordination to their fathers and then, when married, to their husbands.

That said, women did enjoy certain rights. Although legally inferior to men in Roman Law (practiced in the Byzantine Empire and often among those peoples who were subjects of the Germanic aristocracies), a wife maintained the right to any property she brought into a marriage. Women often played a strong economic role in peasant life, and, as with their aristocratic counterparts, peasant women often managed the household even if men performed tasks such as plowing and the like. And the Church gave women a fair degree of autonomy in certain circumstances. We often read of women choosing to become nuns, to take vows of celibacy, against the desires of their families for them to marry. These women, if they framed their choices in terms of Christian devotion, could often count on institutional support in their life choices. Although monasticism was usually limited to noblewomen, women who became nuns often had access to an education. Certain noble-women who became abbesses could even become powerful political actors in their own right, as did Gertrude of Nivelles (c. 621 – 659), abbess of the monastery of Nivelles in what is today Belgium.

7.13 CAROLINGIAN COLLAPSE

Charlemagne's efforts to create a unified empire did not long outlast Charlemagne himself. His son, Louis the Pious (r. 814 – 840), succeeded him as emperor. Louis continued Charlemagne's project of Church reform; unlike Charlemagne, who had had only one son to survive into adulthood, Louis had three. In addition, his eldest, Lothar, had already rebelled against him in the 830s. When Louis died, Lothar went to war with Louis's other two sons, Charles the Bald and Louis the German. This civil war proved to be inconclusive, and, at the 843 Treaty of Verdun, the Carolingian Empire was divided among the brothers. Charles the Bald took the lands in the west of the Empire, which would go on to be known first as West Francia and then, eventually, France. To the East, the largely German-speaking region of Saxony and Bavaria went to Louis the German. Lothar, although he had received the title of emperor, received only northern Italy and the land between Charles's and Louis's kingdoms.

This division of a kingdom was not unusual for the Franks—but it meant that there would be no restoration of a unified Empire in the West, although both the king of Francia and the rulers of Central Europe would each claim to be Charlemagne's successors.

---

4   Tertullian, *On the Apparel of Women, 1:1.*

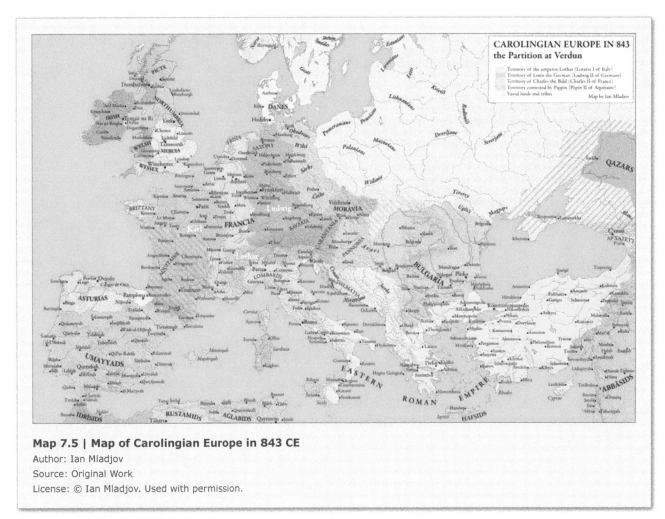

Map 7.5 | Map of Carolingian Europe in 843 CE
Author: Ian Mladjov
Source: Original Work
License: © Ian Mladjov. Used with permission.

Western Europe faced worse problems than civil war between the descendants of Charlemagne. In the centuries following the rise of the post-Roman Germanic kingdoms, Western Europe had suffered comparatively few invasions. The ninth and tenth centuries, by contrast, would be an "age of invasions."

In the north of Europe, in the region known as Scandinavia, a people called the Norse had lived for centuries before. These were Germanic peoples, but one whose culture was not assimilated to the post-Roman world of the Carolingian west. They were still pagan and had a culture that, like that of other Germanic peoples, was quite warlike. Their population had increased; additionally, Norse kings tended to exile defeated enemies. These Norsemen would often take up raiding other peoples, and when they took up this activity, they were known as **Vikings**.

One factor that allowed Norse raids on Western Europe was an improvement in their construction of ships. Their ships were long, flexible, and also had a shallow enough draft that they did not need harbors so could be pulled up along any beach. Moreover, they were also shallow enough of draft that they could sail up rivers for hundreds of miles. What this feature of these ships meant was that Norse Vikings could strike at many different regions, often with very little warning.

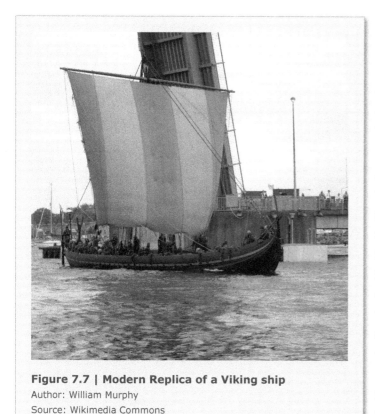

Figure 7.7 | Modern Replica of a Viking ship
Author: William Murphy
Source: Wikimedia Commons
License: CC BY-SA 2.0

Even more significant for the Norse attacks was that Western Europe in the ninth and tenth centuries was made up of weak states. The three successor kingdoms to Charlemagne's empire were often split by civil war. Although King Charles the Bald (r. 843 – 877) enjoyed some successes against the Vikings, his realm in general was subject to frequent raids. England's small kingdoms were particularly vulnerable. From 793, England had suffered numerous Viking raids, and these raids increased in size and scope over the ninth century. Likewise, to the west, Ireland, with its chiefs and petty kings, lacked the organization of a state necessary to deal with sustained incursions.

The result was that not only did Viking raids on the British Isles increase in scope and intensity over the ninth century, but also the Norse eventually came to take lands and settle.

To the south and west, al-Andalus suffered fewer Norse attacks than did the rest of Europe. A sophisticated, organized state with a regular army and a network of fortresses, it was able to effectively deal with raiders. The Spanish emir Abd-al Rahman II defeated a Viking raid and sent the Moroccan ambassador the severed heads of 200 Vikings to show how successful he had been in defending against them.

To the east, the Norse sailed along the rivers that stretched through the forests and steppes of the area that today makes up Russia and Ukraine. The Slavic peoples living there had a comparatively weak social organization, so in many instances they fell under Norse domination. The Norsemen Rurik and Oleg were said to have established themselves as rulers of Slavic peoples as well as the princedoms of Novgorod and Kiev, respectively, in the ninth century. These kingdoms of Slavic subjects and Norse masters became known as the **Rus.**

Further to the south, the Norse would often move their ships over land between rivers until finally reaching the Black Sea and thus Constantinople and Byzantium. Although on occasion a Norse raid would have great success against Byzantine forces, in general, a powerful and organized state meant that, as with al-Andalus, the Norse encountered less success.

Norse invaders were not the only threat faced by Western Europe. As the emirs of Muslim North Africa gradually broke away from the centralized rule of the Abbasid Caliphate (see Chapter Eight), these emirs, particularly those of Tunisia, what is today Algeria, and Morocco turned to legitimate themselves by raid and plunder; this aggression was often directed at southern Francia and Italy. The Aghlabid emirs in particular not only seized control of Sicily, but also sacked the city of Rome itself in 846. North African raiders would often seize territory on the coasts of Southern Europe and raid European shipping in order to increase their own control of trade and commerce. In addition, the emirs of these North African states would use the plunder from their attacks to reward followers, in another example of the pillage and gift system.

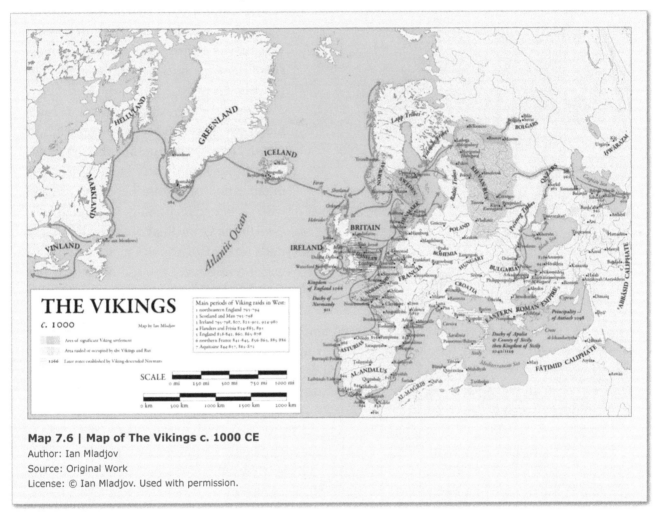

Map 7.6 | Map of The Vikings c. 1000 CE
Author: Ian Mladjov
Source: Original Work
License: © Ian Mladjov. Used with permission.

Central Europe also faced attacks, these from the Magyars, a steppe people. The Magyars had been forced out of Southeastern Europe by another steppe people, the Pechenegs, and so from 899 on migrated into Central Europe, threatening the integrity of East Francia. As was the case with other steppe peoples, their raids on horseback targeted people in small unfortified communities, avoiding larger settlements. They eventually settled in the plains of Eastern Europe to found the state of Hungary; although they made Hungary their primary location, they nevertheless continued to raid East Francia through the first part of the tenth century.

7.13.1 An Age of Invasions in Perspective

Norse, Magyar, and Muslim attacks on Europe wrought incredible damage. Thousands died, and tens of thousands more were captured and sold into slavery in the great slave markets of North Africa and the Kievan Rus. These raids furthered the breakdown of public order in Western Europe.

But these raids had effects that also brought long-term benefits. Both Norse and Muslim pirates traded just as much as they raided. Indeed, even the plunder of churches and selling of the gold and silver helped create new trade networks in both the North Sea and Mediterranean. These new trade networks, especially where the Norse had established settlements in places like Ireland, gradually brought about an increase in economic activity.

All told, we should remember this "age of invasions" in terms both of its human cost and of the economic growth it brought about.

7.13.2 New States in Response to Invasions

In response to the invasions that Europe faced, newer, stronger states came into being in the British Isles and in Central Europe. In England, Norse invasions had destroyed all but one of the Anglo-Saxon kingdoms. The only remaining kingdom was Wessex. Its king, Alfred the Great (r. 871 – 899), was able to stop Norse incursions by raising an army and navy financed by a kingdom-wide tax. This tax, known as the **geld,** was also used to finance the construction of a network of fortresses along the frontier of those parts of England still controlled by the Norse. This new system of tax collection would eventually mean that England, a small island on the periphery, would eventually have the most sophisticated bureaucracy in Western Europe (although we must note that in comparison with a Middle Eastern or East Asian state, this bureaucracy would be considered rudimentary and primitive).

Likewise, in Central Europe, the kings of East Francia, the region made up of those Saxon territories the Carolingians had conquered in the eighth century as well as various peoples to the south and east, gradually built a kingdom capable of dealing with Magyar invaders. Henry the Fowler (r. 919 – 936) took control of East Francia after the end of the Carolingian Dynasty. He was succeeded by Otto the Great (r. 936 – 973), whose creation of a state was partially the result of luck: his territory contained large silver mines that allowed him to finance an army. This army was able to decisively defeat the Magyar raiders and also allow these kings to expand their power to the east, subjugating the Slavic peoples living in the forests of Eastern Europe.

7.14 THE TENTH-CENTURY CHURCH

As a result of endemic chaos in Western Europe, the Church suffered as well. The moral and intellectual quality of bishops and abbots declined sharply, as church establishments fell under the domination of warlords. These warlords would often appoint members of their families or personal allies to positions of leadership in the Church, appointments based not on any competence or sense of dedication to duty, but rather on ties of loyalty. This was the case even in Rome, when families of Roman nobles fought over the papacy. Between 872 and 965, twenty-four popes were assassinated in office.

7.15 BYZANTINE APOGEE: THE MACEDONIAN EMPERORS

For Byzantium, however, the ninth and tenth centuries represented a time of recovery and expansion. In the first place, the height of the Macedonian Renaissance took place in the later ninth and tenth centuries, resulting in a growth of learning among both clergy and lay elites. This growth of learning took place against the backdrop of military success by the emperors of the Macedonian Dynasty (867 – 1056). The first emperor of this dynasty, Basil I (r. 867 – 886), a soldier and servant of the emperor, had come from a peasant background. He seized control of the Empire when he murdered the reigning emperor and took the position for himself.

Basil was an effective emperor. To the east, as the Abbasid Caliphate broke down, he inflicted several defeats on the Arab emirs on the border, pushing the frontiers of the Empire further east. Although unsuccessful in fighting to maintain control of Sicily, he re-established Byzantine control over most of southern Italy.

It was under the Macedonian emperors that the Eastern Orthodox culture of the Byzantines spread north beyond the borders of the Empire. In 864, the Bulgar khan, whose predecessors had been building a state of their own, converted to Christianity and was baptized. This conversion allowed the Bulgar state to be legitimated by the Church in the same manner as had the Byzantine Empire and the kingdoms of Western Europe.

Figure 7.9 | Basil II
Author: User "Tokle"
Source: Wikimedia Commons
License: Public Domain

In the ninth century, Cyril and Methodius, missionaries from the city of Thessalonica, preached Orthodox Christianity to the Slavic peoples of Eastern Europe and devised the alphabet that we today call **Cyrillic** in order to write the Bible and liturgy in their own language, **Slavonic**. By bringing Orthodox Christianity to the Slavic peoples, the Byzantines brought them into the culture of the Byzantines.

Subsequent emperors maintained this record of successes. John Tzimisces (r. 969 – 976) established Byzantine control over most of Syria. Basil II (r. 976 – 1025) achieved further successes, crushing and annexing the Bulgar state that had grown up in the lands south of the Danube and further subordinating the Armenian kingdoms to the Byzantine emperor. By the end of his reign, the Byzantine territory encompassed about a fourth of what had been the Roman Empire at its height under Augustus.

Basil II had further diplomatic triumphs. He allied with the princes of the **Kievan Rus**, a state that had grown up in Eastern Europe along the rivers between the Baltic Sea and the Black Sea. The Rus was a people group made up of a largely Slavic population, with rulers who were ethnically Norse and who had established themselves as rulers of both Slavic and Turkic subjects when they sailed down the rivers of Eastern Europe from their Scandinavian homeland. This was a hybrid culture already, combining Norse and Slavic. An alliance with the Byzantine Empire also brought Greek elements into the cultural mix. In 988, Kievan Grand Prince Vladimir (r. 980 – 1015) was baptized into the Christian religion and became a close ally of Basil II, sealing the alliance by marrying Basil's sister, Anna. The elite culture of the Rus would come to reflect both Greek, Slavic, Norse, and also Turkic elements. Allying with these people had brought Basil II to the height of the Byzantine state's power.

Figure 7.10 | Baptism of Grand Prince Vladimir
Author: Viktor M. Vasnetsov
Source: Wikimedia Commons
License: Public Domain

Despite its successes during the reign of the Macedonian emperors, the Byzantine state faced weaknesses. The *theme* system had gradually broken down. Increasingly, soldiers came not from the themes, but from the ranks of professional mercenaries, to include those made up of Norsemen. The

Map 7.7 | Map of the Byzantine Empire at the Death of Basil II in 1025 CE
Author: User "Bigdaddy1204"
Source: Wikimedia Commons
License: CC BY-SA 3.0

soldiers of the themes received less training and served mainly as a militia that would back up the core of a professional army, known as the **Tagmata**. Whether this smaller *tagmata* would be up to the task of defending an empire the size of Byzantium would remain to be seen.

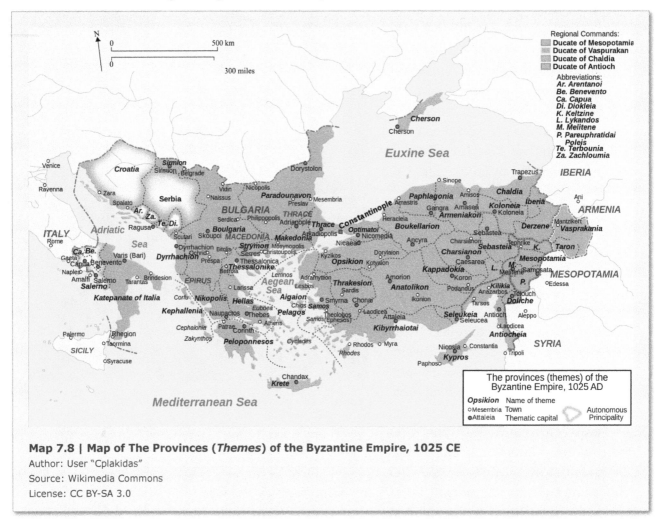

Map 7.8 | Map of The Provinces (*Themes*) of the Byzantine Empire, 1025 CE
Author: User "Cplakidas"
Source: Wikimedia Commons
License: CC BY-SA 3.0

7.16 CONCLUSION AND GLOBAL PERSPECTIVES

In many ways, the period between 500 and 1000 was as transitional for Western Europe and Byzantium as it was for East Asia and the Middle East and North Africa. Just as the Han State had fragmented politically in the third century and given rise to smaller states ruled by warrior aristocracies, so too had Rome fragmented into its eastern half and a series of Germanic kingdoms, themselves ruled by warrior aristocracies. Just as Mahayana Buddhism had arrived in post-Han China, so too had Christianity become the dominant faith of the Roman Empire and its successors.

And yet, these similarities in the end are superficial. All of China's successor states maintained a continuity of bureaucracy and literacy to an extent that Western Europe did not. Moreover, although Mahayana Buddhism would become a key element of East Asian culture, it would never come to enjoy a monopoly of power that Christianity enjoyed in Western Europe and Byzantium and that Islam enjoyed in Spain, the Middle East, and North Africa. The less exclusivist nature of Mahayana Buddhism would mean that it would always be one set of practices among many.

And the greatest difference is that China eventually saw a return to a unified empire under the Sui and then Tang Dynasties. In spite of Charlemagne's efforts to create a new Empire in the west, the story of Western Europe would be one of competing states rather than an empire claiming universal authority.

7.17 WORKS CONSULTED AND FURTHER READING

Backman, Clifford R. *The Worlds of Medieval Europe.* 2ⁿᵈ ed. Oxford: Oxford University Press, 2009.

Fouracre, Paul, ed. *The New Cambridge Medieval History, Volume 1: c.500 – c.700.* Cambridge: Cambridge University Press, 2005.

McKitterick, Rosamond, ed. *The New Cambridge Medieval History, Volume 2: c.700 – c.900.* Cambridge: Cambridge University Press, 1995.

Ostrogorsky, George. *History of the Byzantine State.* Translated by Joan Hussey. Revised ed. New Brunswick, NJ: Rutgers University Press, 1969.

Rautman, Marcus. *Daily Life in the Byzantine Empire.* London: Greenwood Press, 2006.

Reuter, Timothy, ed. *The New Cambridge Medieval History, Volume 3: c.900 – c.1024.* Cambridge: Cambridge University Press, 2000.

Wickham, Chris. *The Inheritance of Rome: Illuminating the Dark Ages, 400 – 1000.* The Penguin History of Europe 2. New York: Penguin, 2009.

7.18 LINKS TO PRIMARY SOURCES

Fordham University's Internet Medieval Sourcebook contains a wide variety of primary source documents from the Middle Ages (that is, 500 to 1500) hosted by Fordham University. From the main page one can find links based on period and category.

The Internet Medieval Sourcebook

    http://legacy.fordham.edu/Halsall/sbook.asp

Georgetown University's The Labyrinth likewise contains a large selection of links to both primary sources and art and art historical materials. Some of the pages have succumbed to "link rot" due to the relative age of the site, but it remains one of the best collections of primary source material available online for free.

The Labyrinth

    https://blogs.commons.georgetown.edu/labyrinth

8 Islam to the Mamluks

Brian Parkinson

8.1 CHRONOLOGY

632 – 661 CE	Rashidun Caliphs
661 – 750 CE	Umayyad Caliphate
750 – 1258 CE	Abbasid Caliphate
909 – 1171 CE	Fatimid Caliphate
1096 – 1487 CE	Crusades
1171 – 1250 CE	Ayubid Sultanate
1250 – 1517 CE	Mamluk Sultanate

8.2 INTRODUCTION

An inveterate adventurer and renowned intellectual, **Ibn Khaldun** was born into a family of ascendant Andalusian Arabs who had immigrated to North Africa. There, present day Tunisia, he received a traditional Islamic education until his parents died from the plague. At the time of their deaths, he was just seventeen years old. On his own, the young and resourceful Ibn Khaldun exploited personal relationships to secure an administrative position at court and thus began a career as an itinerant statesman. Time and time again, Ibn Khaldun landed in prison for his role in conspiracies against various ruling dynasties, only to be released by their heirs. Envoys and grandees recognized his remarkable intelligence and the value of his council. His reputation preceded him, and many dignitaries openly entreated him to join their court. Serving various dynasties, Ibn Khaldun held many important offices, like diplomat, court advisor, and prime minister. But he eventually grew weary of the hazards of palace intrigue and sought instead a more reclusive lifestyle.

Ibn Khaldun retired to the safety of a Berber tribe in Algeria, where he composed **al-Muqaddimah**, or *Prolegomenon*, an outstanding work of sociology and historiography. Published in 1377, he theorized in *al-Muaqddimah* that tribal **'asabiyah**, roughly translated as "social solidarity," is often accompanied by a novel religious ideology that helps a previously marginalized group of people, usually from the desert, rise up and conquer the city folk. Once ensconced in power, these desert peoples evolved into a grand civilization, but *'asabiyah* contained within it destructive elements that could precipitate their collapse. Known for this **Cyclical Theory of History**, Ibn Khaldun posited that, seduced by the wiles of urban culture, the dominant group would over time become soft and enter into a period of decay, until a new group of desert peoples conquered them, when the process would begin anew. This theory applies to the development of Islamic history discussed throughout this chapter.

8.3 QUESTIONS TO GUIDE YOUR READING

1. How does geography play a role in Islamic history?

2. Why were the concepts defined by *muruwah* so important to the early development of Islam?

3. What are the Five Pillars of Islam, and why are they important to the religion?

4. What were the five roles that the Prophet Muhammad played in Medina?

5. What factors led to the rapid expansion of Islam?

6. How did the Umayyads come to power following the Rashidun caliphs?

7. How do you account for the rise of the splits in the Islamic community, like the rise of the Kharijis and Shi'a?

8. Describe the transition from the Umayyads to the 'Abbasids. Compare and contrast the two caliphates.

9. The Fatimids marked the end to the High Caliphate. How did Egypt gain its autonomy from the 'Abbasids? How did the Fatimids take over Egypt?

10. How did the Crusaders gain a foothold in the Middle East? What did it take for Salah al-Din to push them out?

11. What led to the establishment of the Mamluk Sultanate? How did the Mamluk Sultanate go into decline?

12. Does North African history move in cycles of birth, renewal, expansion and decadence? Ibn Khaldoun says that nomads come from the frontiers, desert, and periphery, settle down, and within 120 years, become decadent and collapse. Do you agree?

8.4 KEY TERMS

- 'Abd Allah al-Mahdi
- Abdul Malik
- Abu al-'Abbas al-Saffah, Caliph
- Abu Bakr, Caliph
- Ahmad Ibn Tulun
- 'A'isha
- Al-Azhar
- Al-Hakim
- 'Ali, Caliph
- al-Ma'mun
- Al-Mansur, Caliph
- Al-Mu'izz
- *Al-Muqaddimah*
- Alexios Komnenos, Emperor
- Alids
- *Amsar*
- *Ansar*
- *Asabiyyah*
- Aybak
- Battle of Ajnadayn
- Battle of Badr
- Battle of Karbala
- Battle of Manzikert
- Battle of Marj Rahit
- Battle of Qadisiya
- Battle of Siffin
- Battle of the Camel
- Battle of the Trench
- Battle of Uhud
- Battle of Yarmuk
- Baybars

- *Bayt al-Hikmah*
- Cyclical Theory of History
- Hadith
- *Hajj*
- Harun al-Rashid, Caliph
- *Hijra*
- Husayn
- Ibn Khaldun
- ibn Zubayr
- Isma'ilis
- *Jihad*
- Jizya
- Ka'ba
- *Kharanj*
- *Kharijis*
- *Majlis*
- *Mamluks*
- Marwan, Caliph
- *Mawali*
- Mu'awiya, Caliph
- Mu'tazila
- *Muhajirun*
- Muhammad ad-Darazi
- *Muruwah*
- People of the Book
- Quran
- Qutuz
- Ramadan
- Salah al-Din
- *Salat*
- *Sawm*

- *Shahada*
- Shajar al-Durr
- Sharia law
- Sunna
- The Battle of Ayn Jalut
- The Battle of Hattin
- Treaty of Hudaybiyyah

- 'Umar, Caliph
- 'Umar II, Caliph
- *Umma*
- Urban II, Pope
- 'Uthman, Caliph
- Yazid
- *Zakat*

8.5 GEOGRAPHY OF THE MIDDLE EAST

Academics have not reached a consensus on the geographical boundaries of the Middle East. However, for the purposes of this chapter, this region will encompass the broadly defined areas known as Persia, Mesopotamia, the Levant, Asia Minor, and the Arabian Peninsula. The Middle East straddles three continents, including Asia, Africa, and Europe. The geography of the area promoted cultural diffusion by facilitating the spread of peoples, ideas, and goods along overland and maritime trade routes. In an area generally characterized by its aridity, climate has influenced settlement patterns. Larger settlements are found in river valleys and well-watered areas along the littoral. In these areas, we see the development and spread of productive agriculture.

Map 8.1 | Map of the Middle East
Author: User "TownDown"
Source: Wikimedia Commons
License: CC BY-SA 3.0

8.6 RISE OF ISLAM

Legend traces the Arabs back to Isma'il, the son of Abraham and his Egyptian maid, Haga, a link that would later help to legitimize Islam by connecting it to the Hebrew tradition. In reality, Arabs inhabited the pre-Islamic Arabian Peninsula and shared socio-linguistic commonalities with such other Semitic-speaking peoples in the area as the Hebrews, Assyrians, Arameans, and even the Amhara of Ethiopia. Most of the population of Arabia prior to the rise of Islam resided in the south of the peninsula, in modern day Yemen, where they practiced terraced agriculture and herded ruminants in a relatively small area.

Farther to the north of Yemen, along the highland spine of western Arabia and up against the littoral of the Red Sea, was the Hijaz, a prominent cultural and economic region. Situated in this remote fastness was the dusty city of Mecca, the holiest place in the peninsula and the location of the **Ka'ba**, or "cube," which contained many of the traditional Arabian religious images, including many Christian icons. So important was the Ka'ba to the religion of polytheistic tribes of Arabia that they negotiated a truce lasting one month every year that allowed for safe pilgrimage to the shrine.

The Hijaz was the most arable part of the Arabian Peninsula north of Yemen and distinguished by irrigated agriculture that supported fruit trees and essential grains. Local traders exported a range of Hijazi agricultural products to Syria in the north in return for imperative imports like textiles and olive oil so the region benefited from robust trade. Regional commerce depended

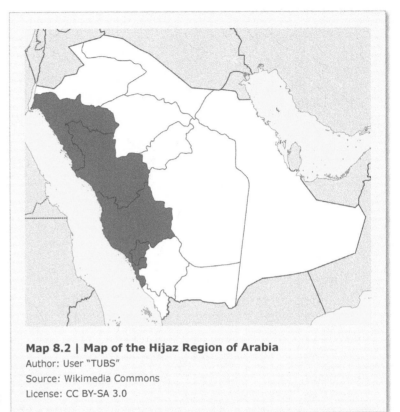

Map 8.2 | Map of the Hijaz Region of Arabia
Author: User "TUBS"
Source: Wikimedia Commons
License: CC BY-SA 3.0

on the security of trade, and piracy on the Red Sea threatened to disrupt business. Under these conditions, merchants diverted their trade overland. Many goods journeyed up the Red Sea Rift from Yemen on their way to the eastern Mediterranean. Caravans of camels carried these goods,

as well as Hijazi exports, to the Levant. Most of the caravans stopped in Mecca, the halfway point up the spine of the peninsula, thus their commerce brought much needed wealth and tax revenue to the city.

The Arabs first domesticated the camel, probably sometime between 3000 and 1000 BCE. Caravan operators eventually availed themselves of these useful dromedaries because they were so adept at crossing the region's massive deserts. Capable of drinking 100 liters of water in mere minutes, they could endure days of travel without needing to replenish themselves again. Moreover, camels instinctively remembered the locations

Figure 8.1 | The Mountains of the Hijaz
Author: User "Salem1990"
Source: Wikimedia Commons
License: CC BY-SA 3.0

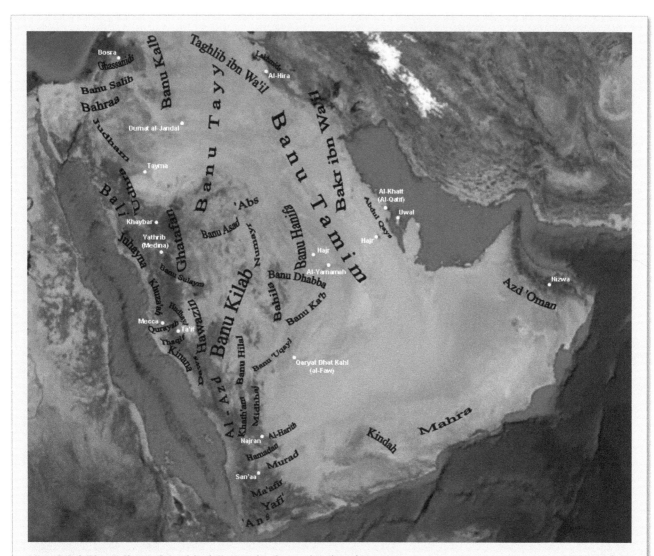

Map 8.3 | The Tribes of Arabia | Notice the Quraysh tribe of Mecca.
Author: User "Slackerlwastudent"
Source: Wikimedia Commons
License: Public Domain

of important, life-sustaining oases. So important were these beasts of burden that the tribes that controlled the camels controlled the trade. And the Quraysh Tribe of Mecca commanded many of the camels in the Hijaz region; therefore, they commanded much of the trade.

Life in the Arabian Peninsula centered around the tribe, which usually consisted of a group of relatives who claimed a shared ancestry. Tribal traditions found meaning in the poetic concept of **muruwah**, which represented the notion of the ideal tribal man. This uniquely Arabian brand of chivalry focused on bravery, patience, persistence in revenge, generosity, hospitality, and protection of the poor and weak. In the absence of formal government, tribes offered physical security to its individual members. Tribes mitigated violence and theft through the shared understanding that retribution for such acts would follow swiftly. Tribes also organized to compete over increasingly scarce resources, as they had a responsibility to provide for the economic needs of their individual members. Nevertheless, tribal traditions had been breaking down prior to the rise of Islam; no longer were the dominant members of society adhering to the principles set forth in *muruwah*.

Into this evolving cultural milieu Muhammad (c.570 – 632) was born in the city of Mecca. Muhammad's father, 'Abdallah, was a member of the Hashimite Clan, a less prosperous branch of the Quraysh Tribe. 'Abdullah died just prior to his son's birth, and Muhammad's mother passed away when he was just six years old. Orphaned at such a young age, his tribe intervened to ensure Muhammad's survival. His uncle, Abu Thalib, the leader of the Hashimite Clan and an important member of the Quraysh Tribe, eventually took custody of the young boy. These early privations influenced Muhammad's later desire to take care of those who could not care for themselves.

In his youth, Muhammad found employment in the regional caravan trade as a dependable herder and driver of camels. During this period, he cultivated a reputation of an empathetic and honest man, one who earned the respect of many Meccans. His upright character soon attracted the attention of a wealthy merchant known as Khadija who hired Muhammad to manage her caravans. Once Muhammad proved his reliability, Khadija, who was fifteen years older than Muhammad, proposed to him, and they married. This marriage afforded Muhammad a financial security that allowed him to begin meditating on religion in the abstract.

Muhammad had been concerned about the direction society had recently been taking and that the concepts defined by *muruwah* were no longer being upheld. He believed that some of the most influential members of society, namely the merchant elite of the Quraysh Tribe, were no longer respecting their traditional responsibilities to the weaker members of society because of their own greed. He thought that the **People of the Book**, specifically, Christians and Jews, might have a better answer for the ills afflicting Meccan society. Muhammad had contact with the Christians and Jews of the peninsula and even traveled to Christian Syria while working in the caravan trade. In this context, the Angel Gabriel appeared to Muhammad at a cave nearby to Mecca in 610, during the holy month of Ramadan. The Angel Gabriel instructed him to "recite," and then he spoke the divine word of God. His revelations became the **Quran**.

At first, Muhammad displayed the very human reactions of fear and distrust to the apparition of the Angel Gabriel. He also expressed embarrassment because he did not want to be associated with the pagan diviners of the region. Fortunately, his wife Khadija had a cousin who was a *hanif*, someone who was neither a Christian nor a Jew, but who believed in a vague concept of a monotheistic god. Her cousin trusted the veracity of Muhammad's revelations. So with trepidation, Muhammad eventually accepted his role as God's vehicle. His wife became the first convert to Islam, with Abu Thalib's son **'Ali** converting soon afterwards.

8.6.1 The Religion of Islam

As a religion of the Abrahamic faith, Islam holds much in common with Judaism and Christianity. Islam grew out of the Judeo-Christian tradition, a link which helped to legitimize the new religion. In fact, Muslims believe in the same God, or Allah in Arabic, as the Jewish and Christian God. Although Muslims trust that the People of the Book had received the word of

God, they believe that it had become distorted over time, so God sent the Angel Gabriel to deliver His word to Muhammad, the Seal of the Prophets, or Khatam an-Nabiyyin, for Muslims believe that he represented God's final word to man. Muhammad never claimed to be founding a new religion, rather he served as the last in a long line of God's messengers, beginning with the Hebrew prophets, and including Jesus. His revelations, therefore, represent the pure, unadulterated version of God's message. The Prophet's followers memorized the revelations and ultimately recorded them in a book called the Quran. Together with the

Figure 8.2 | The Birmingham Quran Manuscript | Dated among the oldest in the World.
Author: Anonymous
Source: Wikimedia Commons
License: Public Domain

Quran, the **Hadith**, traditions of Muhammad used to illustrate a concept, and the **Sunna**, the teachings of the Prophet not found in the Quran, helped guide and inform Muslims on proper behavior. And with that knowledge came great responsibility, as God held His people to a high standard of behavior, based on their obedience, or submission to His will. In fact, the word Islam means submission in Arabic, and a Muslim is one who submits (to God).

Figure 8.3 | Pilgrimage to Mecca | Notice the prominently featured Ka'ba.
Author: User "BotMultichillT"
Source: Wikimedia Commons
License: CC BY-SA 2.0

Derived from a Hadith, the Five Pillars of Islam are essential, obligatory actions that serve as the foundation of the faith. The first pillar, known as the witness, or **shahada**, is a profession of faith, in which believers declare that "There is no God but God, and Muhammad is His messenger." Prayer, also called **salat**, is the second pillar of Islam. Islam expects faithful Muslims to pray five times a day, kneeling towards Mecca, at dawn, noon, afternoon, sunset, and evening. One should perform ritual ablutions prior to their prayers in order to approach God as being symbolically clean and pure. The third pillar is almsgiving, or **zakat** in Arabic. Islam requires Muslims to contribute a proportion of their wealth to the upkeep of the Islamic community. This proportion, or tithe, accorded with the size of one's wealth; therefore, the rich should expect to contribute more than the poor. Fasting, or **sawm**, is the fourth pillar of Islam and takes place during Ramadan, the ninth month of the Islamic lunar calendar. For the duration of **Ramadan**, believers consume neither food nor drink from dawn to dusk. This practice is meant to remind them of what it is like to be poor and go hungry. The fifth and final pillar of Islam is pilgrimage, or **hajj**. Islam expects all able-bodied Muslims to make a journey to Mecca at least once in their lifetime. All five pillars combine to unite the Islamic community.

8.7 THE EXPANSION OF ISLAM

The Prophet Muhammad started publically preaching his strict brand of monotheism in the year 613, by reciting the Quran, quickly convincing some of the commoners of Mecca to believe in him. Most of his early converts belonged to groups of people who had failed to achieve any significant social mobility, which, of course, included many of the poor. His followers memorized his recitations and message that called for the powerful to take care of the weak, a message that resonated with many of these economically and socially marginalized. Islam served as a binding force, replacing tribal solidarity, or *'asabiyah*.

Muhammad's message challenged the Umayyad Clan's leadership of society. The most powerful branch of the Quraysh Tribe, the Umayyads had been enriching themselves from the lucrative caravan trade while, at the same time, ignoring the privations of the needy. Prodding his tribal brethren, Muhammad had also spoken out against the traditional pagan gods. Tribal tradition dictated that the polytheistic Arabs of the peninsula worship their tribal gods; they also believed in *jinns*, or nature spirits. As custodians of the Ka'ba, which contained all of these traditional Arabian religious images, the Umayyad Clan augmented their income by collecting revenue from the traditional pilgrimage to Mecca.

The political implications were clear. The Muslims threatened to disrupt a delicate equilibrium. The Prophet's message jeopardized the social and economic standing of the elite members of society, who accused the Muslims of serving as agents of unwelcome change. Tensions grew, and conflict spilled into the streets of Mecca, dragging the two respective camps into the fray. The more that Muhammad's followers grew in number, the more opposition they encountered from the Umayyad Clan. To avoid this conflict, some Muslims fled to the Kingdom of Aksum, located in Ethiopia, at this stage in the early history of Islam, where they received protection from Muhammad's enemies under the Christian King Armah. Indeed, the first Muslims went by the name of **muhajirun**, meaning "emigrants," for they would soon be forced to leave Mecca under pain of severe Umayyad persecution.

During this period, Muhammad's wife Khadija died in 619. With her death, Muhammad lost his source of emotional support and fell into depression, thus enduring a personal crisis. That same year, the Prophet's uncle Abu Thalib passed away. Already bereaved, Muhammad further suffered the loss of his personal protector in the Quraysh Tribe. Now cut off from the tribal leadership and accused

Figure 8.4 | The Quba Mosque of Medina | The oldest mosque in Islam.
Author: User "Abderlrhman 1990"
Source: Wikimedia Commons
License: CC BY-SA 3.0

of stirring sectarian tension, Muhammad was on his own and vulnerable to Umayyad harassment in Mecca.

While Muhammad endured harsh reprisals from the Umayyads for his public preaching, a conflict was boiling in Yathrib, later called Medina, a trade city located a few days to the north of Mecca. Some individuals from Medina had traveled to Mecca in 620, where they heard the Prophet preach and soon adopted Islam. Impressed by his reputation as an honest man, the leaders of Medina invited Muhammad to their city in 622 to act as a mediator of tribal infighting over a shared oasis. As opposition in Mecca had become too intense for Muhammad and his followers to remain there, they migrated to Medina in 622, a seminal event known as the *hijra* that marks the first year of the Islamic calendar. The Prophet rapidly converted many of the city's inhabitants to Islam. These new Muslims came to be identified as the *ansar*, meaning "helpers." Together with the muhajirun, the ansar helped the Prophet institutionalize the religion of Islam and develop an *umma*, or community of believers, that would dominate the social and political life of Medina.

Muhammad assumed five different roles in Medina. First and foremost, he was the Prophet of Islam; therefore, he was the religious leader of the community. Second, he acted as the political leader of the *umma*. Because his followers agreed with him politically, they agreed with him religiously as well. Third, Muhammad served as a judicial leader, using the Quran as the basis of law. Fourth, the Prophet functioned as a legislator, working with the *majlis*, or council of elders, to enact laws. He therefore governed his capital, Medina, with no separation of church and state. Finally, Muhammad was a military leader who ensured that statehood would prevail for the Muslims.

A major concern of Muhammad's leadership was to determine how the Muslims could contribute to the Medinan economy. He received a revelation during this period that suggested the Muslims should raid the caravans coming north out of Mecca. (Qur'an 22:39) In 624, the Medinans engaged a caravan of Meccans along a popular trade route bypassing Medina. In the ensuing **Battle of Badr**, named after a nearby oasis, 300 Muslims defeated nearly 1000 Meccans and seized their caravan. They considered their signal victory a sign from God that he was on their side. Their success enhanced Muhammad's prestige and that of the Islamic community among the Arab tribes in the peninsula.

Unwilling to cede control of the lucrative caravan trade to the upstart Muslims of Medina, the Umayyads confronted the Muslims in 625 in the **Battle of Uhud**, which referred to a local mountain. Foot soldiers in the vanguard of the Muslim forces led their defense. Meanwhile, a group of ambitious archers, ignoring the Prophet's command to remain stationary, joined the battle. Their imprudent action let the Meccan cavalry strike the unprotected flank of Muhammad's warriors. The Meccans failed to capitalize on their victory, however, and were unable to take Medina, a failure that leads some historians to consider the battle an ultimate success for the Muslims.

In 627, the Umayyads of Mecca and the Muslims of Medina met in a final confrontation in what became known as the **Battle of the Trench**, or *khandaq* in Arabic; this battle ended in another triumph for the Muslims. In preparation for a foreseeable Umayyad attack, a Persian engineer named Salman had suggested that the Medinans build defensive works around the city. So the Muslims survived the Meccan assault by entrenching themselves behind a near-impregnable barrier. In 628, the Umayyads finally realized that they were unable to vanquish the Muslims so sent a delegation of Meccans to sue for peace. The resulting **Treaty of Hudaybiyyah** symbolized their desire to extricate themselves from a losing situation, as Mecca ultimately compromised so their merchant elite would not lose any more trade to the Medinans. The treaty provided for an official tolerance of Islam and for the Muslims to return to Mecca the following year, free from persecution.

In 630, two years before his death, the Prophet Muhammad advanced on the city of Mecca with an army of some 10,000 Muslims. Encountering only limited resistance, the army of Muslims took control of the city, an act that symbolized the idea of Islamic expansion. Muhammad cleansed the Ka'ba of its purported 360 religious images and dedicated it to God. The prestige of the Muslims extended with their victory over the Meccans. As tribes learned of this triumph, they soon followed the lead of the winners, both politically and re-

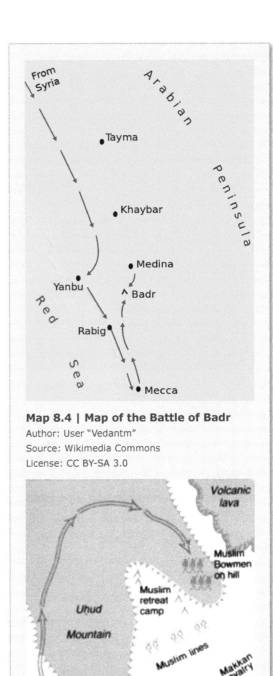

Map 8.4 | Map of the Battle of Badr
Author: User "Vedantm"
Source: Wikimedia Commons
License: CC BY-SA 3.0

Map 8.5 | Map of the Battle of Uhud
Author: User "Warda99"
Source: Wikimedia Commons
License: CC BY-SA 1.0

ligiously, sending delegations to forge alliances with the Prophet. By the time that Muhammad passed away, most of Arabia had converted to Islam. The religion provided the Muslims of the peninsula with a new 'asabiyah, or social solidarity, endowing the movement with a unity of purpose.

In the absence of the Prophet, Muslim leaders had to develop a body of law to deal with important legal questions. Over time, **Sharia law** became a legal system in which Islamic principles provided an accepted means to regulate all features of daily life, including, but not limited to, economics, politics, family life, and society. Sharia law is based on the Quran, Hadith, precedent, and interpretation. In fact, the capacity for various interpretations of the law has led to the development of several schools of Islamic jurisprudence.

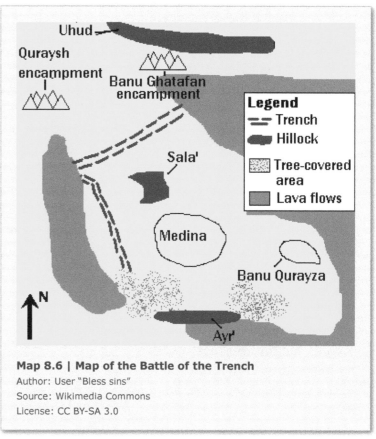

Map 8.6 | Map of the Battle of the Trench
Author: User "Bless sins"
Source: Wikimedia Commons
License: CC BY-SA 3.0

8.8 THE RASHIDUN CALIPHS

Muhammad did not formally appoint a successor, or *khalifa* in Arabic, and no clear replacement arose to lead the Muslim community forward at the time of his death. In fact, the *umma* divided into three groups, with each willing to appoint their own successor to the Prophet. Emerging as a vocal leader at this critical juncture, 'Umar, one of Muhammad's closest companions, convinced the *majlis*, or elders of the community, to elect **Abu Bakr** by consensus as a compromise candidate. Abu Bakr had been Muhammad's closest friend; Muhammad's marriage of political alliance to **'A'isha**, Abu Bakr's daughter, further solidified their relationship.

The election of Abu Bakr (632 – 634) brought much-needed stability and an almost democratic form of government to Islam. As caliph, Abu Bakr held together the converts to Islam by deploying the forces at his disposal, thus cementing his authority among the Arabian tribes. He prevented any rebellious Muslim tribes from reverting to the worship of their traditional tribal gods, as they were wont to do. Abu Bakr died in 634, two years after the Prophet Muhammad had died.

The *majlis* chose **'Umar** (634 – 644), a close friend of Abu Bakr, to be the next caliph. 'Umar had been the military power behind Abu Bakr. A dynamic and uncompromising leader, 'Umar recognized the necessity of expansion northward to achieve various ends. First, he sought to subdue the security threat of raiding nomads, many of which remained a law unto themselves. Second, in his struggle to contain discontent, he used the cohesive element of *jihad* to unite the Muslim community against unbelievers and expand God's dominion. (The Arabic term of *jihad* actually refers to a "struggle," usually against spiritual impurity, often known as "greater *jihad*," and is associated with fulfilling God's objectives here on earth. The "lesser *jihad*," alternatively, is a physical struggle against the unbelievers of the *Dar al-Harb*, or Abode of War, until it is absorbed into the *Dar al-Islam*, or Abode of Islam, where believers were free to practice their faith as members of the predominant faith. Of note is the fact that Muhammad did not consider jihad important enough to make one of the pillars of Islam.) Third, 'Umar understood the importance of plunder for the nascent caliphate. Troops received four-fifths of the loot from conquest; the remainder of the revenue went to him to be dispersed amongst the neediest members in the Islamic community.

'Umar directed the full might of Islam northward against the Eastern Roman Empire, sometimes referred to as the Byzantine Empire. In 634, their first encounter took place in southern Palestine. The ensuing **Battle of Ajnadayn** was a decisive victory for the Muslims and a major loss for Emperor Heraclius. Two years later, an outnumbered Muslim army defeated the Eastern Roman Empire yet again at the **Battle of Yarmouk**, located on the eponymous river, somewhere between Damascus and Jerusalem. In both instances, the Byzantines relied on their slow, heavy cavalry, whereas the Arabs capitalized on their light armor and their superior mobility. The Muslims realized that they could not just charge the East Roman lines; they showed their tactical superiority by flanking the Byzantines and executing a successful rearguard action instead. These victories opened up greater Syria to Muslim conquest. Antioch, Aleppo, and Jerusalem fell to

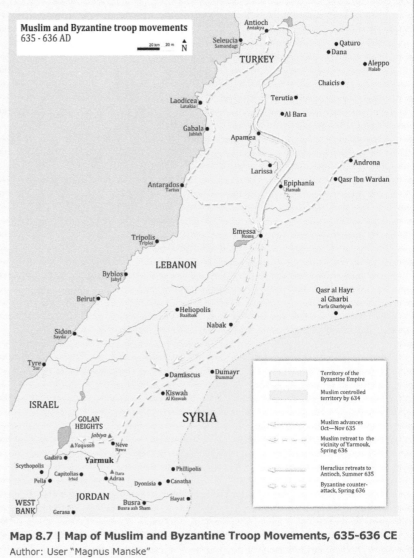

Map 8.7 | Map of Muslim and Byzantine Troop Movements, 635-636 CE
Author: User "Magnus Manske"
Source: Wikimedia Commons
License: CC BY-SA 3.0

the Muslims not long thereafter. 'Umar appointed Mu'awiya, a member of the Meccan Umayyad aristocracy to govern Syria at his behest.

Once he dealt with the increasingly vulnerable Byzantines in the Levant, 'Umar directed his army to the east against the Sasanian Empire of Persia. In 636, fighting along the banks of the Euphrates River, a smaller Arab force triumphed over the Persians, at the **Battle of Qadisiya**. After successive days of exhaustive combat, the Muslims took advantage of environmental conditions and their light cavalry's mobility when they chased a dust storm and took the Sasanids by surprise.

To save their empire, the Persians mounted a failed counterattack. In 642, Umar's army eventually defeated the forces of the Sasanian Emperor Yazdagird III at the Battle of Nahavand, situated deep in Iran's Zagros Mountains. Yazdagird fled to the east as a fugitive, and, in 651, met his death at the hands of a local miller who killed the emperor in order to rob him of his belongings.

In 639, General 'Amr petitioned 'Umar for permission to invade Egypt and eventually persuaded the caliph that he could easily take Egypt so gained his reluctant consent. In 641, he received a message from 'Umar recalling his forces. The general ignored the order and seized Egypt with just a few hundred soldiers. With promises of toleration, 'Amr convinced the Egyptian Coptic majority to

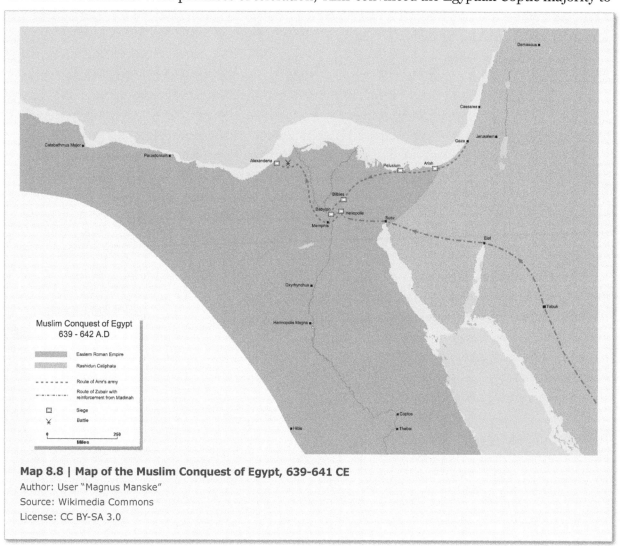

Map 8.8 | Map of the Muslim Conquest of Egypt, 639-641 CE
Author: User "Magnus Manske"
Source: Wikimedia Commons
License: CC BY-SA 3.0

side with him against the Greek Orthodox ruling minority, whose Patriarch Cyrus had been actively persecuting the Copts as followers of a Christian heresy that failed to recognize the Holy Trinity.

Clearly outnumbered Muslim armies thus successfully defeated two long-standing empires in the span of just a few decades. Several explanations help us understand the rapid expansion of Islam during this period. One concept, termed the vacuum theory, posits that the Byzantine and Persian empires had been severely weakened from near-continuous fighting, dating back decades prior to the rise of Islam, so they both suffered from the fatigue of war. Islam, therefore, occupied the vacuum of political power resulting from the collapse of these two exhausted empires.

The success of Muslim military strategy offers a second explanation. While Byzantine forces adopted a defensive stance on the battlefield, the Arabs employed more aggressive tactics, making use of their mobile light cavalry against their enemies' heavily armored armies. Once victorious, the Arabs populated garrison cities on the frontier, called **amsar**, with Muslims. These military settlements provided security, served as logistical loci, and discouraged Muslim troops from mingling with the locals. The caliphs thereby prevented their warriors being assimilated into the communities of the conquered while also preventing soldiers from disturbing the peace. Fustat in Egypt, as well as Kufa and Basra in Iraq, were the largest of the *amsar*. From bases like these, the Arabs could expand and consolidate their hold over the frontier.

Religion also provided an impetus for the expansion of Islam. Fearing that internal tribal divisions threatened the early Islamic state, 'Umar united the Muslims through their common Islamic theology and faced them against a common enemy. Dedicated to the expansion of Islam, Muslims used the concept of *jihad* as a way to unify the *umma*, or Islamic community, against a foreign foe. Faith motivated the troops, who were zealous and determined to fight.

Simple economics also served as a primary motivating factor in the expansion of Islam. For one, Muslim rulers applied the **jizya**, an annual tax levied on non-Muslims, to newly-conquered lands. The money derived from conquest functioned as a driving force in the growth of the caliphate. With the expectation of material reward, soldiers could earn money for their service. While the practice of dividing the spoils of war amongst the soldiers continued under 'Umar, he also started offering salaries to his troops, determining salaries according to the length of service.

The Muslims further exploited the internal divisions of targeted societies, as exemplified in Egypt, where the Coptic Christian majority, together with a large Jewish minority in Alexandria, had suffered under the rule of an oppressive Greek Orthodox Christian minority but gained autonomy and toleration within an Islamic state. And in Syria, another monophysite Christian minority called the Syrian Orthodox Church, or Jacobites, collaborated with the Muslims and hastened the collapse of the Byzantines. All these factors led the early Islamic state to expand exponentially.

In 644, an Iranian captive from the Persian campaign stabbed 'Umar to death. His successor, **'Uthman** (644 – 656), was an elderly man from the Umayyad Clan who won a contentious election over 'Ali. 'Ali possessed all of the 'Alid bona fides. 'Ali was not only son of Muhammad's early protector, Abu Thalib; he was also the Prophet's cousin and son-in-law. He had married Muhammad's daughter Fatima; together, they had two sons, Hasan and Husayn. 'Ali had also earned a well-deserved reputation as a virtuous Muslim. One of the first converts to Islam, he had

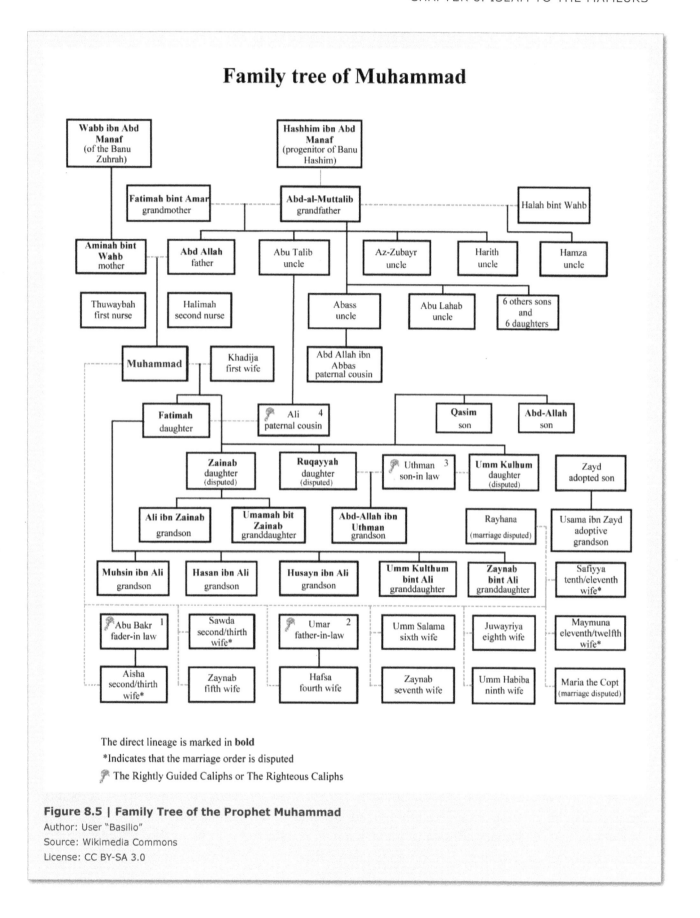

Figure 8.5 | Family Tree of the Prophet Muhammad
Author: User "Basilio"
Source: Wikimedia Commons
License: CC BY-SA 3.0

journeyed with Muhammad on most of his expeditions and fought against the Meccans. Finally, 'Ali also served as a valued advisor to the early caliphs on questions of dogma.

Two factions formed in the wake of questions over 'Uthman's succession, thus initiating the development of a division within Islam. One faction was a group of **'Alids** who believed that 'Ali should inherit the mantle of Islam and referred to traditions suggesting that Muhammad had proclaimed to the faithful that 'Ali should be his successor. The *amsar* followed the 'Alids and later adopted the Shi'a appellation. The other faction, the Umayyads contended that the method of appointing successors should be by consensus, as was done with the first caliphs. Mostly based in Mecca, they later identified as Sunnis. Over time, these factional differences became increasingly difficult to bridge.

Although 'Uthman, one of the Prophet's first converts, was a pious Muslim, he was a corrupt administrator. He displayed nepotistic tendencies that gave precedence to the Meccan elite, a practice that diverged from 'Umar's policies of favoring soldiers who had been the first to respond to the call to action. 'Umar's beneficiaries had usually originated from lesser tribes, those too weak to constitute a coherent threat to the establishment; by contrast, 'Uthman's appointees were members of the Meccan elite who generally pursued policies benefiting the Umayyad merchants of Mecca.

Government also began to disintegrate under 'Uthman's rule, as opposition and instability plagued his tenure as caliph. He managed to offend three separate groups of Muslims. The first of these were the older, pious Muslims, who hailed from Medina. They resented how the hated Umayyads had taken over the same *umma* that they had previously persecuted and had once tried to destroy. Second were the Quran reciters. When 'Uthman commissioned and authorized a single official version of the holy text, an act for which he received many accolades, the Quran reciters lost the opportunity for gainful employment. Third were a disgruntled contingent of 'Alids who called for 'Uthman to resign and advocated the election of 'Ali. Their discontent culminated in 656, when resentful devotees of 'Ali from Egypt broke into 'Uthman's home in Medina and assassinated him, purportedly while he was reading the Quran. They then hastily arranged for the election of 'Ali as 'Uthman's successor.

Thrice rejected by the *majlis* in favor of the first three caliphs, **'Ali** (656 – 661) reluctantly accepted the position of leader of the Islamic community. His selection represented a victory for the faction of legitimists disappointed in the earlier choice of 'Uthman. 'Ali assumed the role of caliph amid high expectations, for he was a pious and generous man. Yet the caliphate suffered under his rule. During this time of instability, he constantly had to suppress revolts. For example, tensions between the supporters of 'Ali and the family of 'Uthman eventually erupted into the first civil war in Islam. In 656, at the **Battle of the Camel**, 'Ali engaged the combined forces of the Prophet's favored wife, **'A'isha**, and her associates, Talha and Zubayr, who were both relatives of 'Uthman. Because 'Ali had failed to bring the dead caliph's assassins to justice; these three together demanded satisfaction for his death.

The conspirators challenged 'Ali near the garrison city of Basra, in southern Iraq, before he had the chance to move the caliphate from Medina to the sympathetic military settlement of Kufa. A first, diplomacy seemed to prevail, as 'Ali sought to avoid bloodshed by negotiating. He succeeded in convincing the three to lay down their arms; however, a group later known as

Kharijis conspired to undermine their reconciliation and set fire to the tents in both camps in the dead of the night. Pandemonium ensued. Because of this single impetuous action, both parties thought the other side had flouted the agreement, committing a violation of trust. During the ensuing battle, 'A'isha was pushed into the middle of the fray on the back of a camel, as was Arab custom. The supporters who rallied to her side were cut down, and 'Ali emerged victorious from a very bloody battle. The repercussions of his victory reverberated across the Islamic world, as older Muslim men castigated 'A'isha for her part in the conflict and suggested that women should not play a role in public life.

Figure 8.6 | 'Ali and 'A'isha at the Battle of the Camel
Author: Unknown
Source: Wikimedia Commons
License: Public Domain

This threat was not the only one 'Ali faced, for he also had to contend with **Mu'awiya**, 'Uthman's cousin and former governor of Syria. Conspicuously absent from 'Ali's new administration, Mu'awiya refused to pay homage to 'Ali and asserted his own independence in Syria. He also echoed the accusations of 'A'isha, Talha, and Zubayr, as members of Mu'awiya's Umayyad Clan had expressed dismay about the quick election of 'Ali, and questions still lingered over the new caliph's part in 'Uthman's death. 'Ali's failure to act against 'Uthman's assassins proved his culpability, Mu'awiya and the Umayyads, and Mu'awiya asserted the traditional Arab custom of exacting revenge on one's enemies.

His conflict with 'Ali culminated in 657 when they met at the **Battle of Siffin**, on the Euphrates River in northern Syria. After months of clashes, 'Ali agreed to arbitration with Mu'awiya. Still preferring negotiation over bloodshed, 'Ali had been of the opinion that Muslims should never take up arms against fellow Muslims. His willingness to negotiate with Mu'awiya, however, caused some of Ali's own soldiers to defect and adopt the appellation of Kharijis, from *kharaja*, meaning "to depart." The first sect in Islam, they departed from Ali because they believed that "judgement belongs to God alone" (Quran 6:57); they saw 'Ali's willingness to negotiate with Mu'awiya as somehow reducing the role of God in determining a successor. In lieu of arbitration, they thought that God would determine the rightful successor by influencing the outcome on the field of battle.

Figure 8.7 | Battle of Siffin, from Balami's Tarikhnama
Author: Bal'ami
Source: Wikimedia Commons
License: Public Domain

8.9 THE UMAYYAD CALIPHATE

In 661, 'Ali suffered the same fate as his predecessor when a Khariji stabbed him to death. And, just like with 'Uthman, the murder of 'Ali took place during prayers. 'Ali's death represented a deep loss for his followers, who saw him as an advocate of an egalitarian version of Islam and a believer in a just and righteous government. His martyrdom came to be regarded as a sacrifice in the service of God and prompted his supporters to pattern themselves after their champion, who, they insisted, had developed spiritual gifts that remained virtually unattainable for others.

The 'Alids encouraged 'Ali's oldest son, Hasan, to succeed his father; however, Mu'awiya threatened the Prophet's grandson with continued warfare and convinced him to renounce his claim to the caliphate. Mu'awiya promised Hasan that he would not appoint an heir so that election of future caliphs would return to the *majlis*. Handsomely compensated by Mu'awiya, Hassan subsequently retired to Mecca and took up religion. He remained there until his death in

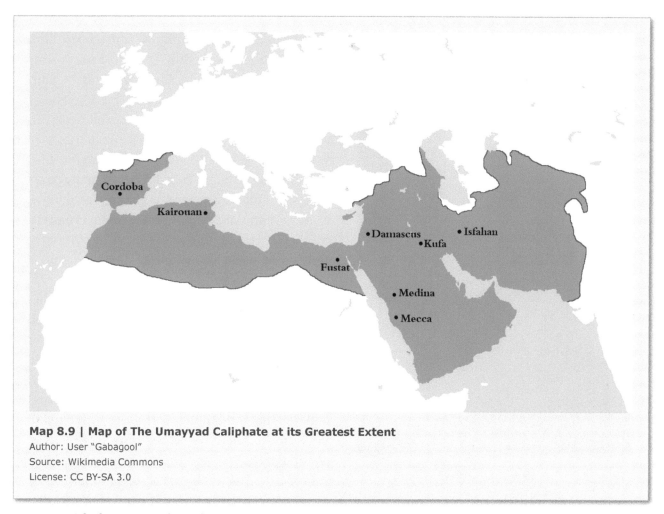

Map 8.9 | Map of The Umayyad Caliphate at its Greatest Extent
Author: User "Gabagool"
Source: Wikimedia Commons
License: CC BY-SA 3.0

669. With this major obstacle removed, Mu'awiya became the fifth caliph, ending the period of the four rightly guided caliphs, also known as the Rashidun Caliphate.

Mu'awiya (661 – 680) founded the Umayyad Caliphate; the tribal *asabiyah* of his Umayyad Clan contributed to their ascendance. And once ensconced in power, the Umayyad Caliphate ended the election of caliphs by consensus and established instead a hereditary principle of succession. Mu'awiya established the caliphate to Damascus, where he previously served as 'Uthman's governor. In Syria, Mu'awiya reformed the bureaucracy by eventually centralizing it. Unable to rely on the Arab tribal system or peninsula traditions to administer to an ever expanding empire, he depended on related Greek merchant families for administrators and adopted the existing administrative machinery of Byzantines, including their imperial customs and bureaucratic practices.

Mu'awiya had received much recognition for his unfaltering determination to seek retribution for 'Uthman's death; however, he had squandered much of that good will in harassing 'Ali. As anti-Umayyad sentiment increased, the rift that existed between the Sunnis and Shi'a continued to expand, for recalcitrant 'Alids continued to harbor resentment against the Umayyads. They remembered when the ruling aristocracy of Mecca had opposed Muhammad and the Muslim community. In fact, Mu'awiya himself had fought against Muhammad until the Treaty of Hudaybiyyah, only to reverse course, convert to Islam, and become the Prophet's secretary.

Figure 8.8 | Hasan fought at the Battle of Siffin, from Bal'ami's Tarikhnama
Author: Bal'ami
Source: Wikimedia Commons
License: Public Domain

Unlike the two caliphs who preceded him, Mu'awiya died peacefully in bed. Prior to his death, he designated his son **Yazid** (680 – 683) as his successor, thus violating his agreement with Hasan. Most notable for his well-deserved reputation as a fierce fighter, Yazid was also known for generally dissolute behavior that offended the religious sensibilities of many pious Muslims. Once ensconced as caliph, Yazid failed to secure an oath of allegiance from **Husayn**, brother of Hasan, one of the most important of Muslim leaders. Their rivalry escalated into a full-scale civil war.

A direct descendent of the Prophet Muhammad and the younger son of the Caliph 'Ali, Husayn rejected the deal that his brother had negotiated, instead pursuing his own claim to the rightful leadership of the Islamic community. His 'Alid supporters loathed the Umayyads and believed that the caliph must be closely related to the Prophet. Husayn's refusal to recognize Yazid as the next caliph and their subsequent conflict culminated in 680 at the Battle of Karbala, located to the west of present day Baghdad. Yazid dispatched a military detachment to Iraq and overwhelmed Husayn's small band of armed followers so that many of Husayn's own men deserted him in his hour of need. The Shi'a perceived this seminal event as a turning point in their history.

Much like the loss of 'Ali, the death of Husayn shocked the incipient Shi'a community, many of whom suffered from intense guilt for failing to assist his little band. Increasing numbers of Shi'a became profoundly affected by his martyrdom, interpreting it as a sacrifice in the best interests of their community; over time, a passion narrative developed that commemorated his last hours. Through this commemoration of the Battle of Karbala on Ashura, the tenth day of the month of Muharram, they remember the terrible suffering and his untimely death and strive to experience an existential intimacy with their martyr.

Yazid had inherited an empire punctuated by civil war and rebellion. Another principle figure among those in revolt was **ibn Zubayr**, grandson of Caliph Abu Bakr. Following the death of Mu'awiya, Ibn Zubayr had sworn allegiance to Husayn. He remained in Mecca, where he stood in opposition to the Umayyads. The general unpopularity of the Umayyads advanced his cause, and many Muslims considered him the rightful caliph. Indeed, much of his support came from Muslims who rejected the idea of hereditary succession and sought a return to the election of caliphs by consensus.

Figure 8.9 | Artistic commemoration of the martyrdom of Imam Husayn at the Battle of Karbala | The focus of the painting is on Husayn's half-brother 'Abbas on a white horse.
Author: Abbas Al-Musavo
Source: Wikimedia Commons
License: Public Domain

Yazid invaded the Hijaz in order to put an end to ibn Zubayr's rebellion, but the caliph's abrupt death in 683 halted the campaign. **Marwan** (684 – 685) followed his cousin Yazid but was not universally recognized as caliph, for many considered ibn Zubayr the legitimate successor. To garner support, Marwan exploited latent tribal animosities that existed between his Kalb Tribe, also known as the Yemen, and the Qays Tribe, who supported ibn Zubayr. At the **Battle of Marj Rahit** in 684, Marwan's Kalb forces defeated the Qays, allowing him to consolidate Umayyad control over Syria and Egypt, thus shrinking ibn Zubayr's rule down to Iraq and the Hijaz. Not until 691 did **Abdul Malik** (685 – 705), heir to Marwan, recover Iraq from ibn Zubayr. In the process, he also had to pacify Khariji and Shi'a areas. Abdul Malik then dispatched

Figure 8.10 | The Mourning of Muharram in Iran
Author: Payam Moein
Source: Wikimedia Commons
License: CC BY-SA 4.0

General Hajjaj to the Hijaz. A brutal military leader, Hajjaj laid siege to the holy city of Mecca in 692 in order to secure the submission of ibn Zubayr's men. He then beheaded ibn Zubayr and crucified his body. Abdul Malik rewarded the brutal general for his loyal service with the governorship of Iraq, where his ruthless reputation persisted.

Once he had assumed the throne, Abdul Malik promoted the Arabization of the caliphate. He rejected the use of Greek, Persian, Coptic, or Aramaic in government, decreeing that all bureaucracy had to be only in Arabic. Non-Arab administrators had to learn Arabic in order to keep their government jobs. Their integration did not lead to the complete Arabization of Umayyad society that Abdul Malik envisioned, however, and the spread of Arabic was not as great as the spread of Islam.

Figure 8.11 | Abdul Malik on One of the New Coins
Author: World Imaging
Source: Wikimedia Commons
License: CC BY-SA 3.0

Many Muslims continued to speak Berber, Turkish, Kurdish, and Persian. Although a separate process, Arabization only accompanied Islamization.

Abdul Malik also sought to Islamize the caliphate. First, he discontinued the earlier Byzantine coinage and created the first Islamic currency. Then he instituted a tax code based on the principles of Islam. Caliphs levied an additional tax on non-Muslims, known as the *jizya*, as was customary in Islam. Christians and Jews in conquered lands also paid a property tax called *kharaj*. By converting to Islam, one could avoid paying the *jizya* and *kharaj* altogether. Most important for ordinary citizens was the fact that Muslims bore lower tax rates than non-Muslims. As one could imagine, the thrust for conversion became primarily economic. Although the process of Islamization was relatively peaceful and gradual, Islam did become the dominant religion of the region. And the parallel processes of Arabization and Islamization helped to reestablish centralized rule after the second civil war.

Figure 8.12 | Early Ottoman Jizya Document
Author: World Imaging
Source: Wikimedia Commons
License: CC BY-SA 3.0

Not all of Abdul Malik's reforms adhered to the egalitarian principles set forth in Islam. Arab tribal elites did not want to recognize the **mawali**, non-Arab Muslims, as social equals, so did not afford them the same rights as Arab Muslims. However, the emerging power and influence of the *mawali* was apparent. They had become the intellectual elite of society and were the bureaucrats and commercial leaders of the *umma*. Nevertheless, they faced social discrimination. For example, Umayyad caliphs taxed the *mawali* as if they were non-Muslims. This inequitable practice became a social problem for the Umayyads, for it stood in stark relief against the values of justice and equality that had originally compelled them to convert.

An extremely devout and pious man, the Caliph **'Umar II** (r. 717 – 720) upended the Umayyad moral order. He considered it immoral to show prejudice against the *mawali* and to favor the Arabs, so he attempted to resolve the lingering hostilities of the *mawali* by advocating the equality of all Muslims. 'Umar II declared an end to the practice of taxing the *mawali* like the Christians and Jews. His advisors warned him against this change because it precipitated numerous conversions of non-Muslims, so he decreased military expenditures to compensate for an expected drop in revenue. His reforms might have ended the official discrimination against the *mawali*, but they alienated the Umayyad privileged class, who paid a servant to poison 'Umar II to death in 720.

8.10 THE 'ABBASID CALIPHATE

For many Muslims, 'Umar II's reforms had come too late. The Umayyads had already managed to alienate three important groups of Muslims, Kharijis, the *mawali*, and the Shi'a, whose combined power and influence were coopted by the 'Abbasids and threatened the internal security of the caliphate. Kharijis eschewed disputes over lineage and advocated a more egalitarian brand of Islam than the Sunni Umayyads. They believed that any Muslim could be the rightful heir to the mantle of the Prophet, so long as that person rigorously adhered to the examples set forth in the Sunna. Kharijis thought that caliphs who diverged from the Prophet's example should be overthrown, as evidenced by their assassination of the Caliph 'Ali. Second, Umayyad authorities had enacted punitive measures against the *mawali*, mostly Persians, but also Kurds and Turks. They treated them like second-class citizens, no different than the People of the Book. Finally, it angered most of the Shi'a that

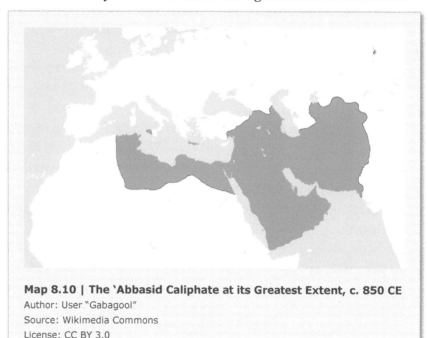

Map 8.10 | The 'Abbasid Caliphate at its Greatest Extent, c. 850 CE
Author: User "Gabagool"
Source: Wikimedia Commons
License: CC BY 3.0

Figure 8.13 | Abu al-'Abbas al-Saffah is proclaimed the first 'Abbasid Caliph, from Balami's Tarikhnama
Author: Bal'ami
Source: Wikimedia Commons
License: Public Domain

the Umayyads could not trace their ancestry to the Prophet Muhammad. They also blamed the Umayyads for the death of their martyr Husayn. The 'Abbasids collaborated with these disaffected groups to incite unrest and rebellion. They particularly cultivated Shi'a anti-Umayyad sentiment, emphasizing their own connection to the Prophet; indeed, the 'Abbasids traced their ancestry to Muhammad's uncle 'Abbas and the Hashimite Clan. They also vaguely promised to adopt Shi'a Islam once in power. Together, these three groups formed a constituency that campaigned on behalf of the 'Abbasids.

A secretive family, 'Abbasids bided their time until the opportune moment to rebel against the Umayyad Caliphate. In 743, the 'Abbasids began their revolution in remote Khorasan, a region in eastern Persia, just as the Umayyads were contending with not only revolts but also the inopportune death of the Caliph Hisham. In that moment of Umayyad disorder, the 'Abbasids dispatched Abu Muslim, a Persian general, to Khorasan to start the revolution. Abu Muslim's early victories against the Umayyads allowed **Abu al-'Abbas**, leader of the 'Abbasid dynasty, to enter the sympathetic city of Kufa in 748. Together, Abu Muslim and Abu al-'Abbas, who adopted the honorific of as-Saffah, or "the generous," confronted the Umayyad Caliph Marwan II in 750, at the Battle of the Zab, in modern day Iraq. Sensing defeat, Marwan II fled, but his pursuers eventually caught and killed him in Egypt. As-Saffah captured the Umayyad capital of Damascus shortly thereafter. The 'Abbasids attempted to eliminate the entire house of the Umayyads so that not one remained to come forth and rise up against them, but one, 'Abd al-Rahman, escaped eminent death and fled to Egypt. The only member of the family to abscond from certain demise, 'Abd al-Rahman fled across North Africa to Spain, where he recreated a Spanish Muslim dynasty in a parallel fashion to the Umayyad dynasty in Syria. Under the Umayyads, Spain became the wealthiest and most developed part of Europe (see Chapter Seven). In fact, it was through Islamic Spain that ancient Greek learning entered Europe.

The change from the Umayyad's Arab tribal aristocracy to a more egalitarian government, one based on the doctrines of Islam, under the 'Abbasids, corresponds to Ibn Khaldun's Cyclical Theory of History. The 'Abbasids officially advocated Sunni orthodoxy and severed their relationship of convenience with the Shi'a. They even went so far as to assassinate many Shi'a leaders, whom they regarded as potential threats to their rule. To escape 'Abbasid persecution and find safety and security, many Shi'a scattered to the edges of the empire. While the Shi'a might have been disappointed with the 'Abbasids for refusing to advocate Shi'a Islam, most Muslims welcomed the 'Abbasid's arrival. They had justified their revolt against the corrupt Umayyads because the latter had digressed from the core principles of Islam. As standard bearers of the Prophet's own family, the 'Abbasids were publicly pious, even digging wells and providing protection along hajj routes.

Caliph al-Mansur (754 – 775) abandoned the Umayyad capital of Damascus and moved the caliphate close to the old Persian capital of Ctesiphon. Construction of the new city of Baghdad began in 762. Situated at the confluence of the Tigris and Diyala rivers, it boasted a prime location that provided access to the sea with enough distance from the coast to offer safety from pirates. Modeled after circular Persian cities, Baghdad rapidly escaped its confines and expanded into its environs. Quickly eclipsing Chang'an, it became the largest city in the world, with over half a million inhabitants. In effect, Baghdad became a public works project, employing 100,000 citizens and stimulating the economy. Al-Mansur's newly-founded city proudly displayed lavish 'Abbasid family residences and grandiose public buildings. It even had working sewers, which dumped raw sewage into the nearby canals and rivers.

Prominently featured in *One Thousand and One Nights*, **Harun al-Rashid** (789 – 809) represented the climax of 'Abbasid rulers; as such, he improved upon the work his predecessors had begun. For example, Harun furthered Baghdad's development into a major economic center by encouraging trade along the Silk Road and through the waters of the Indian Ocean. He also made marginal agricultural land more productive, taking advantage of technological advances in irrigation to cultivate borrowed crops like rice, cotton, and sugar from India, as well as citrus fruits from China.

Harun al-Rashid's reign coincided with the so-called Golden Age of Islam when Baghdad developed into a preeminent city of scholarship. He began construction of the **Bayt al-Hikmah** (House of Wisdom), the foremost intellectual center in the Islamic world. The complex boasted of several schools, astronomical observatories, and even a giant library, where scholars translated scientific and philosophical works from neighboring civilizations, including works from Persian, Hindi, Chinese, and Greek.

As a result of this move from Damascus to Baghdad, Persia increasingly influenced the Islamic world, with a synthesis of Arab and Persian culture beginning under the 'Abbasids. For instance,

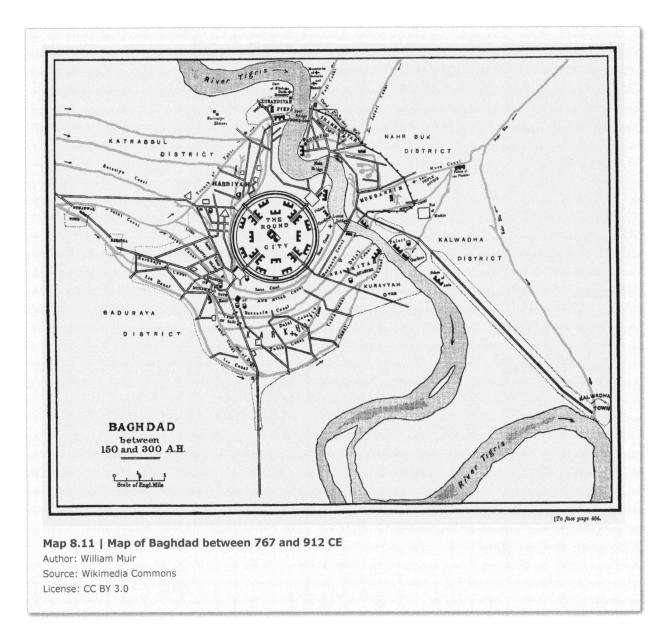

Map 8.11 | Map of Baghdad between 767 and 912 CE
Author: William Muir
Source: Wikimedia Commons
License: CC BY 3.0

the Persian Sibawayah (d. c. 793) responded to the need for non-Arab Muslims to understand the Quran by systematizing the first Arabic grammar, titled *al-Kitab*. The greatest poet of the period, Abu Nuwas (d. c. 813), was of mixed parentage, Arab and Iranian. The avant-garde themes of his poems often emphasized dissolute behavior. Although ibn Ishaq (d.768), a historian of sorts, was born in Medina, he relocated to Baghdad, where he too came under the influence of Persian culture. At the behest of Caliph al-Mansur, he composed the first authoritative biography of the Prophet Muhammad. Another important Persian scholar, al-Tabari (d. 923) wrote the *History of Prophets and Kings*, a great resource on early Islamic history.

Inheritors of Sasanian court traditions that emphasized ceremony, the 'Abbasids slowly distanced themselves from their subjects. The harem embodied this spatial separation. A forbidden place, the caliph's family made the harem their personal residence. Caliphs controlled the empire through family, solidifying political alliances by marrying many powerful women.

Page | 322

Figure 8.14 | John the Grammarian as Ambassador Before Theophilos and Mamun | The Embassy of John the Grammarian in 829, between the Byzantine emperor Theophilos on the right and the Abbasid caliph al-Ma'mun on the left.

Author: Unknown

Source: Wikimedia Commons

License: Public Domain

The harem bestowed power to women, and they played an important role in influencing 'Abbasid politics, particularly in terms of questions over succession. In the late 'Abbasid period, various women selected and trained the successors. Young men who were to rule resided in the harem, and much scheming over which son the caliph preferred occurred there. The mother of the caliph, however, dominated internal politics of the space. Harun's mother played a significant role in his reign, for example. The second most powerful woman in the household was the mother of the heir apparent. She could be any woman, even a concubine, for young, beautiful women were highly sought after at a time when the harem became more important under the 'Abbasids.

Riven apart by palace intrigue, the 'Abbasid Caliphate eventually succumbed to internecine warfare. In fact, Harun al-Rashid himself divided the caliphate when he designated his eldest son, al-Amin, as his heir, for he had already bequeathed the province of Khorasan to his younger son, al-Ma'mun. Upon their father's death in 809, al-Amin demanded his brother's territory and obeisance. Of course, al-Ma'mun refused, and a catastrophic civil war ensued. In 812, al-Ma'mun's army, under the command of his Persian general, Tahir, laid siege to Baghdad. Tahir caught al-Amin attempting to escape from the city and decapitated him. Al-Ma'mun succeeded his brother as caliph, but remained in Merv, his former capital. He ultimately relocated to Baghdad in 819, by which time, years of sporadic violence and lawlessness had severely damaged the city.

Al-Ma'mun (r.813 – 833) continued his father's tradition of sponsoring scholarship. He completed the *Bayt al-Hikmah* that his father had begun. He also expressed a love for philosophical and theological debate and encouraged the Islamic doctrine known as the **Mu'tazila**, a rationalist formulation of Islam that stressed free will over divine predestination. Influenced by Aristotelian thought, the Mu'tazila attempted to solve the theological question of evil. It asserted that human reason alone could inform proper behavior. Condemned as a heresy for incorporating extra Islamic patterns of thought into their belief system, many Muslims concluded that the Mu'tazila's rationalism exceeded the holy doctrines of Islam.

The 'Abbasids began their long, slow decline under al-Ma'mun, who was the first caliph to confer greater freedom upon his emirs, or provincial governors, initiating a process of decentralization that eventually unleashed uncontrollable centrifugal forces. This process began when al-Ma'mun first awarded his general Tahir with the governorship of Khorasan, where Tahir raised his own revenue and directed his own affairs. The Tahirid dynasty dominated the politics of the region, resisting Abbasid attempts to restrain them. From Khorasan, Tahir's family represented an existential threat to the caliphate.

Internal problems continued under al-Muʿtasim (833 – 842), the successor to al-Ma'mun, who replaced undependable tribal armies with **mamluks**. The *mamluks* played an increasingly important role in the fate of the caliphate. They were part of an elite slave system that imported young boys from various backgrounds, though usually Turkic, and trained them in the military arts. Because the enslavement of Muslims was not permitted in Islam, caliphs obtained slaves by raiding outside of the Islamic world or by trading for them. Indoctrinated at a young age, *mamluks* remained loyal to their leaders, serving as their personal bodyguard. Once emancipated, however, they entered into a contractual relationship with their former masters and benefited from certain property and marriage rights. Although often portrayed as slaves in the popular imagination, *mamluks* actually formed a proud caste of soldiers who considered themselves superior to the rest of society. As the elite bodyguards to the caliph, they supplanted the traditional ethnic hierarchy of the 'Abbasids, a shift which led to much class conflict often resulting in unrest and civil disturbances. In order to remove the *mamluks* from the volatile situation in Baghdad, the caliph moved the capital to Samarra, some 60 miles to the north, a measure that only delayed the inevitable, as subsequent caliphs could not control the rising tensions that resulted in social instability and contributed to the decentralization and fragmentation of the empire.

The transition from tribal armies to *mamluks* had profound repercussions for the 'Abbasids. *Mamluks* like **Ahmad ibn Tulun** (835 – 884), a slave from Circassia, most exemplified this pattern of decentralization and fragmentation that had disastrous consequences for the 'Abbasid Caliphate. He had been sent by the 'Abbasids to Egypt in order to restructure and strengthen it on their behalf. An intellectual and religious person, ibn Tulun founded schools, hospitals, and mosques in Egypt, the most famous being

Figure 8.15 | Mamluk Lancers on Horseback
Author: Nick Michael
Source: Wikimedia Commons
License: Public Domain

the eponymous ibn Tulun Mosque. However, he saw weakness back in Baghdad, as the 'Abbasids suffered from instability, including palace intrigue, disorderly *mamluks*, and revolts like the Zanj Rebellion, a slave rebellion that threatened the fate of the caliphate. The 'Abbasids could not control ibn Tulun, and, as the caliphate broke down, he managed to secure almost complete autonomy from Baghdad. By the end of his reign, he was so independent that he kept his own tax revenue and raised his own *mamluk* army, for he, too, depended militarily and politically on his loyal *mamluks* to stay in power.

Figure 8.16 | The Ibn Tulun Mosque, Cairo, Egypt
Author: Berthol Werner
Source: Wikimedia Commons
License: CC BY-SA 3.0

Ibn Tulun's autonomy in Egypt portended the decline of the 'Abbasids, whose real authority came to an end in 945. The Buyids, an Iranian dynasty, overthrew the 'Abbasids and relegated them to the status of mere religious figureheads; the caliphate continued in name only. Following the collapse of the Abbasids, the centralization and political unity of the lands formerly under their control broke down; however, economic, cultural, and religious unity remained.

8.11 THE FATIMID CALIPHATE

While Egypt grew increasingly independent of Baghdad under the Tulunids, the rule of the 'Abbasids over their broad empire generally declined. From this vacuum of power, the Fatimids (910 – 1171) emerged. Members of the Isma'ili sect of Shi'a Islam, the Fatimids traced their genealogy to the relationship between Fatima, the Prophet's daughter, and 'Ali. **Isma'ilis** believe that the divinely ordained spiritual leadership of the Islamic community, or caliphate, descended from 'Ali down to Isma'il, the son of Jafar al-Sadiq. They refused to recognize the legitimacy of the 'Abbasids and sought to convert the masses of Sunnis to their own schismatic brand of Islam. To do so, Isma'ili missionaries spread out to the far flung fringes of the empire and preached a religious revolution. These emissaries achieved their greatest success in the North African Maghreb.

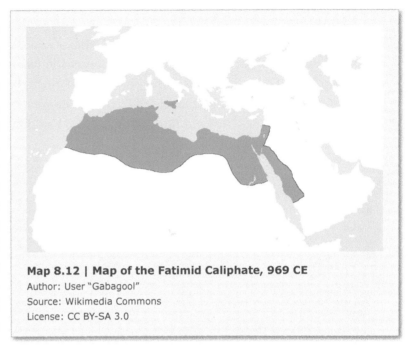

Map 8.12 | Map of the Fatimid Caliphate, 969 CE
Author: User "Gabagool"
Source: Wikimedia Commons
License: CC BY-SA 3.0

'Abd Allah al-Mahdi, founder of the Fatimids, proclaimed himself the *mahdi*, the precursor to the final judgement, representing an ideology that compelled people to change. Hounded by 'Abbasid agents of persecution who sought to uphold Sunni orthodoxy, he fled from his family's homeland in Syria and, disguised as an ordinary merchant, traveled westward through the Maghreb to Sijilmasa, where he went into hiding. In 909, local Isma'ili missionaries rescued him from Sijilmasa. By 920, he had consolidated power and made his capital at Mahdiya, located in present day Tunisia. As the *mahdi* and a catalyst for change, he converted tribal troops and inspired them to fight on his behalf. 'Abd Allah al-Mahdi endowed the Fatimids with a new *'asabiyah*, providing them with the unity of purpose necessary to defeat the 'Abbasids in North Africa. Within forty years, 'Abd Allah al-Mahdi had conquered the whole of Northwest Africa. He aimed his expansion at Egypt but failed to seize it. His grandson, al-Mu'izz, however, succeeded in this aim.

Al-Mu'izz (953 – 975) used a combination of *mamluk* and tribal armies to capture Egypt in 969. Rather than contend with older, possibly rebellious cities like Alexandria, al-Mu'izz founded Cairo, the City of the Conqueror. He developed Cairo into the preeminent cultural and economic center of the Islamic world, taking over from a Baghdad in decline. Al-Mu'izz established **al-Azhar**, the largest and most famous mosque in Egypt, which also served as a religious center that focused on the theological development of Shi'a Islam. Once in power, the Fatimids changed the official state religion of Egypt from Sunni orthodoxy to Shi'a heterodoxy, though the majority of the population in Egypt remained Sunni Muslims.

Al-Hakim (991 – 1021) ascended to the throne of his father, al-'Aziz, at the age of eleven. As a young man, he quickly displayed a pattern of unpredictable behavior. Just four years after taking command of the empire, he had his regent, the eunuch Barjawan, murdered. Additionally, al-Hakim earned a place in infamy by targeting Christians and Jews, worsening the generally amiable relations with the People of the Book that the Fatimids had previously enjoyed. For instance, in 1004, al-Hakim prohibited Christians from celebrating Epiphany and Easter. He also forbad the use of wine, a prohibition which caused religious difficulties for Christians and Jews alike. In 1005, al-Hakim decreed the Law of Differentiation, requiring all of the People of the Book to prominently display religious icons indicating their particular religious adherence. In 1009, he became infuriated by some of the Orthodox Church's religious practices and consequently razed the Church of the Holy Sepulchre in response. A few years later, he ordered the destruction of thousands of churches and synagogues in Palestine. Al-Hakim even made Western pilgrimage to the Holy Land difficult. During this period, pilgrimages to Palestine had been increasing, and many pilgrims returned home complaining of Muslim treatment of Christians in the Holy Land. His behavior towards Christians elicited a strong Western reaction, for Europeans used his conduct as a way to encourage support for the Crusades.

Around the year 1010, **Muhammad ad-Darazi**, an Isma'ili preacher, began teaching that al-Hakim was a manifestation of God. Ad-Darazi believed that universal rationality was made incarnate in the person of Adam and then passed down through the prophets to the family of 'Ali and his descendants, including the Fatimids. His doctrines eventually spread to the Levant, where these ideas found reception amongst the Druze, a cognate of Darazi, although they viewed Ad-Darazi as a heretic. A follower of Isma'ilism, al-Hakim did not want to be associated with ad-Darazi and his teachings, so he had the preacher executed in 1018.

Al-Hakim continued his tendency to display erratic behavior when he walked out into the desert in 1021 and never returned. While his disappearance has remained a mystery for the ages, those who worshiped the caliph believe that he went into Occultation, later to return as the messianic *mahdi*.

Figure 8.17 | The Al-Azhar
Author: User "Buyoof"
Source: Wikimedia Commons
License: CC BY-SA 3.0

Figure 8.18 | Al-Hakim
Author: Al-Ahram
Source: Wikimedia Commons
License: Public Domain

8.12 THE CRUSADES

In 1071, the Great Seljuq Empire, under the leadership of Alp Arslan, defeated the Byzantines at the **Battle of Manzikert**, near Lake Van, taking the Eastern Roman Emperor, Romanus I, prisoner in the process. This defeat was crushing for the Byzantines, allowing waves of Turkmen *ghazis*, or raiders, to press deep into the heartland of Anatolia, eventually establishing the Sultanate of Rum, with its capital at Nicaea. A series of weak emperors succeeded Romanus I with **Alexios Komnenos** (1081 – 1108) eventually ascending to the throne ten years later. As the new emperor, he made peace with the Seljuqs of Rum, and the two states eventually adopted cordial relations. They began to trade with each other and even lent one another military support when needed. Alexius needed this military support in order to secure his borders from groups of Turkic marauders. To that end, he appealed to **Pope Urban II** (1088 – 1099) for help recruiting mercenary soldiers, namely Frankish knights. An effective cavalry, the Frankish knights had earned an impressive reputation for how they acquitted themselves on the battlefield.

Meanwhile, European leaders had been searching for creative ways of expelling society's troublemakers and were not averse to sending their soldiers abroad, for the region was suffering from overpopulation and endemic violence. They believed that it was better for the martial groups in their society to fight against the Muslims than amongst themselves. In this way, the Crusades externalized continental violence and promoted European peace.

In 1095, Urban II launched the first crusade from Clermont, a city in southern France. He had benefited from recent church reforms, renewed religious fervor, and a concomitant increase in papal power. While traveling through France, he made an argument for the recovery of the Holy Land: because it belonged to Jesus, it should be controlled by his followers. He also appealed to the greatness of the Franks, promising potential pilgrims a land flowing with milk, honey, and riches. And he offered them well-designed spiritual rewards. For example, salvation applied to those who died on campaign, and anyone who invested in a crusade secured themselves a place in heaven.

The Crusades started in 1096 and were part of a larger process whereby Muslims ceded territory to non-Muslims, sometimes permanently. Provoked by al-Hakim's treatment of Christians in the Holy Land, as well as the Turkic invasion of Anatolia, Europeans commenced several centuries' worth of armed crusades against the Muslim states of the eastern Mediterranean and North Africa. Save for the first crusade, in which the Christians established the Crusader states of Edessa, Antioch, Tripoli, and the Latin Kingdom of Jerusalem, all of their campaigns ended in disaster. In fact, they were either looting expeditions or responses to the loss of Crusader states to Muslims. The success that the Latin knights did enjoy related to not only the political fragmentation of the Seljuqs in the eastern Mediterranean, but also the general disinterest of the Fatimid Caliphate in Egypt, which had been dealing with both the repercussions of a religious schism and the consequences of famine and plague. Slow to respond to the challenge posed by the Christians, the Fatimids watched the Crusaders from afar with indifference.

The Muslim counterattack eventually came under the direction of **Salah al-Din** (Saladin) (d. 1193), a unifier of various Muslim factions in the eastern Mediterranean. An ethnic Kurd, he hailed from a family of soldiers of fortune in the employ of the Zengid Dynasty's Nur al-Din, a vassal of the Seljuq Turks. Salah al-Din set off in his twenties to fight battles for his uncle, Shirkuh, a Zengid general. A dynamic leader and tactician, he helped his uncle dispatch with the Fatimid opposition in Egypt and solidified Nur al-Din's rule there. His uncle dying soon thereafter, Salah al-Din eventually became the vizier, or senior minister, to Nur al-Din in 1169. For five years, Salah al-Din ruled Egypt on behalf of Nur al-Din. Then Nur al-Din died in Damascus in 1174, leaving no clear successor.

8.12.1 The Ayyubid Sultanate

In the absence of a formal heir to Nur al-Din, Salah al-Din established the Ayyubid Dynasty (1171 – 1260), named after his father, Ayyub, a provincial governor for the Zengid Dynasty, a family of Oghuz Turks who served as vassals of the Seljuq Empire. Once in power, Salah al-Din established a Sunni government and insisted that the mosque of al-Azhar preach his brand of Islam. He used the concept of *jihad* to unify the Middle East under the banner of Islam in order to defeat the

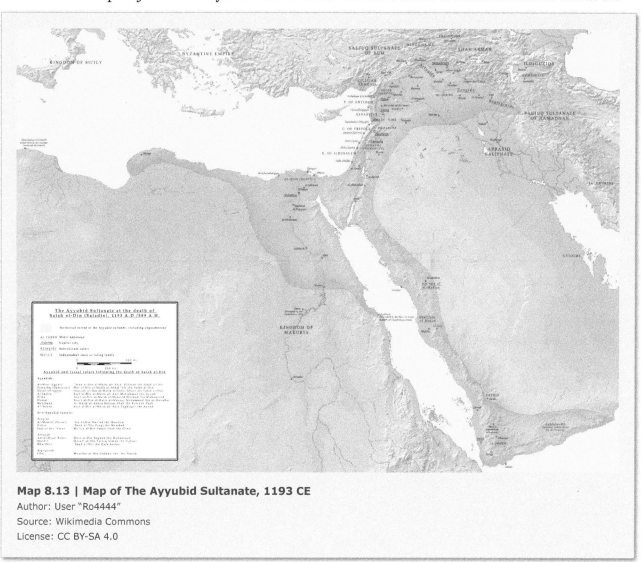

Map 8.13 | Map of The Ayyubid Sultanate, 1193 CE
Author: User "Ro4444"
Source: Wikimedia Commons
License: CC BY-SA 4.0

Christians, but he did not principally direct *jihad* towards them. A champion of Sunni Islam, he believed that his religion was being threatened mainly from within by the Shi'a. Like most of their predecessors, the Ayyubids also benefited from tribal *'asabiyah*, or dynastic consensus. Ayyubid 'asabiyah included a Kurdish heritage, as well as a strong desire to return to Sunni orthodoxy. It was as champions of Sunni Islam that they purposely recruited leading Muslim scholars from abroad, ultimately culminating in Egypt becoming the preeminent state in the Islamic world.

Initially, Salah al-Din displayed no particular interest in the Crusader states. He had clashed with the Crusaders, and King Baldwin IV of Jerusalem; also, Raynald de Chântillon even had handed him a rare defeat at the Battle of Montgisard in 1177. But the Crusaders ultimately brokered an armistice with Salah al-Din. Eventually, Raynald broke their truce when he started attacking Muslim pilgrims and trade caravans in the 1180s. Ensuing skirmishes between the forces of Salah al-Din and Guy de Lusignan, the new King of Jerusalem, presaged a forthcoming battle. In 1187, the two sides met near Tiberias, in modern day Israel. Salah al-Din intentionally attacked the fortress of Tiberius in order to lure the Crusaders away from their well-watered stronghold. His plan worked, and the Christians quickly ran out of water. On the night before the battle, Salah al-Din set brush fires to exacerbate their thirst. He coerced the parched Latin Knights down through the Horns of Hattin towards the cool waters of Lake Tiberius. Salah al-Din bottlenecked the Crusader forces, with the double hill of Hattin acting as a choke point.

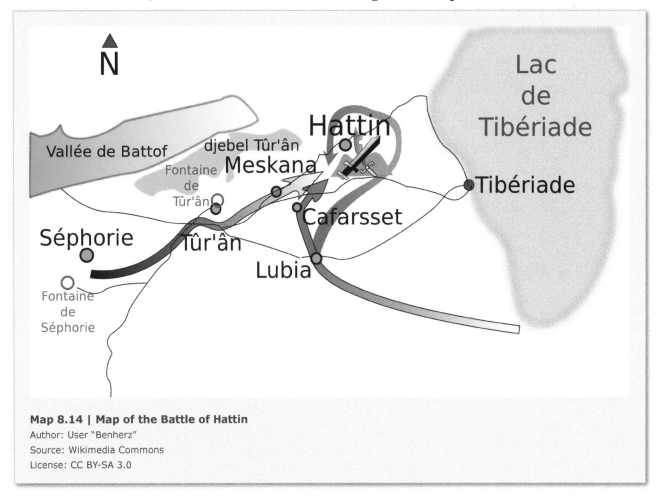

Map 8.14 | Map of the Battle of Hattin
Author: User "Benherz"
Source: Wikimedia Commons
License: CC BY-SA 3.0

The Battle of Hattin represented a smashing victory for Salah al-Din and a major loss for the Crusaders. Tradition dictated that Salah al-Din hold most of the leaders for ransom. Unlike the Crusaders, he treated the defenders of cities with understanding. He showed tolerance of minorities, and even established a committee to partition Jerusalem amongst all the interested religious groups. In this way, he proved his moral superiority to the Crusaders.

With most of their important leaders either killed in battle or captured, no unified Christian leadership remained to fight against Salah al-Din. Deprived of the backbone of their organization, the Crusaders were left with only a few defenseless fortresses along the coast. Salah al-Din pressed his advantage. Increasingly isolated and relying on ever dwindling numbers of Latin Christians willing to remain permanently in the Holy Land, the Latin Crusaders were eventually expelled from the region in 1291.

Although Salah al-Din had maintained direct control over Egypt, he intentionally distributed control over wide swaths of the empire to loyal vassals and family members, whose governance became increasingly autonomous from Cairo. Salah al-Din's sons and grandsons, who did not have the same ability as their forefather, had trouble managing an increasingly decentralized empire. Widespread *mamluk* factionalism and family disputes over the control of territory contributed to the weakening of the sultanate. In this vacuum of power, the *mamluks* came to the fore.

8.13 THE MAMLUK SULTANATE

The year was 1249, and Louis IX's seventh crusade had just gotten underway when as-Salih, the last Ayyubid ruler, took to his deathbed. Under the eminent threat of a Crusader invasion, as-Salih's wife, **Shajar al-Durr**, a Turkish concubine, agreed to take over the reins of government until her son, Turanshah, could assert himself. But he had never truly gained the trust of his father, and a cabal of *mamluks* loyal to as-Salih murdered Turanshah. They then raised Shajar al-Durr to the throne. Her rule resulted in much controversy and suffered from many internal problems. According to tradition, she sought recognition as sultana from the figurehead 'Abbasid Caliph, but he refused to pay homage to her. The *mamluks* responded by installing into power one of their own, a certain **Aybak**. He married Shajar al-Durr, and she abdicated the throne. The most powerful *mamluk* in Egypt, Aybak placated some of the opposition to Shajar al-Durr's rule and also dealt with Louis IX's crusade to Egypt. While *mamluks* did not possess a tribal *'asabiyah* in the traditional sense, they did constitute a proud caste of elite warriors who had an exaggerated sense of group solidarity. As a social group, their former status as slaves provided them with enough group cohesion to overthrow the Ayyubids.

Shajar al-Durr remained unsatisfied in her new role, however. In fact, she saw herself as another Cleopatra and wanted to rule in her own right. She also feared the consequences of Aybak's potential marriage alliance with the daughter of the Ayyubid Emir of Mosul. In 1257, Shajar al-Durr had Aybak strangled and claimed that he had died a natural death. However, **Qutuz**, a leading *mamluk*, did not believe her story. Under duress, her servants confessed to the murder. Qutuz arrested Shajar al-Durr and imprisoned her in the Red Tower. Not long thereafter, Aybak's fifteen year old son, al-Mansur 'Ali, had Shajar al-Durr stripped and beaten to death. He

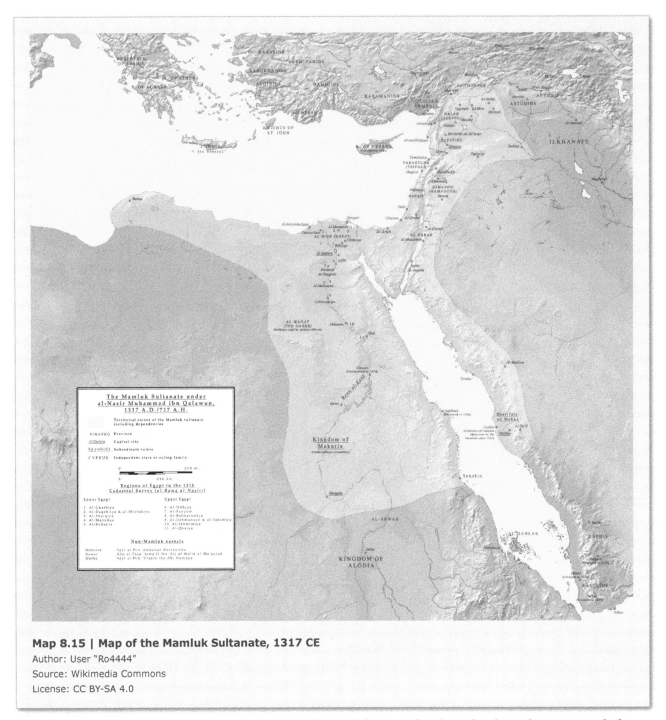

Map 8.15 | Map of the Mamluk Sultanate, 1317 CE
Author: User "Ro4444"
Source: Wikimedia Commons
License: CC BY-SA 4.0

reigned as sultan for two years until Qutuz deposed him, as he thought the sultanate needed a strong and capable ruler to deal with the looming Mongol threat.

The Mamluk Sultanate appeared to be on a collision course with Hulagu's Ilkhanate, one of Mongol Empire's four khanates, whose forces were advancing through the Mamluk-held Levant. Then in the summer of 1260, the Great Khan Möngke died and Hulagu returned home with the bulk of his forces to participate in the required khuriltai, or Mongol assembly, perhaps expecting to be elected the next Great Khan. Hulagu left his general Kitbuqa behind with a smaller army to fight the Mamluks. In July of that year, a confrontation took place at **Ayn Jalut**, near Lake Tiberias. During the ensuing battle, the Mamluk General Baybars drew out the Mongols with a feigned retreat. Hiding behind a hill, Aybak's *mamluk* heavy cavalrymen ambushed the unsuspecting Mongols and defeated them in close combat, securing a rare victory over the Mongols. The Mamluks captured and executed Kitbuqa, and forced the remnants of the Mongol forces to retreat.

Just days after their signal victory over the Mongols, **Baybars** (1260 – 1277) murdered Qutuz, continuing a pattern of rule in which only the strongest Mamluk rulers could survive. Too clever to be deposed, Baybars developed a strong military oligarchy that rested on the iqta' system, a centralized system of land tenure based on money that, by the thirteenth century, had been perfected in Egypt. Under the iqta' system, individual *mamluks* received a percentage of profit from the sale of crops for their upkeep. Baybars owned all of the land, so *mamluks* only received the right to collect taxes from the land, a right akin to usufruct in feudal Europe.

Baybars relocated the 'Abbasid Caliph from Baghdad to Cairo in order to present a veneer of legitimacy to *mamluk* rule. Since the Ptolemys, Egypt had been ruled by foreigners. In fact, the only impact native-born Egyptians had was in religion. The Mamluk Sultanate practiced Sunni Islam and emphasized Sufism. Sufis believed that traditional, orthodox Islam lacked compassion, and their Sufism helped conversion efforts because of its emphasis on love and making a closer connection to God, as opposed to a strict adherence to the dictates of the Quran. Sufis desired something more from religion and emphasized integrating the reality of God into man. Sufis thought that they could achieve a union with God based on love, a notion that contrasted sharply with the general perception of orthodox Islam which denied believers a direct experience to God because Muhammad represented the Seal of the Prophets and all understanding of God came through the prophet. They set up new religious schools to pass on this Sufism. These *madrasa* consisted of a complex, with a mosque, school, hospital, and water supply for each community.

The fourteenth and fifteenth centuries witnessed the decline of the Mamluk Empire. Several internal and external factors help explain their decline. Domestically, the Black Death ravaged Egypt for years. In fact, it continued in North Africa longer than it did in Europe. This plague caused economic disruption in the sultanate. With fewer people available, labor, or human capital, became much more expensive. Further, plague-related inflation destabilized the economy, as the value of goods and services also rose. The *mamluks* responded to inflationary pressures by increasing taxes, but their revenue from those taxes actually decreased. This decrease made it difficult for the *mamluks* to maintain their irrigation networks and, without irrigation, agricultural productivity decreased.

Externally, plague was not the only cause of inflation. Columbus's discovery of the New World began a process in which gold began filtering through Europe and into North Africa. Egypt's weak economy could not absorb this massive influx of money, thus causing more inflation. New trade routes, like the one pioneered by Vasco de Gama, offered Europeans direct sea routes to Asia. No longer was Egypt the middleman for long-distance trade between Europe and Asia, thereby losing out on valuable revenue from tariffs. The profits from commerce transferred to the ascending states of Portugal and Spain. The decline of the Mamluks set the stage for the rise of the Ottomans.

8.14 CONCLUSION

A contemporary historian who served the Mamluk Sultanate, Ibn Khaldun astutely recognized the applicability of his Cyclical Theory of History to the evolution of Islamic history during the period covered in this chapter. By the eighth century, Islam became the predominant social and political unifier of the Middle East. And for the next nine hundred years, various caliphates used family and religion as tools to rule the region. However, these caliphates faced religiously-inspired revolts that challenged their authority. Quelling these revolts weakened the regimes, often leading to greater decentralization and the fragmentation of empires. Into these vacuums of power, new families armed with tribal 'asabiyah and a novel religious ideology came forth to supplant a once dominant group who had succumbed to the wiles of civilization and whose influence gradually waned in the face of insurgent desert peoples.

8.15 WORKS CONSULTED AND FURTHER READING

Berkey, Jonathan P., *The Formation of Islam: Religion and Society in the Near East 600 – 800*. Cambridge: Cambridge University Press, 2003.

Donner, Fred, *The Early Islamic Conquests*. Princeton: Princeton University Press, 1981.

Esposito, John L., *Islam: The Straight Path*. Oxford: Oxford University Press, 1998.

Halm, Heinz, *The Empire of the Mahdi: The rise of the Fatimids*. Leiden: E.J. Brill, 1997.

Lassner, Jacob, *The Shaping of Abbasid Rule*. Princeton: Princeton University Press, 1980.

Kennedy, Hugh, *The Prophet and the Age of the Caliphates: The Islamic Near East from the Sixth to the Eleventh Century*. London: Longman, 2004.

Lewis, Bernard, *The Arabs in History*. Oxford: Oxford University Press, 1993.

Momen, Moojan, *An Introduction to Shi'I Islam*. New Haven: Yale University Press, 1985.

Powell, James M., ed. *Muslims Under Latin Rule*, 1100 – 1300. Princeton: Princeton University Press, 1990.

Watt, W. Mongomery, *Muhammad: Prophet and Statesman*. Oxford: Oxford University Press, 1974.

8.16 LINKS TO PRIMARY SOURCES

Ancient Accounts of Arabia 430 BCE – 550 CE
> https://legacy.fordham.edu/halsall/ancient/arabia1.asp

Ibn Ishaq (d. c. 773 CE): Selections from the Life of Muhammad
> https://legacy.fordham.edu/halsall/source/muhammadi-sira.asp

The Prophet Muhammad: Last Sermon
> https://legacy.fordham.edu/halsall/source/muhm-sermon.asp

Muhammad Speaks of Allah
> http://www.mircea-eliade.com/from-primitives-to-zen/040.html

Muhammad's Call

http://www.mircea-eliade.com/from-primitives-to-zen/231.html

Muhammad is the Messenger of God

http://www.mircea-eliade.com/from-primitives-to-zen/232.html

Muhammad Proclaims the Prescriptions of Islam

http://www.mircea-eliade.com/from-primitives-to-zen/122.html

The Sunnah, (traditions of the Prophet Muhammad), excerpts

https://legacy.fordham.edu/halsall/source/sunnah-horne.asp

Abu Hamid al-Ghazali (1058 – 1111 CE): The Remembrance of Death and the Afterlife

https://legacy.fordham.edu/halsall/source/alghazali.asp

The Battle of Badr, 624 CE

http://web.archive.org/web/19980119194508/http://www.islaam.com/ilm/battleof.htm

Al-Baladhuri: The Battle of The Yarmuk (636 CE) and After

https://legacy.fordham.edu/halsall/source/yarmuk.asp

Accounts of the Arab Conquest of Egypt, 642 CE

https://legacy.fordham.edu/halsall/source/642Egypt-conq2.asp

Yakut: Baghdad under the Abbasids, c. 1000 CE

https://legacy.fordham.edu/halsall/source/1000baghdad.asp

Abul Hasan Ali Al-Masu'di (Masoudi) (c. 895? – 957 CE): The Book of Golden Meadows, c. 940 CE

https://legacy.fordham.edu/halsall/source/masoudi.asp

The Seven Voyages of Sinbad the Sailor story from the Thousand and One Nights

http://www.sacred-texts.com/neu/lang1k1/tale15.htm

Ibn Rushd (Averroës) (1126 – 1198 CE): Religion & Philosophy, c. 1190 CE.

https://legacy.fordham.edu/halsall/source/1190averroes.asp

Firdausi: The Epic of Kings, c. 1000 CE

http://classics.mit.edu/Ferdowsi/kings.html

Sa'di (1184 – 1292 CE): Gulistan, 1258 CE

http://classics.mit.edu/Sadi/gulistan.html

African History to 1500

Charlotte Miller

9.1 CHRONOLOGY

200,000 – 100,000 BP (Before Present)	First behaviorally modern human emerged in Africa
c. 7000 BCE	Beginnings of the Agricultural Revolution in Africa
c. 3000 BCE – 1500 CE	The Bantu expansions
900s BCE	Rule of Queen Makeda (Ethiopia)
c. 800 BCE – 300 CE	Kingdom of Da'amat (Ethiopia)
c. 250 BCE	Founding of Djenne-Jeno, one of Africa's first cities (Western Sudan)
c. 100 – 950 CE	The Empire of Aksum
c. 300 CE	Ghana emerged as a state (Western Sudan)
c. 325 – 350 CE	The rule of King Ezana (Aksum/Ethiopia)
c. 800 CE	Ghana became an empire (Western Sudan)
1000 – 1500 CE	Height of Swahili society (East Africa)
1200 – 1450 CE	Height of Great Zimbabwe (southern Africa/ Zimbabwe Plateau)
1235 CE	Sundiata Keita founded the Mali Empire (Western Sudan)
1324 – 1325 CE	Mansa Musa performed the hajj (Western Sudan)
Early 1400s CE	Portuguese began to explore the Atlantic coast of West Africa; beginnings of the Age of Exploration
1460s CE	Sunni Ali built the Songhai Empire (Western Sudan)
1493 – 1528 CE	Askia the Great ruled during the Golden Age of the Songhai Empire (Western Sudan)
Early 1500s CE	The Portuguese built a Trading Post Empire in the Indian Ocean (East Africa)
1591 CE	Moroccans invaded the Songhai Empire (Western Sudan)
1699 CE	The Omanis (allied with some Swahili rulers) seized Swahili city-states from the Portuguese (East Africa)

9.2 INTRODUCTION

Adventurously sailing the Indian Ocean in the early 1500s CE, Duarte Barbosa, a Portuguese naval officer, was confident that he was helping to forge a new, enduring era of Portuguese dominance. As he passed through several Swahili city-states on the East African coast, Barbosa noted the brisk trade and the riches of these African settlements where he saw a "great plenty of gold" that would serve Portuguese interests.[1] In his mind, God had destined these stashes of gold for the Portuguese and the local Swahili rulers acted unwisely and arrogantly to defend themselves. In the conflict that followed, the Portuguese plundered the Swahili city-states, burning buildings and enslaving African men and women. Barbosa boasted that when the Portuguese looted the settlements, they slaughtered many people and took a "great spoil of gold and silver and goods."[2] Barbosa's description highlights the violence of Portuguese conquest and also his expectation that he and his countrymen were creating a new Portuguese empire that would make a lasting mark in East Africa and the wider Indian Ocean world. However, less than 100 years later, Portuguese influences were noticeably absent in most of East Africa and their power in the Indian Ocean was fading rapidly. Barbosa, himself, had traveled with his brother-in-law, Ferdinand Magellan, and met an untimely end (in his early 40s) in the Philippines.

Writing about the coast of East Africa, Barbosa paid little heed to the hundreds of years of Swahili history that preceded his visit. Therefore, his narrative gives us minimal information about Swahili civilization. This chapter will fill in some of the silences in the written historical record as it describes Africa's major contributions to World History.

Figure 9.1 | Kibo Summit of Mt. Kilimanjaro | Is this the image of Africa you have? The picture shows the famous snow-capped peak, Kibo summit, of Mt. Kilimanjaro, which is located in Tanzania (East Africa). The African continent has great geographic and climatic diversity.
Author: Muhammad mahdi Karmi
Source: Wikipedia
License: GNU Free Documentation License (email author before using)

---

1 Quoted in "The East Coast of Africa: Duarte Barbosa," *Aspects of World Civilization, vol. 1*, Ed. Perry M. Rogers, (Upper Saddle River, NJ: Prentice Hall, 2003): 376.
2 Ibid, p. 377.

Since information readily available in the U.S. tends to focus on issues like drought, famine, and war, Americans have many common misconceptions about Africa. In addition to associating Africa with extreme hardships, a plethora of western-made TV shows focus on wildlife and the rainforests. However, these popular images don't give an accurate portrayal of the everyday experiences of most Africans or tell us much about the history of the continent.

One of the main points glossed over by these popular images is that the African continent is large and diverse. Africa is the second largest continent in the world. Today, it has over 50 independent countries. You can also find just about every imaginable environment, from savannahs, rainforests, and deserts, to glaciers and snow-capped mountains in Africa. Its over 1,000 languages (or about one-third of the world's languages) also demonstrate the continent's diversity.[3] Africa is home to more than a billion people, who are living, working, and raising their families.

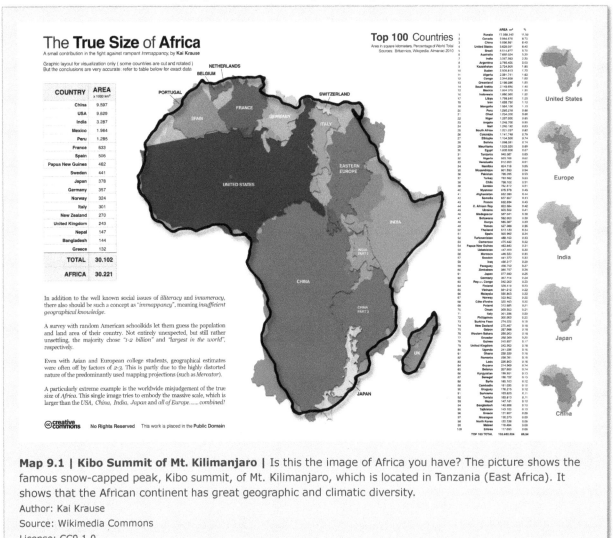

Map 9.1 | Kibo Summit of Mt. Kilimanjaro | Is this the image of Africa you have? The picture shows the famous snow-capped peak, Kibo summit, of Mt. Kilimanjaro, which is located in Tanzania (East Africa). It shows that the African continent has great geographic and climatic diversity.
Author: Kai Krause
Source: Wikimedia Commons
License: CC0 1.0

3   African Language Program, Department of African and African American Studies, "African Languages," Harvard University, http://aaas.fas.harvard.edu/greetings-director-african-language-program.

Historically, Africans faced significant environmental challenges that limited population growth. There are exceptions, but overall, African soils are poor and rainfall has been unpredictable. Soils are comparatively unfertile, due in part to the geologic age of the continent. Also, the more temperate climates in a number of regions slows the decomposition of organic materials in the soil, meaning that the soil in many regions has few minerals and nutrients. The areas that are exceptions, such as the highlands of Ethiopia, Rwanda, and Burundi, have seen much higher population concentrations. Rainfall also tends to be concentrated in just two or three months a year, while disease has been yet another challenge.

Considering the past 5,000 years of African history, malaria, yellow fever, and trypanosomiasis (also known as sleeping sickness) have made the biggest impacts on population growth and settlement patterns. Even today, all three diseases affect the continent. Both **malaria** and **yellow fever** are spread to people by mosquitos. According to the World Health Organization (WHO), despite preventative measures and great efforts to extend the availability of treatments, malaria was responsible for almost 600,000 deaths in 2013. Children in Africa account for most of the fatalities, and the WHO estimates that currently one African child dies from malaria every minute of every day.[4] Those who have suffered through malaria multiple times as adults will attest that malaria, with the exception of its most virulent strains like *plasmodium falciparum,* is usually more of a nuisance than an emergency for healthy adults. It causes symptoms like headaches, fever, and chills. Even though it does not usually constitute a medical emergency for adults, malaria does decrease productivity and has significant treatment costs. On the other hand, yellow fever has a high mortality rate—about 50%—even amongst healthy adult populations.[5] While malaria and yellow fever have historically taken the

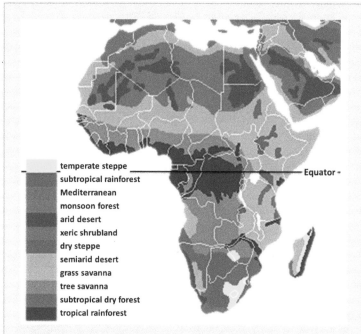

Map 9.2 | Climatic Map of Africa | Here you can see the present-day climatic map of Africa. There is great variation from the Mediterranean climate of the north and southern tips (think: olives, grapes for wine, and citrus fruits), to the second largest desert in the world (the Sahara Desert), through the savannas, grasslands, and the more forested regions. Today, we see a general drying trend on the continent, leading to increasing conflict over things like water rights and pastureland. However, although there has been some contraction and expansion of rainforests over the past millennia, the continental climatic map has remained fairly stable for about 5,000 years.

Author: Ville Koistinen
Source: Wikimedia Commons
License: CC BY-SA 2.5

4   World Health Organization Media Centre, "Malaria: Fact Sheet," http://www.who.int/mediacentre/factsheets/fs094/en
5   World Health Organization Media Centre, "Yellow Fever: Fact Sheet," http://www.who.int/mediacentre/factsheets/fs100/en

largest toll on human populations, one of the main effects of **trypanosomiasis** (or sleeping sickness) has been to limit the practicality of keeping certain types of livestock in Africa. Horses and many breeds of cattle are especially susceptible to trypranosomiasis, which is spread by the tsetse fly and can lead to either chronic illness, characterized by weight loss, fever, anemia, cardiac lesions, and other symptoms in animals, or to a more immediate death. Until the past fifty years or so, in many parts of the continent, these noteworthy challenges with disease, alongside the low fertility of the soils and the unpredictable rainfalls, were significant constraints on human population growth. Environmental challenges and disease also affected settlement patterns as, for example, people avoided more forested and wetter areas because of the prevalence of mosquitoes. Additionally, Africans continuously adapted their herding and farming techniques to overcome these challenges.

9.3 QUESTIONS TO GUIDE YOUR READING

1. Describe the environments of Africa.

2. Which environmental challenges and diseases have historically limited population growth in Africa?

3. Discuss the methodological challenges of studying Ancient and Medieval African History.

4. Identify commonly used terms that are potentially problematic for scholars of Africa. Explain why these terms are potentially problematic.

5. What was distinctive about the agriculture of the Ethiopian Highlands?

6. Explain the legend of Queen Makeda and King Solomon and why it remains significant for Ethiopians.

7. How were the states in this region shaped by trade and inter-cultural relationships?

8. Describe the spread of Christianity into Aksum.

9. What characteristics were shared by the Western Sudanic States?

10. How did the location of the Western Sudanic states have an impact on their history?

11. Describe the relationship between the Western Sudanic States and the Islamic World.

12. How did nineteenth century European scholars depict the Bantu Migration? What factors influenced their view?

13. How have post-colonial scholars challenged nineteenth century depictions of the Bantu Migration?

14. How did the ruling classes of Great Zimbabwe generate wealth and demonstrate their elite status?

15. How are oral traditions, such as the one recounted here about Kilwa Kisiwani, important to Swahili identity?

16. Describe the urban style of Swahili city-states.

17. Compare the trans-Atlantic and Indian Ocean slave trades.

18. How did the Portuguese impact the East African coast?

9.4 KEY TERMS

- African diaspora
- Aksum
- Bantu expansions
- Bantu Migration
- Catalan Atlas
- Ghana
- Great Zimbabwe
- griots
- Indian Ocean World
- *Kebra Nagast*
- Kingdom of Da'amat
- King Ezana
- malaria
- Mali Empire
- mansa
- Mansa Musa
- monsoon winds
- Queen Mekeda
- Sahel
- Songhai Empire
- stelae
- Sundiata Keita
- Swahili city-states
- syncretism
- Timbuktu
- Trading Post Empire
- tribe
- trypanosomiasis
- Western Sudan
- yellow fever
- Zanj Rebellion

9.5 WRITING THE HISTORY OF ANCIENT AND MEDIEVAL AFRICA

Scholars of Africa, particulary those working in the last two generations, have employed all sorts of methods to describe the ancient African past. They have necessarily been on the forefront of methodological innovation because of the limited availability of written primary sources, meaning sources recorded by ancient Africans themselves. Therefore, scholars have turned to a wide range of materials to complement the available written records.

Before about 1800 CE, many African societies kept their records orally, as opposed to in written form. These societies have rich, complex histories that some past historians, relying primarily on written records, ignored when they studied the African continent.

The professionalization of the study of history in the West (meaning primarily in Europe and the United States), which entailed the transition from writing about the past out of personal interest to writing about the past as a profession with established methodologies, mainly occurred in the 1800s. European and American views of Africans during that era were generally derogatory and prejudiced. These nineteenth century professional scholars tended to portray Africans as primitive, meaning unchanged from time immemorial. Western methodologies, with their reliance on written sources, backed up European views of Africans as unchanged. Two general results of the nineteenth century scholarship in the West were the assumptions that Africa, which was commonly referred to as "the dark continent," lacked a history prior to European arrival on the continent and that any urban developments or complex state structures in Africa were the achievements of outsiders. For example, as you will see in this chapter, there were nineteenth century European scholars who credited people from Yemen with building the Axum trading empire and attributed the archaeological findings at Great Zimbabwe to Phoenicians. Especially since the 1960s, there has been a strong movement to reclaim these (and other) developments as African. As part of this effort, scholars employ new methodologies, including the study of oral sources, archaeology, climate change, linguistics (the study of languages), and paleoarchaobotany (the study of ancient plant materials), to gain more accurate, multi-faceted information about the African past.

Perhaps most contested and also potentially the most revealing are the available oral sources. Many ancient African societies had special people tasked with orally transmitting official histories and preserved traditions. For example, **griots** in parts of West Africa memorized chronologies, cultural traditions, and legal precedence to advise kings and state leaders. Griots also traveled and performed theater and praise-songs throughout empires to spread cultural values and communicate news from governments. Griots held honored places in their societies, reflecting their importance to both rulers and people's everyday lives. Locally produced proverbs and oral teachings also played vital roles in many ancient African societies. Additionally, African communities honored older generations for their knowledge of the past, leading Amadou Hampate Ba, a famous author from Mali, to write, "In Africa, when an old man dies, it's a library burning."[6] These examples are just some of the ways that ancient peoples used oral traditions. Since the 1960s, scholars of Africa have recognized the importance of studying these oral sources as they convey a great deal of information about the past. Using oral sources is not without its challenges, but their inclusion has broadened the scholarly understanding of African societies.

9.5.1 Terminology

Especially due to nineteenth-century tendencies to portray Africans as inferior, current scholars of Africa have a whole host of stereotypes to correct. One of the main stereotypes they

---

6   Quoted in Ann Badkhen, *Walking with Abel: Journeys with the Nomads of the African Savannah* (New York: Riverhead Books, 2015): 20.

encounter is the common perception that African societies are timeless, that they have not changed in hundreds or thousands of years. The movie *The Gods Must Be Crazy* encapsulates this stereotype. *The Gods Must Be Crazy* (1980) is a fictional account that follows the San people in the Kalahari Desert in southern Africa. The movie portrays the San as untouched by and unaware of the modern world until one member of their community finds a Coke bottle discarded from an airplane. In the movie, adventure ensues.

Movies, television shows, and other media often show us an Africa that is rural, a landscape dominated by wild animals, and a continent isolated from the rest of the modern world. However, these images do not accurately represent the continent in either our present time or the past. In 2010, one-third of Africa's population lived in cities, and it is likely that one-half of Africa's population will be urban dwelling by 2030.[7] Lagos (Nigeria) is Africa's largest city south of the Sahara Desert, with population experts estimating that it is home to 21 million people. With this estimate, Lagos is on a par size-wise with cities like Beijing, Cairo, and Mexico City. Urbanization on this scale is a fairly recent phenomena. However, this chapter will introduce you to some Medieval cities, including the famous city of Timbuktu, to discuss African urban cultures. We will also explore the trade routes that connected Africa to much of the world, emphasizing that Africa has been connected to the Arabian Peninsula, Asia, and Europe for millenia.

Even if we do not intend it to, some of the language that we use on an everyday basis can perpetuate assumptions that Africa is isolated or behind the rest of the world. One example of a potentially problematic term is "**tribe**." As African historian Christopher Ehret has pointed out, the use of "tribe" in reference to Africans often carries the underlying judgement that the people who are "tribal" are exotic, wild, backwards, and potentially dangerous. In common useage, "tribesmen" are not modern citizens of nation-states, but instead remnants of the past. To highlight the descriminatory use of the term, Ehret asks us to consider why African wars are often referred to as "tribal" wars instead of as the civil wars they actually are, and,

> ...Why is Shaka, the famous nineteenth-century ruler, called the king of the Zulu "tribe" when he was actually the king of a centralized and military powerful state? Why are Africans in "traditional" dress said to be engaging in "tribal" dancing, when Europeans garbed similarly in the clothes of an earlier time are said to be performing "folk" dances?[8]

Ehret makes the case that the way that we commonly use "tribe" perpetuates a lot of the negative stereotypes Europeans had of Africa in the nineteenth century. Furthermore, many historians question the idea that African "tribes" even existed prior to European colonization of the continent one hundred and fifty years ago. Instead, scholars discuss much more fluid, adaptive, or inclusive ethnic identities and suggest that nineteenth century Europeans tried to harden divisions and create "tribes" to suit their own administrative purposes. Dismissing Africans as "tribal" also allowed European to legitimize the trans-Atlantic slave trade (in the fifteenth through nineteenth centuries) and colonizaton of the continent (in the nineteenth

---

7   "Growth Areas: the urbanisation of Africa," *Economist* (Dec. 13, 2010), http://www.economist.com/blogs/daily-chart/2010/12/urbanisation_africa

8   Christopher Ehret, *The Civilizations of Africa: A History to 1800* (Charlottesville, VA: University Press of Virginia, 2002): 7.

century). Today, people often fall back on "tribe" and "tribal" instead of trying to understand the complexities of African politics and social organization.

There are a handful of other terms that modern scholars scrutinize to show that they are based on similar prejudices. Two such terms are "stateless society" and "bushmen." Many written sources from the nineteenth century produced by Europeans did not recognize the existence of states in Africa that had more democratic, less centralized, or less hierarchical leadership structures. These written sources assumed that all states had kings or other centralized authority figures. They denied the existence of states organized in other ways. Some African societies were centralized under the rule of monarchs, but others used, for example, councils of elders, had more decentralized, egalitarian systems, or relied on age-sets to mobilize labor and manage government affairs. These latter examples had functioning governmental structures, but nineteenth century Europeans usually did not recogize these alternative forms of state organization and claimed that Africans were incapable of ruling themselves without European intervention. The use of the phrase "stateless society" was one way that Europeans claimed to be more advanced and thus destined to colonize Africa in the nineteenth entury.

According to this same nineteenth-century ideology, the "bushmen" and "pygmies" of Africa were hopelessly behind and isolated from modern times. The San people featured in *The Gods Must Be Crazy* are an example of a society sometimes referred to as "bushmen." Scholars now consider "bushmen" and "pygmy" to be derogatory when used in reference to Africans because of the history of the terms. Over the past two hundred years, the terms have been coupled with assumptions of a lack of historical development, isolationism, and a lack of participation in modern economies. These assumptions do not reflect the reality of hunter-gathering societies. Instead, scholars have shown that hunter-gathering societies have long been in regular contact with pastoralists and people living in agriculturally-based societies in Africa. Most people,who in the past would have been labeled bushmen or pygmies, prefer to be referred to by their linguistic or ethnic identities in order to avoid the stigmas attached to these terms and to avoid being lumped in with people with whom they share very little. If we understand how words like tribe, stateless societies, and bushmen have been used in the past, then we can avoid perpetuating some of the problematic stereotypes about Africa.

Overall, as you read this chapter, keep in mind that Africa has been a continent of innovation and change since the first behaviorally modern humans emerged there between 200,000 and 100,000 years ago. Africans were some of the first farmers and some of the first iron-workers. Africans developed their own artistic traditions (see Figure 9.2, Map 9.3, Figure 9.3) and unique state structures. With such a big, diverse continent to consider, this chapter examines four civilizations (states of larger scale and complexity) to show major changes impacting the continent. Each of these states was also connected to the rest of the world. The chapter starts with ancient Ethiopia in Northeast Africa (300 to 700 CE) and moves to the Western Sudanic Empires in the Sahel of West Africa (800 to 1591 CE). In the second half, it discusses Great Zimbabwe (1200 to 1450 CE) and, finally, the Swahili states in East Africa (1000 to 1500 CE).

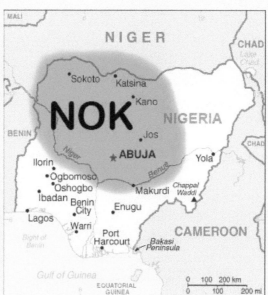

Figure 9.2 | An Example of a Terra-Cotta Statue Produced by the Nok Culture, c. 550 BCE | The Nok people lived in what is today Northern Nigeria.
Author: User "Daderot"
Source: Wikimedia Commons
License: Public Domain

Map 9.3 | Map of Nok Culture | The Nok were just one innovative community in ancient Africa. They were a sophisticated Iron-Age civilization (c. 1000 BCE) now known for their terra-cotta sculptures.
Author: Locutus Borg
Source: Wikimedia Commons
License: Public Domain

Figure 9.3 | A lifesize bronze head found at Ife (Nigeria) | Created by a Yoruba artist in the thirteenth century CE, it may represent a member of the royal family.
Author: Locutus Borg
Source: Wikimedia Commons
License: Public Domian

9.6 AKSUM AND ETHIOPIA

Aksum, which was at its most powerful in the fourth through sixth centuries CE, was located in what are today Ethiopia, Eritrea, and parts of Sudan. At its high point, Aksum extended its influence beyond Africa into parts of the southern Arabian Peninsula as shown on the map below. Aksum was a great trading empire, with its own coinage, its own language, and its own distinctive Christian church. If you are familiar with accounts of the Queen of Sheba, you know pieces of the story that Ethiopians use to explain the origins of the Ethiopian Solomonic Dynasty and their possession of the Ark of the Covenant. (Visit the following link to view a map of the Kingdom of Aksum: http://www.earlheinrich.com/Ancient%20Nubia/Aksum_Empr-Map-72dpi.jpg. The capital of the kingdom was the city of Aksum and its most important port was Adulis. You can see that the kingdom stretched into the Sudan and Yemen at its height in the sixth century.)

Unlike some other regions in Africa, Ethiopia had very fertile, volcanic soils that supported large populations. Climatic variation found at the different elevations throughout Ethiopia also encouraged agricultural diversification and trade. Around 7000 BCE, there was population growth in the region that corresponded with the Agricultural Revolution. While some domesticated animals and crops were introduced from Northeast Africa and the Fertile Crescent, Ethiopians domesticated other crops themselves. Most notably, Ethiopians domesticated teff, a grass, and nsete, known as the "false banana," that they ground to make bread and porridge. We also have Ethiopians to thank for coffee! Since the Neolithic Revolution, Ethiopia stands out for its agricultural productivity and innovation, both of which sustained large populations in the region.

The **Kebra Nagast** ("The Glory of Kings"), a 700 year old text that is sacred for Ethiopian Christians and Rastafarians, traces the origins of the Ethopian royal family back to the Queen of Sheba and King Solomon of Jerusalem. The *Kebra Nagast* identifies the Queen of Sheba as an Ethiopian ruler known locally as **Queen Mekeda**. According to the text, in approximately 950 BCE, the newly enthroned Queen Mekeda traveled to study with Jerusalem's well-known king, King Solomon. Queen Mekeda wanted a capable mentor for leadership advice and spiritual guidance. Charmed by her, King Solomon played these roles and Queen Mekeda, flattered by his attentions, was a hardworking tutee who eventually converted to Judaism. As their lessons continued, King Solomon planned the seduction of Queen Mekeda, which, as described in the text, occurred when Solomon tricked and cornered her. Their sexual union produced a child, Menelik I, to whom Queen Mekeda gave birth on her journey home to Ethopia.

As time passed, King Solomon remained haunted by a dream that Menelik was his rightful sucessor and was delighted when his son, as an adult, returned to Jersusalem. According to the *Kebra Nagast,* King Solomon intended for Menelik to follow him as the next king of Jerusalem, but Menelik refused and instead returned to Ethopia. In an unexpected twist, when leaving Jerusalem, part of Menelik's entourage stole the Ark of the Covenant, which held the Ten Commandments. When King Solomon discovered the theft, he sent soldiers to recapture the Ark of the Covenant. However according to the *Kebra Nagast*, God helped Menelik and his men evade capture by lifting them up over the Red Sea. In the end, Menelik and the Ark of the Covenant made it safely to Ethopia. For Ethiopian Christians, the *Kebra Nagast* partially explains the formation of the Ethopian Orthodox Church (the Tawahedo Church). Through today, the Ethopian Orthodox Church claims possession of the Ark of the Covenant, which it says is housed in the Church of Our Lady Mary of Zion in Aksum, Ethiopia.

Figure 9.4 | The Queen of Sheba |
The Queen of Sheba as illustrated by Conrad Kyeser in the early fifteenth century.
Author: Conrad Kyeser
Source: Wikimedia Commons
License: Public Domain

According to the *Kebra Nagast*, early Ethiopian rulers were descendants of King Solomon through Menelik I. More than two thousand years after King Solomon's rule, a thirteenth century Ethiopian king, Yekuno Amlak (r. 1270 – 1285 CE), reclaimed this legacy by tracing his origins back to King Solomon and Queen Mekeda. He founded what became known as the Solomonic Dynasty, which ruled Ethiopia for about 500 years from 1270 to 1769 CE. Members of

Ethiopia's royal family continued to claim descent from King Solomon up through the last Ethiopian emperor, Haile Selassie, who was overthrown in 1974. Therefore, the link back to King Solomon and Queen Mekeda is part of Ethiopian religious beliefs and has also legitimized claims to political power.

From the era of the rule of Queen Mekeda in about the tenth century BCE and Yekuno Amlak's revival of the Solomonic Dynasty in the thirteenth century CE, the largest kingdoms in Ethiopia were Da'amat and Aksum. The **Kingdom of Da'amat** was the first to emerge in northern Ethiopia in about the tenth century BCE. In the 1960s and 1970s, archaeologists excavating

Figure 9.5 | The Building that Allegedly Houses the Ark of the Covenant | It is part of the Church of Our Lady of Zion, built in the fifth or sixth entury CE in Aksum, Ethiopia.
Author: Adam Cohn
Source: Wikimedia Commons
License: CC BY-SA 3.0

the Kingdom of Da'amat unearthed evidence of the region's role in trade and its connections to Southern Arabia. Archeological finds show that, by the seventh century BCE, ivory, tortoiseshell, rhino horn, gold, silver, and slaves were brought from interior regions of Africa and traded through Da'amat for imported cloth, tools, metals, and jewelry. Inscriptions, imagery, architectural styles, and even overlaps in historical traditions (such as those associated with the Queen of Sheba) also suggest close connections between the Kingdom of Da'amat and Saba (Yemen) in Southern Arabia. For example, the Kingdom of Da'amat used religious symbols in its monumental architecture, including the disc and

Figure 9.6 | The Temple at Yeha, Located in Northern Ethiopia |
Yeha was likely the first capital of the Kingdom of Da'amat.
Author: User "JialiangGao"
Source: Wikimedia Commons
License: CC BY-SA 3.0

crescent, also found in Southern Arabia. The oldest standing building in Ethiopia, the Temple at Yeha (c. 700 BCE), had an altar with these symbols. Up until several decades ago, some scholars used evidence of these connections to argue that people from Saba founded the civilization at Da'amat. Now, in line with the trend to reclaim African civilizations, very vocal scholars push us to acknowledge the African origins of the Kingdom of Da'amat and view it as a precursor to the trading empire of Aksum.

The Kingdom of Da'amat weakened in the fourth century BCE as Red Sea trade became more important than some of the previous northern overland routes. It gave way to the state of Aksum, with its important cities of Adulis and Aksum. Adulis, positioned on the coast, rose in prominence and grew wealthy. It served as a safe harbor for ships traveling from Southeast Asia. The growing capital city in the interior, Aksum, was a stopover point for land-based trade routes into the Sudan and especially Sub-Saharan Africa. Ivory, slaves, tools, spices, gold, silver jewelry, copper, and iron were eventually traded through the capital city of Aksum to the coast. The state of Aksum began minting its own gold and silver coins in the third century CE, demonstrating how important long-distance trade was to its economy.

In addition to its role in inter-regional trade, Aksum was also known for its early conversion to Christianity. Ethiopian tradition traces the establishment of Christianity in the region back to two shipwrecked Syrians. One of the Syrians, Frumentius, was particularly influential because he became the first bishop of Ethiopia in 303 CE and guided the king of Aksum, **King Ezana** (r. 325 – 350 CE),

Figure 9.7 | The Church of Debre Damo | In the sixth century CE, Christians exiled due to doctrinal diputes sought refuge in Ethiopia. Once there, they founded the Ethiopian Orthodox Church. Subsequently, one group of Orthodox monks built a monastery at Debre Damo. Debre Damo is located on an isolated mountain top in northern Ethiopia. To this day, it is accessible only by rope ladder and no women (or female animals) are allowed up the rope.
Author: User "Giustino"
Source: Wikimedia Commons
License: CC BY-SA 2.0

in his conversion to Christianity. Some of the coins minted in Aksum actually attest to King Ezana's conversion as the coins from the first half of Ezana's reign have the disc and crescent symbols of earlier Ethiopian rulers, while coins from the later decades of Ezana's reign have a Christian cross. As bishop, Frumentius also encouraged Christian merchants to settle in Aksum. About a century later, Christianity in Ethiopia grew further as the state offered refuge to Christians fleeing persecution due to doctrinal disputes within the Church. Nine priests, breaking with the Church in Jerusalem, settled in Ethiopia and founded the Ethiopian Orthodox Church. They maintained ties with the Coptic Church in Egypt and developed a distinct liturgy using Ge'ez, the local language. Members of the Ethiopian Orthodox Church also incorporated local beliefs, such as the legendary connection to King Solomon, into their religious traditions.

The ruling family, coastal elites, and military leaders amassed significant wealth during the height of Aksumite power. Like the Aksumite kings before him, Ezana amassed wealth by collecting tribute from surrounding states and taxing trade. Aksum and its surrounding states were agriculturally productive with fertile soils and effective irrigation systems. Their agricultural productivity meant that the work of peasants and the wealth generated through foreign trade supported the ruling classes and elites. Building a powerful miitary, King Ezana expanded the empire and claimed control over most of Ethiopia, Nubia, and Saba (Yemen). He also used his assets to showcase his power with, for example, "conquest stones" that commemorated his victories. In addition to celebrating Ezana's military strength and commitment to ruling fairly, the "conquest stones" also proclaimed that God had ordained his reign. The stones impart Ezana's edicts and Christian beliefs. One section reads:

> [...] The Lord of Heaven strengthens my dominion!
> And as he now has conquered my enemy, (so)
> May he conquer for me, where I (but) go! As
> he now has given me victory and has over-
> thrown my enemies.
> (So will I rule) in right and justice, doing no
> wrong to the peoples. And I placed
> The throne, which I have set up, and the Earth
> which bears it, in the protection of the Lord
> of Heaven, who has made me king...[9]

Ezana is known to us because of archaeological findings, including the aforementioned conquest stones. He and other Aksumite kings also famously commissioned the construction of **stelae** (singular: stele). Stelae were tall rectangular pillars with rounded tops set up to mark the underground grave sites of Aksum's royalty and elite. The most ornate stelae were elaborately carved into a marble-like material with faux doors at the bottom and multiple stories, as indicated by windows etched into each level. They have been described as "ancient skyscrapers," with the

---

9   As quoted in Esperanza Brizuela-Garcia and Trevor Getz, *African Histories: New Sources and New Techniques for Studying African Pasts* (Boston: Prentice Hall, 2012): 33-36.

largest being one hundred and eight feet tall. Most stelae have fallen in the over 1700 years since their construction, but several do remain standing. One stele even caused international uproar as the Italians took it during their occupation of Ethiopia at the onset of the Second World War and just recently returned it at great expense.

The stelae demonstrate the wealth of Aksum's ruling classes and links between the ruling generations. Unfortunately, the graves marked by the stelae have been cleared out by tomb robbers in the intervening years. However, small remnants of glass, pottery, furniture, beads, bangles, earrings, ivory carvings, and objects gilded in gold attest to the wealth buried with affluent Aksumites. These artifacts also show the availability of trade goods brought from long distances. Furthermore, the architecture of the stelae is suggestive of connections back to earlier kingdoms. For example, the rounded top of the stelae is reminiscent of the disc symbol found in the region as far back as the Kingdom of Da'amat. Ezana was the first Christian king in the region; however, the architecture that he commissioned maintained ties to Aksum's pre-Christian past.

Aksum's power began to wane at the end of the sixth century CE. First, the Persian Empire interrupted Aksum's trade with parts of southern Arabia in the late sixth century. Then, Muslims increasingly dominated trade along the Red Sea coast and the most profitable trade routes shifted from the Red Sea to the Persian Gulf. In response, Aksum shrank as Ethiopia's Christian rulers turned away from coastal trade and became more dependent on the tribute they collected from agriculturally productive regions to their south.

As Muslims in coastal areas became more powerful and Christian rulers shifted their attentions away from the coast, the relationship between Ethiopian Muslims and Christians remained complex. In the seventh century CE, one king of Aksum, al-Najashi Ashama Ibn Abjar, gave sanctuary to some of the first followers of Islam before he himself converted. In subsequent years, Muslims traders and Christian elites oftentimes cooperated. For example from the tenth through fourteenth centuries, Muslims set up trading settlements in the interior that facilitated the

Figure 9.8 | A Stele Built during the Height of the Aksum Empire in Ethiopia
Author: User "Zhiem"
Source: Wikimedia Commons
License: CC BY-SA 3.0

conspicuous consumption of Christian elites who desired imported goods. However, there were also periods of conflict, especially after Muslims unified to form the Adal Sultanate in the fourteenth century. The Adal Sultanate militarily extended its influence over much of the region and for several centuries supported a thriving, multi-ethnic state. In the sixteenth century, Ethiopian Christians allied with the Portuguese to fight against the Adal Sultanate. After the fall of the Adal Sultanate, Ethiopian Christians rejected Portuguese attempts to convert them to Catholicism and forced Portuguese missionaries out of the region in 1633 CE.

9.7 THE WESTERN SUDANIC STATES

Who comes to mind as the richest person *ever*? Many economists and historians propose a person who might surprise you: Mansa Musa. Mansa Musa was an emperor in the Western Sudan during the Middle Ages. He was so rich that the people of his own time could not even fathom his wealth. Unable to put a dollar amount on Mansa Musa's bewilderingly large fortune, Rudolph Ware, a current professor at the University of Michigan, instructs us to "imagine as much gold as you think a human being could possess and double it..."[10] Other sources estimate that, adjusted for inflation, Mansa Musa was worth $400 billion.[11] How did Mansa Musa become so wealthy? Like the other Western Sudanic rulers, he controlled much of the world's access to gold during a period when gold was in very high demand.

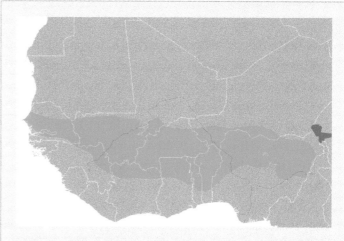

Map 9.4 | Map of Western Sudan | The area highlighted in green is the Western Sudan. In the Middle Ages, African kings used their monopoly over west African gold to build a series of large empires in the Western Sudan.
Author: User "Alatoron"
Source: Wikimedia Commons
License: Public Domain

Map 9.4 shows the large area in West Africa commonly referred to as **the Western Sudan**. The Western Sudan does not correspond with a modern-day African country; instead, it is a region. Arabic-speaking travelers gave the region its name, calling it *bilad-al-Sudan* or the "Land of Blacks." The Western Sudan encompasses the Sahel and some of its surrounding grasslands from the Atlantic coast in the east through Lake Chad in the west. The **Sahel**, which in Arabic means "the shore," is a transition zone between the Sahara Desert to its north and the more forested regions to its south. Much of the Sahel is grassland savannah. Straddling regions with different climates, the people of the Western Sudan developed productive agriculture, trade networks, and an urban culture. The architecture of the Western Sudanic states stands out for its use of mud (adobe) to construct its monumental buildings, such as the Great Mosque in Djenne (Figure

10   Jacob Davidson, "The 10 Richest People of All Time," *Time* (July 2015) http://time.com/money/3977798/the-10-richest-people-of-all-time/
11   "Musa's Money." BBC. http://www.bbc.co.uk/programmes/p02f9r6g

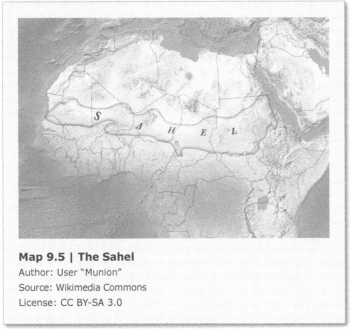

Map 9.5 | The Sahel
Author: User "Munion"
Source: Wikimedia Commons
License: CC BY-SA 3.0

9.9) and Aksia the Great's tomb in Gao (Figure 9.11). From roughly 800 to 1600 CE, the people of this region organized and supported—sometimes under duress—the large states that dominated the Western Sudan. Three of the best known of these states became the empires of Ghana (800 – 1070s CE), Mali (1230s – 1430s CE), and Songhai (1460s – 1591 CE).

The leaders of Ghana, Mali, and Songhai came to dominate the region because they controlled access to West African gold. An increase in the demand for West African gold corresponded with the rise of these empires. The spread of Islam and rise of new states along the North African coast and in Europe gave the biggest boost to the demand for gold. Monarchs in Europe and North Africa wanted West African gold to mint coins. To meet the demand, Berber traders used newly introduced camels to carry gold north across the desert. Then, they loaded up their camels with big slabs of salt to return south. The people in many parts of West Africa considered salt a valuable commodity due to their distance from the ocean and the time required to extract salt from plant, animal, and other resources. While the demands for gold and salt drove the trade, weapons, manufactured goods, slaves, textiles, and manuscripts also passed through the desert. With the flow of all of these goods, the Western Sudanic states emerged at the nexus of the trans-Saharan trade routes.

The North African Berber traders crossing the Sahara Desert were early converts to Islam, and they introduced Islam to market towns of the Western Sudanic states. With continuing trade, the region's connections with Northeast Africa and the Middle East grew through the Middle Ages. Growing urban areas, like Timbuktu, attracted Muslim scholars. In later centuries, the kings of Mali and Songhai deliberately fostered these connections with the larger Islamic World due to their religious beliefs and, sometimes, to enhance their status and secure their positions. For example, Askiya Muhammad, the king of Songhai from 1495 to 1528, successfully sought recognition as the "caliph of Sudan" from Egyptian rulers. The new title brought him prestige within the Islamic world and Africa. Therefore, trans-Saharan trade brought Islam to the Western Sudan, and many of the kings of Mali and Songhai cultivated their relationships with Muslims in Northeast Africa and the Middle East. As a result, Islam influenced the culture and lifestyle, particularly of urban residents, in the Western Sudan.

9.7.1 Ghana

We associate the first powerful empire, **Ghana** (800 – 1070s CE), with people who spoke the Soninke language and lived in the area between the Niger and Senegal Rivers—parts of present day Mauritania and Mali. In this region, agricultural productivity supported labor specialization, urban areas, and eventually state formation. From as early as 300 BCE, the region's farmers used iron tools to grow an abundance of crops. Archaeological evidence found at Djenne-Jeno, one of the earliest urban areas in the Western Sudan, which has been dated to approximately 250 BCE, suggests that people had access to plenty of rice, millet, and vegetables. Iron technologies also allowed craftsmen to make iron spears and swords so people could protect themselves. Probably for defense purposes, Soninke speakers began joining together to form the ancient state of Ghana around 300 CE. Then, as the populations continued to grow, the state expanded its territory.

Even before Ghana was a state with a clearly defined centralized administration, Soninke speakers had been involved in extensive systems of trade using the region's complex river systems. They often acted as middlemen, trading in fish from the rivers, meat from herders, and grains from farmers. After 300 CE, Ghanian leadership began collecting tributary payments from neighboring chiefdoms. In the centuries that followed, Ghana's leaders used their ability to tax trade to build an empire. By 800 CE, they had consolidated their control over trade, their authority over urban areas, and their reign over tributary states.

Especially in the minds of the Arab scholars chronicling the history of this period, the gold trade defined Ghana. They heard about the large caravans with hundreds of camels passing through the Sahara Desert on their way to and from Ghana. To build their fortunes, the Ghanian kings taxed trade goods twice. They taxed gold when it was initially brought from the forested regions in the south to their market towns and again right as the Berber traders departed for the north. News of Ghana's wealth spread to the extent that Medieval Arab scholars who had never even traveled to Africa wrote about the Ghanian kings. In one manuscript, Al-Bakri, an eleventh century geographer based in Muslim Spain, described how a Ghanian king was adorned in gold and guarded by dogs wearing gold and silver collars. According to Al-Bakri, the king demonstrated his power having his subjects "fall on their knees and sprinkle dust on their

Map 9.6 | Map of the Trans-Saharan Trade Routes | Note how the routes crossed to settlements, like Koumbi Saleh, Gao, and Timbuktu, that began as market towns before growing into state capitals and cities of Muslim scholarship. The map also shows the origins of the gold in the region's southern forested areas. The sites where the gold originated are appropriately shaded to indicate the gold mines at Bambuk, Boure, and Lobi.
Author: User "As77zz"
Source: Wikimedia Commons
License: CC0 1.0

heads" upon entering his presence.[12] The kings shored up their power through their ostentatious displays of gold and their monopoly over trade. Al-Bakri recognized the centrality of gold to the finances of the Ghanian kings. According to him, the kings claimed all of the gold nuggets for themselves, leaving only gold dust for everyone else. By this time, the Ghanian kings had also used their wealth to build strong armies, with archers and calvary, to collect tribute and carry out the empire's expansion.

Al-Bakri's depiction of Ghana's capital city, Koumbi Saleh, also evidences the introduction of Islam to the region. He described two separate sites within the capital city, Koumbi-Saleh. To trade their wares, the merchants used one site, which was clearly Muslim with mosques, while the king lived in a royal palace six miles away. The separation between the sites and lack of mosques near the royal palace suggest that Islam had primarily impacted the market towns; the leadership and masses of Ghana did not convert.

9.7.2 The Mali Empire

Due to attacks from the Muslim Almoravids from the North, issues with overgrazing, and internal rebellions, Ghana declined in the eleventh century, opening up an opportunity for the rise of Mali. The origins of the **Mali Empire** (see Map 9.7) are associated with the king **Sundiata Keita** (c. 1217 – 1255 CE). An epic, recounted orally by griots for centuries and written down in various forms in the twentieth century, relates the story of Sundiata's rise. One version written by Guinean D. T. Niani in 1960 follows Sundiata as he overcomes a number of challenges, like being unable to walk until he is seven years old, being banished by a cruel stepmother, and facing tests given by witches. With

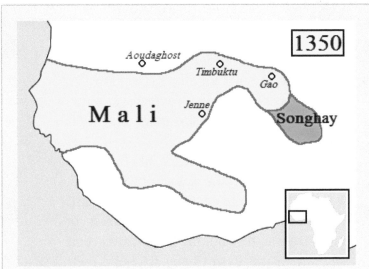

Map 9.7 | The Mali Empire, c. 1350 CE | The empire encompassed over 400,000 miles, including territory in the Sahara Desert, through the Sahel, and into some of the coastal forest. The empire's control over such a large area meant access to a wide range of crops, facilitating agricultural specialization and trade.
Author: User "Astrokey44"
Source: Wikimedia Commons
License: CC BY-SA 3.0

loyal followers and the attributes of a born leader, Sundiata overcomes these and other challenges in the epic to found the new empire. Under Sundiata, some of Mali's leadership converted to Islam; however, even with conversion, they maintained important pre-Islamic traditions. The epic demonstrates the prevalence of **syncretism** or the blending of religious beliefs and practices in West Africa. For instance, the epic traces Sundiata's background back to Bilali Bounama, one of the early followers of the Muslim prophet Muhammad, and the powerful pre-Islamic, local

---

12   Quoted in "Kingdom of Ghana: Primary Source Documents." African Studies Center. Boston University Pardee School of Global Studies. http://www.bu.edu/africa/outreach/k_o_ghana

clans of the lion and the buffalo. According to oral tradition, Sundiata's ability to draw from both Muslim and traditional African sources of strength allows him to overcome adversity and defeat his less worthy opponents.

Like Sundiata, most of the subsequent kings of Mali combined Muslim and local religious traditions. For example, they often completed the "Fifth Pillar" of Islam by performing the hajj, the pilgrimage to Mecca required of all able Muslims. In the meanwhile, they continued to use pre-Islamic amulets, maintain their animistic beliefs, and consider pre-Islamic sacred sites to be important. Similarly, when they converted, the people living within Mali's cities and those involved in trans-Saharan trade also blended Muslim and traditional beliefs and practices.

Sundiata built the Mali Empire in the thirteenth century and the empire reached its height under Mansa Musa (c. 1280 – 1337 CE), in the early fourteenth century. Through diplomacy and military victories, Sundiata swayed surrounding leaders to relinquish their titles to him. Thus, Sundiata established a sizeable empire with tributary states and became the **mansa**, or emperor, of Mali. Most of the subsequent mansas of Mali maintained their control over the gold-salt trade, the basis of their wealth. Mali also developed a more diversified economy and was recognized in Europe, North Africa, and the Middle East as a prosperous trading center.

Mansa Musa, who was likely Sundiata's grandson or grandnephew, further developed the empire and made it one of the crossroads of the Medieval Islamic World. Mansa Musa used a large army of approximately 100,000 soldiers to reunify the empire after several tumultuous decades. Under Mansa Musa, Mali stretched much farther east, west, and south than had its predecessor kingdom, Ghana. With its access to very diverse environments, trade in agricultural produce became more important in Mali than it had been in Ghana. Farmers specialized in regional crops and the state operated farms where slaves grew food for the royal family and the army. Mansa Musa also developed the empire's administration, dividing the territory into provinces and appointing competent governors. With all of these achievements, Mansa Musa is best remembered for going on the hajj from 1324 to 1325 CE. He attracted a great deal of attention traveling in a huge caravan made up of almost 100 camels, 12,000 slaves, and an estimated 30,000 pounds of gold. Local lore claims that he gave out so much gold during his three month stay

Figure 9.9 | The Great Mosque in Djenne | The Great Mosque in Djenne demonstrates the regional architectural style of the Western Sudan. The original structure was likely built in the thirteenth century. The current mosque was rebuilt in the early twentieth century. The wooden scaffolding gives the structure support and also helps men replaster the exterior, which they do every year. The exterior of the mosque is plastered in mud (adobe).
Author: User "Ruud Zwart"
Source: Wikimedia Commons
License: CC BY-SA 3.0

in Cairo that the price of gold dropped by 25%. Likewise, reportedly after he passed through Alexandria, the value of gold in the city stayed low for a decade. Mansa Musa's impressive display in Northeast Africa and the Middle East boosted Mali's standing in the Islamic World. After his return to Mali, Mansa Musa further cultivated Islamic connections by building new mosques and schools. He hosted Muslim scholars and made cities, including **Timbuktu**, Djenne, and Gao, into centers of learning. Mansa Musa also encouraged the use of Arabic, and the libraries, especially of Timbuktu, became repositories of Islamic manuscripts. The **Catalan Atlas** (Figure 9.10) demonstrates Mansa Musa's preeminence. Commissioned by Charles V of France, the 1375 map shows Mansa Musa ruling his empire. He sits atop a gold throne, wearing a gold crown, carrying a gold sceptre, and gauging (or perhaps

Figure 9.10 | Mansa Musa | An image from the Catalan Atlas that demonstrates Mansa Musa's reputation as the gold-laden king of Medieval Mali. The description reads, "This Black lord is called Musa Mali, Lord of the Black people of Guinea. So abundant is the gold which is found in his country that he is the richest and most noble king in all the land." (The British Museum. The Wealth of Africa: The Kingdom of Mali, Presentation. https://www.britishmuseum.org/pdf/KingdomOfMali_Presentation.pdf.)
Author: User "Olivierkeita"
Source: Wikimedia Commons
License: Public Domain

admiring) a gold nugget. Awash in gold in the Catalan Atlas, Mansa Musa paid for his various projects by collecting tribute from surrounding states and taxing trans-Saharan and inter-regional trade.

Several factors, such as weak leadership, foreign invasions, and rebellions within the tributary states, led to the decline of Mali after Mansa Musa's death. The empire got increasingly smaller through the early fifteenth century. With the decline of Mali, leaders in one of its breakaway tributary states, Songhai (alternatively spelled Songhay), expanded militarily and encroached on Mali's territory. By the late 1460s when

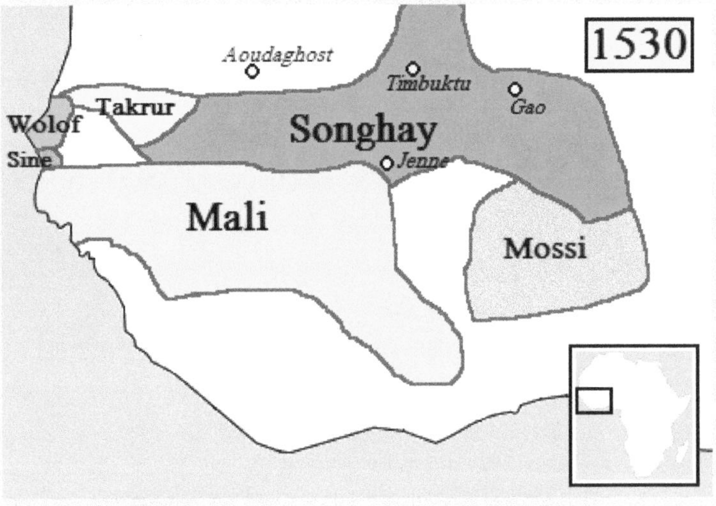

Map 9.8 | The Songhai (alternatively spelled Songhay) Empire, c. 1530 | Note that by the early sixteenth century, the Songhai Empire encompassed the important trading and religious centers of Timbuktu, Djenne (sometimes spelled Jenne), and Gao.
Author: User "Olivierkeita"
Source: Wikimedia Commons
License: Public Domain

he captured Timbuktu, Songhai's leader Sunni Ali had begun to build a new empire, the Songhai Empire, through military conquest.

9.7.3 Songhai

The **Songhai Empire** is most closely associated with the Sorko people who lived alongside the Niger River, southeast of Gao. By about 800 CE, the Sorko had created their own state, Songhai, trading along the river and building a military that used war canoes. With the growth of trans-Saharan trade and eventually the discovery of new gold fields, the Sorko and other ethnic groups in the area established market towns in Songhai. Most of the people who moved to these market towns converted to Islam by the eleventh century. In the early fourteenth century, the Mali Empire collected tribute from Gao, though other parts of the Songhai state remained in-dependent. Using his military to pick off pieces of Mali in its waning years, Sunni Ali built the Songhai state into an empire in the 1460s.

During its Golden Age, the Songhai Empire was ruled by Askia Mohammad I (r. 1493 – 1528). Referred to as Askia the Great, Askia Mohammad I was a devout Muslim, who centralized the empire's administration, encouraged agriculture, and further expanded the state. Askia rose to power as the general-in-chief of the army of Gao. He won a military victory over Sunni Ali's son to found a new dynasty, the Askia dynasty. As a devout Muslim, Askia went on the hajj to Mecca from 1496 – 1497. The pilgrimage brought him international recognition and reinforced his claims to power especially because the Sharif of Mecca bestowed Askia with the title "the Caliph of the Sudan." Upon his return, Askia used Islam to validate attacks on neighboring states, like the Mossi in 1498. He also rebuilt Islamic centers. Leo Africanus, originally from Granada (Spain), traveled through Timbuktu in 1526 and wrote,

> [...] There are in Timbuktu numerous judges, teachers, and priests, all properly appointed by the king. He greatly honors learning. Many hand-written books imported from Barbary [the coastal regions of North Africa] are also sold. There is more profit made from this commerce than from all other merchandise.[13]

Under Askia, Timbuktu, Djenne, and Gao, once again, beckoned scholars and people with com-mercial aspirations. Taxing gold remained an important source of revenue for the king, but trade expanded to incorporate items such as manuscripts, kola nuts, prisoners of war (who were sold as slaves), horses, and cowry shells (which were used as an internal currency). Additionally, to cen-tralize his administration, Askia appointed loyal Muslim governors to new provinces, replacing hereditary rulers. After his death, Askia's sons, particulary his last son, Askia Dawud (r. 1549 – 1582 CE) continued to generate wealth by taxing trans-Saharan trade. Like their father, they also tended to invest in Songhai's Islamic centers. For example, during the reign of Dawud, there were approximately one hundred and fifty Islamic schools operating in Timbuktu. Askia Dawud's death in 1582 saw the reemergence of power struggles amongst competing rulers and rebellions within

---

13   "Leo Africanus: Description of Timbuktu." From *The Description of Africa* (1526). http://public.wsu.edu/~brians/world_civ/worldcivreader/world_civ_reader_2/leo_africanus.html

Figure 9.11 | The tomb of Askia the Great built in 1495 in Gao | Note the use of mud (adobe) architecture common in the cities of the Western Sudanic states. People still use the prayer rooms and meeting space at the site.
Author: User "Olivierkeita"
Source: Wikimedia Commons
License: Public Domain

tributary states, signaling the end of the Golden Age of Songhai.

Then, the biggest blow to the crumbling Songhai Empire came from the invasion by Morocco in 1591. The Moroccan army used new technology, muzzle-loading firearms, to defeat the Songhai troops. The Songhai state limped along until 1737, but after 1591, it was no longer a unified empire with control over numerous tributary states. For almost 1,000 years, large empires had dominated the Sahel. The leaders of Ghana, Mali, and Songhai, each in turn, taxed trans-Saharan trade and grew powerful. They built their empires with urban centers, strong militaries, and numerous tributary states. However, the Moroccan invasion eroded their power. Furthermore, the Age of Exploration, begun by the Portuguese in their progress down the West Africa coast in the fifteenth century, redirected trade. Trans-Saharan trade diminished and was largely replaced by trade up and down the Atlantic coast of West Africa.

9.8 THE SPREAD OF AGRICULTURE AND GREAT ZIMBABWE

Most of the languages indigenous to Africa belong to one of the major language groups shown in Map 9.9. Over the past several decades, historians of Africa have started to pay more attention to these language groups. They use comparisons of core vocabulary words in related languages to examine the spread of ancient technologies and the interaction between peoples. Using linguistics (the study of languages), historians corroborate information found in other sources, like oral traditions of dynastic origins and archaeological findings.

Today's scholars are not the first ones to notice linguistic similarities on the continent. During European colonization one hundred and fifty years ago, anthropologists grouped Africans into "tribes" based on presumed physical, cultural, and linguistic similarites. Involved in this classification, anthropologists and others noticed striking similarities amongst the languages spoken by about 400 different ethnic groups in the southern and eastern third of the continent. They found that people in most of Sub-Saharan Africa spoke languages that used the root *−ntu* to refer to person, with the prefix *ba-* added in the plural. Combining the root and the plural prefix, nineteenth-century colonial anthropologists referred to people in these communities as *Bantu* and later traced Bantu languages back to a root, a mother language spoken in parts of Cameroon and Nigeria. To explain the similarities in the languages, European scholars hypothesized that about 2,000 years ago there was a **Bantu Migration**, a massive departure of thousands of Bantu speakers from the Bantu homeland. As they described, Bantu-speakers imposed iron technology and traditions of agriculture on the peoples they encountered in eastern and southern Africa. Influenced by their own conceptions of colonization, nineteenth century anthropologists portayed the Bantu Migration as a rapid conquest of Sub-Saharan hunter-gatherer societies by the technologically advanced, Iron Age Bantu speakers.

Since the 1990s, historians of Africa have used linguistics to reject some pieces of the nineteenth-century description of the Bantu Migration. Referring instead to **Bantu expansions**, they generally agree that the movement of Bantu speakers was more of a slow diffusion of languages and technologies that lasted about 4500 years, from roughly 3000 BCE to 1500 CE. Bantu speakers took multiple routes, and sometimes their

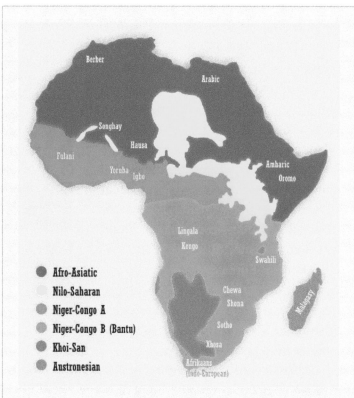

Map 9.9 | Map showing the Distribution of the Six Major Language Families in Africa | While it is not marked, the Bantu homeland was in parts of Nigeria and Cameroon. From 3000 BCE to 1500 CE, Bantu (or Niger-Congo B) languages spread slowly and unevenly from the Bantu homeland through most of southern and eastern Africa.
Author: Mark Dingemanse
Source: Wikimedia Commons
License: CC BY-SA 2.5

movement occurred on the scale of a single family, as opposed to a mass of thousands. From the linguistic evidence, historians also suspect that both Bantu speakers and those they settled amongst contributed ideas and technologies; there was mutual "teaching and learning from one another."[14] The current view of the Bantu expansions is much more complex as it recognizes give and take between Bantu newcomers and indigenous populations. For example, some indigenous populations rejected Bantu languages, while others repackaged Bantu technologies incorporating their own innovations. There was no Bantu migratory conquest of indigenous communities. Instead, the study of linguistics seems to confirm that Bantu languages, iron-working, and agriculture slowly spread through eastern and southern Africa in the early centuries CE.

These corrections are important because they allow scholars to much more accurately discuss state formation in southern Africa. In the colonial era, European scholars sometimes jumped to misleading conclusions when they encountered evidence of early African states. For example,

---

14   As quoted in Brizuela-Garcia, Esperanza and Trevor Getz, *African Histories: New Sources and New Techniques for Studying African Pasts.* Boston: Prentice Hall, 2012: 43.

in 1871 when the German geographer Carl Maunch saw the ruins of an impressive civilization, Great Zimbabwe, he concluded that people from Yemen must have built the grand structures. Biased by nineteenth-century racism, Maunch assumed that Africans were incapable of statehood and the skilled masonry techniques evident at Great Zimbabwe. Subsequent Europeans reached similar conclusions upon viewing the site, attributing the civilization to Phoenecians and Arabs. Some white supremicists in southern Africa clung onto this fabricated history of Great Zimbabwe's foreign origins until the early 1990s.

Figure 9.12 | The Ruins of the Great Enclosure at Great Zimbabwe in the Mosvingo Province of present-day Zimbabwe
Author: User "Macvivo"
Source: Wikimedia Commons
License: CC BY-SA 3.0

In the meantime, a number of scholars had confirmed the African origins of Great Zimbabwe. Archaeologists showed that Great Zimbabwe had features, like stone masonry and rituals involving cattle, found in nearby African kingdoms. Historians used oral tradition and linguistics to track African state formation in the region and show that Great Zimbabwe was a Bantu civilization. Archaeologists and historians concluded that from approximately 1200 to 1450 CE, **Great Zimbabwe** was the thriving commercial and political center of a rich southern African state.

Figure 9.13 | The Hill Complex at Great Zimbabwe
Author: Jan Derk
Source: Wikimedia Commons
License: Public Domain

During the Middle Ages, a prosperous elite based in Great Zimbabwe ruled over about 300 settlements on the Zimbabwe Plateau. Great Zimbabwe and the linked settlements had similarly constructed walled enclosures, practiced mixed farming (they grew crops and kept livestock), and used iron, copper, and bronze. The 300 settlements paid tribute in the form of ivory, gold, cattle, and crops to the rulers in Great Zimbabwe. The wealth generated through the collection of tribute helped Great Zimbabwe become a center of trade and artistry. Great Zimbabwe exported gold and ivory to cities like Sofala and Kilwa Kisanwani, on the East African coast. From the coast, these goods were carried to the Persian Gulf, India, and China. In exchange, Great Zimbabwe's elite imported luxury items like stoneware, colored glass beads, and cotton. Out of these imports, artisans based in Great Zimbabwe made jewelry, ornaments, and cloth for elite consumption.

The architectural evidence of Great Zimbabwe's social hierachies is one of the most dramatic elements of the site's ruins. Covering three square miles, the ruins of Great Zimbabwe consists of many clusters of stone buildings. The most famous structures are the Hill Complex (Figure 9.13) and the Great Enclosure (Figure 9.12). The stone buildings were constructed with local granite, and the stones were stacked without mortar. Scholars hypothesize that the ruling elite resided and performed ceremonies on the Hill Complex, symbolically demonstrating their authority with the height and separation of the complex. From about 1300 CE, more than 15,000 people lived in the valley below them in small, circular homes with thatched roofs and walls made of clay and gravel. The Hill Complex overlooked a number of other structures, including the famous Great Enclosure. With its stone walls up to thirty-five feet tall, the Great Enclosure was the largest structure in precolonial sub-Saharan Africa. The Great Enclosure was a ceremonial site, perhaps used by religious leaders or as a site for the initation of youth. Scholars disagree about its exact function, but suggest that the Great Enclosure further demonstrated the status and wealth of the capital city and the ruling classes.

Great Zimbabwe declined in the fifteenth century and was abandoned by 1450 CE. Some scholars suggest that the site deteriorated because it was supporting up to 30,000 people and thus became too crowded, deforested, and stripped bare of resources through overuse. Surrounding gold mines may have also been depleted. In any case, trade shifted to support the rise of two new kingdoms, Batua to the west and Mutapa to the east. Both kingdoms built stone walls like those seen in Great Zimbabwe and practiced mixed agriculture, using cattle for ceremonies and as symbols of the ruling elite's power. From the fifteenth through seventeenth centuries, the kingdoms also faced the Portuguese and the influx of other African populations. The Mutapa Kingdom lasted the longest, enduring until 1760. Overall, this rewritten history of southern African statehood acknowledges the significance of the Bantu expansions that brought agriculture and iron to many regions. It also celebrates the African origins of great civilizations and demonstrates how Africans shared technologies and cultural practices across the Zimbabwean plateau.

9.9 THE SWAHILI CITY-STATES (EAST AFRICA)

In the tenth century CE, a grand Persian sultan, Sultan Ali ibn Sulaiman al-Shirazi sailed to Kilwa Kisiwani, an island off the East African coast. When he arrived, he was generous and people liked him, which enabled him to marry the daughter of Mrimba, the local headman. The newlyweds were set up to live more or less happily ever after. However, Sultan Ali and Mrimba made a deal, brokered by Mrimba's daughter. The deal gave Sultan Ali control of the island in exchange for enough cloth for Mrimba to "walk on it from the island to his new abode on the mainland."[15] The deal went through and Mrimba moved to the mainland, but then Mrimba regretted relinguishing

---

15   John Middleton, *The World of the Swahili: An African Mercantile Civilization*, (New Haven: Yale University Press, 1994): 31-32.

his position and plotted to militarily retake the island from his son-in-law. In response, Sultan Ali used magic from the Qur'an to stop Mrimba's plot. By reading the Qur'an in a special way, Sultan Ali kept the sea levels high, which confined Mrimba to the mainland, where he gave up and retired. Upon Mrimba's death, his mainland territory passed to the son of Sultan Ali who also ruled Kilwa Kisiwani. In this oral tradition, the union of Mrimba's daughter and Sultan Ali forged a new Muslim family, with Persian and African ancestry, that ruled Kilwa Kisiwani and the mainland coast.

The above version is just one account of Kilwa Kisiwani's origins; nevertheless, it conveys some very important elements of Swahili identity. Starting at least by the thirteenth century CE, in response to resident Arab merchants who scorned non-Muslims and some African practices, African elites in East Africa claimed descent from Shirazis (Persians) and to have been early converts to Islam. In some cases, the connections may have been exaggerated or inaccurate from a historical standpoint. However, regardless of their accuracy, these stories demonstrate some of the defining features of Swahili identity.

As it controlled gold coming from Great Zimbabwe, Kilwa Kisiwani became one of the

Map 9.10 | The Swahili Coast of East Africa | From 1000 to 1500 CE, numerous Swahili states emerged along this 1,000 mile stretch from Mogadishu in the north (present-day Somalia) to Sofala in the south (present-day Mozambique).
Author: George McCall Theal
Source: Wikimedia Commons
License: Public Domain

most prosperous of the Swahili city-states. From 1000 to 1500 CE, **Swahili city-states** were wealthy urban areas connected both to the African interior and the larger Indian Ocean World. Dozens of Swahili city-states running down the East African coast from Mogadishu to Sofala, and including islands off the coast, were commercial centers, tied together by a shared identity, not an overarching political structure. In addition to Islam and claims to Persian ancestry, Swahili identity also became associated with Indian Ocean trade, an urban style, and a shared language (Swahili).

Historians of Africa trace the origins of the Swahili city-states to the Bantu expansions, explaining that by the first century CE, Bantu farmers had built communities along the East African coast. They traded with southern Arabia, southeast Asia, and occasionally Greece and Rome. Although trade contracted after the fall of the Roman Empire, it rebounded several hundred years later. At that time, residents of the Swahili city-states played a pivotal role as middlemen, selling gold, timber, ivory, resins, coconut oil, and slaves from the interior regions of Africa to traders arriving from throughout the Indian Ocean World. In return, Swahili elites bought imported glass, porcelain, silk, spices, and cloth. The seasonal **monsoon winds** that allowed trade between the Swahili coast and southern Arabia, the Persian Gulf, and southeast Asia also facilitated cultural exchange. Blowing towards the East African coast three to four months of the year and reversing several months later, the monsoon winds stranded traders for months at a time, encouraging intermarriage and cultural exchange. Furthermore, the wealth of the Swahili coast attracted Persian and Arab immigrants. With African, Arabian, and southeast Asian influences, Swahili culture became a blended culture as, for example, the Swahili language incorporated loan words from Arabic and Hindi.

One of the quintisessential features of the Swahili city-states from 1000 to 1500 CE was their urban style. A few families made up the elite, ruling classes, while most people in the cities were less wealthy, working as craftsmen, artisans, clerks, and sailors. People in villages along the coast could also identify as Swahili. Claimants of Swahili identity spoke the Swahili language and were Muslim. Archaeology shows that emerging Swahili cities had mosques and Muslim burial grounds starting in the eighth century CE. By their height, the Swahili city-states were distinctly Muslim; they had large mosques built of local coral stone. The Swahili, regardless of their economic status, drew a distinction between themselves as Muslims and the "uncultured," non-Muslim Africans of the interior.

The elite families played a role in fashioning Swahili urban style. In addition to tracing their descent back to some of the earliest Muslim settlers from Persia, they embraced Islam, financing mosques, practicing purdah (the seclusion of women), and hosting large religious celebrations. Their Muslim identity stimulated trade, as visiting Muslim merchants felt comfortable extending credit to them and living with their Swahili host families while waiting for the winds to turn. By 1350 CE, the urban style of Swahili city-states exhibited a distinguishing architecture. Many of the cities became "stone towns" with wealthy Swahili families constructing multi-level homes out of the coarse coral. The Swahili elite

Figure 9.14 | The Great Mosque at Kilwa Kisawani | Sultan Suleiman ibn Muhammed (r. 1421 – 1442 CE) improved the mosque. The mosque was constructed of coral blocks, which became a defining feature of urban Swahili architecture.
Author: Claude McNab
Source: Wikimedia Commons
License: Public Domain

used their stone houses to establish themselves as prominent, creditworthy citizens. They wore imported silk and cotton and ate off imported porcelain to further display their status. Like other Swahili, the ruling classes distinguished themselves from non-Muslims of the interior. They may have been partially moved to draw this distinction by their desire to sell as slaves people captured in the neighboring, non-Muslim communities.

Slavery within the **Indian Ocean World**, the zone of contact and interaction connecting people living adjacent to the Indian Ocean, began well before the spread of Islam in the seventh century CE. During the high point of the Swahili city-states, Muslim traders controlled the slave trade within the Indian Ocean World. Slaves tended to be captives of war sold to the Arabian Peninsula and regions near the Persian Gulf. Slaves were put to work as sailors, agricultural laborers, pearl divers, domestic workers, concubines, and musicians. Our information about the everyday lives of slaves in this region is very limited.

In one famous revolt, slaves from East Africa (the Zanj), who were forced to work on sugar plantations and salt flats near Basra (in present-day Iraq), seriously challenged the power of the Abbasid Caliphate. Led by Ali ibn Muhammad, the Zanj rose up in the **Zanj Rebellion**, a guerrilla war against the Abbasids. For fourteen years, the Zanj and their supporters, altogether an estimated 15,000 people, raided towns, seized weapons and food, and freed slaves. They captured Basra and came within seventy miles of Baghdad, the Abbasid capital. The rebels created their own state with fortresses, a navy, tax collection, and their own coinage. At enormous cost, the Abbasids finally put down the revolt in 883 CE using a large army and by offering amnesty to the rebels. Scholars have used the Zanj Rebellion to examine the scope of the Indian Ocean trade in East African slaves, the conditions of slavery in the Indian Ocean World, and the agency (the ability to exert their own will) of slaves. Some of these scholars suggest that the Zanj Rebellion led Muslims in Arabia to largely abandon the practice of using East African slaves as plantation laborers. The rebellion helps them explain why the Indian Ocean slave trade developed differently than the trans-Atlantic slave trade.

While there were some similarities between the trans-Atlantic trade that brought slaves to the Americas and the slave trade within the Indian Ocean World, there were important differences. Both slave trades took Africans, contributing to an **African diaspora**, or a dispersal of African peoples and their descendants, all over the world. The trans-Atlantic slave trade, which lasted approximately 300 years and reached its peak in the eighteenth century CE, forced approximately 12 million people, mostly from West Africa, into the Americas. The slave trade within the Indian Ocean lasted much longer, about 2000 years, and was generally smaller in scale. Scholars suggest that African slaves in the Indian Ocean World had more social mobility, especially since many of them were skilled soldiers. Also, according to Islamic precepts, slaves had some basic rights and could be incorporated into the households that they served. Theoretically, a freeborn Muslim could not be enslaved. Unlike slavery in the Americas, slavery within the Indian Ocean World was not racially codified, so freed slaves did not automatically face racial discrimination. And due to their reproductive capacities, women were more sought after as slaves within the Indian Ocean World, while the trans-Atlantic slave trade had the highest demand for young men. Despite these general trends, there was great individual variation within the slave experience.

Moving up the East African coast in the late fifteenth and early sixteenth centuries, the Portuguese sacked some Swahili cities and tried to tax trade. In 1498, when they happened upon the Swahili coast, the Portuguese were trying to establish a direct sea route to the riches of India and China. After using an East African guide to reach India, the Portuguese began to set up a **Trading Post Empire**, which intended to tax trade within the Indian Ocean. The Trading Post Empire consisted of a series of forts along the Indian Ocean coast where Portuguese administrators collected taxes and issued trade permits. In the early 1500s, the Portuguese returned to the Swahili city-states to enforce their will. As the Swahili city-states did not have a unified political structure or large armies, the Portuguese successfully looted and destroyed some Swahili cities. However, the Portuguese cultural influence and their ability to enforce tax collection was very limited north of Mozambique. The Portuguese did not move inland beyond the coastal cities and, by and large, trade within the Indian Ocean continued without a great deal of Portuguese interference. However, the Portuguese presence encouraged Swahili leaders to ally with the Omanis from southern Arabia. In 1699, the Omanis, working with some Swahili rulers, seized Mombasa from the Portuguese, and began an era of Omani dominance of the Swahili coast.

9.10 CONCLUSION

These African states showcase the continent's connections to the rest of the world, a multitude of African innovations, and the importance of using a variety of methodologies to interrogate long-held assumptions about Africa.

Africa was not isolated. Instead, oceans and deserts were "highways" in these periods. Aksum, the Western Sudanic states, Great Zimbabwe, and the Swahili coast were all commercially linked to Europe, the Mediterranean, the Arabian Peninsula, the Persian Gulf, southeast Asia, and even China. Although there were local differences, the ruling classes in each of the states collected tribute from outlying areas and participated in long-distance trade. The wealth of these states supported labor specialization, urbanization, and other innovations.

African states contributed to great cultural change. As just one case in point, Ethiopia, the Western Sudanic states, and the Swahili city-states all experienced religious transformations. Not only did Ethiopia serve as a sanctuary for both Christians and Muslims, but Ethiopians also established their own Church, the Ethopian Orthodox Church. Starting in the thirteenth century CE, Western Sudanic rulers converted to Islam, maintaining some of their pre-Islamic beliefs while building their connections with the rest of the Islamic World. Medieval African cities like Timbuktu benefitted from these connections. They attracted traders as reports of African gold circulated far and wide. Taxing the gold trade, Western Sudanic rulers developed these cities as both trading depots and places of scholarly learning. The Swahili in coastal East Africa also embraced Islam as one of the defining features of their identity. Their urban style reflected the centrality of Islam, which they believed distinguished them as cultured and refined. All four states also developed numerous other innovations, such as those in art, architecture, metal-working, agriculture, and political organization.

Before the twentieth century, foreigners recorded much of Africa's written history. There are limitation to their accounts, meaning that a number of written documents about Africa are misleading, at best. Many African societies remembered their own histories orally, using professionalized classes of historians, storytellers, and musicians, in addition to proverbs and the teachings of elders. Over the past fifty years, historians of Africa have done more to incorporate Africa's oral traditions into their examination of the ancient past. They have also used linguistics and archaeology to create a more accurate written history of the continent and reclaim African civilizations.

9.11 WORKS CONSULTED AND FURTHER READING

Ali, Omar. *Islam in the Indian Ocean World: A Brief History with Documents*. Boston: Bedford/St. Martin's, 2016.

Asante, Molefi Kete. *The History of Africa: The Question for Eternal Harmony*. 2e. New York: Routledge, 2015.

Brizuela-Garcia, Esperanza and Trevor Getz. *African Histories: New Sources and New Techniques for Studying African Pasts*. Boston: Prentice Hall, 2012.

Center for Food Security and Public Health. "African Animal Trypanosomiasis." College of Veterinary Medicine, Iowa State University. 2009 http://www.cfsph.iastate.edu/Factsheets/pdfs/trypanosomiasis_african.pdf

Collins, Robert O. and James Burns. *A History of Sub-Saharan Africa*. Cambridge: Cambridge University Press, 2007.

Conrad, David. "Oral Tradition & Perceptions of History from the Manding Peoples of West Africa." In *Themes in West Africa's History*. Ed. Emmanuel Kwaku Akyeampong. Athens, Ohio: Ohio University Press, 2006: 73-96.

Ehret, Christopher. *The Civilizations of Africa: A History to 1800*. Charlottesville, VA: University Press of Virginia, 2002.

Garlake, Peter. *Early Art and Architecture of Africa*. Oxford: Oxford University Press, 2002.

Gilbert, Erik and Jonathan Reynolds. *Africa in World History: From Prehistory to the Present*. 3e Upper Saddle River, NJ: Pearson, 2012.

Hall, Martin. *Farmers, Kings, and Traders: The People of Southern Africa*, 200 – 1860 Chicago: University of Chicago Press, 1990.

Horton, Mark and John Middleton. *The Swahili*. Oxford: Blackwell Publishers, 2000.

Keim, Curtis. *Mistaking Africa: Curiosities and Inventions of the American Mind*. 3e. Boulder, CO: Westview Press, 2013.

Marcus, Harold. *A History of Ethiopia*. Berkeley: University of California Press, 2002.

Niane, D.T. *Sundiata: An Epic of Old Mali*. Trans. G.D. Picket. Harlow, England: Pearson Longman, 2006.

Nurse, Derek and Thomas Spear. *The Swahili: Reconstructing the History and Language of an African Society, 800 – 1500*. Philadelphia: University of Pennsylvania Press, 1985.

Ranger, Terence. "The Invention of Tradition in Colonial Africa." In *The Invention of Tradition*. Ed. Eric Hobsbawm and Terrence Ranger. 211-262. Cambridge University Press, 2012.

Shillington, Kevin. *History of Africa*. 2e. Oxford: Macmillan Education, 2005.

UNESCO. "Tomb of Askia." http://whc.unesco.org/en/list/1139

Wiley, David. "Using 'Tribe' and "Tribalism' to Misunderstand African Societies." http://www.africa.upenn.edu/K-12/Tribe-and-tribalism-Wiley2013.pdf

10

The Americas

Eugene Berger

10.1 CHRONOLOGY

18,000 – 15,000 BCE	First humans migrate to the Americas
c. 13,000 BCE	Big game hunters inhabit the Great Plains
c. 10,000 BCE	Mesoamericans begin to cultivate squash
10,000 – 3,500 BCE	Paleo-Indian Period
5600 – 3000 BCE	Early Plains Archaic Period
2000 BCE – 250 CE	Preclassic or Formative period in Mesoamerica
c. 1900 BCE	Mesoamericans begin to make pottery
1800 – 800 BCE	Late Initial Period in Peru
1500 – 400 BCE	Middle Formative Period in Mesoamerica. Peak of Olmec statue carving
c. 1000 BCE	Maize becomes widespread in North America
400 BCE – 100 CE	Late Formative Period in Mesoamerica
200 BCE	The Moche begin their conquest of Peru's north coast
200 BCE – 400 CE	The Hopewell culture flourishes in North America
100 BCE – 600 CE	The Nazca culture flourishes in Peru
400s CE	Tiwankau founded
550 CE	Teotihuacán reaches 125,000 residents
700 CE	The Huari Empire reaches its height
700 – 1400 CE	Cahokia
750 CE	Tikal reaches 80,000 residents
800 CE	The Toltec city of Tula reaches a population of 35,000
1000 CE	The Chimu establish the capital city of Chan Chan
1050 CE	The population of Chaco Canyon's five great pueblos reaches 5,000 inhabitants
1325 CE	Tenochtitlán founded
1471 CE	Death of Inca Pachacuti

10.2 INTRODUCTION

This city has many public squares, in which are situated the markets and other places for buying and selling. There is one square twice as large as that of the city of Salamanca, surrounded by porticoes, where are daily assembled more than sixty thousand souls, engaged in buying, and selling; and where are found all kinds of merchandise that the world affords, embracing the necessaries of life, as for instance articles of food, as well as jewels of gold and silver, lead, brass, copper, tin, precious stones, bones, shells, snails, and feathers. ...There is also an herb street, where may be obtained all sorts of roots and medicinal herbs that the country affords. There are apothecaries' shops, where prepared medicines, liquids, ointments, and plasters are sold; barbers' shops, where they wash and shave the head; and restaurateurs, that furnish food and drink at a certain price. There is also a class of men like those called in Castile porters, for carrying burdens....Painters' colors, as numerous as can be found in Spain, and as fine shades; deerskins dressed and undressed, dyed different colors; earthenware of a large size and excellent quality; large and small jars, jugs, pots, bricks, and an endless variety of vessels, all made of fine clay, and all or most of them glazed and painted; **Maize**, or Indian corn, in the grain and in the form of bread, preferred in the grain for its flavor to that of the other islands and terra-firma; pâtés of birds and fish; great quantities of fish, fresh, salt, cooked and uncooked ; the eggs of hens, geese, and of all the other birds I have mentioned, in great abundance, and cakes made of eggs; finally, everything that can be found throughout the whole country is sold in the markets, comprising articles so numerous that to avoid prolixity and because their names are not retained in my memory, or are unknown to me, I shall not attempt to enumerate them.[1]

The above is from Hernán Cortez's description of **Tenochtitlán**, the Aztec capital he and his Tlazcalan allies conquered in 1521. As the Spanish explorers in the Americas, and later the French, English, and Dutch, saw monetary gain from reporting their exploits to their respective monarchs, we often end up with a stilted or incomplete version of the Americas before 1500. Part of this can be attributed to the bias of European explorers, and misinterpretation of Native American beliefs and practices.

Undoubtedly the most misunderstood practice was that of human sacrifice witnessed by the Spanish conquerors of the Aztec Empire. Among Mesoamerican and Andean peoples alike there was a belief that all life, cosmic, human, animal, and plant alike, grew beneath the soil and sprung forth above the surface. Furthermore, humans had a role in nurturing that life cycle. In many of the cultures we will discuss, shamanism was an important religious tradition whereby shamans or religious specialists could control the forces of the natural world. Often shamans would conduct ceremonies requiring sacrifice from members of his community to ensure cosmic and earthly order. While the Spanish (and Hollywood) tend to focus on more dramatic ceremonies where hearts are

---

1   Hernán Cortez. Second letter to Charles V, Mexico, 1520. https://www.historians.org/teaching-and-learning/classroom-content/teaching-and-learning-in-the-digital-age/the-conquest-of-mexico/letters-from-hernan-cortes/cortes-describes-tenochtitlan

cut from living warriors, other kinds of sacrifices in Mesoamerica and the Andes were integrated in hundreds of ways into daily life. For many cultures ritual bloodletting was a widespread practice, but one where the injured party survived to perform the ceremony the next year. Often times, human-shaped grain cakes would serve as stand-ins for actual human participants. Most sacrifices in fact were actually offerings or prayers to Mesoamerican or Andean deities. For example a Nahua newborn might be named in honor of Maya rulers. Or the first corn tortilla of the day might be consumed in honor of the sun.[2] These beliefs would eventually be manifest in physical structures like a cave under Teotihuacán's Pyramid of the Sun in Mexico or sunken plazas at Chavín de Huantar in Peru and Tiwanaku in Bolivia. These sacred spaces were constructed beneath the earth's surface to allow the cultures aboveground easier access to the Earth's creative capacity.

As historians, it also is helpful to point out some of our myopic tendencies regarding the peopling of the Americas. In Chapter One we talked about discrepancies regarding the date at which *Homo sapiens* arrived in the Americas. While there is evidence supporting an overland migration from Beringia, and geographically speaking the Beringia migration is the most logical explanation, some scholars argue that this approach has become "dogma" and even "ideology," leaving no room for evidence that may challenge this explanation. While we cannot argue that we are close to abandoning the Beringian migration as the most likely theory, there is mounting evidence that suggests a seaborne migration from Asia or even a "Solutrean" migration from Europe ten thousand years before an ice-free corridor opened up in North America.[3] Considering new theories may help us explain how the Americas came to be populated and how civilizations developed so quickly here.

A third weakness in our narrative of the Americas involves the demographic collapse of the indigenous population that occurred after the arrival of European diseases. Especially in the Circum-Caribbean, millions of indigenous peoples succumbed to European disease and overwork in the first decades of the sixteenth century, giving them little opportunity to construct their own historical narrative apart from the one that Europeans were writing.

Keeping these limitations in mind, our task in this chapter is to admire a pre-Columbian history where in a little over 15,000 years migrants from Asia (probably) populated the Americas by foot, built hundreds of major cities, supported a population in the tens of millions, and constructed two of the most impressive empires the world has ever known. Fortunately recent advances in archaeology and calendrics have helped us uncover much of this pre-Columbian past that had been largely clouded by our obsession with the triumph and tragedy of the European conquest.

10.3 QUESTIONS TO GUIDE YOUR READING

1. What crops were first domesticated in the Americas and where?

2. What did we learn from the **Olmec** about the transition from chiefdoms to states?

3. How did the Maya support such rapid urbanization?

---

2   Kay Almere Read and Jason J. Gonzalez, *Handbook of Mesoamerican Mythology* (Santa Barbara: ABC-CLIO, 2000), 25-26.
3   Bruce Bradley and Dennis Stanford, "The North Atlantic Ice-Edge Corridor: A Possible Palaeolithic Route to the New World," *World Archaeology* 36:4 (December 2004):460.

4. What were some of the features of urban life in **Teotihuacán** and **Tenochtitlán**?

5. How did **The Moche**, **Huari,** and **Chimu** build their regional influence?

6. How did the Inca use local resources to build their empire?

7. What was the role of Macchu Picchu within the Inca Empire?

8. How were cultures of the North American West able to overcome limited rainfall?

9. What traits did mound building cultures of North America share?

10.4 KEY TERMS

- Aspero
- Ayllu
- Cahokia
- Chaco Canyon
- Chan Chan
- Chavín de Huantar
- Chiapas
- Chumash
- Coricancha
- Cuzco
- Great Bison Belt
- Hopewell
- Huaca de la Luna
- Huaca del Sol
- Huari
- Huayna Capac
- La Venta
- Machu Picchu
- Maiz de Ocho
- Maize
- Mesoamerica
- Norte Chico
- Olmec
- Pachacuti
- Pithouses
- San Lorenzo
- Tenochtitlán
- Teotihuacán
- The Aztec Empire
- The Chimu Kingdom
- The Moche
- The Nazca
- Tikal
- Tiwanaku
- Toltec

10.5 MESOAMERICA

This discussion of the Americas before 1500 begins in the "middle." Although scholars believe that man migrated to Beringia and hence North America first, **Mesoamerica** was the first section of the Americas where scholars have found evidence of large settlements, agriculture, and unique cultural traditions, so this chapter starts there. The Mesoamerican culture area is found in what are now the modern countries of Guatemala, Mexico, Belize, El Salvador, and eastern Honduras. The region's frequent volcanic eruptions, earthquakes, and hurricanes gave it quite a staggering amount of ecological diversity including mountains, coastal plains, and a peninsular limestone platform (the Yucatán). The region's climatic diversity is attributable to the fact that it sits in both tropical and subtropical latitudes.

Less is known about migration to Mesoamerica than for North and South America during the Paleoindian period, but many scholars put people in the region by 15,000 BCE. These early residents hunted large and small game alike and consumed a wide range of plant resources. The Archaic period in Mesoamerica stretched from 8000 to 2000 BCE, during which scores of cultures adapted to the region's ecological diversity by domesticating wild food sources like "beans, squash, amaranth, peppers, and wild Maize (*teosinte*)."[4] The maize of large kernels of today took thousands of years of domestication for Mesoamericans to produce, but by the formative period it was a staple crop supporting tens of thousands. Groups living closer to the coast could also take advantage of wetland crops, such as manioc.

10.5.1 Early Farming in Mesoamerica

Just as early farmers in Southwest Asia turned wild plants into domestic crops, so too did their contemporaries in Mesoamerica with maize, squash, and tubers. Foragers in the southern Mexican highlands lived on a diverse diet of plants and animals, including cactus fruit, corn, squash, beans, fish, deer, and rabbits. Their contemporaries in the tropical lowlands further south consumed tubers like manioc, sweet potato, arrowroot as well as fruits like avocadoes. While Mesoamericans did domesticate most of these crops, they did so before becoming sedentary, a fact revealing the existence of regional variations in the path to agriculture. Around 10,000 years ago, Mesoamericans began to cultivate squash, both as a food source and as storage containers. Rather than staying near their cultivated land, however, early planters formed mobile "agricultural bands" that still hunted and would return to harvest mature squash or chilies. Over time, these bands planted more and hunted less until eventually they formed sedentary agricultural villages. But that process took at least 2,000 years. In fact, it may have been in the much denser tropics in and around Panama where residents first left foraging behind for agriculture. Around 10,000 BCE, after the extinction of megafauna, these tropical peoples begun to cultivate their forest environment. Tropical cultivation tended to be cramped, but tropical residents did manage to domesticate the tubers like manioc, sweet potato and arrowroot that we mentioned above.[5]

Over the next several centuries, village dwellings themselves revealed a growing emphasis on permanence and increasing sophistication. Brick walls and plaster floors began to replace hides and sticks. Unlike round huts, new rectangular houses allowed for expansion by extending walls and adding a perpendicular end wall. Expanding permanent dwellings allowed villages to grow through natural population increase. Permanent dwellings also helped establish distinc-

---

4   Michael E. Smith and Marilyn A. Masson, eds., *The Ancient Civilizations of Mesoamerica: A Reader*, (Hoboken, NJ: Wiley-Blackwell, 2000), 8.

5   Ristvet, 43-46.

tions between public and private space and public and private activities, effecting communal and private property. Not only did villages have to decide where and how to build, they also had to organize around when to plant, where to settle, when to harvest, and where to store the food. The invention of pottery during this period served storage needs tremendously. Tasks in construction, gathering, defense, and food production became more specialized and supervised, leading to the beginnings of class. The elite developed, a strata usually comprising warriors, priests, and administrators.

10.5.2 The Formative Period

By the beginning of the Formative Period around 2000 BCE, most residents of Mesoamerica were sedentary, many living in small bands that moved only seasonally.[6] However, by 300 CE many of these small bands had been replaced by quite common large urban centers. This was a rapid transition, to say the least. This rapidity was possible because of greater use of domesticated crops and storage and improved technology, like pottery vessels. Pottery appeared between 1900 BCE and 1750 BCE on the Pacific coast of **Chiapas** in highland valleys and on the Gulf coast. After about 1400 BCE, scholars start to see widespread sharing of obsidian, shell, jade, and iron artifacts, a sharing which denotes significant interaction by this point. A social hierarchy also began to develop in Chiapas, where there was a two-tiered settlement hierarchy of small centers and villages. In other words, the elite had bigger houses. Over time and in more areas, plastered floors and dirt floors appeared in different dwellings and altars in others. Burials too indicated social differentiation.

The **Olmec** were the earliest civilization in Mesoamerica and, therefore, drove much of this rapid development. The Olmec developed along the Gulf of Mexico and flourished during the Early Formative and Middle Formative (1500 – 400 BCE), while the Late Formative (400 BCE – 100 CE) saw their evolution and transformation. Scholars use this timeline with the caveat that Mesoamerica houses a number of unique cultural traditions, and there are variations within this timeline in terms of when they developed urbanization, states, agriculture, and certain technologies. The Olmecs' most

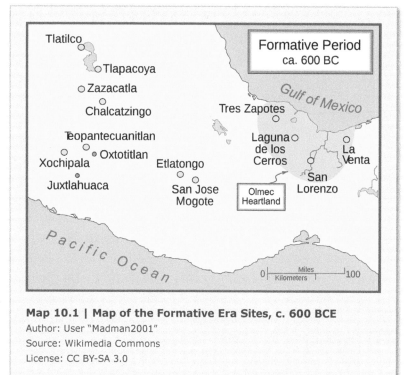

Map 10.1 | Map of the Formative Era Sites, c. 600 BCE
Author: User "Madman2001"
Source: Wikimedia Commons
License: CC BY-SA 3.0

6   Christopher Pool, **Olmec Archaeology and Early Mesoamerica**, (Cambridge: Cambridge University Press, 2007), 7.

notable accomplishment was their monumental stone sculpture. Other Mesoamerican cultures had stone monuments, but the Olmec versions were unique in their sophistication, size, and number. A common theme occurs during the coherent tradition spanning 1400 BCE to 400 BCE. Statues were carved out of thrones or in low relief on stelae. The largest of them weighed over forty tons. Stones had been transported as much as ninety km from their sources. The labor required to do this demonstrates the power of these rulers. Aside from statue carving, Olmec elites also commissioned carved columns, drains, and embellishments in large houses. An inordinate amount of iron trade also occurred, and objects like polished iron mirrors were found in the tombs of high-ranking individuals. The import of jade sculptures was perhaps even more prominent with thousands of tons of "serpentine blocks" buried in massive offerings at the Olmec center of **La Venta** in southern Mexico.[7]

Many of these monuments were commissioned by or for elite members of an increasingly sophisticated socio-economic hierarchy first seen in the Early Formative Olmec of **San Lorenzo.** San Lorenzo itself stood at the apex of a three- or four-tiered settlement hierarchy which included subordinate centers, villages, and special purpose sites. This increasing sophistication became solidified through Olmec politics as well. Early in the Formative Period most groups were organized in tribes, but the Olmec soon began to form a set of chiefdoms that allowed for organized leadership across generations, albeit through kinship ties. The Olmec also became the first civilization in the region to develop a state, where the same hierarchy became more stratified and institutions became more specialized.

Some scholars even call the Olmec an "empire," but most say it falls short for a few important reasons. First, the Olmec never had a large enough population at their disposal to form a conquering army. Second, while there existed a number of significant urban Olmec sites, such as La Venta and San Lorenzo, none of them has been identified as an Olmec capital. Finally, the art and archeological records of surrounding societies don't indicate an Olmec domination but rather the existence of something of a theocratic state, as elites seemed to have both political and religious authority and a considerable amount of influence.

Final questions related to our understanding of the region are: Why did the Olmec evolve at all, and why did they evolve when they did? One theory involves the ecological relationship to Mesoamerica's lowland environment. Another holds that increasing productivity led to high population growth, which caused a pressure to organize politically. Control of these resources as well as the limited use of warfare accounted largely for the authority of individual chieftains. Other scholars have added to this observation, pointing out that the abundance but lack of diversity of Olmec area agriculture forced them to develop a competitive advantage vis-à-vis societies that lived closer to obsidian, salt, and stone deposits. (The Olmec would need to trade for these resources that were central for hunting and food production). A more sophisticated society would have that advantage.

Once the Olmec did manage to organize as states, they began to plan for their permanence. From the above-mentioned stone deposits, the Olmec produced their cultural hallmark: monumental stone sculpture. Around 1650 BCE, the Olmec began to produce stone effigy bowls, but these are much smaller than the monumental sculptures that followed. Over 200 known monumental

---

7   Pool, 15.

Figure 10.1 | Olmec Colossal Head, La Venta, Mexico
Author: User "Hajor"
Source: Wikimedia Commons
License: CC BY-SA 3.0

stone sculptures remain; one-third are from San Lorenzo and the surrounding area. The colossal heads are the largest; some stand up to three and a half meters tall. Each head is unique, containing its own ear ornaments, headdress, specific facial features, and expressions. Most scholars think they are portraits. Table top altars have been found in a range of sizes across Olmec sites. Most now believe they served as thrones but others believe they served as altars as well. They often show humans emerging from a niche in front of the monument. The Olmec also crafted smaller sculptures in the round. These sculptures incorporated human and supernatural themes or humans in ritual or symbolic postures. A fourth sculptural style, one that corresponds to later periods, was stelae. These stelae often depicted supernatural beings and elaborately dressed individuals engaged in specific actions. These stone sculptures would be impressive for modern humans to achieve but are made more impressive considering the fact that the Olmec possessed no metal tools with which to cut them.

The purpose behind these sculptures, outside of their artistic value, seems to have involved monumentality. Stone as a whole gave a sense of order, stability, and equilibrium. The harmonic proportions in the works enhanced those ideas. The sculptures also contained a good enough mix of naturalism and abstraction to give a nod to the spiritual world as well. For the Olmec as shamanists, a direct connection existed between order on earth and order in the spiritual world. Olmec shamans, through ritual and through the assistance of their *nagual* (also referred to as *nagualo*) or "animal spirit companions," could travel to the supernatural world or guard against spirits who desired them harm.[8] Therefore, a number of altars and smaller sculptures show human-jaguar or human-dragon anthropomorphs, particularly those that reflect the existence of a gateway or portal between worlds. La Venta Altar 4, for example, had an earthly purpose as a throne and a symbolic one as a cosmological model. When the Olmec ruler sat on the throne he could be present in both the natural and supernatural realms. This journey between worlds was aided by the intercession of the ruler's animal spirit companion (in this case a jaguar).[9]

The Olmec undoubtedly left a lasting legacy on the Caribbean coast of Mesoamerica, but the legacy can be difficult to trace, as much of it has been subsumed into a debate about its being a "mother" culture for the Aztec and Maya. (Recent scholarship has given less credence to the

---

8   F. Kent Reilly III, "Art, Ritual and Rulership in the Olmec World," In Smith and Masson, eds., 374.
9   Ibid., 393.

Olmec as a "mother culture" and argues that it developed independently of Maya and Valley of Mexico cultures). Hopefully as scholars and students examine the Olmec as an independent cultural entity, its legacy will continue to become clearer.

10.6 THE MAYA

The importance of the influence of the Olmec on the Maya may seem superficial, but it is quite important, as the Maya's rise to sophistication was so fast and so complete that it almost defies explanation. After settling at the base of the Yucatán Peninsula around 1000 BCE, the lowland Maya learned how to deal with drought, feed tens of thousands of people, and organize politically—all before 250 BCE.

The Late Classic period was one of tremendous growth. The city of **Tikal**, in present day Guatemala, had reached a population of 80,000 by CE 750, while the population of its rival Calakmul reached 50,000. To support these large populations, the Late Classic Maya had almost a totally engineered landscape that included water management projects, flattened ridge tops, and terraced hillsides. The population was fairly dense in cities and in surrounding countryside. Their leaders had tombs built in their honor, imported luxury items like jade statues, feathers, cacao, and other items from the Mexican Highlands. These activities all demonstrate real sophistication.

The Late Classic Maya also had an advanced numerical annotation system of dots and bars and used zero. Maya writing began as pictographs and blended into quite artistic symbolism. In addition to their more than seven hundred carved monuments, the Maya culture produced wooden carvings, incised jades, and pottery.

Politically speaking, the Maya were never unified under one ruler or even a set of rulers. Instead, the Maya were a civilization that shared a set of cultural traits, a language family, but no single ruler or sense of common identity. Individual Maya Kingdoms rose and fell, but none was ever able to dominate the entire Maya area.

While their rule was perhaps not widespread, Maya rulers did hold tremendous power and prestige within their kingdoms. Rulers were kings at the top of a "steep" social hierarchy that was reinforced by religious beliefs. The king was a hereditary ruler chosen by the gods and a member of one of several elite bloodlines. The Maya priestly class organized a complex pantheon of both gods and deified ancestors.

This ancestor worship required not only ceremony and temple building, but a complex understanding of calendrics as well. Both the Maya and the Olmec

Figure 10.2 | Mayan Stela | Stela with Mayan Script, Anthropological Museum in Mexico City.
Author: User "Wicki"
Source: Wikimedia Commons
License: Public Domain

understood time as "a set of repeating and interlocking cycles instead of the linear sequence of historical time,"[10] much as the concept is understood today. Long cycles alternated with short cycles; the long periods involved the repeated creations and destructions of the world in their creation stories—with an emphasis on repeated. Since cycles are by definition repeated, certain dates are more important than others because they are attached to good and bad events in the past. Calendar priests determined what those dates were and so had considerable power. They also had the power to rewrite the course of events if this benefited the ruler. [11]

10.6.1 Teotihuacán and the Toltec

While the Olmec and Maya accomplished incredible things, urbanization to the north in Mexico's central valley may have left the most permanent legacy. To the north of the Maya culture area, the Valley of Mexico was the most "agriculturally desirable" zone in Mesoamerica. Climate was temperate, and rainfall, although not abundant, was predictable—in contrast to the drenching rains of tropical Mesoamerica. Lesser amounts of rainfall of course required aqueducts, reservoirs, and canals if a city were to thrive. Cuicuilco was such a city that rose to prominence in the Valley of Mexico by 150 BCE, only to be badly damaged by a volcanic eruption around 400 CE. The subsequent decline of Cuicuilco allowed a competing city, **Teotihuacán**, to rise to prominence in the area, and by 100 CE, its population reached 60,000 inhabitants. By 550 CE, Teotihuacán was one of the six largest cities in the world, with a population of 125,000. Teotihuacán covered more than 20 square kilometers, had a marketplace, an administrative center and several different types of housing. Its largest buildings seem to have had both a functional and a spiritual use. The Pyramid of the Sun, the largest building in the city was built over a sacred cave likely connected with creation myths. By the fourth century CE, Teotihuacán had the modern equivalent of neighborhoods; new houses were laid out on a rough grid with many homes organized into apartment compounds.[12] The dwellings were constructed of volcanic rock, mortar, and wood for the roofs. The compounds also had a system of underfloor drains. Many of the dwellings in these complexes are decorated with "polychrome wall murals" containing multiple religious themes and military themes, some depicting play or everyday life, while others being much more abstract.[13]

To support its massive population, Teotihuacán needed to secure supplies and tribute from surrounding areas. Many neighboring areas were conquered through a combination of trade and military conquest. Force was used to secure trade routes to the south and thus have access to goods as diverse as cacao beans, tropical bird feathers, salt, medicinal herbs, and honey. Once the city's influence had expanded and they had become the region's undisputed merchant power, its subsistence base increased to include the entire Basin of Mexico and some neighboring peoples like Tlazcala. The reach of Teotihuacán's leadership even extended into Maya kingdoms like Tikal where it influenced, and may have even ousted, a Maya ruler in the late

---

10   Matthew Restall and Amara Solari, *2012 and the End of the World: The Western Roots of the Maya Apocalypse.* (Lanham, MD: Rowman and Littlefield, 2011).

11   Ibid.

12   Adams, 46-49.

13   Ibid.

fourth century. Tikal's position within its own region may in fact have been strengthened by this subordination to Teotihuacán.[14]

Teotihuacán was able to sustain impressive growth and expansion for more than five centuries, but ultimately its size and complexity seemingly contributed to its decline. At about 650 CE, roughly half of Teotihuacán's public buildings and a number of temples, pyramids, and palaces were burned. Many were knocked down and torn apart as well. This does not seem to be the work of invaders, but instead internal and external groups who attacked declining symbols of power.

The Late Classic Maya would also experience a collapse of their cultural systems around 840 CE. Years of population growth and demands on and from the elite came to a head with a period of prolonged drought in the early ninth century. Resulting famines and infighting caused population losses in Maya settlements nearing eighty-five percent and in many areas abandoned farmlands were retaken by the forest.[15]

While many of these Late Classic Maya sites would never recover from their demographic decline, Mesoamerica remained fertile and southern Mexico remained temperate, so a number of polities rose to prominence in the area after the abovementioned declines. Tula, which had been founded by Teotihuacán leaders as an administrative center, emerged in the Valley of Mexico after 650 CE. Tula would become the capital of the Toltecs, who saw their principal city grow to a population of 35,000 by 800 CE. Like all Mesoamerican cities at the time, Tula would expand its influence through trade. Toltec ceramics were found in regions ranging from Costa Rica to Guatemala; while Toltec style I-shaped ball courts and rain dances were adopted by cultures like the Anasazi and Hohokam in modern day Arizona and New Mexico. One of these ball courts still sits near the modern city of Phoenix, Arizona.[16] While much of the Hohokam culture area sits in what is now the United States, it was heavily influenced by the culture of Mexico. Not only did the Hohokam build ball courts, they also erected platform mounds and dug irrigation canals like those found in Mexico.

One important difference that the Toltec developed from their predecessors was their desire to conquer. Perhaps influenced by the rapid decline of Teotihuacán, the Toltec wanted to rise to prominence quickly. Their construction of Tula was hasty and conflict with neighbors went beyond typical captive taking or territorial gain. The Toltec viewed their conquest as a "sacred war" where man would aid the gods in their fight against the powers of darkness. The Toltec eventually merged their sacred war with that of the northern Maya in the Puuc Hills of the Yucatán. The northern Maya elites had already adopted "divine war" when the Toltec invaded the Yucatán city of Chichén. Chichén would become the Toltec administrative center in the peninsula in the late tenth century but they did not completely drive out the city's Maya founders. In fact, the Itza Maya ruled the region under the Toltec and continued to do so well into the post-Columbian period.[17]

---

14   Adams, 48-49.
15   Ibid., 60-65.
16   Ibid., 69-71.
17   Ibid., 69-75.

10.7 THE AZTEC

While the Itza were one of the last unconquered native civilizations in the New World, another post-classic kingdom drew the most attention from Mexico's Spanish conquerors: the Aztec. The Aztec capital was the magnificent city of **Tenochtitlán**, founded around 1325 CE by a Nahuatl-speaking, previously nomadic group called the Mexica. Tenochtitlán was composed of a network of dozens of smaller city states who used the lake environment to plant wetland gardens and used raised causeways to separate the gardens and move around the city. Some fields were raised as well, a feat which drained them and helped them contribute to supporting a population that totaled around 300,000 people (including the population of the neighboring city of Texcoco). Eventually a network of canals was created that drained fields, fed crops, and provided for navigation with canoes. Not only were these raised fields a source of multiple crops, but also the lake provided wildfowl, salamanders, and algae.

However, as the population grew to over a million, other means of support were needed, so the people looked to outside tribute. Beginning in 1428, the Mexica sought independence from their Tepanec patrons and allied with other outlying towns to form the Triple Alliance, which

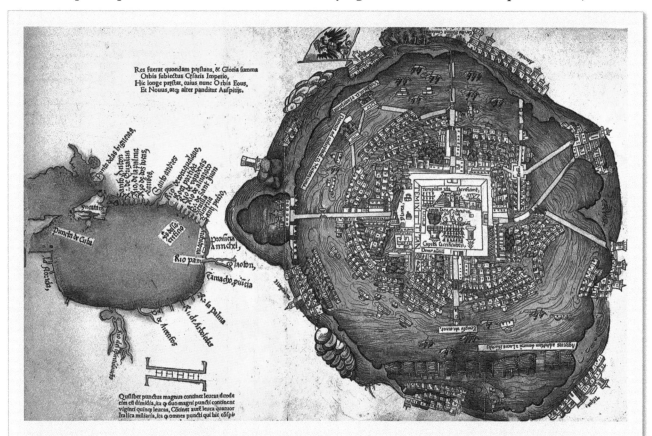

Figure 10.2 | Map of Tenochtitlán and Gulf of Mexico | Drawn by member of Hernán Cortés expedition, 1524.
Author: User "Lupo"
Source: Wikimedia Commons
License: Public Domain

by 1431 dominated the basin where they made their home. The unified Aztec people were led by the Mexica ruler Itzcoatl and his advisors. In making an alliance with Texcoco, the Aztec were able to build a causeway between the cities and help improve the infrastructure of Tenochtitlán. They then began construction on the Great Temple, a central market, and a larger network of gardens or *chinampas*. The Great Temple would become the orienting point for the entire city and would become the site of thousands of human sacrifices.

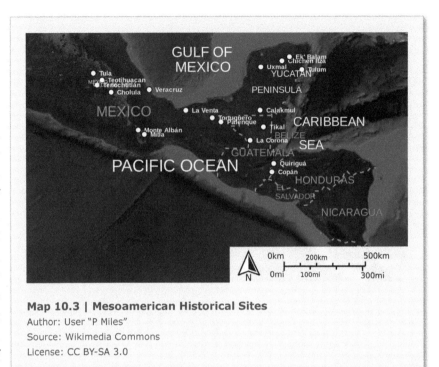

Map 10.3 | Mesoamerican Historical Sites
Author: User "P Miles"
Source: Wikimedia Commons
License: CC BY-SA 3.0

The Aztec are perhaps best known, and may even have grown infamous (like the Toltec and others before them), for practicing human sacrifice. However, the context in which these sacrifices take place reveals that they were not conducted in a wanton or random manner. First of all, for the new Aztecs, there was little tradition of and, therefore, little opportunity for community building to draw upon. Their rise to power had to have been quick and dramatic. Furthermore, they possessed a worldview that held that even though they had achieved greatness, decline was inevitable. This view was present in their philosophy and their ceremonies—including those of sacrifice. This view was also important for ritual victims, because upon their death, they believed that they would be freed from the burdens of the uncertain human condition and become a carefree hummingbird or butterfly.

For the Aztec, ritual provided a kind of protection against excess; there was order in it, even if it was violent. Men had no independent power, and gods were very abstract in their doling out of gifts. Finally, in the Mexica worldview, the earth receives rather than gives, much like it does in the Judeo-Christian tradition. Through fertility and death, humans satisfy that hunger. The process of birth and death is not "dust to dust" but the transition from one form of flesh to another. All man can do is order his portion of this natural cycle.

10.8 EARLY ANDES

Humans arrived in South America after migrating through North and Mesoamerica; they began to craft small campsites and fishing villages along the Pacific coast. Around 3,000 BCE, the small campsites villages were replaced by residential and ceremonial centers. This transition was made possible through a new focus on irrigation and communal agriculture.

These Pacific coast and Andean cultures left an incredible amount of material culture (much of it well-preserved because of the dry climate) for archeologists to analyze. Their work shows that parts of the Classical Andes—modern Peru, Chile, Ecuador, Bolivia, and Colombia—possessed the same level of cultural complexity as did China, Persia, and India during the same period. Through this material culture, the Classical peoples begin to separate themselves from their ancient and often less complex ancestors.

While it is tempting to lean heavily on artifacts for knowledge of the period, there is a danger of overreliance. For example, pottery of the Moche culture (see Figure 10.3) is well known for its often quite graphic images of female fertility and sexuality. These pieces are important works for archaeologists and historians alike, but one must keep in mind that little is known about how much these representations of Moche female sexuality in art actually tell us about gender relationships in their society. In other words, "shock value" or aesthetic quality should not be confused with universality.

This section begins with the end of the archaic period and the rise of a group of civilizations referred to as the **Norte Chico**.

10.8.1 Norte Chico

The Pacific coast developed large ceremonial and residential centers, which were organized around distinct status and rank among citizens. This area resembles other "crucible" areas like the Deh Luran Plain of Iraq, the Nile in Egypt, and the Olmec heartland. While similarities with the aforementioned early civilizations exist, the Norte Chico stands out for three reasons. First, it was politically "pristine." Scholars find no evidence that any outside polity influenced its development. Second, it endured for more than 1,300 years. This longevity gave the Norte Chico great influence in what would ultimately become a distinct Andean civilization. For example, large platform mounds of Norte Chico would also appear later in the highland center of **Chavín de Huantar**. The final reason Norte Chico stands out from other early civilizations is its development happened very quickly. By 2800 BCE, there were a number of similar large sites all with residential complexes, plazas, and platform mounds.[18]

The **Aspero** site is the archetype of these large sites. It covers fifteen hectares and contains six platform mounds. While there are a number of large sites like Aspero, there doesn't seem to have been a central Norte Chico chiefdom or state. There was no Norte Chico capital and no real evidence of conflict or warfare. This absence of conflict may be connected with the fact that scholars find no indication of differentially-distributed sumptuary goods, such as jewelry, clothing, and exotic trade materials, in Norte Chico. Even shell beads and stone are extremely rare to find in these sites so near to the Pacific.

Usually a cultural area requires some centralization and large scale agriculture before scholars refer to it as a civilization. The Norte Chico earns that distinction, however, because the level of cultural complexity indicates that they at least tried to centralize. Complexity is tricky. In the Norte

---

18   Jonathan Haas and Winifred Creamer, "Crucible of Andean Civilization: The Peruvian Coast from 3000 to 1800 BC" Current Anthropology 47:5: October 2006, 746.

Map 10.4 | Map of Peru Site Locations |
Archeological Site Locations Within Peru,
including El Paraiso, Caral, and Aspero
Author: User "Ontrvet"
Source: Wikimedia Commons
License: CC BY-SA 3.0

Chico, there occurred episodic attempts at non-egal-itarianism which were eventually abandoned. Many scholars also argue that Norte Chico did in fact become sophisticated and sedentary, not through agriculture but through fishing; this argument is known as the maritime theory. While unique, the maritime theory has trouble supporting the idea that the Norte Chico advanced merely through fishing, as insufficient archaeological evidence of communal labor sites centered on fishing exists to support it. Instead, a more likely explanation of Norte Chico complexity involves agriculture and fishing meeting at the middle, in a "shared labor" theory. A number of coastal sites contain not only remnants of cotton fishing nets, but other inland products like avocadoes and corn as well. These remnants mean that the canal building that took place between 4,000 and 3,000 BCE in the interior was likely only possible with the assistance of the coast's more plentiful labor force. This assistance was paid for with cotton nets and other agricultural products that in turn helped the coastal population feed itself and grow year after year. A larger temporary labor force would produce more canals and aqueducts, a cycle that explains much of the Norte Chico's economic expansion. Some of this cooperation may have even taken the form of pilgrimages to Norte Chico sites and the construction of monuments within Aspero, Caral, and other sites to commemorate them. The dry season of July and August presented a lull that would have been a good time for such pilgrimages. Evidence of communal cooking and eating exists, along with that of communal building.

10.8.2 Chavín de Huantar

While the Norte Chico is the oldest identifiable civilization along the Pacific Coast, Chavín de Huantar has also captured much attention as a crucible site for Andean culture. **Chavín de Huantar** is the iconic representation of The Late Initial Period (1800 – 800 BCE), where Peru saw the beginnings of a mix of Andean, coastal, and Amazon cultures. Chavín is located at an altitude of more than 3,000 meters in the Callejon de Conchucos, the easternmost basin between the Cordilleras Negra and Blanca in the Peruvian Andes. It is also midway between the coast and jungle, giving it access to the culture and resources of the greater Andean region. This access made it a pilgrimage center, an importer of luxury goods, and a disseminator first unifying Andean style.[19] Chavín's "Old Temple" is 330 feet across the back and more than fifty feet high at its highest. The

---

19   Rebecca R. Stone, *Art of the Andes: From Chavin to Inca*: 3rd ed. (New York: Thames & Hudson, 2012).

temple is U-shaped with a sunken court in the middle, and harpy eagle, jaguar, and parading shamans surround it. The temple is also built around the *lanzón* (great lance) which was a kind of supernatural conduit. The lanzón is similar in style to the Tello Obelisk which was found in a corner of the Old Temple courtyard. The obelisk contains carvings on all of its sides, carvings which primarily represent tropical and mythical origins or "gifts of the cayman."[20] Many dualities appear on the obelisk: male-female, plant type, ecological zone, sky-water, life-death, etc. These dualities and their meaning were reinforced by the pilgrimages made to Chavín and the ceremonies contained within them. It seems that Chavín architects used all of the symbolic value of the site available to them. The mixed human-animal features of the sculptures, the ingestion of hallucinogenic San Pedro cactus (also represented in sculpture), and even including acoustic symbolism were all important parts of the pilgrimages. Archaeologists have found marine shell trumpets in the tunnel complex under the city and have attempted to replicate how sound would contribute to the mind-altering rituals undertaken at the complex.[21]

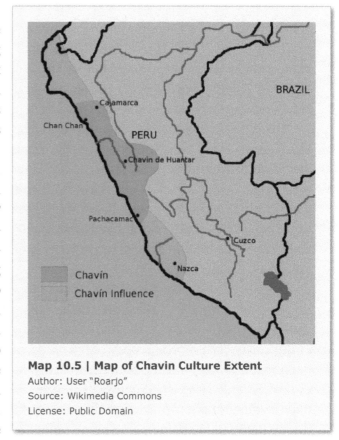

Map 10.5 | Map of Chavin Culture Extent
Author: User "Roarjo"
Source: Wikimedia Commons
License: Public Domain

The images and rituals at this site help establish what scholars refer to as the "Chavín cult."[22] The Chavín cult presents a universalist message based on the combined elements of coast and highlands that helped bring people to sites like this for ceremony and construction. In other words, these ideas helped move the Andes into the state phase. At Chavín, it also seems that there was a leader/priest, like in Egypt. It was, therefore, through spiritual power that the state congealed and grew, as well.[23]

10.8.3 Moche

Chavín de Huantar was not a developed civilization, but it did help create the importance of religion and ceremonial life in the Andes, both in every day practice and in sacred sites. Later, other groups in Peru, groups like the **Moche**, would build on religion and ceremony to help with state formation. The Moche began to conquer the North coast valleys in 200 BCE and, by 250 CE, had begun to construct the **Huaca del Sol** or temple of the sun and the **Huaca de la Luna** or temple

---

20   Rebecca R. Stone, *Art of the Andes: From Chavin to Inca*: 3rd ed. (New York: Thames & Hudson, 2012).
21   Ibid.
22   Ibid.
23   Ibid.

of the moon at their capital, which bore the same name. The Huaca del Sol seems to have been a royal residence and the Huaca de la Luna a place of worship. The Huaca del Sol contained over 143 million bricks, arranged into columns and marked with symbols perhaps of who made them.[24] Each column probably represented a tax-paying **Ayllu** (kinship-based community), meaning that the Huaca or temple was a literal representation of how the empire was held up by its individual units.

There is still some debate about how much centralization there was at the upper echelons of Moche politics, but there was undoubtedly a leadership class with several administrative levels. The first administrative level was that of the divine kings who are depicted in murals and ceramics from this period. The second was of noble administrators. Below that were bureaucrats who organized the already extant clan system. Below them were the long-standing clan leaders. The lowest level was composed of commoners, many of whom lived in single story adobe houses. Most commoners mastered some craft like metallurgy or weaving. Others were highly skilled and perhaps worked exclusively for the rulers.

Residents living outside of the capital were almost exclusively farmers who lived along the Moche's extensive irrigation canals—in the Chicama Valley, there is a 120 km long canal still in use today. The Moche found a very practical application of the previously mentioned coastal-mountain symbiosis through the llama. The llama is a domesticated mountain pack animal that the Moche used to journey to the coast and gather guano at the Chincha Islands for fertilizing their valley farms.

By 600 CE, the city of Moche covered an area of a square kilometer and probably had a population of 15,000. Each conquered valley outside of the capital had its own huaca, and each one was connected to Moche by relay runners who carried messages written in the form of lines and dots on Lima beans.

Perhaps the most notable Moche legacy was their art. Their buildings, their murals, and their pottery alike reflected their great skill and the high level of societal stratification. The Huaca del Sol at Cerro Blanco for example contained millions of bricks and more than 100 types of geometric symbols. Moche murals contained a unique series of squares depicting both abstract and mythological concepts involving themes of creation, combat, sacrifice, and men-jaguars. As already mentioned, this sacrifice may not have always been violent, may not have been literal, and always has a functional explanation. In this case, sacrifice is

Figure 10.3 | Stirrup-spout Vessel, Peru North Coast, Moche Culture, 100-500 CE
Author: Unknown
Source: Wikimedia Commons
License: Public Domain

designed to terrify or at the very least impress a subject population. While it is important to contextualize this sacrifice, we must also remind ourselves that this is not a modern civilization with a middle class or even a democratic tradition. It was archaic in the sense that a small group of people was supported by a large population underneath them. This kind of relationship required brutality.

---

24   Adams, 106.

10.8.4 Huari

While the Moche were notable because of their art and material culture, their use of violence to achieve and hold power threatens to cloud our image of the north coast peoples. The **Huari**, on the other hand, were able to build a successful empire in nearby areas combining intimidation and militarism with diplomacy, trade, and ideology. The Huari ruled over more territory than any previous Andean polity, partially by coopting neighboring groups through taxation, distribution of goods, feasting and religious ceremonies. There is also evidence that the Huari used sacred mummy bundles or trophy heads to incorporate outgroups and maintain a ritual relationship with these outgroups. Huari textiles and ceramics were found far from the capital, and Huari architecture was highly influential throughout the region.[25] The Huari Empire carved out a centralized state in a region where none had previously existed by coordinating local irrigation and labor systems. By 700 CE, Huari maintained a population of 25,000 and an over 700 kilometer-wide "zone of influence" connected by a road network that may have been the model for the Inca road system. In fact, it was ultimately Huari diplomacy and organization, rather than Moche violence in ritual killings, that provided a more useful precedent for the Inca.[26]

10.8.5 Chimu

The **Chimu** Kingdom was perhaps influenced more directly by remnants of the Moche, occupying as they did more or less the same geographic area. The Chimu capital of **Chan Chan** was established at about 1000 CE. Through their system of split inheritance, the Chimu forced the newly-ascended ruler to build his own material wealth. This expectation meant conquest of new territory and an increase in taxes. It also meant

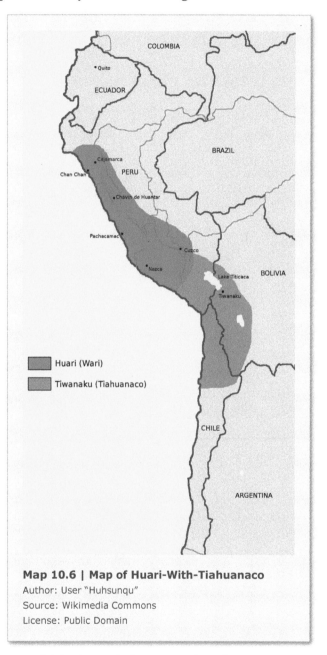

Map 10.6 | Map of Huari-With-Tiahuanaco
Author: User "Huhsunqu"
Source: Wikimedia Commons
License: Public Domain

the construction of a new palace where each ruler would be buried along with hundreds of his attendants and llamas who were sacrificed to accompany him in the afterlife. A Chimu ruler was

25   Tiffany Tung, *Violence, Ritual, and the Wari Empire: Bioarchaeological Interpretations of the Human Past: Local, Regional, and Global Perspectives* (Gainesville: University of Florida Press, 2012), 24-25.
26   Adams, 113.

also buried with a sample of the wealth he had accumulated in his lifetime in the form of textiles, wood carvings, pottery, or jewelry. While earthquakes meant that the Chimu had to work hard to reclaim or make any use at all of Moche irrigation canals, they did manage to revive and extend the Moche system to eventually provide Chan Chan with diverse agricultural products from maize to cotton to peanuts. The Chimu also employed violence in their rise to power; however, their conquest by the Inca cut short any means for scholars to see if they intended to follow or rather eventually break from the Moche legacy.[27]

10.8.6 South Coast peoples

The south coast of Peru developed somewhat distinctly because it is extremely arid. In certain areas along the coast there has never been recorded rain. Surviving there meant accessing and controlling Andean runoff that sometimes went underground. As a result, the south coast's population was much smaller, but in many ways was culturally richer.

The **Nazca** carved out their civilization along the south coast between 100 BCE to 600 CE. There was a large center at Cahuachi as early as 200 BCE, but it was largely ceremonial rather than residential. Forty huacas were also built in the areas surrounding Cahuachi but also were without large permanent populations. The Nazca maintained a regular pilgrimage to Cahuachi involving music, feasts, and fertility rites. There was some captive sacrifice, but it is not clear of whom. Nazca leadership was probably a confederacy of clans, making the forty huacas the hubs of political and sacred activities. Huacas are further explained in section 10.8.8.

The Nazca are well known for their pottery and textiles. Their pottery depicted mythical feline or otter figures, many of which were associated with water and fertility—in this climate, water essentially is fertility. The same figures are represented on the Nazca lines/geoglyphs that were created by clearing the desert floor of stone and leaving the motifs. The straight lines were probably "ritual walkways." Others argue that the Nazca Lines were an astronomical calendar centered around the agricultural cycle. Overall, the Nazca had an impressive but brief florescence which came to an abrupt end after a prolonged drought in the 550s CE.[28]

Figure 10.4 | Nazca Lines Hummingbird
Author: Unukomo
Source: Wikimedia Commons
License: CC BY-SA 3.0

27   Adams, 114-116.
28   Adams, 109.

10.8.7 Tiwanaku

Tiwanaku was a ceremonial center and administrative city near Lake Titicaca established in the fifth century CE. At its height, more than 40,000 people lived in the city itself; they were supported by a population of 365,000 in the subjected outskirts. Surrounding farmlands produced high crop yields with abundant quinoa and potatoes supported by meat and legumes. They used canals, ridged fields, and raised fields, and they even created a series of ditches that created fog and prevented frost in the colder months.

Figure 10.5 | An Inca Quipu, from the Larco Museum in Lima
Author: Clause Ableiter
Source: Wikimedia Commons
License: CC BY-SA 3.0

In the city itself, several large platform mounds connected by causeways were used by the administrators of this complex system. From subordinate colonies hundreds of miles away, they received corn, coca, tropical birds, and medicinal herbs. Many of these goods were carried by llamas. Alpacas also provided high grade wool for textiles.

Tiwanaku contained many ethnic and linguistic zones and "vertically integrated" many areas of the Andes for the first time. Tiwanaku was relatively stable until its downfall around 1,000 CE, perhaps falling victim to its own success. Saline deposits from long term irrigation may have reduced the fertility of the soil, leaving Tiwanaku without its most distinct advantage.

In general, comparing these three more recent civilizations to the first civilizations of Norte Chico reveals increased complexity in all cases with class structure developing, warfare, and religion, even though their methods of survival were quite different.

10.8.8 The Inca

The Huari and Tiwanaku built on local resources to construct their states. While the Inca are the best known of these Andean civilizations, they began in the same way by building on the Ayllu kinship system.

In some ways, the Ayllu system was ready-made for empire. Ayllus were networks of families and individuals who traded in labor and subsistence and ritual activities.[29] This system meant built-in labor obligations existed, as did rules about marriage and ancestor worship. All of these rules were reinforced through ritual, allowing the Inca to build upon Ayllu rituals to increase his power, authority, and divine claim to the throne. Future Incas were only eligible to rule if they descended from the royal allyu.

---

29   Michael A. Malpass, *Daily Life in the Inca Empire, 2nd ed.* (Westport, CT: Greenwood Press, 2009), 32.

After the Inca had established their legitimacy, their expansion would begin during the reign of **Pachacuti**. By the time of his death in 1471, he conquered not only the Chanca and Quechua ethnicities of the southern Andes, but also the coastal Chimu. Topa Inca continued his father's conquests; he was succeeded by **Huayna Capac**. The Inca used **Cuzco** as their imperial capital, expanding it around several huacas into the shape of a puma. They also built the Sun Temple in honor of the god Inti who was all-powerful, benevolent and from whom Inca rulers claimed to descend.

Not only did the Ayllu help the empire take shape, but it also became its main administrative units once it had expanded. Local Ayllu nobility reinforced their connection to the empire through the mummification and consecration of ancestors. Mummies or other sacred bundles would become "huacas," venerated in Cusco by Inca nobility to establish a sacred connection between local Ayllus and the empire. (See map for the connections between Cuzco and surrounding areas). Labor obligations were the primary form of taxation organized through the Ayllu and closely recorded on quipus. Through Ayllu labor, the Inca were able to collect taxes, store and distribute food, and build their road system. The Inca road system eventually covered over 5,500 kilometers, stretching from Ecuador to Chile. Counting all of the sub-systems, the roads covered brings that amount closer to thirty-two thousand aggregate kilometers. The roads varied in sophistication and width, depending on conditions and need, but could include staircases, causeways, and suspension bridges. This complexity had added elements of efficiency through the Inca network of messengers that would operate twenty-four hours a day and carry a message from one location in the empire to another in a matter of a few days.

The Inca also used religion extensively to keep their empire strong. Each Ayllu had a huaca connected to it with multiple meanings, including as an origin point. The sun, on the other hand, was the royal progenitor, and the temple Coricancha located in Cuzco was the most important temple to the sun. From Coricancha radiated forty-one sacred lines or ceques connected to 328 huacas in the Cuzco valley. Many huacas were connected to water or rain, giving a sacred importance to some drains, fountains, baths, and libations.

An empire of this size would not have been possible without an effective army as well. Inca arms reflected the landscape. Their armor was light, they used lots of projectiles, and they protected their fortresses with boulders that could be rolled down hills.

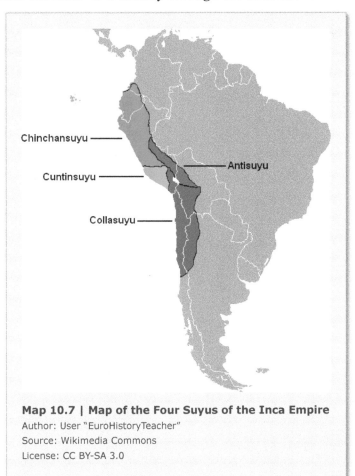

Map 10.7 | Map of the Four Suyus of the Inca Empire
Author: User "EuroHistoryTeacher"
Source: Wikimedia Commons
License: CC BY-SA 3.0

All these defenses used the advantages the mountains offered. Some archers were even recruited from the Amazon. Their strength was in their combination of mobility and superior numbers. There was very little siege tradition; battles would commence as soon as the armies arrived.

All empires would collect taxes, have armies, and build temples. The Inca were so successful, it seems, because they considered the most fundamental elements of Andean culture to strengthen their hold on power. Pre-Inca Andean society was a uniquely parallel one in which both men and women were important contributors to Andean religious, economic, and political life. In forming their empire, the Inca were very cognizant of Andean understanding of gender. To garner the support of the female sphere (some scholars say to undermine it), the Incas *created* a revered class of *aclla* women; these were attractive girls who would represent their newly conquered home Ayllu as elites of the glorious Inca Empire. These "chosen women" not only solidified Inca imperial bonds through marriage, converting a political entity into a family, but also expanded Inca religious legitimacy when a chosen few were periodically sacrificed and converted into the "divine custodians" of their communities.

10.8.9 Machu Picchu

Nestled in the Peruvian Andes, **Machu Picchu** is undoubtedly the most well-known Inca site by modern tourists. The site is located at 8,000 feet above sea level, in a forested area. It is framed by the Urubamba River and sits on a ridge between two peaks. The site itself must have been spectacular before construction began, but the complex itself is nothing short of extraordinary.[30]

Figure 10.6 | Peru Machu Picchu at Sunrise
Author: Allard Schmidt
Source: Wikimedia Commons
License: Public Domain

Despite its iconic status, much less is known about its fifteenth century role. Its construction seems to have been ordered by Pachacuti, who used it as a royal retreat of sorts from Cuzco. The most attractive time for travel would have been during the winter when Machu Picchu was much warmer than Cuzco. There is evidence of the same skilled craftspeople and retainers that accompanied the Inca in Cuzco maintaining a presence in Machu Picchu as well. Macchu Picchu did have tracts of surrounding land to feed the court, the emperor, and visiting dignitaries, and to supply the ceremonies connected with their arrival. However, this was not a city. Only a few year-round residents inhabited it, and even at its

30   Ibid., 108-09.

seasonal height, the population only reached about 750. There are agricultural terraces which grew potatoes and maize, and a spring for bathing and drinking that was connected by aqueducts to a fountain between the Temple of the Sun and the residences. There are one hundred and seventy-two structures at the site in total, including residences for the Inca's elite retinue and smaller dwellings for the servants. Also thirty buildings are dedicated to ceremonial purposes, including the Temple of the Three Windows; the Intihuatana, an oblong rock at the head of a large staircase; and The Temple of the Condor. The construction is not only visually impressive, but also structural engineers have remarked at its sophisticated drainage and foundation work that have allowed it to stand mostly intact for more than 500 years[31].

10.9 NORTH AMERICA

While most evidence points to human migration through North America to South America, the hallmarks of civilization would arrive later in what are now the United States and Canada. Many of us refer to the areas connected by Panama simply as "The Americas," but the Panamanian land bridge first linked the two continents only two million years ago. This was prior to human arrival in the Americas, but this separate development meant that North and South American flora and fauna experienced millions of years of separate development and evolution. This distinct development would influence the pace and patterns of human settlement in the Americas a great deal.

10.9.1 The West

The arrival of maize, beans, and squash from northern Mexico helped mark the transition to sedentary culture in the Southwest of what is now the United States. There is some evidence of primitive maize dating back to the middle of the second millennium BCE, but it would not become widespread until about 1000 BCE. A newer, drastically different maize, "**Maiz de Ocho**," is believed to have been the key to the flourishing of sedentary villages across the Southwest and to the eventual appearance of large pithouse villages around 500 BCE. Maiz de Ocho is better suited to arid conditions and yields larger kernels which are more easily milled. **Pithouses**, dwellings whose name indicates that its walls were in fact the sides of an excavated pit, became widespread across the Southwest because they were "thermally efficient." They lost less heat than aboveground structures in winter and, as they were built into the ground, were cooler in the summer. Pithouses remained in wide use in the area until about 700 CE, when more complex exchange networks and social organization led to more diverse settlement patterns.[32]

One of these new settlement patterns was the "great pueblo" that appeared as part of the "Chaco Phenomenon" around 900 CE. To deal with unpredictable summer rainfall, the Chaco Anasazi people of New Mexico built three "great houses"—Peñasco Blanco, Pueblo Bonito, and Una Vida," a large structure situated at natural drainage junctions. The semi-circular town of Pueblo Bonito grew out of a pithouse village to eventually form a semi-circular network of more than 600 rooms and reached a height of five stories along the canyon's rear wall. The complex's walls were built of

---

31   Ibid., 112-114.

32   Brian M. Fagan, *Ancient North America: The Archaeology of a Continent*, 3rd ed. (New York: Thames and Hudson, 2000), 306.

sandstone blocks whose surfaces and cracks were smoothed and shored up by a clay-sand mortar. Construction of the high ceilings also involved complicated ashlar masonry patterns that could be covered with "adobe plaster or matting."[33]

Each of the larger **Chaco Canyon** sites also had at least one great kiva. Kivas were subterranean gathering places which were used by individual kin groups for work, for education, and for ceremonies. Larger kivas were gathering places for more formal ceremonies where political decisions affecting the entire community were often made.

By 1050 CE, five great pueblos in Chaco Canyon supported a total population of around 5,000 people. While most lived within the relatively compact canyon area, the influence of this populace reached well beyond the immediate pueblo complex. Evidence indicates that the Chaco Canyon people may have had exclusive access to sources of turquoise all over New Mexico and used the stone in their workshops where they produced vases, human effigy vessels, incense burners, bells, trumpets and painted tables. By the early twelfth century, Chaco Canyon's influence extended to much of northwest New Mexico and southern Colorado, where more than seventy outlying sites contained kivas, Chaco pottery, and similar architecture to what was found in Pueblo Bonito. The

Figure 10.7 | Chaco Canyon Pureblo Bonita Doorways
Author: User "Saravask"
Source: Wikimedia Commons
License: Public Domain

Chaco also developed a road system that may have been for the distribution of resources or pilgrimages. Either way, the road construction involved considerable cooperation to craft, at different stages, stairways and ramps carved out of bedrock and other pathways lined with boulders. After 1130 CE, drought and growing population densities led to a 100-year decline of the Chaco sites. By the 1200s most of the pueblos of the Chaco system were empty, their population dispersed and away from the canyon.[34] While this was the height of Anasazi village life, they continued to thrive culturally and are recognized as the precursors of the modern Pueblo peoples.

10.9.2 The Pacific coast

Further west, cultures along North America's Pacific coast were also sedentary, but did not derive their existence from farming. Instead, multiple Pacific coast cultures took advantage of abundant ocean resources, such as various fish species, sea mammals, timber, shellfish, waterfowl, game, and wild plants. The abundance of these resources often suggests that coastal cultures were less complex than their contemporaries in the interior, but the ravages of climate required tremendous adaptation over time. During the Late Holocene period alone, from 2000 BCE to the present, periodic colder episodes may have led to consequences as disparate as lakeside flooding, lowering

33   Ibid., 301.
34   Ibid., 323-329.

of tree lines, drought, and a reduction of available marsh areas. Northwestern Coastal peoples, for example, addressed this volatility by never putting their eggs in one basket. While they may have primarily eaten acorns or salmon, they made sure to always maintain a secondary food source. Further south, the **Chumash,** a people inhabiting the central and southern California coast, developed ceremonial centers, provinces incorporating several villages, sophisticated "watercraft," and vibrant trade with the interior. In fact, this trade helped the Chumash avoid scarcities as well.[35]

10.9.3 The Plains

The Great Plains represented perhaps the largest area of pre-Columbian North America, but it is also one of the least understood. The Wild West shows of the nineteenth century produced the lasting yet erroneous impression that the Plains Indian culture remained unchanged for centuries. Big game hunters in the Clovis Culture first inhabited the area as early as 13,000 years ago. As big game became extinct around 9000 BCE, Paleo-Indian groups on the plains turned to foraging and fishing in river valleys and to hunting of primarily bison as well as deer and fowl. By 9000 BCE, the Ice Age had left behind a vast expanse of "arid grassland" from Alaska to the Gulf of Mexico, an expanse known as the "**Great Bison Belt**." Long before European explorers introduced horses, people on the Great Plains had developed sophisticated processes of hunting bison on foot that involved some hunters disguised as bison, others orchestrating movements among hunting groups, and others shouting to drive the bison toward pre-selected "traps" or "jumps." Dozens of bison would fall over a precipice to their deaths. By 6000 BCE, plains hunters had more sophisticated projectiles that could penetrate the skin of a surrounded animal or one that had become stuck in mud or sand. Findings at the

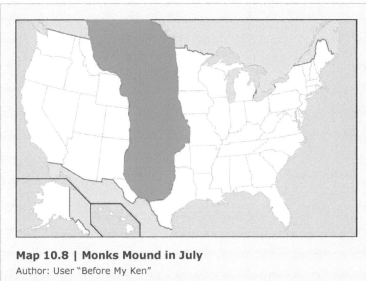

Map 10.8 | Monks Mound in July
Author: User "Before My Ken"
Source: Wikimedia Commons
License: Public Domain

Olsen-Chubbock site in Colorado indicate that by 6500 BCE, Paleo-Indians had also begun to butcher seventy-five percent of the animals they killed, which could sustain a group of 100 people for more than a month.[36] Early Plains Archaic (5600 – 3000 BCE) activity, while still largely dependent on bison, shows some increasing reliance on fish, fowl, and berries, possibly indicating warmer and drier conditions that "diminished grass cover throughout the Central Plains." Middle Plains Archaic peoples (2900 BCE to 1000 BCE) adapted their bison hunting to allow for a more sedentary existence, returning to the same hunting ground year after year, and making much of

35   Ibid., 222, 248.
36   Ibid., 93-96.

the bison meat into pemmican (a brick of pounded flesh and fat), that could be stored for seasons when bison were less plentiful (Fagan 123). By 550 CE, the Late Plains Archaic people had fully incorporated the bow and arrow into their hunts, which tended to be less frequent but more productive, often incorporating "mass kill sites" that were used for hundreds of years in some cases.[37]

10.9.4 The Eastern Woodlands

The term 'Middle Woodland' is occasionally used to refer the period between 200 BCE and CE 400; this coincided with the influence of the **Hopewell** culture over much of eastern North America. Previous to the Hopewell ascendance, the Adena people built hundreds of burial mounds in and around central Ohio (2300 – 2100 BCE). Accompanying the burials were dozens of types of "grave goods" including spear points, stone pipes, and sculptures of animals and human hands. Hopewell mound building (1000 – 200 BCE) and culture as a whole certainly had antecedents in the Adena and early Woodland cultures as a whole, but the Hopewell tradition stands out in its grandiosity. With their center in the Ohio Valley, the Hopewell created hundreds of hectares of earthworks with regionally specific styles of craftsmanship. Copper, shells, obsidian, and shark and alligator teeth were all used to create personal adornments, containers, pipes, and figurines. Much of this artifact diversity can be attributed to the size and vitality of the Hopewell exchange zone which extended across much of eastern North America from Florida to the Great Lakes. While there is evidence that areas as far away as North Dakota participated in this exchange network, the so-called "core areas" were in the Mississippi, Illinois, Scioto, and Miami river valleys in Illinois and Ohio. As trade picked up, so did the ceremonial and political significance of the artifacts received by local leaders and ultimately included in burial mounds. Some artifacts were buried with their owners at death as symbols of their power in life. The expansion of ceremony through these objects also meant that many of the Hopewellian centers shared physical characteristics such as both platform and conical mounds, structures for cremation, and burial vaults. The local populations who participated in these ceremonies seem to have lived near, but not in, the ceremonial centers themselves in single or multiple family households. Although close to other residents, Hopewell communities were scattered across the area, subsisting through a mix of foraging and horticulture.[38]

10.9.5 Cahokia

Other North American mound builders established their center at **Cahokia**, across the Mississippi River from present day Saint Louis. Cahokia was inhabited from about 700 to 1400 CE. At its peak, the city covered nearly six square miles and 10,000 to 20,000 people lived there. Over 120 mounds were built over time, and most of the mounds were enlarged several times. Houses were arranged in rows and around open plazas, and agricultural fields were cultivated nearby. Other mound centers and communities were located in the contiguous "American Bottom" region. Centralization and the beginning of the Mississippian period happened around 1050 CE, and the transition to the Moorehead phase—marked by decreasing mound building—happened about 1200.[39]

37   Ibid., 122-127.
38   Ibid., 417-422.
39   Mary Beth D. Trubitt, "Mound Building and Prestige Goods Exchange: Changing Strategies in the Cahokia Chiefdom,"

What scholars still don't know about Cahokia is why there was decreased mound building after 1200, during the so-called Moorehead Phase. While scholars usually associate decreased construction with societal decline, recent scholarship suggests that the opposite may be true for Cahokia. Instead of declining, Cahokia might have gone through a transition to a lesser focus on staples and storage and greater focus toward prestige goods and economic power. Their decreased mound building may have coincided with their energy being more focused on controlling trade across the Mississippian Southeast. Scholars see evidence of this shift with an increase in nonlocal raw materials and "prestige goods" at Cahokia during this period, such materials and goods as minerals, igneous rock for axeheads, ceramics, marine shell, quartz crystal, and copper.[40]

Figure 10.8 | Monks Mound in July
Author: User "Skubasteve834"
Source: Wikimedia Commons
License: CC BY-SA 3.0

American Antiquity 65:4 (Oct., 2000): 669-690

40   Ibid.

10.9.6 The Arctic

The Arctic's harsh climate meant that it was one of the last areas in the Americas to be permanently settled. The first Paleo-Eskimo populations appeared around 4,000 years ago emanating from Eastern Siberia. They were left behind by the original American colonists. The Arctic colonists expanded rapidly across Alaska, through Canada, and into Greenland as they all possessed arctic small tool kits including the important toggle headed harpoons to kill walrus and seal. In general, their evolution was from reindeer hunters to seal hunters, but both types of societies continued to exist side by side.

10.10 CONCLUSION

Humans migrated to the Americas by 15,000 BCE and perhaps as many as 3,000 years before. The earliest recognizable civilizations in the Americas were in Mesoamerica and began during the Archaic period, ten thousand years ago. Farmers in Mesoamerica began to cultivate crops such as corn, squash, beans, chilies, manioc, and sweet potatoes. During Mesoamerica's more recent Formative Period, the rise of the Olmec Civilization occurred. They would be followed by several others, most notably the Maya, and further to the north the Aztec Empire that was at its height when the Spanish arrived in 1519.

Around 3,000 BCE, small campsites and fishing villages began to appear in Peru. These were eventually replaced by more permanent structures and agriculture communities which would be the antecedents to the incredibly complex cultures of the Classical Andes in Peru, Chile, Ecuador, Bolivia, and Colombia. Among these Pacific Coast cultures were the Moche, the Huari, the Chimu, and the Nazca. Many of these cultures had their political and cultural centers in large urban areas like Tiwanaku, which had a population of about 40,000 people around 100 CE. More than 1,000 years later, it was the Inca Empire that would build on these cultural traditions, extending its rule over more than 5,000 kilometers from Ecuador to Chile.

Sedentary culture first began in North America when people in the desert southwest of the continent began to cultivate maize about three thousand years ago. Groups like the Chaco Anasazi in New Mexico would eventually construct massive complexes of aqueducts, homes, and ceremonial spaces by about 1000 CE. There were other major cultural areas all over North America, from Florida to the frigid Arctic.

Despite (or perhaps because of) their late arrival in the Americas, humans developed at an incredible pace all across the region. The residents of the Americas developed remarkable political sophistication, infrastructure, religion, art, economic integration, and technology that Europeans marveled at when they arrived in the late fifteenth century.

10.11 WORKS CONSULTED AND FURTHER READING

Adams, Richard E.W. *Ancient Civilizations of the New World*. Boulder: Westview Press, 1997.

Bourget, Steve and Kimberly L. Jones, eds. *The Art and Archaeology of The Moche: An Ancient Society of the Peruvian Coast*. Austin: University of Texas Press, 2008.

Bradley, Bruce and Dennis Stanford. "The North Atlantic Ice-Edge Corridor: A Possible Palaeolithic Route to the New World." *World Archaeology* 36:4 (December 2004) 459-478.

Clendinnen, Inga. *Aztecs: An Interpretation*. Cambridge: Cambridge University Press, 1995.

Fagan, Brian M. *Ancient North America: The Archaeology of a Continent, 3rd ed*. New York: Thames and Hudson, 2000.

Haas, Jonathan and Winifred Creamer. "Crucible of Andean Civilization: The Peruvian Coast from 3000 to 1800 BC." *Current Anthropology* 47:5 (October 2006).

Malpass, Michael A. *Daily Life in the Inca Empire, 2nd ed*. Westport, CT: Greenwood Press, 2009.

Mithen, Steven. *After the Ice: A Global Human History, 20,000 – 5000 BC*. London: Weidenfeld & Nicolson, 2003.

Pool, Christopher. *Olmec Archaeology and Early Mesoamerica*. Cambridge: Cambridge University Press, 2007.

Reilly III, F. Kent. "Art, Ritual and Rulership in the Olmec World." In Smith and Masson, eds.

Read, Kay Almere and Jason J. Gonzalez. *Handbook of Mesoamerican Mythology*. Santa Barbara: ABC-CLIO, 2000.

Restall, Matthew and Amara Solari. *2012 and the End of the World: The Western Roots of the Maya Apocalypse*. Lanham, MD: Rowman and Littlefield, 2011.

Silverblatt, Irene Marsha. *Moon Sun and Witches*: Gender Ideologies and Class in Inca and Colonial Peru. Princeton: Princeton University Press, 1987.

Smith, Michael E. and Marilyn A. Masson, eds. *The Ancient Civilizations of Mesoamerica: A Reader*. Malden, MA: Blackwell Publishing, 2000.

Stone, Rebecca R. *Art of the Andes: From Chavin to Inca: 3rd ed*. New York: Thames & Hudson, 2012.

Trubitt, Mary Beth D. "Mound Building and Prestige Goods Exchange: Changing Strategies in the Cahokia Chiefdom." *American Antiquity* 65:4, Oct., 2000, pp. 669-690.

Tung, Tiffany. *Violence, Ritual, and the Wari Empire: Bioarchaeological Interpretations of the Human Past: Local, Regional, and Global Perspectives*. Gainesville: University of Florida Press, 2012.

10.12 LINKS TO PRIMARY SOURCES

Mesoamerica

The Aztecs and the Making of Colonial Mexico
http://publications.newberry.org/aztecs/

Maya Hieroglyphic Writing: The Ancient Codices
http://www.famsi.org/mayawriting/codices/index.html

Popul Vuh: Creation account of the Quiché Mayan People
http://www.mesoweb.com/publications/Christenson/PV-Literal.pdf

The Andes

Moche Decorated Ceramics

    http://www.metmuseum.org/toah/hd/moch/hd_moch.htm

Tiwanaku

    http://whc.unesco.org/en/list/567

Nazca

    http://whc.unesco.org/en/list/700

Machu Picchu

    http://whc.unesco.org/en/list/274

North America

Chaco Canyon

    https://www.nps.gov/museum/exhibits/chcu/index1.html

Hopewell Ceremonial Earthworks

    http://worldheritageohio.org/hopewell-ceremonial-earthworks/

Cahokia Mounds

    http://cahokiamounds.org/explore/

11 Central Asia

Brian Parkinson

11.1 CHRONOLOGY

1206 – 1368 CE	Mongol Empire
1240s – 1502 CE	Khanate of the Golden Horde
1225 – 1370 CE	The Khanate of Chagatai
1265 – 1335 CE	The Khanate of the Ilkhans
1370 – 1507 CE	Timurid Dynasty

11.2 INTRODUCTION

The year was 1216 CE, and a detachment of Mongols campaigned westward out of Mongolia and into Central Asia. They were in aggressive pursuit of the leader of the neighboring Naiman tribe, a certain Küchlüg, who had the misfortune of allying with Jamukha, the principle rival of Genghis Khan. The khan had quickly dispatched with their combined armies, forcing Küchlüg to seek refuge among the Qara Khitai, located to the southwest. In the intervening years, Küchlüg somehow managed to usurp the Qara Khitai throne. Not long thereafter, he attacked a

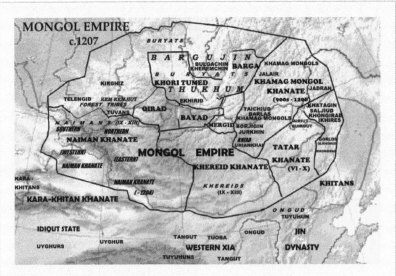

Map 11.1 | Map of the Mongol Empire c. 1207 CE
Author: User "Khiruge"
Source: Wikimedia Commons
License: CC BY-SA 4.0

Karluk tribal confederacy that appealed to Genghis Khan for protection. The Mongol leader deployed 30,000 troops to track down this troublesome renegade. By 1218 the inveterate adventurer had fled south towards the Pamir Mountains in modern day Afghanistan. Eventually, the Mongol general Jebe, along with the help of some local hunters, caught up with Küchlüg and executed him. And yet it was the pursuit of the fugitive Küchlüg that inadvertently brought the Mongols into Central Asia. Their conquest of the region was one without the forethought of empire, yet the area absorbed, adopted, and integrated the Mongols, just as it had incorporated external forces many times before.

Central Asia displayed a remarkable ability to embrace foreign influences, such as the Turkic migrations, expansion of Islam, and Mongol conquest, internalizing them and making them its own, much like an interesting stew. Situated at the crossroads of many empires, Central Asia was tucked in between the Chinese, Europeans, Arabs, and Indians. There, in the middle of these grand civilizations, just along the Great Silk Road, the region connected the Orient to the Occident and linked it to major patterns in world history. It was from there that these external forces saturated the area and shaped the course of its history.

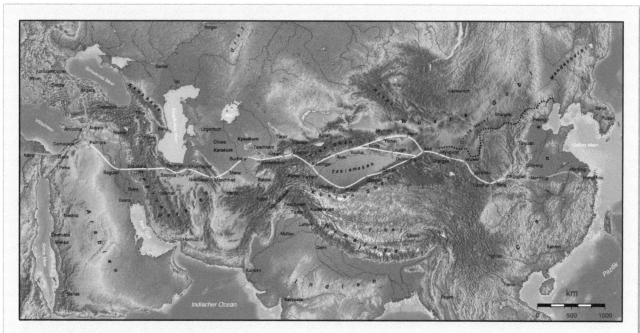

Map 11.2 | Map of the Silk Road
Author: User "Captain Blood"
Source: Wikimedia Commons
License: CC BY-SA 3.0

11.3 QUESTIONS TO GUIDE YOUR READING

1. How did the geography of Central Asia have an impact on its history?

2. In what way did the Turkic migrations change the culture of Central Asia?

3. How did the nomadic way of life facilitate the Turkic conquest of the region?

4. The process of Islamization took place over centuries. What helped to expedite the conversion process?

5. How did Genghis Khan differ from his predecessors? What enabled him to unite all of the Mongol tribes?

6. What was the significance of Inju to the history of the Chagatai Khanate?

7. What role did religion play in the Ilkhanate?

8. Why did Timur attempt to externalize the violence of the steppe?

9. Has Central Asia been an interesting stew of foreign influences, or has it been the product of internal forces?

10. Should the modern day states of Afghanistan and Iran be considered a part of Central Asia? Going back to the Mongol conquest of the region, what similarities do these states share with the core of Central Asia? What are some of the differences?

11. Should the conflict that has existed between nomadic and sedentary societies be considered the primary force determining the course of Central Asian history?

12. What has been the legacy of the conquests of Central Asia? How have the various empires shaped the region since the Turkic migrations?

11.4 KEY TERMS

- Abaga Khan
- Battle of Talas River
- Batu
- Berke Khan
- Börte Üjin
- Chagatay
- Chaghatay Khanate
- Gaykhatu Khan
- General Jebe
- General Sübedey
- Genghis-Khanid Legitimacy
- Golden Horde
- Grand Duchy of Moscow
- Great Hunt
- Güyük
- Heights of Baljuna
- Hülegü Khan
- Inalchuq
- Inju
- Islamization
- Jalal al-Din Manguburti
- Jin Dynasty
- Juchi
- Jurchen

- Kublai Khan
- Khuriltai
- Khwarazmshah Ala al-Din Muhammad II
- Küchlüg
- Mahmud Ghazan
- Möngke
- Mongol Horse
- Naqshbandi Order
- Nasir-ud-Din Mahmud Shah Tughluq
- Nomad Battle Strategy
- Ögedey
- Orkhon Steppe
- Pastoral Nomadism
- Qaghan
- Qutayba ibn Muslim
- Rashid al-Din Hamadani
- Recurve Bow
- Samanids
- Shihihutug
- Silk Road
- Sufism
- Tax Farming
- Temujin (Genghis Khan)
- The Khanate of the Ilkhans
- Thumb Ring
- Timur
- Tokhtamysh
- Toluy
- Transoxiana
- Turkification
- Ulus
- Xiongnu
- Yasa
- Yasaviyah Order

11.5 GEOGRAPHY OF CENTRAL ASIA

Unlike many other regions of the world, Central Asia lacks the distinct topographical features necessary to delineate boundaries. There are several broad geographical zones in Central Asia nonetheless. Perhaps the most well-known topographic area in Central Asia is the great Eurasian Steppe, a latitudinal belt of grassland that stretches from Eastern Europe through Mongolia. It was there that nomadic horse cultures flourished. Located to the south of the steppe was the core of Central Asia, an area known as Transoxiana. This is a dry region that lies beyond the Oxus River, known today as the Amu Darya. In Transoxiana

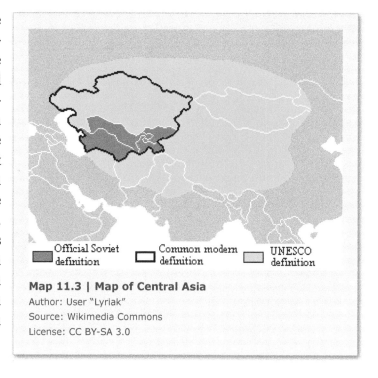

Map 11.3 | Map of Central Asia
Author: User "Lyriak"
Source: Wikimedia Commons
License: CC BY-SA 3.0

trade settlements and irrigated agriculture developed along the Amu Darya and Syr Darya watersheds. Finally, located to the far south, lies the mountainous area of Khorasan, the cultural capital of Persia prior to the appearance of the Mongols.

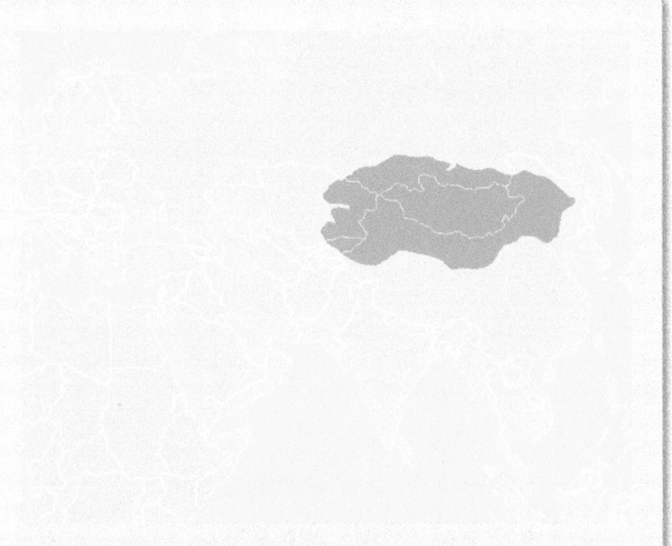

11.6 TURKIC MIGRATIONS

Nomadic migration was the first major external influence that would be integrated into the culture of the region, as steppe peoples imparted a lasting impression to Central Asia. Beginning with the **Xiongnu** (209 BCE – 93 CE), a long-term exodus of steppe peoples spread out of Mongolia and into Central Asia. For millennia prior to the rise of Genghis Khan, the winners of the

Map 11.4 | Map of the Xiongnu Empire in 205 BCE
Author: User "Postmann Michael"
Source: Wikimedia Commons
License: Public Domain

tribal battles for predominance on the **Orkhon Steppe**, prime pastureland located in western Mongolia, forced the vanquished off to the west. These periodic mass departures of Turkic tribes out of the area progressed southwest into Central Asia in a migration conquest, not a trade diaspora, as happened to Africans during the slave trade. These new arrivals forever altered the ethnic makeup of Central Asia. Previously, the region had been predominantly Persian and Indo-European; when the waves of Turkic tribes penetrated into the area, though, they occupied the great steppe and agricultural basin of Central Asia and pushed these Persian groups to the fringes. Over time, they slowly Turkified the area, endowing it with a more nomadic character.

Map 11.5 | Map of the Great Eurasian Steppe
Author: User "Shattered Gnome"
Source: Wikimedia Commons
License: Public Domain

These Turkic tribesmen divided their society into five strata. Members of the royal tribal clan presided over the social order. This dominant group bestowed its name on the tribal confederation, a collection of tribes. Positioned below them were their allies and associated tribes. Next were the common herders who did not participate in struggles for power. Lower still were the artisans, such as blacksmiths and leatherworkers. And finally, we find slaves at the bottom of the hierarchy. They usually acquired their lowly position in society by means of capture in times of war.

These Turkic wanderers belonged to an unstable confederation of clans and tribes roaming the steppe, loosely bound under a **khagan**, a charismatic monarch who laid claim to some sort of divine providence. Khagan made use of their personal charisma, as well as their political and military smarts, in order to maintain group cohesion and ward off challenges to their authority. Under strong khagans, tribal confederations were capable of wielding incredible power, but, more often than not, they were notoriously volatile and often imploded upon the death of their leader, collapsing into a brutal struggle for power. The winners in this struggle forced the losers out of the area, and while many went to the north or south, most to the west. Victorious tribes remained in Mongolia on the highly-prized Orkhon Steppe, located near Lake Baikal.

Although the khaganate was a diarchy, or system of dual rule, with the oldest son controlling half of the land, it lacked a clear transition of power, like hereditary succession. Because the khagan theoretically ruled over a series of tribal confederations, any member of the tribal confederation could ascend to the position of monarch by demonstrating their personal charisma and martial skills on the battlefield. This often resulted in a fight to prove oneself that could erupt into broader inter-tribal strife.

Periodic Turkic migrations into Central Asia transformed the sedentary culture of the region. These steppe peoples lived by practicing **pastoral nomadism**, a way of life centered around herding that most likely predated the Turks but was eventually adopted by them. Their culture was utilitarian in nature and provided all the necessities for life on the great plains of Central Asia, including food, clothing, shelter, and transportation. In order to maintain their pastures, these horsemen followed a fixed, seasonal pattern of migration because they did not want their flocks to overgraze. During the winter, for instance, they camped in foothills and mountain valleys, where it was warmer at lower altitudes. There they built fixed shelters with one main objective: survival. The oral tradition, which included songs, epic narratives, and parables, flourished during the inhospitable winter months.

Figure 11.1 | A Naadam Boy Riding a Mongol Horse on the Mongolian Steppe
Author: User "invictsHOG"
Source: Wikimedia Commons
License: Public Domain

In the spring, the nomads made a ten-day trip to the prairieland to graze their herds on fresh grass that just emerged from mountain runoff. There the women and children erected a central camp, usually comprising four yurts, while the men divided the flocks into their specific pastures. They established about ten satellite camps around the central camp, with each herd positioned about ten to twenty miles from the center. This separation of camps minimized the potential threat that their enemies posed to their herds. During the summer, they traveled to mid-mountain fields, where it was cooler and offered access to water. Covering about ten miles per day, it took them approximately fifty days to reach this campground. Finally, in the fall, they returned to the steppe in order to make provisions for the harsh winter. These preparations included drying and preserving their meat, and taking milk from their animals.

Enhanced mobility was the key to the survival of pastoral nomads. They actually spent a good portion of their lives on horseback and were accustomed to moving over long distances, taking all of life's necessities with them. This allowed them to retreat quickly from rival attacks or areas afflicted by natural disaster. Though their way of life appeared seemingly innocuous, it enhanced the ability of these horsemen to expand rapidly and conquer neighboring groups. It was in this manner that pastoral nomadism accorded its practitioners certain martial advantages. The annual **Great Hunt** served as a military proving ground that helped them hone their fighting skills. In preparation for winter, tribes deployed groups of mounted men, who dispersed in different directions, with the intent of driving every animal within a set perimeter inwards to converge at a pre-established central point. With great co-ordination taking place over vast distances, these migrants learned how to coordinate their movements based on a color scheme of arrows and whistling patterns. Their herding tactics easily translated to military tactics and proved devastating in combat.

Nomad society was certainly capable of waging war. Their ability to shoot from horseback provided them with a mobile and lethal means to overcome slower, infantry-based armies. These horsemen carried portable, three-foot-long **recurve bows** capable of piercing enemy armor from over 450 meters. Metal **thumb rings** enabled a rapid rate of fire without damaging the archer's fingers. Raised hunting and herding from horseback, nomads even learned how to sleep in the saddle of the **Mongol Horse**, their indigenous horse. Though not tall in stature,

Figure 11.2 | Archers on the Mongol Horse
Author: Sayf al-Vâhidî
Source: Wikimedia Commons
License: Public Domain

these sturdy mounts displayed impressive endurance and allowed groups to traverse great distances, often up to 160 kilometers per day. The speed with which they could cover territory on their steeds often confused sedentary forces and multiplied the terror factor. Native to the region, these horses were able to forage for themselves and survive on their own. Nomads did not require supply lines and could, therefore, remain on campaign for an average of three years. The combination of the skills acquired from herding, the double-compound bow, and the Mongol Horse, translated to a formula for political domination of Central Asia, at least until the arrival of Genghis Khan and the Mongols.

Turkic domination of the region began on the battlefield, where the strategies of steppe warfare proved devastating to infantry-based armies. The first stage of the **nomad battle strategy** often commenced with a feigned retreat, in which a group of their cavalry engaged the adversary, retreated, and encouraged their opponents to follow them. This technique lengthened the lines of their challengers, as they pursued the "retreating" Turkic cavalrymen, who were busy shooting backwards from horseback. The next stage of battle involved outflanking the enemy and enveloping them. They then showered their foes with arrows, the objective being to pin the opponent in place. This alone was often enough to break a sedentary power. When fighting against another steppe power, their reserves charged the opponent's lines so as to break their forces into pieces and finish them off piecemeal. Most importantly, because of their limited numbers, the Turkic horsemen were reluctant to risk fighting an enemy that they did not believe they could defeat, instead, they would poison water wells, scorch the earth, and retreat. The Mongols would later employ similar battle tactics that allowed them to conquer the whole of Central Asia.

11.7 ISLAM

Islam was not the first foreign religion to arrive in Central Asia. In fact, the region had already been exposed to many foreign systems of belief prior to the coming of Islam in the seventh century. Local merchants conducting long-distance trade along the Silk Road came into contact with many different religious doctrines; the trade route served as a conveyor of not only goods but also concepts. Generally, intellectual diffusion is not a one-way street, as western ideas traveled eastward and eastern concepts filtered into the west. In this manner, the Silk Road carried Buddhism, Judaism, Zoroastrianism (an Iranian religion with both monotheistic and dualist elements), Siberian Shamanism, and even Nestorian Christianity to Central Asia. The great number of religions found in the area at the introduction of Islam testified to the great tolerance of the region. By the tenth century, however, all of the non-monotheistic faiths had disappeared from Central Asia in the aftermath of Islamic conquest.

It was **Qutayba ibn Muslim** (669 – 716) who expanded the presence of Islam in Central Asia during the eighth century, as the general's forces swept into the area, defeated the Persians, and by 715 CE completed their conquest of **Transoxiana**, the region located beyond the Oxus River. A decisive Arab Muslim victory over the Chinese at the **Battle of Talas River** in 751 secured Central Asia and repulsed the only major challenge to Islamic rule. The triumph over the Chinese made it possible for Islam to become entrenched in the region. The Persian **Samanids** (819 – 999) made Islam the official state religion and established a school of theology in Bukhara.

But **Islamization** did not take place overnight; instead, it took centuries. Transoxiana slowly Islamicized, though it never Arabized. The peoples in the area remained culturally Turkic and Persian. Central Asia retained its Turkic and Persian languages, albeit with a heavy Arabic influence in religious vocabulary.

It took generations for Islam to become fully ingrained in the culture of Central Asia. Unlike other places, where the religion filtered into society from the bottom up, as was the case in Southeast Asia, Islamization in the region occurred from the top down. The process incorporated native peoples, who took part in the process of conversion. Local leaders submitted to the faith in order to maintain their social status and elite position in society. The conquerors offered the Central Asian nobility important positions in the administration so long as they professed Islam, providing the opportunity for the native elite to rule in their own right.

Islam also displayed a remarkable ability to assimilate indigenous Central Asian frontier customs as it advanced through the area, allowing some traditional practices to remain so long as it accelerated conversion. By accepting certain harmless practices in order to Islamicize Central Asia, these Muslims mirrored Christian efforts to Christianize Eastern Europe.

11.7.1 Sufism

The Islam of Central Asia differed greatly from that which originated in the Arabian Peninsula. This vast region embraced Islam, remaking it into a syncretic faith that was culturally its own. Essentially a sort of mysticism, or folk Islam, Sufism in the area emerged from the fusion of Islamic sedentary civilization and Buddhist nomadic culture. Central Asians were generally receptive and tolerant of foreign beliefs, but in order for the faith to take root in the area, missionaries had to make some concessions to the native, specifically pastoral-nomadic culture. The urban-dwelling and agricultural populations of the region generally accepted Sunni Islam and the law of the Sharia; however, the culture and lifestyle of the itinerant peoples of the steppe did not readily conform to the rigors of Islamic law. Sufism helped convert these tribes to Islam, in part due to its doctrinal flexibility. What arose from the mix of orthodox Islam and Turkic pastoral nomadism was a uniquely Central Asian brand of Sufism.

In this context, Sufis evangelized to groups on the frontier of Central Asia. Actually, Sufi merchants were largely responsible for bringing Islam to the region. Central Asian Sufi orders such as the **Yasaviyah** established themselves along trade routes in order to reach out to travelers. These missionaries also proselytized to the Turkic communities on the steppe. Meanwhile, the **Naqshbandi Order**, operating in travel lodges, spread Sufism by ministering to Iranian and Tajik peoples. The followers of these Sufi orders believed that they could better disseminate a form of the faith that was more loving and caring.

11.8 THE MONGOL ERA

The Mongols greatly expanded into Central Asia during the thirteenth century. There they reunited with the Turkic groups who had been expelled from the Orkhon Steppe over the course of a millennia. The Mongols confronted many Turkic peoples who had radically altered their existence since their days on the plains and adopted a stationary way of life.

At this point in time, forces indigenous to the region shaped the world around it; foreign influence waned as a consequence of nativism. The Mongols created the largest empire in history, as Central Asia externalized the violence of the steppe, yet it was with enormous difficulty that they even united as a people. Perhaps the greatest obstacle for them to overcome was their own divisiveness. Inter-tribal strife was commonplace, but once they united, the Mongols expanded deep into Russia, China, India, and the Middle East.

11.8.1 A New System for Unity

It was **Temujin** (1206 – 1227), later known as **Genghis Khan**, who brought this fractured people together and developed a method of governance and expansion that lasted long after his death. Born into the aristocratic Borjigin Clan, most likely in 1167, Temujin's success related to his convictions. Inspired by oral tales of past glory, his personal charisma and sense of fate enabled him to survive a youth of life-threatening privation, eventually bringing the various Mongol tribes together.

With a keen awareness of his own destiny, Temujin was inspired to achieve greatness. He had a clear vision that God predestined him to function as His temporal ruler on Earth and exhibited a desire to claim universal lordship. Through a series of fights, he eventually subjugated local clans in eastern Mongolia. He then expanded his political control of the region through a marriage alliance to **Börte Üjin**, a member of the Olkhonut Tribe, which maintained friendly relations with Temujin's Khiyad Tribe. The Merkit Tribe kidnapped his wife not long thereafter. Temujin heroically rescued her from this rival tribe, but she had been held in captivity for eight months and soon gave birth to their first son Juchi, who suffered from an uncertain parentage. Some historians believe that Temujin acquired the notion of conquering all of the Mongols from his liberation of Börte.

Despite his early successes, Temujin remained greatly outnumbered by his opponents and was forced to retreat to the **Heights of Baljuna**, located in modern day Manchuria, where he convinced his followers to swear an oath of total allegiance to him who called for them to fight unto death for him. For their unwavering loyalty, he promised his supporters

Figure 11.3 | Temujin (Genghis Khan)
Author: Anonymous
Source: Wikimedia Commons
License: Public Domain

a share in his glory upon their victory. Some Mongol tribes yielded to Temujin by 1204 and agreed to recognize him as their leader, thus paving the way for a period of final unification of the Mongols.

Temujin demanded a high level of commitment from his people, endowing his forces with a coherency and unity of purpose. He also promoted allies based on merit, rather than by the traditional Mongol method of advancement based on position within the tribal hierarchy. His opponents, on the other hand, lacked his force of will and entered into a series of squabbles. Temujin took advantage of their internal fights, emerging victorious by 1206. The culmination of his ascendency took place that year at a Mongol assembly, or **khuriltai**, which appointed him as the first undisputed ruler of the Mongols, uniting them under the authority of his position. Temujin adopted the name of Genghis Khan, or universal ruler in this context.

Genghis Khan presided over peoples who had experienced near-constant warfare since 1160. Previously, tribal confederations were loose alliances held together under charismatic khagans and punctuated by tribal warfare. He consolidated all of these diverse tribes and reshaped them into a single "nation," endowing Mongol society with more cohesiveness, a key element to future expansion. He did this by developing a new political order that deviated from tradition.

Restructuring Mongol society into new administrative military units that provided the necessary impetus for expansion, Genghis Khan charged each of his commanders with a tribal unit that was responsible for controlling a particular pasture and fielding soldiers when needed. His system had the added effect of assuaging previous conflicts by assigning the members of one tribe to military detail with other rival tribes, thus emphasizing collective responsibility. By forcing the men from one tribe to stand guard over the pastures of other tribes, he weakened loyalty to ancestral lines and homelands, thereby reinforcing his own leadership.

Genghis Khan represented the ultimate source of justice in his newly-formed state, consolidating his position and making it more authoritarian. By embodying autocracy in the position of the khan, he made the title of khan institutional, not personal, building a new foundation for legitimacy. Previously, tribal leadership rested on charisma. Furthermore, the great khan could not be self-proclaimed but had to be recognized at a khuriltai.

His law, known as **Yassa**, originated as decrees delivered during war. Yassa remained secret, which allowed Genghis Khan to adapt it to changing circumstances. For example, he later incorporated cultural elements indigenous to Mongol society into the law. He based his code on shamanist principles, and it served as the social and political formula binding all Mongols together. It also strengthened Mongol, rather than clan or tribal identification. It is believed that Genghis Khan himself directed the law, while his stepbrother **Shihihutag** served as the high judge, and his son **Chagatai** administered its execution.

11.8.2 Expansion

Genghis Khan encouraged Mongol expansion and the conquest of Central Asia. After subduing inter-tribal warfare, he followed tradition and exported the violence of the steppe. He offered incentives to his soldiers; the spoils of victory went to those who followed him into battle. Genghis Khan received ten percent of the loot and divided the remaining ninety percent between his commanders, who, in turn, distributed their portion amongst their retinue. This plunder also included the inhabitants of all subjugated lands, which resulted in the dramatic depopulation of conquered territory, as the khan received his share of artisans and craftsmen to be sent back to the itinerant Mongol capital.

In 1208, Genghis Khan targeted northern China for pillaging, but he quickly encountered considerable difficulties overcoming well-fortified Chinese municipalities. The Chinese had ringed their principle metropolises with moats and connected these major urban centers to several smaller satellite towns via underground tunnels. The Mongols had attempted to starve these cities into submission, but they lacked the military technology necessary to overcome walls forty-feet high and fifty-feet wide. To counter these challenges, they imported the technology necessary to defeat Chinese cities. Genghis Khan also compensated for a lack of native talent by incorporating foreign engineers into their army. He utilized Arab, Persian, and Chinese experts to solve the problem of defeating Chinese municipalities. Their knowledge of siege warfare enabled them to construct the siege engines capable of subjugating cities.

Adding these new sedentary peoples to the khan's army inevitably caused problems, for these men hailed from distinctly different cultures and did not interact well with the Mongols.

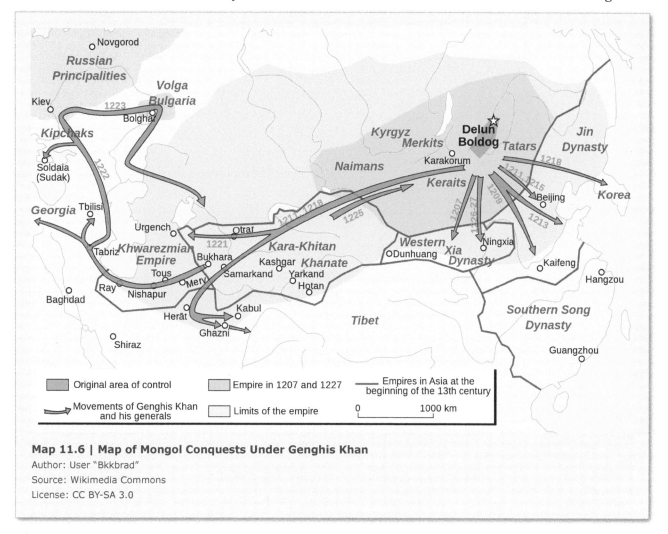

Map 11.6 | Map of Mongol Conquests Under Genghis Khan
Author: User "Bkkbrad"
Source: Wikimedia Commons
License: CC BY-SA 3.0

Genghis Khan, therefore, combined the mobility of his forces with the slow, bulky siege engines of the sedentary armies. While he kept his cavalry independent from the foreign engineers, mostly comprised of mercenaries, he blended these two disparate groups on the battlefield to his strategic advantage.

For the Mongols, building an empire proved much easier than maintaining one. The nomads possessed an inherent need to loot and plunder cities, and Genghis Khan took advantage of this innate desire by remaining on campaign. But the Mongols had difficulty understanding settled civilization and did not know how to maintain order in that new and different cultural milieu. Although they were able to instill fear in their enemies and easily forced many cities to capitulate, the Mongols co-opted local officials to ensure that taxes and tribute flowed freely back to their capital.

With his newly-constructed army, Genghis Khan returned to northern China again in 1210 and began a continuous campaign of destruction, primarily directed against the **Jin Dynasty** (1115 – 1234), an empire ruled by a **Jurchen** minority, a Tungusic people from Manchuria who would later call themselves the Manchu. In an early battle, the Jin put their Turkic cavalry up front to confront the Mongol horsemen. The Mongols managed to convince the Jin Dynasty's cavalry to defect to their side. Genghis Khan subsequently advanced on the Jin capital of Zhongdu and entered into a prolonged siege. In November of 1211, the khan withdrew his troops to their winter pastures, only to return again in 1212. Genghis Khan attempted a rash assault of the city. He failed and was wounded in the process. His Mongols had to retreat once again.

Genghis Khan returned a fourth time in March of 1213, this time with the goal of conquering Korea, Manchuria, and all of northern China. Early difficulties campaigning against the Jin Dynasty prompted him to adjust his strategy. By laying waste to all of northern China, he aimed to annihilate their way of life, turning the region into vast pastureland for his herds. The Mongol leader surrounded Zhongdu and starved the city's inhabitants into submission. He systematically obliterated everything in order to send a message to the inhabitants that it was futile to resist him. He even considered taking the city, brick by brick, and dumping it into the Yellow River. Fortunately for the residents of Zhongdu, a captured Chinese bureaucrat intervened and convinced Genghis Khan that it would be better to "sack" them every year through the collection of tribute. Mongol interest in rebuilding the city began soon thereafter, as Genghis Khan incorporated northern China into his state and opened the region to trade. This campaign represented the first significant addition of territory to the Mongol Empire.

As this chapter began, it was with the tenacious pursuit of the fugitive **Küchlüg** in 1216 that originally brought the Mongols into Central Asia. There they aroused the disdain of the local ruler in the area, **Khwarazmshah Ala al-Din Muhammad II**. Ruling over a loose confederation of disparate peoples, Ala al-Din Muhammad lacked security in his position as the Khwarazmshah. Even his own mother was in intrigue against him. It was he who provoked the wrath of the Mongols. It all began when Genghis Khan sent a trade caravan, which probably included some spies dressed incognito as merchants, to the frontier post of Otrar, located along the Syr Darya. The shah believed that the trade mission was a mere deception meant to obscure an eminent invasion. **Inalchuq**, uncle of Ala al-Din Muhammad and governor of Otrar, improvidently convinced the

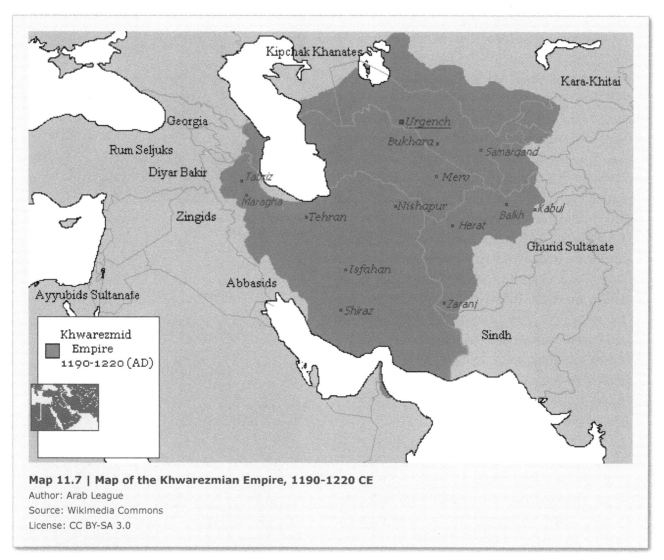

Map 11.7 | Map of the Khwarezmian Empire, 1190-1220 CE
Author: Arab League
Source: Wikimedia Commons
License: CC BY-SA 3.0

Khwarazmshah to have the entire party executed. An enraged Genghis Khan quickly dispatched another envoy and demanded that the governor of the city be put to death and have his head sent back to Mongolia as proof that Genghis Khan's wishes were fulfilled. The shah executed this emissary too, a rash decision that precipitated the Mongol onslaught of Central Asia, which resulted in brutal massacres and a drastic depopulation of the region.

Ala al-Din Muhammad prudently fled the area, leaving the citizens of Khwarazmia to defend themselves against the forces of Genghis Khan. A total of five Mongol armies approached the Khwarazm capital of Samarkand from different directions, converging in 1220. The Mongols slayed the inhabitants of the city and constructed pyramid-like edifices out of their severed skulls. In 1221, they seized the city of Urgench and dumped it into the Amu Darya, piece by piece, diverting the course of the waterway. And yet, Khwarazmshah Ala al-Din Muhammad still inexplicably escaped capture and absconded south. Genghis Khan deployed another force of some 30,000 troops under the generals **Jebe** and **Sübedei** to track him down and put him to death. The shah eventually sought refuge on an island in Caspian, where he died of pleurisy.

Meanwhile, **Jalal al-Din Manguburti**, the son of the Khwarazmshah, assembled an army of resistance. Genghis Khan sent his stepbrother Shihihutug to apprehend Jalal, but he escaped to the Hindu Kush Mountains of Afghanistan. Jalal's forces managed to defeat the Shihihutug-led Mongols on the field of battle at Parwan in the spring of 1221, a rare loss. The Mongols actually respected Jalal for his display of valor and willingness to resist them. Jalal fled to India via the Khyber Pass with his pride intact. The khan headed south himself and defeated Jalal al-Din along the banks of the Indus River. Following their defeat of Jalal, the Mongols descended into India but quickly found the hot and humid climate inhospitable; they decided to return to Mongolia, arriving home by 1225. The Central Asia campaign had started as a punitive expedition but in the process had wiped out any type of resistance in the region.

In the interim, Genghis Khan had ordered Jebe and Sübedei to explore and reconnoiter the west. Between 1221 and 1223 the two most gifted of the khan's generals traveled towards Russia. In the course of their journey, they defeated the Georgians, Armenians, princes of Rus, and Kipchak Turkic tribes. Then they abruptly returned home. The purpose was not to annex the territory but to gather intelligence, which proved to be important to their campaign against the princes of Rus between 1236 and 1240. Meanwhile, Genghis Khan had died on expedition in southern China in 1227. Upon his death, the Mongols participated in a year of mourning, halting expansion.

11.8.3 Succession

The Mongols were the only steppe tribes whose empire actually expanded upon the death of its founder. In fact, most of the Mongol

Figure 11.4 | Death of Khwarazmshah Ala al-Din Muhammad II | From *Jami' al-tawarikh* by Rashid al-Din Hamadani
Author: Sayf al-Vâhidî
Source: Wikimedia Commons
License: Public Domain

Figure 11.5 | Jalal al-Din Fords the Indus River While in Flight from the Mongols
Author: Banwarí Khúrd and Dharm Dás
Source: Wikimedia Commons
License: Public Domain

conquests actually transpired after the passing of Genghis Khan. Unlike previous tribal confederations, it did not implode because Genghis Khan had invented a safe and reliable means of transferring power. He also stabilized Mongol society and made it less fractious, constructing a framework for subsequent generations to follow. To maintain political legitimacy and inherit the throne under this new system, one had to trace their ancestry back to Genghis Khan through his wife Börte and her four sons, Juchi, Chagatai, Ögedei, and Tolui. This

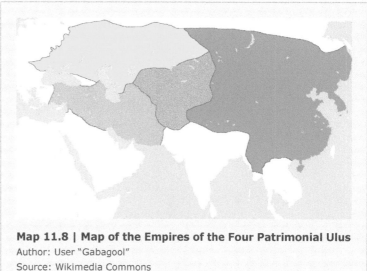

Map 11.8 | Map of the Empires of the Four Patrimonial Ulus
Author: User "Gabagool"
Source: Wikimedia Commons
License: CC BY-SA 3.0

concept dramatically limited contenders for the khanate, mitigating future competition for succession. Only they possessed the required **Genghis-Khanid legitimacy**.

The khan's plan to transfer power upon his death also fused older steppe traditions with his new vision. He bequeathed to his sons parts of the world yet unconquered, so that they had to win these new areas. This stipulation produced an incentive for his sons to cooperate in order to collect their patrimony. Genghis Khan had divided the four patrimonial **ulus**, or states, amongst his sons. The four subsequent empires that grew out of these ulus included the Golden Horde, who were the descendants of **Juchi** and controlled Russia; the Chagatai Khanate, which traced its lineage to **Chagatai** and governed Central Asia; the Mongol-founded Yuan Dynasty in China, the progeny of **Tolui**; and the Ilkhanate of Persia, inheritors of the House of Hülegü and also the successors of **Tolui**.

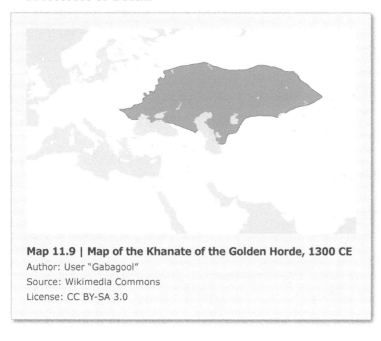

Map 11.9 | Map of the Khanate of the Golden Horde, 1300 CE
Author: User "Gabagool"
Source: Wikimedia Commons
License: CC BY-SA 3.0

Prior to his death in 1227, Genghis Khan expressed a desire that his son Ögedei succeed him, a decision that affronted **Juchi**, his eldest, whose lineage was questioned. Fortunately for the Mongols, Juchi's death preceded that of his father's, narrowly averting a potential civil war. A khuriltai in 1229 confirmed the khan's wishes, and it was under Ögedei that the Mongols realized their destiny of world domination. Between 1230 and 1233, Ögedei's troops defeated the remnants of the Jin dynasty in central China. Then they focused their attention on Russia, as they had

Figure 11.6 | Güyük at the Partyc | From *Tarikh-i Jahangushay-i* by Juvaini
Author: User "Bahatur"
Source: Wikimedia Commons
License: Public Domain

Figure 11.7 | Audience with Möngke | From *Tarikh-i Jahangushay-i* by Juvaini
Author: User "Bahatur"
Source: Wikimedia Commons
License: Public Domain

actionable intelligence on the divisions among the Russian principalities dating to a 1223 reconnaissance mission that utterly crushed a coalition of Russian and Kipchak princes. In 1236, Ögedei launched his campaign in the dead of winter and used rivers as frozen ice highways. By end of 1237, they had taken the Black Steppe, Vladimir, and Riazan. It was only some fortuitous flooding that prevented the complete destruction of Novgorod. The Prince of Novgorod was, however, sufficiently impressed by the Mongol onslaught so voluntarily agreed to pay their tribute. The Mongols commenced a devastating attack on the city of Kiev in December of 1240, culminating in a nine-day siege. They ultimately destroyed the city as retribution for its resistance. The Mongols steamrolled the Hungarians soon thereafter and left the region in ruins en route to Vienna. By December of 1241, their forces were approaching the outskirts of the city. No military power in Europe was capable of withstanding a Mongol attack.

Fortunately for the Viennese, Ögedei died that very same month, and a one year period of mourning ensued. The Mongols were summoned home in order to choose the next great khan. What was supposed to be a quick election turned into a five-year ordeal because **Batu**, son of Juchi and grandson of Genghis Khan, refused to return to Mongolia for the khuriltai. This founder of the Golden Horde believed that he would not be chosen and knew that his relatives could not officially convene a khuriltai without him, thus preventing the body from proclaiming the next great khan. It was Ögedei's death and Batu's independence of thought that saved Europe from Mongol conquest.

The khuriltai finally proclaimed **Güyük**, eldest son of Ögedei, the next khan in 1246. This was not a legitimate election though because of Batu's conspicuous absence. Güyük quickly dispatched an army to punish Batu for meddling in the political process of succession, but Batu had already arranged for his cousin's assassination in 1248. Güyük's death led to another period of paralysis. A khuriltai eventually nominated **Möngke**, Tolui's oldest son, as the next great khan in 1251. Now Möngke had to deal with the problem that Batu presented. He was willing to allow for Batu's autonomy so long as he recognized Möngke as the legitimate khan. It was at this point that Batu's horde become the **Golden Horde**. He adopted the moniker of "golden" because he was asserting his independence.

Batu died in 1256, and his younger brother **Berke** became the first khan of the Golden Horde to accept Islam. This sudden conversion to Islam caused systemic problems in the Mongol Empire because different parts of the four lines of Genghis Khan would adopt different faiths, resulting in political divisions that aligned with religious divisions. As a Muslim, Berke spurned his Buddhist cousins and established firm links with the Turkic Mamluk Sultanate in Egypt, thus making an alliance based on faith with a power outside of the Mongol Empire.

Genghis Khan's empire had exceeded normal steppe expectations, and, with potential fault lines emerging already, his vision of a politically unified empire was never truly realized. A series of civil wars erupted not long thereafter that fractured the Mongol Empire. First came the Toluid Civil War (1260 – 1264), then the Berke-Hülegü War (1262), and finally the Kaidu-Kublai War (1268 – 1301). These three wars had the combined effect of undermining the great khan's authority, and the empire ended up breaking apart on along the lines of the patrimonial ulus, with each moving in their own direction. In fact, the successors of **Kublai Khan** (1260 – 1294), who presided over the Yuan Dynasty in China, could not even convene a khuriltai to appoint a great khan following his death. By 1294, there was neither fiction nor façade of a unified Mongol Empire. It was the end of a unified political unit.

11.9 THE KHANATE OF CHAGATAI

Chagatai (1226 – 1241), the second son of Genghis and his wife Börte, had participated in his father's campaigns, and in 1227 he claimed his patrimonial territory designated as between the Caspian Sea and the Tarim Basin. The origins of the **Chagatai Khanate** shaped its political and demographic character; Chagatai obtained the core of Central Asia, a personal pasture-land located along the Kazakh steppe. He also received the settled lands to the south in modern day Uzbekistan. Chagatai never demonstrated ambition for the position of great khan; rather, he played an important role helping his brother Ögedei exercise authority and uphold Yassa. In doing so, Chagatai served as the glue that helped hold the Mongol Empire together.

As was the case with his father, Genghis Khan, Chagatai had trouble coping with the

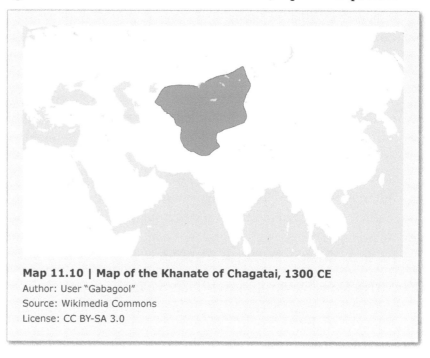

Map 11.10 | Map of the Khanate of Chagatai, 1300 CE
Author: User "Gabagool"
Source: Wikimedia Commons
License: CC BY-SA 3.0

Page | 415

cultural differences that existed between steppe and settled societies. His solution to the conflict between these two civilizations was known as **Inju**, a dual-administrative system and a form of indirect rule. Inju was a political concession designed to separate the two incompatible cultures, allowing both to maintain their own traditional laws yet remain subject to the authority of Chagatai and his descendants. Chagatai was conscious not to force Yassa on sedentary Muslim cities; however, it continued to be exercised on the plains. In agricultural and urban areas, a bureaucratic tradition with a Muslim administration persisted. So long as these Muslims did not openly resist Mongol control, they could go about their daily business, free from Mongol interference in their life. It was in this way that the steppe continued to abide by customary Mongol law, while in the south the people of the cities lived according to the Sharia, or Quranic law.

Inju was also an economic arrangement granting the Mongols a share of the resources produced in sedentary lands. The Mongols rewarded those who cooperated in governance with a portion of the profits; those who participated in Inju were entitled to their allotment of the common imperial settled possessions. At first, all of the conquered towns remained the property of the khan, but over time access to the wealth of the urban areas extended to the nomads who took part in Inju.

Although Inju was a practical solution to the difficulty of governing the two separate societies, it ultimately did not resolve the problem of uniting the sedentary Turkic population and the nomadic Mongols since it failed to accommodate the needs of either society. Actually, it encouraged friction between the two civilizations because it placed hardships on both peoples. While the horsemen benefited handsomely from Inju, they considered it incompatible with their traditional practices because it forced them to climb down from their steeds and settle down in the cities. Yes, the Mongols did receive tribute, slaves, and status as compensation for the inconvenience of ruling over settled lands, but the costs of sustaining this empire were heavy. It was just too demanding for them to uphold. First, the maintenance of empire disrupted the nomadic way of life because they often had to join in exhaustive campaigns, lasting years at a time. Second, the nomads were unaccustomed to a considerable amount of government interference in their daily routine. Increasingly, they viewed the prospect of governing an empire as a burden and preferred to revert to a pastoral lifestyle on the prairie. They sought more independence and stability, so they consciously began to defect from the system and return to their pastures.

Those living in the settled lands to the south chaffed under Inju as well. Though they recognized that government remained an essential part of life, Inju encumbered urban-dwelling and farming peoples too. The Mongols stressed this population by raising additional taxes in an unpredictable and disruptive manner. This annoyed the city folk, who were accustomed to more regular taxation. Ultimately, Inju did not mesh well with either lifestyle. The practice rested on force, not utility. The Mongol state sustained two different societies that often remained in conflict, so it stayed in a state of permanent instability.

11.9.1 Turko-Mongol Fusion

The Mongols were the first to unify the Eurasian steppe, and their occupation of the region corresponded to a wholesale takeover. As they migrated southwest down the steppe, they failed to displace the Turkic peoples already established in Central Asia. Early on, the dominant Mongols offered these Turkic groups a deal to either merge with them or suffer harsh reprisal. So as the Mongols progressed westward, their armies gained strength, as more and more of the Turkic tribesmen joined them, resulting in armies that were mostly comprised of Turkic peoples, not Mongols. In this manner, the Turkic groups absorbed and assimilated the invading Mongols, a process known as **Turkification**; the conflict between the two cultures faded over time and eventually led to a fusion of Turkic and Mongolian societies. Over time, these Mongol pastoralists presiding over a sedentary Islamic culture slowly Turkified. They quickly became a Mongol minority governing a Turkic majority.

There were numerous points of contention between the two groups but also many commonalities. Both societies had originated on the steppe in modern day Mongolia, and, while the Turkic groups had settled down over the years and adopted more of a sedentary existence, many of the principles of pastoral nomadism still lingered in their culture. Both adhered to a patrimonial distribution of inheritance. Also, both the Turkic groups and the Mongols organized along tribal lines, and each followed a pattern of co-opting one tribe into another, thus facilitating a fusion of the Mongols with their Turkic hosts. For this system to work though, the Mongols had to speak the idiom of the people they ruled. So instead of the Mongols imposing their language on the majority of the population, the Mongol elite learned Chagatai, a Turkic tongue.

For many years, religion remained the only major distinction between the two societies, but once the Chagataids converted to Islam in 1333 this conspicuous difference disappeared. While the Mongols adopted the creed and language of the Turkic Chagatai, these Turkic peoples incorporated the Mongol political concept of Genghis-Khanid legitimacy.

11.10 THE KHANATE OF THE ILKHANS (1265 – 1335)

Hülegü Khan (1256 – 1265), grandson of Genghis Khan and son of Tolui, served his brother Möngke (1251 – 1259), the great khan, and campaigned through the Middle East, where he whipped out the Assassins, a secret order of schismatic Shia entrenched in the mountains of Gilan province in 1256. He also destroyed the Abbasid capital of Baghdad in 1258, putting an end to the Caliphate. By 1260 Hülegü controlled parts of Armenia, Iraq, Anatolia, all of Azerbaijan, and all of Iran. Kublai Khan (1250 – 1294) had awarded his brother Hülegü the title of

Figure 11.8 | Hülegü Khan and Dokuz Khatun | From Rachid Ad-Din's "History of the World"
Author: Rachid Ad-Din
Source: Wikimedia Commons
License: Public Domain

Ilkhan, a secondary khan who remained subordinate only to the great khan in Mongolia. This portion of the empire became known as the Khanate of the Ilkhans.

The Ilkhans were a Mongol minority ruling over a Muslim majority; religious problems plagued the Ilkhanate for much of its existence. To begin with, Hülegü, a Nestorian Christian, who later converted to Buddhism on his deathbed, had sacked Baghdad, one of the most politically important cities in the Islamic world, an act that alienated him from his Muslim cousin Berke Khan, ruler of the Golden Horde. The conversion of the Golden Horde to Islam had presented a real problem, for the Ilkhans had initially championed Buddhism in Iraq and Iran. As animosity continued to mount between the two parts of the Mongol Empire over religious differences, we see growing ties of alliance between the Muslim Golden Horde and their coreligionists, the Mamluk Sultanate of Egypt, against the Ilkhans. Belief transcended blood, as one part of Mongol Empire allied against another with an outside source. Faith-based civil wars consumed much of the reign of Abaga Khan (1265 – 1282). These wars were rooted in the Ilkhanate's inappropriate treatment of their Muslim population. The Golden Horde's alliance with the Mamluks threatened the Ilkhanate, and yet no longer could Abaga rely on the full might of centralized Mongol power; he was forced to appeal to Kublai Khan to assuage the hostilities between the Ilkhans and the Golden Horde.

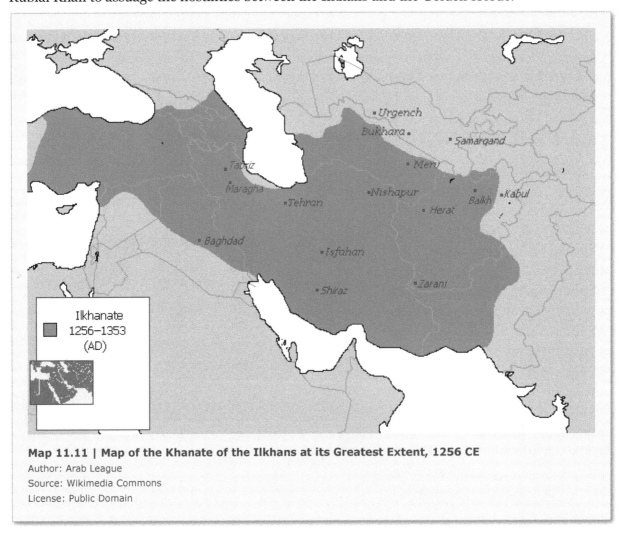

Map 11.11 | Map of the Khanate of the Ilkhans at its Greatest Extent, 1256 CE
Author: Arab League
Source: Wikimedia Commons
License: Public Domain

Figure 11.9 | Conversion of Ghazan to Islam |
From Rashid al-Din "History of the World"
Author: Rachid Ad-Din
Source: Wikimedia Commons
License: Public Domain

Much of the religious conflict during the early Ilkhanate related to doctrinal differences between Islam and the traditional Mongol way of life. The most stubborn problem for the two was the contradiction between the traditional Mongolian method of animal slaughter, which required that no blood be spilled, and the Islamic code of cleanliness, which necessitated that all blood be drained. Each side was appalled by the other's customs. Furthermore, as practitioners of rigid monotheism, Muslims found the Mongol worship of religious images repulsive, a ritual strictly forbidden in Islam.

While spiritual troubles remained a persistent problem for the Ilkhans, the economic situation deteriorated too. **Gaykhatu Khan** (1291 – 1295) practically emptied the royal treasury with profligate spending. He experimented with paper money recently adopted from China to compensate for his wasteful expenditures, but overprinting resulted in massive inflation. The Ilkhans also tried to extract the maximum amount of tribute from the countryside to offset declining revenues. This led to an abuse in tax gathering, known as tax farming, in which rulers sold contracts for the collection of revenues to the highest bidder. This method of tax collection provided a strong incentive to despoil peasants.

It was **Mahmud Ghazan** (1295 – 1304) who solved the Ilkhanate's continued religious and economic problems. He was the first Ilkhan to convert to Islam, thus rehabilitating their image in the eyes of their Muslim subjects and making their rule much more acceptable. Their new public stance towards Islam moderated persistent conflict and paved the way for cultural flourishing. Ghazan patronized Ilkhanid art, scholarship, and science. Ilkhanid art reflected Chinese influence and helped contribute to Persian artistic development. In terms of scholarship, the first true history of the world was completed under the sponsorship of Mahmud Ghazan. Written by **Rashid al-Din Hamadani** (1247 – 1318), the book was richly illustrated with watercolors and portraiture in the Chinese style. Through his travels in the service of the Mongols, Rashid al-Din had become perceptively aware of Ilkhanid Persia's cosmopolitan culture. It was Rashid al-Din, a Jewish convert to Islam, who had convinced Mahmud Ghazan to adopt the faith in order to be more attuned to the beliefs of his peoples. Regarding science, the Ilkhands attempted to amass large amounts of astronomical data from China to Europe. With unprecedented accuracy, they became very good at predicting lunar eclipses. Their data was used throughout Eurasia.

Despite the early looting and plundering indicative of a Mongol conquest, the Ilkhans eventually reactivated the Silk Road and promoted transcontinental trade. The newfound safety of the route throughout Eurasia stimulated trade and encouraged many different kinds of cultures to come together. Ghazan attempted to reform the tax policies that had led to the maximization of taxation. Cities did revive, but the long term negative consequence of conquest continued to be felt by the peasants who suffered from prolonged violence.

Much like the Mongols in Chaghatai Central Asia, eventually Ilkhans went native too. Here we see a Persian-Mongol fusion, as they began to identify with Persian culture and speak the Persian language. As they bonded with Persia, they adopted Islam and began to promote Persian as the written language of their land.

11.11 TIMUR

It was under **Timur** (1370 – 1405) that Central Asia moved to the fore of world events. He attempted to soothe the persistent differences that existed between the steppe and sedentary societies and actually developed a political arrangement that could harness the best attributes of each society, without the dangerous side effect of communal violence associated with combining the two civilizations. He also constructed a new political and military machine that was deeply ingrained in the political background of the Chagatai Khanate, even while he acknowledged that Inju satisfied neither the nomad nor the settled society and eliminated the practice. Astutely recognizing that serious conflict existed between these two incongruent cultures under his control, Timur provided a framework for both societies to live in harmony.

Born in 1336 near Kesh in modern day Uzbekistan, Timur came out of Central Asia and was a product of the Turko-Mongol fusion. He descended from an aristocratic Mongol clan, but he was raised as a Muslim and spoke a Turkic language. Although Timur himself was a native to Transoxiana, he could not assert Genghis-Khanid legitimacy. Unable to trace his ancestry to Genghis Khan, he could not take the title of khan in his own right. Timur understood that because he did not have the correct pedigree, he would have to earn it. His solution was to take the title of emir, meaning commander, and rule through a Chagatayid puppet khan acting as a figurehead. The emir also married into the family of Genghis Khan. While the law of descent was not intended to work this way, Timur changed it to accommodate his children, who would be able to claim Genghis-Khanid legitimacy.

To strengthen the security of his position as emir, he constructed a system of support that ordered his political connections in a series of concentric rings. In his primary circle resided his family and close allies.

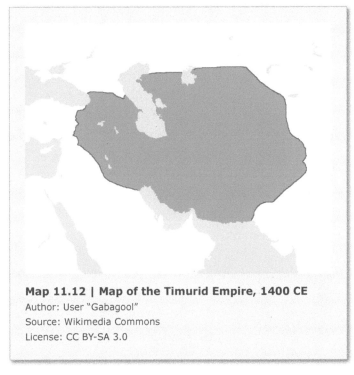

Map 11.12 | Map of the Timurid Empire, 1400 CE
Author: User "Gabagool"
Source: Wikimedia Commons
License: CC BY-SA 3.0

The second ring consisted of loyal tribes and Timur's own Barlas Clan, from which he traced his lineage. The third circle was made up of those peoples Timur had defeated on the battlefield; the second and third rings balanced one another. The outermost bands included Timur's hereditary professional administrators and bureaucrats, soldiers from the plains serving in his cavalry units, and finally the Persian urban and agricultural populations, from which he recruited his infantry and siege units.

Like many transitional figures in history, such as Suleiman the Magnificent, Timur bridged the medieval and modern worlds. He attempted to imitate Genghis Khan's success in the field and designed a novel military machine that was well adapted to the environment in which he lived. His military was the product of a Turko-Mongol fusion, employing Turkic siege techniques and the Mongol cavalry. Unlike Genghis Khan, however, Timur increasingly combined his cavalry, siege, and infantry units, placing his heavy cavalry at the center of formations. His army also utilized an early form of artillery. He ventured to monopolize the market on gunpowder technology so that other powers could not benefit from it.

Figure 11.10 | Timur Facial Reconstruction |
Forensic Facial Reconstruction by M. Gerasimov, 1941
Author: Shakko
Source: Wikimedia Commons
License: CC BY-SA 3.0

Timur was determined to keep his volatile army occupied, so they would not be a burden to the sedentary population in his realm. It was in this context that he developed a formula for success that promoted peace at home and war abroad, a policy that best served the interests of the merchants and townspeople. He externalized the violence of the steppe and destroyed all of the other trade routes that bypassed his territory. Timur attempted to reactivate and dominate the Silk Road and diverted trade to his lands in order to help rebuild the cities that had been damaged from years of Mongol and nomad rule. He did not aim at permanent occupation or the creation of new states; he just wanted to devastate, even going so far as to campaign against the Golden Horde, Delhi Sultanate, and the Ottoman Empire, all in an effort to redirect trade in his direction.

Timur began his military campaigns attempting to secure the back door of the steppe. During this period, which lasted from 1370 to 1385, he conquered and subdued Mogholistan to the northeast, with the aim of securing the core central land route of the Silk Road. (The Chagatai Khanate had already been divided into two parts by the 1340s, Transoxania in the west, and Mogholistan in the east.) Then he engaged the Golden Horde between 1385 and 1395. The Golden Horde had been the master of the northern trade route that bypassed Timur's territory. In order to eliminate this option, he went to war against them in order to divert trade to toward his lands. Timur showed his strategic genius in these expeditions. He defeated a steppe power on the steppe. He put the pieces of his army together in such a way so that he could take his enemies on in their arena and on their terms. In this manner, Timur crushed **Tokhtamysh**, leader of the Golden Horde, in 1395. During the course of this campaign, Timur destroyed their principle trade cities of Astrakhan and Sarai. An interesting byproduct of Timur's campaign against the Golden Horde was that it precipitated the rise of the **Grand Duchy of Moscow**. He had weakened the Golden Horde to such an extent that it made it possible for Moscow to throw off the Mongol yoke.

Timur raided into India from 1398 to 1399 and dealt a blow to the southern sea route that connected the Occident to the Orient. This expedition was primarily for looting, since he never intended to conquer and annex the territory of **Nasir-ud-Din Mahmud Shah Tughluq**, the last member of the Tughluq Dynasty of the Delhi Sultanate. During this campaign, Timur's tactical brilliance was on full display; he had an uncanny ability to adapt to any martial environment that he confronted. For instance, when threatened with a cavalry of war elephants, Timur responded by unleashing a pack of camels laden with incendiary material to charge the enemy lines. Shrieking dromedaries with their backs ablaze incited utter pandemonium among Nasir-ud-Din's cavalry of elephants, who rampaged through the sultan's own lines. Timur easily routed the sultan's forces. When faced with the townspeople of Delhi rising up against their aggressors, Timur brutally sacked the capital of the sultanate and justified the violence in religious terms. His was a Muslim victory over the Hindu unbelievers of India.

In Timur's final period of conquest, which lasted from 1400 to 1404, he campaigned against the Islamic far west, directing his army against the Ottomans. Actually, Timur had initially attempted to avoid conflict with the Ottomans, whose forces had earned an impressive reputation on the battlefield. In fact, Timur had even tried to negotiate with Bayezid I, the Ottoman Sultan, offering him part of Golden Horde's territory west of Dnieper River. But these two expansionist realms inevitably came into conflict in eastern Anatolia. The conflict between the two empires began as the Ottomans expanded to the east and took control of some Turkmen tribes in eastern Anatolia already under the protection of Timur. The emir responded by taking some other Turkmen tribes under Ottoman suzerainty. Offensive missives replete with insulting incriminations ensued. Timur bided his time, waiting for the perfect moment to attack the Ottomans. In 1402, he launched a devastating attack into the heart of Anatolia, as the Ottomans were preoccupied with campaigning against the Hungarians. During the Battle of Ankara in 1402, Timur managed to convince many of the Ottoman forces to defect to his side. He captured the Ottoman sultan, who died in captivity three months later. Timur had not attempted to conquer the Ottomans; he just wanted to punish them for their unwillingness to cooperate. His Levantine expedition also seems to have been designed to weaken the western terminus of the Silk Road in Aleppo, Syria.

Timur died in 1405 while on a campaign against the Ming Dynasty. He had built an empire that spanned the breadth of Central Asia. Unlike Genghis Khan, whose empire continued to expand after his death, the sons of Timur and their followers squabbled over succession, leading to a series of internecine battles. Members of the Timurid Dynasty competed among themselves, with commanders switching loyalties. The empire consequently fragmented. The successors of Timur could not manage the difficulties of governing an empire, and it withered away quickly. The political situation resembled that which Chagatayids had to contend with, the steppe military that had been redirected, but with Timur's death, they returned. A number of Timurid rulers followed; a weak state emerged from all this strife.

11.11.1 Terror and Destruction

Timur certainly committed what we would describe today as war crimes; there definitely was an element of terrorism to his campaigns. In fact, as an admirer of architecture, he is known to have constructed pyramids of human skulls. Extant accounts describe him slaughtering 100,000 Indian prisoners following the Delhi uprising. But not all destruction was the same; and there was a definite difference between that of Genghis Khan and Timur. The emir's annihilation of the region was not meant to serve a utilitarian purpose so much as to inflict suffering. Genghis Khan's used terror as a method to protect his troops, whereas Timur engaged in terror and destruction for pleasure.

11.11.2 Legacy

A product of the Turko-Mongolian fusion, Timur had been the first to reunite the eastern and western parts of the Chagatai ulus. His empire represents the construction of the political boundaries passed down to posterity; the maintenance of this space would define boundaries of modern day Central Asia up to the twentieth century. Under Timur we see growing political and cultural distinctions between Iran, Central Asia proper, and India begin to cement. In this context, we see a split taking place on the steppe that will lead to a differentiation of the Uzbeks and Kazaks. By the late fourteenth century, the tribes on the steppe to the north will become known to Muslim writers as Kazaks, whereas the tribes to the south will be increasingly referred to as Uzbeks, a differentiation that has continued to persist and helped to delimit modern borders.

11.12 CONCLUSION

Three forces combined to shape the course of Central Asian history: the Turkic migrations, expansion of Islam, and the Mongol conquest. Beginning in the second century BCE, waves of Turkic migrations entered the region. It is debatable whether or not they Turkified the original Iranian inhabitants or permanently changed the ethnic makeup of the area. Turkic tribes occupied the great steppe, Turkifying the region and endowing it with a more nomadic character. They also populated the agricultural basin of Transoxiana, displacing the original Iranian inhabitants of the area. Many of these Turks slowly settled down over time. These Turkic peoples displayed a unique ability to absorb the Islamic faith and internalize the Mongol conquest.

Islam transformed the religious adherence of Central Asia and left a lasting mark on the region as well. Transoxiana gradually Islamicized, but Turkic and Persian cultures persisted.

Islamization incorporated native peoples in the process of conversion. As Islam spread through the area, the faith demonstrated an extraordinary capacity to incorporate local traditions, permitting some customs to linger so long as doing so accelerated conversion. Sufi missionaries made some compromises with the Turkic nomadic culture in order to establish the religion in the area. Sufism's inherent flexibility helped to promote conversion, and the blend of orthodox Islam and Turkic pastoral nomadism created a uniquely Central Asian brand of the faith.

The Mongol conquest of Central Asia had the most immediate impact on the history of the region. Although the Mongols eventually Turkified over time, the legacy of Genghis-Khanid legitimacy remained. Genghis Khan had developed a secure and dependable means of transferring power, for Genghis-Khanid legitimacy reduced the number of contenders vying for the throne; the Mongols did not collapse as a "nation" following the death of their founder. Genghis Khan bequeathed a legacy of political legitimacy to the region that would last until 1920.

11.13 WORKS CONSULTED AND FURTHER READING

Adshead, S.A.M., *Central Asia in World History*. New York: Palgrave, 1993.

Allsen Thomas T., *Culture and Conquest in Mongol Eurasia*. Cambridge: Cambridge University Press, 2001.

Christian, David. *Inner Eurasia from Prehistory to the Mongol Empire*. Oxford: Blackwell, 1998.

Findley, Carter Vaughn, *The Turks in World History*. Oxford: Oxford University Press, 2005.

Halperin, Charles J., *Russia and the Golden Horde: The Mongol Impact on Medieval Russian History*. Bloomington, IN: Indiana University Press, 1987.

Khan, Paul. ed., *The Secret History of the Mongols: The Origin of Chingis Khan*. Boston: Cheng and Tsui, 1985.

Morgan, David, *The Mongols*. Oxford: Wiley-Blackwell, 1996

Soucek, Svat, *A History of Inner Asia*. Cambridge: Cambridge University Press, 2000.

11.14 LINKS TO PRIMARY SOURCES

Scott C. Levi and Ron Sela eds, Islamic Central Asia: An Anthology of Historical Sources

https://muse.jhu.edu/books/9780253013590

Medieval Sourcebook:

Ibn Battuta: Travels in Asia and Africa 1325 – 1354

http://legacy.fordham.edu/halsall/source/1354-ibnbattuta.asp

Sacred Texts

http://www.sacred-texts.com/asia/index.htm

William of Rubruck's Account of the Mongols

http://depts.washington.edu/silkroad/texts/rubruck.html

Description of Mongol warfare from Friar John of Plano Carpini

http://www.deremilitari.org/RESOURCES/SOURCES/carpini.htm

The Book of Dede Korkut

https://en.wikisource.org/wiki/Book_of_Dede_Korkut

Ibn al-Athir: On The Tatars, 1220 – 1221CE

https://legacy.fordham.edu/halsall/source/1220al-Athir-mongols.asp

Marco Polo: On the Tartars

http://legacy.fordham.edu/halsall/source/mpolo44-46.asp

Jalal ad-Din Rumi (1207 – 1273 CE): from The Masnavi, c. 1250 CE

https://legacy.fordham.edu/halsall/source/1250rumi-masnavi.asp

Jalal-ad-Din Rumi (1207 – 1273 CE): The Fairest Land, c. 1250 CE

https://legacy.fordham.edu/halsall/source/1250rumi-poems2.asp

Jalal ad-Din Rumi (1207 – 1273): Poems from the Divan-I Shams-I Tabriz, c. 1270 CE

https://legacy.fordham.edu/halsall/source/1270rumi-poems1.asp

Hafiz (1325 – 1389 CE): Verses in Praise of God, c. 1370 CE

https://legacy.fordham.edu/halsall/source/1370hafiz.asp

12 Western Europe and Byzantium circa 1000 - 1500 CE

Andrew Reeves

12.1 CHRONOLOGY

962 CE	Otto I crowned Holy Roman Emperor
987 CE	Hugh Capet elected king of France
c. 1000 – 1100 CE	Emergence of Western European feudalism
1031 CE	Fall of the Cordoba Caliphate
1049 CE	Pope Leo IX begins papal efforts at Church reform
1054 CE	Schism between the pope and the patriarch of Constantinople
1066 CE	Norman Conquest of England
1071 CE	Battle of Manzikert annihilates Byzantine field army
1077 CE	Henry IV repents to Pope Gregory VII at Canossa
1085 CE	Fall of Muslim Toledo to the Christian kingdom of Leon-Castile
1088 – 1231 CE	Foundation of Universities of Bologna, Paris, Oxford, and Cambridge
1091 CE	Norman conquest of Muslim Sicily complete
1095 CE	Council of Clermont, calling of the First Crusade
1099 CE	Fall of Jerusalem to Christian Crusaders, establishment of Crusader States
1100 – 1135 CE	King Henry I rules England
1118 – 1143 CE	Emperor John II rules the Byzantine Empire
1122 CE	Concordat of Worms
1125 – 1152 CE	Raymond is archbishop of Toledo, begins sponsoring the translation of Muslim and Greek philosophy from Arabic into Latin
1143 – 1180 CE	Emperor Manuel Komnenos rules the Byzantine Empire
1154 – 1189 CE	King Henry II rules England
1176 CE	Frederick Barbarossa defeated by Lombard League at the Battle of Legnano; Manuel Komnenos defeated by Saljuq Turks at the Battle of Myriokephalon
1187 CE	Kingdom of Jerusalem defeated by Saladin at the Battle of Hattin, fall of Jerusalem, Pope Gregory VIII issues *Audita tremendi*, calling the Third Crusade

1189 – 1192 CE	The Third Crusade, a rump (remnant of a larger government) Christian Kingdom of Jerusalem is re-established, but Jerusalem remains in Muslim hands
1203 – 1226 CE	France's Capetian kings extend the control of lands directly ruled by the crown
1204 CE	Crusaders sack Constantinople, break-up of the Byzantine Empire
1212 CE	Almohad Caliphate defeated by Spanish Christian kingdoms at the Battle of Las Navas de Tolosa
1215 CE	Magna Carta
1215 – 1250 CE	Frederick II is Holy Roman Emperor
1224 – 1274 CE	Life of St. Thomas Aquinas
1229 CE	A treaty between Frederick II and Egyptian sultan al-Kamil returns Jerusalem to Christian rule
1240 CE	Mongol Conquest of Kievan Rus
1241 CE	Mongol invasion of Hungary
1244 CE	Jerusalem falls to Ayyubid Egypt
1248 – 1254 CE	The Seventh Crusade, France's King Louis IX defeated by Egypt, Egyptian Mamluk *coup d'état*
1250 – 1273 CE	There is no Holy Roman Emperor
1261 CE	Restoration of the Byzantine Empire
1291 CE	Last Crusader territory in the Levant falls to Mamluk Egypt
c. 1300 CE	Genoese sailors begin exploring the Atlantic Ocean
early 1300s CE	Genoese sailors are visiting the Canary Islands
1309 CE	Beginning of Avignon papacy
1314 – 1326 CE	Civil war in the Holy Roman Empire
1315 – 1322 CE	The Great Famine
1324 CE	Mansa Musa's *hajj*
1331 CE	Nearly all Byzantine territory in Asia Minor has fallen to the Ottoman Turks
1337 CE	The Hundred Years' War begins
c. 1350 CE	Beginning of Italian Renaissance and Humanism
1347 – 1351 CE	The Black Death, nearly a third of Europe's population dies
1356 CE	The Holy Roman Empire becomes an elected monarchy
1358 CE	French peasant revolt
1378 CE	Beginning of Great Schism
1385 CE	Lithuania united with Poland, Lithuanian monarch converts to Christianity
1396 CE	Ottoman Turks conquer Bulgaria
1397 CE	Union of Kalmar unites Sweden, Denmark, and Norway under a single crown
c. 1400 – 1500 CE	Renaissance Humanism spreads throughout Europe
1404 CE	Castilian effort to conquer the Canaries begins

1415 – 1417 CE	Council of Constance resolves the Great Schism
1440 CE	Lorenzo Valla shows the Donation of Constantine to be a forgery
mid 1400s CE	Iberians are settling the Azores, a plantation economy worked by African slaves begins to flourish in the Canaries and Azores
1453 CE	Ottoman conquest of Constantinople, final fall of the Byzantine Empire; End of Hundred Years' War and English attempts to conquer France
1454 CE	Treaty of Lodi brings nearly a half century of peace to Italy
1455 – 1485 CE	Wars of the Roses in England
1459 CE	Final Ottoman conquest of Serbia
1479 CE	Marriage of Queen Isabella of Castile and Ferdinand of Aragon creates a united Spanish monarchy
1492 CE	King Ferdinand and Queen Isabella complete the *Reconquista* with the conquest of Granada, Christopher Columbus, sailing for the Spanish crown, makes landfall in the Western Hemisphere
1494 CE	France invades Italy

12.2 INTRODUCTION

15 July 1099: The Al-Aqsa mosque looked down on the city of Jerusalem, the light of the sun reflecting off of its golden dome. Down below the hill on which the mosque stood, a scene of slaughter was unfolding. Up against the northern wall of the city stood a wooden tower laboriously rolled into place hours earlier, over the top of which had poured a desperate band of European knights, the first over the walls of the Holy City.

Within the walls, the narrow, winding streets between the ancient stone buildings of the city rang with the clash of steel on steel and the cries of the dead and dying. Smoke from fires breaking out within the city mingled with the smell of death. In parts of the city, its defenders, Muslim Egyptians, were still fighting, going down under the sword strokes of the Christian soldiers fighting their way through the streets. In the southwest, a small group of defenders had retreated into the more heavily fortified citadel where they were negotiating a surrender with Count Raymond of Toulouse, a shrewd but irascible noble from the south of France.

Elsewhere in the city, the killing of the soldiers was giving way to a more horrific slaughter, as the mail-clad knights cut down men, women, and children where they stood, torturing some with fire, and threatening others with worse if they did not turn over their valuables. By the end of the day, the Christian soldiers hacking their way through the city streets waded through blood up to their ankles.

As the day went on, soldiers pushed through the piles of dismembered corpses to the golden-domed Al-Aqsa Mosque. The mosque stood where Solomon's temple had been millennia before, and the knights, smeared with the blood of slaughter, fell to their knees in prayer, grateful that God had delivered their enemies into their hands.

These men had traveled more than two thousand miles by land and sea. Tens of thousands of their comrades lay dead along the way from starvation, thirst, disease, or battle. But these warriors had made it from their European homelands to seize control of the city of Jerusalem, a city sacred to Jew, Christian, and Muslim, and bring it under Christian rule for the first time in more than four centuries.

An army made up of many of the soldiers of Western Europe had managed to successfully make war on its Muslim enemies and seize territories in the Middle East, near the heart of Muslim culture and political power. How had they done so? And why? To understand, we must look to the how the European Christian world had developed over the eleventh century.

In the years between about 1000 and 1500, the culture and institutions of Western Europe took on a form that was distinct from the post-Roman Germanic kingdoms of the early Middle Ages and which would, in many ways, lay the foundations of Europe (and the Americas) into modern times. At the end of this period, thinkers seeking to bring about a new birth of ancient learning would look back on the thousand years that had come before as the Middle Ages, a period between the world of the Ancient Greeks and Romans and their own. But although these thinkers ostentatiously rejected the Middle Ages, they were in many ways its heirs. To see how this culture developed, we shall begin in Western Europe in the chaotic years of the early eleventh century.

12.3 QUESTIONS TO GUIDE YOUR READING

1. Who held most political and military power in a feudal system?

2. What were some reasons that European towns started to grow in the eleventh century?

3. Why did Europe's agricultural output increase in the eleventh century?

4. What were some lasting results of the eleventh-century popes' attempts to reform the Church?

5. What did Pope Urban II call on Western Europe's nobles to do in 1095?

6. How did the thirteenth-century Capetian kings of France strengthen their authority?

7. Why did Frederick Barbarossa and Frederick II ultimately fail to establish control over Italy?

8. What was the *Reconquista*?

9. How did noble and peasant diets differ?

10. What caused the death of a third of Europe's population between the years 1347 and 1351?

11. Why were Genoese merchants in the service of Iberian kings exploring the Atlantic and western Africa in the fourteenth and fifteenth centuries?

12. Why did Christopher Columbus think he could sail directly from Europe to Asia?

12.4 KEY TERMS

- Albigensian Crusade
- Alchemy
- Babylonian Captivity of the Church
- Bourgeois
- Capetian
- Chain mail
- Christendom
- Commune
- Concordat of Worms
- *Cortes*
- Council of Constance
- Crusade
- Crusader States
- East Francia
- Exchequer
- Feudalism
- Fiefs
- *Filioque* Controversy
- Great Schism
- Holy War
- Humanism
- Investiture Controversy
- *Iqta*

- Italian Renaissance
- Just War
- Legate
- Magna Carta
- Malthusian limits
- Papal bull
- Parliament
- Patriarch
- Pilgrim
- Population sink
- *Portolan* chart
- *Pronoia*
- *Reconquista*
- Scholasticism
- Simony
- *Taifa* states
- Thing
- Three-field System
- Tournament
- Twelfth-century Renaissance
- University
- Vassal States
- West Francia

12.5 THE EMERGENCE OF A FEUDAL ORDER IN WESTERN EUROPE

Out of the chaos and mayhem of the tenth and eleventh centuries, **East Francia**—the eastern third of Charlemagne's Empire that is in roughly the same place as modern Germany—and England had emerged as united and powerful states. In the aftermath of the Abbasid Caliphate's political collapse and the gradual weakening of Fatimid Egypt (see Chapter Eight), the eleventh-century Byzantine Empire was the strongest, most centralized state in the Eastern Mediterranean, and indeed, probably the strongest state west of Song China.

Most of the rest of Christian Western Europe's kingdoms, however, were fragmented. This decentralization was most acute in **West Francia**, the western third of what had been

Charlemagne's empire. This kingdom would eventually come to be known as France. Out of a weak and fragmented kingdom emerged the decentralized form of government that historians often call **feudalism**. We call it feudalism because power rested with armed men in control of plots of agricultural land known as **fiefs** and Latin for fief is *feudum*. They would use the surplus from these fiefs to equip themselves with weapons and equipment, and they often controlled their fiefs with little oversight from the higher-ranked nobles or the king.

How had such a system emerged? Even in Carolingian times, armies in much of Western Europe had come from war bands made up of a king's loyal retainers, who themselves would possess bands of followers. Ultimate control of a kingdom's army had rested with the king, and the great nobles had also exercised strong authority over their own fighting men. The near constant warfare (both external attacks and civil wars) of the tenth and eleventh centuries, however, meant that the kings of West Francia gradually lost control over the more powerful nobles. Further, the powerful nobles often lost control of the warlords of more local regions. West Francia had little governmental authority and much war.

As a result of constant warfare (albeit warfare that was usually local in scope), power came to rest in control of fiefs and the ability to extract surplus from their occupants and to use this surplus to outfit armed men. The warlords who controlled fiefs often did so by means of armed fortresses called castles. At first, especially in northern parts of West Francia, these fortresses were of wood, and might sometimes be as small as a wooden palisade surrounding a fortified wooden tower. Over the eleventh and twelfth centuries, these wooden castles came to be replaced with fortifications of stone. A castle had two roles: it would protect a land from attackers (such as Viking raiders), but it would also serve as a base for the control and extortion of a land's people.

The castle represented Europe's feudal order in wood and stone. Corresponding to the physical structure of the castle was the figure of the knight. Knights in the eleventh century wore an armor called **chain mail**, that is, interlocking rings of metal that would form a coat of armor. The knight usually fought on horseback, wielding a long spear known as a lance in addition to the sword at his side. With his feet resting in stirrups, a knight could hold himself firmly in the saddle, directing the weight and power of a charging horse into the tip of his lance.

Knights and castles came to dominate West Francia and then other parts of Europe for several

Figure 12.1 | A Wooden Castle of the Type that was Common in the Eleventh Century
Author: Julien Chatelain
Source: Wikimedia Commons
License: CC BY-SA 3.0

reasons. The technology of ironworking was improving so that iron was cheaper (although still very expensive) and more readily available, allowing for knights to wear more armor than their predecessors. Moreover, warfare of the tenth and eleventh centuries was made up of raids (both those of Vikings and of other Europeans). A raid depends on mobility, with the raiders able to kill people and seize plunder before defending soldiers can arrive. Mounted on horseback, knights were mobile enough that they could respond rapidly to raids. The castle allowed a small number of soldiers to defend territory and was also a deterrent to raiders, since it meant that quick plunder might not be possible.

Figure 12.2 | Rochester Castle | A stone castle built in the twelfth century.
Author: User "Prioryman"
Source: Wikimedia Commons
License: CC BY-SA 4.0

A knight's equipment—mail, lance, and horse—was incredibly expensive, as was the material and labor to construct even a wooden castle. Although knights had originally been whichever soldiers had been able to get the equipment to fight, the expense of this equipment and thus the need to control a fief to pay for it meant that knights gradually became a warrior aristocracy, with greater rights than the peasants whose labor they controlled. Indeed, often the rise of knights and castles meant that many peasants lost their freedom, becoming **serfs**, unfree peasants who, although not property that could be bought and sold like slaves, were nevertheless bound to their land and subordinate to those who controlled it.

Figure 12.3 | Eleventh-Century Knights
Author: User "Myrabella"
Source: Wikimedia Commons
License: Public Domain

The regions of West Francia controlled by powerful nobles were nearly independent of the crown. But even at the Frankish monarchy's weakest, these nearly independent nobles were understood to hold their territories from the king and to owe allegiance to him if he called on them for military service. In this way, feudalism of the European Middle Ages resembled Western Zhou feudalism. The smaller fiefs that made up the territories of these great nobles likewise were understood to be held from these nobles; the knight who held a fief was, at least in theory, required to render military service to the lord from whom he held it. In practice, though, the kingdom of West Francia (and other regions of Western Europe where such a system held sway) had little cohesion as a state, with most functions of a state like minting money, building roads and bridges, and trying and executing criminals in the hands of the powerful nobles.

12.5.1 Global Context

Thus far, we have discussed feudalism in eleventh-century Western Europe, but a decentralized state dominated by a warrior aristocracy could emerge anywhere that central authority broke down. A similar system emerged in Heian Japan of the twelfth and thirteenth centuries, when mounted soldiers (in this case samurai rather than knights) came to occupy the social role of a warrior aristocracy (see Chapter Four). Such an arrangement would emerge at the same time in the Middle East: the Great Saljuq Empire was dominated by mounted warriors in control of **iqtas**, units of land whose revenues (often from taxation) would fund these warriors, who in turn held their iqtas from the sultan.

12.6 GROWTH OF TOWNS AND TRADE

Although the eleventh century was in many ways Western Europe's nadir, it would also see the beginnings of Western Europe's re-urbanization. One reason for these beginnings was that in those lands that had been part of the Western Roman Empire, city walls often remained, even if these cities had largely emptied of people. During the chaos and mayhem of the tenth and eleventh centuries, people often gathered in walled settlements for protection. Many of these old walled cities thus came to be re-occupied.

Another reason for the growth of towns came with a revival of trade in the eleventh century. This revival of trade can be traced to several causes. In the first place, Europe's knights, as a warrior aristocracy, had a strong demand for luxury goods, both locally manufactured products and imported goods such as silks and spices from Asia. Bishops, the great lords of the Church, had a similar demand. As such, markets grew up in the vicinity of castles and thus caused the formation of towns that served as market centers, while cathedral cities also saw a growth of population. Moreover, Viking raids had also led to a greater sea-borne trade in the North Sea and Atlantic. Often, Viking-founded markets served as the nucleus of new towns, especially in those lands where the Romans had never established a state and which were not urbanized at all. The Irish city of Dublin, for example, had begun as a Viking trading post.

Further south, in the Mediterranean, frequent raids by pirates (most of whom were Arab Muslims from North Africa) had forced the coastal cities of Italy to build effective navies. One of

Figure 12.4 | Medieval Market, Fifteenth Century
Author: Nicole Oreseme
Source: Wikimedia Commons
License: Public Domain

the chief of these cities was Venice, a city in the swamps and lagoons of northeastern Italy. Over the eleventh century, the city (formerly under Byzantine rule but now independent) had built up a navy that had cleared the Adriatic Sea of pirates and established itself as a nexus of trade between Constantinople and the rest of Western Europe. Likewise, on the western side of Italy, the cities of Genoa and Pisa had both built navies from what had been modest fishing fleets and seized the strongholds of Muslim pirates in the islands of Corsica and Sardinia. This clearing of pirates from the Mediterranean led to an increase in maritime trade and allowed the renewed growth of the old Roman towns that had in many cases remained since the fall of the Western Empire. The cities of Genoa and Venice were able to prosper because they stood at the northernmost points of the Mediterranean, the farthest that goods could be moved by water (always cheaper than overland transport in premodern times) before going over land to points further north.

As goods moved north and south between the trade zones of the North Sea and the Mediterranean, nobles along that north-south route realized that they could enrich themselves by taxing markets. They thus sponsored and protected markets in regions of West Francia like Champagne, which themselves would serve as centers of urbanization and economic activity.

The people living and working in towns came to be known as the **bourgeois**, or middle class. These were called a *middle* class because they were neither peasant farmers nor nobles, but rather a social rank between the two. Kings and other nobles would frequently give towns the right to self-government, often in exchange for a hefty payment. A self-governing town was often known as a **commune.**

12.7 GROWTH IN AGRICULTURE

Eleventh-century Europe's economy was primarily agricultural. The eleventh and twelfth centuries saw a massive expansion of agricultural output in the northern regions of Europe, which led to a corresponding growth in the economy and population. The same improvement in iron technology that allowed the equipping of armored knights led to more iron tools: axes allowed famers to clear forests and cultivate more land, and the iron share of a heavy plow allowed farmers to plow deeper into the thick soil of Western Europe. In addition, farmers gradually moved to a so-called **three field system** of agriculture: fields would have one third given over to cereal crops, one third to crops such as legumes (which increase fertility in soil), and a third left fallow, i.e., uncultivated either to serve as grazing land for livestock or simply rebuild its nutrients by lying unused. More iron tools and new agricultural techniques caused yields to rise from 3:1 to nearly 8:1 and in some fertile regions even higher. Another factor in the rise of agricultural yields was Europe's climate, which was becoming warmer in the eleventh, twelfth, and thirteenth centuries. As a result of both climate and new agricultural tools and techniques, food supplies increased so that Western Europe would go through the majority of the twelfth century without experiencing a major famine.

We should note that at the same time that agricultural yields were rising in Europe, so too were they on the rise in Song China (see Chapter Four). Indeed, compared to China, Europe's agricultural production was still relatively meager. It was nevertheless enough to bring about a dramatic growth in Europe's population.

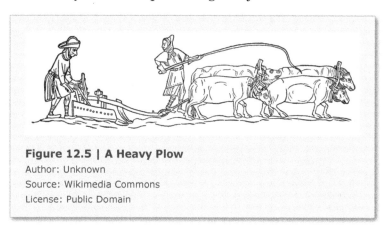

Figure 12.5 | A Heavy Plow
Author: Unknown
Source: Wikimedia Commons
License: Public Domain

12.8 A ROMAN EMPIRE?

Although the Carolingian Empire had collapsed in the ninth century and West Francia remained fragmented, in Central Europe, the rulers of East Francia formed a new empire on the wreck of Charlemagne's. King Otto I of East Francia had defeated the Magyars in 955 (see Chapter Seven), and both Otto and his powerful nobles further subordinated the Slavic peoples to the east to his rule, forcing them either to submit to his direct rule or acknowledge him as their overlord. He followed up on the prestige gained from his victory over the Magyars by exercising influence in Northern Italy, intervening in a dispute between Pope John XII (r. 955 – 964) and Berengar, a petty king. On 2 February 962, Pope John XII crowned Otto as Roman Emperor in a ceremony meant to echo Pope Leo III's crowning of Charlemagne over a century and a half before. Further, Otto deposed Berengar and added Italy to his domains.

Otto was the most powerful ruler in Europe besides the Byzantine emperor. His empire covered most of the German-speaking lands of Central Europe: indeed, Otto and its subsequent emperors would be Germans and the power base of this empire would be firmly Central European. This empire also encompassed northern Italy and much of the territory west of the Rhine. The rulers of this empire would call themselves Roman Emperors and consider themselves the successors to Charlemagne and thus to the Roman Empire. This empire, however, was more modest than Charlemagne's. Although its emperors would claim that all Christian kings owed them obedience, most other realms of Western Europe were independent, especially West Francia (which we shall hereafter refer to as France). Likewise, this empire's control of Northern Italy was always somewhat tenuous, since its rulers' power was based in Germany, far to the north of the Alps.

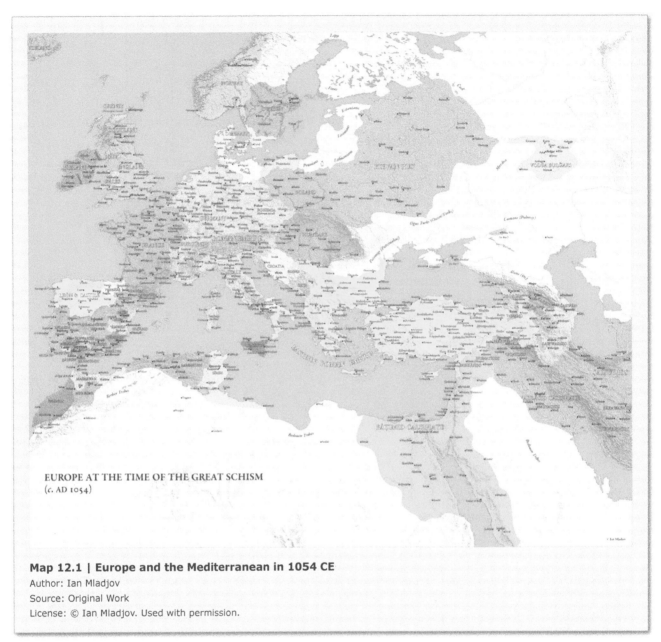

EUROPE AT THE TIME OF THE GREAT SCHISM
(c. AD 1054)

Map 12.1 | Europe and the Mediterranean in 1054 CE
Author: Ian Mladjov
Source: Original Work
License: © Ian Mladjov. Used with permission.

Because these emperors considered themselves to be Roman Emperors and also protectors of the Church—indeed, Otto I eventually deposed Pope John XII for improperly fulfilling his papal duties—historians call their empire the Holy Roman Empire and its emperors Holy Roman Emperors. The reader should carefully note that these emperors did not use either of those titles. They simply referred to themselves as Roman Emperors and their empire as the Roman Empire. We call the Empire the Holy Roman Empire and the emperors Holy Roman Emperors for the convenience of modern readers, so that they will know that they are reading about neither the Roman Empire, which dominated the entirety of the Mediterranean world in ancient times, nor the Byzantine Empire, a regional power in the Eastern Mediterranean for most of the Middle Ages.

12.9 THE HOLY ROMAN EMPIRE'S PERIPHERIES: SECONDARY STATE FORMATION

Anthropologists speak of **secondary state formation,** a process by which people who live in a tribe or chiefdom on the periphery of a state will gradually adopt statehood and the ideological trappings associated with statehood. Oftentimes this state formation happens because a people will need to match the resources of a state for raising armed forces, or because a chief will seek the greater prestige and power that comes from being recognized as a king.

In Scandinavia and in Eastern Europe, state formation occurred on the margins of the Holy Roman Empire. In the late tenth century, the Danes, the Poles (a Slavic people), and the Magyars formed the kingdoms of Denmark, Poland, and Hungary, respectively. These kingdoms were often **vassal states** (i.e., subordinate states) of the Ottonian emperors, but they just as often fought to maintain their independence when they had the capability to do so. Another key factor in the move from chiefdoms to states was the adoption of Christianity: the Christian religion, as we have seen earlier (see Chapter Seven), often legitimated a king. The Christian Bible says that a prince is God's instrument of executing justice.[1] In exchange for their legitimation, monarchs would protect the institutional Church. We can see this relationship between Christianity and secondary state formation when King Stephen I of Hungary received his crown from the papacy in the year 1000.

Far to the north, in Norway, a land of narrow fjords and valleys surrounded by pine-covered mountains, King Olaf II was following a similar set of policies. A Christian who had converted in 1013 while fighting in France, he spent his reign as king of Norway (1015 – 1030) both consolidating Norway into a kingdom that recognized royal authority and converting that kingdom to Christianity.

12.9.1 Global Context

In Northern and Eastern Europe, secondary state formation had gone hand in hand with the adoption of Christianity, which legitimated kings and whose clergy, familiar with the written word, provided the skills of literacy to monarchs. A similar pattern occurred elsewhere in the world, particularly in the African Sahel (see Chapter Nine). In Africa's Sahel, between the tenth and thirteenth centuries, as Ghana and then later Mali consolidated into states, their rulers converted their people to Islam, which provided a similar aid to state-building that Christianity did to the rulers of Northern and Eastern Europe.

12.10 EXPANSION OF CHRISTENDOM

In the Middle Ages, the people of Western Europe did not think of Europe as a geographic and cultural area. Rather, they thought of **Christendom,** those peoples and nations of the world that embraced the Christian religion, as a community sharing common ideals and assumptions. We might compare it to the Muslim notion of Dar al-Islam (see Chapter Eight). And in the eleventh century, Christendom expanded. Not only had the peoples to the north and east embraced

1   Romans 13:4

Christianity, but also Christian peoples and kingdoms in the Western Mediterranean expanded militarily at the expense of Islam. In Spain, the movement of the Christian kingdoms of northern Spain to expand their territory at the expense of Muslim al-Andalus would come to be known as the **Reconquista**, the reconquest. It was known as the *re*-conquest because there had been a Christian kingdom in Spain in the sixth and seventh centuries that had fallen to Muslim invaders in 711. Christians would thus have assumed that Spain, even though much of it might be Muslim ruled, was rightfully Christian. The effort by the Christian kingdoms of the Iberian Peninsula to dominate, conquer, and re-Christianize al-Andalus would become a key element in how Spanish Christians understood their identity both as Christians and Spaniards.

How did the *Reconquista* begin? From the Muslim conquest of Spain in 711 through the early eleventh century, al-Andalus was the dominant military power of the Iberian Peninsula, with Christian kingdoms confined to the marginal, mountainous regions of the peninsula's north (see Chapter Eight). But in 1008, Abd al-Rahman (also known as Sanjul), the caliph's chief adviser, sought to make himself caliph and replace the Umayyad dynasty with his own. The result was nearly three decades of civil war. The Cordoba Caliphate collapsed in 1031, fracturing into what we refer to as the **taifa** states, a set of small, politically weak states. These states were much weaker than the centralized Cordoba Caliphate and so were easy prey for potential conquerors from both the Christian north of the Iberian Peninsula and the Islamic Maghreb.

The Christian kingdoms of Spain had several strengths that enabled them to expand at the expense of the *taifa* states. In the first place, the *taifa* states were not only politically weak, but they were also at odds with each other. In addition, the construction of stone castles in newly-conquered territories allow the Christian kings to secure their conquests. Moreover, the Christian kingdoms of Spain could draw on much of the rest of Western Europe for manpower. By the eleventh century, the knight who inherited a fief would usually be the oldest son of the fief's lord. This arrangement meant that Western Europe had many knights who, as younger sons, had not inherited from their fathers (inheritance nearly always passed to males). These landless knights were looking either for employment or fiefs of their own. New conquests along the frontier of Muslim Spain thus gave them the perfect opportunity to seize their own lands. As a result, French knights flowed south in a steady stream across the Pyrenees.

Figure 12.6 | Twelfth-Century Spanish castle
Author: User "Superchilum"
Source: Wikimedia Commons
License: CC BY-SA 3.0

In Southern Italy, a group of knights from the region of France known as Normandy (and who were thus called Normans) had fought in the employ of the Byzantine emperors against the Muslim rulers of North Africa and Sicily. They eventually broke with the Byzantine Emperors and created the Kingdom of Sicily, a kingdom comprised of Sicily and Southern Italy, the lands that they had seized from both the Byzantines and Sicilian Muslims, with the last Muslim territory in Sicily conquered in 1091. These knights too had come south to the Mediterranean in search of new lands.

The Christian kingdoms of both Spain and Sicily were relatively tolerant of their Muslim subjects. Although Muslims under Christian rule faced civil disabilities similar to the *dhimmi* status of Jews and Christians in Muslim-ruled lands, they had a broad array of rights and protections. Indeed, the Christian kings of Sicily often employed Muslim mercenaries in their military service.

These victories by Christian forces over Muslims would be of great interest to the popes, who were seeking to reform the Church and to find ways that knights could be made to serve Christian society.

12.11 CHURCH REFORM IN THE ELEVENTH CENTURY

By the eleventh century, Europe suffered from frequent violence and the Church itself was in a sorry state: Pope John XII, for example, the man who had crowned Otto I, was so infamous for his immorality that it was said that under his rule the papal palace (called the Lateran) was little better than a brothel. From the mid-eleventh century, both popes and other clergymen would seek to reform both the institutional structures of the Church and Christian society as a whole.

The Holy Roman Emperor Henry III (r. 1039 – 1056) set the reforming papacy into motion. In 1049, he had traveled to Rome to be crowned emperor. When he arrived in the city, he found three men claiming to be pope, each supported by a family of Roman nobles. The outraged emperor deposed all three and replaced them with his own candidate, Pope Leo IX (r. 1049 – 1054). Leo IX would usher in a period in which reformers dominated the papacy.

These popes believed that to reform the Church, they would need to do so as its unquestioned leaders and that the institutional Church should be independent from control of laypeople. The position of pope had long been a prestigious one: Peter, the chief of Jesus Christ's disciples had, according to the Christian tradition, been the first bishop of Rome, the city in which he had been killed. Eleventh-century popes increasingly argued that since Peter had been the chief of Jesus's followers (and thus the first pope), the whole Church owed the popes the obedience that the disciples had owed Peter, who himself had been given his authority by Christ.

Such a position was in many ways revolutionary. In the Byzantine Empire, the emperors often directed the affairs of the Church (although such attempts frequently went badly wrong as with the Iconoclast Controversy). Western European kings appointed bishops, and the Holy Roman Emperors believed that they had the right to both appoint and depose popes. To claim the Church was independent of lay control went against centuries of practice.

Moreover, not all churchmen recognized the absolute authority of the pope. The pope was one of five churchmen traditionally known as **patriarchs**, the highest ranking bishops of the Church.

The pope was the patriarch of Rome; the other four were the patriarchs of Constantinople, Antioch, Jerusalem, and Alexandria. With Jerusalem and Alexandria (and often Antioch) under Muslim rule, the patriarch of Constantinople was the most prestigious of the Eastern Orthodox patriarchs, dwelling in a city that was Rome's successor. The patriarchs of Constantinople believed that the Roman pope had a place of honor because Peter had resided in Rome, but they did not believe he had any authority over other patriarchs.

12.11.1 The *Filioque* Controversy and the Split between Rome and Constantinople

This difference of opinion as to the authority of the pope would eventually break out in conflict. The church following the pope (which we will refer to as the Catholic Church for the sake of convenience), had a creed in its liturgy that said that God the Holy Spirit proceeds both from God the Father and from God the Son. The Eastern Orthodox version of this creed spoke of God the Holy Spirit as proceeding only from God the Father. Representatives of both churches quarreled over this wording, with the popes attempting to order the Orthodox Churches to state that the Holy Spirit proceeds from the Father and from the Son in their creed. We thus call this controversy the **Filioque Controversy**, since Latin for "and from the Son" is *filioque*.

On 16 July 1054, Humbert of Silva Candida, the pope's **legate** (i.e., ambassador) together with his entourage stormed into the Hagia Sophia as the patriarch was celebrating Communion and hurled a parchment scroll onto the altar; the scroll decreed the patriarch to be excommunicated. In response, the patriarch excommunicated the pope. Catholic and Orthodox churches were now split.

12.11.2 Simony and the Investiture Controversy

In spite of the schism between Catholic and Orthodox Churches, the popes turned to reforming the Church in the Catholic west. Two pressing concerns of the popes were the elimination of **simony**, the buying and selling of Church offices, and the protection of the Church's independence from laypeople. The fight of the reforming popes to assert the Church's independence led to the **Investiture Controversy**, the conflict between the popes and Holy Roman Emperors (and other kings of Western Europe) over who had the right to appoint churchmen.

To understand the Investiture Controversy, we need to understand the nature of a medieval bishop's power and authority. A bishop in medieval Europe was a Church leader, with a cathedral church and a palace. A medieval bishop would also hold lands with fiefs on these lands (and military obligations from those who held these fiefs), just like any great noble.

The Holy Roman Emperors believed that they had the right to appoint bishops both because a bishop held lands from the emperor and because the emperors believed themselves to be the leaders of all Christendom. The reforming popes of the eleventh century, particularly Pope Gregory VII (r. 1073 – 1085), objected to this belief. These popes believed that, since their authority as popes came from God, their spiritual authority was superior to the earthly authority of any king or prince. They further claimed their right to be independent rulers of the Papal States in Central Italy, based on the Donation of Constantine (see Chapter Seven).

Gregory VII was up against a man just as strong willed as he in the person of Emperor Henry IV (r. 1056 – 1106). From 1075, their relationship became increasingly adversarial as each claimed the exclusive right to appoint and depose bishops. Eventually, this conflict burst into open flame when Henry claimed that Gregory was in fact not rightfully pope at all and attempted to appoint his own pope. In response, Gregory proclaimed that none of Henry's subjects had a duty to obey him and encouraged his subjects to rise in rebellion.

Without the Church to legitimate Henry IV, his empire collapsed into civil war. As a result, Henry took a small band of followers and, in the dead of winter, crossed the Alps, braving the snowy, ice-covered passes to negotiate with the pope in person. In January, he approached the mountain castle of Canossa where the pope was staying and begged Gregory for forgiveness, waiting outside of the pope's castle on his knees in the snow for three days. Finally, Pope Gregory forgave the emperor.

In the end, though, after a public ceremony of reconciliation, Henry returned to Central Europe, crushed the rebellion, and then returned to Italy with an army, forcing Gregory VII into exile. This Investiture Controversy would drag on for another four decades. In the end, the Holy Roman Emperors and popes would reach a compromise with the 1122 **Concordat of Worms**. The compromise was that clergy would choose bishops, but that the emperor could decide disputed elections. A bishop would receive his lands from the emperor in one ceremony, and the emblems of his spiritual authority from the pope in another. Other kings of Western Europe reached similar compromises with the papacy.

The results of half a century of papal reform efforts were mixed. The Catholic and Orthodox Churches had split with one another, and tensions remain between the two to this day. Although the popes failed to achieve everything they sought, they did gain limited independence of the Church, and they succeeded almost completely in ending the practice of simony. Indeed, one contrast between Western Europe and much of the rest of the world is a strong sense of separation between secular and sacred authority. That separation of Church and state owes much to the troubled years of the Investiture Controversy.

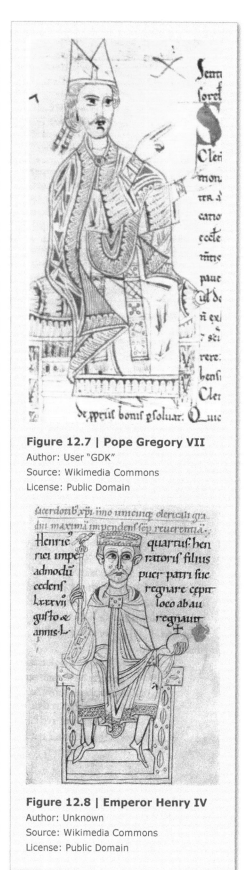

Figure 12.7 | Pope Gregory VII
Author: User "GDK"
Source: Wikimedia Commons
License: Public Domain

Figure 12.8 | Emperor Henry IV
Author: Unknown
Source: Wikimedia Commons
License: Public Domain

The successes of the papacy in their efforts at Church reform, together with the military successes seen by Christians in the Western Mediterranean against Muslims, would inspire the popes to an even more ambitious effort: the Crusades.

12.12 THE CRUSADES

12.12.1 Background: Disaster at Manzikert

On the surface, the Byzantine Empire of the eleventh century looked like one of the world's great powers. It dominated the Eastern Mediterranean, with its emperors reigning from Constantinople, a city full of magnificent churches, splendid palaces, and centuries-old monuments of an ancient empire.

Map 12.2 | The Eastern Mediterranean in 1096 CE
Author: Ian Mladjov
Source: Original Work
License: © Ian Mladjov. Used with permission.

But these outward signs of strength concealed several weaknesses. In the first place, the *theme* system (see Chapter Seven) had begun to break down. The plots of land used to equip soldiers had gradually given way to large estates held by powerful aristocrats. These powerful aristocrats often paid less and less in taxes, starving the state of key resources. The *theme* soldiers themselves were used less often (and when they did fight, they were often poorly trained and equipped), with the emperors relying on mercenaries for most of their fighting. The civilian aristocracy and the military were often at loggerheads.

The Byzantine emperors of the later eleventh century were nevertheless able to hold their own against external threats until the arrival of the Saljuq Turks in the Middle East (see Chapters Eight and Eleven). Both the Byzantine emperor Romanos IV (r. 1068 – 1071) and the Saljuq sultan Alps Arslan (r. 1063 – 1072) sought to control the Caucasus Mountains, whose passes controlled access to the Middle East from the Central Asian steppes. Control of this route was especially important as the steppes served as a source from which the Turks in the Middle East could recruit more fighters.

Byzantine and Turk finally clashed. Romanos sought to break the Turkish threat on his eastern flank and so mustered an immense army. This army consisted both of soldiers of the *themes* and mercenary units drawn from many different peoples: Western Europeans, Cumans and Pechenegs from the steppes, Scandinavians, and Turks. Both the heterogeneity of this army and the dysfunctional politics of the eleventh-century Byzantine Empire would prove to be Romanos's undoing.

On 19 August 1071, the forces of the Byzantine Empire met those of the Great Saljuq Empire at the Battle of Manzikert near the shores of Lake Van in Armenia. The thematic troops were of indifferent quality, but worse for the emperor was the treachery of both the Byzantine commander Andronikos Doukas and the Byzantine force's Turkic mercenaries. The Byzantine field army was annihilated. The emperor himself was surrounded and taken captive after his elite guard of Norse mercenaries went down fighting in his defense.

The result was a catastrophe for the Empire. Not only had most of the Byzantine Army been wiped out, but also competing Byzantine nobles took the opportunity of the emperor's captivity to launch their own bids for power. During the decade of civil war that followed, the Empire's holdings in Asia

Figure 12.9 | Alexios Komnenos
Author: User "Eloquence"
Source: Wikimedia Commons
License: Public Domain

Minor almost all fell under the dominion of the Saljuq Turks. What had been the world's most powerful Christian state now faced destruction.

Eventually, Alexios Komnenos (r. 1081 – 1118) would seize control of the Byzantine Empire and laboriously rebuild its military strength. Alexios was an able and clever military commander who also possessed good long-term sense. He used the tax base of the Empire's Balkan possessions to fund a new army, one composed largely of foreign mercenaries and a small core of Greek soldiers. These indigenous soldiers were often granted out blocks of lands known as ***pronoiai*** (singular ***pronoia***) whose revenues they would use to equip themselves and their soldiers; a *pronoia* was similar to a fief in Western Europe. He also recruited steppe peoples, such as the Cumans and Pechenegs, into his forces. Another group of peoples from which he recruited mercenaries was Western Europeans, particularly from the Holy Roman Empire and West Francia. In March of 1095, he sent a request to the pope for military assistance. The long-term consequences of this request would be earth-shaking.

12.12.2 The First Crusade

The pope who received Alexios Komnenos's request for help was Urban II (r. 1088 – 1099), an associate of reformers like Gregory VII. Churchmen seeking to reform society had looked to quell the violence that was often frequent in Western Europe (especially in France): this violence was usually the work of knights. These reformers were considering how knights could turn their aggression to pursuits that were useful to Christian society rather than preying upon civilians. Fighting against Muslims in Sicily and Spain showed the popes an example of knightly aggression directed towards Christendom's external enemies (see Chapter Eight).

In addition, the Church had long recognized Roman Law's concept of **Just War**: a war could be moral as long as it was defensive, declared by a rightful authority, and likely to cause less damage than if the war had not occurred. By the eleventh century, certain churchmen had further formulated this idea into one of **Holy War**, that is to say, that a war fought in defense of the Church was not only morally right, but even meritorious.

The final element that led to Pope Urban II's turning much of the military might of Western Europe to the Middle East was the idea of Jerusalem. The city of Jerusalem was where Jesus Christ was said to have been crucified, to have died, and to have risen from the dead (see Chapter Six). As such, the Church of the Holy Sepulcher, built on what was said to be the empty tomb from which Christ had risen was the holiest Church in the Christian world—and this Church had been under the control of Muslims since Caliph Umar's conquest of Palestine in the seventh century (see Chapter Eight). The city remained important to Christians, however, and, even while it was under Muslim rule, they had traveled to it as **pilgrims**, that is, travelers undertaking a journey for religious purposes.

Pope Urban thus conceived of the idea of turning the military force of Western Europe to both shore up the strength of the flagging Byzantine Empire (a Christian state), and return Jerusalem and the Church of the Holy Sepulcher to Christian rule after four centuries of Muslim domination.

On 27 November 1095, he gathered several of the major nobles of Western Europe (as well as many lower-ranked knights) to an open-air sermon at Clermont, where he was presiding over a

Church council. In this sermon, he proclaimed that it was the duty of these warrior aristocrats, as Christians, to defend the Byzantine Empire and to put the city of Jerusalem under Christian rule. The result was an enthusiastic response by those knights, who are said to have cried out, "God wills it!" and to have vowed to set off to Jerusalem and bring it under Christian rule. Furthermore, as word of Pope Urban's admonition spread throughout Western Europe, more and more of the knightly class answered the call, mustering under the leadership of several powerful nobles.

This movement of the knights of most of Western Europe to fight against Muslims in the Middle East is generally known as the first of a series of **Crusades.** A crusade was a war declared by the papacy against those perceived to be enemies of the Christian faith (usually, but not always, Muslims). Participating in a crusade would grant a Christian forgiveness of sins. We ought to note that such a concept in many ways superficially resembled the Muslim notion of the Lesser Jihad (see Chapter Eight).

As these forces mustered and marched south and east, the religious enthusiasm accompanying them often spilled out into aggression against non-Christians other than Muslims. One group

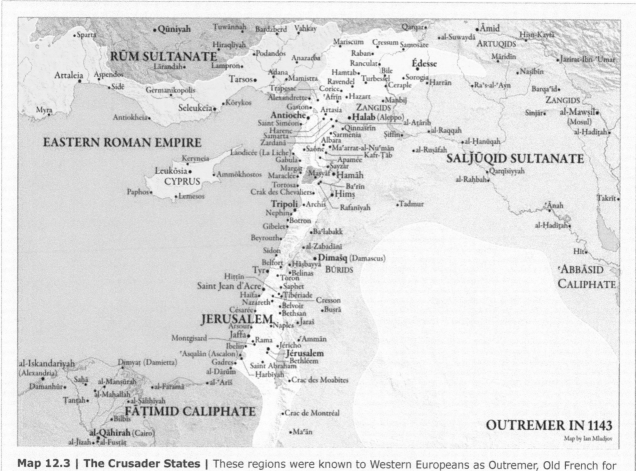

Map 12.3 | The Crusader States | These regions were known to Western Europeans as Outremer, Old French for "across the sea"

Author: Ian Mladjov

Source: Original Work

License: © Ian Mladjov. Used with permission.

of Crusaders in the area around the Rhine engaged in a series of massacres of Jewish civilians, traveling from city to city while killing Jews and looting their possessions before this armed gang was forced to disperse.

The Crusaders traveled in two main waves. The first traveled to the Byzantine Empire, and was ferried across the Bosporus but was wiped out by a Turkish army. The second wave, however, was better planned and coordinated, and, upon its arrival in the Byzantine Empire, reached an uneasy truce with the Alexios Komnenos (who had been expecting a modest force of mercenaries and not the armed might of most of Western Europe). The

Figure 12.10 | Crusader Castle at Byblos
Author: User "Heretiq"
Source: Wikimedia Commons
License: CC BY-SA 2.5

Crusaders were fortunate. After Nizaris had assassinated Nizam al-Mulk and the Fatimid caliph of Egypt had died (both in 1092), the Middle East fell into political chaos (see Chapter Eight). When the Crusaders marched east in 1096, they encountered not a unified Great Saljuq Empire, but a collection of independent and semi-independent sultans and emirs.

The Crusaders moved east, winning a string of victories in Asia Minor: when they could not be outmaneuvered, the armored knights of Western Europe often stood at an advantage against the lightly armored or unarmored mounted archers that mostly made up the bulk of Turkish forces. Following the path of the crusading army, Alexios was able to restore much of western Asia Minor to the control of the Byzantine Empire, although the central Anatolian plateau would remain under the dominion of the Saljuq Turks. The Crusaders advanced on Antioch, the largest and most prosperous city of the Levant, and, after a siege of nearly a year, both seized control of the city and defeated a Turkish army that attempted to relieve it. The army then marched south to Jerusalem and into territory controlled by the Fatimid caliphate—itself a Shi'ite state that was no friend of the Sunni Saljuq Turks. Venice and Genoa, meanwhile, transported supplies to the Crusaders by sea. The Crusaders rejected Fatimid overtures for a negotiated settlement and, in June of 1099, arrived outside the walls of Jerusalem. The Crusaders stormed the city's walls, and, as the city fell, it was subject to a brutal sack, with both the city's defenders and its civilian population subject to a bloody slaughter. We must note that there was nothing particularly unique about this massacre. The custom among most pre-modern peoples was that if a city resisted an attacking army, then it would be subject to sack and massacre of its population were it to fall.

After the fall of Jerusalem, the Crusaders established four states in the Levant: the County of Edessa, in northern Mesopotamia, the Principality of Antioch, centered on the city of Antioch and its environs; the County of Tripoli, in what is roughly Lebanon today; and the Kingdom of Jerusalem, which occupied Palestine and whose capital was the city of Jerusalem. These states were ruled by men (and often women) who were Catholic in religion and ethnically Western European. The religion and institutions of these **Crusader States** were nearly the same as those of Western Europe.

These states attracted some settlers, in both their warrior aristocracy and even merchants and peasants. But many of the subjects of the Christian rulers of these kingdoms were Muslims (or Christian Arabs, who had special privileges over their Muslim counterparts, but fewer rights than Catholic, ethnically Western European Christians). Indeed, the Crusader States would consistently suffer from a lack of manpower: although the pope had spoken of rich lands for the taking in Palestine, most of the knights who had gone on the First Crusade (and survived) returned to Western Europe. The Crusader States relied on extensive networks of heavily fortified stone castles for defense. They were fortunate that the Middle East was politically fragmented and Fatimid Egypt was weak. Whether these states would be sustainable in the face of stronger Muslim powers remained to be seen.

12.13 THE TWELFTH CENTURY IN WESTERN EUROPE

In the twelfth century, many of Europe's kingdoms saw a gradual centralization of state power. England had long been Western Europe's most centralized state. In 1066, a group of Normans under their Duke, William the Bastard, invaded England. William defeated the English army, making himself the king of England: he was thus known as William the Conqueror. This conquest of England by French-speakers moved the culture, language, and institutions of England closer to those of France. Although England looked more feudal, it nevertheless retained a centralized bureaucratic apparatus. William was able to use this bureaucracy to conduct a nationwide census, a feat of which no European state outside of the Byzantine Empire was capable. Although England would suffer a civil war of nearly a decade and a half in the twelfth century, for the most part, its monarchs, particularly

Figure 12.11 | King Henry II and his wife, Eleanor of Aquitaine
Author: Anonymous
Source: Wikimedia Commons
License: Public Domain

Figure 12.12 | Dover castle, built by King Henry II
Author: Jake Keup
Source: Wikimedia Commons
License: CC BY 2.0

Henry I (r. 1100 – 1135) and Henry II (r. 1154 – 1189), were innovative and clever administrators, creating a network of royal courts and a sophisticated office of tax collection known as the **Exchequer**.

France had entered the tenth and eleventh centuries as the most loosely-governed kingdom of Europe. In 987, France's nobles elected Hugh Capet, the count of Paris, as king, effectively replacing the Carolingian dynasty. The **Capetian** Dynasty's kings, however, directly controlled only the lands around Paris. In addition, after the Norman conquest of England in 1066, the Norman kings of England were also dukes of large French territories. Thus, for the first part of the twelfth century, much of France was under the effective control of the English crown.

In spite of these challenges, the Capetian monarchs gradually built their kingdom into a functional state. They cultivated a reputation as defenders of Christianity in order to gain legitimacy from the Church. They also sought to enforce the feudal obligations that the powerful nobles owed to the crown, often calling on them to serve militarily so as to create a habit of obedience to the king.

To the southwest, the rise of the Muslim Almoravid Empire under the rule of aggressively expansionist Muslim religious reformers in North Africa briefly put the *Reconquista* in jeopardy, but, by the early twelfth century, it had resumed, with the Muslim stronghold of Zaragoza falling to Christian armies in 1118. After the First Crusade, those knights

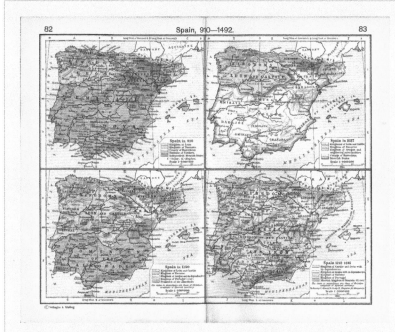

Map 12.4 | Spain, progress of the Reconquista
Author: William R. Shepherd
Source: Wikimedia Commons
License: Public Domain

who traveled to Spain to help its Christian kings fight Muslims received the same forgiveness of sins that the papacy granted to crusaders in the Levant. Over the twelfth century, four major Christian kingdoms would emerge in the Iberian Peninsula: Portugal, Leon-Castile, Navarre, and Aragon. These kingdoms would develop a sophisticated system of taxation in order to fund the *Reconquista*. In the later twelfth century, they faced the challenge of the Almohad Empire that emerged from the Islamic Maghreb to unite Muslim Spain and North Africa. By the 1150s, Christian Spain was on the defensive once again.

In Scandinavia, too, a set of strong monarchies had emerged in Denmark and Norway by the end of the twelfth century.

12.14 EMPIRES: RECOVERY AND COLLAPSE

12.14.1 Frederick Barbarossa and the Holy Roman Empire

The Investiture Controversy had weakened the power of the Holy Roman Emperors. In the early part of the twelfth century, power in the Holy Roman Empire decentralized in the same way that it had in tenth- and eleventh-century France, while the cities of northern Italy were increasingly governing themselves with little direct authority exercised by the Holy Roman Emperors. The Holy Roman Emperor Frederick Barbarossa (r. 1152 – 1190) sought to arrest this decline and make his subjects adhere to his authority.

Frederick's two overriding goals were to ensure that the great princes of Central Europe and the city-states of Northern Italy acknowledged and submitted to his authority. Northern Italy was a particularly vexing challenge. By the middle of the twelfth century, many of the cities of northern Italy had gradually moved from rule by an urban nobility or bishops to self-government by an elected commune, and these communes were often reluctant to acknowledge imperial authority, especially with respect to the taxes that Barbarossa believed were owed him. Shortly after beginning his reign, Barbarossa sought to implement this authority.

Barbarossa had a great deal of initial success, but eventually the city-states of Northern Italy united into an organization called the Lombard League, and this League allied with the popes, who lent their moral authority to the cause of the northern Italian city-states. Indeed, part of the difficulties faced by Barbarossa was that any pope would be more likely to try to keep northern and central Italy as far from direct control of the Holy Roman Emperors as possible. If the emperors were too powerful in Northern and Central Italy, then they would threaten the papacy's independence, jeopardizing everything the eleventh-century reforming popes had struggled to accomplish. Eventually, this coalition of the papacy and Lombard League inflicted a military defeat on Barbarossa at the 1176 Battle of Legnano, after which Barbarossa was forced to concede a great deal of self-rule within the Empire to the Italian city-states.

Near the end of his reign, Barbarossa would lead an immense army on a crusade. In 1187, the kings of Western Europe found themselves forced to respond to a great catastrophe for Christendom: the city, and, indeed, most of the Kingdom of Jerusalem had fallen to a Muslim army under the sultan Saladin. These kings responded with the effort known as the Third Crusade.

12.14.2 The Komnenoi in Byzantium

The other empire claiming (with somewhat more justice) to be the rightful heir of the Roman Empire was the Byzantine Empire, and, after the disaster of Manzikert, the Komnenos emperors had managed to rebuild a Byzantine army based on the system of *pronoiai* and mercenary forces. Emperor John II (r. 1118 – 1143) followed up on Alexios's work and established effective Byzantine control over much of Western Anatolia, consolidated imperial hold on Southeastern Europe, and, indeed, forced the Crusader States to acknowledge him as their overlord.

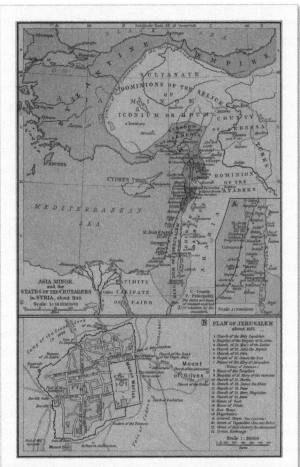

Map 12.5 | The Eastern Mediterranean in the reign of John II
Author: Alexander G. Findlay
Source: Classical Atlas of Ancient Geography
License: Public Domain

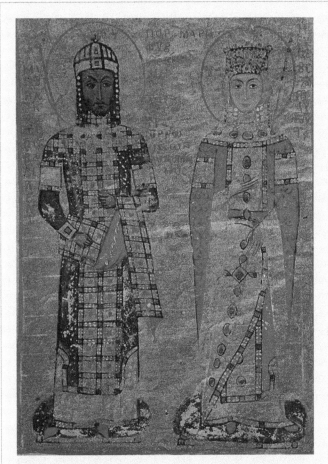

Figure 12.13 | Manuel Komnenos and his wife, Maria of Antioch
Author: Anonymous
Source: Wikimedia Commons
License: Public Domain

At the same time that Barbarossa sought to build the Holy Roman Empire as a credible power, in the east, Manuel Komnenos (r. 1143 – 1180) sought to do the same with his Empire. He managed to suppress the growing power of Venice in the Eastern Mediterranean, form an alliance with the growing kingdom of Hungary, and temporarily force the Turks of central Anatolia to acknowledge his overlordship. In the end, however, the emperor's reach exceeded his grasp. His attempt to conquer Fatimid Egypt in alliance with the Kingdom of Jerusalem failed when the military commander of Damascus, Saladin, outmaneuvered both Byzantium and Jerusalem and instead added Egypt to the territory of Damascus, which created a Muslim Empire in the Middle East that menaced the Crusader States (see Chapter Eight). And the emperor's effort to return central Anatolia to Byzantine rule ultimately failed when his army was defeated by the Saljuq Sultanate of Rum at Myriokephalon in 1176. Ultimately, the Byzantine Empire's undoing was not necessarily in individual battles, but rather in that the loss of the wealthy agricultural land of Central Anatolia to the Turks meant that its emperors never quite had the tax base necessary to put their ambitions of a restored Roman Empire into practice.

In the end, the Komnenoi had managed to restore the Byzantine Empire as a regional power, but it was left with structural weaknesses that would eventually prove to be its undoing.

12.15 THE TWELFTH-CENTURY RENAISSANCE

The twelfth century in Western Europe was a time of renewed vibrancy in intellectual activity, and much of this activity centered on Europe's towns and cities. We call this renewal of intellectual activity the **Twelfth-Century Renaissance** in order to separate it from both the Carolingian Renaissance of the eighth and ninth centuries and the Italian Renaissance of the fourteenth and fifteenth centuries. Both monasteries and cathedrals were centers of education in Western Europe, even during the dark days of the tenth century. Over the eleventh century, thinkers in the monasteries of Western Europe had increasingly sought to apply the tools of logic (in particular Aristotelian logic) to the study of the Bible. But Western Europeans were familiar with very little of Aristotle's work aside from a small number of logical writings that had been translated from Greek into Latin in the sixth century. The twelfth century would see a massive shift, with an immense growth of interest in philosophy on the part of those men (and a few women) who had a formal education. The spur to this interest would come from events in Southwestern Europe.

Al-Andalus had been a major source of Muslim intellectual activity. As early as the tenth century, Christian scholars, such as Gerbert of Aurillac (who eventually became Pope Sylvester II[2], r. 999 – 1003), had visited Muslim-ruled Spain to read the works of ancient Greek thinkers that were unavailable elsewhere in Western Europe. Gerbert's writings show him to be particularly fascinated with Euclid, Arabic numerals, and the concept of zero.

When Toledo fell to Christian armies in 1085, its libraries became available to the larger Christian world. Muslims had translated most of the philosophy of Aristotle into Arabic in addition to writing extensive original works that engaged with the thought of Aristotle and Plato. Once these books were in Christian hands, Raymond, archbishop of Toledo (r. 1125 – 1152), set up translation teams. People who spoke Arabic and the Romance languages of Spain would first translate these books into Spanish, and these books would then be translated into Latin, which would thus make Aristotle and Ptolemy (as well as the works of Arabic philosophers) available to educated people throughout Western Europe. The availability of texts that had been largely known only by reputation to the thinkers of Western Europe spurred an intellectual revolution,

---

2   Between the sixth and eleventh centuries, a practice emerged whereby the pope would adopt a distinct name from the name he was born with upon ascension to the papacy. The practice continues to the present day.

Figure 12.14 | Latin Manuscript of Aristotle's Physics
Author: Jean-Christophe Benoist
Source: Wikimedia Commons
License: Public Domain

as the Christian thinkers sought to understand how to reconcile an understanding of the world based on Christianity with the approach of the non-Christian ancient Greeks.

Such translations on the Christian/Muslim frontier continued through the twelfth and thirteenth centuries. Christendom thus had access to the writings of Muslim philosophers. Western Europeans read natural philosophy, such as al-Haytham's writings on optics and the Aristotelian commentaries of Ibn Rushd (whose name they pronounced as Averroës). This movement saw the translation not only of philosophy, but also of medicine—indeed, in the Muslim world, philosophers often served as physicians—so the medical works of philosophers and physicians such as Ibn Sina (whose name Western Europeans pronounced as Avicenna) were read avidly by Christians in Western Europe.

Philosophy and medicine were not the only fields of study to receive new interest. Western Europeans were also showing a renewed interest in law. Although the kingdoms that had grown up in Western Europe after the fall of the Western Roman Empire had incorporated some elements of Roman Law as well as the oral law of the Germanic peoples into their legal systems, law codes were for the most part unsystematic. Starting from the eleventh century, scholars, particularly those based in the schools of Bologna, began subjecting The Justinian Code (see Chapter Seven) to intense study, using logical analysis to create a body of systematic writing on the interpretation of law. These men who studied Roman Law would often go to work for kings and emperors, with the result that much European law would often draw its inspiration from Justinian.

Most schools were still attached to cathedral churches—indeed, these schools in which medicine, law, and philosophy flourished as disciplines of study might be compared to the madrassas of the Muslim world—so the chief field of study in these schools was theology, that is, the interpretation of the Bible. And theologians increasingly drew on logical analysis and philosophy of language to understand what they believed was God's revelation to humanity.

Eventually, many of these cathedral schools gained the right to organize as self-governing institutions. We call these institutions **universities**. By the end of the twelfth century, the universities of Bologna, Paris, and Oxford had become self-governing institutions and would serve as the foundation of the university system of the Western world that exists to the present day.

12.16 THE THIRD CRUSADE

The Crusader States had endured from 1099 to 1187 because the Muslim Middle East was politically fragmented. Once Saladin had overthrown Egypt's Fatimid Caliphate and united Egypt to Muslim-controlled Syria and northern Iraq (see Chapter Eight), he was able to turn his resources to destroying

Map 12.6 | Europe and the Mediterranean in the Third Crusade
Author: User "Roke"
Source: Wikimedia Commons
License: Public Domain

the Crusader States. Eventually, at the 1187 Battle of Hattin, his forces met the combined forces of the Kingdom of Jerusalem. The result was a complete victory for Saladin. With the manpower of most of the Kingdom of Jerusalem killed or captured—knights and noble prisoners would be held for a hefty ransom, while lower-ranked soldiers would go to slave markets—he was easily able to capture most of the castles and cities that made up the kingdom, to include the city of Jerusalem itself.

The result shocked the Christian world, and Pope Gregory VIII quickly issued the **bull** (that is, an official papal pronouncement) *Audita tremendi*, which called on the Christian world to retake Jerusalem. The kings of England and France, Richard I (known as Lionheart, r. 1189 – 1199) and Philip Augustus (r. 1180 – 1223), respectively, took vows to launch a crusade, as did Holy Roman Emperor Frederick Barbarossa. (As usual, the Christians of Iberia took little part in crusades in the Levant, as their efforts focused on the *Reconquista*.)

Although Frederick Barbarossa died en route (he drowned in a stream in the mountains of Anatolia), both Richard I and Philip Augustus eventually arrived in the Levant by sea. Although Philip soon returned to France, King Richard battled Saladin over the course of two years, to results that were mostly inconclusive. The crusading army seized most of the castles and cities on the coast, and these became the center for a restored, but smaller Kingdom of Jerusalem, but the Crusaders ultimately failed to take Jerusalem itself. The Crusade finally ended in a truce in which both parties ratified this state of affairs, with Christian pilgrims allowed to visit the city of Jerusalem, even though it remained under Muslim rule.

12.17 THE FOURTH CRUSADE

While Jerusalem remained under Muslim control, the papacy's goal was to retake it, especially as, in 1198, the man elected pope was one of the most ambitious men to wear the papal crown of the Middle Ages: Pope Innocent III (r. 1198 – 1216). Innocent's goals were to morally reform society and to launch a crusade for retaking the holy city of Jerusalem. In the year of his election, he issued a call to crusade that ended up as a disaster.

Between 1185 and 1204, the Byzantine Empire had drastically weakened. After the death of Manuel Komnenos with his heir still a child, the Empire faced a string of catastrophes. The child-emperor was murdered, his successor was eventually overthrown, and the next emperor after that was likewise overthrown. During this political infighting, the Empire's peripheral territories of Serbia, Cyprus, and Cilicia all seceded. Closer to the center, the Bulgars rose in rebellion in 1186 and re-established an independent Bulgaria within only a few days' march of Constantinople itself. In addition, the chain of emperors, regents, and usurpers reigning between 1185 and 1204 had allowed the Byzantine navy to gradually disintegrate.

In 1202, a group of crusaders (with kings notably absent) contracted with the government of Venice to transport them to fight in Egypt, now ruled by Saladin's heirs. When these crusaders proved unable to pay, the Venetian government requested their military assistance. The son of the deposed emperor (whose eyes had been gouged out) approached the crusaders and Venetians. He offered the crusaders military and financial assistance and for Venice to gain trading privileges in the Empire if crusaders and Venetians would help him regain his throne. The end result was that, in 1204, after a series of misadventures, a crusader army stormed the walls of Constantinople and put the city to a brutal sack; then, the crusaders parceled out much of the territory of the Byzantine Empire amongst themselves. The most advantageous ports went to Venice, which would use them as the basis of a Mediterranean trading empire that would endure for centuries. The Crusades, which had begun as a result of an appeal for help by the Byzantine Empire, ultimately resulted in its destruction.

Although the Byzantine Empire had been broken up, three states survived that claimed to be legitimate heirs to the Byzantine State. One was established in Western Anatolia with its capital in Nicaea, another, in Epirus, in what is today the country of Albania, while the third was based on the city of Trebizond, on the northern coast of Anatolia. The Nicene Empire would eventually retake Constantinople in 1261, although the restored state would never be the regional power that the Empire had been under the Komnenoi.

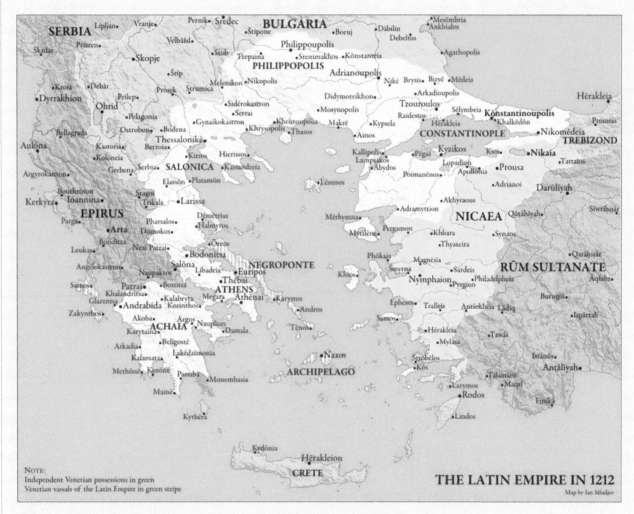

Map 12.7 | The Latin Empire in 1212 CE | The Latin Empire of Constantinople (the state established by crusaders after 1204) and Byzantine successor states
Author: Ian Mladjov
Source: Original Work
License: © Ian Mladjov. Used with permission.

12.18 THE STATES OF THIRTEENTH-CENTURY EUROPE

12.18.1 Eastern Europe

The thirteenth century would prove catastrophic for both Hungary and the Kievan Rus, for the same Mongols who laid waste to much of Asia would eventually arrive from the steppes of Asia and into the plains of Eastern Europe (see Chapter Eleven). In 1240, the Mongols shattered the Kievan Rus, destroyed the city of Kiev, and left the plains around the city littered with dead bodies stretching out to the horizon. The Ruses would remain Mongol vassals for the rest of the Middle Ages. The Mongol advance continued. In 1241, at the Battle of Mohi, a Hungarian army was annihilated, and the Mongols subsequently slew half the kingdom's population before Batu Khan, the Mongol commander, returned to Mongolia for the election of a new Great Khan (see Chapter Eleven).

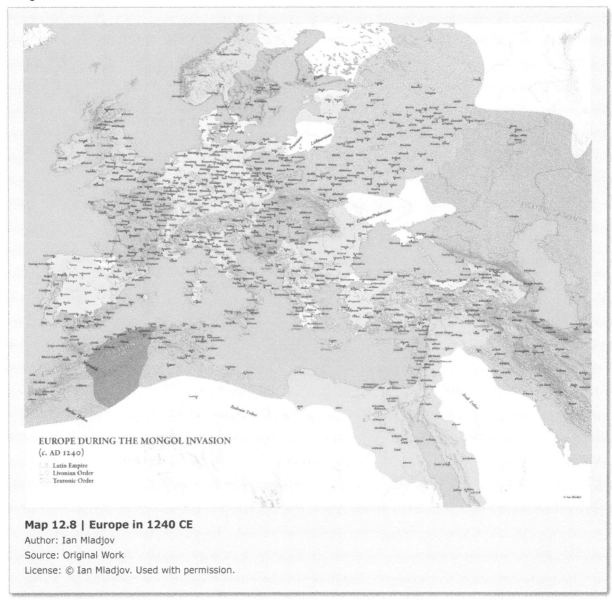

Map 12.8 | Europe in 1240 CE
Author: Ian Mladjov
Source: Original Work
License: © Ian Mladjov. Used with permission.

12.18.2 The Holy Roman Empire: Failure of Frederick II

The Holy Roman Empire remained Europe's dominant power in the first half of the thirteenth century in spite of Barbarossa's incomplete success. The Empire would, however, be fatally undermined by the struggles between Emperor Frederick II (r. 1215 – 1250) and a series of mostly forceful and able popes. The dispute was the same as that which had occupied his grandfather, Frederick Barbarossa. Unlike Barbarossa, the base of Frederick II's power was in Sicily, for his father, Henry VI (r. 1190 – 1197), had married Constance, queen of Sicily, thus making Frederick II ruler of both the Holy Roman Empire and the Kingdom of Sicily. Like his grandfather, he sought to create an empire that ruled both Italy and central Europe. And for the same reason that the popes had opposed Barbarossa, they, together with the cities of northern Italy, opposed Frederick II. In the end, when Frederick died, the Holy Roman Empire collapsed as a unitary state. For nearly twenty years, it had no emperor, as the papacy's allies hunted down and brutally slaughtered Frederick's heirs, and then, by the time an emperor was elected from the Austrian nobles of the Hapsburg family in 1273, the Empire was more a loose collection of states than a centralized empire.

12.18.3 Expansion of Christendom on the Frontiers

To the northeast, Christendom continued to expand. In the forests and bogs around the Baltic Sea, German-speaking crusaders (as well as Danes) conquered the heathen[3] peoples, converting them to Christianity and settling the territory with Germans and Danes. These efforts were recognized by the popes as crusades. By the end of the thirteenth century, all of Europe except for Lithuania was Christian. The kingdom of Lithuania would remain resolutely heathen and militarily resist German Crusaders until 1385, at which time the Lithuanian kings finally converted to Christianity when their kingdom was combined with Poland.

In thirteenth-century Spain, the most significant accomplishment of the Christian monarchs was that, on 16 July 1212, at the Battle of Las Navas de Tolosa, the combined armies of Castile, Aragon, Portugal, and Navarre met those of the Almohad Caliphate and won a victory so crushing that the power of the Almohads was forever broken. In the decades that followed, Aragon, Portugal, and Castile conquered all of Muslim Iberia, save for Granada.

12.18.4 France and England

Perhaps the most successful thirteenth-century monarchs were the Capetian kings of France. In the years between 1203 and 1214, King Philip Augustus managed to dispossess the English king of almost all of his territory held in France. He was also increasingly successful in using a set of recognized laws to enhance his legitimacy. So he made sure that he had a strong legal case drawn up by expert lawyers before he dispossessed England's King John. Likewise, he created a royal court that was a court of final appeal—and that meant that, even in parts of the kingdom where great lords exercised their own justice, the king had increasing authority. In 1208, Pope Innocent III had called a crusade against the semi-independent territories of southern France because of

---

[3]   Generally, we refer to the followers of the Greco-Roman religion that prevailed before Christianity as pagans and the followers of the northern European religion that prevailed before Christianity as heathens.

the presence there of a group of heretics known as the Cathars. In the resulting crusade (called the **Albigensian Crusade** because much of the fighting happened around the town of Albi), crusaders from the north crushed the power of the great nobles of southern France. King Louis VIII (r. 1223 – 1226) then extended the direct rule of the French crown into areas where, for centuries, the French kings had ruled only indirectly.

France's King Louis IX (r. 1226 – 1270) was perhaps its most effective Capetian king. He continued the process of establishing the royal courts as supreme in the kingdom. It was in Louis IX's reign that we can see the beginnings of a sophisticated and accurate royal budget.

When England's King John (r. 1199 – 1216) lost to Philip Augustus, his outraged nobles rebelled, resulting in a civil war from 1215 to 1217. One temporary treaty of this civil war, a treaty known as **Magna Carta** (signed in 1215), would have a much further-reaching impact than anyone who had drafted it could have foreseen. One particular provision of Magna Carta was that if the king wanted to raise new taxes on the people of England, then he needed to get the consent of the community of the realm by convening a council. The convening of such councils,

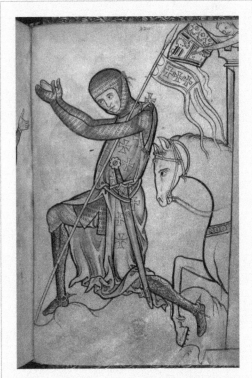

Figure 12.15 | A Knight in Thirteenth-Century Armor
Author: British Library
Source: Wikimedia Commons
License: Public Domain

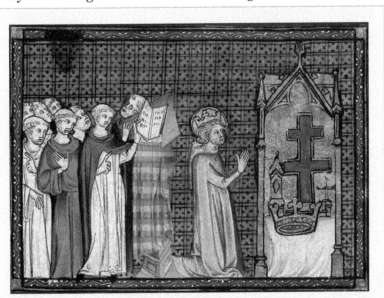

Figure 12.16 | France's King Louis IX
Author: Guillaume de Saint-Pathus
Source: Wikimedia Commons
License: Public Domain

known as **parliaments**, would come to be systematized over the course of the thirteenth century, until, by the reign of Edward I (r. 1272 – 1307), they would have representatives from most regions of England and would vote on whether to grant taxes to the king.

Parliaments were not unique to England, however. Most Spanish kings would consult with a body known as a **cortes**, with representatives of both Spain's towns and nobility, and the Scandinavian kings had assemblies called **things.** Indeed, by 1356, the Holy Roman Emperor would be elected by an assembly of the Holy Roman

Empire's greatest nobles, known as electors. England's parliaments, however, would gradually evolve from assemblies convoked when a king wanted to raise taxes to a regular assembly that gave representative voice to the people of England.

As stated earlier, of thirteenth-century Europe's monarchs, France's Capetian kings were some of the most successful. Indeed, King Louis IX's French state was well-administered enough that he was able to manage the logistics of a military campaign fought at the opposite end of the Mediterranean: the war that modern historians often call the Seventh Crusade.

12.19 LATER CRUSADES AND CRUSADING'S ULTIMATE FAILURE

After the Third Crusade, the re-established Crusader States managed to survive and even expand in power for the next several decades. Syria and Egypt were split between Saladin's heirs, and the crusader kingdoms often enjoyed good relations with Ayyubid Egypt: indeed, a truce worked out between Holy Roman Emperor Frederick II and the Egyptian sultan al-Kamil in 1229 resulted in the city of Jerusalem itself returning to Christian rule.

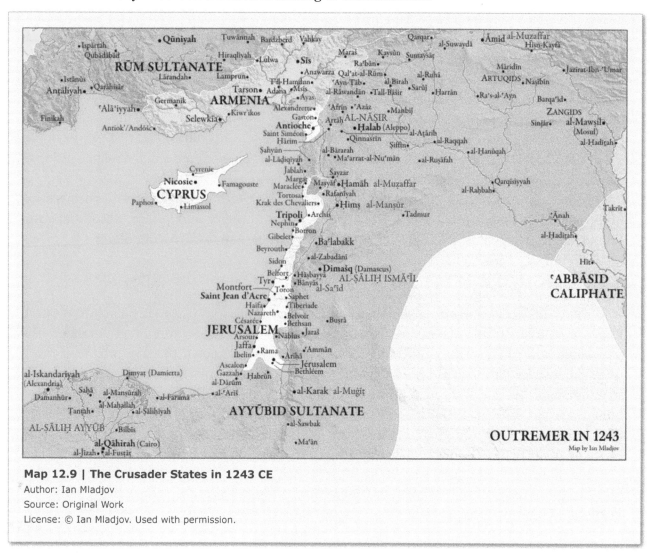

Map 12.9 | The Crusader States in 1243 CE
Author: Ian Mladjov
Source: Original Work
License: © Ian Mladjov. Used with permission.

In the 1240s, however, forces far from the Levant brought down the Kingdom of Jerusalem. As the Mongols gradually conquered Central Asia (see Chapter Eleven), the Khwarazmian Turks were driven from their realm in the steppes into Syria and northern Iraq. They ended up allying with Ayyubid Egypt against the Crusader Kingdom of Jerusalem, and, in 1244, the combined armies of Damascus and Jerusalem were defeated by an Egyptian/Khwarazmian army. Jerusalem fell under Muslim rule, under which it would remain until 1917.

In response to the fall of Jerusalem, Pope Innocent IV (r. 1243 – 1254) called a crusade that would be led by King Louis IX. While it had contingents from other Western European kingdoms, this effort was primarily an effort of the French crown. Although King Louis IX was able to manage the impressive logistical feat of organizing and equipping an army that seized the northern Egyptian port of Damietta, the effort to take all of Egypt was ultimately unsuccessful. Over the course of 1250, the French army was surrounded in the swamps of the Nile Delta outside of Cairo and forced to surrender, with Louis himself captured. The only lasting result in the Middle East was that, during the fighting, the Ayyubid sultan's Mamluks launched a coup d'état and seized power in Egypt, thereby creating in Egypt a military power that would dominate the Levant for nearly three centuries (see Chapter Eight).

Indeed, in the four decades after Louis's failure in the Nile Delta, the Mamluk sultans of Egypt would eventually conquer all of the Crusader States, with the last crusader stronghold in the Levant, the city of Acre, falling in 1291. Although Popes would still call crusades for military efforts against Muslim forces (and indeed, still make calls to retake the city of Jerusalem), crusading had failed. One reason for crusading's ultimate failure was that, as Western European kings consolidated their power, they often had priorities other than crusading. England's Edward I, for example, spent a few months fighting in the Levant in 1271; however, he spent most of his reign fighting to subdue England's neighboring kingdoms of Wales and Scotland.

In the end, the Crusades failed, and their greatest long-term impacts were the destruction of the Byzantine Empire and the growth of the sea power of Genoa and Venice, whose ships and sailors had transported people and supplies between Europe and the Crusader States.

12.20 SCHOLASTICISM

As more and more works of ancient Greek and Muslim philosophy became available to Western European Christians, the question of how to understand the world acquired more urgency. The philosophers of the ancient Greek and Muslim worlds were known to have produced much useful knowledge. But they had not been Christians. How, asked many thinkers, were Christians to understand the world: through divine revelation, as it appeared in the Bible, or through the human reason of philosophers? Indeed, this question was reminiscent of similar questions taking place in the Islamic world, when thinkers such as al-Ghazali questioned how useful the tools of logic and philosophy were in understanding the Quran (see Chapter Eight).

This controversy had raged since at least the twelfth century, when certain devout monks had said, "Whoever seeks to make Aristotle a Christian makes himself a heretic." Out of this controversy, medieval Europe produced its greatest thinker, St. Thomas Aquinas (1224 – 1274). St. Thomas was a Dominican **friar**. Friars were those churchmen who, like monks, took vows of chastity, poverty, and obedience. Instead of living in isolated monasteries, though, friars spent much of their time preaching to laypeople in Europe's growing towns and cities. These friars, whose two major groups were the Franciscans and Dominicans, had schools in most major universities of Western Europe by the early thirteenth century. Aquinas, a philosopher in the Dominican school of the University of Paris, had argued that human reason and divine revelation were in perfect harmony. He did so based on the techniques of the disputed question. He would raise a point, raise its objection, then provide an answer, and this answer would always be based on a logical argument. Aquinas was only part of a larger movement in the universities of Western Europe. We generally call the movement to reconcile Christian theology with human reason through the use of logic **scholasticism**.

Figure 12.17 | St. Thomas Aquinas | Note that the artist shows him defeating the non-Christian Aristotelian philosophy of Ibn Rushd.
Author: Benozzo Gozzoli
Source: Wikimedia Commons
License: Public Domain

Aquinas and the scholastics can be compared to Zhu Xi and the neo-Confucians of Song China. Just as Zhu Xi had sought to integrate Confucian thought with Buddhist and Daoist philosophy, so also Aquinas sought to integrate both Aristotelian logic and Christian theology.

The period not only saw successes in the field of speculative philosophy and theology, but also in the practical application of science. The master masons who designed Western Europe's castles and cathedral churches built hundreds of soaring cathedrals that would be the tallest buildings in Europe until the nineteenth century. We call these cathedrals' architecture **Gothic**. Gothic cathedrals were well known for their use of pointed arches (which may have been copied from Middle Eastern styles) that allowed taller buildings and for stained-glass windows that admitted a dazzling array of light. These cathedrals were in many ways made possible by the prosperity of Europe's towns, whose governing councils often financed the construction of these magnificent churches.

Thirteenth-century Europe showed other developments in technology as well. In 1269, Pierre of Harincourt first came to understand the principles of magnetic poles based on an analysis of the magnetic compass (in use since the twelfth century). At the same time, between 1286 and 1306, based on the pre-existing technology of lens-grinding (much of which had come from the Muslim world), Western Europeans invented eyeglasses. Water clocks had been known throughout the world since ancient times, but, in the years between 1271 and 1300, Western Europeans invented the mechanical clock.

In the twelfth, thirteenth, and fourteenth centuries, Western Europeans gradually adapted the art of **alchemy**, the art of changing (or attempting to change) one element into another, from the Muslim world. Eventually, alchemists (and natural philosophers who studied alchemy) would find new techniques of refining and compounding chemicals, although their ultimate goal, the ability to turn base metals into gold, would never succeed.

In addition to these technologies invented or improved in medieval Europe, the Mongol Empire's opening of trade routes had allowed the importation of East Asian technologies such as gunpowder.

Figure 12.18 | Lincoln Cathedral in England, built in the Gothic style in the thirteenth century | Note the pointed arches and the stained glass. The seats in the church were added in modern times: medieval worshipers stood.
Author: Andrew Reeves
Source: Original Work
License: CC BY-SA 4.0

Figure 12.19 | Late medieval eyeglasses
Author: Conrad von Soest
Source: Wikimedia Commons
License: Public Domain

12.21 DAILY LIFE AT THE MEDIEVAL ZENITH

Even at the height of medieval Europe's prosperity, most people were peasant farmers, living like their ancestors in the Carolingian or Byzantine Empires. They often lived in villages in one- or two-room houses with separate space for livestock. Only the richest of peasants—and some free peasants did prosper—could afford a bed. Most people slept in straw. The most furniture in a peasant household might be a table and stool. The peasant diet was mainly grain, both bread and porridge, and peasants got their protein from both legumes and eggs. The occasional meat came from chickens, those sheep that were too old for shearing, and sometimes pigs. Beef was reserved for nobles.

Figure 12.20 | Peasants Keeping Pigs
Author: User "Pannage"
Source: Wikimedia Commons
License: Public Domain

Nobles often lived in large rural houses. They were sometimes attached to castles, but many castles were unoccupied in times of peace. The noble diet was heavy in meat; indeed, nobles often suffered from gout, a painful swelling of the joints from too much meat in the diet. Meat dishes were lavishly cooked in spices, like cardamom, cinnamon, cumin, pepper, and saffron (chilies were unknown in the Eastern Hemisphere in pre-modern times).

Peasant recreation might include ball games, wrestling, and, of course, drinking. Beer was northern Europe's commonest drink, while, in southern Europe, people drank wine. The best quality wines were a luxury, with nobles throughout Europe drinking the wines of Italy and southern France.

Noble recreation included chess (introduced from the Muslim world around the eleventh century), hunting (usually forbidden to peasants), and the **tournament**, in which knights would form into teams and fight each other, sometimes with blunted weapons, but sometimes with regular weapons, relying on their armor to protect them. Accidental fatalities in hunting and tournaments were common.

Europe's growing cities had narrow, unpaved streets with pools of waste, through which pigs, dogs, and other animals would wander. Paris, whose streets King Philip Augustus had ordered paved and lined with ditches to carry away waste water, was the exception rather than the rule. Likewise, although London had a network of pipes to carry water from springs by 1236, the inhabitants of most cities got water from wells, and these were often contaminated. Indeed, the disease from parasites and contaminated water meant that cities were **population sinks**, with more people dying than were born. Their population increased largely because of people migrating from the countryside,

Figure 12.21 | Thirteenth-Century Knights Fighting in a Tournament
Author: Unknown
Source: Wikimedia Commons
License: Public Domain

since by the twelfth century, most towns of Western Europe recognized a runaway serf as legally free if he or she had resided within the walls of a town for a year and a day.

Medieval Europe remained a patriarchal culture. The division of labor in peasant, middle-class, and noble households, however, meant that women played an active part in economic life. Women peasants would often labor alongside men in the fields, and women often ran taverns. Likewise, among nobles, women usually managed the household and might direct the economic activity of the great agricultural estates.

But women remained subordinate. Although they could be nuns, women could not be ordained as clergy. Legally, a woman was subordinate to her husband. And even though nobles increasingly read love poetry that placed women in a position of honor and devotion (and this poetry may originally have been modeled on the Arabic love poetry common in al-Andalus), this very devotion emphasized the woman as a prize to be sought after rather than as a partner.

12.22 FOURTEENTH CENTURY CRISES

As the thirteenth century drew to a close, Europe began to run into its **Malthusian limits**, i.e., how many people a land's resources can support before food starts to run short. At the same time, the previously-warm climate began to cool, making conditions less suitable for agriculture. Famine returned to Europe.

Between 1315 and 1322, a set of extremely rainy, wet summers—accounts written at the time speak of castle walls being washed away in flood waters—caused crops to fail, resulting in massive famines and starvation. At the same time, livestock throughout western Europe died in droves from outbreaks of Rinderpest, Anthrax, and other diseases.

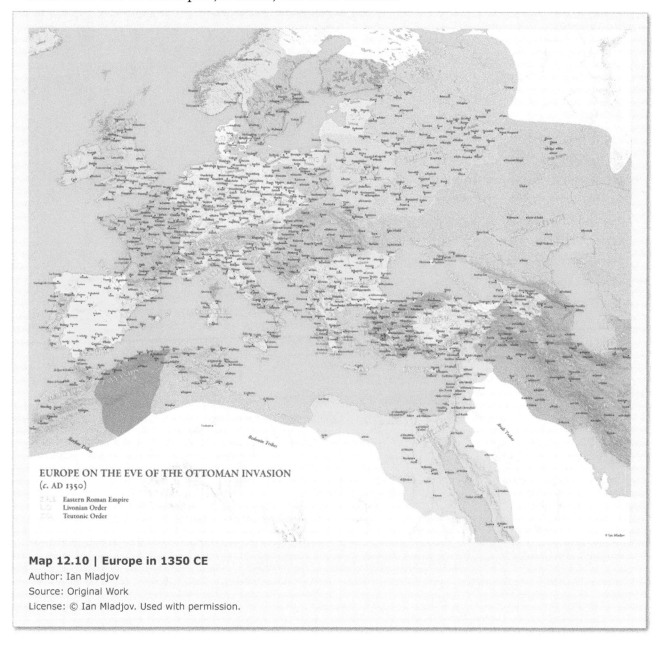

EUROPE ON THE EVE OF THE OTTOMAN INVASION
(c. AD 1350)

　　　Eastern Roman Empire
　　　Livonian Order
　　　Teutonic Order

Map 12.10 | Europe in 1350 CE
Author: Ian Mladjov
Source: Original Work
License: © Ian Mladjov. Used with permission.

Many peasants starved. Many more suffered from malnutrition. Contemporary accounts refer to hungry peasants resorting to cannibalism. Like all other crops, cash crops also failed, so that those who did survive were poorer.

Scarcely a generation had passed after the Great Famine when Europe was hit by a global pandemic: the Black Death. The Black Death was almost certainly an outbreak of Bubonic Plague, caused by the bacterium *Yersina pestis*. This disease has an extremely high mortality rate—certain varieties can have a mortality rate of over ninety-nine percent, and even the more survivable varieties usually kill the majority of the infected. The Plague acts in three ways: the variety called Bubonic Plague results in painful, swollen lumps around the armpits, crotch, and neck (locations associated with the lymph nodes); when they burst, a foul-smelling pus emerges. The septicemic variety results in skin turning black and dying all over the body, and the pneumonic variety—almost always fatal—shows no visible symptoms, but affects the lungs, and can cause a victim to go from healthy to dead in the space of twenty-four hours.

The pandemic began in the Yuan Empire (see Chapter Eleven). Unfortunately for the rest of the world, the trade routes opened by

Figure 12.22 | Victims of the Black Death | Note that above, we can see St. Sebastian in heaven praying to God on behalf of the Plague's victims. He was known for having been executed by arrows during the reign of Diocletian, and so Christian art usually pictured him as being covered in arrows.
Author: Jose Lieferinxe
Source: The Walters Art Museum
License: CC0

the Mongols meant that not only could ideas and technology travel, but that disease could as well. The Plague began in the East and Central Asia, but it quickly spread to the Middle East and North Africa, to the Swahili Coast, and eventually to Western Europe.

Its impacts were calamitous. A little over half of Europe's population died. After the first outbreak of the Plague, between 1347 and 1351, less virulent outbreaks continued to strike Europe nearly every year until 1782. Europe's population began a long decline; it did not start recovering until the fifteenth century. It did not return to its pre-Plague levels until the seventeenth (and in some regions, the eighteenth) century. Casualty rates among clergy were as high as sixty percent, with some monastic houses having casualty rates as high as ninety-nine percent, as monks living in communal environments were more likely to spread disease.

In the aftermath of the Plague, however, living conditions for those peasants who survived improved in many ways. Because there were fewer people, those who survived had access to more lands and resources. In addition, the need to find peasants to work the lands of the nobility meant that nobles often offered better wages and living conditions to those who would settle on their lands. As a result, peasant wages rose and serfdom in Western Europe gradually vanished. Although in some kingdoms, monarchs and their assemblies attempted to create legislation to reinforce the social status of the peasantry, these efforts were often unsuccessful. This failure to maintain pre-existing status distinctions stood in contrast to Mamluk Egypt, where, in the aftermath of the Plague, Egypt's ruling class of largely Turkic Mamluks managed to keep the peasantry in a firmly subordinate role and prevent the rise of peasant wages.

12.23 WAR

Famine and disease were not the only disasters to strike late medieval Europe. The four-teenth century also saw an increase in both civil wars and wars between states. The Holy Roman Empire saw nearly a decade of civil war (1314 – 1326) between rival emperors and, because of the close relations of their kings, Sweden, Denmark, and Norway experienced frequent combinations of civil and interstate war until the 1397 Union of Kalmar brought the three together under one crown.

The longest-running of these wars was between England and France, the so-called Hundred Years' War (1337 – 1453). In 1328, the French king Charles IV died without a direct heir. England's king, Edward III (r. 1327 – 1377), related to the French royal family, claimed to be rightful heir to the crown of France. The resulting war would last over a century, although it was broken by frequent, lengthy truces. Although France had many more people than England, the kingdom of England was often able to defeat it. The main reason was that the English kings made increasing use of trained, disciplined infantry armies. Horses are effective in battle against raiders or other horsemen. A horse, however, is less effective when

Figure 12.23 | England's King Edward III Surveying the Dead after the Battle of Crécy | Note that by the fourteenth century, a knight's armor was a combination of chain mail and metal plates.
Author: Jean Froissart
Source: Wikimedia Commons
License: Public Domain

an infantry formation is able to present a solid front against the horses and use missile weapons on those horses before they can close with their enemy. Using a combination of archers and infantry, the English were able to inflict severe defeats on the French at both Crécy (26 August 1346) and Poitiers (19 September 1356).

The war was particularly hard on the civilians of the French countryside: the method of waging war of a pre-modern army often involved invading enemy territory and burning crops, looting villages, and murdering civilians. French peasants, who had suffered first from the Plague and then from war, rose in rebellion in 1358, but this rebellion was ruthlessly crushed, with the peasants slaughtered and leaders brutally executed.

The Hundred Years' War would spill over into Spain, which itself was suffering from a vicious war between Castile and Aragon that eventually caused a Castilian civil war, with both French and English intervening.

The wars of the fourteenth and especially fifteenth century saw not only an increasing use of trained, professional armies, but also the employment of gunpowder weapons, invented in Song China and first seen in Europe in the early 1300s. At first, firearms were limited to heavy, cumbersome artillery pieces that were deployed from fixed points. Their use on the battlefield and in sieges was limited, although by the fifteenth century, cannons could blast open the gates of most existing fortifications. By the mid-1400s, the harquebus, a man-transportable firearm, appeared on the battlefield in Spain, bringing gunpowder to the individual infantryman.

12.24 SOUTHEASTERN EUROPE IN THE LATE MIDDLE AGES

Meanwhile, in Eastern Europe, the restored Byzantine Empire was unable to fully re-establish itself even as a regional power in the Aegean. The warring Italian city-states of Genoa and Venice controlled many of the best ports of the Aegean and Black Sea, and a new Turkic power, that of the Ottomans, was rising in Central Anatolia in the aftermath of the Mongol destruction of the Saljuq sultanate. Emperor Andronikos II (r. 1282 – 1328) hired a company of mercenaries from the region of Spain called Catalonia, but this Catalan Company, although it won some victories against the Turks, eventually turned on its employer and established a state in Athens that would last for seventy years. With the failure of the Catalan Company to shore up Byzantine defenses in Anatolia, by 1331, nearly all Byzantine territory in Asia Minor had

Figure 12.24 | Late Medieval Serbian Monastery
Author: Petar Milosevic
Source: Wikimedia Commons
License: CC BY-SA 3.0

fallen under Turkish rule; shortly thereafter, the nascent Ottoman Empire began expanding into southeastern Europe.

The disintegration of the Byzantine state did allow for the fourteenth-century flourishing of Serbian and Bulgarian Empires, whose cultures emerged as a melding of both Greek and Slavic elements to create a unique synthesis of cultures and institutions. In the end, though, these Empires would eventually be overwhelmed by the Turks, with the Ottomans conquering Serbia between 1389 and 1459 and Bulgaria in 1396. But even as the Byzantine state crumbled, intellectual activity flourished in the Orthodox Church. Greek intellectuals of the fourteenth century sought to engage with the thought of Aquinas and experiment with new forms of prayer and meditation.

In the end, Ottoman power swept away all resistance, Bulgar, Serbian, and Byzantine, and in 1453, the Turkish army conquered Constantinople. After two thousand years, the last remnant of the Roman Empire was gone. In the meantime, though, the fall of the Byzantine Empire would also be one factor eventually contributing to Europe's Renaissance.

12.25 THE LATE MEDIEVAL PAPACY

In 1250, the papacy looked like it was at its high point. After nearly two centuries of struggle, the popes had definitively broken the power of the Holy Roman Empire. Within less than a century, however, the power and prestige of the papacy would be heavily damaged.

The first major blow came when Pope Boniface VIII (r. 1294 – 1303) clashed with King Philip IV (r. 1285 – 1314) of France. When King Philip attempted to tax French clergy, Pope Boniface resisted strongly, claiming not only that a king had no right to tax any clergy, but also that all earthly authority was subordinate to the authority of the popes, who were rightful lords of the earth. This conflict ended when King Philip had a gang of mercenaries kidnap and abuse the pope. Even though Boniface himself escaped, he died of the shock shortly thereafter.

In order to avoid further antagonizing the French crown, the College of Cardinals (those churchmen in Rome who elect the pope) elected Clement V (r. 1305 – 1314), a Frenchman, to succeed him. Clement, however, never took up residence in Rome. In 1309, he settled the papal court in

Figure 12.25 | The Kidnapping of Pope Boniface VIII
Author: Giovanni Villani
Source: Wikimedia Commons
License: Public Domain

Avignon, a city owned by the papacy which sat just across the border of the Kingdom of France. To many observers at the time, it looked as though the papacy had been relocated to France under the thumb of the French monarchy.

The Italian poet Petrarch referred to the period when the papacy resided at Avignon as the **Babylonian Captivity of the Church**. He was referring metaphorically to the account in the Old Testament (also referred to as the Hebrew Bible) in which the people of Judaea had been held captive in the city of Babylon. Petrarch was insinuating that God's community was now held captive in a foreign land rather than occupying Rome, the city of St. Peter and thirteen subsequent centuries of popes.

Figure 12.26 | The Papal Palace at Avignon
Author: Jean-Marc Rosier
Source: Original Work
License: © Jean-Marc Rosier. Used with permission.

The crisis would only grow worse. In 1377, Pope Gregory XI (r. 1370 – 1378) moved the papal court back to Rome. At his death, the cardinals, pressured by an angry Roman mob, elected Urban VI, an Italian. Urban, however, soon proved to be erratic and abusive, so many cardinals fled Rome to Avignon, where they elected another pope. The result was that the Catholic Christian world now had two popes, each one claiming to be the rightful representative of Jesus Christ on earth. This period, lasting from 1378 to 1417, is known as the **Great Schism**; it resulted in a divided church, with different bishops following different popes. A 1409 council convened to depose both popes and appoint a single pope instead resulted in three popes, as neither Rome nor the Avignon papacy recognized this new pope.

In the end, although the conflict was resolved with the **Council of Constance** (1415 – 1417) deposing all three popes and selecting a new one, the prestige of the papacy had been tarnished. The popes spent much of the later fifteenth century attempting to rebuild the Church's authority and prestige, although whether they would fully succeed remained to be seen.

12.26 THE EUROPEAN RENAISSANCE

No intellectual movement can be traced to a single cause. An idea has many parents and even more children. But if we look to the Mediterranean world of the fourteenth century, we can find at least a few causes of an intellectual and cultural movement historians generally call the **Italian Renaissance**. Renaissance comes from the French word for rebirth. It was an intellectual movement whose ideals were to return to the art, literature, and culture of Ancient Greece and Rome.

Figure 12.27 | Manuel Chrysoloras
Author: Paolo Uccellp
Source: Wikimedia Commons
License: Public Domain

Northern Italy was well-suited to allow for the emergence of the Renaissance. Thanks to Mediterranean trade, it was one of the wealthiest and most urbanized regions of Western Europe. It was also politically fragmented so that the princes of its many courts all offered sponsorship to artists and intellectuals. Moreover Italy's education system had focused more on the literature of Ancient Rome than the rest of Europe, whose scholastic curriculum often focused on logic and philosophy.

In this environment, the Italian poet Francesco Petrarch's (1307 – 1374) writings prompted a greater interest in the literature of Ancient Rome. This focus on studying literature rather than philosophy and theology is often known as **humanism**, since poetry and literature were called humanistic studies in medieval schools. Another key element of the humanistic movement was that its proponents believed in studying the ancient texts themselves rather than the centuries of commentaries that had grown up around these texts. These values of returning to the original texts shorn of their commentaries also led to an increase in the study of how the writers of ancient Rome had used the Latin language and even of how Latin style had altered during different times in the Roman Empire's history.

Originally, humanistic scholars had focused on the study of Latin. But other circumstances soon brought about a greater emphasis on the study of Greek. As the Byzantine Empire crumbled before the Ottoman Turks, many Greek-speaking refugees fleeing the Aegean area settled in Italy, particularly in the city-state of Florence. These refugees brought Greek books with them and founded schools for the study of Greek. In Western Europe after the fall of the Western Roman Empire in the fifth century, the study of Greek had declined.

Figure 12.28 | Santa Maria del Fiore
Author: User "Enne"
Source: Wikimedia Commons
License: Public Domain

As a result, most readers had known of the literature of Ancient Greece, but they had usually only known it in Latin summaries. By the twelfth century, Western Europeans had read the philosophy of Aristotle and the science of Ptolemy, but usually they knew these philosophers only in translations—which had often been translated from Greek to Arabic to Latin.

So a return to the study of Greek meant that scholars were now reading Greek literature in its original language. Manuel Chrysoloras (*c.* 1350 – 1415) established a school for the study of Greek in Florence. Western Europeans now had direct access to most of the writings of Plato and Homer for the first time in centuries.

This interest in the culture of the ancient world also led to an interest in the art and architecture of Greece and Rome. Churches, such as Santa Maria del Fiore in Florence (built between 1420 and 1436), sprang up in imitation of the domed temples (and churches) of ancient Rome, while sculptors such as Donatello (1386 – 1466) produced naturalistic sculptures the like of which had not been seen in more than a thousand years.

Figure 12.29 | Donatello's David
Author: Donatello
Source: Wikimedia Commons
License: Public Domain

Figure 12.30 | Niccolò Machiavelli
Author: Santi di Tito
Source: Wikimedia Commons
License: Public Domain

Figure 12.31 | Desiderius Erasmus
Author: Holbein
Source: Wikimedia Commons
License: Public Domain

This intellectual movement was not simply an affair of scholars and artists. Indeed, its impacts would be far-reaching throughout Western Europe. The children of princes and wealthy merchants gradually came to be educated along humanistic lines, and the fashion for a humanistic education would eventually spread from Italy to the elites of all Western Europe.

Humanism's political impacts would be broad ranging as well. Since the eighth century, the popes had relied on the text of the Donation of Constantine in their struggles with the Holy Roman Empire and to demonstrate their right to rule as earthly princes as well as to spiritually direct the Church. In 1440, the humanist scholar Lorenzo Valla (1407 – 1457) analyzed the Donation of Constantine—and showed definitively that it was a forgery. Its Latin writing style was most certainly *not* the Latin of fourth-century Rome. Valla had shown that one of the foundational documents by which the papacy claimed legitimacy as an earthly power was a fraud.

Even the ideals of how a ruler should govern came under the influence of Renaissance humanism. In his analysis of the historical writings of Ancient Rome, the humanist Niccolò Machiavelli (1469 – 1527) argued that the circumstances of history show that a prince should not necessarily attempt to rule virtuously, but instead should ruthlessly set aside ethics and morality in order to accomplish the goals of the state. One should note that in many ways rulers already behaved this way, but Machiavelli gave an intellectual justification for doing so.

And, of course, an intense study of the language of ancient texts would lead to an intense study of the ancient text that was most important for Western Europe of the later Middle Ages: the Bible. Humanists such as the Dutch scholar Desiderius Erasmus (1469 – 1536) used the tools of linguistic investigation to analyze the Greek text of the New Testament. Other scholars also began looking at the Bible not with the intellectual tools of logic and philosophy, but with linguistic analysis. They began to look at such a text as it had been written, and not at the intervening fourteen centuries of commentary. The results of such reading were explosive.

12.27 STATES IN THE LATE MIDDLE AGES AND RENAISSANCE

As Europe transitioned into the fifteenth century, two of Europe's most organized states remained locked in destructive warfare. England's king Henry V (r. 1413 – 1422) came close to conquering all of France, aided largely by the fact that France itself was riven by a civil war between two powerful houses of nobles, the Armagnacs and Burgundians. Eventually, however, when France's rival houses ended their differences, the unified nation was able to expel English troops, using trained and disciplined infantry funded by a centralized apparatus of taxation. The Hundred Years' War thus ended in 1453. England's loss in France was followed by a civil war (usually known as the Wars of the Roses because the rival factions used a red and a white rose, respectively, as their emblems) that lasted from 1455 to 1485.

In Northern Italy, at the same time as the brilliant artistic achievements of the Italian Renaissance, the city-states of Italy were locked in near-continual warfare until the 1454 Treaty of Lodi brought almost half a century of peace to the Italian peninsula. That peace would come to an end, however, in 1494, when King Charles VIII of France (r. 1483 – 1498) turned the power of the newly consolidated French state to an invasion of Italy. In the wars that followed, the cannons used by the French army were able to effortlessly batter down the Italian cities' and castles' medieval walls. A new era of warfare was beginning.

12.28 IBERIA AND THE ATLANTIC: NEW WORLDS

To the southwest of Europe, events in Iberia would eventually bring about several changes that would usher in the end of Europe's Middle Ages and the beginnings of modern times.

Portugal, Castile, and Aragon were steeped in the traditions of the *Reconquista*, of expanding the dominion of the Christian world by force of arms. The *Reconquista* had established a habit in the Iberian kingdoms of conquering Muslims lands and reducing their Muslim and Jewish inhabitants to subordinate status (or in some cases to outright slavery). By the fifteenth century, these kingdoms had nearly completed the *Reconquista*. As stated earlier, only Granada remained under Muslim rule.

Meanwhile, over the fourteenth century, both Venice and the Ottoman Empire had forced the Italian city-state of Genoa out of the Eastern Mediterranean, so its sailors and ship owners turned their focus to the western half of the Mediterranean Sea. Constantly on the lookout for new markets, Genoese merchants already knew from trade with the Islamic Maghreb that West Africa was a source of gold. In 1324, Mansa Musa's *hajj* to Mecca (see Chapter Nine) had put so much gold into circulation that the price of gold fell by twenty-five percent in the Mediterranean market. If the Muslim rulers of Morocco controlled the overland routes by which gold traveled from Mali to the Mediterranean, then perhaps certain sailors could bypass the overland route by sailing into the Atlantic and around the Sahara and arrive at the source of Africa's gold.

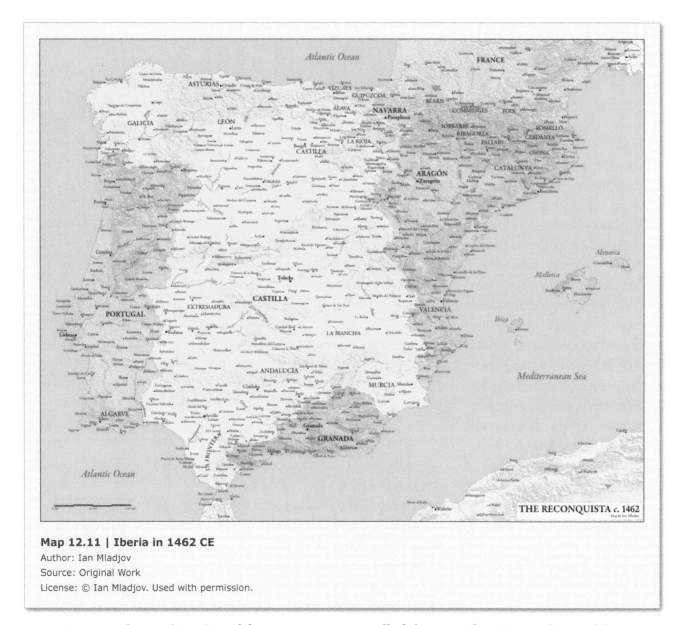

Map 12.11 | Iberia in 1462 CE
Author: Ian Mladjov
Source: Original Work
License: © Ian Mladjov. Used with permission.

By 1300, the combination of the compass, a map called the **portolan** (a map that could accurately represent coastlines), and ships that by operating on sails rather than oars needed fewer people meant that European navigators could begin venturing into open waters of the Atlantic that the Arabs and Ancient Romans had largely avoided.

Genoese merchants began tentatively sailing into the Atlantic. In the early 1300s, they were regularly visiting the Canary Islands. These merchants (and others from Western Europe) increasingly served in the employ of Iberian kings. In 1404, King Henry III of Castile (r. 1390 – 1406) began Spanish efforts to conquer the Canaries and convert their indigenous peoples to Christianity. Over the next century, the Spanish would conquer and settle the islands, driven by the *Reconquista* ideal of the military spread of the Christian faith. In the mid-fifteenth century, the kingdom of Portugal began the conquest and colonization of the Azores, nearly 700 miles to the southwest of Iberia in the Atlantic.

Genoese merchants established sugar plantations on these chains of islands, and those plantations were worked by slave labor. Earlier, in the thirteenth century, Venetian merchants had begun to grow sugar (long cultivated in the Muslim world) in their island colonies in the Mediterranean, and labor for these colonies came from the Mediterranean slave trade. Genoese merchants copied this economic model first in Sicily and then, when they began to operate in the Atlantic, in the Canaries and Azores. Often they would purchase the slaves for these

Map 12.12 | A Portolan Map of Europe and Africa from 1375 CE | Note the depiction of Mansa Musa holding a gold nugget on the bottom of the map and the Azores and Canaries on the bottom left
Author: Cresques Abraham
Source: Wikimedia Commons
License: Public Domain

plantations from Africans on the continent's Atlantic coast. Thus began a slave trade that would be as lucrative for its operators as it was brutal for its victims.

The lure of African gold drew mariners serving Iberian monarchs south and west. By 1482, the Portuguese had established the fort and trading post of São Jorge da Mina on the coast of Guinea. And in the Iberian peninsula, in 1479, Isabella, the Queen of Castile, married King Ferdinand II of Aragon, creating a united Spanish kingdom. In 1492, these monarchs, devout Catholics both, completed the *Reconquista*, conquering Granada, the last Muslim territory in Spain. All of Spain was now under Christian rule, and the king and queen were eager to continue spreading the Catholic religion.

They sponsored a voyage by the Genoese sailor Christopher Columbus. Columbus had miscalculated the size of the world, so he believed that it would be possible to sail to Asia by traveling west across the Atlantic Ocean. European mariners knew the world was a sphere but believed that it was impossible to carry adequate supplies to sail around the world due to the sheer distance between Europe and Asia. When Columbus made landfall in 1492, it was not in East Asia (for he had in fact been wrong, drastically underestimating the size of the world), but rather in a set of lands previously unknown to the peoples of the Eastern Hemisphere. The world was about to be forever changed.

12.29 CONCLUSION

Over the eleventh and twelfth centuries, a rise in agricultural production led to an increase in Western Europe's wealth and population. The chaos of the tenth and eleventh centuries had brought about the origin of a feudal system dominated by knights. Feudal Europe was thus able to respond to the Byzantine Empire's requests for help when its field army was annihilated by Saljuq Turks, resulting in the First Crusade and establishment of a set of Crusader States in the Eastern Mediterranean, but these Crusader states were gradually conquered by Muslim powers over the next two centuries. An army of Crusaders would eventually defeat and break up the Byzantine Empire, and although that empire would be re-established, it was never strong enough to resist the pressure of the Ottoman Turks, who finally conquered it in 1453.

As Western Europe grew in population and urbanized, the urban cathedral schools became the center of an increase in intellectual activity over the twelfth century known as the Twelfth-Century Renaissance. Thinkers of the Twelfth-Century Renaissance used the philosophy of the Ancient Greeks and Arabs to understand the world, and in the thirteenth century the intellectual movement known as scholasticism would seek to reconcile Christianity with Arabic and Ancient Greek Philosophy. By the end of the Middle Ages, Europe's intellectuals would seek to study the writings of the Ancient Greeks and Romans, and not the commentators of the previous thousand years. This movement was known as Renaissance humanism.

Europe's states—with the notable exception of the Holy Roman Empire—gradually consolidated, but the fourteenth and fifteenth centuries saw increasing interstate warfare. The states that emerged out of this endemic war, however, were more militarily powerful and more centralized. At the same time, sailors in the service of Spain and Portugal were exploring the Atlantic and West Africa until the close of the fifteenth century, when Western Europeans discovered the existence of the continents of the Western Hemisphere.

12.30 WORKS CONSULTED AND FURTHER READING

Backman, Clifford R. *The Worlds of Medieval Europe*. 2nd ed. Oxford: Oxford University Press, 2009.

Fernández-Armesto, Felipe. *Before Columbus: Exploration and Colonization from the Mediterranean to the Atlantic, 1229 – 1492*. Philadelphia: University of Pennsylvania Press, 1987.

Grafton, Anthony. *Renaissance Europe, 1350 – 1517*. New York: Penguin, forthcoming.

Jensen, De Lamar. *Renaissance Europe: Age of Recovery and Reconciliation*. 2nd ed. Lexington: D.C. Heath and Company, 1992.

Jordan, William Chester. *Europe in the High Middle Ages*. New York: Penguin, 2001.

Maurer, Armand. *Medieval Philosophy*. Revised ed. Toronto: Pontifical Institute of Mediaeval Studies Press, 1982.

Ostrogorsky, George. *History of the Byzantine State*. Revised Ed. New Brunswick: Rutgers University Press, 1969.

Tyerman, Christopher. *God's War: A New History of the Crusades*. Cambridge, MA: Harvard University Press, 2006.

12.31 LINKS TO PRIMARY SOURCES

Fordham University's Internet Medieval Sourcebook contains a wide variety of primary source documents from the Middle Ages (that is, 500 to 1500) hosted by Fordham University. From the main page one can find links based on period and category.

The Internet Medieval Sourcebook:

http://legacy.fordham.edu/Halsall/sbook.asp

Georgetown University's The Labyrinth likewise contains a large selection of links to both primary sources and art and art historical materials. Some of the pages have succumbed to "link rot" due to the relative age of the site, but it remains one of the best collections of primary source material available online for free.

The Labyrinth:

https://blogs.commons.georgetown.edu/labyrinth

CPSIA information can be obtained
at www.ICGtesting.com
Printed in the USA
LVHW070953030722
722663LV00009B/217

9 781940 771106